THE PEAK, MASSANUTTEN MOUNTAIN

Photo by Dean

A History of
Rockingham County
Virginia

By John W. Wayland, Ph. D

HERITAGE BOOKS
2010

HERITAGE BOOKS
AN IMPRINT OF HERITAGE BOOKS, INC.

Books, CDs, and more—Worldwide

For our listing of thousands of titles see our website at
www.HeritageBooks.com

Published 2010 by
HERITAGE BOOKS, INC.
Publishing Division
100 Railroad Ave. #104
Westminster, Maryland 21157

Copyright © John W. Wayland, Ph.D

All rights reserved. No part of this book may be reproduced or transmitted in any form or by any means, electronic or mechanical, including photocopying, recording or by any information storage and retrieval system without written permission from the author, except for the inclusion of brief quotations in a review.

International Standard Book Numbers
Paperbound: 978-1-55613-325-1
Clothbound: 978-0-7884-7628-0

OUTLINE OF CONTENTS.

LIST OF ILLUSTRATIONS.

INTRODUCTION.

CHRONOLOGICAL TABLE.

PART I.—Chronological.

CHAPTER.
I. Geography of Rockingham County.
II. Geological Features.
III. First White Settlers: 1727-1738.
IV. Rockingham as Part of Augusta: 1738-1777.
V. The New County and the New Nation: 1777-1820.
VI. A Growing Community: 1820-1860.
VII. Rockingham in the Civil War: 1861-1865.
VIII. The Days of Reconstruction: 1865-1876.
IX. From 1876 to 1912.
X. Rockingham To-Day.

PART II.—Topical.

XI. Towns and Villages of Rockingham.
XII. Roads and Railroads.
XIII. Race Elements and Population.
XIV. Churches and Religious Life.
XV. Education and Schools.
XVI. Charitable Institutions.
XVII. Writers and Printers: Books and Periodicals.
XVIII. Singers of Rockingham.
XIX. Rockingham Statesmen and Jurists.
XX. Farms and Farmers.
XXI. Domestic Arts and Manufacturing Enterprises.
XXII. Banks and Banking.
XXIII. Health Resorts.
XXIV. Natural Curiosities.
XXV. Hunting in the Western Mountains.
XXVI. Boating on the Shenandoah River.

XXVII. Court Days of Long Ago.
XXVIII. Some Interesting Incidents:
Spotswood's Expedition of 1716 and the University Pageant of 1909.
The Coming of the Lincolns.
Daniel Boone on Linville Creek.
Valentine Sevier's Sale Bill.
The Influenza of 1806-7.
A Case of Body-Snatching.
A Visit to Philadelphia in 1847.
Death of Ashby: 1862.
Stonewall Jackson at Port Republic.
Killing of John Kline: 1864.
Death of Meigs: 1864.
The Thurman Movement.
Sidney Lanier at Rockingham Springs.
A Fence Corner Council.

CONCLUSION.

APPENDIX.

Sheriffs of Rockingham.
County Judges and Circuit Judges.
County Clerks rnd Circuit Clerks.
Commonwealth's Attorneys.
Superintendents of Schools.
County Surveyors.
Members of House of Delegates.
Members of State Senate.
Marriages in Rockingham, 1778-1720.
Landowners in Rockingham in 1789.
Muster Rolls of Rockingham Soldiers.
Business and Professional Directory of Rockingham County: 1912.
Bibliography: A list of books, magazines, and newspapers containing information concerning Rockingham County and Rockingham People.

INDEX.

LIST OF ILLUSTRATIONS.

Frontispiece, The Peak	
District Map	16
Geological Map	24
General John Sevier	32
Site of First Court House	48
Bear Lithia Spring	48
Suter Wheat Field	48
Steam Plow	48
Court House of 1833	64
Court House of 1874, two views	64
Court House of 1896	64
Chesapeake-Western Bridge	80
Bridgewater Bridge	80
Confluence of the Rivers, Port Republic	80
Lethe	96
Lincoln Homestead	96
Miller Farm Scene	96
Mt. Clinton	96
State Normal School	112
Senator John F. Lewis	128
Etching, 10th Va. Regt. Camp Equipment	138
Battle-Flag 10th Va. Reg.	144
Flag of Chrisman's Boy Company	144
Flag Saved at Appomattox	144
Port Republic Battlefield	144
Hon. John T. Harris	160
Fort Lynne	176
Conrad's Store	176
Funk Printing House	176
Madison Hall	176
Smithland	176
Old Stone Fort	176

Bowman's Mill	176
Bogota	176
Waterman House	192
Chinkapin Tree	192
Town Hall, Bridgewater	192
Farm Lands on Cook's Creek	192
Historical Map	198
District Sunday School Map	198
Bridgewater College	204
Elkton Hotel	208
Singer's Glen	208
First Postoffice	208
Stonewall Jackson's Headquarters	208
View of Harrisonburg	224
Site of Salyards School (McGaheysville)	224
Singers Glen High School	224
Orphans' Home	224
Old Elk Run Church	224
Blosser Hatchery	224
Henry Tutwiler	240
Bishop James Madison	256
Big Spring	272
Ashby's Monument	272
Olden Days on Court Square	272
Asbury's Chapel	272
Old St. Peter's Church	272
Bridgewater Graded and High School	288
Waterman School	288
Harrisonburg High School	288
McGaheysville Graded and High School	288
Shenandoah Collegiate Institute	296
Joseph Salyards	304
U. S. Court House and Postoffice	312
Rockingham Memorial Hospital	312
Rockingham County Almshouse	312
Old Folks' Home	312
Dr. Gessner Harrison	320
Etching, Oldest Known Number Rockingham Register	336
Title-Page Genuine Church Music	342
Judge Daniel Smith	352

Hon. Chas. T. O'Ferrall	359
Judge John Paul	360
Senator I. S. Pennybacker	368
Hand-Woven Coverlets	384
Rawley Springs	394
Massanetta Springs	394
Washington's Profile	400
Giant's Grave	400
Cedar Cliff Falls	400
Formation in Massanutta Cave	400
Diamond Lake, New Market Endless Caverns	400
Sidney Lanier Cottage	416
Keezletown School Building	416
A Rockingham Orchard	416
First Piano Brought Into Rockingham	416
Pageant, Knights of Golden Horseshoe	426
Mt. Vernon Furnace	432
Where Meigs Fell	432
The Falls, Bridgewater	432
Brock's Gap	432
Lincoln Graveyard	432
Silver Lake, Dayton	432
Sidney Lanier	434

INTRODUCTION.

In this volume we present to the public the results of the first serious attempt ever made to write and publish a comprehensive illustrated history of Rockingham County, Virginia. That the task herein essayed has not been undertaken before is remarkable, in view of the broad scope and inviting character of the field; for the sons of Rockingham, both at home and abroad, have been making history for many generations. They have made this fair land between the mountains to blossom as the rose; they have cleared farms and enriched them; they have founded homes and kept them in the light of sacred fires; they have builded altars and worshiped before them; they have erected schools and trained their children; they have sought peace and pursued it, yet in the hour of battle they have set their bravest and best in the forefront; they have borne loss and disaster without flinching, and in the midst of wasted fields and homesteads have raised again the standards of a free and prosperous people. Not only have the brave gone forth for defense, and the strong to arduous labor, but the fair have also done faithfully their noble part. In peace or war, in prosperity or adversity, the women of Rockingham have risen always to their high destiny. Their invincible spirit has given motive to soldier and farmer and scholar; their hands have ministered to sick and wounded, their prayers have soothed the dying; the memorials raised by their toil and patience enhance the past and inspire the future. We give them honor.

It has been the author's purpose in this history (1) to give due recognition to all the important phases of Rockingham life, interests, and enterprises; (2) to emphasize those particular interests and activities that have given the county its distinctive character and influence; (3) to find and preserve some treasures lost, or nearly lost, in the lapse of time and the obscuring din of busy days.

Inasmuch as Rockingham is a great county, mine has been a great task. How well it has been performed, the intelligent reader must judge. No one more than the author will realize the lacks and deficiencies in the result, but he hopes and believes that all will at least credit him with a sincere purpose and an earnest effort. No opinion, however adverse, and no criticism, however sharp, can take from him the joy that he has found in the work. To him it has been indeed a labor of love. The splendid achievements and resources of the county have been appreciated as never before, and things in her history have been found—often by seeming chance or rare good fortune—that were before undreamed of.

At the laying of the corner stone for the new Court House in 1896, Judge John Paul delivered an address that contains much valuable information concerning the courts and civil officials of Rockingham. This address has been found very helpful by the author of this book. In 1885 Mr. George F. Compton, now of Charlottesville, Va., published an extended and interesting series of historical articles on the county in the *Rockingham Register;* in 1900 Mr. John H. Floyd of Dayton wrote a series of ten historical papers concerning Rockingham, and published them in the *Harrisonburg Free Press;* in addition, many historical pieces, in books, magazines, and newspapers have appeared from time to time. To all these, so many as he has seen, the author makes due and grateful acknowledgement; all that he has found published, in any available form, he has listed, and in many cases described, in the appended Bibliography; at the same time he begs leave to state that the bulk of the matter presented in this volume has been collected and prepared by himself, with the generous aid of many friends, from sources that may in a large measure be termed original. It would of course be impossible to enumerate all the sources from which materials have been obtained; but some of the more important ones are herewith indicated.

First in natural order and importance are the official records to be found in the land office at Richmond and in the county clerks' offices of Orange, Augusta, and Rockingham County. The records of marriages, of land sales, and of court proceedings are rich in facts and interest and significance. Of almost equal importance with these original records, are the many printed volumes of Hening's Statutes and the Acts of the General Assembly of Virginia. Old almanacs and files of old newspapers have been found to contain circumstantial accounts of important events that could scarcely be obtained from any other source. Old files of the *Rockingham Register* have proved of special value in this respect. Containing as they do particular and contemporary accounts of practically every notable happening in the county within the past ninety years, the successive issues of the *Register* are a very treasure-house to the student and antiquarian. A complete and well-preserved file of the *Register*, from the first issue in 1822 to the present, would be sought after eagerly by any of the great libraries of the country, and would command almost any price. Although the writer has not seen any complete file of this paper, he has been exceedingly fortunate in securing what is perhaps the best file in existence. Through the generous kindness of Mr. R. B. Smythe, manager of the News-Register Company, Harrisonburg, Va., he now has in his possession *Register* files covering many years. These have been found most helpful in the preparation of this book. Miss Hortense Devier, whose father, Giles Devier, was for many years editor of the said paper, has made a generous loan of extended files. In addition to these files, many fugitive copies of the *Register*, some dating back almost to the first issue, have been put into the author's hands by his friends, as either a gift or a loan. Special acknowledgement is made to Hon. Geo. E. Sipe for access to files of the *Old Commonwealth*. For all these favors he is duly grateful.

He has also had put at his disposal files of other periodicals, old ledgers and day books, and even personal manuscripts and diaries. A manuscript account of Harrisonburg, its people, and the activities centering in it as the countyseat, written in 1892 by a lady who was born in the town in 1812, and giving realistic descriptions of days and doings nearly a century ago, should be specially mentioned. The records of the Methodist church, dating back in their beginning more than a hundred years, have been a source of much information having a general as well as a particular interest. Photographers have contributed pictures, authors have given their books, publishers have opened their presses in hearty and generous co-operation. The librarians at Richmond and at the State University, as well as at other places where the author has gone gathering facts, have been obliging and helpful; hundreds of persons all over the county, and in many other parts of our great country, have responded cheerfully to personal letters requesting particular information. It is indeed an embarrassment of riches that has confronted the author; the task has been one of selection rather than of collection, though he has sought far and long for some things herein presented. He feels, therefore, that he may be justly criticised, not so much for what he has given in this book as for what he has been obliged to leave out. It has been deemed wiser, on the whole, to keep the volume within reasonable size and cost than to include so much as to make it cumbersome in bulk or expensive in price. We have tried to make a book for the average reader, for every citizen, as well as for the scholar and antiquarian.

Grateful acknowledgement is made to special contributors and others who have given aid in supplying materials or suggesting lines of choice, and the names of many of these will be found in the proper connections throughout the volume.

Special mention is yet due in this place, and is gratefully made, of the uniform courtesy extended to the author by Col. D. H. Lee Martz, clerk of the circuit court in Rockingham, and by his assistants, Mr. C. H. Brunk and Mr. J. Frank Blackburn.

CHRONOLOGICAL TABLE.

1716—September—Spotswood visits the Valley—East Rockingham.
1727—Adam Miller settles on the Shenandoah River.
1738—November—Act of Assembly passed creating Frederick and Augusta Counties.
1745—September 23—John Sevier born in Rockingham.
1749—August 27—James Madison, first Protestant Episcopal bishop of Virginia, born at Port Republic.
1751—Thomas Lewis and Gabriel Jones buy land in East Rockingham.
1753—May 11—Valentine and Joannah Sevier sell land to Andrew Byrd, on or near Smith's Creek.
1758—April 28—Massacre at Fort Seybert.
1763—April 18—Valentine Sevier sells his personal property to Andrew Byrd.
1769—Lutheran and Reformed congregations at Peaked Mountain agree to build a union church.
1773—August 15—Valentine and Joanna Sevier sell land in Long Meadow to Michael and David Holsinger.
1775—October—John Alderson installed as pastor of the Linville Creek Baptist church.
1777—October—Act of Assembly passed creating Rockingham County.
1778—April 27, 28—First court held for Rockingham County.
1779—August 5—Thomas Harrison sells lot for county buildings.
1780—May—Act of Assembly passed establishing Harrisonburg.
1780—First Presbyterian preaching in Harrisonburg, according to tradition.
1782—Abraham Lincoln goes from Rockingham County to Kentucky.

A HISTORY OF

1784—First court house for Rockingham completed.
1787—December—Act of Assembly passed creating Pendleton County.
1789—October 29—Rockingham Union Lodge, No. 27, A. F. & A. M., chartered.
1791—December—Act of Assembly passed establishing Keezletown.
1794—Bishop Asbury organizes Methodist school in Harrisonburg.
1801—McGaheysville named for Tobias Randolph McGahey.
1802—January 14—Port Republic established by Act of Assembly.
1804—January 5—New Haven established by Act of Assembly.
1805—Robert Gray locates at Harrisonburg.
1807—November 16—Henry Tutwiler, first M. A. of University of Virginia, born in Harrisonburg.
1807—December—Dr. Peachey Harrison writes of Rockingham for *Philadelphia Medical Museum*.
1809—George Rockingham Gilmer of Georgia visits Rockingham.
1809—Bishop Newcomer (U. B.) confers with Bishop Asbury (M. E.) at Harrisonburg.
1811—February 20—Dr. Asher Waterman sells 35,000 acres of West Rockingham land for $13,125.
1813—Daniel Bryan publishes the "Mountain Muse."
1816—Rockingham Methodists prepare memorial against slavery.
1818—Brown's "Circular" published.
1818—Harrison's Cave discovered.
1820 (?)—Garber's Church built.
1822—Trissel's Church built.
1822—*Rockingham Register* founded by Lawrence Wartmann.
1824—January 26—Timothy Funk born at Mountain Valley.
1825—Mt. Crawford established by Act of Assembly.
1826—February 18—Act of Assembly passed chartering Rockingham Academy.

—10—

ROCKINGHAM COUNTY

1828—Linville Creek Church (of the Brethren) built.
1831—March—Act of Assembly passed creating Page County.
1832—Dunker Annual Meeting held in Rockingham County.
1832—First edition of Joseph Funk's "Genuine Church Music."
1833—January 7—Great Anti-Nullification meeting held in Harrisonburg.
1833—January Court—Old courthouse sold.
1833—March—Dayton established by Act of Assembly.
1834—Valley Turnpike Company authorized to construct toll road from Winchester to Harrisonburg.
1835—February—Bridgewater established by Act of Assembly.
1839-40—Extraordinary snows in Rockingham County.
1840—December 19—Joseph Salyards advertises the resumption of school at McGaheysville.
1844—Sons of Temperance organize at Harrisonburg.
1844—Liberty Springs Company buys land.
1847—Joseph Funk and Sons open printing office at Mountain Valley.
1847—October 5—Cyclone near Friedens Church.
1848—Mt. Vernon Furnace in Brown's Gap built.
1850—Rockingham Parish reorganized and put in charge of Rev. James B. Goodwyn.
1850—Death of Judge Daniel Smith.
1858—Jed Hotchkiss publishes description of Northwest Rockingham.
1861—Dunker Annual meeting held in Rockingham.
1861—October—Girls' school at Harrisonburg turned into a Confederate hospital.
1862—May 8—Col. S. B. Gibbons killed at McDowell.
1862—June 6—Gen. Turner Ashby killed near Harrisonburg.
1862—June 8—Battle of Cross Keys.
1862—June 9—Battle of Port Republic.
1862—December 24—Joseph Funk dies at Singer's Glen.
1864—May 5—Col. E. T. H. Warren and Maj. I. G. Coffman killed in the Wilderness.

A HISTORY OF

1864—June 15—John Kline killed in Rockingham.
1866—John W. Taylor begins teaching at Lacey Springs.
1866—School for colored children organized in Harrisonburg by Misses Martha Smith and Phoeby Libby, of Augusta, Maine.
1868—February—Lutheran Church in Harrisonburg rededicated.
1868—July 13—Old Waterman home near Harrisonburg burns.
1868—Thurman movement in Rockingham culminates.
1869—Rockingham Home Mutual Fire Insurance Company organized.
1869—First railroad opened to Harrisonburg.
1869—New stage line opened from Harrisonburg to Shenandoah Iron Works.
1870—January—*Musical Million* established at Singer's Glen.
1870—January—Navigation opened on Shenandoah River in Brock's Gap.
1870—October—Destructive Floods.
1870—December 25—Destructive fire in Harrisonburg, south side of Public Square.
1871—Harrisonburg graded school organized under new public school system—J. S. Loose, principal.
1871—U. S. District Court located at Harrisonburg.
1872—January 6—West Rockingham Mutual Fire Insurance Company organized.
1872—April—Redivision of Rockingham County into 5 townships.
1872—John Cover builds tannery near Conrad's Store.
1873—September 29—Valley Normal School at Bridgewater opened.
1874—March—First train over Valley Railroad from Harrisonburg to Staunton.
1874—November—Grading on Narrow Gauge completed from Harrisonburg to Bridgewater.
1874—Third Court House erected.
1875—Shenandoah Collegiate Institute at Dayton founded.

ROCKINGHAM COUNTY

1876—May—Catholic church in Harrisonburg consecrated.
1876—Monument to soldiers erected in Woodbine Cemetery by Ladies' Memorial Association.
1877—November—Destructive floods.
1878—Ruebush-Kieffer printing house moved to Dayton.
1879—June—Dunker Annual Meeting at Broadway.
1879—August-September—Sidney Lanier at Rockingham Springs.
1879—New Market Endless Caverns discovered.
1880—Bridgewater College started at Spring Creek.
1880—March—Broadway established by Act of Assembly.
1881—April 18—First through trains from Hagerstown to Waynesboro on Norfolk & Western Railway.
1881—September—A. C. Kimler begins teaching at McGaheysville.
1881—A. S. Kieffer publishes "Hours of Fancy."
1885—Lake's Atlas of Rockingham County published.
1885—G. F. Compton begins history of Rockingham in the *Register*.
1887—Shenandoah Normal College located at Harrisonburg.
1889—Dunker Annual Meeting at Harrisonburg.
1892—February—Shendun established by Act of Assembly.
1892—March 1—Old Folks' Home at Timberville opened.
1892—Harrisonburg synagogue dedicated.
1892—Emma Lyon Bryan publishes "A Romance of the Valley."
1893—Massanutta Cave, near Keezletown, discovered.
1894—February—Timberville established by Act of Assembly.
1895—July 31—Chesapeake & Western Railway completed to Dayton.
1895—September 13—C. & W. Railway completed to Bridgewater.
1897—Fourth Court House erected.
1897—Cross Keys Home Mutual Fire Insurance Company organized.
1898—New water system for Harrisonburg put in operation.
1898—Harrisonburg *Daily News* established.

A HISTORY OF

1899—April 18—Valley Telephone Company absorbed by the Rockingham Mutual System.
1899—May 20—President McKinley in Harrisonburg.
1899—July 1—Rockingham County Medical Association organized.
1903—Nettie Gray Daingerfield publishes "That Dear Old Sword."
1905—Harrisonburg *Daily Times* established.
1906—April—Fravel Sash and Door Company moved to Harrisonburg.
1906—J. C. Paxton builds lime kiln at Linville.
1907—J. W. Wayland publishes the "German Element of the Shenandoah Valley of Virginia."
1911—Harrisonburg and Rockingham County adopted compulsory education law.
1908—March—Elkton incorporated.
1909—June—Great Dunker Annual Meeting at Harrisonburg.
1909—September—State Normal School at Harrisonburg opened.
1911—Waterman School opened.
1911—Rockingham Memorial Hospital built.
1911—L. J. Heatwole publishes his perpetual calendar.
1911—Rockingham *Daily Record* established.
1912—Legislature changes the name of Shendun to Grottoes.
1912—State Sunday-School convention held in Harrisonburg.
1912—E. U. Hoenshel publishes the "Crimson Trail."

CHAPTER I.

GEOGRAPHY OF ROCKINGHAM COUNTY.

Rockingham County, Virginia, extends from the Blue Ridge on the southeast entirely across the great valley to the first Alleghany ranges on the northwest, and has an area of 870 square miles. Only two counties in the State, Augusta and Pittsylvania, are larger. Excepting a great notch, cut out of the east corner in 1831 in the formation of Page County, Rockingham is nearly a square, and lies on the map as if its corners were approaching the cardinal points of the compass in a right-hand turn. The corner farthest north extends nearly up to the 39th parallel of latitude, the south corner being almost as near to the 38th. As to longitude, the 79th meridian cuts it almost in half.

A line drawn due east from the north corner of Rockingham, and measured in that course 107 miles, would end in sight of the Washington Monument, on the south side towards Alexandria. One drawn southeastward from the south corner, and measured 87 miles, would end at a point near enough to Manchester and Richmond to be in sound of the chiming bells in those cities beside the James.

The northeastern half of the great valley of Virginia, comprising now the ten counties of Augusta, Rockingham, Page, Shenandoah, Warren, Frederick, Clark, Jefferson, Berkeley, and Morgan (the last three being in West Virginia), may properly be termed the Shenandoah Valley, since it is drained into the Potomac by the Shenandoah River through its several branches. Prior to the year 1738 the entire Shenandoah Valley, with much more territory west and southwest, was a part of Orange County. In 1738 it was cut off from Orange, and divided into two counties, Frederick and Augusta. In 1777 a large part of Augusta was cut off and erected into

A HISTORY OF

the county of Rockingham. These successive steps are shown in detail by the following copies of the respective Acts of Assembly authorizing them:

An act (passed November 1738), *for erecting two new Counties and Parishes; and granting certain encouragements to the Inhabitants thereof.*

I. Whereas, great numbers of people have settled themselves of late, upon the rivers of Sherrando, Cohongoruton, and Opeckon, and the branches thereof, on the north-west side of the Blue Ridge of mountains, whereby the strength of this colony, and it's security upon the frontiers, and his majesty's revenue of quit-rents, are like to be much increased and augmented; For giving encouragement to such as shall think fit to settle there,

II. *Be it enacted, by the Lieutenant Governor, Council, Burgesses, of this present General Assembly, and it is hereby enacted, by the authority of the same,* That all that territory and tract of land, at present deemed to be part of the County of Orange, lying on the north west side of the top of the said mountains, extending from thence northerly, westerly, and southerly, beyond the said mountains, to the utmost limits of Virginia, be separated from the rest of the said county, and erected into two distinct counties and parishes; to be divided by a line to be run from the head spring of Hedgman river [1] to the head spring of the river Potowmack: And that all that part of the said territory, lying to the northeast of the said line, beyond the top of the said Blue Ridge, shall be one distinct county, and parish; to be called by the name of the county of Frederick, and parish of Frederick: And that the rest of the said territory, lying on the other side of the said line, beyond the top of the said Blue Ridge, shall be one other distinct county, and parish; to be called by the name of the county of Augusta, and parish of Augusta. [2]

An Act (passed October 1777) *for forming several new counties, and reforming the boundaries of two others.*

Whereas it is represented to this present session of assembly, by the inhabitants of Augusta and Botetourt counties, that they labour under many inconveniences by reason of the great extent of the said counties and parishes: *Be it therefore enacted by the General Assembly,* That from and after the first day of March next the said county and parish of Augusta shall be divided by a line beginning at the north side of the North Mountain, opposite to the upper end of Sweedland Hill, and running a direct course so as to strike the mouth of Seneca creek, on the north fork of the

---

[1.] Hedgman River must be what is now called Conway River, forming part of the line between the counties of Madison and Greene.

[2.] Hening's Statutes, Vol. 5, pp. 78, 79.

ROCKINGHAM COUNTY

south branch of Potowmack river, and the same course to be continued to the Alleghany mountain, thence along the said mountain to the line of Hampshire county; and all that part of the said county and parish of Augusta which lies to the northward of the said line shall be added to and made part of the said county and parish of Hampshire. And that the residue of the county and parish of Augusta be divided by a line to begin at the South Mountain (Blue Ridge), and running thence by Benjamin Yardley's plantation so as to strike the north river below James Byrd's house, thence up the said river to the mouth of Naked creek, thence leaving the river a direct course so as to cross the said river at the mouth of Cunningham's branch, in the upper end of Silas Hart's land, to the foot of the North Mountain, thence fifty-five degrees west to the Alleghany Mountain, and with the same to the line of Hampshire; and all that part which lies north eastward of the said line shall be one distinct parish (county and parish), called and known by the name of Rockingham. [3]

Other parts of the same Act establish the counties of Green Brier and Rockbridge; fix the fourth Monday of every month as court day for Rockingham, the first session to be held at the house of Daniel Smith; establish the town of Lexington; change the name of Dunmore County to Shanando, etc.

As at first constituted in 1777, Rockingham County embraced the greater part of what is now Pendleton County, W. Va., and about a third part of what is now Page County, Va. Pendleton County was established in 1787: this transferred the northwest boundary of Rockingham some 25 miles southeastward—that is, from the Alleghany Mountain to its present position on the Shenandoah Mountain. Page County was established in 1831: this cut out from the east corner of Rockingham the big notch already mentioned.

The present boundaries of Rockingham may be indicated as follows: Beginning at the south corner, at a point on top of the Blue Ridge above Black Rock Springs, draw a line, straight throughout the greater part of its course, N. about 55 degrees W., some 32 miles to the top of Shenandoah Mountain; this gives the southwest boundary, separating from Augusta County; turn north about 30 degrees east, and fol-

---

3. Hening's Statutes, volume 9, pp. 420-424.

A HISTORY OF

low the top ridge of the Shenandoah Mountain some 30 miles, to a point opposite Peru, in Hardy County, W. Va.; this gives the northwest boundary, separating from Pendleton and Hardy; turn south about 50 degrees east, and measure a straight course some 26 miles to the top of Massanutten Mountain, above New Market; this gives the northeast boundary, separating from Hardy and Shenandoah. This is part of the original line between Frederick and Augusta, and is frequently called the Fairfax Line, since it marks the southwest limit of the famous Northern Neck, as claimed by Thomas Lord Fairfax. Turn now southwest and follow the crest of the Massanutten Mountain some 9 miles, then turn southeast and go about 12 miles to the top of the Blue Ridge, between Elkton and Shenandoah City; this gives the boundary about the notch, separating from Page County; finally, turn southwestward and follow the crest of the Blue Ridge about 20 miles to the beginning, above Black Rock; this gives the southeast boundary, separating from Greene and Albemarle.

The boundary line of Rockingham around the notch is given more specifically in the Act of 1831, creating Page County, as follows:

> Beginning at a point in the line of the counties of Rockingham and Orange, on the top of the Blue Ridge, opposite to the head waters of Naked creek, in the county of Rockingham; thence, a straight line to the head waters of said creek; thence, with the meanderings of said creek, to its junction with the South river; thence, down the bed of said river, to the upper end of Michael Shuler's island; thence, a straight line to the mouth of Shuler's run; thence, with the main branch of said run, to its source; thence, a straight line, to the top of the Massanutten mountain; thence, with the top of said mountain, . . .

The boundary line between Rockingham and Augusta was described in an address delivered October 15, 1896, by Judge John Paul, as follows:

> Beginning at the South Mountain (Blue Ridge), thence by a direct line past Benjamin Yardley's plantation (now Mohler's) so as to strike North River below James Byrd's house (James *Beard* is the way it is now spelled). The point is at Diehl's ford, about one mile and a half above the junction of Middle and North rivers. Thence up North River to the

ROCKINGHAM COUNTY

mouth of Naked Creek; thence by a direct line so as to cross North River at the mouth of Cunningham's branch (now Thorn Run). This point is at Mr. Sanger's house. Thence, same course, to the foot of North Mountain.

It will be observed from the foregoing statements that two streams by the name of Naked Creek appear in the geography of Rockingham. One of these heads in Augusta County, and forms a small part of the boundary line between the two counties, near Mt. Crawford; the other heads in Page County, and forms several miles of the boundary between that county and Rockingham, in the vicinity of Shenandoah City. Wholly within the county are two streams with the name of Dry River. Both head around the bases of Tomahawk Mountain, near the Pendleton line. One flows northeast and becomes part of the North Fork of the Shenandoah River at Fulk's Run; the other flows southeast and unites with North River at Bridgewater.

The most conspicuous, and perhaps the most wonderful, feature in the physical geography of Rockingham is the southwest promontory of the Massanutten, known as Peaked Mountain, or the Peak. Rising gradually to a great height, it juts out into the wide valley, then sinks down into the plain as completely and almost as abruptly as the rock of Gibraltar into the sea. From the east side it presents an appearance that strongly reminds one of Gibraltar.

The view from the Peak is one of the finest in the world. Behind one is the great hollow in the Peak itself, know as the Kettle; and beyond it are the triple ridges of the range, flanked on the west by the towering bulk of Laird's Knob. To the east is the billowy outline of the Blue Ridge; far to the west are the first ranges of the Alleghanies; halfway between the Peak and Harrisonburg is the long, wooded range of hills known as Chestnut Ridge; and farther back, thrown around the Peak in a great semicircle, are the seven huge, wooded cones that rise out of the plain to a height varying from 300 to 500 feet: Green Hill, beyond Linville; Round Hill, near Singer's Glen; Mole Hill, at Dale Enterprise; Round Hill, at

A HISTORY OF

Bridgewater; Wise's Hill, above Mt. Crawford; Shaver's Hill, near Friedens; and Long's Hill, toward Port Republic.

Beyond Green Hill, the North Fork of the Shenandoah River comes out of the Alleghanies, through Brock's Gap; is joined by Linville Creek at Broadway; flows on past Timberville; and, after receiving the waters of Long Glade Run, Smith's Creek, and other Rockingham streams, continues its meandering course down the Valley, west of the Massanutten range.

Beyond Round Hill at Bridgewater, North River comes out of the Alleghanies, through Briery Branch Gap and other gaps; is joined on its way by Dry River, Cook's Creek, Naked Creek, and many other streams; combines with Middle River near Mt. Meridian, on the line between Rockingham and Augusta; then receives the waters of South River at Port Republic. Here it surrenders its name, the big stream from Port Republic on being called the South Fork of the Shenandoah River. This, having swept down between the Blue Ridge and the Massanutten Peak, and having been augmented by Cub Run, Madison Run, Elk Run, and other Rockingham streams, continues down the Valley, east of the Massanutten Mountain, uniting with the North Fork of the Shenandoah River fifty miles below, at the northeast end of the Massanutten range.

Rockingham County is divided into five magisterial districts, namely, Ashby, Central, Linville, Plains, and Stonewall. The first is named for the great cavalry leader who fell, in 1862, just outside of Harrisonburg; the second is named from its position; the third bears the name of the creek that drains its fertile vales; the fourth has adopted the distinguishing term that has long been applied to the broad, level bottoms that skirt the North Fork of the Shenandoah between Timberville and New Market; and the fifth, with much appropriateness, is named for the hero of First Manassas, of Second Manassas, and of Port Republic. It was in Stonewall District, of Rockingham County, that Stonewall Jackson began and ended his brilliant Valley Campaign.

ROCKINGHAM COUNTY

Of these five districts, Plains is the largest. Its western half is the famous Brock's Gap country. In 1858, Jed Hotchkiss, a few years later renowned as Stonewall Jackson's chief topographical engineer, wrote of this country as follows:

"The region of Brock's Gap, inside, is large enough for a county by itself. I was not prepared to find as large a stream of water there as we did find, nor so much romantic scenery. All 'Germany' is inside, and it is some ways from the Gap."

The sturdy German race prevails all over Rockingham, particularly so, it seems, in the Brock's Gap country; hence the expression just quoted. In years past the region was frequently styled "Little Germany"; and one of the streams that drain it is called German River.

There has been a good deal of interesting speculation as to how Brock's Gap got its name. One tradition is to the effect that "General Brock," while on his way to relieve Fort Seybert, camped in the Gap, and thus gave it his name. If there was a General Brock in the Gap at the time referred to, it evidently was not the "Hero of Upper Canada." Fort Seybert was destroyed in 1758, and the general just designated was not born till 1769. It is most likely that the name was received from some resident of the Gap. In 1748, as the Augusta County records show, Daniel Holman and Peter Gartner became guardians for Julia, George, and Elsie Brock, orphans of Rudolph Brock, deceased. This shows that there were Brocks in this part of the Valley at a very early date. In 1752, as shown by the same records, Christian Funkhousa and Henry Brock sold to Jacob Bare 400 acres of land "on ye south fork of the North River of Shanando above the gap in ye mountain." The property was warranted specially against John P. Brock and his heirs. The witnesses were Peter Scholl, Samuel Newman, and John Bare. This seems to show conclusively that the Brock name was familiar in the Gap as early as 1752, or earlier.

With this brief outline of the geography of Rockingham County, let us proceed to the following chapters, in which, under the various heads, will be found many other facts that might properly be included here.

CHAPTER II.

GEOLOGICAL FEATURES OF ROCKINGHAM COUNTY.

BY

JUSTUS H. CLINE, M. A.,
Assistant Geologist, Virginia State Geological Survey.

On the basis of both geological and physiographic features the state of Virginia is divided into three great provinces: the Coastal Plain on the east, the Piedmont Plateau in the central part, and the Appalachian Mountain province on the west. Rockingham County lies entirely within the latter province.

The Appalachian Mountain province is further divided into three sub-provinces, each of which shows more or less marked differences in the topographic types represented, the Old Appalachians, or Blue Ridge, on the east; the Great Valley, in the centre; and the New Appalachians, or Alleghany Ridges, on the west. Each of the three subdivisions is well represented within the borders of the county.

The topography of the county, in keeping with that of the Appalachian Mountain province in general, is varied and picturesque; and with the exception of the main part of the Blue Ridge may be defined as the parallel ridge and valley type; the ridges being generally parallel with each other and extending in a northeast and southwest direction, in keeping with the strike of the underlying rock-structure.

The Blue Ridge, which forms the eastern boundary of the county, is distinct topographically from the rest of the area in that it presents an uneven and knobby crest, and shows an absence of the parallel ridge type in its main part, which is so well developed both in the valley and the ridges to the west. The foothills, or lower ridges, which flank the Blue Ridge on its western slope, being made up of rocks similar both in origin and structure to those of the west, partake

ROCKINGHAM COUNTY

more nearly of their topographic characters and really belong to the New Appalachian type. The highest point in the Blue Ridge in Rockingham County is High Knob, which attains an elevation of over 3600 feet above sea level.

The Shenandoah Valley province, which makes up the greater part of Rockingham County, when viewed from an elevation appears as a broad, undulating plain, traversed by a series of low ridges which barely appear above it. In these ridges the cherty beds of limestone, which are more resistant than the surrounding rocks, have given rise to a series of round, conical hills which dot the landscape at intervals of a few miles, and have an elevation of from two hundred to three hundred feet above the plain. Good examples of these are Round Hill near Bridgewater and Mole Hill near Dayton. The Shenandoah plain slopes gently toward the southwest as a rule and attains an elevation of about 1500 feet at Harrisonburg. The most conspicuous feature of the Valley province within the county is the Massanutten Mountain, which divides the northern part into two unequal divisions. This peculiar mountain, while only within a few miles of the Blue Ridge and parallel with it, shows no geological kinship with it, for it is in reality an outlier of the New Appalachian ridges about eighteen miles to the west. The mountain ends abruptly in a fine peak which is locally known as Peaked Mountain, 2900 feet above the sea. Laird's Knob, a few miles northward, attains an elevation of more than 3400 feet. The topography of the Massanutten Mountain is identical with that of the Alleghany ridges.

The Alleghany ridges and valleys embrace the western third of the county. These ridges show a more or less even crestline, and are arranged with a decided parallelism. The most elevated part of the county is within this province. High Knob in the Shenandoah Mountain has an elevation slightly more than 4200 feet. Practically all types of ridges found in an eroded region of folded sedimentary rocks occur here: the monoclinal, anticlinal, and synclinal. These ridges are frequently cut by gaps through which streams are now

A HISTORY OF

flowing or have flowed in a former period. The valleys between the ridges are narrow.

The drainage of Rockingham county belongs entirely to the Shenandoah system. The two master streams are the North Fork, which flows west of the Massanutten Mountain, and the main part of the Shenandoah, which flows through the Page valley east of the same mountain. These streams and their tributaries have cut the Shenandoah plain into a deep intaglio, and they now flow in channels from 100 to 300 feet below it. The streams of the county have for the most part adjusted themselves to the underlying structural conditions, and consequently they tend to flow in a northeasterly direction. The chief exception to this is the North River, which flows eastward near the southern border of the county. This stream, instead of flowing parallel with the strike of the rock formations, takes a course at right angles to the strike and maintains it till its influx with the main Shenandoah near the foot of the Blue Ridge. This is explained by the fact that its course antedates the folding of the rock strata which has occurred in the Appalachian province. The county is exceedingly well watered, and springs of large size are frequent.

The rocks of the county fall under the two great lithologic types, igneous and sedimentary. Both types occur in all three of the sub-provinces. It is understood that igneous rocks are those which have solidified from a molten condition, while the sedimentaries are those which are composed of material derived from the waste of land and redeposited in the form of mud, sand, gravel, chemical precipitants, etc., chiefly in lakes and seas.

The only dominantly igneous area in the county is the main part of the Blue Ridge. The formations of the rest of the county are sedimentary, with very minor exceptions. Certainly less than one per cent. of the rocks of the county which outcrop at the surface are of igneous origin, and all these with the few noted exceptions are entirely in the Blue Ridge.

The igneous rocks of the Blue Ridge in Rockingham County are of the basaltic type, which represent material

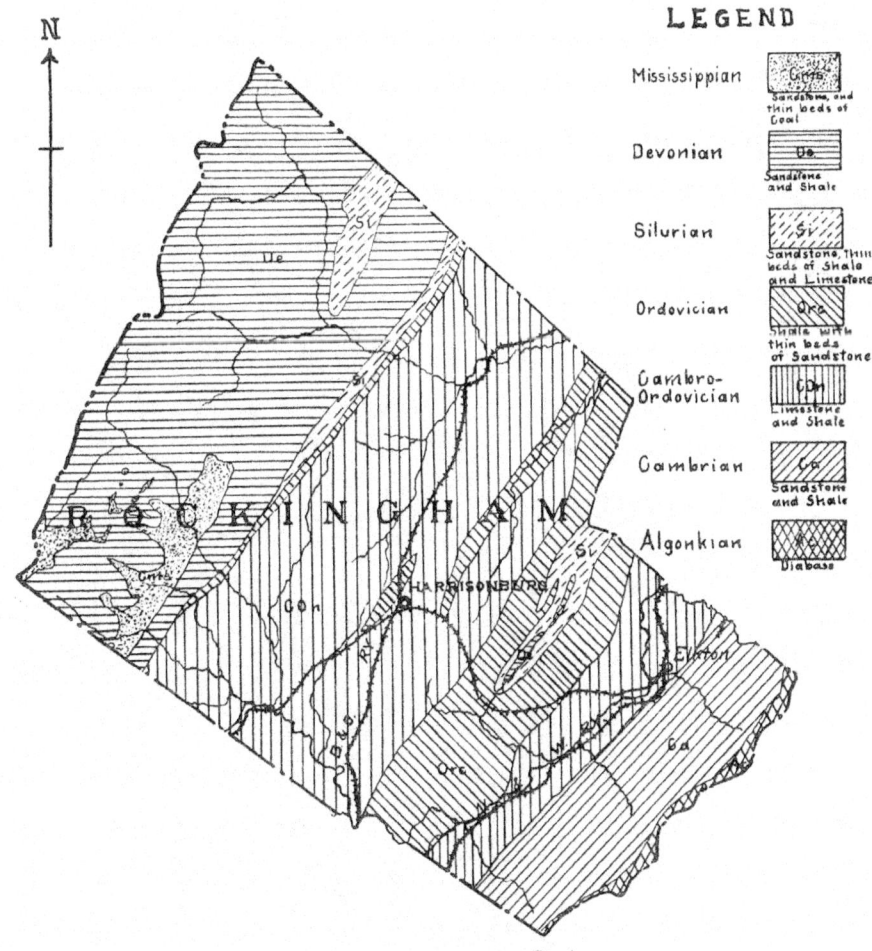

Geological Map of Rockingham County

ROCKINGHAM COUNTY

thrown out on the surface by the extrusive action of ancient volcanoes. The material in its original form was dark or almost black in color, but subsequent alterations and metamorphic changes have usually converted it into rock varying in color from a dark bluish-green to a light green, dependent on the secondary mineralogical constituents. Where these minerals are secondary amphibole and chlorite the rock is bluish green in color; and where epidote is the dominant alteration product the color is light green. There are all gradations between these different colors depending on the proportions of these minerals. Originally the essential minerals which made up the basalt was plagioclase feldspar, magnetite, and pyroxene, but subsequent alterations have almost entirely broken down the original mineral components giving rise chiefly to the three above mentioned, so that at present the rock may properly be termed an epidosite where the dominant mineral is epidote, an amphibolite where the dominant mineral is amphibole, and a chlorite-schist where the dominant mineral is chlorite. For all practical purposes the two latter types may rightly be thrown together and termed amphibolite-chlorite schists. The general name for this basaltic formation wherever it occurs in the Blue Ridge and the Piedmont plateau is Catoctin Schist, so called because it usually presents a slaty or schistose structure, induced by the folding of the earth's crust and the development of the secondary minerals contingent upon such conditions. The rock frequently shows material picked up by the liquid lava streams as they flowed over the ancient land surface covered with the material of older flows; and gas bubbles, or amugdules, are common in the upper surfaces. These cavities have since been filled by percolating waters carrying mineral matter in solution, the resulting minerals being usually epidote, calcite, and quartz. It is within the Catoctin Schist that the copper deposits of the Blue Ridge occur. The rock has been assigned to the Algonkian Period and is therefore one of the oldest formations occurring in the state, and certainly the oldest in the county.

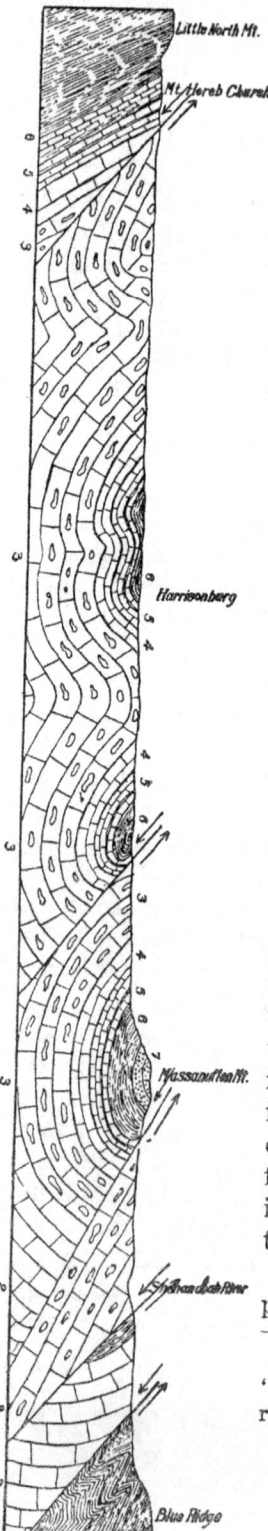

Late investigations have revealed that igneous rocks also occur in the county within the Valley province, in limited quantity, in the form of dikes. These rocks outcrop in the vicinity of Cross Keys and at intervals entirely across the county; the most westerly outcrop reported being in the vicinity of Brock's Gap. A characteristic exposure of these rocks is found near Harrisonburg, where the road leading from Harrisonburg to Keezletown crosses the Chesapeake - Western Railway tracks. The rock is of dark color and medium to fine grained. It weathers to rounded boulders, which are broken only with great difficulty. It is a typical diabase and is composed of the minerals magnetite, augite, olivine, and plagioclase feldspar as essential ingredients. The rock is comparatively fresh, and is probably the youngest of the rock formations in the county, having been forced while in a molten condition into the fissures of the limestone and shale formations of the mountains. While the exact age of the rock cannot be determined, on lithological grounds it may be assigned to the Triassic.[1] The rock, owing to its high lime and iron content, makes road material of the first quality, since it has the necessary ingredients to bind and is far superior to limestone in lasting qualities.

The sedimentary rocks of the county present every phase of sedimentary

---

[1.] Thos. L. Watson and Justus H. Cline, "Dikes of the Shenandoah Valley," in preparation.

ROCKINGHAM COUNTY

possibilities, and rocks of every age occur from the beginning of the Cambrian to the Lower Coal period. Starting with the oldest rocks of this type in the county we find sandstones, which are frequently conglomeritic, and shales of Cambrian age making up the foothills or lower ridges which flank the Blue Ridge on its western slope. This formation rests on the Catoctin Schist as a base and the material of which they are composed was probably derived from it and from other igneous and sedimentary formations to the east of the Blue Ridge. The thickness of the Cambrian sandstone and shale formation may be estimated at from 2000 to 3000 feet. The lower part of the formation is dominantly sandstone, and the upper part shaley. The age of the formation has been determined by the remains of animal life which are preserved extensively in one of the sandstone beds in the form of worm borings by the species *scolithus linearis*, characteristic of the Cambrian.

The Cambrian shales grade into Shenandoah limestone, which succeeds them without break in the sedimentary record, the lower part of the limestone formation also being Cambrian.

The thickness of the Shenandoah limestone is from 1500 to 2500 feet. The upper part is definitely known to be Ordovician in age, from the fossils it contains, but there is no definite line of division marked between the known Ordovician and the known Cambrian. Five distinct divisions of this limestone in central western Virginia have been described by Prof. H. D. Campbell. These are, in ascending order, (1) Sherwood Limestone of Lower Cambrian age, (2) Buena Vista shales of Lower or Middle Cambrian age, (3) Natural Bridge limestone of Middle and Upper Cambrian and Lower Ordovician, (4) Murat limestone, and (5) Liberty Hall limestone of Middle Ordovician age. The Murat and Liberty are probably absent in Rockingham County, and their places occupied by the above and dolomitic limestones of Stones River age and the pure and argillaceous strata designated as the Chambersburg formation. Fossils found near Harrisonburg have identified both these formations at that place.

A HISTORY OF

The Shenandoah limestone varies in color from a grey to dove color and blue. It contains frequent cherty beds, the weathering of which gives rise to the ridges and gravelly hills common in the county. Shaley beds also occur within the limestone of varying thickness. The most prominent of these are the Buena Vista shales of Cambrian age, which are easily recognized by their reddish color. In composition the rock varies from an almost pure limestone to dolomite, in which the lime is replaced largely by magnesia. The rock also shows widely varying percentages of clayey material and silica. The Chambersburg and Stones River formations and the associated Trenton shales afford splendid material for the manufacture of Portland cement.

In the upper part of the Shenandoah limestone shaley beds appear, which increase in frequency and thickness till the formation entirely gives way to the Martinsburg shale. This shale formation occupies a prominent synclinal trough extending entirely across the county. This syncline is known as the Massanutten syncline, since its position is partly occupied by the mountain of the same name. The syncline is very persistent, and extends far beyond the limits of the mountain both to the northeast and southwest. There are also other minor areas of the shale formation which may be seen on the accompanying map. The thickness of the formation is about 2000 feet. The fine blue slate lands of the county are underlain by the lower beds of this formation. The weathering of the shale gives rise to the characteristic rounded hills with oval crests, often very similar in form to the drumlins of glacial origin in the northern part of the United States. The contact between the shale and limestone can readily be detected by the abrupt change in the topography.

The Martinsburg shale is succeeded by the Massanutten sandstone, so called from its occurrence in the mountain by that name. It is to the resistant character of this rock that the Massanutten mountain owes its existence. The thickness of the sandstone is about 500 feet. It varies from a reddish sandy shale to a coarse conglomerate and light grey massive

ROCKINGHAM COUNTY

bedded quartzite. A typical exposure of this quartzite is found at the nose of Peaked Mountain. The formation also occurs in the Alleghany ridges. Its age is Silurian.

The rocks of the Alleghany ridges are as follows, given in order of age: (1) the Martinsburg shale and (2) Massanutten sandstone, which have been described above; (3) Rockwood formation of Silurian age, composed of reddish micaceous sandstones, which grade upward into reddish and brown shales capped with a bed of greyish to yellowish quartzite. The thickness of the formation is about 200 feet. (4) Lewistown limestone of Silurian age, containing numerous fossil corals and braciopods and remains of sponges and microscopic organisms. Its thickness is about 100 feet. (5) Monterey sandstone of Silurian and Devonian age, in part calcareous. The thickness is about 300 feet. (6) The dark colored Romney shales of Devonian age, which were deposited on the eroded surface of the Monterey sandstone. This nonconformity represents the only break in the sedimentary cycle within the bounds of Rockingham County. The thickness of the formation approaches 1000 feet. (7) Jennings formation, also of Devonian age, which is made up of olive to buff colored shales interstratified with massive fine-grained sandstones. Its thickness is about 3000 feet. It is succeeded by the (8) Hampshire formation, made up of thinly bedded grey and reddish sandstone and thick bedded sandstone, all interbedded with thin layers of shale. The formation is as thick as 1400 feet, and it is of Devonian age. (9) The Pocono sandstone of Mississippian age, which is the youngest of the sedimentaries in the county. It is composed of light grey sandstones of a rather coarse texture, which are interbedded with thin layers of semi-anthracite coal. It is about 700 feet in thickness.

The structure of the rocks of Rockingham County can best be understood by reference to the accompanying structure section. It will be remembered that the sedimentary rocks of the county were originally laid down by water in the order in which they now occur, but in a horizontal position. The

A HISTORY OF

beds are rarely found in this position, but have been folded into anticlines and synclines and frequently broken by great overthrust faults and also by simple gravity faults.

Since the folding and faulting of the region, erosion has been active, so that now the mountain ridges frequently occupy the position of the synclines, as in the case of the Massanutten mountain; and the river valleys in the same way occupy the position of the anticlines. The Valley province is not a structural valley, but it is entirely the product of erosion. The material which once occupied its position, being less resistant to the forces of degradation, was disintegrated by chemical and mechanical forces and carried by the streams to the sea. The streams which have been responsible for this work have suffered likewise many changes, and now in a small measure only resemble their early ancestors. The drainage of the county at the beginning of the long cycle of erosion which developed its present land forms seems to have been controlled by two master streams. One of these streams occupied a position similar to North River, in the latitude of Bridgewater, and the other a position similar to the North Fork, in the latitude of Brock's Gap; the North River flowing across the Valley and Blue Ridge, possibly through Brown's Gap, and the North Fork across the Valley and the Massanutten Mountain at New Market and the Blue Ridge opposite Luray. Since the limestones of the Valley were more easily eroded than the harder rocks of the Blue Ridge, and since the Potomac came to be the master stream because of its size, tributaries of the Potomac flowing northward over the soft rocks of the valley were finally able to intercept these streams, first the North Fork at Luray and later the North River at Port Republic. Subsequently to these captures the Valley has been lowered many hundred feet below its level at the time the captures took place.

The limestones of the Valley province are responsible for the numerous beautiful limestone caverns and bold springs which are so common, as well as for the remarkable fertility of the soils of the county, which has made her one of the

ROCKINGHAM COUNTY

most desirable agricultural districts in the entire country. The hand of Providence working through long ages has prepared a habitation for men, which in the beauty of topography and landscape, fertility of soil, excellence of water, delightfulness of climate, luxuriance of vegetation, and all natural environment that makes for human happiness, can hardly be excelled in the entire world.

MASSANUTTEN MOUNTAIN.

By Miss Ruth Conn.

Where the peak of old Massanutten
    Doth bare his broad dome to the skies,
And clad with the strength of Creation
    Unmindful of ages doth rise,

He guards day and night our green valley;
    For Nature who made it so fair,
Grew alarmed for her beautiful treasure,
    And placed him as sentinel there.

When the gray morning mists of the Valley,
    That are wont to encircle his crest,
Have long faded into the sunlight,
    And wandering winds are at rest,

When from off of his summit has faded
    The glow of the evening bars,
He brings from the worlds shining o'er him
    Sweet dreams to our "Child of the Stars."

This sacred trust of Creation
    He kept since the world began,
Till he smiled on the red man's wigwam
    And the hut of the first white man.

And oft in the struggles that followed,
    He echoed the martial tramp,
And sheltered the fires where our fathers
    Lay waiting with Stonewall in camp.

He has stood with us in every struggle,
    Though burdened methinks with our pain;
He has pointed to courage and patience,
    And helped us new visions to gain.

Oh, fairer than Italy's mountains,
    Or Switzerland's snow-crowned towers,
He is to the sons of the Valley—
    This rugged old mountain of ours!

Dear old Peak, thou art guarding thy treasure:
    May men to their trust prove as true!
Not one of Virginia's blue mountains
    Is so dear to our hearts as are you.

McGaheysville, Rockingham County,
    Virginia, May, 1912.

GENERAL JOHN SEVIER
(Pages 348, 349)

CHAPTER III.

THE FIRST WHITE SETTLERS.

1727—1738.

From the best information at hand, it appears that the settlement of Rockingham and adjacent sections of the Valley of Virginia began in or about the year 1727. As in all similar cases, exploration preceded permanent settlement. First, therefore, let us take a preliminary survey of the earliest known explorations.

In 1669, the same year that La Salle came down to the falls of the Ohio, John Lederer, a German of education, said to have been once a Franciscan monk, came up from Jamestown and entered the Valley at or near Waynesboro; in 1670 he crossed the Valley at or near Front Royal and Strasburg. Once above, once below the present boundaries of Rockingham, this German thus seemed to be marking out the district in which his fellow-countrymen should in the years to come build their homes and till their fruitful fields. Lederer's journal, giving an account of his explorations, with accompanying map, was printed in an English translation at London in 1672, and again at Rochester, N. Y., in 1902.

In 1705 the Governor, Council, and Burgesses of Virginia offered a monopoly of trade to any person or persons who should thereafter "at his or their own charge, make discovery of any town or nation of Indians, situate or inhabiting to the westward of, or between the Appalatian mountains."[1] This was an act obviously intended to encourage pioneering west of the Blue Ridge. What response it elicited we do not know, but it may well be imagined that not many years passed before

---

1. Hening's Statutes, Vol. III, page 468.

A HISTORY OF

some adventurous trader fared westward upon the heels of the hope it engendered.

In 1716 Governor Spotswood made his famous expedition into the Valley, coming across the Blue Ridge, as we judge, at Swift Run Gap, and finding a land of "seek-no-farther" in the broad river plains about or above Elkton. We generally look upon Spotswood as doing for the Virginians, in respect to the Valley, what Caesar did for the Romans, in respect to Britain: as discovering it for them: and even as it was a century before the Romans followed Caesar westward, so it was at least a decade before the Virginians began to follow Spotswood. In the meantime Germans occasionally came in from the northeast. More of Spotswood and his knights at another place.

In 1722 Michael Wohlfárth, a German sectarian, is reported to have passed down through the Valley of Virginia going from Pennsylvania to North Carolina;[2] Dr. J. A. Waddell, after investigating various sources of information, is satisfied that in or about the year 1726 John Salling and John Mackey explored the Valley, both settling therein later;[3] and it is likely that other white men, Germans, Scotch-Irish, and English, at other times before as well as after, walked in this great highway of nature from north to south.

We are now coming to the time of permanent settlement, which we are able to fix some five years earlier than 1732, the date so long accepted as marking the beginnings in the Valley. In 1732 Jost Hite, with a number of other Germans, settled in the section now marked by Winchester; and in the same year John Lewis, with a number of other Scotch-Irish, located at or near the place where Staunton now stands; but it appears that as early as 1727 Adam Miller, a German, perhaps with a few others of his own nationality, was staking out claims on the south fork of the Shenandoah River, on or near the line that now divides Rockingham County from Page.

[2.] Sachse's German Sectarians, Vol. II, page 332.

[3.] Waddell's Annals of Augusta, edition 1902, page 24.

ROCKINGHAM COUNTY

On March 13, 1741-2, Adam Miller received from Governor William Gooch a certificate of naturalization, which recites that the said Miller had been a resident on the Shenandoah for the past fifteen years. This fixes the date of his first settlement in 1726-7.[4] In 1733, eight men, Adam Miller being one, addressed Governor Gooch in a petition, praying him to confirm their title to 5000 acres of land in Massanutting, purchased about four years past for more than 400 pounds from Jacob Stover, reciting that they had moved upon the said land from Pennsylvania immediately after the purchase, and that they had located thereon at the time of the petition nine plantations and 51 people.[5] This would fix the date of settlement of the Massanutting colony in 1729 or 1730.

On June 17, 1730, Jacob Stover, a native of Switzerland, was granted leave by the colonial council to take up 10,000 acres of land on the south fork of the Shenandoah, for the settlement of himself and divers Germans and Swiss whom he proposed to bring thither within the next two years, the said land to be laid off in such tracts as he should judge fitting.[6] Stover selected his grant in two tracts, of 5000 acres each, one along the river between the present Luray and Elkton, the other along the same river, higher up, between

---

4. The certificate is in the possession of Adam Miller's great-great-granddaughter, Miss Elizabeth B. Miller, of Elkton, Va. It was printed in the William and Mary College Quarterly, October, 1900, and in Wayland's "German Element," pages 37, 38, in 1907.

5. The full text of this petition may be found in Palmer's Calendar of State Papers, Vol. I, pp. 219, 220, and in Wayland's "German Element," pp. 35, 36. It bears no date, but the date has been conclusively determined, by various circumstances, to be 1733.

6. From records of the proceedings of the Council. These records, particularly such as refer to the settlement of the Valley of Virginia, were published in 1905-6 in the Virginia Magazine of History and Biography, Richmond, with valuable supplementary notes by Mr. Chas. E. Kemper, of Washington, D. C.

Jacob Stover was an interesting character—enterprising to a fault, it would seem. It is charged that some of his representations in

A HISTORY OF

Elkton and Port Republic.[7] The conditions upon which Stover received his grant were that he should actually locate a family of settlers upon each thousand acres within two years. These were the conditions usually imposed upon those receiving large grants of land at that time. Upon satisfactory proof that these conditions had been discharged, a permanent title was given.

The names of the eight petitioners of 1733, who had bought land in Massanutten of Jacob Stover in 1729 or 1730, were as follows:

Adam Miller[8]   Philip Long   Hans Rood[10]
Abram Strickler Paul Long   Michael Kaufman
Mathias Selzer[9] Michael Rhinehart

The family names of all these men, with perhaps one or two exceptions, are to-day familiar and widely distributed, not only in the counties of Rockingham, Page, and Shenandoah, but also in many quarters beyond the limits of Virginia.

It is quite probable that Adam Miller at first pre-empted his claim on the Shenandoah by squatter right, later meeting properly the requirements of advancing governmental authority. It is possible, moreover, that the enterprising Stover sold him and his friends the Massanutten tract before the said Stover himself had a grant for it, since, as we have seen, the latter did not receive his grant until June 17, 1730. The alarm of the eight petitioners of 1733 arose from fear

---

securing grants of land were worthy of Machiavelli. See Kercheval's History of the Valley of Virginia, reprint of 1902, page 46.

[7.] Mr. Chas. E. Kemper fixes the location of Stover's lower tract of 5000 acres, likely the same purchashed by Adam Miller and others in 1729, between Bear Lithia Spring, two miles below Elkton, in Rockingham County, and Newport, a village 12 miles further down the river, in Page County. See Virginia Magazine of History and Biography, January, 1906, pp. 295-297. It should be stated, however, that the little vale and the village that still retain the name of Massanutten are a few miles farther northeast, beyond Newport.

[8.] Adam Miller, who appears to have been the first settler of Rockingham and adjacent sections of the Valley, was born probably at Schrei-

ROCKINGHAM COUNTY

that William Beverly had an earlier or better claim than Stover. They had learned that Beverly was bringing suit against Stover for the land in question.

On May 5, 1732, William Beverly, son of Robert Beverly the historian of Virginia, had received a grant of 15,000 acres on the Shenandoah River, including "a place called the Massanutting Town," provided the same did not interfere with any previous grants made in that section. Obviously

---

sheim, Germany, the native place of Alexander Mack, about the year 1700. He came early in life to Lancaster County, Pa., with his wife and an unmarried sister. Later, going to Williamsburg, Va., he heard of the beautiful valley between the mountains from some Spotswood knights, and followed their path westward, crossing the Blue Ridge at Swift Run Gap. Having seen and desired the goodly land in the river plain below, he brought his family thither. He secured first the "uppermost of the Massanutten lots," near the present Page County line, but probably in Rockingham; in 1741 he purchased 820 acres, including the great lithia spring near Elkton, and was living thereon in 1764 when he sold 280 acres thereof to his son-in-law, Jacob Bear. Here Adam Miller lived till he died about 1780, and here the Bear family still resides, the spring being known as Bear Lithia Spring. He was a soldier in the French and Indian War, as shown by the military schedule for 1758 in Hening's Statutes. In religion he was a Lutheran, and was probably buried at St. Peter's Church, four miles north of Elkton. Among his descendants are the Millers, Bears, Kempers, Yanceys, Gibbons, Hopkins, Mauzys, Harnsbergers, and other prominent families of East Rockingham. A descendant, Hon. Chas. E. Kemper of Washington City, deserves special mention for his valuable publications regarding the pioneer.

9. Mathias Selzer of "Missinotty" is referred to by Gottschalk, a Moravian missionary, in his journal of 1748 as "the son-in-law of Jacob Beyerly, of Lancaster"; as rich, generous, and respected in the whole region, but as bitter against the Moravians. He was evidently a Lutheran. In 1751 he was one of the justices of Augusta County (Summers' History of Southwestern Virginia, p. 821), a fact which shows that he lived southwest of the Fairfax line.

10. Hans Rood (John Rhodes) was doubtless the Mennonite preacher visited at Massanutten by Gottschalk in 1748, and, with his family, massacred by Indians in 1766. See Virginia Magazine of History and Biography, July, 1904, page 69, and Kercheval's History of the Valley of Virginia, reprint of 1902, pp. 101, 102. It is likely that Abram Strickler and Michael Kaufman were also Mennonites.

—37—

there was an interference of this grant with the one made to Stover in 1730. On December 12, 1733, Beverly entered a caveat against Stover, but the latter was sustained in his title, and given deeds for his two tracts of 5000 acres each on the 15th of December, 1733.[11] The fears of the eight petitioners, who held their title from Stover, were thus evidently set at rest.

Recalling now the fact that Stover's upper tract of 5000 acres, as well as the lower one, was granted upon the condition that at least one family should be located on each 1000 acres within two years, and observing that he got full title for both tracts in December, 1733, we may safely conclude that no less than five families were settled by that date along the river between the points now marked by Elkton and Port Republic. Beginning, therefore, at or near the Fairfax line, which marked the northeast boundary of Rockingham till 1831, and following up the south fork of the Shenandoah River past the places now known as Shenandoah City, Elkton, and Island Ford to Lynnwood and Port Republic, we may say that at least fifteen families, all probably German or Swiss, were settled in that district by December, 1733. Counting five persons to a family, there were likely no less than 75 individuals; and among these we know the names of nine: Adam Miller, Abram Strickler, Mathias Selzer, Philip Long, Paul Long, Michael Rhinehart, Hans Rood, Michael Kaufman, and Jacob Stover—all doubtless heads of families.

On April 23, 1734, the colonial council received a petition from a number of the inhabitants living on the northwest side of "the Blue Ridge of Mountains," that is to say in the Valley, praying that some persons in their section be appointed magistrates to determine differences and punish offenders. These petitioners lived so far away from Fredericksburg, the county-seat of Spotsylvania, and consequently so far from

---

11. See records of the colonial council; also extracts therefrom printed in the Virginia Magazine of History and Biography, October, 1905, and January, 1906.

ROCKINGHAM COUNTY

the regular administration of justice, that the reasonableness of their request was obvious. Accordingly, Joost Hyte, Morgan Morgan, John Smith, Benjamin Bourden, and George Hobson were appointed justices within the limits aforesaid— that is, in the Valley. Hite and one or more of the others lived in the lower Valley, but it is likely that one or two of the five either lived in the upper Valley, or were frequently prospecting in that section. Burden later had large holdings of land in what is now Rockbridge County and adjacent sections.

Moreover, in August, 1734, just a few months after the aforesaid petition was presented, the county of Orange was formed. This was an act likely intended to be a still more satisfactory response to the request and desire of the Valley settlers for the efficient administration of law and justice. It shows the growth of political organization westward, and also indicates that the settlement of the Valley had reached a somewhat general stage by 1734. The rapid development from 1734 to 1738 is implied in the fact that in 1738 an Act was passed providing for the organization of the Valley and the country westward therefrom into the counties of Frederick and Augusta.

Let us now give attention to a number of items that show the progress of settlement from 1734 to 1738 in more detail.

On October 28, 1734, John Tayloe, Thomas Lee, and William Beverly obtained a grant of 60,000 acres of land on the Shenandoah River, beginning on Stover's upper tract. This grant accordingly must have extended southwest from the vicinity of Port Republic, up the river past Grottoes, and a considerable distance into the present limits of Augusta County. It was bestowed upon the usual conditions, that one family be located upon each thousand acres within two years.[12]

From Deed Book No. 1, Orange County, the following items have been selected:

[12.] See Virginia Magazine of History and Biography, April, 1906, pp. 360-362.

A HISTORY OF

September 17, 1735, Jacob Stover sold 550 acres of land to Christian Clemon, the said land being on a small run, on the south side of the Shenandoah River, adjoining the "upper corner of Stover's lower 5000-acre tract." Two of the three witnesses to this conveyance were Thomas Hill and W. Russell; the name of the third witness appears to be G. Home.

November 11, 1735, Jacob Stover sold two tracts of land to George Boone, the said tracts containing 500 and 1000 acres respectively, and being situated "near the end of North Mountain,[13] so called, on a small branch of Sherando River": part of 5000 acres laid out for Stover by the Virginia Council, June 17, 1730.[14] Mordecai Simon and S. Hughes were witnesses. Boone is put down as having come from Oley, Pa.

December 16, 1735, Jacob Stover sold 1100 acres, in three tracts, on Gerundo River,[15] to Ludwick Stone. On the same date he sold three tracts, aggregating 500 acres, on the same river, to Mathias Selser.

At least three more men bought land of Stover on this date: (1) John Prupecker, two tracts, of 300 acres and 200 acres, respectively; both on Gerundo River, the larger adjoining the land of Selser; witnesses, John Bramham, Gideon Marr,

---

13. The Massanutten at this time was commonly referred to as the North Mountain, and the Blue Ridge as the South Mountain.

14. Boone's Run is probably the small branch referred to, likely bearing its name from George Boone. It flows southeastward out of Runkle's Gap, in the Massanutten, directly toward Elkton, then turns northeastward and enters the river two miles below Elkton. One can hardly determine whether Stover sold this land from his upper or lower tract. One would at once say, From the lower, were it not likely that he had sold the lower tract entire to Adam Miller and his friends in 1729 or 1730.

15. "Gerundo" is merely another form of Shenandoah. This name has been found in no less than twenty different spellings. See Wayland's "German Element," page 3. No attempt is made herein to reduce the spelling of proper names, of either places or persons, to uniformity. The diverse forms in which they appear are part of the material of history, and have a value.

ROCKINGHAM COUNTY

William Ferrell; (2) Abraham Strickler, 1000 acres, at "Mesenutten on Gerundo"; (3) Henry Sowter, 300 acres, on the south side of Gerundo, near the mouth of Mesenutten Creek.

Some of these tracts, sold by Stover, in December, 1735, were possibly never within the limits of Rockingham County, but all were evidently near the Fairfax line, on one side or the other.

We may place the following land sales, made in 1736, in the same locality. The complete records may be found in Orange County Deed Book No. 1.

February 24, 1736, Ludwig Stein sold 517 acres, in three tracts, on Gerundo River, to Michael Cryter of Pennsylvania; witnesses, Gideon Marr, John Newport. On the same date Ludowick Stein sold 217 acres, on Gerundo River (part of land formerly granted to Jacob Stover), to Michael Coffman.

September 21, 1736, Jacob Stover sold 400 acres, on the west side of Sherundo River, to Peter Bowman; witnesses, G. Lightfoot, Thomas Nichols.

September 26, 1736, Henry Sowter sold about 300 acres, on Gerundo River, to Ludwig Stine.

In Orange County Deed Books 1 and 2 are to be found records of the following land sales on the South Shenandoah in 1737:

February 24, three tracts; Ludwig Stein to Martin Coffman of Pennsylvania: 300 acres on the south side of the river; 217 on the north side; and 100 acres on the north side, at Elk Lick.

October 22, 400 acres; Peter Bowman to Christian Redlicksberger. This was probably the same tract that Bowman had purchased of Jacob Stover in September of the preceding year.

Several transactions of special interest appear in the year 1738. On March 21 Jacob Stover sold to Christopher Franciski 3000 acres, with the mansion house, adjoining Peter Bowman on the river: part of 5000 acres patented to the said Stover, December 15, 1733. The same day Jacob Stover

A HISTORY OF

and his wife Margaret gave a bond to Franciski for £700. At another time within the year they gave him another bond for £1000. To secure the payment of these bonds, Stover and his wife mortgaged 5000 acres on both sides of the Shenandoah River.[16]

How Stover could keep on selling his 5000-acre tracts, and still have them seven or eight years after the first sale, is a mystery. Possibly he took back some land on default of payment; or he may have obtained more than two 5000-acre grants.

March 23, 1738, Ludwig Stein sold two tracts of land aggregating 1005 acres, on the Shenandoah River, to Philip Long; witnesses, John Newport and Christian Kleman.[17]

December 13, 1738, Jacob Stover obtained a grant of 800 acres. This land was on the Shenandoah River, below Port Republic, and was at least in part on the south side of the river, opposite the "Great Island." This island, containing about 60 acres, was purchased of the Franciscos on August 31, 1751, by Thomas Lewis. Two days earlier, August 28, 1751, Lewis had bought of the Franciscos a tract of 470 acres, on the south side of the river, part of the 800-acre tract granted to Stover in 1738.[18]

Christopher Franciscus—"the old Stopfel Franciscus," as he was termed in 1749 by one of the Moravian missionaries who passed through the Valley—[19] had large holdings of land in what is now East Rockingham. He appears to have located in Lancaster County, Pa., in 1709.[20] It is not certain that he ever located permanently in Virginia himself, but he evidently was in the Valley frequently, and his sons, Christopher and Ludwig, were permanent residents.[21]

---

16. See Orange County Deed Book No. 2, pp. 229-234.
17. Idem, page 260.
18. Augusta County Deed Book No. 4, pp. 58-65.
19. Virginia Magazine of History and Biography, October, 1903.
20. Rupp's Thirty Thousand Names, page 436.
21. For more particulars concerning Franciscus and his sons, see Wayland's "German Element," pp. 54-56.

ROCKINGHAM COUNTY

It is evident, from the foregoing particulars, that a considerable number of settlers had located within the present boundaries of Rockingham within the decade following the first known settlement in 1727. The earliest settlements were in the eastern side of the county, though it is quite likely that the tide of immigration that was creeping up the north fork of the Shenandoah had also reached and passed the Fairfax line, west of the Massanutten, by 1734 or 1735. As early as April 30, 1732, William Beverly wrote that the "northern men" were fond of buying land on the upper Shenandoah, because they could get it there six or seven pounds cheaper a hundred acres than in Pennsylvania, and because they did not care to go as far as Williamsburg.[22] It should be remembered also that John Lewis located at or near Staunton in 1732, and that a number of his fellow-countrymen came into the upper Valley with him, or soon after he came. These facts are recalled here in addition to what is definitely known concerning the first settlers and settlements, to show that a large number of persons, Germans, Scotch-Irish, and others, had located in and about the present limits of Rockingham by the year 1738. The majority of these settlers had come up the Valley from Maryland and Pennsylvania, but a few had come across the Blue Ridge from East Virginia.

The first grants of land were sought and secured along the main watercourses, though it is said that in many cases the settlers in a little while sought dwelling places on the higher lands toward the hills and mountains, because of the malaria that infested the bottom-lands. It is not likely, however, that such conditions caused any one to relinquish permanently his fertile holdings along the rivers; and with the development of civilization—the clearing of lowland thickets, the draining of swamps and marshes, the erection of better dwellings—the malaria gradually disappeared.

---

22. Waddell's Annals of Augusta, 1902 edition, page 21.

CHAPTER IV.

ROCKINGHAM AS PART OF AUGUSTA.

1738—1777.

When the first white settlers located in what is now Rockingham County, the whole district west of the Blue Ridge was a part of the county of Spotsylvania. It was thus until 1734, when Orange was formed so as to include within its limits the country west of the Ridge. The Valley thus continued a part of Orange till 1738, when, by an Act of the colonial government, that part of Orange west of the said mountain was divided into the two new counties of Frederick and Augusta. The text of this Act has already been given in Chapter I. The district later organized as Rockingham County fell within the limits of Augusta, according to the division of the Valley made in 1738. The complete organization of Frederick and Augusta was delayed for several years, the first courts being held for the former in 1743, and for the latter in 1745. In 1739 the inhabitants of the lower Valley, impatient at the delay, petitioned Governor Gooch, requesting that the said county of "Frederica" might immediately "take place." About fifty men signed the petition, but none apparently from the upper part of the Valley.[1] We have already seen, however, in Chapter III, that in Augusta, particularly in that part later to become Rockingham, settlement was going rapidly on. From various sources we are enabled to get occasional glimpses through the heavy curtain of years, and recognize some of the figures moving upon that far-off, pioneer stage.

---

1. For a list of the names signed to this petition, see Wayland's "German Element," pp. 57, 58.

ROCKINGHAM COUNTY

A few years years ago, Mr. Charles E. Kemper, a native of Rockingham, and Rev. William J. Hinke, a native of Germany, discovered in the archives of the old Moravian church at Bethlehem, Pa., a series of diaries that had been kept by Moravian missionaries who traveled through the Valley and adjacent parts of Virginia during the years from 1743 to 1753. Mr. Hinke translated these diaries from the German, Mr. Kemper edited them by supplying historical and geographical notes, and then the annotated translations were published in the Virginia Magazine of History and Biography. In these matter-of-fact records, made by zealous heralds of the cross more than a century and a half ago, we find many things of interest relating to persons and conditions in what is now the county of Rockingham.

On July 21, 1747, the Moravian brethren, Leonard Schnell and Vitus Handrup, were in the vicinity of Linville and Broadway, and staid over night with an Irishman who must have lived somewhere below Timberville. They had come across the mountains from what is now Pendleton County, West Virginia, and were traveling on down the Valley toward Winchester. The next spring Brother Gottschalk, who appears to have followed thus far the general course taken by Schnell and Handrup, likely fell in with the same son of Erin. He writes:

> At night [about April 1, 1748] I lodged in a very disorderly, wicked and godless house of an Irishman, who kept an inn. The Saviour helped me through.

Who this Irish innkeeper was cannot now be determined; but he lived near the site of Timberville.

Under date of April 2 Brother Gottschalk writes:

> I continued the journey on foot to the Germans. I crossed the Chanador,[2] which was pretty deep, cold, and had a rapid current. If the Lord had not supported me in the water by his angels, the rapid stream would have carried me off, for I was hardly twenty feet above a fall.

Having gone down the Valley to Cedar Creek, Gottschalk

---

2. The north fork of the Shenandoah.

turned southeastward, crossed the Massanutten Mountain through the picturesque Powell's Fort, and came up the south fork of the Shenandoah to the Massanutten settlements. One night he lodged with John Rhodes, the Mennonite preacher, who was doubtless one of the pioneer settlers. The next day he went to the home of Matthias Selzer, of whom he speaks as follows:

> He is a rude and hostile man towards the Brethren. I was compelled to stay with this man all afternoon, because I wanted to make inquiries about the people in that district and because I was surrounded by water and terribly high mountains on all sides. He treated me very rudely, called me a Zinzendorfian, threatened me with imprisonment, and referred to the travels and sermons of the Brethren in a very sarcastic manner. He said if I should get to the upper Germans they would soon take me by the neck, for he did not know what business I had among those people. In the first place we had been forbidden to travel around through the country, and then again they had such an excellent minister, that if the people were not converted by his sermons, they would certainly not be converted by my teaching. But soon afterwards he related of the excellent Lutheran minister that he got so drunk in his house that on his way home he lost his saddle, coat, and everything else from the back of his horse. I was silent to all this, but prayed for the poor man that the Lord might open his eyes.

Having staid over night with Mr. Selzer, Brother Gottschalk set out eastward to cross the Blue Ridge. His host, with no mean courtesy, speeded the parting guest, the latter being witness:

> I started early. Matthias Selzer saddled two horses and took me not only across the South Branch of the Chanador, but even five miles farther so that I could not go astray.[3]

Having crossed the Blue Ridge, Gottschalk descended into the beautiful valley of the Robinson River, now in Madison County, and became the guest of Rev. George Samuel Klug, pastor of Hebron Lutheran Church from 1739 to 1764. Mr. Klug was at this time extending his ministerial labors to the German communities in Rockingham and adjacent sections of the Valley, and was doubtless the "excellent Lutheran

---

[3]. See Virginia Magazine of History and Biography, July, 1904.

ROCKINGHAM COUNTY

minister" of whom Matthias Selzer had spoken. After a day and a night in association with him, Brother Gottschalk gave him a fair report.[4]

In July, 1748, Brethren Spangenberg and Reutz were in the vicinity of Brock's Gap and Timberville. On the 26th of the month they were at the home of Adam Roeder, for whom it is probable that Rader's Church, just west of Timberville, was named. The Brethren made note of the fact that Adam Rader's mother was at that time eighty-six years old, and that she was living in Lehigh County, Pa., a member of the Macungie [now Emmaus] congregation. Crossing the Valley toward the east, the missionaries came to the Massanutten settlements, where they reported Germans of "all kinds of denominations—Mennonites, Lutherans, Separatists, and Inspirationists."[5]

Early in December, 1749, Brethren Schnell and Brandmueller were on a missionary tour in Virginia. They came down from the vicinity of Staunton, into what is now East Rockingham, and made record of their goings and doings in the following interesting narrative:

> On December 2nd we continued our journey the whole day, because we wished to be with the Germans on Sunday. Once we lost our way. But our desire to preach to-morrow strengthened us in our journey. In the evening we attempted to hire a man to go with us part of the way, but none was willing. We continued for a time down the Tschanator, and arrived rather late at the house of the sons of the old Stopfel Franciscus, who kept us over night.
>
> On Sunday, December 3rd, the young Franciscus went very early with us to show us the way to Matthias Schaub's,[6] who, immediately on my offer to preach for them, sent messengers through the neighborhood to announce my sermon. In a short time a considerable number of people assembled, to whom I preached. After the sermon I baptized the child of a Hollander. We staid over night with Matthias Schaub. His wife told us that we were always welcome in their house. We should always

---

4. For an extended account of Mr. Klug's life and labors, see Huddle's History of Hebron Lutheran Church, pp. 31-38. See also Virginia Magazine of History and Biography, January and July, 1904.

5. Virginia Magazine, January, 1904, pp. 238-240.

come to them whenever we came into that district.

Towards evening a man from another district, Adam Mueller,[7] passed. I told him that I would like to come to his house and preach there. He asked me if I were sent by God. I answered, yes. He said, if I were sent by God I would be welcome, but he said, there are at present so many kinds of people, that often one does not know where they come from. I requested him to notify his neighbors that I would preach on the 5th, which he did.

On December 4th we left Schaub's house, commending the whole family to God. We traveled through the rain across the South Shenandoah to Adam Mueller, who received us with much love. We staid over night with him.

On December 5th I preached at Adam Mueller's house on John 7: "Whosoever thirsteth let him come to the water and drink." A number of thirsty souls were present. Especially Adam Mueller took in every word, and after the sermon declared himself well pleased. In the afternoon we traveled a short distance, staying over night with a Swiss.[8] The conversation was very dry, and the word of Christ's sufferings found no hearing.

On December 6th we came to Mesanoton. We staid with Philip Lung,[9] who had his own religion. I intended to preach, but he would not let us have his house, assuring us that none would come, since Rev. Mr. Klug had warned the people to be on their guard against us. We had soon an opportunity of seeing how bitter the people are towards us. Hence we concluded to leave, which we did, wishing God's blessing upon

---

[6]. Schaub (Shoup) died a month or two after Schnell's visit. On February 26th, 1750, Jacob Nicholas and Valentine Pence qualified as executors of his will. See Augusta County Will Book No. 1, pp. 312, 313. He evidently lived on the west side of the river, somewhere between Port Republic and Elkton.

[7]. Adam Miller, the first settler.

[8]. Mr. Chas. E. Kemper thinks that this "Swiss" was likely Jacob Baer, Sr., a native of Zurich, and at this time a resident of East Rockingham.

[9]. Philip Long was one of the first Massanutten settlers. The Long family is still numerous and prominent in upper Page County. A member of this family was the wife of Gen. Sterling Price, of Missouri. Philip Long was born in Germany in 1678, and died in Page or Rockingham County, Va., May 4, 1755.

Bear Lithia Spring
(Page 37)

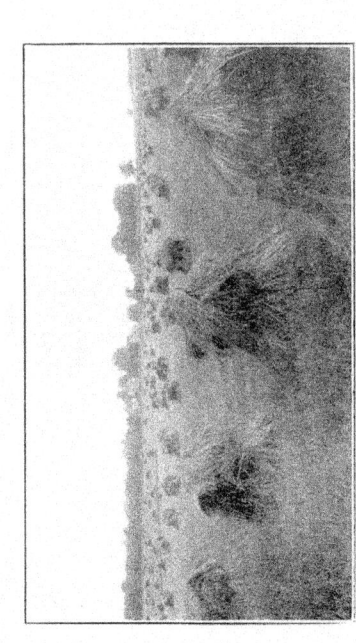

Steam Plow (first in County) in East Rockingham

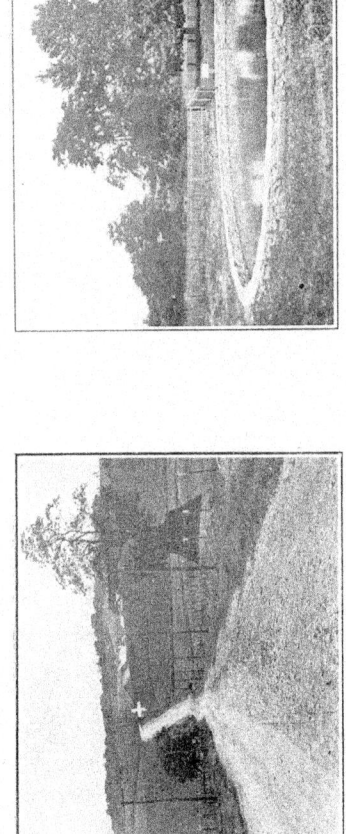

Smithland (p. 68) Looking Toward Harrisonburg. The white cross marks site of original Court House. Photo by J. J. Reilly

Suter Wheat Field, near New Erection

ROCKINGHAM COUNTY

the district. An unmarried man, H. Reder, took us through the river. He told us that eight weeks before he had visited Bethlehem.[10]

On their tour through Virginia in the fall and winter of 1749, to which reference has just been made, Brethren Schnell and Brandmueller made out a table of distances over which they travelled, beginning at Bethlehem, Pa., crossing Maryland into what is now West Virginia, following up the South Branch of the Potomac through what are now the counties of Hardy and Pendleton, and going beyond, even to the valleys of the James and New River, then returning to Pennsylvania through the Shenandoah Valley. Beginning about Staunton, the following distances show the route taken through Rockingham and Shenandoah:

[From N. Bell] To Franciscus at the Soud Schanathor,	30
To Matthias Schaub,	4
To Adam Mueller and back again across the river,	8
To Philip Lung and Mesanothen,	16
To Captain John Funk,	20[11]

In the autumn of 1753 a colony of the Moravian Brethren migrated from Pennsylvania to North Carolina. Their way led up through the Valley. In their record they mention the Narrow Passage and Stony Creek (in Shenandoah County), and speak of camping alongside the "Shanidore Creek," at a place that must now be located between Hawkinstown and Red Banks. Five miles further on they crossed the "Shanidore," and camped close to the bank to observe Sunday (October 21, 1753). They were now in the famous Meem's Bottoms, between Mt. Jackson and New Market. Brethren Loesch and Kalberland were bled, because they were not well, and all gave themselves a treat by drinking tea. The next day, coming on up the Valley, they found, in the vicinity of New Market or Tenth Legion, a tavern-keeper named Severe. This was evidently Valentine Severe, father of General John Sevier, and a relative of Francis Xavier. The next part

---

[10]. Virginia Magazine of History and Biography, October, 1903, pp. 126-128.

[11]. Idem, July, 1904, page 82.

of the narrative gives so many realistic touches relating to the Rockingham of that day, that it is quoted herewith verbatim:

> We inquired about the way, but could not get good information. After traveling three and a half miles, we found two passable roads. Bro. Gottlob and Nathanael preceded us on the left hand road. They met a woman, who informed them about the way. Then they came back to us again and we took the road to the right. We traveled ten miles without finding water. It was late already and we were compelled to travel five miles during the dark night. We had to climb two mountains, which compelled us to push the wagon along or we could not have proceeded, for our horses were completely fagged out. Two of the brethren had to go ahead to show us the road, and thus we arrived late at Thom. Harris's plantation. Here we bought feed for our horses and pitched our tent a short distance from the house. The people were very friendly. They lodge strangers very willingly.

The "two mountains" above mentioned were probably spurs of Chestnut Ridge; and "Thom Harris" was probably no other than Thomas Harrison, founder of Harrisonburg. It is likely that Harrison had already (1753) erected his stone mansion house, now occupied by Gen. John E. Roller as a law office, and, according to the present lay-out of the town, situated on Bruce Street, just west of Main; and that the wayfaring brethren pitched their tent beside the big spring that was for so many years a familiar rendezvous at the west side of Court Square. Harrisonburg still has the habit of being hospitable to strangers.

We follow the brethren a few miles further, as they go on toward "Augusti Court House, a little town of some twenty houses, surrounded by mountains on all sides."

> On October 23 we started at daybreak [from Thomas Harrison's]. We had bought a small barrel of milk to use for dinner, but it broke and we lost all. Two miles farther we bought some meat, and then traveled six miles farther to North River, where we ate our dinner. This creek is half as large as the Lecha [Lehigh], but it is impassable at high water, nor is a canoe in the neighborhood.[12]

The brethren had thus come in their journey to the

---

12. Virginia Magazine of History and Biography, October, 1904, pp. 144-147.

ROCKINGHAM COUNTY

vicinity of Mt. Crawford. They tell of their dinner there of meat and dumplings, and of their experiences farther on, at Middle River, at Robert Bohk's, and at "Augusti Court House"; but having followed them to the borders of Rockingham, we bid them farewell.

Samuel Kercheval, the old historian of the Valley, says:

From the best evidence the author has been able to collect, . . . the settlement of our Valley progressed without interruption from the native Indians for a period of about twenty-three years. In the year 1754, the Indians suddenly disappeared, and crossed the Alleghany Mountains. The year preceding, emissaries from the west of the Alleghany Mountains came among the Valley Indians and invited them to move off. This occurrence excited suspicion among the white people that a storm was brewing in the west, which it was essential to prepare to meet.[13]

Kercheval dates the beginning of Valley settlement in 1732. Counting thence twenty-three years would give 1755, the year of Braddock's defeat. The war with the French and Indians began in 1754, and continued till 1763. During this time Indian raids into the Valley from the west were frequent, particularly in the two or three years following the defeat of Braddock. Occasionally the bands of red men were led by French officers. It was in April of 1758 that the massacres at Upper Tract and Fort Seybert took place, in which more than forty persons were killed, some twenty-odd others being carried into captivity. The Indians at Fort Seybert were led by the famous chief Killbuck. From 1777 to 1787 both Upper Tract and Fort Seybert were within the boundaries of Rockingham County, the site of the latter being west of Brock's Gap, only a few miles beyond the present Rockingham line.[14]

---

13. Kercehval's History of the Valley of Virginia, reprint of 1902, page 49.

14. For detailed accounts of the massacres at Upper Tract and Fort Seybert, see Kercheval, pp. 89-91, and Morton's History of Pendleton County, West Virginia, pp. 42-50.

A HISTORY OF

During this war with the French and Indians the legislature of Virginia passed numerous Acts for the defence of the frontiers, for paying the troops called into service, and for supplying the army with provisions. The frontier counties naturally furnished the largest numbers of men for this war. In the seventh volume of Hening's Statutes is found a schedule, appended to an Act passed in September, 1758, giving the names of soldiers to whom pay was due, together with the names of other persons who held accounts against the Colony for work done for the army, for provisions furnished, for horses sold or hired, etc. In this schedule lists are given from 39 counties. Some of these lists are very short, a few are very long. The longest four, named in order of length, are those of Augusta, Bedford, Lunenberg, and Frederick. Inasmuch as what is now Rockingham was then a part of Augusta, it is possible to find in the Augusta list a number of Rockingham names. The following, copied from the list of Augusta soldiers, are almost certainly names of Rockingham men:

Christopher Armentrout
Henry Benninger
George Capliner
John Cunrod
Walter Cunrod
Woolrey Coonrod
Hugh Diver
Roger Dyer
William Dyer
Abraham Earhart
Michael Erhart
Michael Earhart, Jr.
Jacob Eberman
John Eberman
Michael Eberman
Jacob Fudge
George Fults
John Fulse
Jacob Grub
John Gum
George Hamer
Stephen Hansburgher
Gideon Harrison
John Harrison
Nathan Harrison
Adam Hedrick
George Hedrick
Samuel Hemphill
Leonard Herron
Archibald Hopkins
John Hopkins (lieut.)
Honicle Hufman
Philip Hufman
Francis Kirtley (Capt.)
Gabriel Kite
George Kite

ROCKINGHAM COUNTY

Jacob Kite
Valentine Kite
William Kite
Daniel Long
Henry Long
John Long
William Long
Ephraim Love, (Capt.)[15]
George Mallow
Michael Mallow
Nicholas Mildebarler
Adam Miller
David Miller
Jacob Miller
John Miller
Peter Miller
Jacob Moyers
Nicholas Null
Jacob Pence

Henry Peninger
Gunrod Peterish
Matthew Rolestone
Samuel Rolston
William Rolestone
John Seller
Edward Shanklin
John Shanklin
Richard Shanklin
Paul Shever
James Skidmore
John Skidmore[16]
Joseph Skidmore
George Shillinger
Isaiah Shipman
Josiah Shipman
Lodowick Slodser
Abraham Smith (Capt.)[17]

---

15. Capt. Love probably lived near the site of Singer's Glen. On July 29, 1748, Jacob Dye and Mary his wife sold to Ephraim Love, late of Lancaster County, Pa., 377 acres of land "on ye head Draughts of Muddy Creek under the North Mountain," adjoining Daniel Harrison. Witnesses, William Carroll, William White, and Peter Scholl. Peter Scholl lived on Smith's Creek. As early as 1742 he was one of the twelve militia captains of Augusta, and in 1745 was one of the first justices of the county. Valentine Sevier, father of Gen. John Sevier, is represented as being a member of Scholl's military company in 1742. See Waddell's Annals of Augusta, pp. 45-47.

16. John Skidmore was one of the original justices of Rockingham County.

17. Abraham Smith, son of Capt. John Smith. A. Smith was a captain of militia in Augusta in 1756. In 1757 he was a prisoner in the French dominions. In 1758 he was court-martialed, but acquitted, his accuser being punished. In 1776 he was colonel of militia; in 1778, one of the first justices of Rockingham County, and county lieutenant. He owned a large estate at the foot of North Mountain, about two miles from North River, which descended to his son Henry.

A HISTORY OF

Daniel Smith (Lt.)[18]
Mathias Tice (Dice?)
Christian Tuley
Gunrod Umble
Martin Umble

Ury Umble
Peter Vaneman
Jacob Wiece
Joseph Wiece
Filey Yacome

Among the persons named in the schedule as having furnished supplies to the the troops, the following were all probably from Rockingham:

James Bruister
Wooley Coonrod
George Coplinger
James Cowan
Charles Diver
Hugh Diver
Roger Dyer
William Dyer
Michael Erhart
Evan Evans
Nathaniel Evans
Rhoda Evans
Lodowick Folk

James Fowler
Felix Gilbert[19]
Ruben Harrison
Alexander Hering
Leonard Hire
Nicholas Huffman
Archibald Huston
Gabriel Jones[20]
Joseph Love
Henry Peninger
Matthew Rolestone
William Rolestone
Ephraim Voss[21]

---

[18]. Daniel Smith, a younger brother of Abraham, was a captain of militia in 1776, and in 1778 was one of the first justices of Rockingham, being presiding justice at the time of his death in 1781. He lived at Smithland, two miles below Harrisonburg, and the first sessions of the county court were held at his house. His wife was Jane Harrison. He had been a justice in Augusta County, and had held the office of sheriff in that county. When the troops returned from Yorktown, in the fall of 1781, he was colonel of militia, and was thrown from his horse and fatally injured in the grand review held in Rockingham to celebrate the victory. See Waddell's Annals of Augusta, pp. 150-152.

[19]. Felix Gilbert was a well known citizen of Rockingham, wealthy, and prominent in many connections.

[20]. Gabriel Jones, "The Lawyer," lived on the river, a mile or two below Port Republic, the place now being known as Bogota.

[21]. Voss may have lived in Southwest Virginia, since Fort Voss (Vause) is said to have been at the head of Roanoke River, in the present county of Montgomery, about ten miles from Christiansburg.

ROCKINGHAM COUNTY

By the favor of Mr. John T. Harris the author has been enabled to go over an old day book used from 1774 to 1777, etc., by Felix Gilbert, who lived and kept a store at or near the place since known as Peale's Cross Roads, five miles or so southeast of Harrisonburg. A number of items, copied from this old book, are given below. They have personal, social, and economic interest, as well as some political significance.

1775

Recd. for the Bostonians

Of Patrick Frazier	-	-	-	1 bus. wheat	
Jos. Dicktom	-	-	-	2 do.	
George Boswell	-	-	-	5½ do.	(5 bus. Retd.)
James Walker	-	-	-	1 do.	Return'd
George Clark	-	-	-	1 do.	
James Beard	-	-	-	1 do.	
Robt. Scott & son	-	-	-	2 do.	

It is evident from the above that contributions were being made in this part of Virginia, as well as elsewhere, for the relief of the patriots of Boston, whose harbor had been closed by Act of Parliament in 1774, as a penalty for the "Boston Tea Party."

Monday, Decr. 5th, 1774

John Alford	(weaver)		Dr.	
To 1 pr. Shoe Buckles	- - - - -		1 [s.]	3 [d.]
To 1 qt. whisky	- - - - - -		1	0
To 1 pr. Compasses	- - - - -			9
To 3 doz. Buttons	- - - - -		2	0

[Same Date.]

Robt. Elliot	Pr. Order	Dr.	
To pd. Schoolmaster	- - - - -	6	0
James Wayt Pr. Order		Dr.	
To pd. Schoolmaster	- - - - -	6	0
Dennis McSwyny (Schoolmaster)		Cr.	
[By above two items and]			
Wm. Ham	- - - - - - -	4	4
Esther Taylor	- - - - - - -	10	0

Wednesday, Decr. 7th, 1774.

Little Jack	- - - - - - -	Dr.	
To 1 pt. Tin	- - - - - - -		9 [d.]
½ pt. whisky	- - - - - - -		

—55—

A HISTORY OF

It is possible that Little Jack was an Indian. Whiskey was a common commodity in the Valley in Revolutionary days, as doth abundantly appear not only from Felix Gilbert's old ledger, but also from the records of the court, a number of which records may be found in the next chapter.

Decr. 13, 1774

Col. Thos. Slaugh'r   Dr.
- To a handsaw — 5   6
- To Drawg Knife — 2   9
- a hammer — 2   —
- 1 augr — 1   3
- 1 pr shears — 1   —
- 200 nails — 2   10
- 2 Gimlets — —   6
- 1 Tin Cup — —   6
- 1¼ yds. flannl — 3   1

Friday, Decr. 23d, 1774.

Capt. Danl. Love   Dr.
- To 1 Gal. Rum — 5   0
- 4 lbs. Sugar — 3   4
- To 4 pr. Garters — 3   0

Colo. John Frogg   Dr.
- To 1 knife & fork — 2   3
- To 1 sack salt — 1   1   0

Saturday, Decr. 24th, 1774

Little Jack   Dr.
- To 6 pipes —

Tuesday, Decr. 27, 1774

Jacob Grubb per self & Frow
- To 1 lb. Lead — 6
- To 1 stamp'd Handhf — 3   6
- To 27½ lbs. Iron at 4 d. — 9   2
- To 6 lbs. Eng. Steel — 6   0
- To ½ lb. Blister'd do. — 4½
- To 2 setts knit'g needles — 8

Tuesday, Jany. 10th, 1775

Jacob Lincoln
- To 24½ lbs. Blistered steel — 18   4½
- To 14½ lbs. Eng. do. — 14   6
- To 1 hank silk — 1   0

ROCKINGHAM COUNTY

Saturday, Jany. 14th, 1775

Jack (bigg)	Dr.	
To ½ pt. whisky		4 [d.]

Were "Big Jack" and "Little Jack" both Indians? It would so appear from the nature of their purchases. Indians were frequently seen in this part of the Valley at a much later period.

Saturday, Feby. 11th, '75

Gawin Hamilton	Dr.		
To 5000 E. nails	1	7	6
To 3 Chizels		3	0
To 1 Rasp		1	3
To 1 pr. saddle strops		1	0

Friday, Feb. 17th, '75

Capt. Rowland Thomas	Dr.		
To 35 lbs. tallow at 6d		17	6
To 237 lbs. Flower at 12-1c	1	9	7½

Monday, Feby. 20th, 1775.

Mr. Thos. Lewis pr Capt. Smiths Cesar		
To makg Ring & Staple & pin for Ox Yoke	3	9

Thursday, March 2d, 1775.

Mr. Gabl. Jones—per Jimm—	Dr.	
To 6 Venison Hams at 1-9	10	6

Thursday, 9th March, 1775.

Doctr. Thos. Walker[22] pr Mr. Gilmer			
To 2 yds Osnabrugs		2	2
Mr. Peachy Gilmer	Dr.		
To 23 yd. wt. linin	3	3	3
To 2 Oz. wt. thread		3	0
To 2 felt Hats		4	0
To 2 qr. paper		3	6

---

22. This was probably the distinguished Dr. Thos. Walker, of Albemarle County, Va.

A HISTORY OF

Friday, March 17th, 1775.

Isaac Zane,[23] pr W. Crow	Cr.		
By 20—0—12 Iron - - - - - -	20	2	2

Tuesday, May 30th, 1775.

Mr. John Madison[24] Senr. pr self			
To 18½ yds. Velveret - - - - -	1	14	0

Saturday, July 1st, 1775.

Danl. Love	Dr.	
To 2 Sickles - - - - - - -	2	3

Thursday, July 6th, '75

Jacob Purky	Cr.	
By 1 day Reaping - - - - - -	2	6
By 1 day do. yr. negro - - - - -	2	6

[No date: Probably 1777:]

    one Davis a preacher has a Hyde of Leather—John wilson owes 3 Dollars—an old Quaker on Stephen jays place—Saml. watts owes something.

    Feby. 16th—1778 Boler Lee has rented ye plantation I had of Thos. Dooley on ye South mountain [Blue Ridge]. he is to have it for one year & to make up ye Fences & pay 400 lbs. of good merchantable Tobo. or 12 Barrils of Corn. if he Dos not keep it more than one year he is to let ye person that sukceeds him put in a fall Crop.

LIST OF TITHABLES FOR 1775.

    Felix Gilbert was probably authorized by the Augusta County court to take the list of tithables in his distirct. At any rate, the following list, dated 1775, is found written in his book. Most of the names herein given are still familiar in Rockingham:

John Coutes	1	Heny. Munger	1
Robt. Heth	2	Jno. Tack	1
Jno. Deneston	2	Henry Tack	1

---

    [23]. Gen. Isaac Zane had iron works on Cedar Creek, the present boundary between the counties of Shenandoah and Frederick. He was perhaps a brother of Elizabeth Zane.

    [24]. John Madison was the first clerk of Augusta County, and was the father of Bishop Madison. He lived at Port Republic.

ROCKINGHAM COUNTY

Jacob Tack	1	Adam Siller	1
Chas. Foy	1	Peter Siller	3
John Foy	1	Heny. Siller	1
John Mungor	1	Jacob Arkinbright	2
John Miller	1	John Rush	1
Paul Lingle	1	Henry Deck	1
John Lingle	1	John Deck	1
Danl. Price	2	Jacob Deck	1
John Futch	1	Lewis Rinehart	1
Fredk. Haynes	3	Geo. Hoofman	1
Heny. Null	3	Michl. Hoofman	1
Heny. Tamwood	1	Fredk. Armontrout	5
Jno. Null	1	Mathias Shooler	1
Jacob Lingle, Jur.	1	Ullry Hushman	2
Mathi's Kersh	1	Ullry Hushman, Jr.	1
Michl. Siller	1	Peter Nasmus	1
Avonas Bowyer	1	Geo. Conrod	1
John Bowyer	1	Conrod Petorfish	2
Jno. Futch, Jur.	2	Jacob Moyer	3
Saml. Magot	1	Peter Brunomer	2
James Madday	1	Anthony Brunomer	1
John Hardman	1	Danl. Sink	1
John Hadrick	2	Heny. Cook	1
Stephen Hansberger	3	Heny. Armentrout	1
Adam Hansberger	1	Heny. Price	2
Geo. Fridley	1	Boler Lee	1
Jacob Hammer	2	Michl. Dofflemire	1
Wm. Summersetts	1	Windal Leverts [?]	1
Geo. Blose	1	Adam Blose	1
Conrad Taylor	1	Conrod Young	1
Martin Doffilmire	1	Wm. Smith, Jr.	1
Christian Teter	1	Mijah Smith	1
Heny. Miller	3	Brustor Smith	1
Boston Noster	1	Wm. Smith	1
Thos. Barnet	1	Jacob Nicholas	4
Matthew Petmus	1	Richd. Welsh	1
Wm. Haney	1	John Lawn	1

A HISTORY OF

Thos. Doolin	1	Robert Hill	3
Wm. Lee	1	Willm. Lee, Jr.	1
Zephaniah Lee	1	David Koch	1
Zachariah Lee	1	Rubin Roch	1
Martin Crawford	1	Willm. Boswell	2
Robert Lynes	1	John Frizor	1
James Raynes [?]	1	Ephraim Wilson	1
Thos. Berry	1	Wm. Coile	1
Jas. Raines Jur.	1	Thos. Huet	1
Jas. Berry	1	William Campbell	1
John Siller	1	Jno. Jackson	1
Christian Miller	1	James Bruster	3
Philip Lingle	1	Felix Gilbert	12
Jno. Armontrout	1	John Craig	9
Augustian Price	3	William Hook	1
Geo. Mallow	3	James Hook	1
Wm. Pence	1	Robt. Hook Irish	1
Jacob Grace	1	James Archer	1
Geo. Pence	[?]	George Shaver	1
John Pence	1	James Scott	1
Chas. Rush	1	Nat Scott	1
John Rush	1	Robt. Scott, Jr.	1
Anthoney Aler	2	Jacob Scott	1
William Oler	1	Nicholas M———	3
Henry Oler	1	Michl. Trout	2
John Oler	1	Margt. Purkey	3
John Fults	3	Jacob Purkey	2
Cutlip Arie	1	John Pence, Jur.	1
Robert Hook, Sr.	2	Henry Pence	1
Evan Evins	1	Adm. Pence	1
John Hooper	1	John Purkey	1
Jonathan Evans	1	Henry Purkey	1
Saml. Twichet	1	Jacob Pence	1
John White, Sr.	5	Elijah Hook	1
John White, Jr.	1		

The evidence is already abundant in the foregoing particulars to show that the settlement of Rockingham was go-

ROCKINGHAM COUNTY.

ing on steadily and rapidly during the whole period now under consideration, that is, the years from 1738 to 1777. The records concerning inn-keepers, military organizations, and well established communities, as well as those concerning numerous individuals widely distributed, indicate conclusively that even as early as the first courts in Augusta (1745) that part of the county now included in Rockingham was dotted over with clearings and homesteads. Additional evidence, if it were needed, might be found in the records of the old churches, some of which can easily trace their organization back into the early 18th century. St. Peter's, below Elkton, Peaked Mountain Church, at or near McGaheysville, Rader's Church, near Timberville, Friedens, near Cross Keys, St. Michael's, above Bridgewater, and Spader's Church, near Pleasant Valley, not to mention others, are all old churches, and in a few of them are well-preserved chronicles of very early days. The most complete and best preserved records are perhaps those found in the Peaked Mountain Church. Parts of these records were translated and published in 1905, by W. J. Hinke and C. E. Kemper, in the William and Mary College Quarterly. A complete translation should be given to the public in convenient form, since dozens of families, not only in Rockingham County, but also in many other parts of the United States, would find therein matter of great interest.

A few of the Peaked Mountain records of births and baptisms go back to 1750 and before, but the regular organization of the congregation must, perhaps, be placed a few years later. The following extract is given from the above-mentioned translation by Mr. Hinke, as containing certain facts of historical interest relating to the period under consideration, together with a number of family names that have been familiar in Rockingham for more than a century and a half.

   Agreement Between the Reformed and Lutheran Congregations Worshipping in the Peaked Mountain Church: Rockingham Co., Va., Oct. 31, 1769.

   In the name of the Triune God and with the consent of the whole

A HISTORY OF

congregation, we have commenced to build a new house of God, and it is by the help of God, so far finished that the world may see it.

We have established it as a union church, in the use of which the Lutherans and their descendants as well as the Reformed and their descendants, shall have equal share. But since it is necessary to keep in repair the church and school house and support the minister and schoolmaster, therefore, we have drawn up this writing that each member sign his name to the same and thereby certify that he will support the minister and school-master and help to keep in repair the church and the school-house as far as lies in his ability.

Should, however, one or another withdraw himself from such Christian work, (which we would not suppose a Christian would do), we have unitedly concluded that such a one shall not be looked upon as a member of our congregation, but he shall pay for the baptism of a child 2s. 6d., which shall go into the treasury of the church, for the confirmation of the child 5s., which shall be paid to the minister as his fee; and further, should such a one come to the table of the Lord and partake of the Holy Communion, he shall pay 5s., which shall go into the treasury of the church; and finally, if such a one desires burial in our graveyard, he shall pay 5s., which shall also be paid into the treasury of the church.

In confirmation of which we have drawn up this document, and signed it with our several signatures.

Done in Augusta County, at the Peaked Mountain and the Stony Creek churches, on October 31st, Anno Domini, 1769.

The present elders:

George Mallo, Sr.	Nicholas Mildeberger
John X Hetrick (his mark)	Frederick Ermentraut

Philip Ermentraut	Jacob Bercke
Henry Ermentraut	Jacob I. E. Ergebrecht (his mark)
Daniel Kropf	
Peter Mueller, Sr.	John Reisch
Adam O Hetrich (his mark)	Jacob Ergebrecht
Jacob Traut	John Mildeberger
Augustine Preisch	John Hausman
George Schillinger	George Mallo, Jr.
Anthony Oehler	Jacob Lingle
John Mann	Peter Niclas
Alwinus Boyer	Jacob Kropf
Charles Risch	Jacob Niclas
Henry Kohler	George Zimmerman
William Long	Christian Geiger

ROCKINGHAM COUNTY.

Augustine Preisch, Jr.
Conrad Preisch
Jacob Kissling
Jacob Bens
Adam Herman
Michael Mallo
Christopher X̲ Hau (his mark)

Peter Euler
William Mchel
Jacob Risch
John Ermentraut
Corad Loevenstein
John Schaefer
Christopher Ermentraut
Martin Schneider
John Bens

In closing this chapter it will be of interest to record the fact that the part of Augusta County now known as Rockingham furnished at least one company of soldiers in Dunmore's War, and that this company took part in the famous battle of Point Pleasant, October 10, 1774. This company was commanded by Captain, later, Colonel William Nalle, who lived in East Rockingham, and was, in 1778, made one of the first justices of Rockingham County.[25] It is also a fact of special interest that it was a Rockingham man, Valentine Sevier, who, with James Robertson, later known as the father of Middle Tennessee, first discovered the presence of the Indians early on that fateful morning at Point Pleasant. Sevier was a younger brother of General John Sevier, and was born in Rockingham in 1747. In 1773 he went to the southwest, and was thus a member of Captain Evan Shelby's company in 1774. He and Robertson went out before day at Point Pleasant to hunt turkeys, and thus discovered the Indian army. He was a captain in the Revolution, and took part in the battle of King's Mountain. After other military services, in which he rose to the rank of militia colonel, he removed to Clarksville, Tenn., where he died in 1800.

Among the other captains who took part at Point Pleasant, as given by Thwaites and Kellogg, were Benj. Harrison, John Skidmore, Joseph Haynes, and Daniel Smith.

Benjamin Harrison (1741-1819) was a son of Daniel Har-

---

25. For a list of the men in Captain Nalle's company, see the muster roll in the Appendix. This muster roll is copied from Thwaites and Kellogg's Documentary History of Dunmore's War, page 405.

rison of Rockingham; father of Peachy Harrison, grandfather of Gessner Harrison. He was a colonel in McIntosh's campaign (1777), and led troops in 1781 to aid Lafayette against Cornwallis. John Skidmore, who was wounded at Point Pleasant, was a soldier in the French and Indian War and one of the first justices of Rockingham County. Daniel Smith, though living at this time in Southwest Virginia, was probably a son of Colonel Daniel Smith of Rockingham. Joseph Haynes was a resident of Rockingham or of some section adjacent. In Felix Gilbert's day book before me, covering several years from December 5, 1774, the names of Capt. Jos. Haynes, Capt. John Skidmore, and Capt. Benjamin Harrison, as well as the name of Capt. William Nalle, frequently appear. Evidently they were all frequent customers at Gilbert's store, which, as shown above, was not far from Harrisonburg. It is reasonable to suppose, therefore, that a number of the men in the companies commanded by Harrison, Skidmore, and Haynes were also from Rockingham, though the rolls of these companies seem not to be preserved.[26]

[26.] For additional particulars regarding Harrison and Smith, the reader is referred to Waddell's Annals of Augusta, Boogher's Gleanings of Virginia History, and Thwaites and Kellogg's Documentary History of Dunmore's War. In the last may also be found a sketch of Valentine Sevier, Jr.

Rockingham County Court House, Erected 1895
Photo by Dean [Page 178]

Front — Views of Third County Court House, 1874-1896 — Rear
[Page 168] Photo by Morrison

Second County Court House. 1833-1874
Photo loaned by Mrs. C. S. Burkholder

CHAPTER V.

THE NEW COUNTY AND THE NEW NATION.

1777—1820.

In October, 1777, the Act providing for the creation of the County of Rockingham from Augusta was passed by the Virginia legislature; and early the next year, to wit, in April 1778, the first court for the new county was held. The board of justices was in session two days, and transacted a great deal of important business, not only in process of civil organization, but also in reference to various personal interests of individual citizens.

The following paragraph, copied from the original minute-book of the court, will get the situation and the several actors on the scene clearly before us:

> Be it remembered that on the xxvii Day of April MDCCLXXviii a Commission of the peace and a Commission of Oyer & Terminer under the Hand of his Excellency Patrick Henry Esq. Governor in Chief, dated the xxiv Day of March MDCCLXXviii directed to Silas Hart, Daniel Smith, Abraham Smith, John Gratten, Josiah Davison, John Skidmore, George Boswell, Thomas Hewitt, John Thomas, William Nalle, Robert Davis, James Dyer, Henry Ewing, William McDowell, Anthony Ryder, John Fitzwater & Isaac Hinckel Gent. Justices for the County of Rockingham being read, Daniel Smith & Abraham Smith having administer'd the Oath of a Justice of Peace as prescribed by Act of Assembly also the Oath of a Justice of Oyer & Terminer to Silas Hart Gent. and then the said Silas Hart administered each of the said Oaths to Daniel Smith, Abram Smith, John Gratten, Josiah Davidson, George Bowell, Thomas Hewitt, John Thomas, James Dyer, Henry Ewing, William McDowell, Anthony Ryder, John Fitzwater & Isaac Hinckle, aforesaid, who were sworn in the Commission of the peace & Justices of Oyer accordingly.

Following out a commission issued March 24, 1778, by Governor Patrick Henry, Silas Hart was sworn in as sheriff, with Gabriel Jones and Robert Cravens as sureties. Gaven

A HISTORY OF

Hamilton qualified as deputy sheriff. Thomas Lewis produced a commission as county surveyor, from the president and masters of "the Colledge of Wm & Mary," and was sworn into the office, having Daniel Smith and Abraham Smith as sureties. Peter Hog was unanimously chosen and appointed clerk of the peace.

On this first day of the court, April 27, 1778, the following justices were present:

Daniel Smith	James Dyer
Abraham Smith	Henry Ewing
John Gratten	William McDowell
Josiah Davidson	Anthony Ryder
George Boswell	John Fitzwater
Thomas Hewitt	Isaac Hinckle
John Thomas	

Various matters in the settlement of estates, etc., were transacted. The minutes are signed by Abraham Smith, but apparently written by someone else.

The court resumed its session the next day, April 28, 1778. At the opening six of the justices were present, namely: Daniel Smith, Abraham Smith, John Thomas, John Gratten, Isaac Hinckle, and John Fitzwater; an hour or two later Thomas Hewitt and James Dyer came in, and later still Josiah Davidson. A great deal of important business was transacted this day, in addition to the formal provisions for the settling of several estates.

The sheriff was ordered to summon 24 freeholders as a grand jury for the county;

William Bush, Jeremiah Beasly, Henry Brewster, George Huston, William Magill son of John, Elliot Rutherford, John Fulton, Jr., John Bryan, Jr., Reuben More, Mathias Leas, Jr., Joseph Custard, William Dever, Beerton Blizard, Samuel Skidmore, and Jacob Ellsworth were appointed constables in their respective districts;

Abraham Smith was recommended to the governor and council as a fit man for the office of county lieutenant; Daniel Smith was in like manner recommended for colonel, Benja-

ROCKINGHAM COUNTY

min Harrison for lieutenant colonel, and John Skidmore for major;

John Gratten, John Thomas, and Daniel Smith were appointed coroners for the county;

It was ordered that Gawen Hamilton, being first sworn, should run the division line between Rockingham and Augusta; also the "Length of the County from the said Line to Lord Fairfax's Line, or run any other Line by the Direction of Mr. Lewis the Surveyor to enable him to make out a plan of the County";

Gawen Hamilton was recommended as a proper man to serve as deputy surveyor under Mr. Lewis, "if he is pleased to appoint him to that office";

Gawen Hamilton was appointed a captain of the militia in the county; Joseph Smith, 1st lieutenant; John Rice, 2d lieutenant; and Wm. Smith (3d lieutenant?); Wm. Herring was appointed 2d lieutenant, and Joseph Dictam, ensign, in Capt. Robert Craven's company; Richard Reagen was appointed 2d lieutenant, and Joseph Smith ensign, in Capt. Daniel Smith's company;

It was ordered that Daniel Smith draw from the treasurer of the Commonwealth 12 pounds, and "lay it out for the Support of Bridget Fowler the distressed Wife of John Fowler a Soldier in the continental Army from this County."

Although Silas Hart had been sworn in as sheriff, under the governor's commission, he was not long permitted to enjoy the office; for in the record of the second day's session of the court we find a minute to the effect that Josiah Davidson, John Skidmore, and George Boswell were recommended to the governor as candidates fit for appointment to the position. This procedure is explained in the same minute. It appears that Silas Hart and Daniel Smith, having been senior justices in Augusta, and having thereby held the office of sheriff before the division of the county, had agreed to relinquish their claim to the office when they should fall within the new county of Rockingham. Accordingly, they now agreed, or were required, to allow the office to be handed

A HISTORY OF

down the line of seniority. Josiah Davidson, one of the three nominees, was commissioned by the governor, and was sworn in as sheriff at the next monthly session of the court.

The court, on the second day of the first session, having taken into consideration the "properest place" for the holding of courts until public buildings could be erected, unanimously resolved to hold court at the house of Daniel Smith, Gent., until the said public buildings were completed. The court at the time of this resolution was doubtless sitting at the home of Mr. Smith; for the Act establishing the county had designated his house as the place for holding the first court.

"Smithland," now the residence of Geo. W. Liskey, stands on the southeast side of the Valley Pike, just a mile or two below Harrisonburg. It is one of the finest old country homesteads in many a mile. Situated near the brow of a lofty eminence, it commands a splendid view of vales, hills, and distant mountains. At the sharp turn of the pike just below the house, on the high bank at the left-hand side, the site of an old building may still be discerned: there, tradition says, the first justices of the county sat in their initial sessions.

At the same time that Smithland was selected as the temporary seat of justice, it was ordered that Daniel Smith and Josiah Davidson be empowered to contract with some person for building a "square Log Jayl or prison 12 feet square, laid with square Logs above & below, 8 inches thick at the least, with one Window & a Door made of Iron barrs so as to suit the public Jayl when built, with a good Lock & a Cabin rooff over the upper flour, to be fixed on the most convenient spott of the sd. Daniel Smith's plantation, and in the meantime that the Sheriff be empowered to hire a Guard to watch such prisoners as are taken into his Custody."

After this action the court was adjourned to the next monthly session.

The minutes of the second day are signed by Daniel Smith. It is likely that he or Peter Hog made the entries on

ROCKINGHAM COUNTY

the pages that are now yellow with age and worn with much handling.

The second court for Rockingham County was held on Monday, the 25th of May, 1778.

Among other transactions, Josiah Davidson was sworn in as sheriff, under a commission from the governor dated May 7, 1778; Gabriel Jones was appointed deputy attorney for the commonwealth for Rockingham County, with a salary of £40 a year.

Under commissions from the governor, Abram Smith took an oath as County Lieutenant; Daniel Smith, as Colonel; Benjamin Harrison, as Lieut.-Colonel; William Nalle, as Major.

Anthony Ryder, Gawin Hamilton, Thomas Hewitt, Thomas Boggs (?), Reuben Harrison, and Daniel Smith, Jr., were appointed captains of militia, and took oath according to law.

Felix Gilbert was bound to the governor in the sum of £1000, with two sureties in the sum of £500 each, for a year and a day, to perform his good behavior towards the State and all the good people thereof, he having been charged by Andrew Skidmore with having uttered "words inimical to the State"—words that tended to "sow sedition among the settlers on the western waters." Gilbert was the wealthy store keeper, east of Harrisonburg, with whom we became familiar in the preceding chapter.

The next day a large part of the business consisted in the appointing of road masters for the new roads that were being marked out in various courses. A more particular account of these proceedings is given in Chapter XII. The sum of £20 was voted for the aid of Elizabeth Pennirey, wife of Thomas Pennirey, a soldier in the army of the United States.

At the court held June 22, 1778, it was ordered that William Nalle, Gent., take the list of tithables[1] in the companies

---

1. The tithables were those persons upon whom the poll tax was levied.

A HISTORY OF

of Capt. Coger and Capt. Frazier; George Boswell, Gent., in those of Capt. Hewit and Capt. Pence; Henry Ewing, Gent., in those of Capt. Cravens, Capt. Hamilton, and Capt. Hopkins; John Fitzwater, Gent., in those of Capt. Lincoln and Capt. Boggs; Anthony Rader, Gent., in those of himself and Capt. Harrison; Daniel Smith, Gent., in that of Capt. Smith; Isaac Hinckle, on the North Fork and South Branch; and James Dyer, Gent., on the South Fork.

In following thus the official proceedings in the organization of the new county, one should keep in mind the cotemporary events that were marking the initial steps in the life of the new nation. It was a great and stirring time. Just a little over a year before the General Assembly of Virginia passed the Act creating Rockingham County, Jefferson, a son of Virginia, had written the Declaration of Independence, upon which thirteen young states rose up before the world in a challenge of hope that was as daring as it was splendid and courageous. The very same year and month (October, 1777) that the said Act was passed, the new nation scored a triumph at a crisis in the surrender of Burgoyne at Saratoga. In February following, just two months before the first court of Rockingham met at Smithland, France recognized the independence of the United States, and thus made a telling contribution to their success in the long struggle for freedom. Through all the first years of the county's history this struggle went on, with Fortune wavering near the point of balance, until finally the political independence of the young states was acknowledged by the mother country in 1783. At that time Rockingham County was six years old; the new nation, counting from 1776, was just two years older.

From the records of the county court, a number of which

The lists included not only the planters and householders, but also their sons, men-servants, and slaves of sixteen years and upwards. The various Acts of the Colonial Assembly relating to tithables may be found in Hening's Statutes. An authoritative discussion of the subject is presented in Philip A. Bruce's Institutional History of Virginia, Vol. II, pp. 548-555.

ROCKINGHAM COUNTY

are reproduced either in form or in substance in the following pages, it will clearly and repeatedly appear that Rockingham contributed in generous measure to the cause of American independence. Her soldiers fought on fields at home and abroad. Her citizens furnished supplies of varied kind and enormous quantity for military use. Her magistrates were liberal in providing for the wives and children of patriot soldiers, and alert in suppressing tories. In these records the student of government will read efficiency and equity; the industrial economist will observe many statistics of kind, measure, and value; the soldier will discern military organization and activity; the sociologist will find a people simple and frugal; and the genealogist will recognize many an ancestor in honorable service.

August 24, 1778, George Rootes, Gent., took the oath of an attorney at law, which was ordered certified by the court. On the same day the court appointed John Hinton to draw £20 and lay it out for Bridget Fowler, wife of John Fowler, a soldier in the U. S. service, and her children.

September 28, 1778, George Boswell and John Thomas were appointed to examine and receive the Jayl house built on Danl. Smith's plantation agreeable to a former order of court; whereupon the said gentlemen reported that they had viewed the said Jayl and found it sufficient, &c., except the iron door and window, which could not be procured.

November 23, 1778, the court ordered £25 to be paid Mary Rupe, wife of Nicolas Rupe, a soldier in the continental army, to relieve the distress of herself and seven children.

At a court held on Monday, March 22, 1779, a "Deed from Robt. Hill to the presbyterian Congregation was proved by the Witnesses & O to be recorded Tho. Brewster to pay fees."

Mary Sybert, widow of Chas. Fred. Sybert, a soldier who died in the service of the Commonwealth, being in indigent circumstances, with one helpless child, was allowed £30.

Elizabeth Shulenberger, widow of Geo. Shulenberger,

deceased, late a soldier in the Continental service from this State, being in distressed circumstances, was allowed £30.

George Ruddle and George Baxter, having produced commissions from the governor, were sworn in as captains of militia.

John Herdman was sworn in as 1st lieut. and Thos. Gordon as 2d lieut.

Upon information lodged by Jacob Plumb, Nicolás Weatherholt was bound in the sum of £2000, with Martin Witsell as surety in the sum of £1000, for the said Weatherholt to appear before the grand jury in May to answer the charge of "conspiring & consulting the Destruction of the Commonwealth."

At the court continued March 23, 1779:

Rachel Cash, wife of Jno. Cash, a soldier in the service of the United States from this Commonwealth, being in distressed circumstances with two small children, was allowed £30.

Henry Peninger was bound in the sum of £5000, with Sebastian Hover and Henry Stone securities, each in the sum £2500, to appear before the grand jury in May to answer to the charge of throwing disgraceful reflections upon the Congress, and of speaking words tending to depreciate the Continental currency; and also to be of good behavior for a year and a day. Thomas Hicks and Nicholas Sybert were at the same time bound, each in the sum of £500, to appear personally before the said grand jury, to give evidence against the said Peninger.

Robt. Davis, Robt. Cravens, Andrew Johnston, and John Rush, having produced commissions as captains of militia, were sworn in.

Joseph Dictums was sworn in as ensign.

The court proceeded to lay the ordinary [tavern] rates as follows, to wit:

Rum by the gallon or French Brandy,	£10 — — —
Whisky, per ditto,	4 — 16 0
Wine, per ditto,	10 — — —

ROCKINGHAM COUNTY

Cyder & Beer, per ditto,	1 — 4 —
Rum Toddy, per quart, with loaf sugar,	1 — 4 —
Whisky ditto, per ditto,	0 — 12 —
Warm Breakfast,	0 — 9 —
Ditto Dinner, with Beer,	0 — 12 —
A Bed, with Clean Sheets, per night,	0 — 5 —
Oats or Corn, per gallon,	0 — 6 —
Stableage, with Hay, a night,	0 — 10 —
Pasturage, a night,	0 — 6 —

Monday, April 26, 1779.

"On the complaint of Henry Brewster agt. Gabl. Jones Gent for threatening to shoot him for taking his Horse by Virtue of Authority of Capt. Rush without showing his warrant on hearing the Complaint & the answer of sd Jones the Court are of Opinion that the sd Brewster acted illegaly & therefore dismiss the Complaint."

April 27, 1779.

"Francis Stevins produced a Certificate of his Freedom from his master James Mcvey who acknowledged the same it is ordered to be certified."

May 24, 1779.

Andrew Bird took the oath "of a Captain of the militia in this County."

Michael Bowyer produced a license from the governor, and took the oath of an attorney.

May 25, 1779.

Michl. Coger was appointed to take the list of tithables in his own company; William Nalle, in Capt. Frazer's company; George Boswell, in Capt. Rush's company; Wm. Herring, in Capt. Hewitt's and Capt. Cravens' companies; Gawen Hamilton, in his own company; Henry Ewing, in Capt. Baxter's company; John Thomas, in Lincoln's company; John Fitzwater, in Capt. Boggs' company; Anto. Reader, in Capt. Ruddle's company; William McDowell, in Capt. Bird's com-

A HISTORY OF

pany; Daniel Smith, in Capt. Smith's company; James Dyer, in Capt. Davis' company; and Isaac Hanckle, in Capt. Johnston's company.

"On a majority of the Justices being present & conformable to a resolution of the Court in March last, for fixing a place for the Court house, the several members having proposed three different places a majority were for fixing it on the plantation of Thomas Harrison near the head of the Spring."

"John Davis, William McDowell, Jno. Fitzwater & Benj. Harrison Gent are appointed Commissioners to let out the building of a Court house of Stone 36 feet Long by 26 in Breadth one Story of 12 feet in higth with a partition at one End twelve feet wide to be divided into two Jury rooms with two angle fire places in each of the Jury rooms as also a prison built with Square Logs 12 Ins. thick in inside, 18 feet Square in the Clear & walled with stone 2 feet thick in the lower Story & the wall 18 Inches thick in the upper Story."

June 28, 1779.

Josiah Davidson, sheriff, being called on to undertake the collection of the taxes for the year, and having refused, was deprived of his office; and Abraham Smith, John Gratten, and George Boswell were recommended to the governor for consideration in filling the office. An express was to be hired to carry the recommendation to the governor, the expense to be paid by the sheriff out of the "Depositum" in his hands.

The commissioners appointed to arrange for the building of the court house and jail were empowered to choose a site of not less than two acres for the public buildings, and take deeds for the same in the name of the justices and their successors from Thomas Harrison, the proprietor, together with the liberty of stone and timber from the said Harrison's plantation for the said buildings.

On August 5, 1779, Thomas Harrison, Sr., and Sarah Harson, his wife, in consideration of the sum of Five Shillings current money of Virginia, conveyed to Silas Hart, Gentleman, first justice "in the Commission of the peace" for Rockingham County, his associate justices, and their successors, a tract of land containing Two Acres and a Half, for the sole use and behoof of the said county of Rockingham, upon which to build the Court House and other public buildings necessary for the said county. The tract of land in question had lately been surveyed by Mr. Gawin Hamilton, one of the deputy surveyors of the county, and was set and bounded as follows:

> Beginning at a Cedar Stump near a Small Cedar thence North ten Degrees East twenty poles to a Stake thence South Eighty degrees East twenty poles to two Spanish Oak Saplins thence South ten degrees West Twenty poles to a post thence North Eighty degrees West Twenty Poles to the Beginning.

At a court held for Rockingham the 23d day of August, 1779, Thomas Harrison acknowledged the deed of bargain and sale for the lot in question, and the deed was ordered to be recorded. Teste Peter Hog, C. R. C. The record was made in Deed Book No. 0, page 291—one of the volumes that were partly burned in 1864.[2]

July 26, 1779.

Abraham Smith was sworn in as sheriff of the county, with John Gratten, Henry Ewing, John Henton, David Ralstone, George Chrisman, Francis Kirtly, and Jesse Harrison as securities. Gawen Hamilton and William Smith were sworn in as deputy sheriffs.

Francis Mcbride was bound in the sum of £1000, with James Colhoon and George Chrisman, securities, each in the sum of £500, to appear before the grand jury in November to answer the charge of speaking "words disrespectful to the Government & present Constitution." John Brown, James Floyd, and John Hinton were bound, each in the sum of £100, to appear in person to testify in the case of the said Mc-

---

[2]. For a copy of the original deed made by Thomas Harrison to Silas Hart and others for the county lot, I am indebted to Capt. Geo. G. Grattan, formerly judge of the Rockingham County Court.

A HISTORY OF

Bride. The bond of John Hinton was to secure the evidence of his wife, Estor Hinton.

The sheriff was ordered to pay the sum of £90 to James Butcher for going to Williamsburg and returning therefrom as express for the sheriff's commission—the said sum to be paid from the "Depositum" in the sheriff's hands.

August 23, 1779.

Upon information of Henry Peninger, Gerard Erwine was bound in the sum of £1000, with John Brown and Thomas Campbell, securities, each in the sum of £500, to appear before the grand jury in November to answer the charge of having "propagated some news tending to raise Tumult and Sedition in the State." The said Peninger was also bound in the sum of £500 to appear as a witness in the examination of Erwine.

"Abraham Smith Gent Sheriff protested against the Sufficiency of the Jayl."

Thomas Harrison acknowledged his deed of bargain and sale to Silas Hart and others, justices, on behalf of the county.

The sum of £50 was placed in the hands of David Harnet for the relief of Bridget Fowler, wife of John Fowler, a soldier from this county "on the Continental Establishment," the said Bridget Fowler, with three small children, being in distressed circumstances.

The sum of £20 was appropriated for Barbara Woolridge, and a like sum for Mary Rylie, wives respectively of George Woolridge and John Rylie, soldiers in the continental army.

H. Dever and John Dever were fined "according to law" for breach of the Sabbath.

August 24, 1779.

William Nalle, with Gabriel Jones and Daniel Smith as securities, gave bond for the due execution of the office of escheator for the county.

ROCKINGHAM COUNTY

The sum of £30 was appropriated for Elizabeth Spikeard, whose husband, Julius Spikeard, and son, George Spykeard, were soldiers in the U. S. army.

Vali. Sevier[3] acknowledged deeds of lease and release to Robt. Rutherford.

The sheriff was ordered to pay to Wm. McDowell £93 15s. for the county seal.

The sum of £40 was appropriated for Ann Gum, the wife of Claypole Gum, a soldier.

The court proceeded to lay the levy:

To James Dyer, for two old wolves' heads,	£1—5—0
" Sebastian Hover, one ditto,	—12—6
" James Davis, one ditto,	—12—6
" James Dyer, 2 old wolves,	1—5—0
" Charles Wilson, one old wolf,	—12—6
" Joseph Kester, two old wolves,	1—5—0
" Gabriel Jones, deputy atto., for his salary,	150—0—0
" the Clerk for services, 1230 [lbs. tobacco?]	
" the Sheriff, for ditto, 1230 [lbs. tobacco?]	
" Gawen Hamilton, surveyor, per acct.,	10—0—0
" Peter Hog, clerk, per acct., 270 [lbs. tobacco?]	
" Daniel Smith, per acct.,	75—0—0
" Joseph Smith, William Crow, and Benj. Smith, as guards, 9 days each, on three tories in the county jail,	54—0—0
" Daniel Smith, for the use of his house, in holding 5 courts "since laying last year's levy,"	100—0—0
" Daniel Smith, jailor, for committing and releasing of the tories, 2790 pounds of tobacco, at £5 a 100-wt.,	139—10—0

---

[3] This was either the father or the brother of Gen. John Sevier.

A HISTORY OF

" a depositum for building the court house,   1783—18—0
" the Sheriff, commission on collecting £2466,
    at 6%,   147—19—6

            Total, £2466—0—0
By 1379 tithables, at six dollars, or 36 shillings,
    per tithable,   £2466—0—0

Ordered that the sheriff collect six dollars, or thirty-six shillings, from each tithable in the county as the levy for the ensuing year.

November 22, 1779.

"The Court taking into Consideration the dangerous & malignant Fever that for some months past has raged in the Family of Daniel Smith Gent. & the Apprehension of the people that there is Danger of the Disorder being contagious, to remove any Obstruction to the Administration of Justice & to quiet the minds of the Suitors & others who may have Business at Court, are of Opinion that the Court should be adjourned to the plantation of Thomas Harrison & it is hereby adjourned accordingly."

            Signed by Daniel Smith.

The sum of £30 was allowed to Anne McCoy, mother of William McCoy, a soldier.

November 23, 1779.

The sum of £20 was allowed Saml. Thornhill, father of John Thornhill, a soldier in the service of the States; and £30 was appropriated for Theodisia Maiden, wife of James Maiden, a soldier in the same service.

It was ordered that the sheriff pay Gawen Hamilton £55 for a bookcase for the clerk's office.

It was proved in court that Robert Menzies was a soldier in Capt. Hog's company of rangers in 1758, and that he had also served in Capt. Gist's[4] company in the campaign of 1760.

---

[4]. Capt. Gist was doubtless the famous scout and ranger, Christopher

ROCKINGHAM COUNTY

It was also established to the satisfaction of the court that John Smith, deceased, had been a lieutenant in Capt. John Smith's company of rangers in 1756, and had been killed at Fort Vause. Lieut. Smith was a brother to Abraham Smith. Claims for land were made upon the military service of Menzies and Smith.

It was ordered that Benj. Harrison, William Herron, and John Davis, or any two of them, "let out the Building of a Courtho. of square Logs with diamond Corners Thirty feet Long by 20 feet wide from out to out with a partition twelve feet in the Clear across the house divided into two rooms one 12 feet wide & the other 8 feet wide, the room 12 feet wide to have a neat stone Chimney inside at the Gavle End of it the whole to be floored with Earth as far as the Lawiers Bar & then to be raised with a plank floor to the Justices Bench which is to be raised three feet above the floor & the Breast of the Bench to be studed with a railed Top, the pitch of the house to be 10 feet clear Ceiling & lofted with Inch plank with two window on each side of the ho. facing the Clks. Table & one in Each of Jury rooms the windows 18 Lights each Glass 8 by 10 Inches, with a Door on — side just Clear of the Jury rooms."

This order was evidently to take the place of the one issued May 25, preceding, as shown above. Accordingly, it appears that the first court house was built of logs instead of stone, and that in size it was 20x30 feet instead of 26x36. Neither the court house nor the jail seems to have been completed before the end of 1783 or the beginning of 1784.

March 27, 1780.

The following were sworn in as captains of militia:
Josiah Harrison, Richard Reagan, Jeremiah Beasley.
The following as lieutenants:
Joseph Rutherford, Stephen Conrod, Robt. Smith.

Gist, who accompanied Washington on his perilous journey to the French forts in 1753.

A HISTORY OF

The following as ensigns:
Jacob Havener and Elliot Rutherford.

An allowance of £120 was made for the relief of Jemima Kelly, wife of Emanuel Kelly, a soldier from Virginia in the army of the United States. This allowance was made in accordance with a recent Act of the State Assembly, and was probably to be reimbursed from State funds.

March 28, 1780.

The court proceeded to rate the ordinary prices, for the articles named, as follows:

West India rum or French brandy, per gallon,	£48—	0—0
Rye liquor or whisky,	" 24—	0—0
Wine,	" 48—	0—0
Strong beer, per quart	1—10—0	
Cyder, "	1—10—0	
Hot dinner,	3—12—0	
Breakfast,	3— 0—0	
A cold ditto,	2— 2—0	
A good bed, with clean sheets	12—0	
Oats, by the gallon,	1—16—0	
Corn, by the gallon,	2— 8—0	
Stableage, with hay, per night,	2— 8—0	
Pasturage, per night,[5]	1—10—0	

David Laird proved that he had served as a corporal in Capt. Hog's company of rangers, from the time the said company was raised until it was discharged at Bedford, and that he had not received any warrant for land under the provisions of royal proclamation in 1763.

George Huston and John Fitzwater were sworn in as captains of militia.

[5.] From the figures in the above schedule, as well as from other items preceding and following, it is easy to see how the purchasing value of the continental currency was decreasing. It thus continued to decrease until it had value only in the proverb: "Not worth a Continental." And yet, by a fateful irony of circumstance, men were being arraigned, even in Rockingham, for speaking words tending to depreciate it.

Chesapeake-Western Bridge across the Shenandoah River near Elkton

The Bridge at Bridgewater

By per. of E. G. Furry

[Page 200]

Port Republic: Confluence of the Rivers, the Bridge, and the Heights toward Cross Keys

ROCKINGHAM COUNTY

Jacob Pence proved that he had served as a soldier in Capt. Hog's company of rangers from the beginning of the said company in 1757 until it was discharged at Bedford, making oath that he had never received any warrant for land, as provided in 1763.

Robt. Minnis made it appear that he had served as a soldier in Collo. Byrd's regiment, &c.

John Stephenson proved that he had been a soldier in the independent company under Capt. McClanahan, and also had served in Boqueter's (?) company, &c.

April 24, 1780.

Geo. Armentrout proved that he had served in Capt. Hog's company of rangers, &c.

Daniel Grubb proved service in the same company.

May 23, 1780.

In the case of the commonwealth vs. McBride, the latter being adjudged guilty, was subjected to a fine of £250 and four days' imprisonment.

June 9, 1780.

At a special session of the court, called for the examination of John Davis, suspected of being guilty of treason against the State, and of "other misdemeanors," Daniel Smith, Henry Ewing, Reuben Harrison, Thomas Hewit, and Benj. Harrison, justices, being present, the said Davis was upon trial adjudged guilty of treason, &c., and was ordered sent to the general court to be tried for the same. Furthermore, Seruiah Stratton, James Rodgers, and William Gregg were bound, each in the sum of £10,000, to appear in the case as witnesses on the 6th day of the general court to be held at Richmond the following October.

June 26, 1780.

"Frederick Price, being bound over on Recognizance taken before Danl. Smith Gent for drinking the King of gt

A HISTORY OF

Britain's health & Huzzas for sd King," was tried and bound over to the grand jury court to be indicted, himself in the sum of £10,000, with Augustine Price and George Mallow, securities, each in the sum of £5000.

John Nicolas, Abraham Hammond, and Jacob Arkenbright were bound, each in the sum of £1000, to appear in the above case as witnesses.

"Ordered that Benja. Harrison & William Herring Gent be empowered to agree with the Undertaker of Courtho to omit the partion of the East End of the house for the Jury rooms & to sink the Joyst of the upper room from Gavel of the sd East end to the Joyst over the front Door so as to make a Jury room above wi a pair of Stairs in the Corner, or two jury rooms if the space will admit of it."[6]

August 29, 1780.

Silas Hart, Henry Ewing, John Davis, and William Herring were appointed commissioners to let the building of a county jail, according to the plan agreed on by the court, to the lowest bidder, "between this & the Nov. Court, & to give publick notice thereof."

October 23, 1780.

"On the application of John Magill setting forth that he has kept Ruth McDonald Daughter of Randall McDonald a soldier from this County in the Army of the United States 18 months by agreement of the sd. Randall which being expired, & her Father still in the Service the Court are of opinion that the said Magill be allowed £35 for a barl of Corn & 200 Dolrs for 50 w of pork for the support of the said Ruth McDonald for 1 year."

"The Court taking into Consideration the distressed Situation of Anne Gum & two young Babes widow & orphans of

---

[6]. Evidently, as the process of building continued, the temple of justice was growing smaller. The burden of war was bearing heavily upon the young county.

ROCKINGHAM COUNTY

Claypole Gum a Soldier from this County who died in the service of the States recommend her to the board of Auditors for such relief as they think proper for her distressed circumstances."

October 24, 1780.

William Herring was sworn in as captain of militia; Joseph Dictam and Andrew Shanklin, as first lieutenants; Robt. Harrison as ensign.

George Boswell, upon commission from the governor [Thomas Jefferson] was sworn into the office of sheriff.

November 27, 1780.

Zeruiah Stratton was sworn in as a captain of militia.

"A sufficient number of the grand jury not appearing [24 had been summoned] O that the be discharged & the following persons being summoned & called & not attending O that they be fined according to Law towit Jas. Beard Jo. Rutherford Zeb Harrison Adam Reader Peter Conrod James Dever Francis Stewart Jacob Lincoln & Nico. Cairn."

November 28, 1780.

"Silas Hart John Davis Henry Ewing & Wm. Herring Gent Commissioners appointed to let the building the County Jayl reported that they had let out the building of the same to Cornelius Cain for Eleven Thousand nine hundred & Seventy three pounds, & retd. a Bond of Said Cornes. Cain wi security for the Due performance of said building."

Abraham Smith, having resigned the office of county lieutenant, on account of "his Disorder & Infirmities," the court recommended Danl. Smith for appointment in his stead.

The court allowed 3 barrels of corn, at £40 a barrel, and 150 pounds of pork, at 30 — —, to Frances Clough, wife of John Clough, a soldier in the service of the States.

The sheriff was ordered to pay Thomas Harrison £100 for holding 3 courts in his house.

A HISTORY OF

March 26, 1781.

Daniel Smith, Gent., was sworn in as county lieutenant of the militia; George Chrisman and Reuben More, as captains; Jacob Lincoln, as a lieutenant.

"It is the Opinion of the Court that John Huston be allowed 60 dollars per Day from the 8th Jany till 18th Feby for acting as Dep. Comiss. to the militia sent down against Arnold."

March 27, 1781.

"O that the Clerk purchase a new Testament for the use of the Court & that the Sheriff pay him out of the Depositum."

"It is the opinion of the Court that James Davis a Commissary for the militia of this County ordered to the Southard in Sept last be allowed 80 Dollars per Day from 22 d Sept till the 3 d Novr. being 51 Days."

"Ordered that the late Sheriff [Abram Smith] pay Robt. Campbell the ballce due him for the original Contract in building the Courtho, being £187."

April 23, 1781.

Stephen Conrad was sworn in as a captain of militia, Capt. Jerema. Beeslie's company being divided.

"Ordered that the Sheriff collect Seven Shillings & Six pence in the pound from every person within this County on each pound tax that the said person is now taxed at in the present assessment as pay for the Waggon found by this County for the State."

"It is the opinion of the Court that Joseph Haines be allowed twenty pounds per day for acting as a Commissary to the prisoners Six Days when marching thro this, to Shandoah County."

May 28, 1781.

"Anderson Moffet an anabist Minister having satisfied

ROCKINGHAM COUNTY

the Court by a certificate from the Elders of his Sect that he is duely qualified to administer the Sacraments is licensed to perform the function of marrying by Banns or License in this County."

"The Court proceeded to alter the Ordinary rates in the following particulars towit

a hot Dinner for one person,	30 Dollars
strong Beer or Cyder, per Quart,	12 Dollars
pasturage, per night,	12 Dollars
Whiskey or Rye Liquor, per Gallon,	£57-12-0."

May 29, 1781.

Silas Hart was appointed to take the list of tithables in the districts of Huston and Young; Josiah Davidson, in the districts of Rice and Harrison; Anto. Reader, in the districts of Fitzwater and Ruddle; William McDowell, in the districts of Harrison and Dunlop; John Davis, in the districts of Herring and Magill; Michl. Coger, of his own company; Thos. Hewit, in Capt. Conrod and Capt. Beeslie's companies; James Dyer, in Capt. Johnson and Capt. Stratton's companies; Robt. Davidson, in his own company.

This appears to be the first instance in which the term "district" is used, referring to a subdivision of the county. The original divisions, recognized for the purpose of listing the tithables, were evidently made according to the localities making up the several companies of militia.

"The Court are of opinion that Henry Ewing be allowed twenty pounds per day for twenty-three Days that he acted as Commissary, of the provision Law & 100 Dollars for his Expences."

August 27, 1781.

Zeruiah Stratton produced an account in court for building a granary, and for receiving the grain tax, which was allowed and certified by the court.

"Thomas Hewit Gent is appointed by the Court to the

A HISTORY OF

Office of Sheriff for the ensuing year. O to be certified to his Excellency the Govr."

"It appearing to the Court that a traveller by the name of Moses Doughty with his wife & child was burnt up in the House of Adam Nelson & no relatives or other Connexions of the sd. Doughty appearing to claim administra. of his Estate consisting of a horse & a mare O that the Sheriff take the same into his possession being now in the Custody of Jno. Thomas Coroner & sell them at publick Vendue & make a return to the Court."

William Nalle was sworn in as lieutenant-colonel of the militia.

September 24, 1781.

Isaac Hankle was sworn in as a captain of militia to succeed Andrew Johnston, resigned. Michael Baker was also sworn in as a captain of militia.

The signature of Daniel Smith, presiding justice, appears under this date for the last time. He died before the next court, held in November. The next records are signed by John Grattan.

November 26, 1781.

"Leave is granted to Samuel Gay to keep Ordinary at his house in Harrisons burg for one year from this Date."

A bill of sale of Moses Dougherty's estate was returned by the sheriff and admitted to record.

The court made out the following budget:

To Gabriel Jones, Deputy Atty.,	4000 lbs. tobacco
To Peter Hog, Clerk, for extra services,	1200 " "
To " " , account,	200 " "
To the sheriff, for extra services,	1200 " "

Total, 6600 lbs. tob. = at 10s. cwt., £33

ROCKINGHAM COUNTY

To Cornelius Cain, for building the Jayl, for the balance due and the depreciation of the currency since it was undertaken, in specie, or in paper money at the depreciation fixed by the Assembly,	£100
To Samuel Parrot, 2 wolves heads,	£ 1— 5—0
To Robt. Campbell, as a gratuity for building the courthouse,	3— 3—0
To Robt. Campbell, for the additional work on the courthouse,	7—19—0
For finishing the Jayl, &c.,	40— 0—0
	£ 152— 7—0
A depositum,	10—13
	£196— 0—0
To the sheriff for collecting, 6%	11—15—0
	£207—15—0

It was ordered that the sheriff collect 3s. in specie on every tithable in the county, as a levy for the ensuing year; or the equivalent value in paper currency, as fixed by the Assembly.

Income from 1450 tithables, £217—10—0

November 27, 1781.

"Ordered that the late Sheriff [George Boswell] pay to Cornelius Cain the Money levied this last County Levy for building the County Jayl being £11973, the Commissioners who let the building of the same having reported that the it is finished according to the plan."

George Boswell, late sheriff, settled with the court, reporting a balance on hand of £580—7—0, on 1459 tithables, 8 supernumeraries, and 51 delinquents.

"O that Andrew Shanklen keep the Courtho for the ensuing year & provide a Stock Lock for the fore Door & an Iron Bolt for the other Door & provide the Court with Fire & Candles."

A HISTORY OF

"Ordered that Robt. Campbell undertaker of the Courtho be allowed the further sum of £3. 8 in Specie on the Depreciation as settled by the Assembly."

"O that Henry Ewing & William Herring Gent be appointed as Commissioners to let out the finishing the County Jayl to the lowest Bidder to [be] finished by the May Court."

February 18, 1782.

The former clerk [Peter Hog] being reported dead, Thomas Lewis was appointed clerk pro tem.

Benjamin Harrison, Bruer Reeves, and John Fitzwater were chosen, according to an Act of Assembly passed the preceding October, as commissioners to value the lands belonging to the sundry landholders of the county.

February 25, 1782.

Richard Matthews was appointed clerk pro tem., and Henry Ewing was elected to hold the office permanently.

March 25, 1782.

William Smith was sworn in as a captain of militia.

At a court opened March 26, 1782, and continued several days for adjusting claims, agreeable to an Act of Assembly passed in October, 1781, the following claims were presented and approved. The services rendered and supplies furnished were for the United States in the War for Independence.

Zebulon Harrison for 39 head of cattle, 24 hours at post, stableage for 2 horses 12 hours, corn and rations. Claim dated Dec. 4, 1781.

Josiah Harrison, for 6 days with his team in conducting British prisoners from the South to "Shanado Courthouse." Claim dated March 1, 1781.

Zebulon Harrison, for 700 lbs. of hay—clover and timothy—Feb. 24, 1781; 200 lbs. of beef for the use of British prisoners and guards, Aug. 20, 1781; for the use of the militia guard with British prisoners from this county to Shanado, 14 bu. of oats, at 1 s. 8 d., Dec. 4, 1781.

ROCKINGHAM COUNTY

Josiah Harrison, for bullock driving, 1 day, Jan. 16, 1781.

Gideon Harrison, for bullock driving, 1 day, Jan. 18, 1781.

Archibald Hopkins, for 2 bags for the use of the militia going to "Tyger Valley," April 30, 1779, 18 s.; and for 1060 lbs. of flour, at 15 s. cwt., for the use of the militia ordered on duty, May, 1779. These two items were charged against the State; all others herein recorded were charged against the United States, unless note is made to the contrary.

Archibald Hopkins for 22½ yds. of "Lining" [linen ?] for a tent for the use of the militia ordered to Richmond on duty, at 2 s. a yard, Jan. 16, 1781; for 7 head of cattle, 3 years old, "Each Extraordinary large of that age Estimated at 400 lbs. Each," at 16 s. 8 d. per cwt., for use of the militia ordered on duty to Carolina, Oct. 3, 1780.[7]

George Baxter, for 24 yds. of "lining" for use of the militia, ordered on duty to Richmond, at 2 s. a yard, Jan. 16, 1781.

John Hopkins, for 4 head of cattle, estimated at 1900 gross, at 16 s. 8 d. per cwt., for use of the militia ordered on duty to Carolina, Oct. 3, 1780.

John Hopkins, for 245 lbs. flour, at 15 s. per cwt., for the militia ordered on duty to "Tygers Valley," May 5, 1779. This item was charged against the State.

John Hopkins, for the making of 7 tents, £2 10 s., for militia ordered on duty to Richmond, Jan. 6, 1781; for 21 4-3 yds. of "Lining," for the militia ordered on duty to Richmond, Jan. 16, 1781; for 1 1-2 bus. corn, at 2 s. a bushel, and pasturage for 7 horses, 1 night, at 6 d. each, Oct. 27, 1780.

Marthew Smith, "for one Black Horse 14 Hands High Well Made five years Old one Halter and Bell at 25£ for the use of ye Mal. Ord. on Duty to tygers," April 29, 1782; charged to the State.

---

[7]. A marked difference in the size of cattle has been registered since the 18th century. In 1710 the average weight of beeves sold in the Smithfield market was only 370 pounds. As late as 1795 the average weight of London beeves was only 800 pounds. See Bogart's Economic History of the United States, page 72. In recent years Rockingham cattle have reached a maximum weight of 2000 pounds or more.

A HISTORY OF

William Hook, for 21¾ yds. "lining," for the militia ordered on duty to Richmond, Jan. 18, 1781; for 3800 lbs. of "good timothy Hay," at 1 s. 6 d. per cwt., for the use of the guard removing prisoners from Albemarle barracks to Maryland, Jan. 20, 1781.—These prisoners were probably some of those taken at Burgoyne's surrender in October, 1777, and quartered for a year or two between Charlottesville and Ivy, in Albemarle County.[8]

James Bruster, for 98 days' service with a team, at 10s. a day, employed for the use of the militia ordered on duty to Richmond; account dated April 25, 1781; for 3 days' service with his team, at 15s. a day, employed in removing prisoners from Albemarle barracks, Jan. 10, 1781.

March 27, 1782.

John Hinton, for acting as forage master 7 days, at 5 s. a day; account dated Jan. 1, 1781; for a balance on a receipt for bacon, 50 lbs., at 1s. per lb., and for wheat, 35½ bus., at 6s. per bu., April 30, 1779. The last two items were charged to the State.

John Hinton was allowed other claims for cattle, flour, rye, flour casks, hay, corn, horse pasture, wagoner's rations, etc.

Thomas Moore, for 1 bullock, weight 440 lbs. neat, at 2½ s. a pound, Febr. 25, 1781; for 18 "Diets" at 6d. each, and 7 horses, 1 night, at good hay, 7½ d. per horse, March 4, 1781.

James Bruster, for 9 days public service with his team, at 10 s. a day; for feeding 1 public horse 3 days, at 1s. 3d. a day; for 1 horse in public service 38 days, at 1 s. 6 d. a day; for 4 flour casks, at 2 s. each; account dated Dec. 22, 1780.

John Davis, for 12 yds. of "Course lin'g," at 2 s. 6 d. a yard, Jan. 16, 1781.

James Dunn, for 19 yds. "Course lining," at 2s. 6d. a yard, Oct. 5, 1780.

---

[8]. For a detailed account of the sojourn of these prisoners in Albemarle, see Edgar Wood's History of Albemarle County, Virginia, pp. 31-44.

ROCKINGHAM COUNTY

Elizabeth Shipman, for making 1 tent, 6 s. 3 d., Oct. 15, 1780.

John Crafford, for 16 yds. "lin'g" at 2 s. 6 d. a yard, Oct. 15, 1780.

William Diver, for "1 Kittle 1 Do 10s. per kittle," Oct. 5, 1780.

Ban. Wheton, for 10 yds. of coarse linen, at 2s. a yard, Jan. 16, 1781.

George Gartner, for 1 blanket, "good in Quality," 20s., Oct. 26, 1780.

Balser Counce, for 1 day public service with his team, Oct. 27, 1780.

Ralph Lofties, for 1 iron pot, 20s., Oct. 9, 1780.

France Ervin, for 919 lbs. flour, at 12s. 6 d. per cwt., Nov. 7, 1780.

Henry Stolph, for 8 yds. of "Wolling not full'd," at 5s. a yard, Nov. 9, 1780.

John Bowman, for 9 yds. of "Do.," at 5s. a yard, Nov. 9, 1780.

John Cring, for 13 yds. of "Do.," at 5s. a yard, Nov. 9, 1780.

Daniel Love, for "4 Dozen of Oats," at 1s. 6d. a dozen, and 4 bushels of [oats?], at 2s. a bushel, Nov. 6, 1780 [?].

Margret Devier, for making 1 tent, 6s. 3d., Oct. 7, 1780.

George Long, for 1½ bus. wheat, at 3s. a bushel, Nov. 14, 1780.

Godferry Hamileton, for 6 yds. cloth, at 5s. a yard, Nov. 9, 1780.

Richard Mathews, for "halfe a bus of allum," £1 10s., Oct. 7, 1780.

Thomas Shanling, for 3 days public service with his team, at 10s. a day, and for 4½ bus. oats, at 1s. 8d. a bushel, Oct. 28, 1780.

Jacob Seth, for 6 days public service with his team, March 1, 1781.

William Devir, for 1 bell and strap and buckle, Oct. 13, 1780.

A HISTORY OF

Robt. Williams, for 6 days public service with his team, March 1, 1781.

Isiah Shipman, for "1 Iron or Dutch oven, 1£," Oct. 6, 1780.

David Harnet, for 200 lbs. hay, at 1s. 3d. per cwt., Nov. 3, 1781; for 300 lbs. hay, Jan. 14, 1781. "To the Above Ord. to be aded 31 Galls. of Corn at 4D per gall., and 30 Diets at 6 per Diet."

"The aforesd. Receipts Granted to Mr. Harnet the Artickles Ware as appear to the Court for the use of the Mal. Called Out By Col. Jno. Smith Lieut. of Frederick County In Order to Repulse the enemy When Makeing their Rout as Was Supposed toward the Albamarle Barricks To Retake the Con-n troops Whence the Immergency that Cased [?] Ocasion Every Man to ride [?] for Which."

David Harnet, for 1100 lbs. hay, Jan. 2, 1782; for 7 rations, 1s. each, Aug. 27, 1781; etc.

Michael Couger, for 1000 lbs. beef, Nov. 20, 1780; for 24 diets, May 27, 1781; etc.

Michael Roarick, for 11 yds. coarse linen, Jan. 19, 1781.

William Donafin, for 1 gun, "Which Gun sd. Dunafin Lost In the Battle of Hot Water[9] Being badly Wounded," £2 12s.

John Harrison, for 26 diets, 6d. each, Nov. 13, 1781; etc.

John Armentrout, for 23 days with team, Dec. 11, 1780.

Peter Sellers, for 5 bus. corn, at 2 s., Nov. 14, 1780; 5 bus. rye, at 2 s. 6d., Nov. 10, 1780.

Robt. Elliot, for 5 bus. corn, Nov. 14, 1780; etc.

Frederick Rob, for 19 bus. corn, Febr. 23, 1781.

Coonrod Fudge, for 96 lbs. pork, at 3d., Jan. 13, 1781. "The Same With Mr. Harnets from Shando."

David Fudge, for 1 bu. corn and 3 suppers, at 6d. each, Jan. 13, 1781.

---

[9]. The battle of "Hot Water" was fought, probably, on the 26th of June, 1781, not far from Williamsburg. If the engagement at the time and place mentioned was the "battle" named, Donafin was distinguished, since the Americans who took part therein were picked men, commanded by a Major Willis. See Waddell's Annals of Augusta, pp. 300, 301.

ROCKINGHAM COUNTY

William Young, for 130 lbs. hay, for 10 sheaves oats, 1s., and for 8 diets, at 6d. each, Jan. 13, 1781.
"Same With Harnets."
Adam Hansberger, for 52 bus. corn, Nov. 15, 1780; etc.
David Fudge, for 1 bag, 6s., Febr. 19, 1781.
John Fudge, for 1 pair "Stilards," 12s. 6d., Sept. 16, 1781.
Coonrod Hansberger, for 87 yds. woolen cloth, colored blue, at 7s. 6d. a yard, Jan. 16, 1781.
Adam Hansberger, for 1 "Waggoner Cover Very Good," 40 shillings, Oct. 8, 1780.
Reis Thomas, for 1 good blanket, £1, Oct. 26, 1780.
John Thomas, for 4 diets, at 6d. each, and 2 quarts whisky, 2s., Febr. 26, 1781.
"Ord. that ye Sheriff summon Wm. Herring to attend Court tomorrow."

March 28, 1782.

Justices present:

John Fitzwater   Reuben Harrison
William Nawl   Wm. Herring
Michael Couger

Claims allowed:

Leonard Herring, for 30 bus. corn, July 3, 1781.
Frederick Armentrout, for 1 bag, and 2 bus. "Spotts," Nov. 15, 1780; for 1 bag, April 24, 1779; etc.
Henry Miller, for 50 gals. whiskey, at 3s. a gallon, and casks, 6s., Sept. 14, 1781; 39 horses 1 night at hay, Jan. 14, 1781; and 1 bu. "Spels,"[10] 1s. 8d.; for 30 morning snacks and 30 gills whiskey, Jan. 15, 1781.
"This under the same Circumstances wt. harnets."

---

10. "Spels" was doubtless spelt, a grain related to wheat and barley, much used for food in Germany and Switzerland. It is also called "German wheat." This is a circumstantial touch reminding us that most of the early settlers of Rockingham came from Germany and Switzerland. The "Spotts" sold by Fred. Armentrout were likely some grain or vegetable, also.

A HISTORY OF

Henry Miller, for 1 ax, 5s., Jan. 19, 1781; for 437 lbs. beef, June 6, 1781.

Jere Besselly, for 1 bu. corn and hay for 27 horses 1 night, Jan. 13, 1781.

"Sam at harnet."

Jere Beazle, for pasturing 5 horses 4 days, Sept. 22, 1781;

Jere Beezly, for 1 gal. salt, 7s. 6d., Jan. 13, 1781.

George Kessle, for hay and oats, Jan. 1, 1782.

George Kelsle, for 6 days with team, March 1, 1781.

Gorge Kessle, for 8 days rations for 2 men, Feb. 23, 1778.

Georg Kezle,[11] for 2 days with team, Feb. 12, 1781.

James Laird, for 99 days public service with his team, acct. dated April 11, 1781.

Alexander Miller, for 725 lbs. beef, Nov. 15, 1780.

Frances Stewart, for pasturing 10 cattle 7 days, Nov. 2, 1781; etc.

Jas. Rutherford, for 6 bus. rye, Nov. 17, 1780.

Sam. Hamphill, for 22½ lbs. bacon, at 9d., and 97 lbs. pork, at 3d., Feb. 4, 1781.

Peter Nicholas, for 10 soldiers' diets, Febr. 25, 1781; to the same, for hay, diets, forage, oats, corn, &c., at various times.

Jacob Nicholas, for 200 lbs. hay, and for pasturing 14 head of cattle, Nov. 12, 1780.

Reuben Harrison, for 99 days public service with his team, acct. dated Dec. 12, 1781.

Banabas Carpenter, for 1 beef weighing 287 lbs., at 2d. a pound, Sept. 16, 1781; and for 1350 lbs. hay, at 1s. 6d. per cwt., Jan. 1, 1782.

Barnabas Simmerman, for public service with his team, Jan. 20, 1781; to the same, for hay, corn, diets, lodging, etc., at various times; and "for Damage Done by Continental troops to the possessions of sd. Simmerm., 8 shillings," Dec. 4, 1780.

---

[11] Kessle, Kelsle, and Kezle were obviously one and the same man, to-wit, George Keezell, for whom Keezletown is named.

ROCKINGHAM COUNTY

John Brown, for 2 bus. rye, at 2s. 6d. a bushel, Nov. 17, 1780.

John Frazor, for 2 bus. rye and 10 bus. corn, Nov. 26, 1780.

Nana Simerman, for 66 lbs. mutton, at 3d. a pound, Febr. 21, 1781.

Pat. Guin, for 3 bus. corn, Dec. 7, 1781.

Daniel Smith, for pasturing 34 troop horses 20 days, for beef, corn, and whiskey, July 21, 1781; for public service with his team, &c., Nov. 30, 1781.

Michael Couger, for making 2 tents, at 6s. 3d., Jan. 18, 1781.

March 29, 1782.

Accounts were allowed for military supplies furnished, for public service with teams, for horses lost in public service, etc., to the following:

Reuben Harrison
John Weir
Peter Miller, Sr.
Ester Stephenson
John Burk
Peter Miller, Jr.
Leonard Miller
Robt. Hook
Jacob Bear
Henry Miller
James Bruster
Coonrod Hulvah
Gabriel Jones
Peachy Gilmore
George Mallow
Adam Sellers
Robt. Slaughter
John Branum
Jacob Peters
Woolry Hershman
Ben. White
Henry Long
Lawrence Slaughter
Ann Field
Jacob Kiblinger
And. Hudlow
Joseph Hannah
Paul Lingal
Hans Magart
George Boswell

March 30, 1782.

Accounts were allowed for linen, making tents, for flour, beef, pasturage, rations, etc., to the following:

William Snoding
Henry Stone

A HISTORY OF

Sebaston Hoover
Henry Dove
Henry Harter
Daniel Smith
William Nall
Edward Williams
Jacob Baer
Woolry Hershman
Jacob Moyers
Darby Ragon
Felex Gilbert (For putting in a new axletree, and other-
        wise repairing a public wagon, 5s.)
To the same, for corn, horse shoes, &c.
John Perky
George Pence
Henry Pence (For 8 flour barrels.)
John Smith (For 7 days wagoning, in assisting with the
        British prisoners from the south, to Shen-
        andoah, March, 1781.)
William Marshall
Lewis Circle
Zeb Harrison (For one "Brown Mare, 14½ hands High.
        Stout made 15 years Old 10£.")
To the same, "By a dutch Clark, ye hand not known, for
        40 head of Bullocks at Pasture one Night at
        3 per Head."
Adam Argabright
Martin Argabright
Danl. Guin (For "1 Bay Mare 14 hands & 1 Inch High 5
        years Old Well Made Lost in Publick Service
        twenty Pounds.")
Brewer Reeves
Isaac Wood
Alex. Miller
William Fitzwater
Sarah Bags
Jeremiah Ragon

Lethe—Present Home of E. B. Hopkins
(Pages 109, 110)

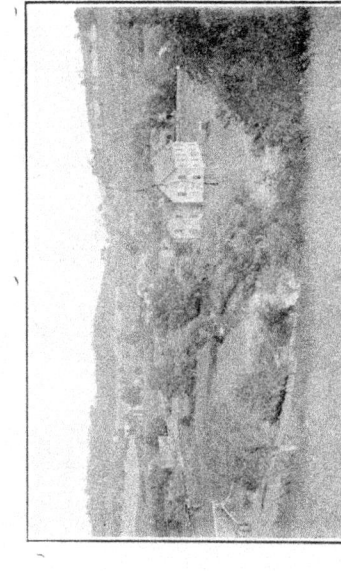

Mt. Clinton: W. C. Academy
(Pages 265, 290)

Lincoln Homestead on Linville Creek. Residence of S. M. Bowman

Farm Home of Miss Lizzie Miller, near Elkton
(Page 35)

ROCKINGHAM COUNTY

John Page
John Ewin
Wm. Stephenson
Frances Erwin
Gawin Hamilton
Jacob Fowland
Johnston Neilson (For "1 Riffel Gun Powder Horn and Shot bag Lost in ye Continental Service In ye year 76 In ye Expedition to Georgia £5 10s.")
Jeremiah Harrison (By assignment from Conrad Smith, for 1 roan mare, with bell and pack saddle, lost in the State service in 1774, "In the Exp. to ye point Under Dunmore," £10.)
Daniel Smith
Handel Vance
Nicholas Curry
Michael Baker
John Fitzwater
Wm. Marshal
Danl. Polser
Wat. Crow
James Elliot
William Magill
John Guin
John Hemphill
James Baird
George Carpenter (For "1 Gun Lost In the year 81 In the Battle at Jas. Town gun Shot poutch and powder horn," £5 5s.)
Wm. Smith (For acting as packhorse master in carrying provisions to "Tyger Valey," 40 days, at 6s. per day, "Who then Acted under the Direction of Wm. Boon accordg appt By Col. Abram Smith C £. sd Boon having someTime ago Retd his Papers By Col. Nawl," etc.)

—97—

A HISTORY OF

Jonathan Shipman
Abijiah Warrin
Jno. McGlahing
Lind. Wade
Jno. Armstrong
Thomas Collick
Jacob Glaspie
William Rice
James Bletcher
John Rice
Jeremiah Harrison
Robt. Craveors
John Deniston
Abram Smith
George Peirce
William Young

April 1, 1782.

Benjamin Harrison took the oath prescribed by law for County Lieutenant of the militia.

April 22, 1782.

Will of Peter Hog, first clerk of the court, written in his own hand, proved by Richard Madison, one of the subscribing witnesses. Gabriel Jones and George Matthews gave bond as executors. Elizabeth Hog is mentioned as surviving widow.

April 23, 1782.

Accounts were allowed for service in the Revolution, as follows:

Sept. 27, 1780.—"To Jas. Carrel for one Waggon, 3 Horses and Geers for four horses All lost in Publick Service Under Comd. of Genl. Stevans In Carolina Being first 52 Days in ye service 7 Day Retg home at 5s. 6d. Day and 10s. 6d. Day for sd. 52 Days in service."

Carrel was allowed for his horses £25, £30, and £15, respectively; for the wagon, gears, &c., £18.

ROCKINGHAM COUNTY

To Wm. Magill, for 15 days serving as quarter master with the militia from this county, to "Head Qt. Mopin Hills," at 6s. a day. No date.

To Wm. Hook, for 1 horse, lost in public service in 1779, £10.

April 24, 1782.

Accounts were allowed for service, supplies furnished, etc., during the Revolution, to the following persons:

George Spears
Sol. Mathews
John Henton
John Hopkins
George Baxter
Jeremiah Ragon
Richard Mathews
Archibald Hopkins
Isiah Shipman
Jonathan Shipman
Archibald Henderson
Silas Hart
James Devier
Hugh Devier
Fred. Armentrout
Mathias Kersh (For 3 beeves weighing nett 1750 lbs., at 2½d. a pound.)
George Weaver
John Weaver
Jacob Perkey
Thos. Care
Henry Monger
Adam Sellers
Col. Wm. Nawl
Robt. Elliot
Henry Armentrout
Wm. White
Martin Petro

A HISTORY OF

Wm. Davis
Wm. Mills
Jacob Nicholas
David Laird
George Mallow
Ann Carpenter
George Carpenter
Adam Fought
William Hook
Thomas Harrison
Frances Stewart
John Miller
George Huston ("For paying for Keeping 1 Horse His Own Property But Lost In the Ctry Service in Mcintosh Expd. Taken Up and Again Rd. to Him For Sixty Days 4 Dollars And pay 1s. 6d. for 106 Days Being ye Time of sd. Expt."
Dated Feb. 18, 1779.)

The sheriff was ordered to collect the window glass tax, agreeable to Act of Assembly passed in May, 1780, "Which Should Have Been Collected In Augt. 81."

May 27, 1782.

Frances Kees [?] took the oath of an attorney "in this Court."

May 28, 1782.

It was ordered that James Montgomery, son of Sam. Montgomery, deceased, be bound according to law, by the church wardens, "To Mr. Jno. Hicks To Learn ye silver smith Trade untill he Comes of ye Age of 21 years he Being 14 year Spt Ensuing and the sd. Hicks Learn him read Wright and Cypher."

Accounts for services rendered, supplies furnished, etc., during the Revolution, were allowed to the following persons:

ROCKINGHAM COUNTY

James Grace
John Davis
Henry Stone
Frances Beaverly
Henry Whisler
Fred. Keiler
George Ruddle
James Magill

Handel Vance
Mary Cravens
Margaret Cravens
John Craig
Wm. Hook
Abram Peters
Nehemiah Harrison

May 29, 1782.

Accounts for services rendered, supplies furnished, etc., during the Revolution, were allowed to the following persons:

John Shipman
Reuben Harrison
Thomas Harrison
Robt. Harrison
Robt. Hook
Walter Crow
Mathew Patton
Robt. Davis
James Dyer
Frederick Kester

Jacob Coofman
John Pence
John Robison
David Robison
John Thomas
George Mallow
Augustine Price
Jacob Harmon
Jno. Bear

May 30, 1782.

Revolutionary claims were allowed to

Bethuell Herring
France Irvine
David Ralston
Robt. Slaughter
Jacob Moyer
Lewis Runckle
Henry Price
John Sword
Hugh Dunahoe
Michael Carns
Thomas Hewitt
Alex. Herring
Frances Stewart

Michael Stump
John Bullet
Charles Rush
Pasley Hover
John Sellers
Stephen Coonrod
Pet. Kize
George Coonrod
Pet. Coonrod
Philip Long
William Pence
Lewis Rhinehart
John Fye

A HISTORY OF

Pet. Runckle
David Laird
John Eddy
Joseph Smith
Thomas Harrison

June 7, 1782.

Revolutionary claims were allowed to

John Herdman
John Hinton
John McWilliams
John Ewins
Chrisly Painter
John Hopkins
Archibald Hopkins
Robt. Dunlap
Ephraim Love
Brewer Reeves
Godfrey Bowman
Wm. Pettejohn
Jacob Bear
Robt. Elliot
James Dier
Easther Stephenson
John Blain
Jacob Warick
Joseph Strickler
Alex. Samples
John McDugal
Henry Ewins
Wm. Hook
Ezekiel Harrison

August 28, 1782.

"Came into Court Benj Crow & made oath that there was a Rifel gun powder horn shot pouch and knife taken from Him When a continental soldier In the year 1777 and put Into the Magn. for which he Recd a certificate Which he Lodged with Walter Crow who also came into Court and Made oath that He Has Lost the sd. Cera. and never Recd any value for ye same the Court Is therefore of the oppinion that ye sd. Benj Crow Be allowed £7 10s for sd gun powder horn shot Pouch and knife and the Same Is ord. to Be Cert."

"Came into Court Walter Crow And Made oath that He Delivered 280 lbs. of Bacon To Mr. Tate Comg. at Albamarle Barricks In April 1779 for Which he has Never Rd. any Valy or Satisfan. the Court Is therefore of ye oppinion that He Be allowed 7½ per lb. and ye same Is ord. To Be Cerd."

"Came into Court Robt. Davis Gent. and Made oath the Hemshire Cty Mal When in this Cty supressing The Tories Red. of Him 30 Diets for Which he Red. no——the Court Is

ROCKINGHAM COUNTY

therefore of ye oppn. that he Be allowed 6 d. per Diet & S ord. To Cert."

September 24, 1782.

"To John Donaphan 1 Gun Lost in Hot water Battle a smooth Rhifle about 3 feet 7 Inches Long Brass mounted with Amidling Lock Vallued To £3 0 & C.

"The Sd. Donaphan was wounded in the Action."—Account dated July 26, 1781.

October 29, 1782.

"To James Reeves for One Rifle Gun Lost in Crossing James River at Sandy Point upon the March Against Genl. Arnold Valued at £5.0.0 Specie."

November 27, 1782.

James Devier was appointed to procure weights and measures for a standard in the county, according to law, "upon the best Terms he can as far as 40£ Will Extend Having Regard To ye Purchassing of the sd. Measures In ye first Place."

March 25, 1783.

"Gawin Hamilton Gent. having advertised the Court of his intentions of removing from this State to the State of Georgia and as he is informed it is necessary for Strangers to carry with them a Certificate of their Character and Conduct from the place where they remove from prayed the Court would Certifie their Knowledge of him, The Court therefore taking the same under consideration and willing to do Justice as well to the said Mr. Hamilton as to their Fellow Citizens in the State where he is about to remove to, Ordered that the Clerk of this Court do Certifie that the said Gawin Hamilton hath been for many years past an Inhabitant of this County that he hath Acted therein in the public Character of an Assistant Surveyor of the aforesaid County, A Magistrate and a Lieutenant Colonel of the Militia, in all which said Capacities he hath demeaned himself with uprightness, integrity Spirit and Resolution, and Show'd by his Actions through the long Contest with Great Brittain that he possessed true Whiggish principles and upon all occasions exerted them for the Advantage of the United States."

On April 29, 1783, certificates were granted to Ezekiel Harrison, Reuben Harrison, and Josiah Harrison, stating that they had been born and brought up in the county, and had behaved themselves as good, faithful citizens and soldiers in the contest with Great Britain, etc. They also were removing to Georgia.

April 29, 1783.

William Dunaphans[12] was allowed £2 for a smooth bore gun lost "in Serving a Tour of Militia Duty under Colo. Naul, sd. gun was lost at Stomen [?] Mill Near Portsmouth in the Year 1781."

May 27, 1783.

"On Application of John Brown Senr. on behalf of James Brown that he is Eldest Brother and heir at Law of John Brown deceased a Soldier in the 8th Virginia Regiment[13] was in the Continental Service at the time of his Death—which is Ordered to be Certified."

June 23, 1783.

"Capt. Stephen Coonrod came into Court and proved that he lost or mislaid a Certain Certificate granted by Col. Wm. Nall to John Fie so that it cannot be found for one old Wolfs Scalp and that the same is Ordered to be Certified."

June 24, 1783.

Agreeable to an order of the court in March preceding,

---

[12]. The Dunaphan family seems to have had a persistent misfortune with guns. This makes three lost by William and John. It is possible, however, that the above item refers to the same gun mentioned in the record of March 27, 1782.

[13]. The 8th Virginia was the famous "German Regiment," commanded first by Muhlenberg, later by Abram Bowman. See Wayland's "German Element," pp. 143, 144.

ROCKINGHAM COUNTY

for the sheriff to let the paving "of that part of the Court House from the Lawyers Barr to the Chimney Ordered that Andrew Shanklin Let the said work with an Addition of two Windows one of each side of the Chair containing Twelve lights each Eight by Ten to be finished in a workmanlike manner with Suitable Shutters &c. by August Court next." On September 23 this work was reported satisfactorily completed.

"O That William Herring and Andrew Shanklin Gent. do lay off the Prison bounds."

Pursuant to the above, Herring and Shanklin made report that the said prison bounds "do begin at a Walnut tree In the Corner of Reeves Lott, from thence to a Stone set up below the South East end of Deviers House, from thence to two black Oak saplins growing from one Root, in the North Side of Lanahans Lott, from thence to a Stone Set up at the West side of Rutherfords Kitchen and from thence to the Beginning."

September 22, 1783.

Daniel McKenley was granted a certificate, stating that he had been a resident of the county for "some years past," had been a person of sober conduct, had manifested true Whiggish principles in the long contest with Great Britain, and had been a good soldier, in the capacity of sergeant, in a long and tedious campaign. Mr. McKenley, like others already mentioned, was going to Georgia.

October 28, 1783.

Henry Ewin, William Herring, and Benj. Harrison, appointed by a former court, reported that they had viewed the work done by James Henton on the "Jayl, Pillory and Stocks," and had found it done according to contract. An order was entered directing the sheriff to pay the said Henton £35 15s. for the said work. Henton was allowed 20s. for a stock lock "now on the inside Door of Jail upon his furnishing a Lock for the Iron Door agreeable to Article."

A HISTORY OF

September 27, 1784.

Gawin Hamilton and Ralph Loftus, having been appointed by a former court to examine Mr. John Lincoln in regard to his abilities as deputy surveyor of the county, reported that they had found nothing to hinder his being admitted to the office.

After the successful close of the Revolution in 1783, Virginia bestowed a northwestern empire upon the new nation in 1784. In 1787 the famous ordinance for the government of the northwest and the new constitution for the nation were both drawn up. Two years later Washington was inaugurated first President, and the "tall young Adam of the West" began to stand erect. In 1793 Whitney invented the cotton gin; in 1798 Virginia and Kentucky passed their fateful resolutions in protest against the Alien and Sedition Acts; in 1803 Jefferson purchased Louisiana; and in 1807 came a trilogy of great events: The passage of the Embargo, the proof of Fulton's steamboat, and the birth of Robert E. Lee. During all this time progress was rapid in Rockingham, notwithstanding the fact that she surrendered a large part of her territory in 1787 in the formation of Pendleton County. The people were subduing the earth and replenishing it; they were clearing forests, building houses, laying out roads, and establishing schools, churches, and towns: they were marrying and giving in marriage. If any one doubts the last, he may abundantly satisfy himself by referring to the list of marriages in the Appendix. At the end of the century Rev. John Walsh, of the Methodist Church, seems to have been best man to Hymen. For the year ending in April, 1798, he reported 30 marriages to the county clerk, and for the next year, ending May 13, 1799, he reported 45.

In 1781 there were about 1500 tithables in the county. Accordingly, the total population was probably about 5000. In 1790 there were about 2100 tithables, and a total population of nearly 7500. By 1810 the figures were about 3000

ROCKINGHAM COUNTY

and 12,500, respectively. There was a variety of race elements: German, Scotch, Irish, English, Dutch, and Negro: but the negroes were remarkably few, compared with the number to be found in the adjacent counties east of the Blue Ridge. The number of negro slaves reported for 1790 was only about 10 per cent. of the total population; the number in 1810 being about 11 per cent. of the total. Most of the taxpayers had horses, while but a few of them had slaves. In 1775 Felix Gilbert reported 12 tithables, and John Craig nine,—more than any one else in their district. The largest slave-holders in the county in 1788 were Peachey Ridgeway, John Mackalls, Thomas Lewis, and William Nall, with 12, 10, 8, and 7 slaves, respectively. At the same time James Dyer had 19 horses and one slave; George Crisman, 17 horses and 4 slaves; Gawin Hamilton, 16 horses and 3 slaves; and Jacob Coonrod, 16 horses and no slaves. Usually, however, those who had a large number of horses also had a considerable number of slaves, and vice versa. Another fact of special significance presents itself in this connection. In 1790 all the negroes in the county were reported as slaves: there were apparently no free negroes; but in 1810 there were 200 or more free negroes. This change was probably the result, in large measure at least, of the work done within this period by the Methodists and other religious bodies in behalf of emancipation.

Particular instances of emigration, about the close of the Revolution, have been recorded. Many other instances might be found. Through the kindness of Mr. H. M. Strickler I am enabled to present the following paragraphs in point from two letters written by Mrs. Ryland Todhunter of Lexington, Mo. Under date of August 26, 1911, she says:

> Almost the entire settlement of Madison County, Kentucky, was made up by a concourse of people who left Augusta, Albemarle, and Rockingham County in a body for that new country about 1785-91.

Again, under date of September 12, 1911, she writes:

> In 1810 there were 100 families who came at one time from Madison County, Ky., to settle in the new Missouri Territory. They were almost

A HISTORY OF

without exception the same names and children of the men who left Augusta and Rockingham County, Va. With them came my Elliott family and the allied families of Glasgow, Wallace, Estill, Trigg, Rodes, Lewis, Turner, Kavanaugh, Oldham, and others. It is possible that Elliott's Knob was named for my family.

August 11, 1911, Maj. W. P. Pence, of Fort Monroe, Va., who has spent much time searching records in the effort to get a complete history of the Pence family, told me that about 1805-1815 there was a notable exodus from Rockingham westward, specially into the northwest territories.

In 1780 Harrisonburg was established as a town; in 1791, Keezletown; from 1801 to 1804 McGaheysville, Port Republic, and New Haven were laid out and named. The first Circuit Superior Court of Law and Chancery for Rockingham County was held in April, 1809, Judge Hugh Holmes presiding. In April, 1811, this court was put in charge of Judge Daniel Smith, to continue under his able direction till his death in 1850. Much of the work done in the magistrates' court during the latter part of the 18th and the early part of the 19th century had for its purpose the improvement of facilities for travel and transportation: the laying out of roads, the clearing of fords, etc. Many details concerning this work may be found in Chapter XII. Educational and religious work was not by any means neglected. The Lutherans, the Reformed, the Mennonites, and the Episcopalians had been in the field from the beginning; the Dunkers, the Presbyterians, the Methodists, and the United Brethren were becoming well established. There were perhaps a few Catholics, Quakers, and Moravians in the county. Particulars regarding these various churches are given in Chapter XIV, while the subject of education receives special attention in Chapter XV.

About 1809 George Rockingham Gilmer, later Governor of Georgia, visited Virginia, the home of his ancestors, and in particular the birthplace of his father in Rockingham County. He came up through East Virginia, stopping in Amelia, Cumberland, Albemarle, and other counties. He was in Charlottesville on the day of the election of members of the State legislature and Congress.

ROCKINGHAM COUNTY

Crossing the Blue Ridge, probably by Brown's Gap, he came into the beautiful Valley. Here I quote from his own account:

I passed that evening the birthplace of my mother—then the residence of my uncle, Charles Lewis—and arrived at Lethe, the birthplace of my father—the residence of my uncle, George Gilmer.

I remained two months at this beautiful place, with the best and kindest people whom I have ever known. The house was of brick, situated upon the descent of a hill, about three hundred yards from the Shenandoah River, which was seen over a beautiful meadow, and through thinly scattered sycamore trees, flowing away with a strong current. From the top of the hill, back of the house, might be seen exceedingly fertile fields, enclosed in a semicircle, formed by the river, and mountains extending in every direction.

In the middle of the valley, between the North Mountain and the Blue Ridge, rose up almost perpendicularly, and to a great height, the Peaked Mountain. In a clear day, many excavations were visible on its side. Upon inquiring about them, I was informed that they had been made by the neighboring Dutch people in search of hidden treasure. A young fellow of the neighborhood, whose father was a man of some wealth and consequence, had a club-foot and was made a tailor of, as fit for nothing else. In following his trade, he went to many places, and became wise in the ways and some of the tricks of the world. After a while he returned to the neighborhood of the Peaked Mountain. The Dutch had heard, and were credulous enough to believe, that a wealthy lord was one of the first settlers of the Shenandoah Valley, had quitted the country a long time before, and returned to Germany, leaving his money behind, hid in the Peaked Mountain. There had been some effort to discover the treasure by digging several places in the mountain side. The tailor told them that, in his travels through Ohio, he had been in a factory of spyglasses, which so added to the power of sight, that he could see several feet into the earth with one of them. Having excited great interest about these glasses and the hidden treasure by his tales, he proposed to the money-hunters that, if they would make up a sufficient sum, he would go with it to this factory, and buy them a glass, by which they could find the concealed gold.

The required sum was collected, and the tailor went to Ohio. Upon his return, he informed his employers that he had purchased a glass better than he had ever seen before; that he had no doubt but that they could have seen through the Peaked Mountain, if he could have got it to them; but unfortunately, as he was traveling home with it, he was obliged to cross a rapid run, which proved more swollen than he supposed. He was washed down by the strong current, lost his saddlebags, with

A HISTORY OF

the glass in it, and came very near losing his life. Another sum of money was made up with which the Irish club-footed tailor left the neighborhood of the Peaked Mountain, never again to be seen there. He laid out the money in the purchase of a tract of land, whilst some had theirs sold to repay the money which they had borrowed to supply the tailor with the means to buy the wonderful glass.

Whilst at Lethe, I witnessed an electioneering scene, equally interesting with the one I had been present at in Charlottesville. David Holmes, who had for twenty years immediately preceding, represented in Congress the district of which Rockingham County made a part, had been appointed Governor of the Mississippi Territory by Mr. Jefferson. A new member had to be elected. The republicans and federalists were very equally divided in the district. Mr. Smith (now Judge Smith) became the candidate of the republicans, and Jacob Swope the candidate of the federalists. The Virginians vote *viva voce*. The candidates seat themselves during the day of the election on the judge's bench, in the courthouse, and as each voter names the person for whom he votes, he is bowed to, and thanked by the candidate voted for. I was in Harrisonburg, the court-house town of Rockingham, on the day of this election, and saw Mr. Smith and Swope, thus seated and occupied. Smith was of an old Virginia family; Swope was German, and could speak the German language. The farmers of the county were mostly Germans; the lawyers, doctors, merchants, sheriffs, clerks, &c., were Virginians. Mr. Smith and Swope addressed the people on the party topics of the day, British orders in council, Napoleon's edict restricting commerce, the embargo, and anti-commercial system of Mr. Jefferson.

After both candidates had spoken, Mr. Swope commenced addressing the people in German, in reply to Mr. Smith. A huge old German rose, and in broken English, said Mr. Swope should not talk German, because Mr. Smith could not talk German, and stopped Swope. Mr. Swope was a merchant, a handsome man, and usually well dressed. He resided in Staunton, Augusta County. He came to Rockingham dressed in German fashion. The German succeeded, though the Smith party had the majority in the district; and Mr. Smith was equal, if not superior to Mr. Swope in qualifications for Congressional service.[14]

The new nation won political independence in the war from 1775 to 1783, but another hard struggle was necessary to secure commercial independence. The conspicuous part taken in the Revolution by the new county of Rockingham has already been indicated, and it may be shown that in the

---

14. From Gov. George Rockingham Gilmer's book on Georgians and Virginians, pp. 243-246.

ROCKINGHAM COUNTY

war from 1812 to 1815 it was not found wanting. In 1813 and 1814 no less than five companies, aggregating nearly 400 men, went into the military service of the nation from Rockingham County. The captains of these companies were Robert Magill, Thomas Hopkins, William Harrison, Robert Hooke, and Daniel Matthews; the names of their men may be found in the muster rolls in the Appendix. It is quite probable that other soldiers from Rockingham, not listed in these rolls, also took part in the second war for independence. For example, Col. Joseph Mauzy (1779-1863), who was for many years a prominent citizen of the county, was in command of a company at Norfolk; and under date of January 11, 1861, the editor of the *Rockingham Register* made this statement:

> In 1812 we furnished more than enough men to form a regiment, yet our men served under strangers.

But peace marks progress while war wins victory. During the war of 1812-15, as well as in the years preceding and following, progress in the new county was steady and substantial. Things intellectual and spiritual were not lost sight of in the growth of things material. As early as 1813 Davidson & Bourne had a printing establishment in Harrisonburg; two or three years later Lawrence Wartmann, whose publications were to become famous, had opened his press in the same town. Daniel Bryan was writing poetry; Joseph Funk was publishing music; John Brown was advocating missions; the Methodists and others were trying to get rid of slavery; the palaces underground were being explored, and the fountains among the hills were being sought for health and pleasure: the day was at the morn in Rockingham.

CHAPTER VI.

A GROWING COMMUNITY.

1820—1860.

The period from 1820 to 1860 was one of varied and far-reaching activities. The new nation had won its political independence by the Revolution, and its commercial independence by the war of 1812: it was now achieving its industrial independence through the development of manufactures, the invention of agricultural machinery, and the improvement of transportation facilities; and was preparing to realize its intellectual independence, as well, by thinking for itself and writing books that were no longer fashioned upon European models. Within this period fall the Missouri Compromise, the enunciation of the Monroe Doctrine, South Carolina nullification, the abolition movement, the economic crisis of 1837, the Mexican War, the Compromise of 1850, John Brown's Raid, and the beginning of secession.

In Rockingham County the main currents of national movements were being felt and registered, and at the same time affairs of State and local interest were riding upon high tides. Population was increasing and being widely distributed by emigration; social institutions were being developed, law systems were being perfected, military organizations were being maintained, and natural resources were being exploited. It was a time frequently marked by sharp political agitation, the constitution of the State being rewritten twice within the period, once in 1829-30, again in 1850-51. Churches were being extended, and not a little attention was being directed toward general education, but the chief local movements of the time appear to have been political, social, and economic, rather than religious or literary. It was a time of "internal improvements"—some railroads

State Normal and Industrial School for Women, Harrisonburg, Va.
(Page 367)

ROCKINGHAM COUNTY

being projected, some towns, perhaps, being "boomed," several banks being established, many roads being constructed, and a large number of bridges being erected. In the decade preceding the crisis of 1837 the building of turnpikes was especially in vogue, the Valley Turnpike and the one leading from Harrisonburg to Warm Springs both being constructed within that time. The Rockingham Turnpike, leading from Harrisonburg eastward toward Swift Run Gap, was not built until some years later, but still within the period under consideration. The roads, good and bad, were being utilized, not only for neighborhood communication and transportation, but also for a great wagon trade with Scottsville, Fredericksburg, Winchester, and other markets; and the Shenandoah River at the same time was a throbbing channel of navigation between the eastern sections of the county and the cities on the Potomac.

Chapters XII and XXVI are devoted specially to roads and the river trade, respectively; further particulars regarding banks may be found in Chapter XXII; and a number of items concerning the bridges of the county will be found here and there—some further on in this chapter.

Rockingham County has always been notable as a distributing center for people. In this respect it resembles those counties of Eastern Pennsylvania, whence most of its early settlers came. Far and wide, over the south, west, and northwest, in Georgia, Alabama, Tennessee, Kentucky, Missouri, Illinois, Indiana, Ohio, and many other States, not only individuals but also communities may be found that trace their ancestry or former places of residence to Rockingham County, Virginia. As already indicated, emigration was common from the first, but so great was the exodus in the period under review that the number of Rockinghamers actually in Rockingham in 1850 was about 300 less than in 1830; and emigration was so rapid in the decade following 1830 that the population (only the white population is included in these figures) was nearly 3000 less in 1840 than in 1830. To cite a single instance, there were nine children in one of the Kaylor fami-

A HISTORY OF

lies, but only one remained in Rockingham; from 1828 to 1833 the other eight moved to Logan County, Ohio, where their descendants are numerous to-day; and with the last of the eight went the mother of them all.

Another reason for the decrease of population in Rockingham between 1830 and 1840 is to be found in the formation of Page County, in 1831, from Rockingham and Shenandoah; but the part taken from Rockingham was small, as may be seen by a glance at the map, not large enough to require of itself the growth of twenty years in compensation. We must reckon still with the steady stream going westward.

The main reason for this movement towards the west is doubtless to be found in the liberal policy adopted by the Federal Government in 1820 for disposing of the public lands. Immediately the movement westward was accelerated, and for a number of years preceding 1837 the land fever was widespread and at high temperature. The population of Ohio, Indiana, Illinois, Michigan, Wisconsin, and Iowa increased from 792,719 in 1820 to 2,967,840 in 1840. Much of the growth of Rockingham in this period must be registered in these States, rather than within her own definite boundaries.

But temporary loss of population did not diminish the fertility of Rockingham fields, or the vigor of her sons and daughters who abode at home. About 1845 Henry Howe traveled all over Virginia, then including West Virginia, and wrote an account of each county in order. Of Harrisonburg he wrote, "The village is handsomely built, flourishing, and is surrounded by a beautiful and fertile country."[1]

Among other towns and villages he mentions specially Mt. Crawford, Port Republic, Deaton (Dayton), and Edom Mills.

One of the features—we might almost say, one of the institutions—of Rockingham life in the early part of the 19th century was the annual Methodist campmeeting at Taylor Springs (now Massanetta). An intimate glimpse into the

---
1. Howe's Historical Collections of Virginia, 1852 Edition, page 460.

ROCKINGHAM COUNTY

conditions frequently prevalent at that time is afforded by a notice that appeared in the *Rockingham Register* of August 11, 1825, in which a committee of the brethren (probably the committee of arrangements) assured the order-loving public that they would spare no vigilance in protecting the meeting of that year against disorder, and that they intended to enforce the law against any who might interrupt the worshipers with liquor-selling, swearing, drinking, or sabbath-breaking. The committee consisted of Peachy Harrison, Stephen Harnsberger, and Edward Stevens.

In the same issue of the *Register* appeared an article, copied with evident approval from the *Alexandria Herald*, which shows that the Methodists and other religious bodies of Rockingham were not alone in their desire to get rid of slavery. The article is as follows:

EMANCIPATION.

In addition to the fact of the emancipation of 70 slaves by Mr. Minge, of Virginia, the Richmond Whig of Friday says that two instances of the triumph (of) philanthropy and patriotism, over the sordid selfishness of our nature, can be recited, equally as meritorious and splendid as that act of distinguished munificence. The Rev. Fletcher Andrew, an ordained minister of the Methodist Episcopal Church, had received from the bounty of a dying relative, twenty slaves, at that time valued at $10,000; shortly after he attained the age of twenty-one years, although they constituted nearly the whole of his worldly property, this amiable and pious man, generously emancipated every one of them. And Mr. Charles Crenshaw, a farmer residing in the neighborhood of Richmond, has recently manumitted all the slaves he owned, amounting altogether to sixty.

An able writer in the *Register* of October 5, 1822, reviews the political condition of the country at large, and deplores the rivalries and dissensions so much in evidence among the different States and sections. He says:

The preservation of our union is unfortunately too deeply connected with this interesting subject—an epoch has appeared in our History, that every federative government must sooner or later experience, an important crisis has arrived; our future prosperity and happiness is wrapped within the events of the next five years, and it rests with us, whether we shall continue to enjoy the blessings of our present happy constitution,

A HISTORY OF

or be subjected to all the vicissitudes, and destructions, of a state of anarchy and confusion. Should one pillar of the Union be removed, the whole Edifice would soon tumble into ruins; and all hopes of a reestablishment will be preposterous. Every state will assume to itself individual sovereignty, the smaller states will feel the encroachment of the greater, and be a prey to every dangerous passion.

There was evidently a strong sentiment in Rockingham and adjacent counties favoring a revision of the State constitution in 1829-30. In Rockingham the vote was 630 for a convention, 125 against a convention; in Augusta, 560 for, 109 against; in Shenandoah, 968 for, 13 against. All the counties of the Valley—perhaps all in the western part of the State—gave large majorities for a convention, while many of those east of the Blue Ridge gave majorities against it. After the convention had done its work, Rockingham gave 457 votes in favor of adopting the new constitution, and only 49 against adoption; in Augusta the vote was 285 and 270, pro and con; in Shenandoah, 671 and 61.

In this connection it will be of interest to see how the famous Nullification Ordinance, passed by South Carolina in November 1832, was received in Rockingham County. The writer has been exceedingly fortunate in securing, through the kindness of Mr. James B. Stephenson of Harrisonburg, a copy of the *Rockingham Register* of January 12, 1833, in which is a full and detailed account of the great mass meeting that was held on Monday, January 7, 1833, to consider the burning questions of the time.

The following editorial note, in the *Register* referred to, will introduce us to the situation:

"In this day's paper we give the proceedings of the meeting held in the Court House on Monday last, pursuant to notice. It will be seen from the preamble and resolutions adopted, that Nullification finds but little favor in this county, and that the President's decided and patriotic course meets with general approbation from all parties."

The meeting referred to in this note was held, as already stated, on January 7, 1833, a large number of citizens of all parties being present. Dr. Peachy Harrison was made chair-

ROCKINGHAM COUNTY

man, and Allan C. Bryan secretary. On motion of Augustus Waterman a committee of seven was appointed to report a preamble and resolutions to the meeting. The following gentlemen composed the committee: Augustus Waterman, David Steele, Henry J. Gambill, Samuel Cootes, Dr. Michael H. Harris, Major Edward H. Smith, and James M. Huston.

A lengthy preamble and extended resolutions under seven heads were reported. The preamble referred to the recent nullification ordinance of South Carolina and acknowledged the crisis thereby impending. Resolution 1 asserted the supremacy of the national government, and denied that it was a compact or league of independent States; Resolution 2 acknowledged the right of revolution as a last resort, but denied the right of any State of nullification or peaceable secession; Resolution 3 deplored the "precipitate, rash, misguided violence of our Sister State of South Carolina," and denounced her conduct as "plainly, palpably, dangerously unconstitutional"; Resolution 4 approved the proclamation of the President; Resolution 5 reprobated the action of the governor of Virginia (John Floyd) in transmitting the ordinance of South Carolina to the Virginia legislature, and declared that the Virginia Resolutions of 1799 could not properly be held as justifying the recent action of South Carolina; Resolution 6 cheered on the Union party in South Carolina; and Resolution 7 ordered that the secretary transmit a copy of the proceedings to the President of the United States, to each of the Rockingham delegates in the General Assembly, and to the following papers: *Richmond Enquirer, Constitutional Whig, Staunton Spectator, Rockingham Register,* and *The Globe.*

The resolutions adopted, particularly Resolutions 1 and 2, followed the constitutional sophistries of Daniel Webster; and on the same page of the *Register* with them is printed Webster's speech in Faneuil Hall, delivered December 17, 1832.

Resolutions 3 and 6 were carried unanimously; the others "with a very few dissenting votes." We may infer that Peachy Grattan, I. S. Pennybacker, and Dr. Moomau were among the dissenting voters; for it is reported that these gentlemen offered substitute resolutions, and supported them in speeches. The defenders of the prevailing resolutions were chiefly Mr. Waterman, Thomas Clark, and Mr. Cootes.

The above-mentioned meeting was perhaps the last notable gathering ever held in the Old Courthouse; for in the same issue of the *Register* that contains the account of the said meeting is to be found a notice, signed by Jacob Rush, David Henton, John Kenney, and Peachy Harrison, commissioners, that on the third Monday of January, 1833, the old building would be sold. It was to be remeved by March 15, in order to clear the ground for the new courthouse.

The attitude of Virginia and Rockingham County toward the political issues of the time may be further illustrated by the following verses, which are the first two stanzas of a song reprinted from the New York *Courier & Enquirer* in the *Rockingham Register* of November 9, 1833.

Save De Union.

A mighty angry quarrel rose
Among de Tariff's friens' an' foes,
An' Souf Calina in a fit,
De Union vows to curse an' quit.
   But save de Union, ole folks, young folks,
     Ole Virginny nevah tire.

Virginny loves her Sistah State,
An' most as much de Tariff hate,
But while de Tariff she despise,
De Union berry much she prize,
   So save de Union, ole folks, young folks,
     Ole Virginny nevah tire.

In 1838 there were six voting places in the county, namely: Court House; Riddle's, in Brock's Gap; Zigler's School House, at Timberville; Richard Pickering's, at Sparta; Conrad's Old Store; Solomon Pirkey's, in McGaheysville. In 1842 there were seven: Harrisonburg; Addison Harper's, Brock's Gap; Schoolhouse of John Zigler, Timberville; Richard Pickering's; Conrad's Old Store; McGaheysville; Bright-

ROCKINGHAM COUNTY

well's old store, on Beaver Creek. In 1858 a precinct was established at the house of Samuel Cootes.

The *Rockingham Register*, in 1840, was ardent in its support of Van Buren. In the issue of August 15 a two-column campaign article appears, aimed, of course, at Harrison and the Whigs, and containing a long list of those gentlemen who constituted the Democratic Vigilance Committee for Central (or Harrisonburg) Precinct. Peachy Harrison was chairman of the committee.

In 1841 the following persons were agents for the *Register*, at the places designated:

Naason Bare—Timberville
Jacob Deck—Brock's Gap
R. Pickering—Spartapolis
Geo. E. Deneale—Smith's Creek
P. A. Clark—Mt. Crawford
John Dinkle—Bridgewater
Joseph Conrad—Conrad's Store
D. Irick—McGaheysville
Reuben Emick—Linvill's Creek
Wesley Bare—Parnassus
Young J. Hiner—Doe-Hill
Wm. McCoy—Franklin
S. Sterling, of Rockh., Gen. Agt.

In 1844 the *Harrisonburg Republican* was in the Presidential campaign, for Clay and Frelinghuysen, and against the *Register*—not to mention Polk and Dallas. The following paragraph is copied from the *Republican* of July 23, 1844.

<blockquote>Our brother of the Fairmount (Va.) Pioneer is correct. "The enterprising Whigs of Rockingham *have* caused a Whig paper to be established in that strong hold of Locofocoism," and what is more to the point, they intend keeping it up.</blockquote>

A few notes relating to military affairs within the period before us are herewith presented. On April 19 (a notable anniversary!), 1822, John Kenny was commissioned colonel (field officer of cavalry) in Rockingham. In 1828 the number of Virginia militia totaled 100,707, Frederick County

A HISTORY OF

standing first with 2569, Shenandoah second, with 2556, and Rockingham fourth, with 2296. In 1835 the General Assembly passed an Act establishing in Rockingham a new and distinct regiment, to be known as the 145th Regiment of Virginia Militia. The commissioners named in the Act were John Cowen, Samuel Cootes, John Allabough, Anderson Moffitt, George Piper, David Lincoln, Samuel Miller, Abram Burd, and David Henton. The next year an Act to apportion more equally the enrolled militia of the three Rockingham Regiments was passed. In the *Register* of April 7, 1838, is found a notice from Wm. Burnside, O. S., ordering the rifle company, commanded by Capt. Speck and attached to the 145th Regiment, to parade on the 2d Saturday of April at Paul's Mill, Beaver Creek. In another copy of the same paper, dated April 8, 1842, are three similar notices: One from J. Billhimer, O. S., to Capt. O. St. C. Sprinkle's company, ordering it to parade in Harrisonburg on the 2d Saturday of April; another, from John A. Hopkins, captain, ordering the artillery to parade at Mt. Clinton on the 2d Saturday; another, from Wm. Burnsides, O. S., ordering the light infantry company, formerly under command of Capt. J. S. Carlile, to parade in Dayton on the 3d Saturday. In the last-named company an election was to be held for captain. The hour appointed for the parade in each of the three notices was 11 o'clock.

Twenty years ago a lady[2] who was born in Harrisonburg in 1812, and who spent her early life there, wrote out her recollections of the olden time. Her account of the "big musters" is given in the following graphic words:

> The annual or general muster was the greatest thing, and was looked forward to for months with the greatest pleasure by all the negroes and children. Training of officers began several days before muster day. It was the most motley crowd that filled the square around the court house. Men of all sorts and sizes, dressed in tow-linen pants and shirts; few had coats and vests; some with old wool hats, and others with straw

---

2. Maria Graham Carr, mother of Gen. C. C. C. Carr of Chicago. For access to copies of her manuscript I am indebted to Mr. R. A. VanPelt and Mrs. Hattie Newman.

ROCKINGHAM COUNTY

hats. I saw one man in this crowd when I was about ten years old; he had on tow-linen pants and shirt, coarse shoes, no stockings; around his waist was a bright red woolen sash: he had a rusty slouch hat on, without band, and torn at the edge. On the front of the hat was a long white feather with a scarlet top—he felt as proud as a general. I saw several soldiers there at one time with bright yellow coats trimmed with black, and green flannel ones trimmed with white or silver. I suppose these uniforms were some of the remains of the War of 1812. My aunt told me that my father had raised a company which he had uniformed at his own expense.

Some men on muster day carried old umbrellas, cornstalks and sticks of wood instead of guns and swords. I suppose the officers were tired of trying to beat sense into these men, and gave up in despair, marching them out to a field in the N. end of town to try to drill them.

After marching the militia out to the field, the Light Horse Company, of about fifty men, under Col. McMahon, went out also. After all the men were on the field the staff officers went out to the Colonel's house to escort him to the field. Not one of them was uniformed. The Colonel had on a blue uniform with metal buttons, a red sash around his waist, and a helmet with a cow's tail on it, hanging down behind. The whisky, beer, and ginger-bread sellers were in their glory, as this was their harvest, many persons taking home a jug full of something and a handkerchief filled with ginger-bread.

I always loved dearly to hear the fife and drum, and got as near to them as I could, listening to them until the tears ran down my cheeks. I was never so affected by any other music.

All the gentlemen of that day ordinarily wore knee breeches with silver buckles, some of these buckles being set with paste; they had shoe buckles to match; silk hose in summer, and black lamb's wool hose in winter.

According to a letter written January 16, 1911, by Mr. D. M. Kaylor of Bellefontaine, Ohio, a famous ginger cake baker of the time was Mrs. Christopher Warvel, who lived near McGaheysville. Mrs. Carr mentions a Mrs. Nye of Harrisonburg who was also noted for her ginger cake, as well as for her molasses-beer and taffy.

Through the favor of Mr. J. L. Argubright, of Dayton, I am able to reproduce the following interesting roll, from the original manuscript. It is a valuable piece of source material in Rockingham military history.

A HISTORY OF

Muster Rool of A Troop of Cavalry Commanded by Capt. John Nicholas for the year 1828

John Nicholas Capt
John Miller 1st Lt
Henry Oungst 2nd Lt
John Albright Cornet
Charles Yancey 1st Sert
(Jacob Frederick 2nd Sert)
Samuel Royer 3th Sert
Joseph Moyer 4th Sert
Jacob Kiblinger
John Royer
Joseph Mahoy
Jonathan Peal
Jonathan Rush
Jacob Armentrout
James Dovel
John Fisher
John Alfred
(Frederick Krahn)
Charles Nicholas miller
David Irick
Tyree R. Brown
Samuel Moor
Michael Rowtz
William Fisher
(William Danner)
Nicholas Miller
Nathan Huston
Peter Miller
Philip Moyer
(Alexa Newman)
Hamilton I Hufman
John Cline
Thomas Reaves
William Reaves
Charles Chandler
David Chandler
(Tandy Dovel)
William Bird
John Anders
David Weaver
George Kaylor

George Nicholas
Philip Deal
Solomon Leonard
Berryman Dorsson
David Royer
Abraham Argebright
James Kook
(John Williams)
David Huston
John Argebright
Jacob Royer
Peter Roler
John May
Jacob Earman
Jacob Allabaugh
John Huffman
Albert Yancey
Francis Kertly
John Dovel
William Youst
(John Wallace)
George E. Craige
William Eater
David Oungst
William Eaton
(Joseph Oungst)
Samuel H. Huffman
David Eitor
Samuel Showalter
Adam Blose Jr
Joshua Snider
Abraham Whitmore
Daniel Rife
Benja Miller
David Eversole
(Jacob Kiblinger Jr)
Henry Conrod
Henry Hansbarger
George Huston
Reuben Propst
Jacob Linaweaver

ROCKINGHAM COUNTY

Wm Peterfish
Ninrod Hitt
Jacob Blose
Isaac Hammer
John Hammer
John Williamson
Westely Bear
St. Clair Kertley

Jacob Conrod
Samuel Gibbons
Thomas Miller
George Kellar
John Swats
George Secrist
John Roberts

Upon special inquiry made not long since of two venerble gentlemen, Mr. Richard Mauzy of McGaheysville and Mr. J. N. Liggett of Harrisonburg, I was informed that Rockingham County, although a stronghold for Polk and his party, took very little interest in the Mexican War, 1846-8. Of Rockingham soldiers in Mexico, the following were all that could be recalled: John P. Brock[3] (1823-1892); N. Calvin Smith[4] (1823-1897); William Smith (brother of Calvin).

In October, 1873, William Ralston died near Linville Depot, aged about 50. It was said that he had been in the Mexican War, as well as in the Civil War. He was known as "Soldier Bill."

Mr. Robert Coffman of Dayton states that Frederick Linhoss, formerly of the same town, was a soldier in Mexico; and Mr. Benj. Long, also of Dayton, agrees with Mr. Coffman in reporting the tradition, received from Mr. Linhoss and Mr. St. Clair Detamore, that a number of men (about a dozen) left Dayton for the Mexican War.

The favorite method for raising money for all "good causes," particularly the building of expensive bridges, was by a lottery. Here is something specific in point:

---

[3]. Born May 17, 1823, near Lacey Springs, died in November, 1892. He was captain of the Valley Rangers in the Civil War.

[4]. Calvin Smith died in Providence, R. I.

A HISTORY OF
COME ON!   COME ON!
THE ROAD TO WEALTH.
ALL HAIL!

Ye elect sons and daughters of the goddess of Fortune, call and buy tickets in the *Shenandoah Bridge Lottery*, where large sums of CASH can be bought for the inconsiderable sum of $4.

This is the heading of an advertisement that appeared in the *Rockingham Register* in January, 1833, regarding the Shenandoah Free-Bridge Lottery, to construct a bridge across the Shenandoah River on the Swift Run Gap road. The drawing was to take place in Winchester, on Tuesday, February 5, 1833. The capital prize was $10,000; other prizes in decreasing amounts were offered, there being finally 18,000 prizes of $4 each. In all there were 18,556 prizes, aggregating in value $108,000. The number of blanks was 17,434. David S. Jones was manager, with his office at Harrisonburg.

At the same time that the above lottery was being promoted, another, with a capital prize of $8,000, was being advertised by Bruffy & Paul, managers, Mt. Crawford, Va. This was being conducted for the purpose of constructing a free bridge across the North River near Mt. Crawford. The drawing was to be held at Strasburg on January 15, 1833. In this there were 30,000 prizes—no blanks; but the small prizes were only $2 each, while the price of a ticket was $4. The aggregate value of the prizes offered was $90,000. This scheme therefore, would have allowed a balance of $30,000 to the managers with which to pay expenses, aid the bridge building, and profit themselves. The gross balance falling to the management under Mr. Jones' lottery would have been $35,960. However, there were repeated drawings for the same bridge—at least in some cases. Mr. Jones states in his advertisement that he had already paid out prizes in the Shenandoah Bridge lottery ranging from $10,000 to $200; and in the same issue of the *Register* he advertises another drawing to be held at Winchester in April, 1833, for a capital prize of $12,000, with smaller prizes in great number.

Among other contemporary lotteries that were authorized or operated in Rockingham were the following:

One in 1831-2 for raising money to construct a road from Harrisonburg to Moorefield; another at the same time for the benefit of the Port Republic and New Haven bridge; in 1833, one to be conducted by Wm. Thompson, Anderson Moffitt, John Zigler, Peter Grim, Saml. Hoover, and Isaac Thomas for erecting a free bridge near Thompson's Store (now Timberville); and one in 1838 for the benefit of the "Mt. Crawford Free Bridge."

In the *Rockingham Register* of November 9, 1833, the following notice appeared:

> The annual general meeting of the Stockholders of the New Shenandoah Company will be held at the house of Mrs. Graham, in Port Republic, on the 15th day of November inst. A general attendance of the Company is requested.
> S. H. LEWIS,
> Treas'r. N. S. Com.

In 1836 the General Assembly agreed to a resolution requesting the board of public works to employ a competent engineer to survey a route for a proposed railroad from Gordonsville, in Orange County, to Harrisonburg, in Rockingham County.

The winter of 1840 in Rockingham was of unusual severity, and is thus described by Joseph Funk in a letter written January 11:

> As our winter weather here has thus far proved to be rather extraordinary, I will state to you something about it. On Saturday night and Sunday before Christmas there fell a snow 14 or 15 inches deep, on a previous snow several inches deep; and on Friday after Christmas, (being on the day of Hannah's infair which was held at Daniel Frank's) there fell another about 10 or 12 inches deep, which drifted, together with the other, in such a manner that many places of roads are impassible either with wagon or horse. Mounds of snow are drifted together from 4 to 6

feet deep. Your sister Elizabeth could not return home from the wedding till the following Wednesday and they were obliged to go through fences and fields to get along: Since then we have had 3 snows several inches deep. Both our lanes and many others, have not yet been passed through by any person since the snows fell. The weather has also been extremely cold, but has now moderated and become more mild and pleasant.

Financial, agricultural, and religious conditions are depicted, in a letter written by Joseph Funk, October 2, 1842, as follows:

Times with us are very pressing in the money way; of which, however, our county has felt less weight than any of the adjacent. But in many respects the times are good. The season has, the past summer, been very good; heavy crops of wheat oats and corn were produced, so that we abound in the provisions of life. But, with regret I mention, that I fear there is too little of true and unfeigned religion among us; which in a great measure, may be owing to the Clergy. If in the room of a pious life—good examples—and warmly preaching the Word of God to our hearts, the preachers read their sermons, and live in conformity to the world, and its vain fashions, I think the church committed to their charge, of course, cannot grow and thrive.

The California gold fever of 1848-9 seems to have affected Rockingham only slightly. Says Mr. Mauzy:

"If any persons from this county went, at that time, to California, I do not know it, though it is probable that a few did so. I know of two who went from Woodstock—John Anderson and a friend of his named Harrison."[5]

Says Mr. Liggett:

"As to gold seekers: On conference with Mr. John Kenney, whose memory of ancient occurrences is more tenacious than mine, the following are recalled: John Higgins, Thomas Fletcher, Jacob Jones, Benj. Miller (probably),—Britt, and John Williams; the last a lawyer. . . . Mr. William Daingerfield emigrated too at an early date, and achieved distinction and fame, ultimately being elevated to the judicial bench. He was a brother of Capt. Daingerfield and Leroy, soldiers celebrated for gallantry in the Confederate army."[6]

[5.] Letter of February 25, 1912.
[6.] Letter of February 24, 1912.

ROCKINGHAM COUNTY

Gen. Samuel H. Lewis,[7] who lived a mile or two below Port Republic, was a wealthy farmer and man of affairs. Like many of his contemporaries, he frequently consulted the almanac in the management of his farm, and was in the habit of recording weather observations and related items at the proper places in the calendar. His almanac for 1852 is before me, and I reproduce from it the following item:

Great Flood.

April 19.—Great flood in the river & runs—Being as high (within two inches) as in 1842.—The Bottom field being recently ploughed, & almost ready to be planted in corn, was very much damaged

In his letter of 1840 Joseph Funk makes reference to a wedding and an infair. In order that present-day readers may know what an infair was, and at the same time appreciate more definitely the social conditions that obtained in the earlier half of the century, I append the following account, written for this work, upon special request, by Mrs. Bettie Neff Miller, of Bridgewater.

I will tell you of the first wedding I ever witnessed. My step-grandmother Neff's maiden sister, Barbara Landes, was united in marriage with David Stemphley (a German) sometime in the forties. I was about 8 years old. (You remember Stemphleytown near Bridgewater; since he was the first settler there the place was named for him.)

I will describe the costumes. The groom was dressed in drab cloth; the bride in a brown merino dress-made petticoat and short gown, with a white apron and handkerchief and a white jaconet cap.

The first relative wedding I ever attended was Uncle Abe Neff's. That was soon after the other—sometime in the forties. He was attired in fine black cloth, the bride in a white dress, with apron of the same material, a beautiful white silk handkerchief and a bobinet cap. The

---

7. Samuel H. Lewis (1794-1869) was the son of Charles Lewis (1772-1832), who was the son of Thomas Lewis (1718-1790). Thomas was the eldest son of John Lewis, pioneer of Augusta. Thomas lived and died at Lewiston, below Port Republic. He was the first surveyor of Rockingham, and had one of the largest libraries in the West. General Andrew Lewis (1720-1780) and Col. Chas. Lewis (1736-1774) were his brothers. Samuel H. Lewis was the father of Sen. John F. Lewis and Samuel H. Lewis (1820-1892).

ceremony was rather long, including a prayer, in which all knelt. When they arose the minister sang a few lines:

> Bless, Lord, this newly-married pair,
> And make the match a blessing prove.

Uncle Abe's was the first infair I attended. All rode on horseback. When they came near the house they galloped the horses, and all alighted in a huddle. The friends came to meet them, and ushered them into the house, where the bride and her attendant dressed for dinner. The bride wore a blue alpaca dress, a black silk apron, and a fancy silk handkerchief. Her bonnet was a white lawn over a whole pasteboard—or half a one, I should have said. Of course, we all thought it was beautiful and tasteful. The table was set with pies, puff cakes, pickles, and different kinds of preserves, with chicken, turkey, and ham on a side table. After eating plenty of meat and chicken, the plates were removed, and pie and cakes were served.

After dinner all went into a room prepared to have them spend their time in playing the oldtime apple-butter plays. We children looked on with delight. Bridal presents were unknown.

I attended several infairs just like the one I have described. In earlier days, while on the road to the groom's home, two young men were sent for two bottles of wine to treat the bride and groom before they arrived at the house. When Aunt Mary Neff was married to William Pence they prepared to send out two bottles of wine—had the bottles trimmed, and looked for the men to come. Old Mr. Pence was an old-fashioned man, and wanted to treat his new daughter-in-law. Your mother and I were in that bridal procession. Times changed somewhat before your mother and I were married. My bridal presents were a home-woven wash line, a home-made linen towel, and a wash-bowl with pitcher. Since then there have been many changes, as you know.[8]

In the four-cornered fight for the Presidency in 1860 the *Rockingham Register* supported Douglas. In the issue of August 3, 1860, the editor disapproves the talk of revolution and declares for the preservation of the Union, yet expresses fear of "black republican fanaticism" and flays the abolitionists. At the same time the division of the Democratic party is deplored. On election day the vote in Rockingham stood as follows: 676 for Breckenridge, 888 for Bell, and 1354 for Douglas. If Lincoln got any votes in the county, the *Register* did not report them; yet it was only 78 years since

---

8. From a letter written September 4, 1911.

SENATOR JOHN F. LEWIS
(Pages 355, 356)

ROCKINGHAM COUNTY

his father and grandfather had left Rockingham, and a number of his relatives were still residing in the county at the time.

By December 14, 1860, the *Register*, while still adoring the Union, showed decided signs of secession sentiment. Evidently it had veered considerably during the last preceding month or two. In the issue of December 28 appears the following, anent the secession of South Carolina:

> We are sorry that the gallant Palmetto State did not continue in the Union until the North had time to retrace its steps and do us justice. There are unequivocal signs of returning reason in many portions of the North, and we at least hope they will yet do what they ought before the rest of the Southern States dissolve their connexion with the Union.

These words have an ominous sound. Coming events were casting shadows.[9]

---

[9]. For letters, almanacs, old newspapers, etc., belonging to the period covered by this chapter, I am indebted, among others, to Mrs. F. Ruebush, Dayton, Va., and to Mr. S. C. Rohr and Hon. George N. Conrad, both of Harrisonburg.

CHAPTER VII.

ROCKINGHAM IN THE CIVIL WAR.

1861—1865.

A consecutive and detailed narrative of a great county in a great war cannot be attempted in a single brief chapter, yet enough may be given to bring those "old, unhappy, far-off things and battles long ago" vividly before us. The rising spirit of early '61 may be felt in the following, copied from the *Rockingham Register* of January 25, 1861:

Military Meeting.

Monday was a proud day for old Rockingham. Notwithstanding the diversity of opinion which exists as to the best mode of settling our present difficulties, all are agreed on arming our Volunteer Regiment. The immense crowd was addressed by Messrs. Warren, Shands, Winfield and Yancey, in patriotic and thrilling speeches, and when the motion was made by Mr. Shands, to ask the County Court to subscribe $2000 in addition to the amount already subscribed, there was not a dissenting voice in the crowd that was audible. The meeting adjourned with three cheers for the Regiment. The arming and equiping of that Regiment is a fixed fact. It was the largest meeting ever convened in our Court-House. Hundreds outside could not gain admittance, but endorsed the action of the meeting.

The voting places in the county at this time were as follows:

District No. 1.

Conrad's Store   McGaheysville

District No. 2.

Taliaferro's Store   Port Republic

District No. 3.

Mt. Crawford   Dayton

ROCKINGHAM COUNTY

District No. 4.
Bridgewater   Ottobine

District No. 5.
Mt. Clinton   Bowman's Mill

District No. 6.
Court House   Keezletown

District No. 7.
Spartapolis   Henton's Mill

District No. 8.
Cootes' Store   Timberville
Mennonite School House

District No. 9.
Sprinkel's Store   Wittig's Store

On February 4, 1861, an election was held to choose delegates to the State convention. S. A. Coffman, John F. Lewis, and A. S. Gray were chosen. An unusually large vote was polled, and was distributed among the several candidates as follows:

Coffman,	2588
Lewis,	2081
Gray,	1999
Woodson,	1120
Newman,	705
Liggett,	503

In reporting the election, the *Register* of February 8 says:

The delegates elect are all conservative *Union* men, and were voted for by the people with the understanding that they are to be the representatives of the strong Union sentiment of the county. Yet while they are all Union men, yet none of them desire to be classed in the category of *"submissionists."* They will go for the Union as long as there is hope of its honorable preservation; but when all just and proper efforts in that direction fail, then they will go, as Virginians and Southern men, for the rights, the honor, and dignity of the old Commonwealth out of the Union.—We hope and pray that such an alternative may not be presented; but if it should, we know enough of the metal of our delegates

A HISTORY OF

to the Convention, to be assured, that Virginia's sacred honor will be safe in their hands.

Politics were ignored in the canvass. In politics, the delegates stand as follows: Two democrats, (Messrs. Coffman and Gray,) and one whig, (Mr. Lewis.) They are all comparatively young men, Mr. Coffman, the foremost man in the race, being the youngest of the three.

Vote for and against referring the action of the convention to the people:

	For Ref.	Against Ref.
Harrisonburg,	474	183
Keezletown,	52	4
Conrad's Store,	144	76
McGaheysville,	77	73
Port Republic,	145	2
Taliaferro's Store,	107	14
Mt. Crawford,	175	38
Dayton,	118	9
Bridgewater,	151	6
Ottobine,	180	20
Mt. Clinton,	93	1
Bowman's Mill,	185	8
Spartapolis,	138	49
Henton's Mill,	82	10
Timberville,	123	3
Trissel's School House,	61	6
Cootes' Store,	100	64
Sprinkel's Store,	13	22
Wittig's	71	00
	2499	593

As shown by the unusually large vote, the people all over the county were intensely aroused. Wednesday morning, March 27, 1861, a Confederate flag was seen floating from the Exchange Hotel in Harrisonburg—three weeks before the Virginia convention adopted the ordinance of secession, and eighteen days before Lincoln's call for troops. "It was," said the next *Register*, "the work of a portion of *the gallant fair ladies of our town,* who are in favor of joining the Confederacy."

On April 17 the convention at Richmond adopted an ordinance of secession by a vote of 88 to 55. Consistently with his declarations before the election, Mr. Lewis voted with the minority, and steadfastly refused to sign the ordinance after it was passed.

The division of opinions and convictions in the convention but reflected the similar divisions over the State—particularly in the western part. In Rockingham the majority agreed with the majority of the convention, but there were also a number who thought differently. For example, in the Blue Ridge sections of East Rockingham, where anti-slavery sentiment and martial spirit were both strong, a number of men went north and joined the Union armies. In other sections of the county the peace principles of large numbers of the people, particularly the Dunkers and Mennonites, kept many from assuming a decided attitude one way or the other; but notwithstanding all these conditions, the attitude of the county as a whole was soon definitely and decidedly for the Confederacy. On April 20, when the "Mountain Guards," from Spring Hill, Augusta County, and the "Rockbridge Rifles" were passing through Harrisonburg the ladies presented them with flags. The firing on Sumter, Lincoln's call for troops, and the action of the Virginia convention had aroused tremendous enthusiasm. Meetings to organize home guards, etc., were held at Bridgewater, Lacey Spring, Harrisonburg, and elsewhere.

Before the war was over, Rockingham men were serving in many different commands; but the organization that is perhaps most frequently thought of in connection with the military history of the county is the 10th Regiment, Va. V. I., made up chiefly of Rockingham soldiers; and we deem our readers fortunate in having presented to them herewith an account of this regiment, written by one who knows its history at first hand.

A HISTORY OF
THE 10TH VIRGINIA REGIMENT, VOLUNTEER INFANTRY.

BY COLONEL D. H. LEE MARTZ.[1]

Written Specially for This Work.

The nucleus of the 10th Regiment Virginia Volunteer Infantry was formed in Rockingham County just prior to the commencement of the Civil War. One company, the Valley Guards, was organized before the John Brown raid at Harper's Ferry, with S. B. Gibbons as captain. This company was sent to Charlestown as part of the military force used as a guard. These events created or aroused a military spirit in Rockingham, resulting in the formation of six other companies, viz., the Rockingham Rifles, captain, James Kenney; Chrisman's Infantry, captain, George Chrisman; Bridgewater Grays, captain, John Brown; Brock's Gap Rifles, captain, John Q. Winfield;[2] Peaked Mountain Grays, captain, William

---

[1]. Col. Martz was born at the old family homestead near Lacey Spring, March 23, 1837. After his early life on the farm he engaged in mercantile business, which was interrupted by the war. He rose from the rank of sergeant in the 10th Virginia Infantry to that of colonel, and at the close of the war he was in command of the 10th, 23d, and 37th Virginia regiments. After a number of years in business again he was elected, in 1887, clerk of the circuit court in Rockingham County, and still holds that office. He has been commander of the S. B. Gibbons Camp, Confederate Veterans, since 1893. On November 14, 1860, he married Miss Mary Nicholas Carter. Mr. Ed. C. Martz, a well-known lawyer of Harrisonburg, is his son.

[2]. Capt. Winfield was born at Mt. Jackson, Va., June 20, 1822, the son of Dr. Richard Winfield. He was a graduate of Washington College, Lexington, Va., and of Jefferson Medical College, Phila. As captain of the Letcher Brock's Gap Rifles, in the 7th Va. Cavalry, he won distinction, and was mentioned as the one likely to succeed Ashby in command of the regiment, but failing health interrupted his military service. In spite of failing health he continued the practice of medicine at his home in Broadway, where he died July 29, 1892. Mr. Chas. R. Winfield, attorney-at-law, is his son.

ROCKINGHAM COUNTY

B. Yancey; Riverton Invincibles, captain, W. D. C. Covington. These seven companies were organized as a regiment just before the war, under the Virginia laws, as State Volunteer Militia, with S. B. Gibbons colonel, E. T. H. Warren lieutenant-colonel, Burke Chrisman and George W. Miller majors. The last two did not see active service.

At the outbreak of the war this regiment was ordered to Harper's Ferry, leaving home on the 18th day of April, 1861, as the 4th Virginia Regiment of State troops. The regiment, as finally organized, became the 10th Virginia Infantry, C. S. A., with S. B. Gibbons colonel, E. T. H. Warren lieutenant-colonel, and Samuel T. Walker major. With the addition of three companies from Shenandoah County—one each from Strasburg, Woodstock, and Edinburg—the regiment remained at Harper's Ferry until some time in June, 1861. Then it moved to Romney, now in West Virginia, by way of Winchester, as part of the 4th Brigade, commanded at the time by Col. A. P. Hill of the 13th Va. On the way back to Winchester the Brock's Gap Rifles were transferred to the cavalry, the regiment being finally composed of eleven companies: six from Rockingham, three from Shenandoah, one from Page, and one from Madison.

The impending battle of Manassas caused the army in the Valley, under Gen. Jos. E. Johnston, to be moved to eastern Virginia, reaching Manassas Junction on the 21st of July. Thence it was hurried to the field of battle. Only four companies, however, of the 10th Regiment (now in Gen. Arnold Elzey's brigade) took part in the battle, having been detached from the regiment and sent to strengthen the Confederate left. These four companies suffered some loss in killed and wounded. After this battle the Confederate army remained around or near Manassas Junction until the following spring, when it was moved to the south side of the Rappahannock River.

Nothing of importance affecting the 10th Regiment occurred in this time until April, 1862, when it was transferred to the Valley, and made a part of Gen. W. B. Talia-

A HISTORY OF

ferro's Brigade, Jackson's Division, then at what is now Elkton. The regiment was composed of the eleven companies aforesaid: A, C, and F from Shenandoah; B, D, E, G, H, and I from Rockingham; K from Page; and L from Madison. While at Elkton Co. C was disbanded, and a new Co. C from Rockingham, Robert C. Mauck captain, assigned to the regiment.

Early in May, 1862, Jackson's command was sent to reinforce Gen. Edward Johnson, in the campaign ending May 8 in the battle of McDowell, with Gen. Milroy in command of the Federals. In this battle the 10th Regiment had the misfortune to lose its colonel, the brave and chivalrous S. B. Gibbons,[3] as well as several men. Soon the command was marched back to the Valley by way of Bridgewater, moved down to New Market, thence over the mountain into the Page Valley, down by Front Royal, thence across to the Valley Pike at Middletown, and on to Winchester after Gen. Banks, who had withdrawn to Winchester and there made a stand. Being so vigorously assailed by Jackson and Ewell as to be completely routed, he hurried on toward the Potomac. The 10th Regiment did not actively engage in this battle, but nevertheless suffered some loss, Capt. Mauck of Co. C being wounded and permanently disabled.

After pursuing Banks several miles, the troops were withdrawn and moved rapidly up the Valley to Harrisonburg, the 3d Brigade going to a point between Port Republic and Cross Keys. While a battle was being fought there, on Sunday morning, June 8, the enemy occupied Port Republic and planted a piece of artillery at the mouth of the bridge, on the Port Republic side of North River. The 3d Brigade was hurried to the bridge, drove the enemy away and took possession of the village.

---

[3]. Simeon B. Gibbons was born May 25, 1833, at Shenandoah Furnace, Page Co., Va., and was educated at the Virginia Military Institute. When put in command of his regiment, he was the youngest colonel in the Confederacy. His father was a Col. Gibbons of Virginia, later of Georgia.

ROCKINGHAM COUNTY

The battle of Port Republic was fought on the next day, June 9, but the Tenth did not become engaged, though hurried to the front to join in the attack upon Shields. A few days after Fremont and Shields had been disposed of, Gen. Jackson was ordered east to join Gen. Lee in the defence of Richmond. Marching to Mechum's River, he went thence by rail to Beaver Dam; thence marched to the scene of the conflict, which culminated in seven days of desperate fighting, McClellan to capture, Lee to save, Richmond. However, from the time the Tenth reached its destination until the end of the struggle, it did not fire a gun, being held in reserve; but it was exposed for a time to damage from the exploding shells of the enemy at Malvern Hill, while supporting a battery, two or three men being slightly wounded.

Soon after the close of this part of the campaign Gen. Jackson with his corps was ordered to Gordonsville to look after the redoubtable Federal general, John Pope. On the 8th of August (1862), a few miles south of Culpeper Court House, near or at Slaughter's Mountain, called by the Confederates Cedar Run, the first encounter took place between Jackson and Pope, resulting in a hard-fought battle, with victory for a time trembling in the balance. The Tenth, under command of Major Stover, was in the fray from start to finish, suffering a considerable loss in killed and wounded. After this battle the troops followed Pope's discomfited army, expecting to give him battle before he could recross the Rappahannock; but this plan failed from some cause. The next move was to cross the Rappahannock and give him battle.

For Jackson, the next thing was to move up the river, cross its two branches, pass around Pope's right, and move on Manassas Junction, thus getting completely in Pope's rear—a very daring and desperate move, resulting in a three days battle, the Second Manassas. In all this the 10th Virginia took an active part, losing heavily in killed and wounded. Among the latter were Lt.-Col. Walker and Major Stover. On the second day, Col. Warren being absent, the command of the regiment devolved upon Capt. W. B. Yancey. Pope's army was routed and driven back with tremendous loss.

The next move was the invasion of Maryland. The Tenth passed through Frederick City, and came back into Virginia by Williamsport to Martinsburg, where it was left on duty with the 2d Va., while Jackson captured Harper's Ferry. The Tenth remained here until the army returned to Virginia, after the battle of Sharpsburg. After remaining in the lower Valley for a time, the army crossed into eastern Virginia, and, moving near Fredericksburg, took position on the hills running parallel with the Rappahannock, back of the town. The Federal general, Burnside, was on the Stafford Heights, on the opposite side of the river.

On the 13th of December (1862) Burnside, having succeeded in crossing the river, fought the desperate and bloody battle of Fredericksburg. The Tenth did not take an active part on the 13th, but was placed on the front line that night, expecting bloody work the next day; but Burnside thought it better not to renew the battle, and withdrew to the north side of the river.

Gen. Lee went into winter quarters at Skinker's Neck, on the south side of the Rappahannock. In the meantime "Fighting Joe Hooker" was placed in command of the Federal army, and in the spring of 1863 began his "on to Richmond" campaign, posting his army about Chancellorsville. Then was planned Jackson's famous flank movement around Hooker's right. The Tenth, being with Jackson, took an active part in the assault upon the enemy, losing many officers and men, on Saturday evening, May 2. Among the wounded were Col. Warren and the writer. On Sunday further heavy losses were sustained, among the killed being Lt.-Col. Samuel T. Walker and Major Joshua Stover.

The next movement was into Pennsylvania, and on to Gettysburg, where the Tenth again participated in some heavy fighting, under the command of Capt. W. B. Yancey. The loss here was not heavy.

After the battle of Chancellorsville the writer was pro-

List of Cooking Utensils required for the use of the 10th. Va. Reg.

	Camp Kettles	Mess Pans	Plates	Knives & Forks	Tin Cups	Buckets	Axes	Hatchets			Remarks
Co. A.	1	2	3	3	2	1	1	1	8	k	
" B.	3	6	24	24	24	1	2	2	1	1	
" C.	2	2	12	12	12	2	1	1		1	
" D.	1	3	17	17	17	1	2	2	1	axe	
" E.	1	1	12	12	10	2	1	1			6 Skillets
" F.	5	4	37	37	37	5	2	2	2	3	10 Kettles
" G.	3	8	20	20	20	6	2	3		1	
" H.	1	4	8	8	10	2	1	2			
" P.	3	5	12	12	25	2	2	2	1	1	
" K.	6	6	36	36	36	4	1	2	2	2	
" L.	2	5	26	26	26	4	2	4	1	1	Haxe
Band	2	2	14	14	14	2	1	1		1	
Total	30	48	221	221	233	32	18	23			

Respectfully submitted,
A. S. Byrd Capt &
A. Q. M. 10th. Va. Reg.

E. T. H. Warren. Col.
10th. Va. Reg.

Aug 27. 1863.

Facsimile of manuscript statement made out by Capt. A. S. Byrd, quartermaster 10th Reg. Va. Vol. Inf., and countersigned by Col. E. T. H. Warren (Pages 138, 139)

ROCKINGHAM COUNTY

moted to the rank of lieutenant-colonel. After Gettysburg the army returned to Virginia, soon moving east of the Blue Ridge and placing itself in front of Gen. Meade, the new Federal commander. The Tenth, now of George H. Steuart's brigade, Edward Johnson's division, engaged in a hot fight with the Federal general, French, on November 27, at Mine Run, losing several men in killed and wounded. This was supposed to be the prelude to a bloody battle, for which great preparations were made, but Meade finally concluded not to risk it. Thus ended the campaign of 1863. The Army of Northern Virginia went into winter quarters near Orange Court House.

About the 1st of May, 1864, Gen. Grant, now in supreme command of the Army of the Potomac, began to move. The first important battle was fought May 5, in which the Tenth again lost heavily in killed and wounded, among the former being Col. Warren[4] and Major I. G. Coffman, leaving the writer the only field officer of the regiment. On the evening of May 10 the enemy captured part of our works, which the Tenth helped to recapture from them. On the 12th of May Gen. Hancock, of the Federals, made his famous assault on our works, capturing nearly all of Johnson's division, including the 10th Va. and the writer. The brave adjutant of the regiment, Whit. Kisling, was killed in this fight. A small remnant of the regiment, under command of that veteran, Capt. W. B. Yancey, took part in several skirmishes until he was permanently disabled by a severe wound.

Shortly after May 12, 1864, the Tenth was made part of a new brigade under Gen. Wm. Terry, being later moved to the Valley, whence, under Gen. Early, it again went into Maryland to threaten Washington, in process of which it took

---

4. Edward Tiffin Harrison Warren was born in Rockingham, June 19, 1829. At Frescati, Orange County, he married Virginia Magruder, December 5, 1855. His son, James Magruder Warren, was a prominent physician in the 80's and 90's at New Hope and Bridgewater. Col. Warren was a practicing lawyer at Harrisonburg at the outbreak of the war.

part in the battle of Monocacy, July 9, 1864, in which Gen. Lew Wallace was defeated.

The writer was exchanged on the 3d of August, 1864, came home, and rejoined his command. In the meantime, however, the regiment, now no larger than a company, took part in the third battle of Winchester, September 19, 1864, when Capt. C. F. Campbell was killed, and at Fisher's Hill, both engagements being disastrous to Early, who came up the Valley as far as Weyer's Cave. In a short time he moved down the Valley, surprising the enemy by a flank movement at Cedar Creek on the morning of October 19, in which the Tenth took an active part, the Confederates driving everything before them. They captured a large number of prisoners, many pieces of artillery, and quantities of supplies, only to lose all except the prisoners, and more too, before the day ended.

In December (1864) Terry's brigade was sent to Gen. Lee, near Petersburg, camping on Hatcher's Run, a few miles south of the city. The Tenth took part in a hotly fought battle in February, 1865, the writer being in command of the 10th, 23d, and 37th Va. Regiments. Later on we were moved to a point in front of the city, where on the morning of April 2, as part of Gen. J. B. Gordon's corps, we stormed and carried the enemy's works, but were finally driven back, the Tenth losing many of its number in killed, wounded, and captured.

Late on the 2d of April we withdrew from the front of Petersburg, in the vain effort to get away from Grant. On the retreat we took part in the fight at Sailor's Creek, with but two commissioned company officers in the Tenth: Lieut. John H. Ralston, who was badly wounded and left in the hands of the enemy, and Lieut. J. G. H. Miller, now commanding the regiment.

On the morning of April 9 we had a skirmish with the enemy at Appomattox, driving them some distance, only to be withdrawn and to furl our banners,—banners never again to be unfurled. But the Tenth did not surrender the

ROCKINGHAM COUNTY

old battle flag, which was hidden under his coat by Lieut. J. G. H. Miller,[5] and which is still preserved in Rockingham by his family.

Lieut. Miller commanded the regiment at Appomattox, now reduced to 8 or 10 muskets. The writer had been put in command of the 10th, 23d, and 37th regiments. Here ended the military career of the noble Tenth Virginia. By April 15 we were home again to start life anew.[6]

We give below Gen. Jackson's own occount of the battle of Cross Keys and Port Republic, June 8 and 9, 1862, as embodied in his report to the Department Headquarters.

We reached Harrisonburg at an early hour on the morning of the 5th, and, passing beyond that town, turned towards the east in the direction of Port Republic. On the 6th, General Ashby took position on the road between Harrisonburg and Port Republic, and received a spirited charge from a portion of the enemy's cavalry, which resulted in the repulse of the enemy, and the capture of Colonel Wyndham and sixty-three others.

Apprehending that the Federals would make a more serious attack, Ashby called for an infantry support. The brigade of General Geo. H. Stewart was accordingly ordered forward. In a short time the fifty-eighth Virginia regiment became engaged with a Pennsylvania regiment called the Bucktails, when Colonel Johnson, of the first Maryland regiment, coming up in the hottest period of the fire, charged gallantly into its flank and drove the enemy, with heavy loss, from the field, capturing Lieutenant Colonel Kane, commanding. In this skirmish our infantry loss was seventeen (17) killed, fifty (50) wounded, and three missing. In this affair General Turner Ashby was killed. An official report is not an appropriate place for more than a passing notice of the distinguished dead; but the close relation which General Ashby bore to my command for most of the previous twelve months, will justify me in saying that as a partisan officer I never knew his superior. His daring was proverbial; his powers of endurance almost incredible; his tone of character heroic, and his sagacity almost intuitive in divining the purposes and movements of the enemy.

---

5. Capt. Miller died at his home in Elkton, June 16, 1889. Upon the old flag he saved may still be read the names of the following battles: Manassas No. 1, McDowell, Winchester No. 1, Port Republic, Cold Harbor, Malvern Hill, Cedar Run, Manassas No. 2, Chantilly, Fredericksburg, Chancellorsville, Winchester No. 2, Gettysburg.

6. Complete muster rolls of the various Rockingham companies are given in the Appendix, as far as possible.

A HISTORY OF

The main body of my command had now reached the vicinity of Port Republic. The village is situated in the angle formed by the junction of the North and South rivers, tributaries of the south fork of the Shenandoah. Over the larger and deeper of those two streams, the North river, there was a wooden bridge, connecting the town with the road leading to Harrisonburg. Over the South river there was a passable ford. The troops more immediately under my own eye were encamped on the high ground north of the village, about a mile from the river. General Ewell was some four miles distant, near the road leading from Harrisonburg to Port Republic. General Fremont had arrived with his forces in the vicinity of Harrisonburg, and General Shields was moving up the east side of the south fork of the Shenandoah; and was then at Conrad's store, some fifteen miles below Port Republic, my position being about equi-distant from both hostile armies. To prevent a junction of the two Federal armies, I had caused the bridge over the south fork of the Shenandoah at Conrad's store to be destroyed. Intelligence having been received that Gen. Shields was advancing further up the river, Captain Sipe,[7] with a small cavalry force, was sent down during the night of the 7th to verify the report and gain such other information respecting the enemy as he could. Captain G. W. Myers, of the cavalry, was subsequently directed to move with his company in the same direction for the purpose of supporting Captain Sipe, if necessary. The next morning Captain Myers' company came rushing back in disgraceful disorder, announcing that the Federal forces were in close pursuit. Captain Chipley and his company of cavalry, which was in town, also shamefully fled. The brigades of Generals Taliaferro and Winder were soon under arms, and ordered to occupy positions immediately north of the bridge. By this time the Federal cavalry, accompanied by artillery, were in sight, and, after directing a few shots towards the bridge, they crossed South river, and dashing into the village, planted one of their pieces at the southern entrance of the bridge. In the meantime the batteries of Wooding, Poague and Carpenter were being placed in position, and General Taliaferro's brigade having reached the vicinity of the bridge, was ordered to charge across, capture the piece, and occupy the town. Whilst one of Poague's pieces was returning the fire of that of the enemy at the far end of the bridge, the thirty-seventh Virginia regiment, Colonel Fulkerson, after delivering its fire, gallantly charged over the bridge, captured the gun, and followed by the other regiments of the

---

[7]. Emanuel Sipe, captain Co. H, 12th Va. Cavalry, later lieutenant-colonel, assigned to command of the 7th Va. Cavalry. He was born in Rockingham, July 5, 1830. Prior to the war he was lieutenant-colonel of the 116th Va. Militia; and both before and after the war was a prominent merchant and man of affairs. He died Sept. 23, 1901.

ROCKINGHAM COUNTY

brigade, entered the town, and dispersed and drove back the Federal cavalry. Another piece of artillery, with which the Federals had advanced, was abandoned and subsequently fell into our hands.

About this time, a considerable body of infantry was seen advancing up the same road. Our batteries opened with marked effect upon the retreating cavalry and advancing infantry. In a short time the infantry followed the cavalry, falling back to Lewis', three miles down the river, pursued for a mile by our batteries on the opposite bank, when the enemy disappeared in the wood around a bend in the road. This attack of General Shields had hardly been repulsed, before Ewell was seriously engaged with Fremont, moving on the opposite side of the river. The enemy pushed forward driving in the fifteenth Alabama, Colonel Canty, from their post on picket. This regiment made a gallant resistance, which so far checked the Federal advance as to afford General Ewell time for the choice of his position at leisure.

His ground was well selected, on a commanding ridge, a rivulet and large field of open ground in front, wood on both flanks, and his line intersected near its centre by the road leading to Port Republic. General Trimble's brigade was posted on the right, somewhat in advance of his centre. The batteries of Courtnay, Lusk, Brockenbrough, and Raines in the centre, General Stewart's brigade on the left, and General Elzey's brigade in rear of the centre, and in position to strengthen either wing. Both wings were in the wood.

About ten o'clock, the enemy threw out his skirmishers, and shortly after posted his artillery opposite to our batteries. The artillery fire was kept up with great animation and spirit on both sides for several hours. In the meantime a brigade of Federal forces advanced under cover, upon the right, occupied by General Trimble, who reserved his fire until they reached the crest of the hill, in easy range of his musketry, when he poured a deadly fire from his whole front, under which they fell back. Observing a battery about being posted on the enemy's left, half a mile in front, General Trimble, now supported by the thirteenth and twenty-fifth Virginia regiments, of Elzey's brigade, pushed forward for the purpose of taking it, but found it withdrawn before he reached the spot, having, in the meantime, some spirited skirmishing with its infantry supports. General Trimble had now advanced more than a mile from his original position, while the Federal advance had fallen back to the ground occupied by them in the morning.

General Taylor, of the eighth brigade of Louisiana troops, having arrived from the vicinity of the bridge, at Port Republic, towards which he had moved in the morning, reported to General Ewell about two, P. M., and was placed in rear. Colonel Patton, with the forty-second and forty-eighth Virginia regiments, and first battalion of Virginia regulars, also joined, and, with the remainder of General Elzey's brigade, was added to the centre and left, then supposed to be threatened. General Ewell having been informed by Lieutenant Heinrichs, of the engineer corps, who had been sent out to reconnoitre, that the enemy was moving a large column on his left, did not advance at once; but subsequently ascertaining that no attack was designed by the force referred to, he advanced, drove in the enemy's skirmishers and, when night closed, was in position on ground previously held by the enemy. During this fight Brigadier Generals Elzey and Stewart were wounded, and disabled from command.

This engagement with Fremont has generally been known as the battle of Cross Keys, in which our troops were commanded by General Ewell. I had remained at Port Republic during the principal part of the 8th, expecting a renewal of the attack. As no movement was made by General Shields to renew the action that day, I determined to take the initiative and attack him the following morning.

Accordingly, General Ewell was directed to move his position at an early hour, on the morning of the 9th, towards Port Republic, leaving General Trimble with his brigade, supported by Colonel Patton with the forty-second Virginia infantry and the first battalion of Virginia regulars, to hold Fremont in check, with instructions if hard pressed to retire across the North river, and burn the bridge in their rear. Soon after ten o'clock, General Trimble with the last of our forces had crossed the North river, and the bridge was destroyed.[8] In the meantime, before five in the morning, General Winder's brigade was in Port Republic, and having crossed the South Fork, by a temporary wagon bridge, placed there for the purpose, was moving down the River road to attack the forces of General Shields. Advancing a mile and a half, he encountered the Federal pickets and drove them in.

The enemy had judiciously selected his position for defence. Upon a rising ground near the Lewis House, he had planted six guns which commanded the road from Port Republic, and swept the plateau for a considerable distance in front. As General Winder moved forward his brigade, a rapid and severe fire of shell was opened upon it. Capt. Poague, with two Parrott guns, was promptly placed in position on the left of the road to engage, and if possible to dislodge the Federal battery. Captain Carpenter was sent to the right to select a position for his battery, but finding it impracticable to drag it through the dense undergrowth, it was brought back, and part of it placed near Poague. The artillery fire was well sustained by our batteries, but found unequal to that of the enemy.

---

8. The squad that burned the bridge was in charge of Courier Geo. H. Hulvey, a native of Rockingham, born at Cross Keys, April 19, 1844. He lost his left arm in the Wilderness, May 6, 1864. For the past 25 years or more he has been superintendent of schools for Rockingham County, and is one of the best known educators in the State.

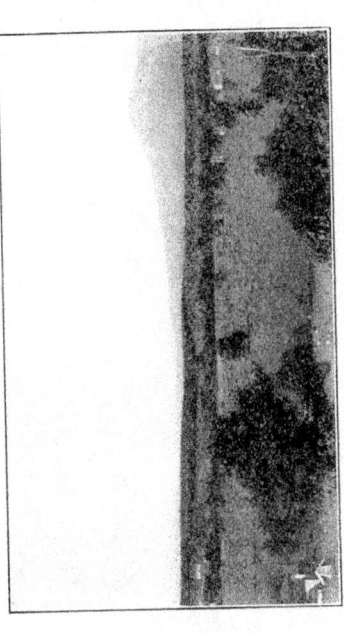

Flag Presented to Chrisman's Boy Company by the Ladies of Winchester (Page 318)

Port Republic Battlefield (Pages 141-147)

Battle-Flag Presented to 10th Va. Regt. Vol. Inf. by the Ladies of Harrisonburg

Battle-Flag Saved at Appomattox by Lt. Miller (Pages 140, 141)

ROCKINGHAM COUNTY

In the meantime, Winder being now reinforced by the seventh Louisiana regiment, Colonel Hays, seeing no mode of silencing the Federal battery, or escaping its destructive missiles but by a rapid charge, and the capture of it, advanced with great boldness for some distance, but encountered such a heavy fire of artillery and small arms as greatly to disorganize his command, which fell back in disorder. The enemy advanced across the field, and, by a heavy musketry fire, forced back our infantry supports, in consequence of which our guns had to retire. The enemy's advance was checked by a spirited attack upon their flank, by the fifty-eighth and fifty-fourth Virginia regiments, directed by General Ewell and led by Colonel Scott, although his command was afterwards driven back to the woods with severe loss. The batteries were all safely withdrawn except one of Captain Poague's six-pounder guns, which was carried off by the enemy.

Whilst Winder's command was in this critical condition, the gallant and successful attack of General Taylor on the Federal left and rear, directed attention from the front, and lead to a concentration of their force upon him. Moving to the right along the mountain acclivity, through a rough and tangled forest, and much disordered by the rapidity and obstructions of the march, Taylor emerged with his command from the wood, just as the loud cheers of the enemy had proclaimed their success in front; and although assailed by a superior force in front and flank, with their guns in position within point blank range, the charge was gallantly made, and the battery, consisting of six guns, fell into our hands. Three times was this battery lost and won in the desperate and determined efforts to capture and recover it. After holding the batteries for a short time, a fresh brigade of the enemy advancing upon his flank, made a vigorous and well conducted attack upon him, accompanied by a galling fire of canister from a piece suddenly brought into position, at a distance of about three hundred and fifty yards. Under this combined attack, Taylor fell back to the skirt of the wood, near which the captured battery was stationed, and from that point continued his fire upon the advancing enemy, who succeeded in recapturing one of the guns, which he carried off, leaving both caisson and limber. The enemy, now occupied with Taylor, halted his advance to the front. Winder made a renewed effort to rally his command, and succeeding, with the seventh Louisiana, under Major Penn, (the Colonel and Lieutenant Colonel having been carried from the field wounded,) and the fifth Virginia regiment, Col. Funk, he placed part of Poague's battery in the position previously occupied by it, and again opened upon the enemy, who were moving against Taylor's left flank, apparently to surround him in the wood. Chew's battery now reported, and was placed in position, and did good service. Soon after, guns from the batteries of Brockenbough, Courtnay and Rains, were brought forward and placed in position. Whilst these movements were in progress on the left and front, Colonel Scott, having rallied his command, led them, under the orders of General Ewell, to the support of General Taylor, who, pushing forward with the reinforcements just received, and assisted by the well-directed fire of our artillery, forced the enemy to fall back, which was soon followed by his precipitate retreat, leaving many killed and wounded upon the field. General Taliaferro, who the previous day had occupied the town, was directed to continue to do so with part of his troops, and, with the remainder, to hold the elevated position on the north side of the river, for the purpose of co-operating, if necessary, with General Trimble, and prevent his being cut off from the main body of the army by the destruction of the bridge in his rear. But finding the resistance more obstinate than I anticipated, orders were sent to Taliaferro and Trimble to join the main body. Taliaferro came up in time to discharge an effective volley into the ranks of the wavering and retreating enemy. The pursuit was continued some five miles beyond the battle-field by Generals Taliaferro and Winder with their brigades and portions of the batteries of Wooding and Caskie. Colonel Munford, with cavalry and some artillery, advanced about three miles beyond the other troops. Our forces captured in the pursuit about four hundred and fifty (450) prisoners, some wagons, one piece of abandoned artillery, and about eight hundred muskets. Some two hundred and seventy-five (275) wounded were paroled in the hospitals near Port Republic.

Whilst the forces of Shields were in full retreat, and our troops in pursuit, Fremont appeared on the opposite bank of the south fork of the Shenandoah, with his army, and opened his artillery upon our ambulances, and parties engaged in the humane labors of attending to our dead and wounded, and the dead and wounded of the enemy. The next day, withdrawing his forces, he retreated down the Valley.

On the morning of the 12th, Munford entered Harrisonburg, where, in addition to wagons, medical stores and camp equipage, he captured some two hundred small arms. At that point there also fell into our hands about two hundred of Fremont's men, many of them severely wounded on the 8th, and most of the others had been left behind as sick. The Federal surgeons attending them were released, and those under their care paroled.

The official reports of the casualties of the battle show a loss of sixteen (16) officers killed, sixty-seven (67) wounded, and two (2) missing; one hundred and seventeen (117) non-commissioned officers and privates killed, eight hundred and sixty-two (862) wounded, and thirty-two missing, making a total loss of one thousand and ninety-six, (1,096) including skirmishers on the 6th; since evacuation of Winchester, one thousand one hundred and sixty-seven, (1,167;) also one piece of artillery. If we add to the prisoners captured on the 6th and 9th, those who were paroled at Harrisonburg, and in hospitals in the vicinity of Port Republic,

ROCKINGHAM COUNTY

it will make the number of the enemy who fell into our possession about nine hundred and seventy-five, (975,) exclusive of his killed, and such of his wounded as he removed. The small arms taken on the 9th, and at Harrisonburg, numbered about one thousand (1,000.) We captured seven pieces of artillery, with their caissons and all of their limbers, except one. The conduct of the officers and men, during the action, merits the highest praise.

I forward, herewith, two maps, by Mr. J. Hotchkiss, one giving the route of the army during the retreat from Strasburg to Port Republic, and the other of the battle-field.

On the 12th, the troops recrossed South river, and encamped near Weyer's Cave. For the purpose of rendering thanks to God for having crowned our arms with success, and to implore His continued favor, divine service was held in the army on the 14th.

The army remained near Weyer's Cave until the 17th, when, in obedience to instructions from the commanding General of the Departmert, it moved towards Richmond.

I am, General, very respectfully, your obedient servant,

T. J. JACKSON,
Lieutenant General.

The following letter, giving additional particulars relating to the battle of Cross Keys, was written in May, 1912, at Frankfort, Indiana, by Capt. William N. Jordan, a native of Rockingham, then nearly ninety-two years of age.

I was born in Mt. Crawford Christmas Day in the year 1820, and my mother died when I was nine days old. I was taken and raised by strangers in the neighborhood of Friedens Church, by a man named Martin Neir, and I staid with him until he died in 1844. Before I was seventeen years old I commenced driving his team of six horses in hauling produce to market,—Fredericksburg and Richmond were the markets at that time. After some time had passed Scottsville became a market for produce, and after a few years more Winchester became a market for the people of Rockingham.

I still remained on the place. On the 5th day of October, 1847, about eight o'clock, we had a cyclone. It tore the barn clear away, and part of the house; and in a large orchard there was not one tree left standing. Wife and I and the girl were in the part of the house that was not torn down. In the part of which the roof was taken off were two boys; but none of us was hurt.

Then Martin Neir's widow and I made sale of the land and property, and I bought me a home near the Cross Keys, and lived there until the Civil War commenced. I was assessor of that district in '59 and '60, and I was captain of the Cross Keys and Mt. Crawford cavalry. I had about

—147—

A HISTORY OF

100 men in the company, and we were mustered into service of the Confederacy on the third day of June, 1861, and were in a number of battles. Among them was the fight at Cross Keys. We were on the left flank of Gen. Ewell's army during the fight.

My farm was just outside of the line of battle. The Yankees broke open my corn crib and took corn to feed their horses, but did not disturb my family. This was on Sunday, and the next morning Gen. Jackson took us across the river and burnt the bridge; and the North River being high they could not follow us; and we went across South River, then down the river, and whipped Shield's forces, and ran them away below the White Post; and on Monday night Fremont began to fall back.

They had made a hospital of a very large two-story house, and set it afire when they left. It was thought by the old people that lived close there that there was a large number of dead and wounded in the house at the time, for they heard some of them calling for help. And they left their dead lying all over the battlefield; and we had to make a big circuit to cross the river to get on the battlefield [of Cross Keys]. We did not get around there until Wednesday morning. Gen. Imboden, who was in command of the cavalry, detailed me and my company to gather up and bury the dead. At one place we buried 81 bodies, and at another 21. They were mostly foreigners, from the looks of them. It has been so long ago that I don't remember how many we lost in that battle.

I had eight children of school age at that time, that I thought ought to be going to school. As there was no free school system then, I thought I would go to a state where they could get an education. So I sold out there and came to Indiana. My wife died January 21, 1911. We were married and lived together nearly sixty-six years. I am now staying with one of my daughters, and expect to stay here what few days may yet be allotted to me.

I voted for James K. Polk in 1844, for President, and I am still a Democrat. So good bye.

(Signed) Capt. Wm. N. Jordan.

In 1860 there were in Rockingham County 2387 slaves; in 1863, 2039: loss, 348. During the same time the number of horses was reduced from 7670 to 6656: loss, 1014; and the number of cattle from 21,413 to 14,739: loss, 6674.[9] But when these statistics were gathered the worst was yet to come.

In the fall of 1864 Sheridan's army was encamped about Harrisonburg and Dayton. One rainy evening Major John R. Meigs, of Sheridan's staff, and two other Federals met three Confederate scouts near Dayton, and attempted to capture

---

[9]. *Rockingham Register*, March 25, 1864.

ROCKINGHAM COUNTY

or kill them, but in the fight Meigs himself was killed. It was reported to Sheridan that Meigs had been shot by a bushwhacker. To administer a gentle reproof to the community, Sheridan ordered that every house within five miles of the spot where Meigs fell should be burned. The work of burning began. A number of buildings in the vicinity were devoted to the torch. The people of Dayton were warned of the impending destruction, and moved out into the surrounding fields, where men, women, and children spent the chill October night as comfortably as they could, waiting to see their homes go up in flames. But sometime the next evening they were told the order to burn the town had been withdrawn, and were allowed to return to their houses.

I have heard several explanations as to why Dayton was not burned. One report has it that a Masonic apron was found by the burners in one of the houses nearby; another, that the many kindnesses extended to the Federals by the people of the community were remembered in the camps. Not long ago I learned that the Federal officer whose task it had been to carry out the order to burn was still living in Ohio, and I wrote to him asking him for information. He is mayor of Clarington, Monroe County, Ohio. His letter follows.

Clarington, Ohio, March 16, 1912.

MY DEAR SIR:

Yours of the 11th recd. In reply will say that I was a main participant in that stirring and heart-rending event of Oct. 5th, 1864, at the town of Dayton, Va., where, at 5 o'clock P. M., by an order issued by our commander, Genl. P. H. Sheridan (order No. 89), I was ordered to take my regiment, the 116th O. V. I., and set the torch of destruction to every building in that beautiful town, for what some foolhardy citizen had done, or was supposed to have done—the killing of Major Meigs of Sheridan's Staff.

Now the reason why the order of Genl. Sheridan was not carried out is, Genl. Thomas F. Wildes of my brigade, at one time colonel of the 116th O. V. I. (my regiment), who was a particularly ideal officer under Sheridan, and suited Sheridan on account of his bravery and fighting qualities, begged and prayed Sheridan to revoke the order, as my regiment, the 116th O. V. I., formerly Genl. T. F. Wildes' regiment, was the regiment detailed by Sheridan to carry out his heart-rending order.

A HISTORY OF

Gen. Wildes prevailed on Sheridan to revoke the order, and I got the order 5 minutes before we were to apply the torch to that beautiful and peaceful town.

When I announced the revoking of the order, there was louder cheering than there ever was when we made a bayonet charge.

I know every foot of ground in that country. I was only 17 years old then, and my heart fairly leaped for joy when the order was rescinded. Brigadier-Genl. Thomas F. Wildes, together with the regimental officers, are the ones who saved those towns, Dayton, Harrisonburg, and Mt. Crawford, from being burned down. We fought quite a hard battle at Piedmont on June 5th, under Genl. Hunter.

Yours very truly,

COL. S. TSCHAPPAT.

It was just a day or two after the incidents above recorded that Sheridan began his wide-spread retreat down the Valley, burning mills and barns, and driving off or killing horses, cattle, sheep, and hogs.

A vivid and realistic conception of the destruction wrought in Rockingham by the "burning" may be obtained by looking over the various items in the following letter, written by a gentleman living at the time in the vicinity of Timberville, and published in the *Rockingham Register* of March 24, 1865.

Near Timberville, Va , February 13, 1865.

Editors of the Register:—I hereby send you a list of losses sustained in this portion of Rockingham county, by Sheridan's army. The prices fixed are those prevailing before the war.

David Cline, one barn, horse stable, 300 bushels of wheat, 34 tons of hay, 9 cattle, 30 sheep, loss about $2,600.

George Moffett, 1 barn, 20 tons of hay, cattle, farming utensils, &c., loss about $1600.

Jonas Early, 1 barn, 150 bushels of wheat, 10 tons of hay, house property, &c., loss $2000.

John Rife, 1 barn, wheat, hay, &c., loss $1000.

John W. Driver, 6 horses, 14 sheep, loss $800.

Widow Driver, 1 barn, horse stable, 200 bushels of wheat, 20 tons of hay, wagon, ploughs, &c., loss $2,500.

S. H. Myers, 1 barn, 325 bushels of wheat, 10 tons of hay, 7 cattle, and other property, $2500.

Thornton Thomas, 5 horses, 10 cattle, 30 sheep, loss $700.

George Lohr and Sons, 3 barns, 1000 bushels grain, 10 tons hay, 7 horses, 10 cattle, farming implements, &c., $5,900.

ROCKINGHAM COUNTY

Philip Lowry, 1 stable, 1 horse, hay, &c., $400.
Jesse Bushong, 2 horses, 3 cows, $225.
A. Bushong, 1 horse, $100.
Albert Flemens, 1 barn, 2 cows, hay, &c., $700.
Matthias Minnick & Son, 1 barn, 225 bushels of wheat, 6 tons hay, 5 horses, 12 cattle, threshing machine, ploughs, &c., $2,000.
George Arehart, 1 barn, 160 bushels of wheat, 10 tons hay, 8 cattle, farming implements, $1,400.
Abram Arehart, 1 barn, horse stable, 200 bushels wheat, 12 tons hay, 11 cattle, sheep, hogs, &c., $2,000.
Jacob Arehart, 3 horses, 4 cattle, 11 sheep, $400.
Moses Tussing, 1 barn, 4 tons hay, 3 horses, 2 cows, $900.
David Bowman, 1 barn, 500 bushels wheat, 10 tons hay, 12 cattle, &c., $2,000.
William G. Thompson, 1 merchant mill, some grain, horse gears, cattle, etc., $4,000.

The above list comprises that portion of the 8th district, north of the Shenandoah River and east of the Timberville road. A number of other persons had small losses which are not mentioned in the above list.

Yours, Respectfully,

B. Hoover.

The losses enumerated by Mr. Hoover foot up a total of $33,725. The district in which this loss was sustained is not over one-sixtieth of the productive portion of the county; therefore, if equivalent loss was suffered all over the county, the grand total would exceed $2,000,000—estimated upon ante bellum prices. Estimated upon contemporary prices in Confederate money, the grand total would be over $20,000-000. A calculation of this sort will obviously justify the following statement found on page 1303 of Garner and Lodge's history of the United States:

"The value of property destroyed in Rockingham County alone was estimated at $25,000,000; thousands of families were reduced to absolute want and on every hand the signs of desolation were pitiable in the extreme."

In the summer of 1864, upon the advance of Hunter's army up the Valley, a lot of the records of the county and of the circuit court were loaded on a wagon and hauled eastward, the aim being to take them through Brown's Gap to a place of safety in or beyond the Blue Ridge. The wagon was

A HISTORY OF

overtaken on the road between Port Republic and Mt. Vernon Furnace by some of Hunter's men, and set afire. After the Federals left, some persons in the neighborhood put out the fire, using for the purpose, it is said, some green hay just cut in a nearby field. The records left at the courthouse were not injured, though the files of the *Rockingham Register*, in the office of that paper, were destroyed. The partly burned records of the county were collected and brought back to the county-seat, where many of them may still be seen. An effort has been made to restore them as fully as possible.

A war always stimulates home manufactures. "Necessity is the mother of invention." In Chapter XXI will be found a number of items showing some of the particular manufactures in Rockingham during the war, as well as during other periods. It is needless to say that a war also raises prices. Here are some illustrations from the case before us:

1861.

"Prices Reduced! Best fine salt at $9 to $9.25. Prime Super Flour $4.75.—Isaac Paul."

Brown sugar 20 cents a pound.

Orleans molasses $1.00 a gallon.

1862.

Cash prices paid by Isaac Paul in August: Butter, 40c; cheese, 40c; lard, 25c; hard soap, 30c; bacon, 27-30c.

In October Isaac Paul was advertising tobacco at 60 cents a pound, and offering to pay the following prices: Wool, $1 to $1.25; flax seed, $1 to $1.25; butter, 40 to 50c; cheese, 40 to 50c; lard, 25c; flour, $8 to $8.50; bacon, 35 to 40c.

In September-October salt was over $15 a sack.

In November ink was $1 a bottle; Isaac Paul was offering 75c for butter and cheese; J. N. Hill was offering to pay $1 a pound cash for 10,000 pounds of good roll butter.

1863.

In April flour was $20 a barrel at the mill; wheat was $4 a bushel; corn, $4; bacon, $1 a pound; hay, $1 a cwt.

1864.

In February the American Hotel in Harrisonburg was advertising board at $150 a month; supper, lodging, and breakfast for $10; board at $10 a day; single meals at $4. "Positively no credit."

The same month D. A. Plecker was urging: "Buy your salt two years in advance when you can get it at 50 cts. per pound"; while Fishback & Long, at Montezuma, were offering "Also, a lot of Salt which we will sell at 60 cents by the sack."

In May Isaac Paul had some salt at 45 cents.

In July $1000 was given or offered for a horse.

In December salt was 80 cents a pound.

1865.

In the *Register* of March 24 the following estray notice appeared: "A White Boar, supposed to be one and a half years old, left ear cut, appraised at $175."

But the flowers still bloomed in Rockingham, though often broken in the strife. In the fall of 1861 the Female Seminary, located where the Main Street school in Harrisonburg now stands, J. Mark Wilson, principal, was turned into a hospital for wounded and sick Confederate soldiers. Early in 1864 there was a general hospital at Harrisonburg, Dr. A. R. Meem, surgeon in charge. More than 300 Confederate soldiers were buried in Woodbine Cemetery, where, every springtime, sweet flowers in fair hands are borne to mark the place.

In Chapter XVI other particulars are given that have application here.

In 1862 Rev. Daniel Thomas, a Dunker minister, sold 1000 gallons of cane molasses at $1 a gallon, Confederate money, to his poor friends and neighbors, when he was offered $2 a gallon in gold or silver, by speculators. At another time he sold several hundred gallons of flaxseed oil at great pecuniary loss, for benevolent reasons.

In the *Register* of April 24, 1863, appeared a fine tribute to the Rockingham farmers. It was shown that they were a sturdy, industrious class of loyal citizens, even in the midst of most aggravating circumstances. When their fields were devastated, their stock driven off, and their buildings burned

A HISTORY OF

by the public enemy, and when their own fellow-countrymen in arms failed to respect their rights—riding down grain and grass in mere wantonness, burning fences, men and officers alike, and even threatening the protesting owners, the farmers of Rockingham County were still loyal, and strove with no less energy to raise supplies for their country at large as well as for their immediate families.

The following paragraphs appeared in the *Register* of February 5, 1864:

Notice.

At a meeting of the Rockingham Medical Association, held in Harrisonburg, January 18th, 1864, the following resolutions were unanimously adopted:

Resolved, That we will practice at old rates, notwithstanding the present high prices of medicines, in all cases where our patrons will pay us in produce at old prices.

Resolved, That in every case where it is not convenient to pay in produce, we will receive a bond at old rates, payable after the war.

Resolved, That in every instance where it is desirable to pay us in money, we will regulate our charges in proportion to the prices of the produce of the country; except for our services to the poor and needy, and especially to families in service, or killed or disabled in the service.

Resolved, That all old open accounts standing upon our books shall be included in the above regulations.

The next meeting will be on the 3d Monday in February, at 10 o'clock.

Geo. K. Gilmer, Secretary.

This chapter must be concluded with another excerpt from the *Rockingham Register*,—that paper true to its name. The following article appeared under date of March, 24, 1865:

Trotter's Stage Line.

One of the "institutions" that has, so far, survived "the wreck of matter" caused by the Yankees in this beautiful Valley, is Trotter's stage line. Notwithstanding the heavy losses of the enterprising proprietor caused by the enemy, he is still in motion, and his teams and his stages still run up and down the Valley as though nothing had occurred to molest them. A stage line requires unusual energy and industry in its proper management, and that is exactly what *"Trotter's line"* (most

ROCKINGHAM COUNTY

appropriate designation!) has. It required great skill and activity to save the stages and teams from the Yankees the last time they came up the Valley; but Trotter has the singular good fortune to have an agent at this end of the line, who may be safely trusted to take care of everything under his control. JOS. ANDREWS is as energetic as the proprietor of the stage line whose interests he so carefully protects and promotes. It is to the energy and industry of Mr. Andrews, (who, by the way, is "an old stager" himself,) that the Valley people are now indebted for the mail facilities and other very great accommodations resulting from the movements of a regular daily line of stages. These can hardly be properly estimated and appreciated. We almost felt as if we were cut off from the outside world and the rest of mankind until the arrival of Trotter's stages disturbed the Sabbath-like stillness of our paralyzed village. With our stores closed, (the merchants fearing that the Yankees might soon come again,) and with our Post Office shut up as if we had entered upon an unending Sabbath, it was really a pleasant sight to us to see *Trotter's* teams coming *trotting* in a week ago as gaily as if there never had been Yankees in the Valley, and as if forage and corn could still be had in abundance. It has, really, been a wonder with us, how the large number of teams have been kept up so well. It is all attributable to the tireless activity and industry of the chief director and agent, Mr. Andrews, who is known to all travellers in the Valley as one of the most accommodating stage agents to be met with. A stage line, under his management, is obliged to go ahead. If ever any stage line deserved encouragement and countenance Trotter's Valley line assuredly does. In fact, we cannot see how the people could possibly do without it.[10]

---

10. For the gift or loan of old papers and other source materials for the period covered by this chapter, I am under grateful obligation to Mrs. Cornelia S. Burkholder, of Harrisonburg, and to the following gentlemen: Joseph E. Shaver, Friedens; C. L. Denton, Pleasant Valley; Joe K. Ruebush, Dayton; A. E. Wyant, Elkton; W. H. Sipe, Bridgewater; Rev. C. W. Stinespring, Baltimore; and Q. G. Kaylor, Marshall Crawford, C. A. Hammer, and Capt. J. H. Dwyer; Harrisonburg, as well as to others whose names have already been given.

CHAPTER VIII.

THE DAYS OF RECONSTRUCTION.

1865—1876.

In no period of our nation's history have so many great problems thrust themselves upon us as during the decade immediately following the Civil War. America continued to be a world stage for the play of giants; and while the full light was upon the center, the great drama, in its subsidiary parts and inevitable accompaniments, was in thrilling action round all the widening circles. Although Rockingham County was more or less remote from the stage's center, it never lost its cue or count from the bitter opening to the better end. It played its part and suffered its share of the tragic years.

In other chapters, under particular topics—roads and railroads, churches and religious life, education and schools, banking, manufacturing, etc.—will be found much of the matter that chronologically falls in this; but enough will doubtless be given here to justify the title: "Days of Reconstruction."

The period was marked first by high prices and financial stringency; later came the rush of enterprise and speculation, attendant upon rising prosperity; then the crash of '73, and the tedious recovery from the shock. In January, 1867, flour was selling in Harrisonburg at $12 and $12.50 a barrel; bacon, hog round, at 11 and 12 cents a pound; butter at 25 cents. In the same issue of the *Register* from which these quotations are taken is found the following paragraph:

At a recent sale in Shenandoah county of the property of Mrs. Hannah Wilkin, dec'd, wheat sold for $3.10 per bushel; corn, 69 cents; cows $25 and $32; beds and bedding each from $30 to $35.[1]

[1.] *Rockingham Register*, January 17, 1867.

ROCKINGHAM COUNTY

One of the most striking features of the time, up to 1870, or thereabouts, was the prevalence of lawlessness. Robbery and vandalism were rife. There was robbing of stores, mills, smoke-houses, and persons. Early in 1870 the street lamps of Harrisonburg were smashed, and a few months later a large number of shade trees about the public square and elsewhere were "belted"—the bark being cut off in a circle all around the trunks. Cattle were killed in the fields —the meat being carried off, the horns and hide usually being left. Hogs in their owners' fields or sties were either butchered there or driven away. Much of this freebooting was done by negroes lately slaves and by poor whites hard pressed by evil times; but it is also known that some of it was done by young white men of respectable families, whose foraging propensities still lacked restraint. War is always demoralizing; and the country fell heir to more than one unwelcome legacy from the years of '61 to '65.

But, as already intimated, depression and stringency were soon overborne by the rising spirit of progress and the onrush of material prosperity. In April, 1866, there were two iron foundries in full blast at Port Republic. Conditions in May are thus graphically portrayed in the *Register:*

> The remarkable display of energy by the people of the Valley, since the close of the war, is the most forcible commentary that could be given of their character. Without a currency, almost destitute of money, their fields laid waste, barns and other farm houses destroyed, stock stolen and driven off, no surplus supplies on hand, and their labor system broken up, yet they have managed to rebuild their fences and barns, repair their premises generally, and [make] progress in improvements heretofore not enjoyed. Throughout the entire Valley steam saw-mills dot almost every neighborhood, factories and foundries are being built, and the slow and imperfect implements of agricultural husbandry heretofore used supplanted by the most improved labor-saving machinery.
>
> .... At Mt. Crawford a large Woolen Factory is in process of construction; also, an Earthen Ware establishment. In Harrisonburg, Messrs. Bradley & Co. have in successful operation their Foundry, and will shortly commence erecting a much larger one, on ground recently purchased for that purpose near the old buildings. At Port Republic and McGaheysville the spirit of enterprize is fully awakened, factories, foundries and mills being put into operation as rapidly as the workmen can

complete their contracts. Carding mills are, also, multiplying throughout the county, and many other improvements are being inaugurated, which we have not space to enumerate.[2]

By June a great many of the barns and mills destroyed by Sheridan in October, 1864, had been replaced. In September the editor of the *Register* wrote:

> Our friends, Henry E. Rhodes and David Weaver, have erected and completed not less than eight large Swisher barns within the last six months. These barns are all in Rockingham, and all, with but one exception, take the places of barns burnt by Gen. Sheridan.[3]

In his issue of October 11 the editor of the same journal devotes a full column to progress in the eastern section of the county: The sawmills of Dr. S. P. H. Miller & Co., near Conrad's Store; the iron furnace of Milnes & Johns, successors of the Forrer Brothers; the chapel erected by the ironmasters for the benefit of the iron-workers, etc.

In the *Register* of December 20 (1866), a correspondent from John J. Bowman's mill, on Linville Creek, says:

> You can count around it [the mill] some fourteen new barns, one extensive tannery, and one first class up-and-down saw mill, all . . . . . . erected during the past summer and the previous autumn.

Among the other features of the year, a find of coal was reported on Briery Branch. During the next decade or more this coal field was a center of interest and speculation.

Early in 1867 it was announced that Philo Bradley & Co., operating the foundry in Harrisonburg, had sold within the past year more than 700 ploughs of their own pattern, and had been obliged to refuse orders for more.[4]

A noteworthy instance of energetic push and practical method in rebuilding material fortunes out the wreck of war was cited at River Bank, two and a half miles east of McGaheysville, where Larkins & Harlow had installed a circular

---

[2]. *Rockingham Register*, May 24, 1866.

[3]. Idem, Sept. 20, 1866.

[4]. Idem, February 7, 1867.

ROCKINGHAM COUNTY

saw, laid the foundations for a large flouring mill, and made other substantial improvements.[5]

By the latter part of 1868 Harrisonburg had made so many important steps upward, and had so many more in contemplation, that we might truthfully declare that it was experiencing a moderate "boom." The same might be said of Bridgewater, Timberville, and other towns of the county.

From 1866 to 1872 John Woods of Shenandoah, the famous bridge builder, had built or rebuilt no less than five bridges in Rockingham: one each at Bridgewater, Mt. Crawford, the crossing above Mt. Crawford, River Bank, and Conrad's Store.

In the last month of 1868 the Manassas Gap railroad was extended to Harrisonburg, and the first train ran into the town. Other railroads were projected, and construction work on some was seriously begun. In 1873 work was begun on the Washington, Cincinnati & St. Louis (narrow gauge) road, surveyed westward past Bridgewater; and in 1874 the Valley road was pushed on to Staunton. Some of the wagon roads were laid out upon new routes, and many were improved one way or another.

There was a revival in things spiritual as well as things material. Soon after the close of the war, about 1867, a county library association was formed, with James Kenney as president. In November, 1867, the Valley Musical Association was organized at Harrisonburg. A great wave of temperance sentiment began to sweep over the country, and friends of temperance associated themselves for aggressive service under different names. In June, 1868, the Ladies' Memorial Association was formed, under the presidency of Mrs. C. C. Strayer, with Mrs. W. H. Ritenour and Mrs. M. M. Sibert, secretaries. In the fall of 1868, and again in 1875, the second coming of Christ was preached in Rockingham and adjacent sections by William C. Thurman and others. In May, 1873, a Young Men's Christian Association was organized at the Episcopal Church in Harrisonburg, with F. A. Berlin, president; and in October of the same year the Rock-

---

5. *Rockingham Register*, May 23, 1867.

A HISTORY OF

ingham County Bible Society was organized at the Methodist Church in the same town, with Philo Bradley, president.

In March, 1866, there was a small squad of Federal soldiers in the county, looking up horses, etc., bearing the United States brand. They also made one or two arrests, under military orders. Later, a number of the civil officers were removed by order of the military governor, but for the most part the military aspects of the reconstruction program were less prominent in Rockingham than in many other sections of the State. On March 18, 1866, a large mass meeting of citizens of the county was held at the court house, and resolutions were adopted expressing hearty approval of President Johnson in his efforts to uphold the Constitution against infringement by Congress, and declaring a cordial loyalty to his administration. On the whole, there appears to have been a good feeling between the two races, and a sensible cooperation between them. An exception to this might have been noted at Bridgewater, on the night of December 24, 1868, when some young white men entered the colored school building, recently opened by an agent of the Freedmen's Bureau, and knocked out the windows, broke the stove, damaged the other furniture, etc.; but this act was not approved by the better judgment of the people at large.[6]

A notable incident of the year 1866 was a violent tornado, which, on the 23d of April, swept in a semi-circle around Harrisonburg, not damaging the town, but blowing down barns and other buildings, uprooting trees, unroofing barns and houses, etc., in the vicinity.

At the time under consideration Harrisonburg was a great distributing point for mail. From July 1, 1867, to June 30, 1871, the mails went out thence into the county and adjacent sections according to the following schedule:

To Waynesboro and intermediate points, 34 miles, and back, twice a week;

To Keezletown, Roadside, and intermediate points, 18 miles, and back, twice a week;

---

6. See the *Old Commonwealth*, January 6, 1869.

HON. JOHN T. HARRIS
(Pages 161, 356, 357)

ROCKINGHAM COUNTY

To Cootes' Store, Broadway, New Market, etc., 33 miles, and back, twice a week;

To Franklin and intermediate points, 43 miles, and back, once a week;

To Bridgewater, Mt. Solon, Deerfield, Bath Alum, etc., 62 miles, and back, twice a week.

E. M. Nuckols got the contract for carrying the mails between Harrisonburg and Waynesboro at $446 a year, for four years; and C. W. Airy secured the job of carrying them between Harrisonburg and Franklin at $300 a year.[7]

The old county court, composed of justices of the peace, continued till 1870. The circuit superior court, held first in 1809, was succeeded by the present circuit court in 1852. The judge of the circuit court from 1866 to 1869, a critical period, was Hon. John T. Harris, a citizen of Rockingham, distinguished in various departments of public service. No truer commentary on the times and no keener analysis of conditions can be found than that presented in his charge to the grand jury, May 11, 1867, and it is accordingly reproduced in full:

I feel it my duty to say a word to you on the changed condition of our public affairs with a view that you may the more fully understand yours.

Since our last meeting a very material and important change has taken place in our State and National relations. For the first time in our history, the civil law has become subordinate to and dependent on the military.—This you may suppose works an important change in your duties, but it does not, as I will presently shew. You who have ever been taught that in peace at least, the civil tribunals are supreme, can scarcely realize that now they are a mere institution of the moment, liable at any time to be superceded or abolished at the will and pleasure of a military commander. It seems anomalous that the power heretofore only secondary and used in aid of the civil law, shall, in the twinkling of an eye, become supreme, and all else to it secondary and only existing by its will and its pleasure. Yet such is the stern reality, and one of the many sad results of the terrible conflict from which we have just emerged. Changes as important and more marvelous than this have been wrought. In a brief space the political institutions of a whole

---

7. See *Rockingham Register*, January 10 and March 28, 1867.

section have been changed. From the greatest and most enlarged liberty compatible with republican government enjoyed by one class, and the most absolute servitude imposed on another, we witness a curtailment of the enlarged liberty of the one and an entire disenthrallment of the latter; and where once existed legal and political distinctions so broad, positive and marked, that it was thought nothing but Providence could remove them, now are seen the entire obliteration of those distinctions and all before the law are placed in a great measure upon an equal footing.

The question recurs, shall we recognize the changes as facts fixed and irrevocable, and conform our actions accordingly, or shall we perversely and stubbornly refuse to do anything to ameliorate the condition of the people?—Wisdom, patriotism, love of family, love of friends and duty to posterity, all combine to enjoin upon us the full recognition of our true condition, and stimulate us to active exertion to do all that is possible to restore as far as may be the countless blessings we once enjoyed. Fault-finding, crimination, recrimination, party strife, uncharitableness of thought and opinion will not promote this much desired result, but only tend to increase our troubles, intensify the feelings of hostility and postpone the end desired, if not sought by all, the restoration of the States to all the rights and powers to which they are now entitled. This consummation so devoutly wished can best be attained by a strict adherence to the appeal made us by the General commanding this State, wherein he says:—"The undersigned appeals to the people of Virginia, and especially to Magistrates and other civil officers, to render the necessity for the exercise of this (military) power as slight as possible by a strict obedience to the laws and by impartial administration of justice to all classes." Strict obedience to the laws and impartial administration of justice to all classes, the cultivation of kindly feeling one for another, a due deference to the opinion of those who differ from us, an honest effort to overcome prejudices of a century, the banishment of visionary hopes of other and better terms of National adjustment, a frank and manly acceptance of the terms and conditions imposed upon us, will tend in a great degree to lighten our burthens and bring us back to other and better days.

Notwithstanding these important revolutions, the Judiciary still exists—still continues to perform its varied functions, and to this time has not been touched even by the hand of the military. And you, gentlemen, are not only permitted but enjoined to perform your time-honored and sacred duties without "fear or favor," only remembering that so far as pertains to your office and duty, that the law has wiped out all distinction of caste, and placed all, in regard to "crime and punishment," on a common footing. I trust, gentlemen, you will prove equal to the occasion.[8]

---

[8]. *Rockingham Register*, May 16, 1867

ROCKINGHAM COUNTY

This authoritative recommendation, so obviously the expression of common sense and prophetic wisdom, must have had a far-reaching influence, and doubtless accomplished much in bringing the people at large to "a frank and manly acceptance" of the results of the war and the actual conditions of the time, and thus in relieving Rockingham from some of the unfortunate experiences that attended reconstruction in so many other places.

The number of white voters registered in Rockingham in 1867,—the first registration under the reconstruction laws of Congress,—was 3228, a very large number considering all the circumstances; and the number of colored men registered was 418.[9] These figures, compared with corresponding ones in other sections of the South, will in large measure explain why the process of reconstruction was accomplished here with so little disturbance.

There were nine voting places in the county at this time (1867), namely, Roadside (near Conrad's Store), Port Republic, Mt. Crawford, Bridgewater, Hopkins' School House, Harrisonburg, Lacey Springs, Bowman's Mill, and Squire Fulk's. The colored voters were lined up in "Loyal Leagues," but of course this made little difference, they being so few. At the election, October 22, 1867, the whites cast 261 votes for a constitutional convention in Virginia, and 1082 votes against such a convention; the negroes cast 304 votes for, and 10 votes against, a convention. At the same time J. N. Liggett and John C. Woodson, Democrats, were elected delegates for Rockingham by decided majorities.[10]

The watchful editors of the *Register*, J. H. Wartman and S. M. Yost, reported what they regarded as a decided movement of immigration into Rockingham from the States north and west during the year 1867, etc.; but at the same time they were obliged to chronicle with regret a continuance of the westward movement on the part of home folks. About the only consolation the loyal editors had in the matter was

---
9. *Rockingham Register*, October 17, 1867.
10. *Rockingham Register*, October 24, 1867.

A HISTORY OF

that many of those who left Rockingham had the *Register* sent after them. Before me is one of the old ledgers used in the *Register* office—the one covering the period from 1857 to 1868; and from it one can determine not only the names of many who had left the county during these and preceding years, but also the places to which they had gone. In this particular ledger there are the names of 1343 subscribers to the *Register*, 214 being in States other than Virginia; and these 214 names are thus distributed:

Illinois,	43	New York,	2
West Virginia,	38	Alabama,	1
Indiana,	30	District of Columbia,	1
Ohio,	23	Florida,	1
Iowa,	21	Georgia,	1
Tennessee,	21	Kansas,	1
Missouri,	14	Kentucky,	1
California,	4	Massachusetts,	1
Pennsylvania,	4	Oregon,	1
Texas,	3	Washington Territory,	1
Maryland,	2		

The following table, showing the number of marriage licenses issued to persons of both races in Rockingham during certain years, will be of interest.

Year.	To White.	To Colored.	Total.
1865	208	1	209
1866	277	4	281
1867	254	13	267
1871	163	22	185
1872			196
1875	186	22	208

In January, 1868, the *Register* paid a handsome compliment to Joseph D. Price, "formerly of Maryland, but now a permanent resident of this place [Harrisonburg]—a gentleman who has done more to stimulate enterprise and business in this part of the State than any other citizen of the Valley." Price was at the time head of a wood-working factory company in Harrisonburg, and a dealer in real estate.

ROCKINGHAM COUNTY

In May, 1868, Mr. Ela, member of Congress from New Hampshire, made a political speech in Harrisonburg, dividing time with Hon. John B. Baldwin. According to the facetious (though I suspect slightly prejudiced) report given in the next issue of the *Register*, the gentleman from New Hampshire was somewhat enlightened and very decidedly outargued.

In September, 1868, it was announced that the people of East Rockingham were to have improved mail facilities—that the mail was to be carried to Keezletown, McGaheysville, and Roadside three times a week instead of twice, as before.

Early in 1870 some changes were made in the political divisions of the county, and the nine townships, according to the new arrangement, had the following names, with the respective areas, as indicated:

	sq. mi.
Brock's Gap,	171.7
Plains,	84.8
Linville's Creek,	91.0
Elk Run,	107.6
Stonewall (including McGaheysville, Port Republic, etc.),	94.2
Ashby (including Cross Keys, Peale's Cross Roads, etc.),	59.8
Harrisonburg,	29.0
Central,	144.8
Franklin (including Mt. Crawford, Bridgewater, etc.),	95.1
Total,	878.0
	(561,920 acres).

Of the total, about 500 square miles were reckoned as mountain land, the remainder, 378 square miles, being comparatively level. Of these 378 square miles, nearly one-fourth was supposed to be in timber in 1870. It is safe to

A HISTORY OF

conclude that practically all the mountain land was in timber.[11]

According to the current edition of Johnson's Cyclopaedia, there were about this time 14 flouring mills in the county. This was doubtless below the actual number; for the *Register* of November 3, 1870, gives the following statistics for the four townships named:

	People.	Productive Industries.
Elk Run,	2341	10
Plains,	3040	30
Brock's Gap,	1366	16
Linville,	3547	17

The most memorable, as well as the most disastrous, incident of the year 1870 was the great flood in October. The Shenandoah River, as well as many others streams of Virginia, rose to an unprecedented height, field crops, fences, bridges, buildings, stock, and even people being carried away in the rush of swirling waters. At Bridgewater, Mt. Crawford, Port Republic, River Bank, Conrad's Store, Shenandoah City, and many other places in Rockingham and Page the damage done was incalculable, and in many cases irreparable.

In the *Register* of September 14, 1871, the following figures of values, prepared by S. R. Sterling, appeared:

Township.	Real Estate.	Personal Property.
Harrisonburg,	$ 930,389.82	$ 377,063.88
Central,	1,127,827.13	372,617.00
Franklin,	1,048,063.47	397,534.00
Ashby,	901,783.07	182,333.00
Plains,	1,276,247.00	349,152.00
Linville,	1,179,022.29	320,132.00
Stonewall,	681,966.21	159,069.00
Elk Run,	545,095.41	92,580.00
Brock's Gap,	91,503.29	43,118.00
Total,	$7,781,897.69	$2,293,598.88
Grand Total,		$10,075,496.57

---

[11]. See *Rockingham Register*, May 5, June 2, and August 25, 1870.

ROCKINGHAM COUNTY

Appended is this note: "Stonewall and Elk Run Township were seriously injured by the flood of 1870, and these assessments were made since then. The re-assessment of the lands in these Townships has greatly reduced their value."

In January, 1872, John E. Roller of Rockingham introduced in the Virginia Senate a bill proposing to re-arrange the townships of the county, reducing their number, etc. On March 2, following, this bill was passed, and the next month George J. Kisling, Henry Neff, and George H. Dinges, commissioners, appointed under the Act, made a division of the county into five townships, or districts, as at present constituted.

Prices of some common necessities and luxuries in June, 1872, were as follows: Flour, $8.50 to $9.75 a barrel; wheat, $1.85 a bushel; corn, 80 cents a bushel; bacon, hog round, 8 cents a pound; chickens, live, $3.00 a dozen; turkeys, 7 cents a pound.

In the Presidential campaign of 1872 Rockingham seems to have been enthusiastic for Greeley and Brown, giving them 2130 votes; but the 735 votes cast for Grant and Wilson at the same time is a surprisingly large number, considering everything.

In 1873 the assessors' books showed the number of horses in Rockingham County to be 7550, and their value $418,297.00. At the same time there were 16,946 cattle, valued at $226,948.00.

As an example of the numerous development enterprises of 1872, 1873, etc., many of which found Black Friday of September, 1873, an unlucky day, the Virginia Improvement Company may be cited. This company was chartered and organized in 1873, with a capital stock of $500,000.00. B. B. Thomas was president; R. N. Pool, vice-president; Robt. C. Thomas, secretary; Eugene Borda, treasurer; and Henry M. Clay, general superintendent. The principal offices were at Philadelphia, Pa., and Bridgewater, Va. The principal objects appear to have been the building of North River Railroad and the booming of Bridgewater.

A HISTORY OF

In the State election of 1873 Rockingham gave 2794 votes to Kemper (Conservative) and 623 to Hughes (Republican). There were at this time 19 voting places in the county, distributed among the five townships as follows:

In Stonewall three: Conrad's Store, McGaheysville, and Port Republic.

In Ashby five: Cross Keys, Mt. Crawford, Dayton, Bridgewater, and Ottobine.

In Central three: Keezletown, Harrisonburg, and Mt. Clinton.

In Linville Creek four: Melrose, Edom, E. Hoover's Cooper Shop, and Singer's Glen.

In Plains four: Tenth Legion, Timberville, Cootes' Store, and Wittig's Store.

In April, 1874, the county supervisors adopted the plans of Julius C. Holmes of Charlestown, W. Va., for a new court house; in May the contract for the building was let to Holmes at $11,450.00; and in December the new building was used for the first time.

I have before me a diary, covering the years from 1873 to 1880, kept in the exact hand of James Kenney, who for nearly four years, 1870 to 1873, was judge of the Rockingham County Court. Two items from this diary are here introduced.

Feb. 8, 1875—Wednesday—7 A. M. 10 degrees below O. Clear & cold. The coal oil in the lamp on the office mantel piece froze. I do not mean solid, but it had that white, milky look like sweet oil when it freezes. This is decidedly the coldest weather I can remember.

Apr. 24, 1875—Saturday—J. R. Jones[12] who owns the old stone Pres. church on East Market St. is now having it pulled down for the erection of a new building for business purposes on the same site. My earliest

---

[12.] John Robert Jones, son of David S. and Harriet Yost Jones, was born in Harrisonburg in 1828. As captain he served the South with distinction in Florida, March, 1861; in April following he enlisted a company of 104 men in Rockingham County, Va., and joined Gen. Johnston at Winchester, his company a little later being made Co. I, 33d Va. Infantry, Stonewall Brigade. In August, 1861, he was made lieutenant-colonel of the 33d regiment, and in July, 1862, was promoted to the rank of briga-

ROCKINGHAM COUNTY

recollection of a church was this one where I went to Sunday school at least 44 years ago.[13]

At the April court, 1875, ten licenses for selling liquor in Rockingham County were granted: five at Harrisonburg, one at Timberville, two at Broadway, one near Airey's still house, and one at Rawley Springs. Applications for four others were refused.

On August 4, 1875, the 10th Regiment, Virginia Volunteer Infantry, the history of which has been given in the preceding chapter, held a reunion at Brock's Springs, and effected a permanent organization.[14]

The Reconstruction Period and this chapter may both be fittingly closed with two more extracts from Judge Kenney's diary, which are herewith presented.

1876 Saturday Jan. 22
I have just returned from a visit to the Soldiers' Monument. It was completed on yesterday, the 21st of January 1876. The monument is quite handsome and speaks well for the taste of those who got up the design and for the skill and workmanship of Anthony who did the stone work and carving and superintended the erection. I had the honor of preparing two of the inscriptions. Shortly after the war which ended in 1865 a Memorial Association was formed by some of the ladies of our town and county. The bodies of the Confederate soldiers who had died or were buried in this Rockingham County were removed to a lot adjoining Woodbine Cemetery, and every year since the war the ladies have designated a day, and with processions, dirges, muffled drums, and tolling bells laid spring flowers and ever greens above the dust of the dead soldiers, and this spring these ladies can point with pride to this beautiful tribute of patriotism and gratitude.

---

dier-general. He was captured at Gettysburg, and held as a prisoner at Johnson's Island and at Fort Warren till July, 1865. For a number of years following the war he was a dealer in agricultural implements, and a writer on agricultural subjects. For eight years or more, from about 1876, he was commissioner in chancery for the circuit court. He died April 1, 1901.

13. I am indebted to the kindness of Mr. Chas. Switzer, of Harrisonburg, for the loan of the Kenney diary.

14. *Rockingham Register*, August 12, 1875.

A HISTORY OF

Mrs. Juliet Strayer[15] is the president of the Association and to her more than any other person belongs the credit of erecting this Monument.

December 31, 1876, Sunday

This is the last day of the year 1876, a year that will be considered in the future history of the nation as remarkable for many reasons. This is the 100th year of our national independence, that is that on the 4th of July, 1776, the colonies through their representatives in Congress assembled at Philadelphia declared their independence of Great Britain and after a seven years war assisted by the French their independence was acknowledged. The anniversary was celebrated by a national exhibition at Philadelphia. It was called the Centennial Exhibition and all the nations of the earth were invited to participate and most of them did. The exhibition was a complete success. I went to the exhibition and was astonished at its magnitude.

This has also been a remarkable year for the Presidential election. It is remarkable in this, that questions have arisen for which there is neither law nor precedent to decide. Hayes, Governor of Ohio, was the administration or Republican candidate, and Tilden Governor of New York the Democratic or Conservative candidate. Soon after the election (which was held on Nov. 7 1876) it was announced that Tilden had received 203 electoral votes and Hayes 163, it requiring 185 electoral votes to decide, but in a short time it was reported that South Carolina, Florida and Louisiana, had gone for Hayes and those the states having 19 electoral votes would change the whole matter give Hayes 186 votes and leave Tilden 184. The Democrats charged that it was a fraud perpetrated by the retiring board all of whom were of the administration party, that they had changed the true vote and counted the Hayes electors in. Affairs were in this situation when Congress met in December, the Democrats having a majority in the house of representatives and the Republicans in the Senate. Both houses of Congress at once appointed committees to proceed at once to those three states examine into the questions of fraud. So far only one committee have reported & they say that South Carolina voted for Hayes by a small majority. The people of the whole country are greatly excited and many persons

---

[15.] Juliet Lyle Strayer, wife of Crawford C. Strayer, lived in Harrisonburg over 40 years, and was president of the Ladies' Memorial Association about 35 years. She was born Nov. 12, 1826, the daughter of Abraham and Martha Reid Smith of Rockingham, and died in Harrisonburg Aug. 31, 1893. On the entrance to the soldiers' section of Woodbine Cemetery is a tablet with this inscription: "To the Memory of Mrs. Juliet Lyle Strayer Founder and for Many Years President of the Ladies Memorial Association."

ROCKINGHAM COUNTY

fear a civil war, but I have no apprehensions. Most persons are willing that the Congress settle the question, and I think they will. The popular vote was Tilden 4,268,207. Hayes 4,027,245. Peter Cooper 82,920, and about 11,000 scattering. The administration is with Hayes and is loth to see the power pass from their party. There are more than 100,000 office-holders, all appointees of the administration and they will do anything they dare to retain their party in power. In South Carolina in addition to the presidential contest they have one for Lieut. Governor, Members of Congress and members of the State Legislature. The Democrats claim the election of their candidates and the Republicans the election of theirs. Both Governors have been inaugurated, and there are two Legislatures, each body claiming to be the Legislature of South Carolina according to the laws and constitution of the state. The administration sides with the republicans and keeps its candidate in power by the aid of the United States soldiers.

In Oregon the Governor refused to certify the election of Hayes electors in full and gave a certificate to one of the Tilden electors. At this date, the 31st of December 1876 no one can forsee the result but I hope the whole matter may be settled without bloodshed. I have been through one war and do not wish to see another. (Added later) On the 25th & 26th January 1877 Congress passed a compromise election bill selecting a committee of 15 to decide all disputed questions as to the electoral vote.

CHAPTER IX.

FROM 1876 TO 1912.

The earlier periods of the history of the County have been presented in chapters of considerable length, but it is not deemed necessary or advisable to make this chapter very long. Accordingly, it is made to consist, for the most part, of a brief chronicle of certain important or significant events.

In 1876 Rockingham County gave Tilden and Hendricks 3444 votes, as against 514 for Hayes and Wheeler; the nation at large gave the former 4,284,885 and the latter 4,033,950. Notwithstanding these facts, and others even more pertinent, the Electoral Commission, by a partisan vote, declared Hayes and Wheeler elected. The South, to use the words of Judge Kenney, had been through one war, and did not wish to see another, and so accepted the ruling. President Hayes, on his part, did the fitting thing by withdrawing the last Federal troops from the South, and Reconstruction, as prepared by Stevens and distributed by carpetbaggers, came to an end. Rockingham had already begun to show, in her own revival and progress, what the whole South was soon to become.

One of the significant things about the county has been that she has always contributed liberally to good causes. Possibly herein is revealed the secret of her growth and prosperity. She has given abundantly, not only in means, but also in women and men. Her part in the development of the great West and Northwest has already been referred to several times. During the years now under consideration the building of the West was going rapidly on, and Rockingham still continued to send forward sturdy helpers. In 1876 there seems to have been a marked immigration from the Valley and other parts of the State. In February of that year a

ROCKINGHAM COUNTY

party of about fifty persons went west from Rockingham. It may have been a loss to Rockingham, but it was certainly a gain to the West.

On Friday, March 9, 1877, Judge Kenney wrote in his diary: "A volunteer company was formed to-night called after my old company, the Rockingham Rifles (the name was subsequently changed). O. B. Roller was elected captain."

In November, 1877, another great flood devastated the river sections of Rockingham and adjacent counties. Of all the floods in the Valley, those of 1870 and 1877 are most frequently referred to as notable for destructiveness.[1]

On January 27, 1878, Judge Kenney wrote: "I notice some 10 or 12 English sparrows in the street. Last fall or winter was their first appearance in this town [Harrisonburg]."

On Sunday, September 29, the same year, he wrote: "Col. A. S. Gray died about 2 P. M. He was in the 65th year of his age. He was the son of Robert Gray, who was born in Ireland. A. S. Gray was born in Harrisonburg. He began life as a lawyer; was a militia colonel; was a member of the convention when the war began, and was opposed to secession. After the war was a Republican, and was marshal of this district for about 8 years."

March 3, 1879, an Act was passed by the General Assembly for the protection of deer in Rockingham County, making it unlawful to kill them from December 1 to August 1.

Three more brief extracts from the Kenney diary are here introduced; natural history, State politics, and agricultural progress being the respective topics.

Friday, May 9, 1879: Birds that I have seen in our yard in the last day or two: the house sparrow, English sparrow, wren, yellow bird, blue bird, cat bird, bee bird, peewit, robin, martin, chimney sweep, house martin, sand martin, & oriole; and the humming bird will come when the trumpet creeper blooms.

Tuesday, Nov. 4, 1879: This is election day for a Senator & two delegates from this county. There is great excitement throughout the

---

1. On the flood of 1877, see the *Rockingham Register*, Nov. 29, 1877.

A HISTORY OF

state in regard to the adjustment of the state debt. One party is called funders and the other party readjusters. The funders support the law known as the McCullok bill, and the other party want a new settlement.

Tuesday, June 22, 1880: I went to Lurty's farm to see a self-binding reaping machine. It works well.

About January 1, 1881, there was intense cold throughout the Valley. The snow in Rockingham and surrounding districts was from 25 to 30 inches in depth. At Harrisonburg the temperature was 20 degrees below zero; at Mt. Clinton and Broadway it was 30, and at Bridgewater 22. In June of the same year a terrific hail-storm swept over Port Republic. In August, 1882, Harrisonburg and vicinity was visited by a destructive flood.

There were at least two notable incidents in 1883. In July John F. Lewis, J. B. Webb, and Henry B. Harnsberger, commissioners, selected the site in Harrisonburg for the new Federal court house. The Baptist Church lot, the Henry Shacklett lot, and the W. C. Harrison lot, lying together in the corner of Main Street and Elizabeth Street, east of Main, were taken at the price of $12,000. In September about 200 Union veterans came in a body to visit the Valley. Harrisonburg and the county turned out in hearty style, and gave them a royal welcome.

In 1884 certain changes were made in two of the lines dividing townships: (1) the one between Ashby and Central; (2) the one between Linville and Plains. The same year the work of restoring the county records, partly destroyed in 1864, was authorized.

In April, 1887, three of the five districts in Rockingham, namely, Ashby, Central, and Linville, voted under the local option law to prohibit the sale of liquor. The vote in each district was as follows:

Ashby, 714 against license; 121 for license.

Central, 692 against license; 451 for license.

Linville, 286 against license; 252 for license.

The vote taken in Plains at the same time resulted in a count of 301 against license, and 329 for license. But there were no bar-rooms in any of the districts except Central (at

ROCKINGHAM COUNTY

Harrisonburg) and Stonewall (one at McGaheysville). The vote taken in Stonewall the following July resulted in a considerable majority in favor of license.[2]

The year 1889 was remarkable for its heavy rainfall. It was thought by Rockinghamers to have broken the record of a century or more. Floods did much damage to crops in various parts of the county. This will be remembered as the year of the Johnstown flood. Other things too were at the flood in Rockingham and neighboring counties; for this year of 1889, with the year or two following, has ever since been called the "Boom Time." Cities were laid out—on paper—and built, too,—on cherished hopes and fair prospects. The farmers of Rockingham almost always know what to do with their money, but at that particular period it soon became painfully evident that some of them, not a few, did not know. Harrisonburg, Shendun, and Elkton were doubtless the Rockingham towns most conspicuous in the booms, but Broadway and other places were also heard from. It is only fair to add that nearly all these towns have ever since had a normal, healthy growth, even if the dreams of boom times have not all come true—yet.

In 1890 the population of the county was 31,299: 28,477 white, 2822 colored. Upon petition of the requisite number of voters, Judge George G. Grattan, of the county court, ordered a new division of the county into voting precincts. A new voting place was established at Swift Run. As finally adjusted, the arrangement was as follows:

Stonewall District: Port Republic, Swift Run, McGaheysville, Furnace No. 2, Elkton.

Ashby District: Moyerhoeffer's Store, Cross Keys, Pleasant Valley, Mt. Crawford, Bridgewater, Dayton, Ottobine.

Central District: Mt. Clinton, Keezletown, Harrisonburg.

Linville District: Oak Grove School House, Singer's Glen, Edom, Melrose, Mountain Valley.

---

[2] See *Rockingham Register*, April 28 and July 14, 1887.

A HISTORY OF

Plains District: Tenth Legion, Broadway, Timberville, Cootes' Store, Wittig's Store.

In 1891 there was much agitation for better roads in Rockingham. The year is especially notable for the death of the pine trees all over the Appalachian region in Virginia, West Virginia, etc.

It is said that Rockingham, in 1892, was the first Virginia county to organize forces to take part in the great world's fair at Chicago. Governor McKinney appointed Dr. S. K. Cox and Mrs. A. E. Heneberger as managers of the Rockingham exhibit at the fair, and they appointed assistant committees in the several districts of the county. Mrs. K. S. Paul of Harrisonburg rendered notable service in the enterprise.

In the Presidential election of 1892, Rockingham gave Cleveland 569 votes more than she gave Harrison. In 1888 she had given 281 more to Harrison than to Cleveland; and in 1884 she had given Cleveland the princely plurality of one vote over Blaine.

In 1891 a dispute had arisen between Rockingham and Augusta concerning the location of the dividing line from North River to the top of the Blue Ridge—past Grottoes and Black Rock Springs. About June, 1893, the matter was settled, according to the Rockingham claims, for the most part, at least, Professor William M. Thornton of the University of Virginia acting as expert arbiter. In August (1893) stones were put up, marking that part of the line that had been in dispute.

On November 11, 1893, the S. B. Gibbons Camp, Confederate Veterans, was organized at Harrisonburg, with the following officers: Captain, D. H. Lee Martz; First Lieutenant, B. G. Patterson; Second Lieutenant, S. H. Butler; Adjutant, J. S. Messerly; Quartermaster, Giles Devier.

The following statistics relating to marriage licenses issued in Rockingham County during certain recent years may be apropos:

1876   total,   208

Stone Barn Built in 1803,
on Burkholder Farm, "Fort Lynne"
[Page 318]

Conrad's Store
[Page 197]

Funk Printing House, Singer's Glen
[Pages 320, 321, 332]

Madison Hall, Port Republic
[Page 255]

Smithland, Home of Geo. W. Liskey

Burtner House at Dayton. Old Stone Fort
[Page 198]

Bowman's Mill, Greenmount
[Page 375]

Bogota, Home of Gabriel Jones
[Page 350]

ROCKINGHAM COUNTY

1877					224
1879	to white	220	to colored,	17	237
1880		193		25	218
1884		217		13	230
1889		201		24	225
1893		225		16	241

In July, 1894, there was a destructive hurricane in the vicinity of Broadway. On August 22 the Kagey family held its annual reunion at Dayton. Former reunions had been held in Ohio, Illinois, and elsewhere. Franklin Keagy, Chambersburg, Pa., published a massive, splendidly illustrated history of the family in 1899.

The assessment for 1895 showed the following real estate values in the several districts of the county:

District.	Whites.	Colored.	Total.
Ashby,	$2,016,723	$ 6,612	$2,023,335
Central,	1,673,229	18,938	1,692,167
Linville,	1,011,660	2,866	1,014,526
Plains,	1,218,112	1,509	1,219,621
Stonewall,	1,241,953	12,209	1,254,162
Totals,	$7,161,677	$42,134	$7,203,811

The values of real estate in the towns are included in the above statement. In Central District most of the property owned by colored persons was located in Harrisonburg, the value of such property there being $15,940.

On September 29, 1896, the northern sections of the Valley were visited by another notable freshet, thought by some persons to have been the worst since 1870. The loss in Rockingham to public roads, bridges, etc., was estimated at $15,000 to $20,000. Mr. S. H. W. Byrd of Bridgewater has recorded four unusual floods at that town, in as many different years, to wit: 1870, 1877, 1889, and 1896. In 1877 North River came up Main Street to Bank Street; in 1896 Dry River broke across the bottom above the town and poured in a torrent diagonally across, passing between the Methodist Church

A HISTORY OF

and the public school, and crossing College Street just east of the Presbyterian Church.

On October 15, 1896, the corner stone of the present splendid court house was laid, the address of the occasion being made by Judge John Paul, an eminent son of Rockingham. The finished building was formally opened on September 28 of the next year, the address on that occasion being made by Senator John W. Daniel. A new jail for the county was completed about the same time. The board of county supervisors, under whose authority the court house was built, was composed of the following men: W. L. Dechert, J. H. Shipp, E. W. Carpenter, C. E. Fahrney, and D. H. Moore. The building committee were W. L. Dechert, E. W. Carpenter, and C. E. Fahrney. W. M. Bucher was superintendent, W. E. Speir, was contractor, T. J. Collins & Son were architects. According to the report made to the supervisors in June, 1898, the cost of the court house was $82,142.77. Including the outlay for approaches, furniture, etc., the grand total was stated as $96,826.24.

At the November election in 1896, McKinley was given 3525 votes, Bryan 2998, Levering 100, and Palmer 27. These figures totaled the largest number of votes ever cast in the county at one election up to that time. A vote distributed like this one affords concrete and striking evidence of the fact that decided changes in political affiliation have taken place since the days when overwhelming Democratic majorities were the rule in Rockingham.

On May 12, 1898, the Harrisonburg Guards, E. W. Sullivan, captain, left for the war in Cuba. Col. O. B. Roller, who accompanied the Guards, was acting colonel of the 2d Virginia Regiment at Jacksonville, Florida, during the summer. On September 23, after an absence of four months, the Guards, now Co. C of the 2d Va. Infantry, reached home. Most of their time away had been spent in camp at Jacksonville, and they were properly chagrinned because they had not been called to the front.[3]

---

[3]. Muster Rolls of the Guards may be found in the *Rockingham Register* of May 13 and 20, 1898.

ROCKINGHAM COUNTY

Fittingly, in view of the events and spirit of the time, it was in the summer of 1898 that the movement, long retarded, to mark the spot where General Turner Ashby fell, June 6, 1862, culminated in the erection of a monument. It is made up of two great stones, a huge pointed granite elevated upon a massive limestone base, and stands a mile and a half south of Harrisonburg, on the wooded hill where the gallant cavalry leader received his death wound. It was unveiled on the 6th of June, 1898, just thirty-six years after the sad day held in memory. The place is visited each year by an increasing number of persons interested in the history of Virginia, as wrought in the valor of her sons. Since the State Normal School was opened at Harrisonburg in 1909, a large number of young women from all parts of the State have visited the Ashby monument, and have carried the story learned there back to their homes and into their schools.

The claims allowed by the county supervisors at their June meeting in 1898, for sheep killed by dogs, amounted to the surprising figure of $678.60. A century earlier the justices' court was paying for the scalps of wolves. It might have been proper for the fathers of 1898 to have considered the advisability of putting a premium on the scalps of worthless and dangerous curs.

In February, 1899, the thermometers in Rockingham registered 23 degrees below zero. There was a big blizzard—the snow was deep and drifted. The editor of the *Register*, shivering still in memory, no doubt, wrote:

It made the deepest snow and the coldest weather we have known, certainly since the famous winter of 1856-7, and possibly since the beginning of the century.[4]

He apparently had overlooked or forgotten the cold of January, 1881. Thermometer readings in rural sections of the county, however, seemed to sustain the editor's conclusion. In the next issue of his paper it was reported that Eld. John P. Zigler's thermometer had registered 40 degrees

---

4. *Rockingham Register*, February 17, 1899.

A HISTORY OF

below zero, and that those of Jack Bradford and Michael J. Roller had registered 40 and 38 degrees below zero, respectively. All these readings were Fahrenheit.

Since these instances of extreme cold have been recorded, it is proper to say that such weather is very unusual in Rockingham. Zero weather is unusual. It is not often that thermometers in this section of the State fall below 10 degrees or 8 degrees above zero.

In May, 1899, it was ordered that certain experimental free delivery mail routes be established in Rockingham; and in June the free delivery service was inaugurated.

The census of 1900 showed a gain of 2228 in ten years in the population of the county, and the increase of property values shown by the assessment of the same year indicated an era of material growth. The next year the tax rate was reduced from $1.25 to $1.10.

In 1902 the first automobile owned in Harrisonburg,—the property of J. L. Baugher,—attracted much attention. At this writing,—ten years later,—the number of machines in the same town is said to be over 40.

Monday, January 8, 1904, marked the opening of the last term, in Rockingham, of the old county court, which has given place to the circuit court under the present constitution.

Three notable events in 1911 marked gratifying progress in educational and benevolent work: The opening of the Waterman School, the building of the Rockingham Memorial Hospital, and the adoption of the law for compulsory school attendance in Harrisonburg and Rockingham County; all of which are noticed in more detail elsewhere in this volume.

Inasmuch as some notice has been given to unusual weather conditions in preceding years, it may be of interest to record that a few days of extreme cold weather were experienced in Rockingham, as well as in many other places, early in January, 1912, the mercury at one time falling 25 degrees below zero. The present summer (1912) has been remarkably cool and agreeable.[5]

---

[5]. For the loan of periodicals falling within the time limits of this

CHAPTER X.

ROCKINGHAM TO-DAY.

Rockingham County, like every other great county, is too big to be seen all at once, and too many-sided to be appreciated fully from any single view-point. The chapters that follow present some of its manifold phases, each in its particular significance, and thus make possible a more definite estimate upon an analytical basis; all that is attempted here is a collection of a few more or less general statements, in the nature of a suggestive, though incomplete, summary.

Rockingham to-day has 35,000 people (34,903 by the census of 1910); no millionaires, very few paupers, and $1000 on the average for every man, woman, and child, white and black; 3528 farmers, and a farm for each of them; 363,042 acres of land in these farms, and 560,640 acres of land altogether; 26,435 cattle; 11,704 horses; 19,754 swine; 25,199 sheep; 2314 colonies of bees; and 236,812 head of poultry. It also has one of the two largest hatcheries in the State. There are seed farms for the planters, thoroughbred flocks and herds for the stockman, and nurseries for the fruit grower; there are hundreds of growing orchards, from which about 1000 carloads of apples are produced every year, not to speak of peaches, pears, cherries, plums,—or watermelons.

There are in the county three noted summer resorts, three splendid caves, and three famous battlefields; there are abundant mineral deposits, of various kinds, including iron and coal; there are numerous spring-fed streams, affording moisture for plants and unexcelled water power; there are 40

---

chapter, grateful acknowledgement is made to Mr. Garnett C. Sites, of Staunton, Bishop L. J. Heatwole, of Dale Enterprise, and Mr. C. L. Matthews, of Harrisonburg.

A HISTORY OF

flouring mills,[1] two large tanneries, brick kilns and lime kilns, plow factories, wood-working factories, creameries, canneries, 9 banks, and a wool mill whose products are recognized as of superior excellence at home and abroad.

In Rockingham to-day 16 religious denominations are represented, and more than 140 Sunday-schools are operated; the churches are served by about 80 preachers and pastors, and the people at large by 34 physicians and surgeons, several of them specialists; there are 14 dentists, 27 lawyers, and about 290 educators and teachers; there is a ministers' union, a medical society, a teachers' association, a ladies' memorial society, a boys' corn club, a horticultural society, a fair for the school children, an annual horse show, a fair for mechanics and farmers, a Sundayschool association, a women's Christian temperance union, and an anti-saloon league; there are farmers' and stockmen's organizations, missionary societies, insurance companies, and benevolent, fraternal, and patriotic societies almost without number.

There is a modern hospital, with hundreds of women working for it; an orphans' home, and an old folks' home; there are two public almshouses, one for the county, one for the county-seat, and two court houses, one for the county, one for the nation. There are 10 incorporated towns, several of which are lighted with electricity, and more than 30 towns and villages altogether; the rural districts, as well as the towns, are supplied with excellent telephone systems, and daily mail delivery; there are about 80 miles of railroad track, operated by four different companies, about 70 miles of macadamized road, with a growing movement for more; dozens of strong bridges spanning streams large and small, 37 postoffices, and 20 regular railroad stations.

Rockingham has to-day a weekly newspaper 90 years old,

[1.] For information on this point I acknowledge special obligation to Messrs. John G. Yancey and W. J. Dingledine, of Harrisonburg. Mr. Dingledine has recently published an attractive booklet giving many interesting statistics concerning Rockingham County and the town of Harrisonburg.

ROCKINGHAM COUNTY

five printing and publishing establishments, three daily papers, and a monthly music journal that is probably the oldest in the United States; there are five or six bands and orchestras in the county, and probably more people, old and young, who can sing, and who love music, than in any other section with the same population in America. There are 142 school buildings, including 11 high-schools, in the public school system; and besides these there are three institutions for higher education, whose combined annual enrollment reaches about 1000 students representing nearly every county in Virginia and many States outside of Virginia.

Rockingham County to-day (1912) has the following staff of county and district officials:

Circuit Judge—T. N. Haas.

Clerk of Court—D. H. Lee Martz; deputies—C. H. Brunk, J. F. Blackburn.

Sheriff—E. J. Carickhoff; deputies—D. E. Croushorn, John Adams, Otho Miller, Chas. Meyerhoeffer, Lurty Koontz, R. E. Pugh, J. J. Branner, Chas. R. Fawley, W. H. Yankey, T. A. Carickhoff.

Commonwealth's Attorney—Chas. D. Harrison.

Treasurer—Peter W. Reherd; deputy—Harry Way.

Superintendent of Schools—Geo. H. Hulvey.

Surveyor—Jos. G. Myers.

Coroner—J. M. Biedler.

County Supervisors.

D. N. Washington, from Ashby District.
Brock T. White, from Central District.
J. Newton Swank, from Linville District.
A. M. Turner, from Plains District.
M. H. Harrison, from Stonewall District.

Ashby District.

Justices of the Peace—J. W. Keiter, J. P. Rauhof, Homer M. Hill.

Constable—I. N. Jones.

Road Commissioner—A. S. Heatwole.

A HISTORY OF

Assessor—C. H. Funkhouser.
Overseer of Poor—J. H. Simmers.
School Trustees—D. C. Graham, C. T. Callender, J. S. Good.

Central District.

Justices of the Peace—D. Wampler Earman, F. J. Argenbright, P. I. Derrer.
Constable—G. R. Black.
Road Commissioner—J. W. Sheets.
Assessor—Frank A. Heatwole.
Overseer of Poor—J. W. Minnich.
School Trustees—E. J. Suter, Frank Ralston, C. A. Crenshaw.

Linville District.

Justices of the Peace—J. C. Cooper, J. P. Howver, Joel Rinker.
Constable—A. A. Frank.
Road Commissioner—C. W. Dove.
Assessor—B. F. Myers.
Overseer of Poor—W. H. Shaver.
School Trustees—John S. Funk, A. A. Howard, S. R. Bowman.

Plains District.

Justices of the Peace—J. W. Pickering, Geo. A. Neff, L. P. Souder.
Constable—T. A. Fansler.
Road Commissioner—E. P. Myers.
Assessor—M. Harvey Zirkle.
Overseer of Poor—C. F. Evans.
School Trustees—E. P. Myers, H. H. Aldhizer, J. Luther Wittig.

Stonewall District.

Justices of the Peace—John W. May, J. A. S. Kyger, John I. Wood.

ROCKINGHAM COUNTY

Constable—G. W. Baugher.
Road Commissioner—C. W. Baugher.
Assessor—E. L. Lambert.
Overseer of Poor—J. F. Life.
School Trustees—A. S. Bader, A. S. Kemper, J. T. Heard.

Representatives in General Assembly.

Senate—John Paul.
House of Delegates—C. H. Ralston, G. N. Earman.

CHAPTER XI.

TOWNS AND VILLAGES OF ROCKINGHAM.

It appears from the "American Gazetteer" that in 1798 there was only one postoffice in Rockingham County. This one was at Harrisonburg, which was put down as "Rockingham Court House."[1] The old postoffice, just west of Harrisonburg, noticed more particularly in the next chapter, had probably been absorbed by the one at the court house by 1798. In 1813 there were only three postoffices in the county: Harrisonburg, or Rockingham C. H., Henry Tutwiller, P. M.; MGaheystown, Tobias R. MGahey, P. M.; Kites Mill, Jacob Kite, P. M.[2] In Martin's Gazetteer of Virginia, edition 1835, the following towns are put down as in Rockingham County: Bowman's Mill, P. O., Brock's Gap, P. O., Conrad's Store, P. O., Cross Keys, P. O., Harrisonburg, Kite's Mills, P. O., Linville Creek, P. O., McGaheysville, P.O., Mount Crawford, Port Republic, and Smith's Creek, P. O.[3] Harrisonburg, Mt. Crawford, and Port Republic are followed by the letters "P.V.," which supposedly stand for "postal village." The population of these three villages is given (1835) as 1,000, 180, and 160, respectively. In 1845, or thereabouts, Henry Howe visited Harrisonburg, Mt. Crawford, Port Republic, Deaton (Dayton), and Edom Mills. He says Mt. Crawford then had a church and about 30 dwellings; Port Republic, a church, and about 35 dwellings; Deaton and Edom Mills he calls "small places." Harrisonburg is cred-

---

[1]. A copy of the American Gazetteer, abridged edition of 1798, was loaned by Mr. E. M. Whitesel, Pleasant Valley, per Mr. Q. G. Kaylor.

[2]. For these items I am indebted to the researches of Mr. Milo Custer, Bloomington, Ill. Kite's Mill was probably on the river below Elkton.

[3]. I am indebted to Hon. Geo. E. Sipe for the loan of Martin's Virginia Gazetteer for 1835.

ROCKINGHAM COUNTY

ited (1845) with 8 stores, 2 newspaper offices, a market, 1 Methodist church, 2 Presbyterian churches, and about 1100 people.[4]

It is quite probable that one of the oldest centers of trade in what is now Rockingham was at Peale's Cross Roads, the point 5 miles southeast of Harrisonburg, where the roads from Swift Run Gap and Brown's Gap come around the end of Peaked Mountain and cross the Keezletown Road. Felix Gilbert had a store at or near this point in 1774, and likely had been located there for a number of years preceding. A tanyard and other productive establishments marked the place later.

With these statements as introductory, let us take up the several towns in more detail.

Harrisonburg, laid out upon 50 acres of land belonging to Thomas Harrison, was legally established in May, 1780, by the same Act that gave recognition to the town of Louisville, in the county of Kentucky.[5] The place in early days was often called Rocktown; for example, Bishop Asbury designates it by that name in his journal, in 1795; and as late as 1818, perhaps later, the name Rocktown was frequently used. It is said that German Street was originally the main street, and what is now Main Street was then called Irish Street or Irish Alley.

In 1797 the town was enlarged by an addition of $23\frac{1}{2}$ acres, laid off in lots and streets, from the lands of Robert and Reuben Harrison; and Thomas Scott, John Koontz, Asher Waterman, Frederick Spangler, and Saml. McWilliams were made trustees. In 1808 an Act was passed enabling the freeholders and housekeepers resident in the town to elect five trustees annually; and by the same Act the trustees were authorized to raise $1000 by taxation for the purchase of a fire engine, hooks, and ladders. All the men of the town were to constitute the Harrisonburg Fire Company.

---

[4]. Howe's Historical Collections of Virginia, 1852 Edition, pp. 460, 461.

[5]. Hening's Statutes, Vol. X, pp. 293—295.

A HISTORY OF

In the *Rockingham Register* of October 5, 1876, appeared a long article entitled, "Harrisonburg Fifty Years Ago," from which we quote the following paragraphs. They present a graphic account of certain interesting conditions in 1826, and thereabouts.

Jos. Cline occupied the Wm. Ott house,[6] and carried on the tanyard now owned by Lowenbach. The house on the corner was built by James Hall, lawyer, fifty years ago. The stone house attached was the first house built in Harrisonburg. It was built by Thomas Harrison. After that house was put up, Mr. Harrison offered Maj. Richard Ragan (the father of 'Aunt Polly Van Pelt'), who was a blacksmith, ten acres of land around the 'big spring' if he would bind himself to put up a shop near the spring. But the Major could not be fooled into any such a speculation, and he declined. At that time the ground around the spring was covered with rocks, many of the cliffs being so tall that a horse could hide behind them. There were but two practical paths to the spring, one running along by Dr. Waterman's house and the other down by the house in which A. M. Effinger lives. Subsequently the rocks and thorn bushes and other undergrowth was cleaned away, and the spring was made a resort of the ladies of the town, who used to do their washing by the spring. Clothes lines made of grape vines were provided along the branch, and after the clothes were dried they were carried home to iron. Subsequently the trustees of the town passed an ordinance forbidding women to do their washing at the 'spring.'

Fifty years ago there were no railroads in all this country. Our merchants went 'below' twice a year only. It required from four to six weeks to go 'below,' lay in goods and return. The goods for Harrisonburg were sent to Fredericksburg by water, and from there brought over in wagons. It took two weeks to make the trip. The wagoners charged from $1 to $1.25 a hundred for hauling. Some goods were brought up the Valley, by way of the 'Keezletown road,' that being at that time the principal thoroughfare of the Valley.

Fifty years ago the mails were carried from Winchester to Harrisonburg in Bockett's two-horse coaches. The mail came once a week, except when the river at Mt. Jackson would be swollen by the rains, or when the roads were very bad, when the mail would not come oftener than semi-monthly. In the course of time the business of the Valley became so important, that the mail route was changed to a s mi-weekly one. It was hard work, but Bockett actually ran from Winchester to Staunton in three days.

---

[6]. The Ewing building, opposite Newman Avenue, occupies the site of the Ott house. The stone house built by Th. Harrison is now Gen. Roller's law office.

ROCKINGHAM COUNTY

Fifty years ago there were but two churches in town, the old Methodist Church, which stood on the hill above the Catholic Church, and the Presbyterian Church.[7] Fifty-five years ago there was no paper published in Harrisonburg. At that time Ananias Davisson, had a small office in which he printed the Kentucky Harmony and other musical works. Shortly after that Lawrence Wartmann commenced the publication of the 'Rockingham Weekly Register,' with 86 subscribers. The REGISTER list now reaches 1800.

On March 31, 1838, Samuel Shacklett, Isaac Hardesty, Jacob Rohr, Jr., Nelson Sprinkel, and Samuel Liggett were elected trustees of Harrisonburg for the ensuing year. All these gentlemen were well known residents of the town for many years, Hardesty and Shacklett being very successful merchants. Before me is an old account book used by Mr. Shacklett, containing entries made from 1851 to 1874. On one of the leaves is a carefully prepared table, of four columns, headed,

Merchants that have done business in Harrisonburg and quit, classed as follows to Wit

Broke	Neither made or Lost	Made under $10,000	Made over $10,000

In the column under "Broke" are written the names of 36 individuals and firms; under the next head, "Neither made nor Lost," are 30 names; three men, A. E. Heneberger, M. Hite Effinger, and Geo. Cline, are put down as having made under $10,000; while in the fourth column are eight names: Thos. Scott, John Graham, Jerry Kyle, Jno. F. Effinger, Isc. Hardesty, S. Henry, M. H. Effinger, and "S. S."[8]

By an Act of March 16, 1849, the boundaries of Harrisonburg were defined as follows:

Beginning at a point on the old Valley road, beyond the gate leading

---

[7]. "The old Methodist church on the hill" stood where the church of the Brethren now stands; the Catholic church referred to stood (1876) opposite the passenger station, on the site now occupied by the large Snell building; the Presbyterian church in 1826 was on E. Market Street.

[8]. This old book was placed at my disposal through the courtesy of Messrs. Sipe & Harris, Harrisonburg.

to Mr. A. C. Bryan's farm, and in a line with the land of J. Hardesty and others; thence westwardly, on a line with the said land, to the head of a lane which intersects with the road leading to Antioch; thence from the head of said lane, in a southern direction, in a line parallel with the present western limits of said town, to a point in the Warm Springs Pike, at or near the old brewery, and on a line with the lands of Mrs. P. Kyle Liggett and others; thence east, in a line with said lands, to a point in the lots of Mrs. E. Stevens; thence northwardly, in a straight line, to the beginning, shall be and continue to constitute the area of the town heretofore known as the town of Harrisonburg, in the County of Rockingham.

The boundaries of the town have been rearranged at various times since the above date; for example, in 1868, 1877, 1894, etc. On February 14 and 15, 1868, J. H. Ralston, county surveyor, made a survey which was defined in the next issue of the *Register* as follows:

The survey commenced at a point near Swanson's residence, about 1 mile East of the Court House. It ran thence in a Northern direction, passing east of Hilltop, R. A. Gray's property, to a point in the line between Gray & P. Liggett, thence in a North-western direction, crossing the Valley Turnpike to the North of David Yeakel's lane, on the Kratzer road. Thence with the Kratzer road, crossing the O., Alexandria and Manassas Gap Railroad, to a point near Capt. D. S. Jones' pond, thence crossing the lands of D. S. Jones to a point West of the Waterman house, thence passing West of Jackson Miller's house, to a spring in Kyle's field, West of the brick dwelling house, thence crossing the H. & W. S. pike to the Toll-gate on the Valley pike, thence with the Port Republic road, to a white oak tree on the top of the hill, (not far from where Gen. Ashby was killed,) thence in a Northeastern direction to the beginning.

The Woodbine Cemetery Company was chartered by the legislature in March, 1850, John Kinney, Ab. Smith, and fourteen others being named in the Act, and given the right to purchase and hold, in or near the town, not more than 15 acres of ground for the purposes specified.

In 1868 the amount of taxes levied in Harrisonburg on personal property was $1659.57, and on real estate, $2885.82; on both, $4545.39. In 1911 the total amount, on real and personal property, at a rate of 65 cents on the $100, was $22,083.80. In 1870 the population of the town was stated as 2828; at present (1912) it is, almost exactly, 5000.

ROCKINGHAM COUNTY

The "boom" period was marked by decided "plants" and prophecies in Harrisonburg, not all of which grew or came true; but, as already indicated, the town has had a constant and healthy growth. It is noted as the best horse market in the Valley. In 1899 Harrisonburg voting precinct was divided into East Harrisonburg and West Harrisonburg.

In August, 1873, Judge James Kenney wrote in his diary: "The necessity of pure water is now felt in our town"; and the question of a good water supply was agitated for a number of years following. In 1883 the city fathers put in a water system, on a small scale, apparently for protection against fire. In 1886 the artesian well which was to supply the town had been put down 455 feet. In 1889 the well of J. P. Houck had been bored to a depth of 600 feet. The same year a system of water works was completed and accepted by the council. In 1890 the town had a water supply from an artesian well 600 feet deep (presumably Mr. Houck's); and the Houck Tanning Company was putting in an electric light plant. On December 22 (1890) the electric lights were turned on for the first time. In 1895 the town took up a proposition for a better water supply, and in 1898 the present splendid system, bringing an abundant supply by gravity from Riven Rock, near Rawley Springs, was installed under the direction of N. Wilson Davis, engineer. In 1904 the town issued $60,000 in bonds for the construction of a municipal light and power plant, which has been in successful operation for a number of years past.

On Christmas day, 1870, about 4 o'clock in the morning, fire broke out on the south side of the public square, and burned all the buildings over to the old stone Waterman house. The loss totaled $50,000 or $60,000.

In 1875 the first town clock for Harrisonburg was put in the court house tower.

In 1887, and thereabout, Harrisonburg had no saloons.

In 1902 the Big Spring, so long a landmark of the town, was covered over.

Among the historic houses of the town are the Harrison

house, now Gen. John E. Roller's office; the Waterman house, south side of the public square; and Collicello, west of the freight station.

Collicello was built about 1812 by the eminent lawyer, Robert Gray; and there his 8 children, one of whom became the distinguished Col. Algernon Gray, were born.

The Waterman house, a low stone structure with dormer windows, was the residence of Dr. Asher Waterman, who built it prior to 1799. Later, it was the home of Sen. Isaac S. Pennybacker (born 1805, died 1847). In 1854 it was the original home of the Bank of Rockingham, the first bank in the county. From 1860 to 1905 it was the residence of Hon. D. M. Switzer. When Mr. Switzer came to Harrisonburg in 1843 this house was occupied by the Rev. Henry Brown, pastor of the Presbyterian church. At that time there was but one pavement in the town: that one was of stone, and lay on the north and east sides of the Waterman house, which then, and until the fire of 1870, stood more than 20 feet in advance of the other buildings on the south side of the public square.

The Harrison house is mentioned in this volume in so many connections that no special sketch is deemed necessary here.

Harrisonburg has had an organized military company throughout many years of its history; and, as already indicated, the beginning of its fire companies must be dated more than a century ago. The Harrisonburg fire companies in recent years have been conspicuous in the State conventions and contests, winning notable honors at Staunton in 1893, at Portsmouth in 1894, at Roanoke in 1912, and at other places at other times. They are doing a fine service in Harrisonburg, and occasionally in neighboring towns.

In July, 1897, shortly after the fire laddies of Harrisonburg had distinguished themselves at Winchester, the following lines by M. J. McGinty, of New York, appeared in the *Register:*

Switzer Building   Waterman House   [Pages 192, 354]

The Chinkapin Tree
[Page 406]

Old Town Hall, Bridgewater
[Page 199]   Photo by Furry

Fertile Farm Lands on Cook's Creek

ROCKINGHAM COUNTY

All hail to the laddies, those knights of the reel,
The quick-sprinting victors, with hearts true as steel;
All hail to the firemen, victorious and brave,
Slaves only to duty—their mission to save.

* * * * * *

All hail to the champions! Our hats off to you;
O, here's to the invincible wing-footed crew!
We drink to your health! may your record remain
As a shaft for all time to your worth and your fame.

* * * * * *

The present municipal officers of Harrisonburg are:
Mayor—John H. Downing.
Recorder—John G. Yancey, Jr.
Assessor—R. Lee Woodson.
Treasurer—Henry A. Sprinkel.
Sergeant—J. E. Altaffer.
Councilmen—J. S. Bradley, A. M. Loewner, T. E. Sebrell, R. Lee Allen, T. N. Thompson, D. C. Devier, V. R. Slater, F. F. Nicholas, J. M. Snell.

Keezletown, or, as it was first written, Keisell's-Town, was laid off on 100 acres of land belonging to George Keisell, and established by law under an Act of Assembly passed December 7, 1791. Seven gentlemen, George Houston, George Carpinter, Martin Earhart, Peter Nicholass, John Snapp, John Swisher, and John Pierce, were made trustees.[9] It is said that a good deal of rivalry had developed between Thomas Harrison and Mr. Keisell in the effort to locate permanently the county-seat, the former championing Harrisonburg, the latter Keisell's-Town. In fact, a rather entertaining story is told of how, on one occasion, the two gentlemen ran (more exactly, rode) a race to Richmond in the interests of their respective enterprises, in which, by the merest chance, Mr. Keisell was outdistanced by his rival.

In 1844 Houck, Hosler & Co. were advertising the opening of a general store at "Huffman's Tavern establishment in Keezletown." Shepp's spring, near the village, is said to

---

9. Hening's Statutes, Vol. 13, page 297.

supply fine mineral water. The people of the community are intelligent and enterprising, and give good support to their schools and churches. The population of Keezletown is about 225.

The following interesting account of **McGaheysville** and the man for whom it was named has been supplied, upon special request, by Mr. Richard Mauzy.

McGaheysville is located eleven miles east of Harrisonburg on the Stanardsville turnpike, and on "Stony Run," appropriately named, which has its source between the main longitudinal ranges of the Massanutten mountain, locally called "The Kettle," and flows through the center of the village, and, two miles below, empties into the Shenandoah River.

This village is, as the Irishman said of his pig, "Little, but ould."

Its name dates from 1801 when the first postoffice was established there with Tobias Randolph McGahey as Postmaster, for whom the village was named.

Among the first, if not the first to settle there, was Thos. Mauzy, (the eldest son of Henry Mauzy of Fauquier Co., Va., by his second marriage,) who settled there in the latter part of the 18th century, and owned the property which he sold in 1805 to his youngest brother Joseph, where the latter did business and reared his family and lived till his death in December, 1863, and where his son Richard now resides, having been owned by the Mauzys for 115 years consecutively.

Thos. Mauzy also owned the farm and mill on the Shenandoah River where the Harrisonburg Electric plant is now located, which he sold in 1822.

Though the population has increased slowly with time, the number and variety of industries have decreased, owing to the combination of capital and to the establishment of factories which made private enterprises unprofitable.

About 75 years ago there were in the village several tailor shops, shoemaker shops, cabinet and carpenter shops, hatter shops, wheelwright-shop, blacksmith shops, a tannery, and one store of general merchandise.

The following are the names of some of the citizens who lived there about that time:

Dr. Darwin Bashaw, Dr. Hitt, Joseph Mauzy, Christopher Wetzel, Peter Bolinger, A. J. O. Bader, Philip Rimel, John Garrett, John and Jacob Leap, Solomon and Jacob Pirkey, John and Augustus Shumate, Zebulon and David Gilmore, David Irick, Allison Breeden, Jacob Fultz, and Geo. Brill.

The following with reference to the man for whom the village was

ROCKINGHAM COUNTY

named, furnished by his granddaughter, Miss Alice McGahey, will be of interest:

Tobias Randolph McGahey was born in Dover, Delaware, March 24, 1765. He came to this valley with a Scotch-Irish colony when a young man. In 1801, when a postoffice was established there, he was appointed postmaster, and the office was called McGaheysville. In 1802 he married Mrs. Eva Conrad, a wealthy widow of one of the first settlers in the Valley, and a resident of McGaheysville. They remained 19 years at this place, when his wife died.

His occupation, when he first came to the Valley, was surveying. He also built flouring mills in Shenandoah, Page, Rockingham, and Augusta counties, and afterwards, in 1827, engaged in the mercantile business at Bonny Brook, on a farm he owned there, one mile northeast of McGaheysville.

His mother (Mrs. Barnes) was a notable character in the village. She taught school, and not only taught the girls to read, write, and cipher, but to sew, knit, and paint. She lived to an old age and did much good in her journey of life.

During his first wife's time, Mr. McGahey lived where A. S. Bader now resides, and reared three nieces and two nephews.

It is said that McGaheysville was first called "Ursulasburg," in honor of a Mrs. Long, a native of Switzerland, who lived near.[10] The present population of the village is about 350. It has one of the best schools in the county.

Port Republic is one of the oldest towns in Rockingham, and in the 20's and 30's, after the South Shenandoah had been made navigable for floatboats, was, in the happy phrase of Mr. Richard Mauzy, a place of great expectations. The following paragraph, from an Act of Assembly passed January 14, 1802, gets us back to formal beginnings:

Be it enacted by the general assembly, That twenty-three acres of land, the property of John McCarthrey, junior, lying between the north and south branches of the south fork of Shenandoah river in the county of Rockingham, shall be, and they are hereby vested in George Gilmer, Benjamin Lewis, Matthias Aman, John Givens, and Henry Perkey, gentlemen trustees, to be by them, or a majority of them, laid off into lots of half an acre each, with convenient streets, and established a town by the name of Port Republic.

Lots were to be sold at auction, the purchaser in each

---

10. See *Rockingham Register,* May 13, 1898.

A HISTORY OF

case being required, upon forfeit, to erect "a dwelling house sixteen feet square at least, with a brick or stone chimney to be finished fit for habitation within ten years from the day of sale."

January 26, 1866, an Act was passed incorporating Port Republic, and on March 31, following, the first election under the new charter was held. John Harper was chosen mayor, and Tobias M. Grove sergeant.

In olden days "Port" was noted for its fights—personal encounters—but in latter times it is as peaceable and law-abiding as other places.

The bridges at Port Republic, specially those across the North River, have had an interesting history. The first one, or one of the first, was burned in June, 1862, by Stonewall Jackson, to prevent Fremont from following him across the river. The next one was built in 1866, by citizens of the community, at a cost of about $3000. This washed away in the great flood of 1870. In January, 1874, the county court appropriated $600 to aid in rebuilding this bridge. The next bridge was washed away in 1877, and was not rebuilt for two or three years. The present bridge is a single-track iron structure.

Mr. Richard Mauzy says that Holbrook, a citizen of Port, is entitled to the credit of making the original McCormick reaper a success, by devising the sickle as it has since been generally adopted on all reapers.

The population of Port Republic is about 200.

In January, 1804, an Act of Assembly was passed establishing the town of **Newhaven** on the land of Gideon Morgan and William Lewis, and appointing Edwin Nicholas, Asher Waterman, George Huston, George Gilmore, Mathias Amon, Benj. Lewis, Henry Perkey, and Henry J. Gambill as trustees. The site of New Haven is on the north side of the rivers, opposite or a little below Port Republic. It will be observed that the two places had several trustees in common, and their names indicate the importance that was attached to their location upon navigable water. We can readily imagine them

ROCKINGHAM COUNTY

upon a "boom" in 1804, and thereabouts, but New Haven seems never to have reached the actual proportions of a town. The name is by this time remembered by only a few persons.

One of the most progressive towns of East Rockingham is **Elkton,** known until 1881 as Conrad's Store. Near the town stood until recently Elk Run church, one of the oldest churches in the county; and the town is built where Elk Run flows into the Shenandoah River. The origin of the name Elkton, therefore, is obvious. Conrad's old store building still remains as one of the landmarks. Another place of historic interest is the old Kite homestead, where Stonewall Jackson had his headquarters in 1862.

In 1867 the postoffice at Conrad's Store was moved out a mile or two to Geo. W. Sanford's shoemaker shop, and named Roadside. In 1881 Elkton postoffice was established, with Jas. H. Shipp as postmaster. One of the promoters of Elkton in "boom" times (1889-90) was Dr. S. P. H. Miller (1835-1895). In March, 1908, the town was incorporated, and J. A. S. Kyger was chosen mayor. The councilmen were J. R. Cover, J. T. Heard, J. E Leebrick, V. C. Miller, W. A. Gordon, and I. L. Flory. Since 1881, when the Norfolk & Western Railway was opened, and especially since 1896, when the Chesapeake-Western was completed to Bridgewater, Elkton has been a railroad center of growing importance.

The river bridges at Conrad's Store and Elkton, like those at Port, have had an interesting, though expensive, history. On June 3, 1862, the Conrad's Store bridge was burned by Co. D, 7th Va. Cavalry, S. B. Coyner, captain, to keep the Federal general Shields from coming across to join Fremont against Jackson. In June, 1868, proposals were solicited by J. H. Kite, president of board, for building the island bridges across the Shenandoah, near Conrad's Store. The bridges were carried away by the flood of 1870. In 1872 a bridge 200 feet long, across the river, and one 100 feet long, across the race, were built by John W. Woods. These probably corresponded to the "island bridges" of 1868. The Conrad's Store bridge fell again in the flood of 1877; was rebuilt in 1878-9 (by John

A HISTORY OF

Woods) and again washed away in September, 1896. In May, 1897, part of the new iron bridge that was being erected was washed down.

The population of Elkton at present (1912) is about 1000, and the town officers are the following:

Mayor—J. A. S. Kyger.
Treasurer—W. H. McVeigh.
Sergeant—W. E. Lucas.
Councilmen—R. B. Wilson, J. F. Taylor, J. R. Cover, J. T. Heard, L. F. Yeager, W. E. Deal.

Dayton is likely one of the oldest "inland" towns in the county. Probably the first house was the one built of stone by the Harrisons, and still standing in fine condition at the northeast end of the town, on the west side of the Warm Springs and Harrisonburg Pike. It is now occupied by the Burtner family. Capt. John A. Herring, whose ancestors were some of the first settlers of the community, says:

It was once surrounded by palisades, and in times of Indian invasion the people around went there with their families for protection. There is a tradition that there was an underground passage dug to the creek [Cook's Creek] nearby, for water, in case of a siege.

A writer in the *Rockingham Register* of January 5, 1894, says that this old house was sold early in the 19th century by Dr. Peachy Harrison to Maj. John Allebaugh.

Prior to the Revolution there was an Episcopal chapel in what is now the north section of the Dayton cemetery; and up the creek a short distance, on the ground now covered by Silver Lake, was "Old Erection" of the Presbyterians. In March, 1833, Dayton was established by law. Rifeville and Rifetown were earlier names. In 1854 John Stinespring was proprietor of Dayton Hotel. Dayton's stirring experiences in 1864 are narrated elsewhere. In 1903 and 1911 the town was visited by destructive fires, but the enterprising spirit of her people seems akin to the phenix essence. Dayton is probably the largest town south of Mason and Dixon's line without a single colored citizen; and likely has the largest business carried on through its postoffice of any town of its size in the

ROCKINGHAM COUNTY

country. The latter condition is due to its publishing houses and schools, referred to elsewhere.

The present (1912) population of Dayton is about 600, and its municipal officers are the following:

Mayor—J. W. Keiter.
Clerk—Henry Beery.
Assessor—J. H. S. Good.
Sergeant—J. A. Shifflett.
Councilmen—P. X. Heatwole, J. W. Heatwole, J. H. Rhodes, J. W. Rhodes, J. N. Shrum, J. A. Stone, G. P. Arey.

The beautiful town on the North River, three miles southwest of Dayton, was first called Dinkletown, after one of the first families in the community, then Bridgeport, because it was a flatboat port at a bridge, and finally **Bridgewater,** because, doubtless, the bridge continued to be a necessity although the place ceased to be a port.

According to Mr. S. G. Dinkle, John Dinkle about 1810 put up a carding machine, a sawmill, and a grist mill on the north side of the river, about a quarter of a mile below the bridge. The grist mill was replaced by a flouring mill about 1835. According to Mr. Dinkle and Mr. S. H. W. Byrd, this flouring mill burned in 1855, and was replaced immediately by the mill now standing there. On February 7, 1835, the town was established by law, on 20 acres of land belonging to John and Jacob Dinkle. The trustees were Jacob Dinkle, Michael Wise, Jesse Hoover, John Dinkle, Sr., and John Dumore. Quoting from the Act: "Liberty st. shall be laid off & established 20 ft; Main st. 55 ft. wide: Grove st. 20 ft. wide & Center alley 12 ft. wide." The old town hall, standing on the west side of Main Street, below the intersection of Commerce Street, is said to have been formerly a church. Mr. S. H. W. Byrd calls attention to the fact that Bridgewater was established by law the same year as Milwaukee, Wis. In 1892 Capt. Philander Herring testified that the town had had no barroom or liquor saloon of any kind since 1854. It has had none since 1892. In 1868 a company was formed and chartered to build an observatory on Round Hill, just west of

A HISTORY OF

town; but this splendid project seems to have failed. In 1873, the period of railroad fevers, Bridgewater and vicinity were on a "boom." In the *Register* of May 9 (1873) it was reported that no less than 33 flouring mills, 2 wool mills, and a number of sawmills were to be found within a radius of five miles of the place. On February 23, 1880, a considerable section of the town was laid waste by fire. In 1904 the corporate limits of the town were extended to their present ample proportions.

Now, a word concerning the Bridgewater bridges. For most of this acknowledgement is made to Mr. S. H. W. Byrd. First, there was an old bridge on posts, low, near the water. In 1853 another bridge was built by Abram S. Williams. This was burned by the Confederates in 1862. The third bridge was erected in 1866—completed in October—by John W. Woods. It had a support in the middle. On September 29, 1870, the northern half of this bridge was swept away by the great flood. The fourth bridge was completed in December, 1870, by Col. Wm. F. Pifer. This, too, had a center support. It was washed away November 24, 1877. The present bridge was finished by Wm. H. Grove in April, 1878. It crosses at a single colossal leap of 240 feet or more, and is said to be the longest single-span wooden bridge in the world.

The population of Bridgewater (1912) is about 1000. The town officers are the following:

Mayor—H. C. Hale.
Recorder—S. H. W. Byrd.
Treasurer—O. W. Miller.
Assessor—E. A. Dinkle.
Sergeant—J. W. Walters.
Councilmen—J. H. Wine, W. H. Miller, C. B. Kiser, L. V. Miller, O. W. Wine, B. H. Beydler.

When the above officers were elected, June 11, 1912, the town voted a bond issue of $25,000 for a water and sewer system.

It is said that **Mt. Crawford** was established by law in 1825. In 1835 an Act of Assembly was passed incorporating

ROCKINGHAM COUNTY

the Mt. Crawford Water Company. In earlier days the place was known as Mt. Pleasant, and perhaps also as Mt. Stevens. In the *Rockingham Register* of October 5, 1822, Dr. Wm. Frey respectfully acquainted his friends and the public generally that he had removed from his former residence to the house of Fred. Hoffman in the village of Mt. Pleasant on the Staunton road, 17 miles from the latter place and 8 miles from Harrisonburg. In Martin's Gazetteer of Virginia, for 1835, this is said concerning Mt. Crawford:

> It contains 25 dwelling houses, 1 house of public worship free for all denominations, 2 common schools, 2 taverns, 3 mercantile stores, 2 tailors, 2 saddlers, 2 boot and shoe factories, 1 smith shop, 1 tin plate worker, 1 cabinet maker, 1 wheelwright, 1 cooper, 1 pottery, 2 milliner and mantua makers, 1 gun smith, 1 wagon maker, 1 manufacturing flour mill, and 1 saw mill. The North river is navigable for flat boats about three miles above this village, . . .

The bridges at Mt. Crawford suffered by the war and by the floods of 1870 and 1877, and their history would make an interesting chapter. In 1895 the town received its present charter. The population (1912) is about 400, with the following municipal officers:

Mayor—O. A. Layman.

Councilmen—J. H. Funkhouser, F. H. Lago, A. M. Pifer, J. C. Wise, M. Dean, W. F. Moyerhoeffer.

Among the various things to the credit of Mt. Crawford, not the least is the reputation it has won for enforcing law—particularly against reckless joy-riders.

The city of **Sparta** (Spartapolis) is ancient and honorable, whether in Laconia or in Rockingham. In 1831 our Sparta was established by law; it was a city 8 years later; that is to say, by an Act of the Assembly in 1839 its name was expanded to Spartapolis. In 1842, perhaps earlier, it was one of the county voting places. In the years leading up to and into the civil war it was frequently a place of muster. The present name is Mauzy, and the population is put down as 12.

A mile or two southwest of Mauzy, on the Valley Pike, is the village of **Lacey Spring**. Mrs. Maria Graham Carr says

—201—

A HISTORY OF

that her grandfather, John Koontz, built a house at Lacey Spring, in 1815, that was afterwards occupied by the Lincoln family: that he had a tanyard, operated by Isaac Hite; and that he also had a sawmill, not far from his house. The great spring that gushes out from the rocky hillside would certainly have afforded an abundant water supply for such establishments. Mrs. Carr also mentions a house of entertainment, first occupied by a Mrs. Patten, later in the hands of the Lincolns. In February, 1898, an old two-story log house at Lacey burned, which, according to the report then published, had been erected in colonial times, and had been kept by David Lincoln as an inn during the early part of the last century. The 100 people who live at Lacey Spring are among the most intelligent and enterprising in the county.

The statements regarding the beginnings of **Timberville** are somewhat complicated. In 1814, when John Zigler located there, a log house, then old, stood on the west bank of the river. In the year mentioned Mr. Zigler opened a tannery, which, at his death in 1856, was said to be the largest in the county. He started a pottery in 1830, and also operated a hemp mill. It is said that Tobias Shull opened a blacksmith shop in 1830 at B. F. Crist's present stand, and that a Mr. Carnes started a mill in 1831. Early in the century, perhaps before 1820, Abraham Williamson, a brother of Dr. J. D. Williamson of Hardscrabble (above New Market), opened the first store, and the place was known as Williamsport. This name would indicate that the river was being utilized for transportation. Another tradition says that Wm. G. Thompson founded Timberville. He was a prominent resident of the community as early as 1833, when he, John Zigler, and others were trying to get a free bridge across the river. The place was then called Thompson's Store. It is said that Thompson, in 1837, built the house now or recently owned by C. Fahrney. About 1850 the place was known as Riddle's Tavern. For many years, however, Timberville has been the accepted name, and the town was thus incorporated in 1884.

ROCKINGHAM COUNTY

with Jacob Garber, Chas. E. Fahrney, Wm. A. Pierce, John A. Roller, and Saml. C. Smucker as trustees.

It is said that one day in early times, a four-horse team and wagon broke down the bridge, at Timberville, with more serious results to the bridge than to the team. The third bridge, erected in 1840, washed away in 1842 or 1843. Then the river was forded till 1884, when the present bridge was built.

The population of Timberville (1912) is about 400. C. J. Smucker is mayor; Milton Whitener, clerk; B. F. Zirkle, treasurer; S. A. Henkel, sergeant; with J. A. Garber, W. B. Fahrney, D. S. Wampler, F. M. Bowman, F. H. Driver, and R. S. Bowers, councilmen.

May 22, 1909, the Harrisonburg *Daily News* printed an elegant illustrated supplement on Timberville.

The town of **Broadway,** at the junction of Linville Creek with the North Shenandoah River, and at the mouth of Brock's Gap, occupies a strategic point for trade. The beginnings of settlement and industry were probably made on the point of land between the creek and the river, at or near the Winfield residence. As early as 1808 the Custers had a mill there, and they were probably at the same time operating the store that for many years was kept in the old stone building adjacent to the Winfield house. The mill that Sheridan burned in 1864 was stone, and was likely the original one. During the period of Reconstruction the brick buildings, now occupying the site, were erected for machine shops.

According to tradition, the name Broadway was adopted from the habit of the merry daredevils, who were accustomed to assemble at the place for carousals, of referring to themselves as on the "broad way."

In March, 1880, Broadway was incorporated with Saml. C. Williams, P. W. Pugh, J. W. Basore, Michael Zigler, and M. B. E. Cline as trustees. Various changes in the charter and boundaries have been made since. The present (1912) population is about 700, and the town officers are the following:

A HISTORY OF

Mayor—J. H. Nave.
Clerk—C. R. Whitmore.
Sergeant—G. W. Beaver.
Councilmen—C. R. Winfield, G. S. Fultz, Claude Knupp, W. N. Williams, C. E. Miller, Oscar Orebaugh.

Cootes' Store stands above Broadway, at the actual mouth of Brock's Gap. The place bears its name from Mr. Samuel Cootes (1792-1882), for many years a prominent citizen of the county. In 1858 the place was made a voting precinct. For many years past it has been a postoffice. The population is about 30.

A short distance southwest of Cootes' Store is the village of **Turleytown,** said to have been founded by Giles Turley, who stopped there on his way to Kentucky—and remained there. In 1903 Dr. John S. Flory, of Bridgewater, published an interesting description of the old Turleytown blockhouse, which was erected in early times. The Turleytown Baptist church also has an interesting history. The population is about 40.

In 1860 a postoffice was established at Mountain Valley, and the name was changed to **Singer's Glen.** Mountain Valley had already become famous as the home of Joseph Funk, father of song in Northern Virginia, as the place of his school, and as the place where he and his sons printed and bound the music books and other publications that were being sent all over the country. The appropriateness of the present name has been proved by both the nature of the work that Joseph Funk & Sons kept up there till the later 70's, and the character of the people who still live there. In March, 1894, Singer's Glen was incorporated, with B. H. Franklin mayor; and S. H. Swank, G. W. Shaffer, Jos. R. Funk, S. W. Brewer, D. M. Hollar, and C. F. Shank, councilmen. The present (1912) population is about 180, and the town officers are: B. H. Franklin, mayor; J. F. Moubray, sergeant; S. H. Swank, P. H. Donovan, W. C. Funk, G. W. Hedrick, D. S. VanPelt, and D. M. Hollar, councilmen.

The name of **Edom** appears as early as 1844, perhaps

Bridgewater College Buildings and Campus, Bridgewater, Va. (Page 260)

ROCKINGHAM COUNTY

earlier. In 1835 Joseph Martin, in his Gazetteer of Virginia, mentions Linville Creek P. O., which may be identical with Edom. Henry Howe, a decade or more later, speaks of Edom Mills. The population of this beautiful village is about 140.

Another Rockingham village, similar in situation to Edom, built upon a never-failing stream and surrounded by sloping hillsides, is **Mt. Clinton.** According to an article printed in the *Register,* October 11, 1883, this place got its name about 1833, by a vote of the people of the community registered at the store of Bowman & Devier. Several names were under consideration, but a certain gentleman authorized Bowman & Devier to give a horn of apple-jack to every man who said "Mt. Clinton." And so Mt. Clinton it came to be. Before this the place was referred to as Muddy Creek, and was already the site of a mill, a tilt hammer, a cooper shop, etc. The meeting-house nearby was known as Gospel Hill. Henton & Burkholder were general merchants at Mt. Clinton as early as 1833, perhaps earlier. About 1895 the village came into prominence as the seat of West Central Academy, mentioned in Chapter XV. The population is (1912) about 225.

Cross Keys is an ancient village, being mentioned by Martin in 1835 as a postoffice. There have been a church and a store at Cross Keys for several generations, and the place was made famous by the battle fought there June 8, 1862, between Fremont and Ewell. The population is about 50.

Spring Creek is a village of about 200 people, situated in a prosperous farming section of western Rockingham. It maintains various local enterprises, and should be remembered as the place where Bridgewater College had its beginnings in 1880.

Ottobine, or Paul's Mill, on Beaver Creek, the site of a mill, a church, a postoffice, etc., has been well known for many years. For example, as early as 1838, possibly before, it was a place of muster. The population is about 60.

Another village of western Rockingham, surrounded by beautiful farms, is **Clover Hill,** with a population of about 70.

A HISTORY OF

Rushville, at the confluence of Muddy Creek and Dry River, with a population of about 60, has been well known in the county for many years.

Stemphleytown, between Dayton and Bridgewater, has borne its name since the 40's or 50's from David Stemphley, the first resident. The population is about 40.

In December, 1866, Jacob Funkhouser, C. E., was laying off a town at Kratzer's Spring, on the Middle Road. This was evidently the village now called **Linville,** located a short distance south of Linville Depot. About 1870 the name Etna was applied to a certain part of Linville. The present population (1912) is about 250.

River Bank, near McGaheysville, should receive special notice, in addition to other things, for the mere fact of its existence, since it has probably been washed away oftener than any other place in the county. The bridge built at River Bank soon after the war was swept away in 1870. In 1873 a mill was erected and plans perfected for the rebuilding of the bridge. The leaders of River Bank industry at that time were J. H. Larkins, W. B. Yancey, R. A. Gibbons, and Henry E. Sipe. In January, 1874, three spans of the new bridge were swept away by a freshet; and in the big flood of 1877 not only the bridge, but also the grist mill and saw mill, went down in the waters. In 1874 a postoffice was established at River Bank, with E. L. Lambert, postmaster.

Grottoes, whilom Shendun, owes its meteoric phases to the "booms" of 1890, its permanent character to the fertility in the soils, the caves in the hills, and the ores in the mountains about it. Mt. Vernon Forge had marked the place of old. In March, 1891, it was alive with industries. Males 430, with females 279, made a total population of 709, showing an increase of 100% in about five months. In February, 1892, an Act of Assembly was passed incorporating the town of Shendun; W. I. Harnsberger was elected mayor, R. T. Miller, E. R. Armentrout, J. W. Rumple, J. G. Hall, J. M. Pirkey, L. D. Patterson councilmen. In March, 1893, receivers were appointed for the Grottoes Company, at Shen-

ROCKINGHAM COUNTY

dun. This year (1912) another Act was passed changing the name of the town from Shendun to Grottoes. The present population is about 400. C. D. Harnsberger is mayor; J. E. Graves, assessor; R. D. Melhorn, treasurer; S. F. Newman, sergeant; J. M. Pirkey, J. W. Lemon, M. D. Eutsler, W. I. Harnsberger, J. M. Bell, and J. L. Leeth, councilmen.

In 1893 street cars were running in Shendun. This, so far as is known, gives the place a unique distinction among the towns of Rockingham. In the *Rockingham Register* of January 30, 1891, the following item of interest appeared:

"The first child born in Shendun was a daughter to Mr. and Mrs. W. I. Harnsberger, and granddaughter of Hon. H. B. Harnsberger, of Port Republic. It was named Shendun Bell, the latter name in compliment of Maj. H. M. Bell, of Staunton, one of the principal promoters of Shendun."

In the following table are given the names of villages, postoffices, etc., of Rockingham not already mentioned, grouped by districts. In column (1) are names that appeared in Lake's atlas of 1885; in column (2) are the names that now appear in Rand McNally's map of Virginia; in column (3) are given figures of present population, as nearly as these can be approximated; in column (4) are given the years in which postoffices were established at some of these places; and in column (5) the names of first postmasters.

Ashby District

(1)	(2)	(3)	(4)	(5)
Meyerhoeffers Store	Meyerhoeffers Store	20		
Goods Mill	Goods Mill	25	1871	Saml. Good
Scotts Ford	Scotts Ford	25		
North River	North River	25	1874	J. J. Roller
Friedens	Friedens	20		
Pleasant Valley	Pleasant Valley	80	Rockingham P.O.	
Berlinton		30		
Coakleytown		30		
Montezuma	Montezuma	30		

A HISTORY OF

	Lilly	25	1885	W. H. Sipe
	{ Spring Creek Station			
	Onawan	15		

Central District

(1)	(2)	(3)	(4)	(5)
Peach Grove		20		
Dale Enterprise	D. Enterprise	50	1872	C. H. Brunk
Karicofe	Hinton	30		
Chrisman	Chrisman	40	1881	W. E. Long
Gladwell				
	Penn Laird	40		
	Chestnut Ridge		1894	John Miller
	Rutherford			
	Pleasant Hill			

Linville District

(1)	(2)	(3)	(4)	(5)
Paulington	Paulington	25		
Mt. Tabor				
Melrose	Melrose	25	1873	R. Armentrout
Cherry Grove	Ch. Grove	20		
Greenmount	Greenmount	60		
	Zenda	30		
	Latona	20		
	Bruce	20		
	Sky	20		
	Ft. Hoover[11]	25		
	Hoover	20		
	Palos -			
	Genoa	10		
	Paul			

---

11. Ft. Hoover, a small structure mainly of stone, used in later times (and likely in earlier times also) as a dwelling, stood at the west foot of Green Hill, on the north bank of Joe's Creek, a mile below Singer's Glen. A low mound, with a few scattered bits of stone, now marks the place.

Elkton Hotel

Mountain Valley—Singer's Glen. An Artist's Dream—Home of the "Harmonia Sacra"

Log House in Center, First Postoffice in Rockingham   (Page 212)

Stonewall Jackson's Headquarters at Elkton. Blue Ridge Mountains in Background
(Page 197)

ROCKINGHAM COUNTY

Plains District

(1)	(2)	(3)	(4)	(5)
Roark	Arkton	20		
Oakwood	Oakwood	20		
Dogtown	Athlone	40		
Tenth Legion	Tenth Legion	30		
Cowans	Daphna			
Mechanicsville				
Honeyville				
Bakers Mill	Bakers Mill	20		
Fulks Run	Fulks Run	50	1873	G. W. Fawley
Yankton				
Criders	Criders	20	1881	W. R. Crider
Dovesville	Dovesville	40		
	Mayland	30		
	Hupp	30		
	Holman			
	Tunis	20		

Stonewall District.

(1)	(2)	(3)	(4)	(5)
Swift Run	Swift Run	25		
Furnace	Furnace	50		
Greenwood				
Millbank	Antelope	75	1877	W. H. Marshall
Inglewood	Inglewood		1873	C. W. Shepp
Yancey	Yancey	25		
Almond	Almond	30		
Montevideo	Montevideo	50	1873	C. M. Killian
Lynnwood	Lynnwood	70	1871	A. L. Wagner
Leroy			1872	S. B. McCommon
Liola				
	(Grottoes)			
	Rainbow	20		
	Model	40		
	Island Ford	30		
	Beldor	50	1894	
	Roadside	30		
	Lewis			

A HISTORY OF

In addition to the foregoing, the following notes may be of interest.

In 1840 Nicholas' Tavern was a well known place in East Rockingham.

In 1842 there was a place, evidently in Rockingham, called Libertyville.

In 1863 Burke's Mill was a postoffice in Rockingham.

In 1870 a postoffice was established at Mt. Vernon Forge, D. F. Haynes, P. M.

In 1873 a postoffice was established at Belton, Rockingham County.

The postoffice at Melrose was *re-established* in 1873.

In 1879 there was a place in northwest Rockingham called "Yankeetown."

In 1890 Mt. Hermon P. O. was established, with J. M. Lam postmaster.

In 1891 Amberly P. O. was established, with J. W. Tate postmaster.

In 1893 a postoffice was established at Bear Lithia, J. T. Taylor, P. M.[12]

---

[12]. In addition to those already named, Mrs. Thos. Kille of Harrisonburg, Mr. J. A. Garber of Timberville, Miss Paulina Winfield of Broadway, and Mr. J. R. Shipman of Bridgewater have given aid on this chapter, and to them grateful acknowledgement is made.

CHAPTER XII.

ROADS AND RAILROADS.

Nothing is of more importance in the economic history of any county or country than the development of facilities for travel, transportation, and communication. In this chapter an attempt is made to chronicle some of the more important steps in the building and supervision of roads and railroads in Rockingham County, together with certain particulars regarding telegraphs and telephones.

In February, 1744, Peter Scholl and others living on Smith's Creek petitioned the court (of Augusta County) for a road. They said they had to work on a road 30 miles distant from their plantations. This sounds as if there were no legally established roads in this part of the Valley at that time. A year later James Patton and John Buchanan reported that they had viewed a way from the Frederick County line, and the court ordered it established as a public road.[1] Whether this road was east or west of the Massanutten Mountain cannot, perhaps, be determined, but it must in either case have been much nearer than 30 miles to Smith's Creek.

In 1753 when the Moravian Brethren came up the Valley with a wagon there were some passable roads west of the Massanutten, along by the places where New Market, Lacey Springs, and Harrisonburg now are; but these roads were not in good order. It is possible that the main thoroughfare at this time and for some years afterward passed, not by Harrisonburg, but by Keezletown. There is an old ford across Middle River, about four miles above Port Republic, known as Pennsylvania Ford. This seems to indicate that travelers and immigrants from Pennsylvania crossed at that

---

1. Waddell's Annals of Augusta, pp. 47, 48.

point; and it may be that this ford was on the main road up the Valley in very early times.

Bishop L. J. Heatwole tells me that there was a very old trail from the Old Fields, in Hardy County, W. Va., to Williamsburg, that came through Brock's Gap, past Joe's Spring at Singer's Glen, past Greenmount, and past the Big Spring at Harrisonburg, and so on across the Valley just above the Peaked Mountain, crossing the Blue Ridge by Brown's Gap.[2] In March, 1910, or thereabout, Mr. Heatwole contributed an interesting article to the Harrisonburg *Daily News* on the first postoffice in Rockingham County, in which he made reference to this old trail. The postoffice, which was likely such only by common agreement of residents, messengers, and travelers, was at the Liskey farm, a mile and a half northwest of Harrisonburg, probably in the old log house still standing over the spring. It stood by or near the old Williamsburg trail.

At a court held for Rockingham County on Tuesday, May 26, 1778, and continued from the preceding day, the following road overseers were appointed:

Henry Lung of the road "from the big hill to the Line of Shanandoe County";

George Huffman of the road "from the big hill to Henry Millers";

Henry Miller of the road "from his own house to the Top of the Mountain over Swift Run Gap";

Paul Ingle of the road "from the fork of the road leading to Swift Run Gap to Casper Haines Shop";

Casper Haines of the road "from his Shop to the main road leading from Staunton to Winchester";

Stephen Conrad of the road "in the room of Frederick Haines";

---

2. Brown's Gap was formerly known as Madison's Gap. The stream flowing out of it is still called Madison Run. The Madisons, it will be recalled, lived just above Port Republic.

ROCKINGHAM COUNTY

John Frazier of the road "from the Augusta Line to John Stephensons run";

Jacob Perkie of the road "from Stephensons run to John Keplingers place formerly Samples";

David Harnett of the road "from John Keplingers formerly Samples to Zeb Harrisons ford on Smiths Creek";

John Philips of the road "from Zebulon Harrisons ford to the Line of Shanandoe";

Jacob Woodley of the road "from the ford on this side of Sebastian Marts to Reuben Harrisons";

Jeremiah Harrison of the road "from Reuben Harrisons to Danl. Smiths Gent.";

Jeremiah Reagan of the road "from Danl. Smiths to the run that comes from Geo. Seawrights field";

Joseph Dictam of the road "from the run that comes from Geo. Seawrights field to the line of Augusta";

John Pence of the road "from the ford of the river at Gabl. Jones's to Felix Gilbert's";

Robt. Elliot of the road "from Felix Gilberts to Danl. Smiths house";

Joseph Lear of the road "from Danl. Smiths to the ford of Linvells Creek at Thos. Brian's";

Marten Gum of the road "from the ford of Linvells Creek at Thoms. Bryans to the fork of the Road on this Side of Jno. Thomas's mill";

John Ruddell of the road "from Chas. Daillys Ford to the upper Ford of Michael Baker";

Paul Gustard of the road "from Michael Bakers upper ford to the County Line on Cacapon";

Marten Witsel of the road "from the fork of the Cacapon road to the top of the mountain by Weatherholts";

John Bear of the road "from Daillys ford down the River to the Line of Shanandoe County";

Andrew Andes of the road "from Chas. Daillys ford under the No. Mountain to the line of Shanandoe";

A HISTORY OF

Rees Thomas of the road "from Daillys ford to Thos. Gordons";

Thomas Fulton of the road "from Thos. Gordons to the Line of Augusta";

Thomas Bowen of the road "from the fork of the road above Thomas's Mill to the Pine Tree between Francis Greens & Thos. Campbells";

John Herdman of the road "from the sd. pine tree to Harrisons Mill pond";

William Herring of the road "from Harrison's Mill pond to the forks of the road below Jno. Fowlers";

Gawin Hamilton of the road "from Rices Cabin in dry river Gap to Benj. Harrisons."

In each case above it was provided that "the usual tithables work thereon." The minutes of subsequent courts show that numerous changes were made from time to time in the personnel of the road masters.

At a court held November 24, 1778, "On the petition of Sundry Inhabitants in the forest for turning the road leading from Brocks Gap to Massenutting, Ordered that Maths. Reader, Jno. More & Nicolas Cairn do view the Conveniencies & Inconveniencies attending turning the road as prayed by the petitioners & report the same."

March 23, 1779.

Benj. Harrison, Joseph Dictam, Danl. Smith, and Jeremiah Reagen were appointed to view a road from Danl. Smith's plantation to James Magill's ford on the North River, and report *pro* and *con* on the same.

Christopher Our was appointed overseer of the road from Danl. Smith's to the dry fork in place of Jeremiah Harrison.

William Chesnut was appointed overseer of the road from Thos. Gordon's to Dry River, the tithables within 3 miles of the said road to work thereon.

G. Hamilton and Jno. Rice were appointed to view the Brock's Gap Road that crosses Dry River and make report.

ROCKINGHAM COUNTY

Saml. Skidmore was appointed overseer of the road from Hampshire Line to Joseph Skidmore's.

April 27, 1779.

On favorable report of viewers previously appointed, the court ordered a road opened from Danl. Smith's to the ford of the North River, by James McGill's; Richd. Reagan was appointed overseer of the same from Smith's to where the new road would cross the Butler Road; Nehemiah Harrison, from the Butler Road to Coll. Benja. Harrison's; William McGill, from Harrison's to the ford of the river: all the tithables within 3 miles to work on their respective portions.

May 25, 1779.

James McVey was appointed overseer of the road from Archd. Hopkins' mill[3] to Nehemiah Harrison's.

November 23, 1779.

Robt. Rutherford, Michl. Warren, and James Reagan were appointed to view and mark the nearest and best ground for a road from mill at the plains to the courthouse at Thos. Harrison's.

Joseph Dictam, Ezekiel Harrison, and John Huston were appointed to view and mark the nearest and best ground for a road from the courthouse to George Huston's.

Nehemiah Harrison, John Rice, and Gawen Hamilton were appointed to view and mark roads from Briary Branch Gap and Dry River Gap to the courthouse.

Joseph Smith was made overseer of the road from Benj. Harrison's to Gawen Hamilton's, and John Rice of the road from Gawen Hamilton's to the feeding trough in the mountain.

March 27, 1780.

Archbd. Hopkins, John Hopkins, and John Harrison were appointed to view the route for a road petitioned for from Hopkins' Mill to the courthouse.

---

3. This mill was likely the one on Muddy Creek, at Chrisman, now operated by H. L. Burtner.

A HISTORY OF

March 28, 1780.

Ab. Hankle, George Teter, and Robt. Minnis were appointed to view and mark a road from the Augusta line to the line of Hampshire, down the No. Fork.

Jo. Dictam, Saml. Hemphill, and William Cravens were appointed to view and mark a road from Ezekiel Harrison's to the Walnut Bottom—"the nearest and best Way."

April 24, 1780.

William Campbell was made overseer of the Rockfish road, from James Bairet's to Jacob Whitmore's, the tithables within two miles on each side of the road to work thereon.

It was ordered that the tithables within four miles on each side of the road from the run at Robt. Rutherford's to the Plains Mill work under Ezekiel Harrison, overseer thereof.

Aug. 29, 1780.

Upon report of the viewers, it was ordered that the roads from Briery Branch and Dry River gaps be opened. Joseph Hinton was appointed overseer from the Briery Branch road in Collo. Smith's land to where it crosses the first fork of the Mole Hill draught; Alex. Miller, Jr., from the said fork to the courthouse.

March 26, 1781.

John Hopkens, Jesse Harrison [?], and Rees Thomas were appointed to view a road from Geo. Baxters, leading to Brock's Gap, to the lower end of Josiah Davison's land.

May 28, 1781.

On its being represented to the Court that the Court of hampshire have order'd persons to view the Ground from Leonard Stumps to the deviding Line between that County & this for a Road to lead from the Courtho of sd County to the Seat of Government, & praying this Court to appoint viewers from this County Line to the foot of the Mountain on this Side in order to effect such a necessary Design, it is ordered that Jno Fitzwater Conrod Humble Martin Witsell & Henry Witsell or any three of them being first sworn do view the Ground from the County Line to the foot of the Mountain leading to the head waters of Cacapon or the Gap Waters as the Ground will best Suit and report the Conveniences

ROCKINGHAM COUNTY

& Inconveniences attending the making of the sd Road & in particular what Labour & Expense may attend the Digging bridging &c of the same.

August 27, 1781.

On the petition of the Inhabitants of Brocks that a convenient Road may be opened to the Courtho O that John Thomas Rees Thomas Peter Hog & George Spiers or any three being first sworn do view the nearest & best Way from the Gap to the road at Michl. Warens.

November 27, 1781.

Capt. James Magill was appointed overseer of the road from Capt. Ben. Harrison's to the county line, "leading to the Iron Works."

O that the Tiths. from the picked Mountain on one side & two miles on the other side of the road work under Jacob Woodly overseer of the road from the forks to the big Spring.

April 1, 1782.

Ordered that Nicholas Karn be appointed overseer of the road in the room of Ezekiel Harrison "from the Plain Mills to opposite Val. Seveyors old House in the Long Meadow including the Branch or Creek."

May 28, 1782.

It was ordered that Felix Gilbert, John Harrison, and Henry Ewin, being first sworn, should view "the Nearest and Best Way from the Courthouse [to] The ford of Cub run By Wm. Young and Mark ye Same and Make Return of their proceedings To Next Crt."

May 27, 1783.

Robt. Dunlap was appointed overseer of the road in place of Henry Ewin, the tithables "This Side of Gap Road" to work thereon "As far as a Crooked Locust where Blain's Road Crosses the sd. Road"; and David Bery was appointed overseer from Hopkins' Mill to the said locust on the said road.

James Devier was appointed overseer to open the road from Harrisonburg "To Where the sd. Road Will fall Into the path Crossing the big Hill and That all Tithables within three miles on each side Work thereon"; and Felix Gilbert was made overseer from Cub Run to the said place on the hill.

In June, 1784, a petition was presented to the court by sundry inhabitants of the county for a road from the county line, by Plain Mills, to Harrisonburg. Brewer Reeves, Ezekiel Harrison, Jeremiah Ragan, and Robert Rutherford, or any three of them, were appointed to view the proposed road and make report. At the next court, July 26, Reeves, Harrison, and Ragan reported that they had laid off the road as follows:

Beginning at the county line, running thence near by George Ruddel's, thence near to John Moor's, thence crossing the river opposite Moor's house, thence to Michael Holsinger's, thence into the former road near John Reeves's, it was to continue thence with the said former road to Harrisonburg. Nicolas Carn was appointed overseer of the new road from the county line to Carn's (or Carr's) Spring. Jacob Lincoln was to be overseer from the said spring to Michael Warrin's, and Benj. Smith from Warrin's to Harrisonburg.

At the August court, 1784, Joseph Dictum, William Fowler, and George Snodding reported that they had laid off a road from Harrisonburg to the line of Augusta, toward Staunton, as follows:

> Keeping the old [road] past Edwd. Shanklins and from thence Crossing the North River below Fowlers Still house from thence past Hugh Campbell and past the three Springs leads to a place called the read Banks near the County line.

In an old almanac, for the year 1788, published at Philadelphia or Baltimore, is found the following table of distances on the road from Philadelphia to the Falls of the Ohio:

Martinsburg to	
Winchester to	20 miles
Newtown to	8 "
Stover's town	10 "

ROCKINGHAM COUNTY

  to
 Woodstock 12 miles
  to
 Shanandoah river 15 "
  to
 North branch 29 "
  to
 Stanton 15 "
  to
 North fork J. riv. 15 "
  to
 James river 18 "
  to
 Botetort C. H. 12 "
  [&c.]

A corresponding table of distances, from Winchester to the Falls of the Ohio, is found in "The Virginia and Farmer's Almanac" for 1792, printed and published at Winchester by Richard Bowen. The name "Stephensburg" appears in Bowen's table in place of "Newtown." Bowen styles himself "The North Mountain Philosopher."

In Benjamin Banneker's Pennsylvania, Delaware, Maryland, and Virginia Almanac for 1794, printed at Baltimore, is a table of places and distances on the road from Baltimore to Knoxville, containing the following:

 Harper's Ferry to Charles-Town 12
    to Stone's Tavern 10
    to Winchester 11
    to New-Town 8
    to Stover's-Town 10
    to Woodstock 12
    to Newmarket 8 [18?]
    to Harnet's 15
    to Keesletown 5
    to Ten-Mile Stage 15
    to Staunton 10

to Miller's 12
to Steel's Mill 6[4]

It will be observed that the route indicated in the table just above goes east of Harrisonburg, past Keezletown, to Staunton and places further on. "Harnet" was probably David Harnet, who is frequently mentioned in the old records of the county. Evidently he lived two or three miles east or northeast of Harrisonburg.

As early as 1789 an Act of Assembly was passed for repairing the Swift Run Gap road. In 1809-10 an Act was passed to incorporate it.

The late Capt. J. S. Harnsberger informed me that one of the first roads built into Rockingham County came down from Staunton to Port Republic, and passed thence on the east side of the river down to Swift Run Gap.

Mr. Geo. F. Compton, in his chapters on the early history of Rockingham, says:

From 1790 to 1800 about $3,000 was appropriated to putting the Swift Run Gap Road in order, and this was at that time the main road of the county.

The road to which Mr. Compton refers was doubtless the one going eastward from Harrisonburg, through Swift Run Gap.

A map of the Waterman lands, made in 1795 (and amended in 1811) shows an old "Road from Frankline to Winchester." It came across the Shenandoah Mountain between Tomahawk Mountain and Brush Ridge, and, after coming on eastward to or toward Little North Mountain, went down on the west side of Little North Mountain, through or past Brock's Gap.[5]

[4.] I am indebted to the kindness of Hon. Geo. N. Conrad, of Harrisburg, for the loan of the above almanacs.

[5.] At the time referred to Dr. Asher Waterman of Harrisonburg owned 93,000 acres in what is now West Rockingham and Pendleton. I was allowed to examine the old map above mentioned through the kindness of Mr. A. G. Waterman, of New York, and Mr. Ed. C. Martz of Harrisonburg.

ROCKINGHAM COUNTY

In the *Rockingham Register* of October 5, 1876, I find a statement that in 1826, and thereabouts, the Keezletown Road was the principal thoroughfare of this part of the Valley.

In 1827-8 and in 1836-7 Acts were passed by the Assembly authorizing the Rockingham County court to make contracts for repairing the Dry River Gap road.

In 1829-30 an Act was passed to incorporate the Warm Springs and Harrisonburg Turnpike Company; the next year the Harrisonburg and Thornton's Gap Turnpike Company was incorporated; and in 1832-3 the powers of the court were enlarged for the purpose of opening roads from Harrisonburg to Charlottesville.

In March, 1834, an Act was passed providing for the construction of a road from Skidmore's Fork, in Rockingham, to South Fork, in Pendleton.

In the same month and year the Act was passed authorizing the construction of the Valley Turnpike, from Winchester to Harrisonburg; and about two years later another Act was passed granting a charter for the Harrisonburg and Staunton Turnpike. These two roads, which soon became one, have since become celebrated, and for two or three generations have constituted the main highway of the Valley. Trotter's stages, Jackson's Foot Cavalry, and Miss Mary Johnston's "Long Roll," as well as the pathfinders of the national automobile highway, have found it good and have left it more famous.[6]

In 1849 an Act of Assembly authorized the spending of a sum of money, not to exceed $333, for the purpose of finishing and improving the mountain part of the road from Harrisonburg, through Brock's Gap, to Moorefield.

In 1850 the Rockingham Turnpike Company was authorized to build a macadamized road from some point at or near Stanardsville, via Swift Run Gap, to some point on the Valley Turnpike. The point chosen was Harrisonburg, and

---

6. For more particulars concerning this road see Wayland's "German Element," pp. 209-212.

the road has been an important highway across the eastern part of the Valley ever since. It has been out of private control for a number of years.

In March, 1851, the Harrisonburg and Franklin Turnpike Company was incorporated.

January 15, 1867, an act was passed authorizing the Warm Springs and Harrisonburg Turnpike Company to charge a toll of three cents on all persons walking over the bridge at Bridgewater. The writer well remembers the first information he had of this provision. It was received about nineteen years ago, this month or next, shortly after he had become a citizen of Rockingham and a resident of Bridgewater. But he has a shrewd suspicion that some of the older residents of the town have not known of it until this day.

In the *Rockingham Register* of January 9, 1868, the following notice appeared concerning the stage lines on the Valley Pike:

> The old and well-known stage line of Trotter & Bro., in the Shenandoah Valley, is now making its regular trips between Staunton and Winchester, twice daily, (Sundays excepted). . . . . the stages leave Staunton and Winchester in the morning as well as in the evening. . . .
> Jos. Andrews, Agt.

Trotter & Bro. co-operated at Staunton with Col. M. G. Harman, who was also a famous master of travel.

In February, 1868, it was announced that Trotter & Co.'s daylight line between Staunton and Winchester had been taken off, owing to a decrease in travel; and that the night line had been quickened. In 1870, after the railroad had come in from Strasburg to Harrisonburg, the Trotters were still operating their stages as connecting links between Staunton and Harrisonburg, at one end, and between Strasburg and Winchester, at the other.

In March, 1868, the editor of the *Register*, evidently having in prospect the completion of the railroad to Harrisonburg, advocated a wagon road from Harrisonburg to Franklin. He says:

> We once had a charter for a road from this place to Franklin, but

ROCKINGHAM COUNTY

through the neglect of those interested and squabbles about routes, the whole thing went down, and we are yet without this necessary and important highway.

At the June court, following, Peter Paul was appointed to confer with the authorities of Pendleton regarding the repairs of a road leading across the Shenandoah Mountain, into Pendleton, and to make report. From time to time the road between the two county-seats (Harrisonburg and Franklin) has been improved, and Harrisonburg has been the chief depot on the railroad for the citizens of Pendleton for many years. About 1907 the road across the mountain, for a distance of four miles,—from Dry River to the top of the Shenandoah Mountain,—was made better than ever before. Joseph G. Myers was surveyor, Hoover & Andes were the contractors. The road from bottom to top was put on a grade of $3\frac{3}{4}$ degrees; the old road at some points had a grade of 9 degrees.

Attention has already been called to the fact, in Chapter VIII, that the great material revival in Rockingham in the half dozen or more years following 1865 consisted in large measure in the building of roads—opening new ones and improving old ones. Generally, this road-making may be accounted for as part and parcel of economic reconstruction; particularly, it is explained by the completion of the railroad to Harrisonburg in the winter of 1868-9. The coming of the railroad stimulated the building and improving of wagon roads.

In September, 1868, a new road from Port Republic to Harrisonburg was surveyed by Harnsberger & Kemper, who thus reduced the distance to $10\frac{1}{2}$ miles,—$1\frac{1}{2}$ miles less than by any old road. An incident of the enterprise was the sending up of rockets one night at Harrisonburg, to enable the engineers to get the exact bearings of the course. But let no one innocently suppose that this road was or is straight. The Valley Pike, the Keezletown Road, the Middle Road (passing Linville, Timberville, etc.), and other roads that run up and down the Valley, parallel with the ranges of mountains and the ridges of hills, follow courses generally direct, and are quite straight for considerable stretches; but the roads that cross the Valley, either at right angles or obliquely, are not straight, and cannot easily be made so.

In July, 1869, Bonds & Mauzy began to advertise a new stage line, running from Harrisonburg to Shenandoah Iron Works on a tri-weekly schedule. This line was opened largely as a result, no doubt, of the completion of the railroad to Harrisonburg.

January 22, 1870, the Harrisonburg and Rawley Springs Turnpike Company organized, making Wm. H. Hamrick president, and David A. Heatwole[7] secretary and treasurer. The directors were Abram Andes, Reuben Swope, Hugh Swope, John Brunk, and Maj. Thos. Shumate. The same day a road meeting was held at Mt. Clinton, looking toward the construction of a turnpike. The pike now connecting Mt. Clinton with Harrisonburg is a much-used road.

In February, 1871, Robert S. Jones began building (or rebuilding) the bridge across North River, on the Valley Pike above Mt. Crawford. The flood of the preceding autumn had destroyed nearly all the bridges in the county. The rebuilding of others is chronicled in other connections.

In 1871 the Virginia legislature granted a charter for a graded road from Rawley Springs to Bridgewater; but one of the commissioners, writing in 1873, intimated that his board had failed to carry out the project for the reason, as he said, that they could not decide where to locate the bridges over

---

7. David A. Heatwole was born in Rockingham, March 9, 1827. He was a man of influence and enlightened public spirit. He served a term as county supervisor for Central District, and frequently as assessor of real estate. For 25 years he was president of the West Rockingham Mutual Fire Insurance Company (organized 1872), and for about the same period was president of the Rawley Springs Turnpike Company. He encouraged the young men of his community in educational and literary work, and was himself a writer and investigator of no mean ability. For further particulars see Heatwole Family History, page 200, and Hardesty's Encyclopedia, Rockingham edition, pp. 409, 410. He died at his home near Dale Enterprise, March 29, 1911.

General View of Harrisonburg (Looking North)

Mr. R. Mauzy at site of Salyards' School
(Page 289)

Singer's Glen High School

Orphans' Home, Timbervile
(Pages 313, 314)

Old Flk Run Church (Page 264).
Photo by Hammers

The Blosser Hatchery, Dayton (Page 372)

ROCKINGHAM COUNTY

Dry River. He declared that the river so often changed its channel that the commissioners were fearful lest any bridge they might erect should in time be left on dry land.

In February, 1872, Acts of Assembly were passed incorporating the Bridgewater and Mt. Crawford Turnpike Company and the Bridgewater and Rawley Springs Turnpike Company. Among the directors of these companies were J. W. F. Allemong, G. W. Berlin, and Dr. J. G. Minor. Neither of the turnpikes contemplated in these Acts were constructed.

It was announced in May, 1873, that "a new and comfortable coach called the Mountain Rover" had been put upon the stage route from Harrisonburg to Shenandoah Iron Works. This line of stages was still in operation the following August. Whether it survived the financial crash of September or not is not known. In July, 1874, Jos. B. Moyers was advertising a new stage line, on a tri-weekly schedule, from Harrisonburg to Roadside and Newman's Cave, at the base of the Blue Ridge, in East Rockingham.

One of the well-known roads of Rockingham is the "Lawyer Road," so called after Gabriel Jones, the famous lawyer. He had it cut through the woods, it is said, as a "near cut" to the county-seat at Harrisonburg. It begins at Bogota, the Jones homestead, on the river near Lynnwood, and comes out on the Rockingham Turnpike at Roudabush's Mill, on Cub Run.[8] Crossing the Shenandoah Mountain, from the Feed Stone on Dry River, above Skidmore's Fork, is an old trail known as the Lawyers' Path. This is probably so called because the lawyers crossing from Harrisonburg to Franklin, and vice versa, used it.

In June, 1878, the bridge on the Valley Pike, across North River above Mt. Crawford, was again being rebuilt. It, with a number of other bridges in the county, had been carried away in the great flood of the preceding November.

In 1877-8 Judge O'Ferrall issued orders in the Rockingham County court directing the road boards of Stonewall and

---

8. For interesting sketches of the Lawyer Road, see *Rockingham Register*, January 23, 1874, and May 3, 1888.

Central districts to take charge of, repair, and keep in order the Rockingham Turnpike, the said road evidently having been abandoned by the company.

In 1891 a bridge was being erected over the Shenandoah River at Island Ford, East Rockingham.

In 1911 or 1912 that part of the Harrisonburg and Warm Springs Turnpike lying in Rockingham was taken over by the county.

One of the unmistakable signs of progress at the present is to be found in the construction of fine macadamized roads, by co-operation of local and State forces, in various parts of the county. It costs money to build good roads, in Rockingham as well as elsewhere; but we are learning that they are a good paying investment, worth as much here as anywhere else.

Referring now to the railroads in Rockingham County, we shall take up first those that have actually been constructed, namely, (1) the one coming up the Valley on the west side of the Massanutten, and passing through Strasburg, Woodstock, Broadway, Harrisonburg, and Staunton; (2) the one coming up the Valley on the east side of the Massanutten, and passing through Shenandoah City, Elkton, Grottoes, and Basic City; (3) the one crossing the Valley from Elkton, through Harrisonburg, Dayton, and Bridgewater. Having spoken of these, we shall next present a few facts regarding certain railroads that have been projected, but not constructed, as yet.

(1) "Under an Act of the Virginia Legislature, passed March 9, 1850, which provided for the organization of a corporation under the style of Manassas Gap Railroad Company, 'for the purpose of making a railroad from some convenient point on the Orange and Alexandria Railroad, through Manassas Gap, passing near the town of Strasburg, to the town of Harrisonburg, in the county of Rockingham,' and subsequent Acts, construction was begun at a connection with the Orange & Alexandria at Manassas, and the line was opened from Manassas to Strasburg in 1854. As indicated

ROCKINGHAM COUNTY

above, the original charter of the Manassas Gap required the company, after crossing the mountains, to extend its line down the Valley of Virginia to Harrisonburg, but the line in the direction of Harrisonburg was not destined to be opened until after the war."

In 1858 the Manassas Gap road had already been surveyed past Broadway, to Harrisonburg; and another railroad had been surveyed through Brock's Gap, to connect Broadway with a proposed line of the B. & O. on the South Branch of the Potomac. In February, 1861, an Act of Assembly was passed authorizing the county of Rockingham to issue bonds for a sum not exceeding $100,000, to be loaned to the Manassas Gap company for the purpose of completing the road to Harrisonburg.

"During the Civil War the Manassas Gap Railroad was entirely wrecked, its rails and rolling stock being carried away for use in other parts of Virginia, where they could better facilitate military movements. The Orange & Alexandria, while it did not suffer the same fate, was, however, left in a condition which demanded a practical reconstruction. It was accordingly proposed that the two properties should be consolidated the better to carry out their common purpose, and an Act passed February 14, 1867, which recited an agreement negotiated between the Manassas Gap Railroad Company and the Orange & Alexandria Railroad Company for consolidation, upon condition that the Orange & Alexandria Railroad Company should reconstruct the Manassas Gap Railroad within two years from February 14, 1867, and should assume the debts of the Manassas Gap Railroad Company, authorized such consolidation under the style of Orange, Alexandria & Manassas Railroad Company."

Rockingham County took $150,000 worth of stock in the Manassas Gap company, which was turned into the consolidation of the O. & A. and M. G. railroads in 1867.[9]

On December 11, 1868, the first passenger train ran into

---

9. The *Rockingham Register*, February 28, 1867.

A HISTORY OF

Harrisonburg.[10] From that date, or shortly afterward, regular travel and traffic began. According to a schedule of the O., A. & M. railroad, between Harrisonburg and Alexandria, advertised in the *Register* of October 14, 1869, passengers could leave Harrisonburg at 9:45 a. m., daily, except Sunday. Samuel Ruth was superintendent of transportation; J. B. Gentry, general ticket agent.

"Under date August 20, 1873, the Washington City, Virginia Midland & the Great Southern Railroad Company leased to the Baltimore & Ohio Railroad Company the line between Strasburg and Harrisonburg, and the Baltimore & Ohio continued in possession of this line under the lease referred to until after the reversionary interest therein had passed to the Southern Railway Company, when on March 1, 1896, default was made in the payment of rental; and subsequently on November 30, 1896, the receivers of the Baltimore & Ohio surrendered the line to the Southern Railway Company, the successor of the Virginia Midland Railway Company which had acquired the property of the Washington City, Virginia Midland & Great Southern Railroad Company."[11]

April 4, 1866, a great meeting was held in Staunton, composed of delegates from Roanoke, Botetourt, Rockbridge, Augusta, Rockingham, Shenandoah, Berkeley, and Alleghany counties and Richmond City, to organize the Valley Railroad Company. Col. M. G. Harman was elected president, with eleven directors.[12]

The Valley Railroad Company was chartered in 1868, to construct a railroad from Harrisonburg to Salem (in Roanoke County).[13] In 1872 that part of the road between Harrison-

---

[10]. The *Old Commonwealth*, December 16, 1868.

[11]. The paragraphs quoted are from a letter written to the author, October 14, 1911, by Pres. W. W. Finley, of the Southern Railway Company.

[12]. *Rockingham Register*, April 13, 1866.

[13]. From letter of Sept. 2, 1911, by C. W. Woolford, secretary, Baltimore, Md.

ROCKINGHAM COUNTY

burg and Staunton was under construction. On March 3, 1874, the cars went from Harrisonburg to Staunton for the first time.[14] For short periods in 1876 and 1877 traffic was suspended owing to the lapsing of leases, etc.

The present status of the road (or roads) under consideration is this: The part from Harrisonburg down the Valley, past Woodstock and Strasburg, is in the hands of the Southern Railway Company; the part from Harrisonburg up the Valley through Staunton, to Lexington, is in the hands of the Baltimore and Ohio Railway Company.

(2) In the later 60's there was in evidence much organized agitation for the construction of a railroad through Page County and East Rockingham. In 1870 Hon. William Milnes subscribed $60,000 to the project.

The Shenandoah Valley Railroad Company was chartered February 23, 1867, and the work of construction was commenced during the year 1870, but was suspended in 1873, after a considerable amount of grading had been done.

Work was not resumed until the spring of 1879, when the construction of the line from Shepherdstown to Waynesboro was commenced. The progress was such that on December 15th, 1879, the contractors having the work in hand were able to run trains from Shepherdstown to the Shenandoah River, a distance of 42 miles, when track laying was suspended to await the completion of the bridge at Riverton. The Northern Division, then known as the Maryland Division, from Hagerstown to Shepherdstown, including the Potomac River Bridge, was commenced in February, 1880, and finished in August of 1880. In May, 1880, work was begun at Waynesboro also, and track-laying was pushed northward from that point until the junction of the rails was effected near Luray in the spring of 1881.

In tabular form the progress is indicated as follows:—

---

14. Diary of Judge James Kenney.

A HISTORY OF

Date of Schedule	From	To
Dec. 15, 1879	Shepherdstown	Shenandoah River.
May 10, 1880	Shepherdstown	Bentonville.
August 19, 1880	Hagerstown	Bentonville.
Sep. 6, 1880	Hagerstown	Milford—76 miles.
Dec. 20, 1880	Shenandoah	Waynesboro

The road was accepted from the contractors in March, 1881, and on April 18th, 1881, the first through schedule of trains between Hagerstown and Waynesboro was put into effect.

The Atlantic, Mississippi & Ohio Railroad was purchased on February 10, 1881, and reorganized as the Norfolk and Western Railroad Company, by parties having a large financial interest in the Shenandoah Valley Railroad. The extension from Waynesboro to Roanoke was undertaken in June, 1881, and prosecuted with such vigor that the first through schedule of trains between Hagerstown and Roanoke was put into effect on June 19th, 1882.

The promoters of the Shenandoah Valley Railroad, also of the Norfolk and Western Railroad, were mainly gentlemen of Philadelphia and Boston. Mr. Upton L. Boyce, of Boyce, Va., was instrumental in bringing this project to the attention of capitalists, and had much to do with furthering the construction of the road. The chief engineer during the construction was Mr. W. W. Coe.[15]

(3) As early as February, 1870, perhaps earlier, a railroad west from Harrisonburg, past Dayton, Bridgewater, and other places in that course was being agitated. In October, 1872, the people of Harrisonburg voted a corporation subscription of $25,000 to the narrow gauge road proposed—vote 222 for, 19 against. In June, 1873, this subscription was increased to $50,000—vote 171 for, 29 against. R. B. Osberne was chief engineer; P. B. Borst of Luray was president.

---

[15]. For most of the above particulars I am indebted to the kindness of Supt. E. A. Blake, of the Norfolk & Western Railway Company.

ROCKINGHAM COUNTY

November 3, 1873, Judge Kenney wrote in his diary:

Cloudy and warm this morning. Yesterday I walked out to where they have commenced work on the narrow gauge railroad. This road has a sounding name, the Washington, Cincinnatti & St. Louis Railroad. They are working about ten hands and two carts. All the capital they have is the subscription of $50,000 by the town of Harrisonburg.

In August, 1874, the *Register* reported work on the narrow gauge "entirely suspended." In November following it was stated through the same paper that the grading from Harrisonburg to Bridgewater had been completed, and that the whole line from Harrisonburg to Sangerville was ready for the ties and iron. For the next ten years the work was in the main suspended, except for hopeful talk on the part of a few individuals, and occasional digging here and there. In 1892 the project was revived with new vigor. In 1895 the old narrow gauge interests were transferred to the standard gauge Chesapeake & Western, and on June 7 work was begun again at or near the point, south of Harrisonburg, where the Chesapeake-Western now crosses the B. & O. The first rail was laid July 1. The old narrow-gauge grade, properly widened, was utilized at some places.

From January to March, 1895, the sum of $150,000 was subscribed, mainly in Rockingham, conditioned upon the completion of the road from Elkton to Bridgewater. Among the chief promoters were E. C. Machen, W. H. Rickard, J. M. Snell, Jacob Meserole, W. H. Ritenour, and P. W. Reherd. O. H. P. Cornell was chief engineer. On March 23, 1896, track-laying was completed between Elkton and Bridgewater; and on April 28 following the road was opened to traffic between those towns. In 1901 the contract was awarded for the extension of the road from Bridgewater to North River Gap. Its present western terminus is Stokesville, Augusta County. C. A. Jewett is traffic manager; C. B. Williamson is superintendent. These gentlemen have their offices at Harrisonburg.

Now, a few words concerning the railroad projects that have not yet materialized.

A HISTORY OF

It will be recalled that in 1858 a road had been surveyed from Broadway, through Brock's Gap, to the South Branch. In 1873 a company that evidently intended to follow the same route in general was chartered: B. Chrisman, president; Dr. Cootes, Dr. Winfield, and Dr. Williams, directors. The road proposed (through Brock's Gap) was to have connections and extensions reaching from the Atlantic to the Great Lakes, and was to be known in its entirety as the Norfolk, Massanetta, & Toledo Railway.[16] In Feburary, 1883, John Q. Winfield and P. W. Pugh, of Broadway, with A. W. Kercheval of Romney, and others, were promoting the Toledo, Massanutta, & Petersburg Railway.

One of the most interesting projects of the early seventies was the one set on foot by the North River Railroad Company, chartered March 21, 1872, and organized at Bridgewater January 9, 1873. J. W. F. Allemong[17] was made president; D. A. Plecker, vice-president; R. N. Pool, general superintendent; John W. Jacobs, secretary; Dr. Harvey Kyle, treasurer. The directors were G. W. Berlin, J. G. Minor, T. M. Hite, D. A. Plecker, G. H. Dinges, J. W. F. Allemong, R. N. Pool, Harvey Kyle, and J. W. Jacobs. The road was to extend from Bridgewater to Port Republic. The charter required that the part from Bridgewater to Berlinton be put under contract within 90 days. In April the enterprise was purchased by Henry M. Clay of Kentucky, who was reported to

---

[16] *Rockingham Register*, September 19, 1873.

[7] John W. F. Allemong, born at Stephens City, Va., Sept. 5, 1828, son of Rev. John and Hannah Payne Allemong; married Sarah C. Hailman, June 7, 1857; moved to Bridgewater, 1863, and until 1889 was one of the most prominent and enterprising citizens of Rockingham, being a merchant, bank president, director in the Bridgewater Wool Mills, Bridgewater Carriage Works, etc. In October, 1889, he moved to Salem, Va., where he took his accustomed place, as a captain of industry, till his death, Oct. 29, 1904. He was a member of the Methodist Church, and served in various responsible offices therein. He was the father of six children, two of whom survive him: Mrs. Ella V. Strayer, of Harrisonburg, and Mr. John Edwin Allemong, a prominent attorney and business man of Roanoke City.

ROCKINGHAM COUNTY

be ready and able to push it. The narrow gauge, with the long name, was also being boomed at Bridgewater at the same time.

June 18, 1873, ground was broken at Bridgewater for the construction of the N. River R. R. A speech was made by Rev. J. S. Loose; the first shovelful of dirt was thrown by Adam Rader, the oldest resident of the town. In July the second mile was let for construction to Wm. H. Kiracofe. H. M. Clay, general superintendent, had bought 7 acres of land at the northeast end of the town, on the turnpike, and had laid out grounds for depot, car shed, machine shops, round house, etc. In August it was announced that the road was to extend westward to the Ohio River. But in September came Black Friday.

In March, 1872, the Harrisonburg, Bridgewater, and W. Augusta R. R. Co. was incorporated. The road was to begin at or near McGaheysville, pass thence via Harrisonburg to Rawley Springs, thence through or near Bridgewater to some convenient point on the C. & O. Ry.

In 1874-5 D. A. Plecker was proposing to build a narrow gauge railway from Mt. Crawford depot to Bridgewater. In 1876 a bill was passed the Virginia legislature incorporating the Harrisonburg & Orange C. H. Ry. Co. In 1890 a railroad was proposed through Shendun Pass (Brown's Gap); a plan was being considered by business men of Elkton and Harrisonburg for connecting those towns with a railroad; a street railway for Harrisonburg was being considered; and the Harrisonburg & Western Ry. Co. was organized at Harrisonburg, Messrs. J. P. Houck, C. A. Sprinkel, T. A. Long, and Jacob Meserole being the chief promoters.

In 1891 a railroad from Shenandoah City to Harrisonburg was projected; another, from Shendun to Weyer's Cave station (on the B. & O.), was projected and surveyed. In 1892 (February 16) an Act was passed incorporating the Harrisonburg & Bridgewater Electric Ry. Co. In 1895 a charter was issued to the Basic City, Bridgewater, & Western Electric Ry. Co. In 1901 an Act was passed incorporating the Central

A HISTORY OF

Railroad of Virginia, Messrs. Wm. H. Rickard, P. W. Reherd, D. C. Reherd, Herman Wise, John B. Peale, H. B. Miller, and A. A. Chapman being named as incorporators.

It is of interest to notice that three periods of conspicuous activity in promoting and building railroads in Rockingham (as elsewhere) coincided with or shortly preceded the years 1857, 1873, and 1893: years of notable economic crises. In 1873, no less than five different roads were being projected or actually constructed: (1) The one from Harrisonburg to Staunton, opened in 1874; (2) the one through Page and East Rockingham, opened in 1881 (now the Norfolk & Western); (3) the narrow-gauge westward, past Bridgewater, opened as a standard-gauge in 1896; (4) the one from Bridgewater to Port Republic, still in possibility; (5) the one through Brock's Gap, also a possibility only, as yet.

Just when the first telegraph line was put up in Rockingham County is not definitely known; but there was one running into Harrisonburg as early as 1863—perhaps earlier. N. M. Burkholder was in charge of the Harrisonburg office from 1863 to 1865, as appears from an original schedule before me. Additional lines were being constructed, or earlier lines were being restored or repaired, in 1872-3. In 1884 the *Bridgewater Journal* said: "If we cannot get a railroad we *must* have a telephone or telegraph connection with Harrisonburg. A telegraph line will cost $300." The next year a telegraph line was completed between Harrisonburg and Bridgewater. It is needless to say that at present telegraph lines are maintained by all the railroads; and there is a Western Union office in Harrisonburg.

No material improvement has had a more rapid development in Rockingham, or has done more to dissipate provincialism in the county, than the telephone systems. In February, 1893, the Valley Telephone and Telegraph Company was chartered by J. W. Click, C. Driver, N. W. Berry, and others. This company succeeded to the possession of the Rosenberger & Shirley lines, but was soon in competition with the Virginia & West Virginia Telephone Company. In

ROCKINGHAM COUNTY

August, 1895, the Valley Telephone Company, centering in Harrisonburg, had nearly 150 'phones in operation. In 1899 a gentleman from Illinois, widely traveled, who spent a couple of weeks in Rockingham, said there were more 'phones here than in any other section he knew.

In 1897 the Rockingham mutual telephone system was organized. The same year connection by telephone was established between Rockingham and Pendleton, from county-seat to county-seat. January 25, 1898, an Act was passed incorporating the Rockingham Mutual Telephone and Telegraph Company, naming D. B. Showalter, Chas. H. Ralston, J. N. Fries, C. H. Brunk, J. R. Bowman, W. J. Lineweaver, C. N. Strickler, C. D. Wenger, M. A. Layman, J. E. Shaver, J. H. Shirkey, and W. C. Switzer. In April, 1899, the Rockingham Mutual and the Valley Company were consolidated.

In 1901 a long distance line between Harrisonburg and Staunton was completed. In March, 1902, an Act was passed incorporating the Harrisonburg Mutual Telephone Company, naming W. C. Switzer, John A. Switzer, S. B. Switzer, G. R. Eastham, and J. P. Mauzy.

At present there are in the county the following telephone companies: (1) Harrisonburg Mutual, with exchanges at Harrisonburg, Bridgewater, and Weyer's Cave; (2) Rockingham Mutual, with exchanges at Dayton, Timberville, McGaheysville, and Goods Mill; (3) Plains District, with exchange at Broadway; (4) Swift Run, with exchange at Elkton; (5) Mayland, with exchange at Mayland.

CHAPTER XIII.
RACE ELEMENTS AND POPULATION.

Five years ago the conclusion was reached, after an analytical study of numerous facts and figures, that at least 70 per cent. of the people of Rockingham County are of German descent, and bear German names.[1] This conclusion has had rather striking confirmation in an additional experiment just carried through. Lake's Atlas of Rockingham County, published in 1885, contains the names of practically all the heads of families outside of the larger towns, then living in the county, geographically distributed on the large-scale maps of the five districts. By inspection of these names, and by actual count, the following tables have been prepared; and while no absolute accuracy can be claimed for the results, they are believed to be generally reliable. The striking coincidence is to be found in the fact that these figures show a German element in Rockingham of almost exactly 70 per cent. Moreover, if we may be certain of anything in the case it is this, that the number of people of German stock has not been put too high. One is constantly confronted with instances in which names originally German have been changed into forms that are not now recognized as German. For example, the county records contain entries in which Zimmerman is changed to Carpenter; Yager to Hunter; Swartz to Black; etc. In an inspection of names Carpenter, Hunter, and Black would not usually be counted as German; and many similar cases may be cited; hence the probability that one is apt to underestimate the number of German families, rather than overestimate it, from an inspection of the names in their present forms.

---

[1] See the "German Element of the Shenandoah Valley of Virginia," pp. 94, 95, etc.

ROCKINGHAM COUNTY

TABLE OF NUMBERS.

Races	By Districts.					Totals
	Ashby	Central	Linville	Plains	Stonewall	
German	560	360	363	510	256	2049
English	113	80	60	88	116	457
Scotch	61	42	41	34	59	237
Irish	35	24	39	32	33	163
French	19	4	2	1	8	34
Welsh	4	0	1	2	7	14
Dutch	6	2	2	0	0	10
Totals	798	512	508	667	479	2964

TABLE OF PERCENTAGES.

Races	By Districts.					Totals
	Ashby	Central	Linville	Plains	Stonewall	
German	70*	70*	71*	76*	53*	69*
English	14*	16†	12†	13*	24*	15*
Scotch	8†	8*	8	5	12*	8†
Irish	4*	5†	8†	5†	7†	5½
French	2*	4-5	2-5	1-6	2†	1*
Welsh	½	0	1-5	⅓†	1½	½
Dutch	1	⅓*	⅓*	0	0	½†
Total						100

Explanation: * indicates plus; † indicates minus.

A HISTORY OF

The first table above shows the numbers of names of the different races or nationalities found in the different magisterial districts of the county; the second table shows a corresponding distribution, stated in percentages.

It is probable that Shenandoah County is even more largely of German stock than Rockingham; and it will be observed from the tables that the largest percentage of German names in Rockingham has been found in Plains District, the district adjacent to Shenandoah County. The strongest Irish element seems to be resident in Linville District; while Stonewall District, lying next to Eastern Virginia, has, as one would naturally expect, the largest infusion of English names.

Practically all the families and family names now found in Rockingham have been here for several generations, and most of them since the 18th century. This is particularly true of the German names and families. Most of these came up the Valley from Pennsylvania and Maryland prior to 1800. Very few of the recent immigrants from Germany have come to the Valley of Virginia. Most of the Germans that have located in Rockingham in recent years have been the Jews, who now make up an important class of tradesmen in Harrisonburg. So far as known, all of these have come to the county since 1850.

Incidental references, from various sources, show that most, if not all, the nationalities named in the above tables have been represented in Rockingham from early times. In 1749 a Hollander was living in East Rockingham (see page 47). Mrs. Carr says that the Scherdlins, who had a vineyard on the hill east of Harrisonburg a century ago, were natives of France; Valentine Sevier, who came to Rockingham prior to 1750, was of French stock; and the Mauzys, who have been in the county more than a hundred years, are also French. In August, 1781, Evan Evans and Jona. Evans, with William Morriss, were appointed to appraise the estate of Philip Conrod. The Evanses lived in East Rockingham, and evidently were Welsh. One of the earliest Scotch names preserved is that of Hugh Douglas, who received a patent for 175 acres of

ROCKINGHAM COUNTY

land just west of Round Hill, above Bridgewater, in 1750. In 1774-5 John Craig, Wm. McGill, John Eadie, Wm. Campbell, John Murry, Saml. Curry, Alex. Curry, James Laird, and Lachlan Campbell were residents of this section, and they were all evidently Scotch. The name Laird is preserved geographically in Laird's Knob, east of Harrisonburg, and in the village of Penn Laird. William Ewing, a native of Glasgow, father of Henry Ewing, who was many years county clerk, came from Pennsylvania in 1742 and purchased 300 acres of land three miles northwest of Harrisonburg.[2]

As to the Irish, it might be sufficient to call attention to the fact that two of the original justices of Rockingham, John Grattan and John Fitzwater, were likely of Irish lineage. Captains Frazier and Ragan of Revolutionary days were evidently Irish, as were James Gillilan, Thomas Doolin, Patrick Guin, John Guin, Daniel Guin, Darby Ragon, and Hugh Dunahoe, of the same period. In Felix Gilbert's old day-book of 1774-5, "Irish" is written after the name of Robt. Hook. A good many Irishmen came into the Valley about 1857 to 1869, as workers on the railroads. In 1866 Michael Flinn was living in Harrisonburg. The schoolmaster, Hugh Tagart, had died there about 1840. Patrick Kelly, carder and fuller, was in the county in 1844. On July 12, 1894, died, at the age of 78, Patrick Flahavan, who had been an employee of the Valley Railroad ever since its construction, and had been watchman at the bluff south of Mt. Crawford station for nearly 20 years. Main Street of Harrisonburg used to be called Irish Alley. On February 11, 1879, Judge James Kenney wrote in his diary:

E. J. Sullivan, Post Master at this place, died this morning in the 55th year of his age. He was born in Ireland. He has been postmaster here ever since the close of the war in 1865.

Robert Gray, the famous lawyer, who located at Harrisonburg in 1805, was a son of Erin, as were likely the Bryans, or O'Brians, distinguished in both earlier and latter days.

No special catalogue of Englishmen and Germans is

---

2. Memoirs of Virginia Clerks, page 346.

attempted here. They must speak for themselves, and are obviously numerous enough to make themselves heard. It may be a matter of interest in this connection, however, to know that along in the later 60's and early 70's there was a Turn-Verein at Harrisonburg. It was organized about March 1, 1867, with Wm. Loeb president, Jonas Loewenback treasurer, and Adolph Shockman secretary. The qualifications for membership were good moral character and German extraction. Meetings were held weekly, and all proceedings were conducted in the German language.

A few people in Rockingham can still speak traditional German—a dialect of the "Pennsylvania-Dutch"; but the number is becoming smaller every year. German has not been much used for the past fifty years, except in the home talk of certain families.

In October, 1822, the Harrisonburg postmaster advertised a list of letters for 82 persons named. Of these, 30 had names that were unmistakably German; 14 were probably Scotch or Scotch-Irish; 3 were apparently Irish; 5 or 6 were likely English; 2 or 3 were apparently Welsh; the rest were of uncertain character.

The negro race is, of course, largely represented in Rockingham County, though the proportion of negroes here is much smaller than in the adjacent counties east of the Blue Ridge. For example, the number of slaves in Rockingham in 1840 was 1899, in a total population of 17,344, or only about 11 per cent., while at the same time the number of slaves in the four counties of Albemarle, Orange, Madison, and Culpeper made up about 57 per cent. of the whole population. In 1880 the total population of Rockingham was given as 29,567. Of these, 29,368 were classed as natives, while only 199 were classed as foreign-born. At the same time the whites numbered 26,137; the blacks, only 3430.

At the November court for Rockingham County, in 1880, James Cochran, colored, was a member of the grand jury. In 1874-5 Harrisonburg had a colored policeman, Joseph T. Williams by name, who was also a barber. Williams had

Tutwiler Bust, University of Virginia Library
(Page 308)
Photo by J. S. Patton

ROCKINGHAM COUNTY

been born free, but had served four years in the Confederate army, as a faithful servant. He is said to be at present a well-to-do property owner in Washington City.

Rockingham families are proverbially large. Many of them number their members by the hundred, and some by the thousand, if we extend the circle beyond the county into the States and countries whither they have gone. Looking through the telephone directory of the county, it appears that the Armentrouts, Bowmans, Clines (Klines), Garbers, Goods, Heatwoles, Holsingers, Longs, Millers, Myerses, Rhodeses, and Showalters, are most numerous. The Millers seem to outnumber all the rest. Family histories have been published by the Funks, the Kageys, the Funkhousers, the Heatwoles, the Shueys, the Beerys, the Wengers, the Kempers, the Koiners, and others; and genealogies of the Pences, Kaylors, and other families are known to be in preparation.

In an old ledger of the *Rockingham Register*, covering the years 1857-1868, there are under the M's 118 names; and, of these, 34 are Millers, 8 are Myerses or Moyerses, 6 are Martzes. Under the N's are 20 names, 6 being Niswander and 4 Nicholas. There are 138 names that begin with H, 9 being Huffman, 6 Heatwole, 6 Hopkins, and 5 Harnsberger. And there are 186 names that begin with S, among which are 14 of the Smiths, 11 of the Showalters, 9 of the Shavers, 7 of the Sengers, and 5 of the Stricklers.

John Detrick, who lived near Greenmount in the early part of the last century, had 13 children. They all grew up, all married, and all had grandchildren before they died. Thirteen may be an unlucky number in some places, but not in Rockingham.

In conclusion, a few words about the longevity of Rockingham people. In February, 1841, died Henry Hammer, aged 88, who had been a soldier in the Indian wars and in the Revolution. In 1868, at Fort Lynne near Harrisonburg, died Martin Burkholder, aged 91; at the same place, in 1898, his son John Burkholder died, at the age of 89. In June, 1874, Mrs. Katie Shepp, living in the Massanutten Mountain near Keezletown, reached the age of 120. Her husband had been a wagoner in the Revolutionary war. She, at the age of 20, had married him in 1774.[3] In 1885 Wm. G. Thompson died at Timberville, aged 86 years and 7 months. February 17, 1894, George Kiser died at Mt. Crawford, aged over 92. He had been born in Mt. Crawford in 1801, and had been a merchant, a miller, and a tanner. June 8, 1895, Elizabeth Funk (*nee* Meliza), a native of Rockingham, died in Harrison County, Mo., aged 92 years, 8 months, and 14 days. In 1897 John R. Funk died in Harrison Co., Mo., aged nearly 89. He had been born near Turleytown, Rockingham Co., Va., in 1808.

In June, 1898, Mrs. Margaret D. Effinger, of Staunton, a daughter of Judge Daniel Smith, of Rockingham, revisited Harrisonburg, at the age of 89. In 1898 Mr. John C. Wetzel, who was born in McGaheysville in 1802, was still living in that village. One of the present hale citizens of McGaheysville is Mr. Richard Mauzy, aged 88. He was a pupil in Joseph Salyards' McGaheysville school in the later 30's. At Frankfort, Indiana, lives Capt. Wm. N. Jordan, a native of Rockingham, at the age of 92. On July 25, 1912, at the reunion of the Funk family in Singer's Glen, Messrs. Samuel Funk of Tennessee and John Funk of Virginia, two hale sons of Rockingham, were present; the latter aged 90, the former aged 93.

---

[3]. The *Old Commonwealth*, July 16, 1874.

CHAPTER XIV.

CHURCHES AND RELIGIOUS LIFE.

In the following pages a sketch, largely in tabular form, is given of each denomination in the county. The several sketches are arranged in alphabetical order, according to the respective headings.

BAPTIST CHURCH.

Baptist Churches in Rockingham (1912).

1. Bridgewater: Constituted 1873; Sundayschool organized 1878.
2. Broadway: Constituted 1892.
3. Harrisonburg: Constituted 1869; present church erected 1886.
4. Mt. Crawford: Constituted 1841. The church originally stood on the east side of the Valley Pike, just at the north end of town; the present church is located near Mt. Crawford Station (North River).
5. Riverview: Near Cootes' Store; constituted 1908.
6. Singer's Glen: Constituted 1876; present church dedicated 1888.
7. Turleytown: Constituted 1859; present church dedicated July 12, 1885.

The following paragraphs are copied from a valuable paper recently prepared by Dr. C. S. Dodd, who for several years past has been a zealous worker in the Baptist churches of northern Rockingham.

As early as 1743 the English settlers had established a Baptist church at Mill Creek (now Page County), and on August 6, 1756, Linville and Smith Creek churches in Rockingham County were constituted.

Linville Creek was disturbed by the Indians in 1757, and

received such cruel treatment that many of the members fled to Eastern Virginia for safety; so some time elapsed before the remnant had service again.

Foremost of these Baptists who came to Rockingham as missionaries was Elder John Koontz, whose brother had preceded him to Rockingham a few years. He and Elder John Alderson, Sr., were preaching here about the same time. This being a new doctrine, it met with opposition from many quarters. Mr. Koontz was severely beaten on several occasions for preaching this faith.

Another co-laborer was Elder Andrew Moffett, who also suffered for this cause as a malefactor and was committed to jail; nor was he the last of his family to be persecuted for his convictions; for Rev. John Moffitt, who fell by the hand of an assassin in 1892, because of his stand against the saloon in the city of Danville, was a relative.

Linville Creek ordained Elder John Alderson, Jr., in 1775, and for two years he served the church as pastor. He then moved to Greenbrier County (now in W. Va.), where he was destined to do a work that few men accomplished.

Conspicuous among the Rockingham Baptists stood the life of Elder John Ireland for being maltreated by the Established Church. He was sent to Culpeper Jail for preaching without a permit. In prison there he suffered many things. From 1838 to 1842 the Baptist church throughout the South was torn asunder over missions. One wing, self-styled Old School, or Primitive Baptist, was and still is anti-missionary in spirit; protests against Sunday school as being without scriptural support, does not have any salaried ministers, etc. This body now separated from the church, causing much confusion and contention over church property. The other body was afterwards known as Regular, or Missionary, Baptists.

When the division was made (about 1840) the Old, or Primitive, Baptists had churches located in this county as follows: one near Dayton; Linville Creek; Mt. Pleasant; and Runions Creek; the latter two being in Brock's Gap. At the time of this writing the Runion Creek Church, in Brock's

ROCKINGHAM COUNTY

Gap, which has a small membership, with Elder Reuben Strickler of Page County as pastor, is the only surviving church of this faith in this county.

Rev. John E. Massie and Rev. V. L. Settle were the first Missionary Baptists to visit this county, and they awakened the missionary spirit in the remnant; and then soon Mt. Crawford, Linville Creek, and Turleytown churches were organized as Regular Baptist churches. Mr. Massie moved the old Linville Creek Church from near Green Hill to a far more convenient site, where it now stands, and for this he was sued in the Rockingham Court by one of the trustees. Mr. Massie plead his own case, and Mr. Jacob Myers, who was present, quotes him as saying: "I admit I moved the building, but I beg to state that I placed it in a more convenient place where more people can and will attend services." He won his case.

Turley Town may truly be called the mother church, since Singers' Glen, Broadway, Cootes' Store (River View), also North Mill Creek and South Mill Creek, of Grant County, W. Va., are her offspring, and many churches in the far west now have in their membership those who joined Turley Town before leaving this state. The first fruits of the evangelical work of these missionaries were Timothy, Solomon, Benjamin, and John Funk, sons of Joseph Funk, a Mennonite layman of Singers' Glen. All except John were called to the ministry of the churches, and for many years they preached in the county and elsewhere. They were lovers of music and taught it as well as preached the Gospel. Rev. Timothy Funk for more than 50 years taught music and preached, going as far east as Orange County, Va.

Mr. Joe K. Ruebush of Dayton has located the site of the Primitive Baptist Church at that place. It stood just out of town, toward the southwest, near the point where the railroad now crosses the Warm Springs Pike.

Silas Hart, a native of Pennsylvania, high sheriff of

A HISTORY OF

Augusta in 1764, and senior justice of Rockingham in 1778, was a Baptist.[1]

The regular Baptist churches in Rockingham now have a total membership of about 600; while there are in the county about 60 primitive Baptists.

BRETHREN CHURCH.

Since about 1882 there has been an organization of the Brethren Church (Progressive Dunkers) in Rockingham. They at present have four houses of worship: One in Dayton; Bethlehem, a mile and a half southwest of Harrisonburg; Mt. Olive, near McGaheysville, and one at Arkton, east of Tenth Legion.

Bethlehem was dedicated in February, 1894, by Eld. E. B. Shaver; John Thompson, Lee Hammer, and J. H. Hall being the building committee.

Among the pioneers of this church in Rockingham were Eld. E. B. Shaver, of Maurertown, Va., and S. H. Bashor. A history of the denomination at large was published in 1901 by Eld. H. R. Holsinger, of Lathrop, Cal. The membership in Rockingham is about 350.

CHRISTIAN CHURCH.

Christian Churches in Rockingham (1912).

1. Antioch: A mile and a half south of Greenmount; organized by Rev. I. N. Walter about 1832; present house erected in 1880.

2. Bethlehem: At Tenth Legion; admitted to conference in 1851; original deed dated Sept. 21, 1844.

3. Linville: Organized June 10, 1871, by Rev. D. A. Long; dedicated 3d Sunday of January, 1873.

4. Concord: Organized in 1891 by Rev. E. T. Iseley; house built in 1893. Located 3 miles north of Tenth Legion.

5. New Hope: Three miles southeast of Harrisonburg; organized in 1895 by Rev. E. T. Iseley; house built in 1896.

---

[1]. See Waddell's Annals of Augusta, pp. 204, 238; Semple's History of Virginia Baptists, 1810 edition, p. 192.

ROCKINGHAM COUNTY

6. Bethel: Four miles northwest of Elkton; organized August 25, 1896, by Rev. J. W. Dofflemyre; house built in 1899.
7. Beulah: Five miles southeast of Harrisonburg; organized in 1898 by Rev. W. T. Herndon; house built in 1899.
8. Mayland: Organized in 1899 by Rev. W. T. Herndon; house built in 1900.
9. Mt. Olivet. Two miles southwest of McGaheysville; organized in 1899 by Rev. W. T. Herndon; house built in 1900.
10. Island Ford: House built in 1905.

For most of the facts embodied in the foregoing statements regarding the Christian Church in Rockingham, I am under obligation to Rev. A. W. Andes, of Harrisonburg. He has also supplied a list of ministers, which will be found in the Directory at the end of the volume.

Mr. C. O. Henton of Harrisonburg has loaned the deed made in 1833 at Antioch. This deed is before me. It bears date of May 4, 1833, and is signed by Martin Croomer, who made his mark. It conveys a lot containing 10,848 square feet of land to John Kratzer, Sr., John Higgens, Peter Paul, Martin Burkholder, and Jacob Burkholder, Jr., trustees, for the use of the Christian Church and all other religious denominations that might obtain consent of the trustees to preach there. The lot was bounded as follows: Beginning on the lands of the said Martin Croomer, near the residence of Martin Burkholder, at a stone where there was formerly a white oak, corner made for the school house lot, by the said Martin Croomer and Molly his wife, in the year 1810, thence with the patent line S. 10 degrees W. 113 feet to a walnut, thence S. 80 degrees E. 96 feet, crossing the big road to a white oak, thence N. 10 degrees E. 113 feet to intersect the line of the school house lot, thence with the said line N. 80 degrees W. 96 feet to the beginning.

The consideration was one dollar; and a building was already erected on the land. Daniel Bowman, Jacob Burkholder, Jr., and David Lawman signed as witnesses.

From the published minutes of the Valley Christian Con-

A HISTORY OF

ference, held in Edinburg, Shenandoah County, and Antioch, Rockingham County, in August, 1869, it appears that Antioch and Bethlehem in Rockingham were represented.

The following items have been gleaned from the files of the *Rockingham Register:*

In June, 1866, a new Christian church was dedicated at Cedar Grove, 2½ miles from Harrisonburg. This must have been in the vicinity of the present New Hope Christian Church.

In August, 1868, the Valley Christian Conference met at Bethlehem. John Burkholder presided; and the following Rockingham churches were represented: Antioch, Bethlehem, and Cedar Green (Grove).

At the organization of the Linville Church in 1871, Rev. D. A Long presiding, DeWitt C. Beery was secretary, H. C. Beery was treasurer, and A. R. Rhinehart, John C. Williams, and H. C. Beery were deacons. The building committee was composed of Col. E. Sipe, Isaac Stone, John C. Williams, Harvey Simmers, John Fridley, and D. C. Rhinehart.

In November, 1874, Eld. Benj. Seever, of the Christian Church, "who used to preach in this part of Rockingham from 1843 to 1849," visited Harrisonburg.

On April 3, 1877, died David Ralston, aged 74, who had been "for more than thirty years a member of the Christian Church at Antioch."

On January 24, 1897, the Christian Church east of Harrisonburg, at Mt. Vernon school house, E. T. Iseley, pastor, was dedicated. This evidently refers to New Hope.

The membership of the Christian Church in Rockingham at the present is about 700.

CHURCH OF THE BRETHREN.

Church of the Brethren (Dunker) Church Houses in Rockingham (1912).

1. Garber's: "The Old Meeting House"; two miles west of Harrisonburg; built about 1820; rebuilt recently.

—248—

ROCKINGHAM COUNTY

2. Linville Creek: One mile east of Broadway; house built in 1828 or 1830.

3. Beaver Creek: First minister, John Brower; Martin Miller made elder April 5, 1855; house burned June 13, 1869; new church used for communion meeting Nov. 13, 1869.

4. Mill Creek: Congregation organized in 1840, Isaac Long (1815-1895) and Daniel Yount being present; new house erected in 1860.

5. Greenmount: Built in 1859; rebuilt 1898. In 1872 at Greenmount died Benj. Bowman, aged 87 years, who had been a minister for 50 years.

6. Pine Grove: Two miles northeast of Linville; built about 1850.

7. Plains: A union house, the Brethren having precedence on fourth Sundays; a schoolhouse as early as 1827; present building erected 1857.

8. Bridgewater: Built in 1878. In September, 1892, Eld. Solomon Garber died near Bridgewater, aged over 80.

9. Dayton: House built in 1851 by the Lutherans, and used by them, the Methodists, and the United Brethren prior to 1861.

10. Timberville: House completed in 1879. The first Dunker meetings in Timberville began about 1820 in John Zigler's barn; his brick house, built in 1832, was arranged for meetings.

11. Mt. Olivet: Three miles northeast of Cootes' Store. On Lake's map (1885) a Dunker church is shown at this point.

12. Montezuma: Old schoolhouse, used as a church for a number of years.

13. Fairview: Two miles north of Mt. Clinton.
14. Fairview: Two miles northeast of Tenth Legion.
15. Newdale: One mile north of Tenth Legion.
16. Bethel: At Mayland.
17. Cedar Run: Two miles west of Broadway.
18. Brock's Gap: Organized in 1895.
19. Oak Grove: Three miles west of Cootes' Store.
20. Mt. Zion: Two miles northeast of Singer's Glen.

A HISTORY OF

21. Melrose.
22. Mt. Pleasant: Near Peale's Cross Roads.
23. Harrisonburg: Mission opened by Eld. P. S. Thomas and others about 1900; church built in 1907.
24. Hinton Grove: Formerly Trinity; present church built at Hinton about 1900.
25. Rawley Springs.
26. Briery Branch.
27. Bridgewater College Chapel: In use since 1884.
28. Pleasant Run: Near Pleasant Valley.
29. Sunnyside: Two miles west of Port Republic.

The Brush Meeting House was erected in 1843, west of Broadway, and an old church used to stand near Ft. Hoover.

On May 10, 1798, Martin Garver, certifying a marriage he had performed, subscribed himself as "Minister of the Duch Babtist Susiety."

In 1875 it was stated in the *Register* that there were at that time 35 Dunker ministers in Rockingham County.

Among the leaders of the church in Rockingham, not already named, may be mentioned Peter Nead (1795-1877), John Kline (1800-1864), Samuel H. Myers (1832-1897), and Daniel Hays (1839).

The anti-slavery and anti-war principles of the Dunkers are well known, and they, with the Mennonites, suffered not a little in Rockingham during the civil war by arrest, imprisonment, etc.

The establishment of a school in 1880, now well known as Bridgewater College, has done much to give efficiency and distinction to the work of the Brethren in the Valley of Virginia and adjacent sections. The membership of the church in Rockingham totals about 2500.[2]

---

[2]. For more particulars regarding the Church of the Brethren, the reader is referred to the following publications: Howard Miller's Record of the Faithful; Wayland and Garber's Bridgewater College, Past and Present; Hays and Sanger's Olive Branch; D. H. Zigler's History of the Brethren in Virginia; Two Centuries of the Church of the Brethren, Chapter II.

ROCKINGHAM COUNTY

Church of Christ.

There are two church houses of the Church of Christ in Rockingham, one on E. Market Street, in Harrisonburg, the other in Dayton.

In July, 1871, a Christian church was organized in Dayton, with 16 members, by Rev. D. A. Long. What the connection is between this organization and the present Church of Christ in Dayton is not known. The present church was dedicated July 15, 1883.[3]

The church in Harrisonburg has been opened more recently. The pastor of both churches is Rev. Geo. C. Minor, who lives in Harrisonburg, and who is an active worker in all departments of religious activity. One of the pioneer workers in Rockingham, as well as in Shenandoah and other counties in Virginia, was Rev. J. D. Hamaker, who is still an active leader. His home is in Strasburg.

There are members of the Church of Christ at Lacey Springs, Keezletown, Elkton, and other places in the county, as well as in Harrisonburg and Dayton, the total number being about 150.

Episcopal Church.

Rockingham Parish in Virginia was organized some years prior to the breaking out of the American Revolution in 1776; the exact year is not known, and up to that time was under the charge of the Rev. Mr. Balmaine, with two houses of worship, one at Dayton, and the other close to the present Union Church near Cross Keys.

During the long weary years of that memorable struggle for American independence the parish seems to have declined, and after the close of the war both of the above mentioned houses of worship were neglected and allowed to go to ruin, and for more than sixty years there is no record of any regularly organized religious work being done in the parish by

---

3. It is assumed that the church dedicated in Dayton, July 15, 1883, by the Disciples of Christ was the same as that now known as the Church of Christ.

A HISTORY OF

Episcopalians, although it is very probable that occasional services were held at or near Port Republic.

In 1850 an effort was made to revive the parish, and the Rev. James B. Goodwyn was placed in charge as minister; and after him the Rev. John C. Wheat, Vice-Principal of the Virginia Female Institute at Staunton, Va., preached regularly in the parish at great cost of labor and inconvenience to himself.

In 1865, after the close of the Civil War, the parish was re-organized at Port Republic, Va., with the Rev. John C. Wheat still serving as minister, and on March 8, 1866, a meeting of the members of the parish and other contributors was held in Harrisonburg with Mr. John F. Lewis, one of the old vestry of Rockingham parish, presiding; when the following named gentlemen were elected as vestrymen; General Samuel H. Lewis, John F. Lewis, Samuel H. Lewis, Jr., Andrew Lewis, John R. Jones, Wm. H. Effinger, Frank Boylan, Joshua Wilton, Foxhall A. Dangerfield, Algernon S. Gray, Dr. George W. Kemper, Jr., and Edward H. Stevens. John F. Lewis of Port Republic and Andrew Lewis of Harrisonburg were elected wardens, and Wm. H. Effinger secretary and treasurer. At this meeting the resignation of Rev. John C. Wheat was accepted, and a resolution of thanks for his untiring efforts and Christian zeal in behalf of the Protestant Episcopal Church here was passed and directed to be communicated by the secretary to Mr. Wheat. The next business in order being the choice of a rector, the Rev. Henry A. Wise (son of Henry A. Wise, ex-governor of Virginia) was called, and a notice in due form, signed by the wardens, was directed to be sent to the Bishop of the Diocese. Mr. Wise accepted the call and was duly installed as rector, holding services on alternate Sundays in Harrisonburg and Port Republic, the services in Harrisonburg being held in the second story of a frane building on Main Street just north of what was then known as the Old School Presbyterian Church. This frame building was then owned by Mr. Samuel Shacklett, the lower floor being used as a wareroom. The upper

ROCKINGHAM COUNTY

story was called Shacklett's Hall, where services were held once a month on Sunday afternoons by the Old School Baptists.

In May, 1867, Mr. Wise resigned to become rector of Christ's Church, Baltimore, and the following October the Rev. Thomas Underwood Dudley, Jr. Deacon, afterwards Bishop of Kentucky, was sent by the Right Rev. John Johns, Bishop of the Diocese of Virginia, to minister during his diaconate. From October 1 to December 1, 1867, services were held on alternate Sundays by Mr. Dudley at the points where Mr. Wise, his predecessor, had previously officiated, till, owing to the severity of the weather, the services at Port Republic were discontinued and then held twice each Sunday at Harrisonburg, the vestry having in the meantime rented at $15.00 per month the brick church on North Main street formerly owned and used by the New School Presbyterians (Rev. T. D. Bell, Pastor). This church stood on the ground now occupied by the Post Office and U. S. Court House.

In March, 1868, a vacant lot on the northeast corner of Main and Bruce streets was purchased from Dr. Geo. K. Gilmer for one thousand dollars for the purpose of erecting thereon Emmanuel Protestant Episcopal Church.

In February, 1868, Rev. Dudley, at the request of the vestry, started on a tour through some of the Northern States soliciting funds for the new church building, and succeeded in procuring about $3500. At the same time subscription papers were circulated in the town and throughout the parish, by which means about $1500 was promised, and the ladies of the parish, ever ready and at all times doing their part and doing it well, had already raised some eight hundred dollars. With these several sums of money in hand and promised, the rector and vestry undertook to build the church, and on the 24th of June, 1868, the corner stone was laid with appropriate Masonic ceremonies by Rockingham Union Lodge No. 27 A. F. and A. M., Mr. Joseph T. Logan acting as Grand Master, on which occasion an appropriate and eloquent address was

A HISTORY OF

delivered by the Rev. James D. McCabe, D.D. On the same day the ladies of the congregation held a dinner and fair in the basement of the Methodist church on German Street, from which they realized the handsome sum of six hundred dollars.

Mr. Dudley having tendered his resignation, preached his last sermon on the last Sunday night in December, 1868, using the same text from which his first sermon was taken, viz: "Except ye repent ye shall all likewise perish"; and to the very great regret of his people removed to Baltimore, where he assumed charge as rector of Christ's Church in that city, as the successor to Rev. Henry A. Wise, deceased.

On the first Sunday in 1869, the Rev. John Cosby, having accepted the call of the vestry, preached his first sermon in the New School Presbyterian Church, and on February 7, 1869, he began to hold regular services in the basement of the new church and continued to use that room as a chapel until August 1, 1869, when the first service was held upstairs in the church proper.

The foregoing paragraphs have been copied from a valuable paper, recently prepared, on the Episcopal Church in Rockingham, by Mr. J. Wilton, of Harrisonburg. The rectors at Harrisonburg since 1869, as recorded by Mr. Wilton, are the following:

Alexander W. Waddell, 1870-1875.
David Barr, 1875-1879.
T. Jervis Edwards, 1879-1881.
O. S. Bunting, 1881-1889.
W. T. Roberts, 1889-1892.
O. M. Yerger, 1893-1899.
W. J. Morton, 1900-1902.
Robert U. Brooking, 1903-1908.
Dallas Tucker, 1908-1909.
John L. Jackson, 1910—

Mr. Wilton refers to the old chapel at Dayton. On May 6, 1911, Mr. Joe K. Ruebush pointed out to me the site formerly occupied by this chapel, agreeing with the following,

ROCKINGHAM COUNTY

copied from a letter written September 10, 1912, by Capt. J. A. Herring:

"My grandmother and grand-aunt told me a great deal about the history and people of the early days. [The Herrings were among the pioneers in the Dayton section.] There was an Episcopal chapel near the north end of the graveyard [north side of Dayton]. Under the English rule it was the established church. Parson Bellmain ministered to the people there. When the war of the Revolution came on he went as a chaplain to the army, and never returned. The old people said there was never any Episcopal service there after he left. I can remember the old building, but it was removed long ago."

In East Rockingham at present there are at least four Episcopal churches or chapels: Sandy Bottom, St. Stephens, Rocky Bar, and Grace Memorial. These are in charge of the Rev. J. R. Ellis, who is also doing a splendid work in the adjacent sections of the Blue Ridge in connection with mission schools. Mr. Ellis informs me that the services of the church in this section of the county have been kept up connectedly since colonial times.

A short distance southwest of Port Republic, on a beautiful situation overlooking the river plain and valley bordered with mountains, is Madison Hall, the birthplace of James Madison, first Episcopal bishop of Virginia. His father was John Madison, cousin of President Madison, and first clerk of Augusta County. His mother was a Miss Strother, whose sisters married Thomas Lewis and Gabriel Jones. He was born August 27, 1749, at Port Republic, and died March 5, 1812, at Williamsburg. He graduated at William and Mary in 1772; studied law; was admitted to the bar, but soon turned to theology and teaching. From 1777 to 1812—for 35 years— he was president of William and Mary College. He had at least three brothers, Thomas, Rowland, and George. Thomas, born in 1746, was a captain, and married Susanna, youngest sister of Patrick Henry. George was a governor of Kentucky.[4]

The membership of the Protestant Episcopal Church in Rockingham in 1906 was reported as 163.

JEWISH CHURCH.

The first Jewish families that settled permanently in Rockingham County emigrated from Austria in 1859. Among them were Messrs. Leopold Wise and Herman Heller, who settled in Harrisonburg; Samuel Loewner, who settled in Dayton; and Jonas Heller, who located in Mt. Crawford.

There may have been Jewish settlers previous to those mentioned above, as the early court records of Rockingham County disclose a certain transaction in which it is expressly mentioned that one of the parties thereto was a Jew; but as to when and where they may have settled, we have no knowledge.

When the civil war broke out, Messrs. Albert and Herman Wise, Emanuel Lowner and Jonas Heller enlisted in the Confederate army, serving under General Jackson. After the close of the civil war the Jewish community was increased by a number of emigrants from Germany and Austria, among whom were Messrs. B. Ney and Joseph Ney, Simon Oestreicher, and William Loeb.

These few families met from time to time at the residence of Leopold Wise on W. Market Street for divine services, which were conducted by Samuel Lowner, Adolph Wise, and Simon Oestreicher in accordance with the orthodox ritual. Later the Jewish community organized itself under the name of the Hebrew Friendship Congregation of Harrisonburg, bought ground for a cemetery, and rented a room in the Liskey building, on W. Market Street, which was used

---

[4.] On Bishop Madison, Madison Hall, etc., see: Appleton's Cyclopedia of American Biography, Vol. 4; Tyler's Williamsburg; Waddell's Annals of Augusta, pp. 112, 113; Cartmell's Shenandoah Valley Pioneers, p. 446; Thwaites and Kellogg's Dunmore's War, p. 280; Virginia Magazine of History and Biography, Vol. 13, p. 360.

Bishop James Madison   (Page 255)
From oil portrait in rooms of Virginia Historical Society,
Richmond   Photo by Cook

ROCKINGHAM COUNTY

for a temporary place of worship as well as a Sunday school for the young.

As the Congregation grew in numbers and became more prosperous, more desirable quarters were secured in the Sibert building on Main Street, the ladies began to take an active interest in the congregation by organizing themselves into an Auxiliary Society, and helping to establish a permanent choir, with the result that the services became more impressive and modern in spirit. The first class was confirmed by Major Hart of Staunton, in the new place of worship.

Thus were continued the activities of the Congregation for two decades, Messrs. Samuel Loewner, Adolph Wise, and Simon Oestreicher devoting their time and energy to promote the spiritual welfare of the Congregation.

In 1890 the Congregation began devising ways and means to erect a permanent House of Worship, and with that end in view, a lot was purchased on North Main Street, and a building committee was appointed, with Mr. B. Ney as chairman.

The members were enthusiastic over the new undertaking, and through the indefatigable labors of the building committee, in conjunction with all the members of the congregation, and the Ladies' Auxiliary Society, funds were realized from the proceeds of a fair given in Harrisonburg, to which the people of the different denominations responded liberally. Additional funds were raised by soliciting some of the prominent Jewish congregations of the East for contributions to the worthy cause. When, in 1892, the Temple was dedicated by Dr. Shoanfarber of Baltimore, it was free and clear of debt. It was a gala occasion for the Jewish community of Harrisonburg; the dedicatory services were attended by the Jewish people of Staunton and Charlottesville, and many of the prominent people of Harrisonburg participated in the festivities.

The new Temple stimulated a keener interest in congregational life, yet the community was not large enough to be

A HISTORY OF

able to procure the services of a Rabbi; so Messrs. Adolph Wise and Simon Oestreicher continued to minister to the spiritual needs of the congregation, and it is principally due to the untiring efforts of these two gentlemen that the congregation continued its spiritual activities.

In 1910 the congregation deemed it advisable to procure the services of a Rabbi; accordingly Rev. J. Schvanenfeld of Baltimore was unanimously elected, and since then the congregation has started on its new career.

The religious status of the congregation had remained unchanged during four decades, from the time of its organization; but in pursuance of the Rabbi's advice, the ritual used by all modern American Hebrew congregations was introduced; a new constitution and by-laws, similar to those in vogue in the prominent American congregations, were adopted. The entire congregational machinery was reorganized with the result that the religious life of the congregation has been reawakened. The congregation is conducted by a Board of Managers consisting of Messrs. Adolph Wise, President; Simon Oestreicher, Vice-President; Joseph Ney, Treasurer; V. R. Slater, Secretary; B. Ney, Bernard Bloom, Abraham Miller, Charles Loewener, and Herman Wise. The President appoints the various committees to look after the material welfare of the congregation; the Rabbi looks after the spiritual welfare of the congregation by conducting services on Sabbaths and holidays; preaching to the old, and teaching the young.

The Ladies' Auxiliary Society is also active in commendable work by having a standing committee to look after the poor and the stranger, to whom financial aid and advice are given irrespective of race or creed. The Auxiliary also proves its usefulness in decorating the Temple on special occasions and providing the Sunday school children with entertainments.

The foregoing excellent account of the Jews in Rockingham was prepared for this work by Rabbi J. Schvanenfeld.

In 1877-8 Rabbi Sterne was with the congregation in

ROCKINGHAM COUNTY

Harrisonburg; and in 1883 Rabbi M. Strauss was called to conduct weekly services and teach a school. Neither of these remained long.

In 1906 the U. S. Census Bureau reported 20 Jews, heads of families, in Rockingham; and in 1910 a religious census of Harrisonburg showed a membership of 87 in the Jewish church.

LUTHERAN CHURCH.

Lutheran Churches in Rockingham (1912).

1. Rader's: Near Timberville; organized, by Lutherans and Reformed, as early as 1762; log house replaced in 1806; present church built in 1878-9; in hands of Lutherans since 1881.

On May 20, 1765, Adam Reider and Alex. Painter deeded 3 acres of land for a church to Peter Scholl, in behalf of the Presbyterian church, and to Michael Neice, in behalf of the Lutheran church. Abram Bird was witness. "Presbyterian" in this case is doubtless "Reformed." In 1872 an Act of Assembly was passed making the above deed valid to the Lutherans and Reformed.

2. Friedens: Organized perhaps as early as 1748; still held jointly by the Lutherans and Reformed; the Dinkles, Shanks, Wises, and Hoffmans were among the organizers.

3. McGaheysville: Peaked Mountain Church, built in 1769, and held jointly by the Lutherans and Reformed, stood at or near the site now occupied by the old union church. The latter is said to have been built about 1800 by Nicholas Leap, and to have been dedicated May 25, 1804, by Christian Streit and John Brown; used only by the Lutherans since 1885.

4. St. Peter's: Four miles north of Elkton; perhaps called in early times Lower Peaked Mountain Church; dedicated in June, 1777; remodeled in 1910.

5. Spader's: Near Pleasant Valley; an old church.

6. St. John's: Near Singer's Glen; present house dedicated in 1887.

A HISTORY OF

7. Harrisonburg: Built before the civil war; used as hospital, barracks, etc., during the war; rededicated in 1868: services conducted by Rev. J. I. Miller, assisted by Revs. Snyder, Holland, McClanahan, and Keller, of the Lutheran Church; A. P. Boude, of the Methodist Churh; and S. Funk, of the Baptist Church: Rev. G. W. Holland installed as pastor.

8. Bridgewater: Dates back to 1866 or before; present house dedicated in 1881.

9. Trinity: East of Melrose.

10. Edom: In 1871, a new church, replacing an old one, was dedicated at Edom for the use of the Lutherans, Southern Methodists, and Presbyterians.

11. St. Paul: Two miles north of Tenth Legion.

In 1851 the Lutherans built the church in Dayton now owned by the Church of the Brethren. In Lake's Atlas (1885) a Lutheran church is located on the Back Road, three miles northeast of Cootes' Store. In the same atlas an "Old Dutch Church" is located at Paulington. This may have been Lutheran.

In 1891 Rev. J. P. Stirewalt organized a Lutheran congregation, 37 communicants, near Hupp P. O. This is identified with St. Paul.

Many of the oldest settlers of Rockingham were Lutherans or Reformed, and a number of the first churches were held jointly by these two denominations.

Rev. Geo. S. Klug (see pp. 46, 47) was perhaps the first Lutheran preacher to labor in what is now Rockingham County. Rev. Paul Henkel (1754-1825) doubtless did much work in Rockingham. The Henkel (Lutheran) Press, established at New Market, so near to Rockingham, in 1806, has had a potent and wide influence.

The eminent Joseph A. Seiss, born in Maryland, preached for a year or so in Rockingham about 1842. Two young men who heard him at Friedens and Cross Keys (Union Church) were Peter and Joseph I. Miller, who were born near Mt. Crawford Depot (as now named), the former September 18,

ROCKINGHAM COUNTY

1828, the latter June 2, 1831. Both, having conquered hard fortune in securing an education, entered the ministry in 1858. Both became distinguished as educators and preachers. Rev. J. I. Miller served churches in Clear Spring, Md., Shepherdstown, W. Va., Staunton, and elsewhere. He was the pioneer in the field of higher education for women in the Lutheran Church in the South; founded and conducted schools for women at Staunton, Luray, and Buena Vista. He died February 26, 1912, full of years and honors. His brother, Rev. Peter Miller, having been a teacher and preacher for more than fifty years, is still about his Father's business among his people at Rio, W. Va.

The eminent Dr. C. Armand Miller, now of Charleston, S. C., is a son of Rev. J. I. Miller.

The Lutherans in Rockingham number between 600 and 700.[5]

MENNONITE CHURCH.

Mennonite Churches in Rockingham (1912).

1. Trissel's: Four miles west of Broadway; first house built in 1822; first ministers, Henry Rhodes, Henry Funk, Henry Shank.

2. Pike: First known as Moyers's; located two miles east of Dayton; house built in 1825; first ministers, Fred. Rhodes and Abram Nisewander.

3. Brenneman's: Two miles west of Edom; built 1826; first ministers, Michael Kauffman and Samuel Shank.

4. Weaver's: Two miles west of Harrisonburg; built in 1827; first called Burkholder's; first ministers, Peter Burkholder, Martin Burkholder, and Samuel Coffman.

5. Bank: One mile north of Rushville; first ministers, David Rhodes and John Weaver.

---

[5] In February and March, 1895, and February and March, 1897, articles appeared in the *Rockingham Register* dealing with the early history of Friedens Church. The published address of Gen. J. E. Roller, made October 25, 1897, at Hagerstown, Md., also presents interesting matter concerning it. The *Shenandoah Valley*, New Market, Va., of January 2, 1908, gives an account of St. John's Lutheran Church.

A HISTORY OF

6. Mt. Clinton: One mile west of Mt. Clinton; house built in 1874; first ministers, David Showalter, Jacob Driver, Jos. N. Driver.

7. Zion: Near Daphna Station; house built in 1885; first minister, Samuel Shank.

8. Lindale: Near Edom; house built in 1899; first minister, Henry Wenger.

9. White Hall: House built in 1875.

Services are also conducted at Newdale, Dry River, Peak Schoolhouse, and Gospel Hill. The total membership in the county is about 600.

There were probably three Mennonites at Massanutten as early as 1730 (see pp. 36, 37). One of the three, Michael Kauffman, is likely the man who, as a minister of that name, settled later on Linville Creek. In 1748 the Moravian missionaries found a number of Mennonites at Massanutten (see page 47). The Mennonites were among the earliest settlers, therefore, in what are now Rockingham and Page counties.

Up to about 1840 the Mennonite preaching and singing were exclusively in the German language. In or about 1816 Joseph Funk, of Mountain Valley (now Singer's Glen), a Mennonite, published a music book in German, entitled, "Choral-Music." It was printed in Harrisonburg, and was doubtless one of the first music books printed in Virginia. In 1832 Funk sent out the first edition of "Genuine Church Music," later famous under the title "Harmonia Sacra." In 1847 he opened at Mountain Valley what is said to have been the first Mennonite printing house in America. Ten years earlier he, with Peter Burkholder, had published a large volume on Mennonite history and doctrine.

Although not many of the early Mennonites in Rockingham favored higher education, it is an interesting fact that provision was made from the beginning at Brenneman's and Weaver's for the erection of a schoolhouse on the church lot.

In the Mennonite Church, as in all other churches, there have been occasional differences of opinion that have resulted in separate organizations. In Rockingham, about ten years

ROCKINGHAM COUNTY

ago, a part of the Mennonite church perfected a separate organization, and erected a church a short distance southeast of Rushville. This church is called Pleasant View, and represents what may be termed the Old Order. The house was built in 1902-3, and the membership numbers 90 or 100.[6]

METHODIST CHURCH.

Methodist Churches in Rockingham (1912).

1. Harrisonburg: Organized as early as 1788; church lot donated by Robert and Reuben Harrison in 1789; first church finished in 1794. The Methodist Mission at the north side of Harrisonburg was established in April, 1899.

2. Bridgewater: Organized prior to 1866, since a Methodist church was in Bridgewater in that year.

3. Dayton: Present church opened April, 1899; the organization ante-dates the civil war.

4. Clover Hill: Church dedicated in November, 1886.

5. Spring Creek: Church dedicated June 14, 1885.

6. Rushville: Present church dedicated in December, 1896. The first church there was likely erected about 1858, since on March 3, 1858, an Act of Assembly was passed authorizing the trustees of Gospel Hill meeting house, on Muddy Creek (now Mt. Clinton), to sell the church for the benefit of the M. E. church to be erected within the Rushville circuit.

Churches 2, 3, 4, 5, and 6 constitute the Bridgewater Circuit.

7. Mt. Crawford: Date of organization unknown. There was a union (or free) church in Mt. Crawford as early as 1835.

8. Fairview: Two miles southeast of Mt. Crawford.

Churches 7 and 8 compose the Mt. Crawford Circuit.

---

6. For more particulars concerning the Mennonites in Virginia and elsewhere, the reader is referred to the following: A History of the Mennonite Conference of Virginia and its Work, by L. J. Heatwole, C. H. Brunk, and Christian Good; Hartzler and Kauffman's Mennonite Church History; C. H. Smith's Mennonites of America; the *Rockingham Register*, June 14, 1895, etc.

A HISTORY OF

9. Keezletown: A new Methodist church was being erected at Keezletown in 1869. In November, 1883, a Methodist church, likely the present one, was dedicated.

10. McGaheysville: It is said that a Mr. Bader built a Methodist church in McGaheysville in 1835.

11. Fellowship: Three miles east of Linville.

12. Linville: Church dedicated in September, 1890.

13. Edom.

Churches 9, 10, 11, 12, and 13 make up the Rockingham Circuit.

14. Elkton: Said to date back to 1821, when Conrad Harnsberger and Col. Miller donated 4 acres of land for church site and cemetery, and Wm. Monger hewed the logs and built the church. This house was evidently the same as the famous old Elk Run Church, which stood until recently opposite (north of) Cover's tannery.

15. Mt. Hermon: Two miles west of Elkton; corner stone laid September 22, 1893.

16. Mt. Pleasant: Two miles east of Elkton.

Churches 14, 15, and 16 form the Elkton Circuit.

17. Port Republic: Date of organization unknown. As early as 1835 there was a union (free) church in Port Republic.

18. Grottoes.

19. Timber Ridge: Three miles northwest of Port Republic.

Churches 17, 18, and 19 constitute the Port Republic Circuit.

20. Broadway: Church dedicated in October, 1881.

21. Lacey Springs.

22. Glass's Church.

Churches 20, 21, and 22 belong to the New Market (Shenandoah County) Circuit.

23. Furnace: Four miles northeast of Elkton.

Church 23 belongs to the Shenandoah City (Page County) Circuit.

In the *Rockingham Register* of January 5, 1866, appeared

ROCKINGHAM COUNTY

the statement that Long's school house, which stood on land in the southern part of Rockingham belonging to the heirs of Ephraim Whitmer, and which had been erected some 50 years before (to wit, about 1816), had been used in early days as a church by the Methodists; later, by the United Brethren.

In 1872 the Baltimore Conference, M. E. Church, South, made appointments to the following charges in Rockingham County: Harrisonburg, Bridgewater, Rockingham, E. Rockingham, and Rockingham Mission.

In the latest available census reports, the membership of the M. E. Church, South, in Rockingham County is given as 2560.

The first Methodist church in Harrisonburg, which was also the first in the county, so far as known, stood on the hill west of the county court house, on the site now occupied by the Church of the Brethren. In this house the school established in 1794 under the direction of Bishop Asbury, noticed more fully in Chapter XV, was conducted. The divisions, etc., incident upon the civil war caused certain changes in organization, and the natural course of circumstances has brought about various changes in the construction and location of church houses. At present the Harrisonburg Methodists are just completing a splendid brown-stone church on the west corner of Main and Bruce streets. When the cornerstone of this structure was laid, September 1, 1911, Rev. H. H. Sherman, pastor, read an extended and interesting paper on the history of Methodism in Harrisonburg, which paper was published in full at the time by the local press.

On September 17, 1821, a meeting was held by the official members of the Methodist Church in the Rockingham Circuit, at which the following resolutions were passed:

Resolved that it Shall be the farther duty of the Same Committee [Peachey Harrison, Joseph Cravens, Geo. W. Harrison, Reuben Harrison, and Gerard Morgan] to prepare a petition to the next General Assembly of this State praying that Body to pass a law for the better protection of Camp meetings and that G. W. Harrison be the Chairman thereof.

JOS. CRAVENS,
  Clerk.

LOUIS R. FECHTIG,
  Presiding Elder.

A HISTORY OF

The campmeetings at Taylor's Springs and other places had been much disturbed by disorder, the sale of liquor, etc. On February 19, 1822, the committee reported to the quarterly conference that a memorial had been prepared and forwarded to the legislature.

Says Mrs. Carr:

> The camp meeting was one of the great features at that time. It was looked forward to with even greater pleasure than general muster day. Everybody that could raise money enough to get materials for a tent was sure to be there with their families. A good many would go if they had to stint themselves for months. For many years it was held on Taylor Spring grounds. The water was so good and healthy that many people stayed there all summer to drink the water. George W. Harrison had a nice two-story frame house on the corner of the campground. Those that did not have a tent would go out in the morning to stay all day, and take their lunch along.

From 1815 to 1820, as the old minute book shows, the quarterly conferences for Rockingham Circuit of the Methodist Church were concerned frequently with the question of slavery. According to the rules of the church and a prevailing sentiment, there were persistent efforts to secure the gradual emancipation of slaves belonging to members of the church; and there was evidently a marked disposition on the part of the Rockingham Methodists to make a test on this point with persons applying for membership. About 1816 an elaborate memorial was draw up, addressed to the General Conference in Baltimore, deploring the existence of slavery among members of the church, together with the fact that the General Conference had authorized the Annual Conferences "to make whatever regulations they Judged proper respecting the admission of persons to official stations in our Church!" The memorial concludes:

> Therefore we most ardently desire that the General Conference would adopt some plan that would enable us to look forward to the day when this great evil shall be removed and the Methodist Church shall become the Glory of all the Churches; If nothing better should be thought of, Permit us, to suggest the following plan; That no person shall be admitted to official stations in our Church, Who holds Slaves, without emancipating them when the Laws of the State shall admit of Emanci-

pation, and in case they cannot Emancipate them in the State where they may live, to give the Slave the offer of liberty by going to some of the States that will receive and protect free people of Colour, whenever he or she may choose to go,—

And that all persons coming forward to Join our societies, holding Slaves, shall be informed, that we will take them on trial for Twelve Months, and offer them every information in our power, on the Subject— And if they will submit to the same plan of Emancipation as in the case of Official Members, we will consider them Acceptable Members, of Our Church; But if not, they can have no place among us—

And also that the General Conference, Strongly recommend to all our members, conscienciously to avoid Hiring Slaves, in all cases where it can be dispensed with, as this practice tends Indirectly to incourage that sin which we long to be delivered from.

Another interesting incident connected with the history of Methodism in Rockingham was the formation of the Armenian Union Church, August 12, 13, 1847, at Dry River Church, by Benj. Denton, a minister of the M. E. Church, John L. Blakemore, formerly of the Lutheran Church, and others. Later, Denton and Blakemore seem to have separated; and Denton, endeavoring to get things more to his notion, organized another synod at Dry River Church in 1849. The members of this body were Benj. Denton, ordained preacher; John D. Freed, licentiate preacher; Algernon E. Gilmer, Madison Tyler, and John Denton, delegates. A house was built at Dry River, near the old one, in 1850, and services kept up for some time. The old Dry River Church was originally Methodist. Denton published a little book on his movement.[7]

Presbyterian Church.

Presbyterian Churches in Rockingham (1912).

1. Cook's Creek: New Erection; organized in the 18th century; called "New Erection" because an older establishment was, or had been, at Dayton; second church at New Erection built in 1834; present one in 1912.

---

[7]. I am under obligation to Dr. H. H. Sherman for the loan of old records of the Methodist Church, of books, etc., and for direct information; to Bishop L. J. Heatwole for access to a copy of Denton's booklet, etc., and to Rev. John W. Rosenberger for aid.

A HISTORY OF

2. Harrisonburg: First preaching by Presbyterians said to have been done about 1780; congregation organized in 1789; first church built (on E. Market St.) about 1793; present church erected (northeast side of Public Square) in 1907-8.

3 Cross Keys: For many years a union church; present church erected about 1872.

4. Broadway: Church dedicated June 5, 1870; Rev. T. D. Bell, D. D., organizer and first pastor.

5. Edom: A new church, replacing an old one, was dedicated in 1871 for use of Lutherans, Methodists, and Presbyterians.

6. Massanutten: At Peale's Cross Roads; dedicated in November, 1874.

7. Bridgewater: Congregation organized in June, 1878; church dedicated in December, 1889.

8. Dayton: Replaces Old Erection.

9. Mt. Olive: On Rawley Pike, 9 miles west of Harrisonburg; dedicated January 3, 1897.

10. Elkton.

11. Mabel Memorial Chapel: Two miles southeast of Harrisonburg; dedicated 1899.

It is probable that Presbyterian ministers were sent into this part of Virginia from Pennsylvania prior to 1750. In 1752 the congregations of North and South Mountain, Timber Grove, North River, and Cook's Creek are mentioned in the records of the Philadelphia Synod. In 1756 the Cook's Creek congregation made application to the synod that Rev. Alex. Miller might be sent them as pastor, and in 1757 he came. He was installed as pastor for Dayton (Old Erection) and Peaked Mountain (probably Cross Keys).

The church at Dayton was finally abandoned, apparently for New Erection; and about 1780 the old church was torn down. Later, a dam was built across the creek below, and the waters backed up and spread out until the site of Old Erection, with the graves about it, was lost in Silver Lake.

The following table will not only give interesting information regarding the history of one church, but will also

ROCKINGHAM COUNTY

show how "division and reunion" have been part and parcel of the experiences of Rockingham Presbyterians.

HARRISONBURG PASTORS.

1789-1808—Benjamin Erwin.
1809-1814—A. B. Davidson.
1818-1821—Daniel Baker, D. D.
1822-1826—Joseph Smith.
1827-1837—Abner Kilpatrick.
1837-1839—J. W. Phillips.

1839—DIVISION.

Old School	New School
1840-1850—Henry Brown.	1837-1839—J. W. Phillips.
1853-1856—J. H. Bocock, D.D.	1840-1841—A.H.H. Boyd, D.D.
1858-1867—D. C. Irwin.	1842-1844—T. L. Hamner.
	1846-1867—T. D. Bell, D. D.

1867—REUNION.

1867-1884—John Rice Bowman, D. D.
1885-1887—J. H. Smith.
1887-1892—L. B. Johnson.
1893-1904—E. P. Palmer, D. D.
1905-   —Benjamin Wilson, D. D.

The following description of the little stone church on East Market Street, and of the services held in it, is copied from the manuscript of Mrs. Carr, whose account of Harrisonburg in olden days is of such rare interest.

Next comes the old stone Presbyterian church. The lot on which it was built was taken from Harriet Graham's part of her portion which her father gave her afterwards. John Graham's land furnished the land on which the church was built. The last ten feet on the W. side was where the principal entrance was; there was also a door on the E. and S. ends. My grandfather paid a great deal more than his share towards the erection of this church.

There were four high pews in each corner of the building, each pew having one a foot or two below it. My grandfather's pew was in the N. W. corner, and Sam Henry had one under it. Mr. Scott had the S. W. corner; and I do not remember who had the pew below his, unless it was

A HISTORY OF

the Herrons. The S. E. corner was Dr. Waterman's, with Robert Gray's below his; the N. E. was Mr. Jerry Kyle's. The pulpit was very high, and half way between the E. and the W. on the N. side of the church. Under it, a little distance from the floor, was the enclosure of perhaps six or seven feet where the elders sat. In front of the pulpit stood a man who led the singing, giving out two lines of the hymn at a time, the congregation joining in the singing. The rest of the seats were on a level with the floor. The high pews were entered by doors. The upper part of the pews were of turned balustrades—two steps leading up to the high pews and one step to the low pews.

The communion was administered twice a year; long high benches were placed in the aisles, in front of the pulpit, with clean white linen placed on them; then on either side were low benches for the communicants to sit on. Every communicant brought a small square piece of copper called a token, and when they were seated at the table laid it before him. The elders came around and took them all up; then a solemn hymn was sung beginning, "On that dark and doleful night." The elders after the singing handed around the bread and wine. Afterwards an address was delivered by the preacher, and a few more verses were sung, when those at the table would retire and make room for others: there were usually four or five tables. It was certainly a more solemn ceremony than at the present day.

The Presbyterians in Rockingham at the present time number between 1000 and 1200.[8]

REFORMED CHURCH.

Reformed Churches in Rockingham County (1912).

1. Friedens: Termed a mother church by Gen. J. E. Roller (Hagerstown address, 1897), and indentified with the "New Germantown" visited in 1748 by the eminent Michael Schlatter. Still held jointly by the Reformed and Lutherans. Repaired and rededicated in 1894.

2. St. Michael's: Three miles south of Bridgewater;

[8.] For aid in securing the foregoing information, I acknowledge special obligation to Mr. Milo Custer, Bloomington, Ill., and Dr. B. F. Wilson and Judge George Grattan, of Harrisonburg.

Reference is made to the following publications: Webster's History of the Presbyterian Church in America (Phila., 1857); Custer's Alexander Miller and Descendants; Year Book of the Harrisonburg Presbyterian Church; and files of the *Young Virginian*, published in 1874-5, etc., by Rev. W. T. Price, pastor at New Erection.

ROCKINGHAM COUNTY

organized (as Lutheran or as Lutheran and Reformed) in 1764; house had dirt floor; Rev. Benj. Henkel (Lutheran) said to have been buried under the chancel, about 1794; in 1830 the old log house was remodeled; in 1876 it was torn down, and present brick church was built.

3. Brown Memorial: At McGaheysville; build in 1885, after a separation of the old Reformed and Lutheran congregation.

4. Mt. Crawford: Congregation organized and church built in 1842.[9]

5. Timberville: Cornerstone laid in 1881; church dedicated June 1, 1884; built by the Reformed congregation that had previously worshiped at Rader's Church.

6. Pleasant Valley.

7. Harrisonburg: Congregation organized 1894-5 by Rev. J. S. Garrison; church built in 1897.

The most famous leader of the Reformed Church in Virginia was Rev. John Brown, preacher, organizer, author, reformer, born in Germany, 1771. Having come to America, he began the study of theology at Chambersburg, Pa., in 1798; about the same time he visited the Reformed churches in the Valley of Virginia. In 1799 or 1800 he came to be pastor of the Rockingham churches—walking all the way from Pennsylvania. He labored at St. Michael's, Friedens, McGaheysville, and elsewhere. In 1818 he had a 400-page book printed in Harrisonburg (intended as a "Circular"), in which he advocated Bible societies, foreign missions, freedom, and peace. In 1850 he died at Bridgewater, having served his people 50 years. No wonder they called him Father Brown.

Another beloved pastor was John C. Hensell, who died March 29, 1894, at Mt. Crawford, aged 85. For many years he had preached at Mt. Crawford, St. Michael's, Friedens, McGaheysville, and other neighboring places.

---

[9]. I am indebted to Mr. S. H. W. Byrd, of Bridgewater, for the particulars given regarding St. Michael's Church and Mt. Crawford Church.

A HISTORY OF

The Reformed Church members in Rockingham number about 600.[10]

ROMAN CATHOLIC CHURCH.

There have doubtless been some Roman Catholics in Rockingham from very early times. The present church organization seems to date from about 1865. In this year, perhaps earlier, the Catholics had a chapel in Harrisonburg. In July, 1866, their chapel was on German Street,—a schoolhouse shortly before occupied by Miss Mary J. McQuaide. Father McGuire, of Maryland, and Father Joseph Bixio held occasional services in Harrisonburg in 1865 and 1866. In 1867 a Sundayschool was conducted, and Father Weed of Staunton held services each 4th Sunday. In November, 1867, Right-Rev. Bishop McGill of Richmond preached in Rev. Mr. Bell's (Presbyterian) church in Harrisonburg. Mass was celebrated in the Catholic chapel at 10 a. m., November 5. In the summer of 1873 Father Kane, of Washington or Baltimore, and Right-Rev. James Gibbons,[11] of Richmond, visited Harrisonburg and stimulated the movement for building a church. The *Rockingham Register* of September 5 and October 31 contains lists of names of those persons subscribing to the enterprise. In June, 1876, it was reported that the Catholics had purchased the church formerly belonging to the Methodists. In August following the church was dedicated, Bishop Gibbons preaching the sermon. In the evening Father O'Keefe preached. Special music was furnished by the St. Francis choir of Staunton.

---

10. On Brown Memorial Church, see *Our Assistant*, May, 1899, published at Mt. Crawford; on Father Brown, *Rockingham Register*, March 29, 1895, and March 12, 1897; on St. Michael's Church, the *Register*, April 26, 1877; on Rader's Church, etc., the Harrisonburg *Daily News*, May 22, 1909, supplement.

I acknowledge information received from Mr. S. H. W. Byrd concerning Father Brown.

Rev. J. S. Garrison, of Harrisonburg, is preparing to publish a history of the Reformed Church in Virginia.

11. Now Cardinal Gibbons of Baltimore.

Big Spring, Court Square, as in Olden Days   Photo by Morrison

Normal School Girls at Ashby's Monument (Page 179)

OLDEN DAYS ON COURT SQUARE
Waterman   Kenny   Catholic
House   House   Church [Pages 272, 273]
High Hill at Left site of First Methodist Church [Pages 263, 265]

Asbury Chapel (Page 284)
Gen. Roller's Library
Oldest House in Harrisonburg

Old St. Peter's Church, near Elkton (Page 259)

ROCKINGHAM COUNTY

The church purchased was the one erected about 1863 by the Northern Methodists. It stood on the bank opposite the B. & O. passenger station, on the site now occupied by the large Snell building. For several years, about 1868 and following, it had been used as a place of worship by the Baptists. This church burned in April, 1905, and about a year later the present handsome Catholic church on Main Street was erected.

The total number of Catholics in Rockingham is about 250.

UNITED BRETHREN CHURCH.

United Brethren Churches in Rockingham (1912).

1. Mt. Hebron: Formerly Whitesel's Church; oldest in the county; located a mile or so southeast of Pleasant Valley. Rededicated in February, 1876, by Bishop J. J. Glossbrenner.

2. Pleasant Grove: On the Valley Pike, two miles south of Mt. Crawford.

3. Dayton Station: Dayton. Church dedications: June, 1878; September, 1904. The congregation was organized prior to the civil war. In 1866 there was a United Brethren Church in Bridgewater, 3 miles south of Dayton.—See *Rockingham Register*, June 28, 1866.

4. Ottobine: About 1½ miles north of Spring Creek.

5. Pleasant Valley.

6. Mt. Horeb: A short distance southwest of Hinton; dedicated in August, 1875.

7. Mt. Clinton.

8. Harrisonburg: Lot on W. Market Street purchased in July, 1894; first service in new church, January 5, 1896.

9. Cedar Grove: A mile and a half east of Harrisonburg. Church dedicated in November, 1886.

10. Mt. Sinai: Three miles south of Harrisonburg.

11. Keezletown.

12. Singer's Glen: Donovan Memorial Church, dedicated in May, 1906. Salem, formerly located one mile north of Singer's Glen, was founded during the civil war, said to have been the only U. B. Church erected within the Confederate States during the war.

13. Herwin: One mile east of Linville.
14. Cherry Grove: Three miles northeast of Singer's Glen.
15. Lacey Springs.
16. Mt. Bethel: On the Keezletown Road, four miles south of Lacey Springs.
17. Mountain Valley: Two miles east of Lacey Springs.
18. Broadway: Church dedicated in 1893.
19. Cootes' Store: Union church.
20. Mt. Carmel: Three miles west of Cootes' Store.
21. Keplinger's Chapel: Near Crider's.
22. Shady Grove: Two miles northwest of Port Republic.
23. Mt. Zion: Three miles northeast of McGaheysville. Church dedicated in 1899.
24. Elkton.
25. East Point: Two miles west of Elkton.
26. Mt. Hebron: Near Beldor.
27. Swift Run: On Swift Run, southeast of Elkton.

In the *Rockingham Register* of Feburary 26, 1864, appeared this paragraph:

"Virginia annual conference of the United Brethren in Christ will meet at Freeden's Church, Rockingham County, Va., on the 11th of March."

Inasmuch as Whitesel's Church is near Friedens, the former may be the one referred to in the above notice.

The United Brethren have been at work in Rockingham for more than a century. In 1809, when the Baltimore Methodist Conference met for the second time in Harrisonburg, Christian Newcomer, who succeeded Otterbein and Boehm as bishop of the United Brethren, was present in the effort to arrange for the union of the two churches. Although the plan for union was never formally consummated, Asbury recieved Newcomer warmly, and cordial relations have always existed between the two bodies. The United Brethren have frequently been called German Methodists. Practically all of their preaching up to 1820 was in the German language, and the teaching is like that of Methodism.

ROCKINGHAM COUNTY

Like the Mennonites, the Dunkers, the Methodists, and at least some of the Lutherans and Reformed, the United Brethren opposed the institution of slavery. Their well-known attitude on this question subjected them to no little unpopularity and to some persecution. In 1830 there were only three church houses in all Virginia, one of these being Whitesel's Church. So heavily did the storms of the civil war fall that Bishop Markwood, in 1865, or thereabouts, is said to have exclaimed, "There is no United Brethren church in Virginia." In view of this statement, and the discouraging situation that warranted it, the present large number of churches in Rockingham and adjacent sections of the State is the more remarkable.

One of the indefatigable leaders in building up the waste places after the war was Rev. John Williams Howe. He was born December 4, 1829; and lived long enough to see much rejoicing in the blessings that followed his labors. He died June 17, 1903. A fitting sketch of his life and work is given in the second volume of "Our Heroes," by W. M. Weekley and H. H. Fout. The same book contains an extended tribute to Rev. James L. Hensley, another leader of the church, a native of Rockingham. The establishment of a church school at Dayton,[12] in 1876, which has since grown to large proportions and influence, contributed greatly to the success of the religious work now so much in evidence. In this connection the influence of the Ruebush-Kieffer publishing house at Dayton should also be mentioned.

The membership of the United Brethren churches in Rockingham in 1906 had reached a total of 2917.[13]

Colored Churches.

So far as ascertained, there are eight colored churches in Rockingham: Two Baptist, two Methodist, and four United Brethren.

[12.] Now Shenandoah Collegiate Institute and School of Music.

[13.] For aid in securing information regarding the United Brethren Church in Rockingham, I am under special obligation to Rev. A. S. Hammack and Mr. Joe K. Ruebush, of Dayton.

A HISTORY OF

The colored Baptists in Harrisonburg have had a church organization for many years. Shiloh Church was dedicated July 11, 1875; and again in June, 1882. The Baptists of Bridgewater erected a church on Mt. Crawford Avenue, near Main Street, about ten years ago.

The colored Methodists of Harrisonburg dedicated John Wesley Church November 25, 1866. In January, 1870, they purchased the "brick church on the hill" shortly before relinquished by the Baptist congregation (supposedly the colored Baptists), for $2500;[14] and in January, 1880, they purchased Andrew Chapel, on the west side of German Street, of the white Methodists.

The colored Methodists of Bridgewater used to meet in an old school house that stood on the southwest side of the river, not far from Warm Spring. In May, 1879, they first used the present house of worship, west of Main Street.

In 1879, Mt. Moriah, the colored M. E. church at Mt. Vernon Forge, was burned.

The four United Brethren churches are the following:

1. Harrisonburg: Organized in April, 1876, by Rev. A. H. Wells.
2. Linville.
3. Long's Chapel: Near Lacey Springs; used as early as 1885.
4. Dungee's Chapel: Near Pleasant Valley.

Reliable statistics of membership of the colored churches have not been available.

The date when and the place where the first Sunday school was organized in Rockingham have not been ascertained; but abundant evidence is at hand to show that ever since the civil war Sunday schools have been numerous.

In the published obituary of John Hinton Ralston, who died in 1874, at the age of 80, it is asserted that he had been one of the first persons in his community to encourage Sunday schools, and to engage earnestly in the work, when many

---

[14]. *Rockingham Register*, February 3, 1870.

ROCKINGHAM COUNTY

good people opposed them on conscientious grounds.—Mr. Ralston was a ruling elder at New Erection.

In June, 1866, it was stated in the *Register* that there were 41 Sunday schools in the county, and 2500 scholars.

At a county Sundayschool convention held in Harrisonburg, October 26, 1866, the following statistical report of certain schools in Rockingham County was made:

	Scholars	Classes	Books
M. E. School, Hbg.,	226	21	188
Presbyterian, "	120	23	585
Episcopal, "	—	—	—
Harmony,	66	11	100
Fellowship,	93	11	—
Linville's Creek,	77	9	—
Cross Roads,	70	10	150
Mt. Crawford (Union),	157	18	500
" (Bap.),	75	15	—
McGaheysville,	104	18	300
New Erection,	40	8	—
Dry River (Union),	75	10	75
Elk Run,	75	13	200
Edom (Union),	92	8	40

Verses Committed.

Edom school,	15,462
Dry River school,	6,669
Harmony school,	10,503[15]

In February, 1867, the following statement appeared:

We learn from Rev. F. W. Stanley, agent for the A. T. S., that there are in Rockingham county over twenty-nine Sunday Schools in operation. In 29, the statistics show 322 teachers and 3016 scholars. Within the past year, in these twenty-nine schools, there have been 200 conversions.

This is a winter report.

In July, 1898, a Sundayschool Union of Harrisonburg and Rockingham County was organized in Assembly Hall, Court

---

15. *Rockingham Register*, Nov. 8, 1866.

House, J. P. Houck being made president, and J. C. Staples, secretary.

This is a summer report.

For several years Mr. Henry N. Whitesel of Harrisonburg, now deceased, was the enthusiastic president of the county Sundayschool organization. He was succeeded in office by Prof. Geo. H. Hulvey, who held the presidency till 1910.

The most remarkable development in efficient organization, extending from the county force to the district officers, and from the latter to the individual schools, has been witnessed during the last two years. Not only has the county association made itself vital in all its parts, but it has also set a pace for other counties of the State. According to the reports of the State officers, based upon careful comparisons of statistics, the Rockingham County Sundayschool Association, for efficiency and thoroughness of work, is now second to none in Virginia. It is also an acknowledged fact that this condition must be credited mainly to Dr. E. R. Miller, of Harrisonburg, who has been president of the organization since 1910. It would be difficult for any one not acquainted with the facts at first hand to appreciate the value of his services, or to realize how much time and labor he has devoted to the work; but the results speak for themselves, and are patent to all. The county convention this year was attended by 1000 people, and practically every school in the county was represented by delegates or letter. From the reports presented it appears that there are in the county 142 Sundayschools, with 1415 officers and teachers, and 12,184 scholars: a total enrollment of 13,599. Of this number, 3972 are in Ashby District; 3349 in Central; 1622 in Linville; 2139 in Plains; and 2517 in Stonewall.

The table on the opposite page has been prepared from statistics collected by the president of the Association during the past two years, and will be convenient for reference. It shows that all the churches are awake to the importance of the Sundayschool work.

ROCKINGHAM COUNTY

DISTRIBUTION OF SCHOOLS, 1911-12.

Denominations	MAGISTERIAL DISTRICTS					Total
	Plains	Linville	Central	Ashby	Stonew'll	
Baptist	2	1	1	2		6
Brethren	1		1		1	3
Christian	3	2	2		3	10
Church of Brethren	8	5	6	10		29
Church of Christ			1	1		2
Episcopal			1		4	5
Lutheran	2	2	1	½		5½
Mennonite		1	4	2		7
Methodist	2	2	3	8	9	24
Presbyterian	1		5	3	1	10
Reformed	1		1	3½	1	6½
United Brethren	3	5	5	6	7	26
Union	2	1	1	3	1	8
Total	25	19	32	39	27	142

The Sundayschool map presents the above conditions in a still more graphic manner.

A HISTORY OF

The present (1912-13) officers of the county Sunday-school association are the following:

Dr. E. R. Miller, president.
Mr. W. J. Dingledine, vice-president.
Rev. J. S. Garrison, secretary.
Dr. W. T. Lineweaver, Treasurer.

SUPERINTENDENTS OF DEPARTMENTS.

Elementary Division, Mrs. P. S. Thomas.
Secondary Division, Mr. J. D. Alexander.
Adult Division, Prof. J. Owen Long.
Home Department, Miss Vada Funk.
Teacher-Training Department, Rev. A. W. Andes.

Y. M. C. A.

In December, 1860, there was a Young Men's Christian Association in Harrisonburg, with Geo. O. Conrad, president, J. B. Odor, secretary; and the organization was preparing to hold its 4th annual meeting in the M. E. Church on January 5, 1861.

In May, 1873, there was another organization of the Y. M. C. A. in Harrisonburg, F. A. Berlin being made president; Jos. T. Logan, vice-president; D. H. Lee Martz, secretary; J. Wilton, treasurer; Frank L. Harris, librarian.

There seems to have been another revival of the organization in 1884; at any rate it was in operation in 1885, and until sometime in 1886, when it was discontinued. For three years it lapsed; but in March, 1889, a new start was taken. E. T. Dadmun of Staunton came down as a special aid: Judge Grattan was made president, J. C. Staples, secretary; and a ladies' auxiliary gave assurance of support. From this revival the work seems to have gone on for 14 years—that is, till March or April, 1903.

As early as 1827 a Rockingham County Bible society, with John Brown as president, was in operation. In September, 1866, a county Bible society was organized at Harrisonburg, in a joint meeting of the several churches. In November, 1874, Col. D. H. Lee Martz was president of the society;

ROCKINGHAM COUNTY

Rev. Cline, of Broadway, and other ministers in the county, were vice-presidents. In 1875 the society was active. J. J. Miller was colporteur for the county, and was expected to visit every family. In the *Register* of February 11 (1875) he made an interesting report.

TEMPERANCE MOVEMENTS.

In March, 1844, Marshall Division No. 3 of the Sons of Temperance, a national order, was organized at Harrisonburg, with Wm. G. Stevens, Jacob R. Stevens, J. M. Conrad, W. McK. Wartmann, John W. Bear, L. W. Gambill, Chas. D. Gray, and Henry T. Wartman charter members. During the next four years 153 men were initiated into the chapter. Some of the well known names that may still be seen upon the roll are these: Alg. S. Gray, Geo. O. Conrad, St. Clair Kyle, Jacob E. Harnsberger, P. Liggett, J. N. Liggett, John H. Graham, Morgan Switzer, and John G. Effinger.

In 1846 Worth Division No. 44, Sons of Temperance, was organized at Port Republic, and was kept going till the civil war. In January, 1873, it was revived and reorganized. On Christmas Day, 1860, the Sons of Temperance at Bridgewater had an elaborate procession, the Mt. Crawford Cavalry under command of Capt. Jordan, taking part.

Mt. Crawford for many years seems to have been a potential center of temperance sentiment. As early as 1838 the village had a live temperance society. On May 20, 1854, a large convention of temperance advocates was held in the Mt. Crawford Reformed Church, Dr. M. H. Harris presiding. C. Coffman Bare and J. B. McGill were secretaries. A committee of gentlemen in each precinct in the county was appointed to obtain signatures to a petition to the court, praying the court not to grant any license for the sale of "ardent spirits" in the county. Frequently during the years of Reconstruction Mt. Crawford was heard from regarding temperance, when the "Friends of Temperance" were organizing councils.

The following paragraph, which appeared in the *Register* of March 19, 1868, will give an idea of what was being done for temperance at that time.

A HISTORY OF

We are gratified to notice that our talented and intelligent young friend, E. Roller, Esq., of Harrisonburg, is exerting himself actively in behalf of the cause of Temperance in the Valley. We see that he has proposed organizing Councils of Temperance in Woodstock, Strasburg, Edinburg, Mt. Jackson and New Market, in our sister county below us. He has already organized a number of flourishing Councils in Rockingham and Augusta counties. This is a new organization with the same objects of the old order of Sons of Temperance, an institution that flourished and did much good before the war.

Mt. Crawford was honored in this tribute, for "E. Roller, Esq.," now well known as Gen. John E. Roller, grew up in the vicinity of Mt. Crawford.

In March, 1868, Harrisonburg Council No. 37, Friends of Temperance, elected J. S. Harnsberger president, and A. Poe Boude chaplain. In July following the same council elected J. Ed. Pennybacker president, J. Wilton associate, T. U. Dudley chaplain, and J. Gassman secretary. In the fall of 1869, at Petersburg, J. Ed. Pennybacker (1844-1912) was elected president of the State council.

During the decade from 1873 to 1883 the Good Templars were active in Rockingham, having organizations in many parts of the county. In January, 1882, a county local option alliance was organized at Harrisonburg. The same year a local option petition, 18 feet long, with a double row of names, was on exhibition at the store of Houck & Wallis. In 1884 a women's temperance reading room was established in the old clerk's office. It was during the later 80's that the saloons in Harrisonburg and certain other parts of the county were closed a little while by local option.

For a number of years past the Women's Christian Temperance Union and the Anti-Saloon League have had active organizations in Rockingham.

Benevolent societies and temperance societies have not been wanting among the colored people of Rockingham. For example, in 1875, 1876, etc., organizations of the Sons of Jonadab, the True Reformers, and the Sons of Purity were effected in various parts of the county.[16]

---

16. General acknowledgment is made to Dr. E. R. Miller, Dr. H.H. Sherman, Rev. L. J. Heatwole, and Hon. James Hay for aid on this chapter.

CHAPTER XV.

EDUCATION AND SCHOOLS.

The desire on the part of the Valley of Virginia people for higher education has become general only in recent years; but from early times most of them have craved for themselves and their children the rudiments of learning—or more; and therefore elementary schools grew up with the first settlements. Frequently the pastor was also the teacher; and in many cases the church house and the school house were built on the same lot. The records are not sufficient to give us many particulars regarding the first schools in Rockingham and adjacent sections, but we know of some that were here more than a century ago; and with these, as well as with others that came later, we shall have to do.

In 1794 the Methodists of Harrisonburg opened a school. It was organized under the direction of no less a person than Bishop Asbury himself. We read on the yellowed page of the minute book:

In conference chamber, the following persons were nominated by the Bishop as Trustees of the Harrisonburg School, viz.

Andrew Shanklin	Samuel McWilliams
Joseph Denny	Robert Harrison
Benjamin Smith	Thomas Harrison
Reubin Harrison	Joseph Cravens
Jeremiah Reagan	William Cravens
George Wells	William Hughs
Benjamin Harrison	

From the thirteen nominated, seven were chosen, as follows:

Andrew Shanklin	Benjamin Harrison
George Wells	Samuel McWilliams
Benjamin Smith	Joseph Cravens
Reuben Harrison	

A HISTORY OF

The elder of the circuit, who appears a few months later as Joshua Wells, was to be president of the board, ex officio; George Wells was made vice-president; Joseph Cravens, clerk; Benjamin Harrison, treasurer.

It is said that Asbury held the conference this year (1794) in the Harrison house, on Bruce Street near Main, which is now Gen. John E. Roller's law office. The log church, which stood on the top of the hill where the Dunker church now stands, was new and likely unfinished; for on June 23 the seven trustees, who looked after the business of the church as well as that of the school, resolved, "that a sum sufficient to finish the Methodist meeting house suitable for said School as well as publick Preaching &c. be raised by Subscription."

So the meetinghouse became also the schoolroom. Brother John Walsh was employed as teacher at a salary of fifty pounds.

If the term "Blue Light" or "Blue Laws" could with propriety be attached to the Methodists, we should certainly be inclined to use them both in describing the rules by which this school for boys and girls was to be regulated. They—these rules—remind us very much of some that John Wesley himself drew up for another school:—but here they are, as formulated by the seven trustees on the 23d of June, 1794.

Rule 1. The Scholars shall attend at Eight O'clock in the Summer and Half Past eight in the winter; and the Teacher Shall regulate the time of attendance in Spring and Autumn, according to the length of the day.

2. They Shall be allowed an hour for recreation in Winter, and two Hours in Summer.

3. They Shall be dismissed at six o'clock in Summer, and at four in Winter; and in Spring and Autumn in proportion.

4. The School Shall always be opened and closed with prayer.

5. The Teacher Shall appoint a weekly monitor out of a Senior Class, who Shall Call the list upon all Occasions, and see that the Scholars be present at all times of Publick worship in the School; and give Information of all misdemeanors in the Teachers Absence. And also that all Scholars of Seven Years old and upwards shall attend at publick service on the Sabbath, wherever his or her Parents Guardians or Master may direct.

ROCKINGHAM COUNTY

6. No gaming of any kind, nor Instruments of Play shall be tolerated.

7. The Tutor shall be judge of all excuses for non attendance, and shall deal with the delinquents accordingly.

8. A strict order of silence shall be observed in School hours.

9. In every case of Sinning against God, the trial shall be very Serious, the facts proved, and the Sinner Properly dealt with, according to the Judgment of the Teacher. If it should be near the time of a Visitation (of the trustees) let it be laid over till the meeting of the Board of Trustees.

10. In a case of rebellion against the rules of the School, or the Authority of the Teacher, Such a Scholar with the concurrence of the Tutor, with the Trustee, Shall be dismissed.

Nevertheless, in Case of Such dismission there shall be a right of appeal to board of Trustees.

11. No Scholar Shall be permitted on any account whatever to wear Ruffles or powder his hair.

12. The Scholars Shall be examined in the "Instructions for Children" Once a week Except the Children of such parents as disapprove the same.

13. There Shall be a Garden procured (if practicable) that those Scholars who choose it may Recreate themselves therein.

14. That no teacher Shall be Eligible for a Trustee.

15. It is Earnestly recommended that no person or persons will send their Children to the School without observing the Strictest punctuality, in making payment Half Yearly; And if Any Subscriber neglects payment one Year, it Shall be determined by a majority of the Trustees, whether he shall be permitted to send the Ensuing Year.

16. Every subscriber is required to give three months notice, if he does not Continue to Send the Insuing Year.

17. There Shall be no more than Forty Scholars admitted into the School and the Subscribers Shall pay to the Trustees the sum of Thirty three Shillings for each Scholar per Year.

18. No Subscriber shall have restitution for the Scholars loss of time, by sending more than the number, or longer than the time subscribed.

The school evidently was continued in session the whole year. The last Fridays in the months of November, February, May, and August were days set apart for visitation. On these days the vice-president of the board of trustees was to call a meeting of the trustees, and they were to "Examine the Scholars in their knowledge of God and progress in Learning."

Subscribers were to have the privilege of sending their

A HISTORY OF

black servants into the school for the first year, "Under these Restrictions viz. They Shall be Classed & Seated by themselves."

A space in the gallery, on the right hand of the pulpit, was to be set apart for the reception of such pupils as attended public worship. The teacher or a trustee was to sit at their right.

If we are disposed to revolt at some of the foregoing regulations, we are certainly gratified at others. On the whole, we must regard the provisions for this school of a hundred and fifteen years ago as remarkably sane and liberal. One or two provisions are surprisingly progressive; for example, who would now imagine that the people of that day were planning for a school garden?

In May of the next year, 1795, Bishop Asbury was again at Harrisonburg; and he gave on that occasion further evidence of his concern for the new school. Under date of Wednesday, May 13, he writes in his Journal: "Rode twenty-four miles to Rock-Town, and preached at three o'clock; and again the next day. Here I met the trustees of our school, to whom I read my Thoughts on Education. In the evening I left the town, and on Friday 15, rode forty miles."

It appears from the records that the teacher for the second year, 1795-6, was a Mr. Spencer. It would seem that early in 1795 the trustees were planning to enlarge the school by having two departments and two teachers—Mr. Walsh and Mr. Spencer. The new department was to be a "grammar school." March 16, 1795, the Board resolved that "the Grammar School Shall be under the same Rules & Regulations which have been made for the English School—except the Two last weeks in April & the Two first in October, which times shall be set apart for Vacation as Common in Grammar schools."

The outcome seems to have been about this—the minutes are very meager—that Mr. Spencer for the second year had a school combining in some measure the two departments contemplated.

ROCKINGHAM COUNTY

After 1796 I find no more references in the records to this school, definitely; but at a quarterly meeting conference held in Harrisonburg on Saturday, January 15, 1820, the matter of securing a school teacher was again under consideration.[1]

Mrs. Carr, whose recollections went back into the first quarter of last century, mentions Richard Fletcher, Rev. Mr. Cole, and Rev. Joseph Smith as among the Harrisonburg schoolmasters of that time; and names Tiffin Harrison, Gessner Harrison, and Henry Tutwiler as pupils of Mr. Smith. She gives the following characteristic account of school life:

The school hours were from eight to twelve, and from two to five. Recess was never known at that time. We were allowed to go out once in the morning and once in the afternoon. A piece of wood shaped like a paddle was hung on the inside of the door by a piece of string; on the one side was written the word OUT, in large letters, and on the other side was written IN. Two girls were allowed to go out together, when the paddle was turned to OUT, and when they came in the paddle was turned to IN. Sometimes the paddle was reversed, when two more girls would go out to meet the others and have a good time playing, until the teacher missed them; he would send for them to come back. Girls were very seldom punished; if ever, very slightly; boys were frequently whipped or kept in after school. We were taught reading, spelling, writing, grammar, and geography. A pupil who had gone through Pike's arithmetic, Morse's geography, Murray's grammar, and could spell a dozen words without mis-spelling three, could write a plain round hand, he was a man that was thought capable of holding any common office. Ladies of that day never followed any profession, or meddled with men's affairs—they could teach small children their alphabet and work samplers.

On January 20, 1806, an Act was passed incorporating the Rockingham Library Company, the said company being authorized to procure a library for the improvement of the inhabitants. In 1818 an Act was passed changing the time of meeting of this company. In 1867 the Rockingham Library Association was chartered, and books opened for subscriptions at $2.50 a share; in November (1867) James Kenney was

---

1. Acknowledgment is made to Dr. H. H. Sherman for access to records.

elected president of the association, J. L. Sibert vice president, O. C. Sterling, Jr., treasurer, Ran D. Cushen secretary, Wm. D. Trout, librarian.

In the summer of 1825 S. M. Hunter and Rich. P. Fletcher were advertising the opening of a school in Harrisonburg, on August 15, in which school Greek, Latin, philosophy, rhetoric, geography, English grammar, mathematics, surveying, reading, writing, and arithmetic were to be taught.

In February, 1826, Rockingham Academy was chartered, with Samuel Moffett, Wm. McMahon, Saml. Newman, Andrew Moffett, Isaac Thomas, Peter Crim, John Hoover, Joseph Cline, and Saml. Hoover as trustees. This school was located between Timberville and New Market, and is now known as Plains (school and church).

In 1827 Miss Anna Moore was conducting a school in Harrisonburg for girls; and at the same time another school, at or near the same town, was going on under the direction of Abner W. Kilpatrick. In November, 1833, Mr. Kilpatrick was preparing to open his school at his home, $3\frac{1}{2}$ miles from Harrisonburg; board and tuition for 5 months for $55.

In 1839 a project was on foot, and was probably carried through, to establish an academy in Harrisonburg. An Act of incorporation was passed by the legislature this year or the next.

For a year or two, beginning about 1838, a school in McGaheysville was conducted by Joseph Salyards, probably the most famous teacher that has ever lived in the Valley of Virginia. Born near Front Royal in 1808, he grew up at New Market, winning by toil an education in spite of poverty and obscurity. After many years of work as a teacher in Rockingham, Page, and Shenandoah, he died at New Market, August 10, 1885, full of years and honors. Roanoke College conferred the M. A. degree upon him in 1872; and he is remembered as scholar, teacher, and poet.[2]

---

[2]. See biography of Salyards by Elon O. Henkel, New Market, Va.; also sketch and selections from his poems in Harris and Alderman's Library of Southern Literature, Vol. X.

Harrisonburg High School. Site of Old Academy, used as Confederate Hospital

McGaheysville Graded and High School

Bridgewater Graded and High School

Waterman School. (Page 304)

ROCKINGHAM COUNTY

Mr. Richard Mauzy, who went to Salyards' school in McGaheysville, thinks he opened it in 1838. After a year or so Salyards became temporarily insane; but in December, 1840, and January and February, 1841, he was advertising the resumption of his school at McGaheysville.

Mr. Mauzy supplies the following list of early McGaheysville teachers:

George Mauzy, about 1830-31.
Miss Jeanetta Conrad, about 1832-33.
Charles Buck, 1833-35.
David Howard, 1836.
Mr. —— Lamb, 1836-37.
Joseph Salyards, 1838-39, etc.

Salyards probably taught at New Market from about 1845 to 1855; from about 1857 to 1860 he was principal of Rockingham Male Academy, located on W. Market Street, Harrisonburg, in a building that now forms part of the residence of James Kavanaugh. Academy Street marks the place. From 1859 or 1860, for two or three years, he was principal of Pleasant Grove Academy, located on the Valley Pike, two miles south of Mt. Crawford. Before me are notices of this school in the *Southern Musical Advocate* of July and August, 1860, and the *Rockingham Register* of Aug. 3, 1860, and Oct. 4, 1861. In 1860 P. S. Roller, J. R. Keagy, and D. Ross were proprietors of Pleasant Grove Academy; and Salyards was spoken of as "one of the oldest and best teachers in the Valley." The branches taught included languages, literature, and mathematics. Mr. S. T. Shank, writing in the Harrisonburg *Daily News* of February 27, 1911, says that Salyards was assisted at Pleasant Grove in 1860-61 by his son.

In August, 1862, Salyards was in charge of Cedar Grove Seminary, near Broadway; and in 1864 he was at Rosendale, on Smith's Creek. The old stone house at Rosendale ("Smith Creek Seminary") in which he taught is still standing. From Rosendale, according to Mr. Thos. L. Williamson, he went to Luray, thence returning to New Market, where he spent the remainder of his life. Mr. Elon O.

A HISTORY OF

Henkel says he went to Woodstock from Luray, coming to New Market in July, 1870.

One of Salyards' advanced pupils at Rosendale was a young man who was blind, but who, in spite of misfortune, has, like his master, achieved distinction. The following paragraphs from his pen are a special contribution to this work.

The writer is glad of the opportunity of paying a grateful tribute of reverent respect to the memory of Joseph Salyards. He was a man of the common people. In early life he developed an extraordinary taste for the higher learning, and, without masters or schools, made himself familiar with the ancient languages to such a degree that he read Latin, Greek, Hebrew, and Sanscrit with the ease and fluency of a master, and not merely the text books in those languages, but their literature with critical discrimination and judgment. He also read and wrote in all the modern languages that had a literature. Besides his wonderful linguistic accomplishments, he was the most profound scholar in mathematics, science, philosophy, history, and literature that Rockingham ever produced, and perhaps the State of Virginia.

He was not appreciated in his day at his true value. He would have adorned any chair in any school or college. The drawback in his life was his own consent to live in the humble sphere to which he had been born, and he never made any effort to rise above it, so far as the writer knows. In early life he was fond of attending the country dances, and not always as careful to avoid the social cup as he should have been. It is said that he lost an eye in consequence of an attempt to go to such a frolic on a dark night, possibly in not perfect command of himself, by striking his face against a fence stake, inflicting an injury which destroyed an eye. With one good eye, which was happily preserved, he learned more than most people, and was at the time at which the writer knew him a perfectly temperate man of most dignified bearing. He spoke elegantly, wrote with a facile pen, and would have commanded attention in any company. He enjoyed the friendship and high respect of the best men in

ROCKINGHAM COUNTY

the valley of Virginia; was known most favorably by John Baldwin, A. H. H. Stuart, and Hugh Sheffy of Staunton, and the prominent men all along the beautiful valley. The acquaintance was not very profitable to him in social life; but they loved and honored him.

During the war between the States I was sent to his little school at Rosendale, on Smith Creek, in the northern edge of Rockingham County, where I found a rare opportunity of prosecuting my studies in the more advanced learning, which could not at that time have been found anywhere else. He was tenderly kind to my infirmity, which made me dependent on the eyes of others, giving me all the encouragement in his vast field of wisdom and learning.

In a stone house, which had in ante-bellum days been a still house, on the beautiful estate of the late George Rosenberger, within a stone's throw of his hospitable home, where I lived for a year or two, Mr. Salyards taught a school composed of the sons and daughters of the surrounding farmers, in the earlier grades, as we would say now. The venerable teacher found time in that school of sixty or more "scholars" to hear me work out my problems in the advanced courses in which I was so busy. I had for my companion a young friend who took the same courses with me, and we enjoyed much of the great teacher's time, both out of school and in the hours of the day's work. We often went to his little log house in the field, only a few hundred yards from Mr. Rosenberger's residence, where, surrounded by his children and their mother, much younger than himself, we enjoyed his elegant conversation, and the treasures of his splendid library, a surprise in such surroundings. He referred to his books with the readiness of one who had them entirely at his command. No time was ever lost in finding the most abstruse references. He seemed with almost an instinctive precision to turn to just what we wanted. I feel that I owe any success I may be thought to have achieved in the course of my life to his instruction and inspiration.

After nearly fifty years, I recall with wonder and astonishment, that he told me with his own lips, that he had had in early life an ambition to write a literary degree after his name, and had sought from the University of Virginia the privilege of standing for examination with a view to such degree; but his request was declined. A finer general scholar, of more varied learning than any one of the faculty, he had to be denied the distinction because, doubtless, of some iron-bound rule of the institution. In later life, however, that institution honored itself not less than him, in bestowing a degree without examination.[3]

This backwoods philosopher for many years frequently contributed to the local press, and is still remembered doubtless by some of the older newspaper people; his articles having appeared in both prose and verse on a great variety of subjects; and possibly also he may have written for some of the magazines. About 1874 he gave to the world a poem of which it was not worthy, and did not appreciate, for it still lingers on the shelves of the publishers, if indeed it is not out of print. "Idothea" is almost an epic, and received a most flattering review from a great English review by a distinguished author of high literary note. My memory is at fault as to the name of the English reviewer. It had also flattering notice from several sources in this country. A. W. Kercheval and the writer reviewed it for the publishers, who issued a pamphlet to advertise the book; but it was all in vain. The rich descriptions of local scenery and personages of note in his community, and the deep philosophy of the work make it a treasure in itself, which may some day, to a more appreciative auditory, bring it into favor and general knowledge. Prof. Salyards, in the last years of his useful life, occupied a chair in the Polytechnic Institute at new Market.

H. H. JOHNSON,
Senior Teacher, Blind Department, School
for the Deaf and Blind, Romney, W. Va.

---

[3]. This is a mistake. Prof. Johnson probably had in mind the degree conferred by Roanoke College. The University of Virginia has never conferred a degree except for residence work.

ROCKINGHAM COUNTY

Mr. S. H. W. Byrd of Bridgewater informs me that a number of the old citizens of his town and vicinity were pupils at an old school house that formerly stood at St. Michael's Church.

In August, 1840, Chas. Viquesney, a native of France, was advertising a night school at Harrisonburg, to teach French; the said school to be conducted during the coming winter. At the same time Julius Hesse was giving notice of a writing school; and Henry Brown was announcing a "School for Females" to open September 1: both in Harrisonburg. On February 22, 1841, the Bridgewater debating society celebrated Washington's birth, with the Harrisonburg band in attendance. In 1844, as I am informed by Rev. A. Poe Boude, Wm. W. Littell was running a school in Dayton—the only 9-months school in Rockingham at that time. Among his pupils were A. P. Boude, Danl. Smith, and John Green Smith; the Smiths being sons of Judge Danl. Smith. The same year (1844) Wm. C. Jennings was preparing to open a school in Harrisonburg, April 29.

In 1851 an Act was passed incorporating Rockingham Male and Female Seminary, to be established in or near Harrisonburg. The trustees were Wm. Kiger, Thomas D. Bell, Robt. Grattan, and ten others named. In 1854 Rockingham Male Seminary was in charge of R. W. Thurmond, principal. In September of the same year Miss Harriet Bear was preparing to open a school for young ladies in one of the basement rooms of Andrew Chapel (Hbg.). About 1856 the "Academy" near Broadway, first in charge of James Wright, was erected.

During the years now under consideration, Joseph Funk, at Mountain Valley (Singer's Glen), was conducting a school to which a number of young men came from various parts of the country. It is probable that he was teaching at his home as early as 1825 or 1830; and his school was continued by his sons for a number of years after the civil war. In the *Southern Musical Advocate* of July, 1859, he and his sons were advertising their school—offering to teach not only music, but also grammar, elocution, and the art of teaching music. Board and music tuition cost $9 a month; instruction in grammar and elocution raised the total cost to $10 a month.

On the first Monday in September, 1860, Rockingham Male Academy, in Harrisonburg, reopened under the principalship of John W. Taylor. Thos. D. Bell was secretary of the board of trustees. Mathematics, natural science, Latin, Greek, French, etc., were offered. On the first Wednesday of September, 1861, the third session of Rockingham Female Institute, in Harrisonburg, began, with J. Mark Wilson principal.

The early days of Reconstruction were fruitful in schools as well as in marriages. In the fall of 1866 the following schools were announced:

Harrisonburg.
Female Institute, P. M. Custer, principal.
Male Academy, E. H. Scott, principal.
School for Children, Miss Alice Houck.
" " Miss Mollie McQuaide.
" " Miss Fannie Lowman.[4]
" " Miss Carrie Harrison.
School for Young Ladies, Rev. A. Poe Boude.
Conrad's Store.

---

[4]. Fannie Lowman was born at or near Rushville in 1840 or 1841, and died in Harrisonburg in November, 1909. In spite of lameness, poor health, and few pecuniary advantages she gained an education in good schools: in Georgetown and Staunton; in the Valley Normal at Bridgewater, the School of Methods at Charlottesville, and elsewhere: and for more than 30 years she was a teacher—two years in Texas, the remainder in Virginia. Some of her first earnings went to aid a younger sister, who also became a teacher. For several years before her death she was entitled to a teacher's pension, but she preferred a meager salary with the work she loved. With characteristic altruism, it was her wish that the very few dollars she left at death be devoted to others rather than to herself or her memory. On learning these facts the Rockingham County Teachers Association undertook to mark her grave, in order that her own small balance might not be thus consumed, but might go to benefit the living. The fund for a monument is growing, and her colleagues and old pupils are embracing a privilege in honoring her.

ROCKINGHAM COUNTY

Classical School, W. K. Jennings.
          Linville Creek.
Classical School, John D. Pennybacker.[5]
          Lacey Springs.
Classical School, John W. Taylor.[6]

Professor Taylor did not, perhaps, designate his as a classical school, but it seems to have been similar to the others that were thus called.

In 1866 there was a Rockingham County teachers' association, H. Handy being secretary.

The first regular session of Harrisonburg Female Institute, A. Poe Boude principal, Mary L. Attkisson teacher of French and music, was advertised to open February 18, 1867, in the basement of the "E. M. Church on the hill."

In April, 1867, B. A. Hawkins opened the first session of Keezletown Academy. In October following B. A. Hawkins and W. T. Brett were principals of Pleasant Grove Academy; at the same time P. M. Custer was principal of Rockingham Female Institute, and B. F. Wade was principal of Rockingham Male Academy, the last named two schools being at Harrisonburg. In this same year (1867) John H. Moore had a large school at Beaver Creek.

In 1868 W. S. Kennedy was advertising a classical school to open September 1, in the town hall at Bridgewater, to

---

[5]. John Dyer Pennybacker (1833-1904) was a son of Sen. I. S. Pennybacker, and a brother of J. Ed. Pennybacker (1844-1912). His wife was Elizabeth Lincoln (1827-1905).

[6]. John W. Taylor was born 76 years ago on the west bank of the Shenandoah River, in East Rockingham, opposite what is now the town of Shenandoah. His father was Zachary Taylor (Scotch-Irish) and his mother Nancy Eppard (German). Winning early education under scant advantages, he taught a school at East Point when 18 or 19. Continuing his studies at Richmond College, Randolph-Macon, and other schools, he received the A. M. degree at Randolph-Macon in 1860. The next session he was principal of the male academy in Harrisonburg. In 1865 he opened his school at Lacey Springs, where he has taught almost continuously to the present. His wife was Virginia C. Lincoln, a daughter of Jacob Lincoln, of Rockingham.

continue 10 months. At the same time J. H. Turner and G. W. Holland were principals of Rockingham Male Academy, and P. M. Custer[7] of Rockingham Female Institute. The buildings of the last, which stood on the site of the present Harrisonburg Main Street School, had been erected a few years before the war; during the war they were used as a hospital by the Confederates. (See page 153).

In 1870 there were at least ten schools for the white children in Harrisonburg.[8] In the fall of 1871 the Harrisonburg graded school was organized, under the new public school system, and Rev. J. S. Loose was elected principal. In 1871 a classical school was opened in Bridgewater, with John H. Barb principal, Richard Halstead intermediate teacher, and Frank Stover primary teacher.[9] In 1872 S. C. Lindsay opened a classical and mathematical school in Harrisonburg, in September, to run till June of the next year.

In 1873 a boarding and day school for young ladies was opened in the home of Rev. W. G. Campbell, his niece and two daughters being teachers. In 1877 the house on Campbell Street, Harrisonburg, now Shaffer's boarding house, was built for a school by the Misses Campbell. As late as 1892 Miss S. L. Campbell was conducting the school. Later members of the family had charge of Westminster School in Richmond.

In 1874 and 1875 B. L. Hodge was principal of McGaheysville Male and Female Academy. The session ran 9 months, and classical as well as English instruction was offered.

At Dayton, in 1875, A. Paul Funkhouser and other progressive leaders in the United Brethren Church founded Shenandoah Seminary, which has grown into the well known Shenandoah Collegiate Institute and School of Music. As in-

---

[7]. Rev. P. M. Custer died in Alabama in 1890, aged 70. For particulars regarding Rockingham Female Institute, I am obliged to Mr. L. H. Ott.

[8]. *Rockingham Register*, June 30, 1870.

This information was given by Mr. S. H. W. Byrd.

Campus Scene, Shenandoah Collegiate Institute, Dayton, Va. (Pages 296, 297)

dicated in the name, music has been much encouraged in the policy of this school. The institution has really inherited the musical traditions and tendencies that so long distinguished the school of Joseph Funk & Sons at Singer's Glen. Since its organization it has grown in favor and popularity at home and abroad, particularly in the Southern States, from all of which a large number of students come annually. It aims to supply the best of instruction by modern methods at lowest possible cost. It exalts the moral above the merely intellectual.

To the older buildings, two new brick structures have recently been added: (1) Howe Memorial Building (1899), occupied exclusively by the School of Music; (2) the Administration Building (1909), four stories, containing laboratories, class-rooms, studios, offices, etc. Separate dormitories are provided for ladies and gentlemen. Reading rooms, literary societies, a Y. M. C. A., a Y. W. C. A., special lectures and entertainments, etc., supplement the work of the class-rooms and chapel. The students publish a handsomely illustrated annual, "The Zynodoa," and maintain athletic organizations. The enrolment for 1911-12 was 259. J. H. Ruebush is general manager; J. N. Garber is president of the board of trustees. The board of control is composed of J. H. Ruebush, C. A. Funkhouser, G. P. Hott, and A. S. Hammack. The faculty comprises 17 regular members.

In March, 1876, State Supt. W. H. Ruffner visited Harrisonburg and made two addresses on education in the courthouse. The specific purpose of his visit (he had been invited by the town council) was the erection of a public school building. In November, 1878, Supt. Ruffner was in Harrisonburg attending a teachers' institute. On October 30, 1879, Judge Kenney wrote in his diary: "The new brick school house for the free school is about finished. Cost $5000." It was used for the session of 1879-80, Clarence H. Urner of New Market being principal of the school. This building is now used for the grades in the Main Street school. The trustees under whose direction it was built were J. L. Avis, G. O. Conrad, and G. F. Compton.

A HISTORY OF

Harrisonburg in 1878-9 had a Shakespeare Club. Traces of the same club, or another like it, were found just twenty years later.

In 1878 and thereabouts North Mountain Academy, near Chrisman, J. W. Jones being principal, was attracting a good deal of attention.

In 1878 there came to Rockingham a man who probably did more than any other to commend the public schools to general favor, to stir up school spirit, and to inspire his pupils with a desire for higher learning. This was A. C. Kimler. From 1878 to 1881 he taught at River Bank; from 1881 to 1889, at McGaheysville. It was at the latter place he did his great work for Rockingham. Says Mr. Richard Mauzy: "He established Oak Hill Academy, and was a successful teacher."

During his eight years at McGaheysville Professor Kimler sent students to Randolph-Macon College, Roanoke, Franklin and Marshall, Nashville Normal School, the University of Virginia, West Point, Richmond Medical College, and Baltimore Dental College. He received letters commending their work from Dr. Smith of Randolph-Macon, Dr. Venable of the University of Virginia, and others. Among those he sent out were the following, many of whom are well known to-day:

William Yancey, Harrisonburg, deceased.
C. N. Wyant, school principal in Pennsylvania.
Dr. J. B. Rush, Woodstock, Va.
R. H. Sheppe, teacher and educator, deceased.
Rev. J. P. Harner, Middlebrook, Va.
C. C. Herring, editor; Harrisonburg.
Rev. Melville Killian.
H. W. Bertram, lawyer and editor; Harrisonburg.
Floyd W. Weaver, county clerk, Luray, Va.
J. H. Bader, educator; McGaheysville.
Rev. John Life.
Fayette Hedrick, McGaheysville.
Luther Hopkins, McGaheysville.

ROCKINGHAM COUNTY

C. L. Lambert, Little Rock, Ark.[10]

Bridgewater College dates its beginnings from 1880, when D. C. Flory, assisted by J. R. Shipman, opened a normal and collegiate institute at Spring Creek. In 1882 the school was located at Bridgewater, where it has since gained wide recognition. It was chartered as a college in 1889. On December 31 of this year the main building burned, but others have taken its place until to-day there are 7 buildings; two frame, five brick. These include a gymnasium and a central heating plant. One of the benefactors of the school was W. B. Yount, who was president from 1892 to 1910. The institution represents especially the educational interests of the Church of the Brethren, and is co-educational. Work is offered leading to the degrees of B. A., M. A., Th. B., etc. The library contains over 10,000 volumes.

The students conduct three literary societies, the Victorian, the Virginia Lee, and the Acme; and publish a monthly magazine, founded in 1896, the *Philomathean Monthly*. A student civic league and other organizations are also maintained. The enrolment during the session of 1911-12 was 184.

John S. Flory is president of the college; Hiram G. Miller is president of the board of trustees. The faculty consists of 17 regular members, with a number of assistants. An active alumni association has been in existence since 1899. Graduates of the institution have taken high rank at the universities, and a large number have entered the Gospel ministry.

At Mt. Clinton, in 1890, a 2-room graded school, offering some high-school work, was built up into a 4-year high-school, and named West Central Academy. It continued in this character till 1902. I. S. Wampler, now fiscal secretary of the alumni association of Peabody College, Nashville, was principal; and among the other teachers were C. J. Heatwole,

---

[10]. Abram C. Kimler graduated from Franklin and Marshall College in 1878. After leaving McGaheysville he went to New Market, Va.; thence to Shepherdstown, W. Va., where he was principal of the State Normal College for several years. At present he is principal of the Waynesboro (Va.) High School, and he is still sending students up higher.

A HISTORY OF

L. R. Dinges (now studying in Germany), D. I. Suter, M. A. Good, and D. B. Wampler. The largest enrolment in high school classes at any time was 170. Public and private funds were combined for maintenance. Graduates entered Washington and Lee, the University of Virginia, and other colleges. The summer normal institutes were a special feature. About 1897 it was ascertained that 65% of all the teachers in Rockingham had at some time been students of this school.

In 1896 Rockingham Military Academy, at Mt. Crawford, was opened under the principalship of Otey C. Hulvey. From the beginning of the second session until the suspension of the school in 1901, Capt. F. A. Byerly, now a prominent teacher in West Virginia, was principal and commandant. The school occupied a handsome three-story building just west of the Valley Pike, at the northeast end of Mt. Crawford. For some time, prior to his connection with the R. M. A., Capt. Byerly had conducted Sunnyside School for Girls at Pleasant Valley.

A Rockingham County historical society was organized in 1898-9. A committee, made up of Maj. George Chrisman, James B. Stephenson, and F. A. Byerly, drew up a constitution and by-laws. Gen. John E. Roller was elected president. There were 16 vice-presidents, an executive committee, a library committee, a committee on Confederate soldiers, and a reception committee. The society was given the use of a room in the courthouse; but in spite of this official recognition, the rich field at hand, and the need of a strong organization to preserve our historical materials, interest in the organization soon fell to a low ebb. A revival of spirit will doubtless come at some time in the future, when many golden opportunities have passed forever. Rockingham County needs a historical society; but such a society to live must have the sympathy of many people.

It is a common misimpression that our present public school system in Virginia is altogether a product of Reconstruction—that we had no free schools before the war. As a matter of fact, there were legislative provisions in Virginia as early as 1780—perhaps earlier—for the establishment of free schools;

ROCKINGHAM COUNTY

and such schools were in actual operation from the beginning of the 19th century up to the civil war. To be sure, these public free schools were inadequate to the general need: they were intended for the poor, and in most cases were used only by the poor. This fact will explain some of the prejudice against free (public) schools in more recent times.

A few statistics from different periods will illustrate general conditions. In 1824-5 the number of free schools in 98 counties and towns of Virginia was 2450; the number of "poor" children was 21,177; the number sent to school was 10,226; the amount expended for their tuition was $49,222.22. Eleven counties made no report.[11] In 1826 $45,000 was appropriated for schools in the different counties; Rockingham's share was $942.12.

According to the census of 1850, there were in Rockingham 2765 persons who could neither read nor write, in a total white population of 17,500. Rockingham's share of the school fund this year was $1399.[12]

The increased allotment ten years later, and its distribution among the several districts of the county, are shown in the following table:

SCHOOL FUND QUOTAS

For Rockingham Co., for the Year 1861.

The following is the apportionment made by the Superintendent of the Literary Fund for Rockingham county, for the year ending September, '61:

Dist. No.				
"	1	C. A. Sprinkel,	Commissioner,	$180 00
"	2	J. W. C. Houston,	"	130 00
"	3	B. F. Lincoln,	"	140 00
"	4	P. P. Koontz,	"	130 00
"	5	Wm. Sellers,	"	100 00
"	6	Madison West,	"	130 00
"	7	Jos. H. Conrad,	"	170 00
"	8	Wm. B. Yancey,	"	120 00
"	9	Y. C. Ammon,	"	150 00

11. From a Virginia almanac of 1827.
12. From a Virginia almanac of 1852.

A HISTORY OF

Dist. No.	10 Geo. W. Kemper,	Commisioner,	$140 00
"	11 Jos. Beery,	"	120 00
"	12 Geo. P. Burtner,	"	120 00
"	13 Jacob Byerly,	"	170 00
"	14 M. H. Harris,	"	130 00
"	15 Peter Wise,	"	50 00
"	16 Wm. Beard,	"	140 00
"	17 G. R. Harrell,	"	140 00
"	18 F. M. Ervine,	"	200 00
"	19 Jesse Ralston,	"	80 00
"	20 Arch'd. Hopkins,	"	230 00
"	21 Jno. Q. Winfield,	"	130 00
"	22 Henry Neff,	"	130 00
"	23 Benj. Trumbo,	"	160 00
"	24 Jacob Caplinger,	"	140 00

CHAS. A. SPRINKEL,
County Sup't of Schools for
Rockingham County.

From the *Rockingham Register* of Dec. 14, 1860.

In the same issue of the *Register* the school teachers of the County are notified that all claims against the Board of School Commissioners must be presented each year by the October Court; the notice being signed by M. H. Harris, president, and Chas. A. Sprinkel, clerk.

Although there was less prejudice against the free school system of 1870 and following years in the Valley than in most other sections of Virginia, many even in Rockingham looked upon it with misgiving, fearing an aggravation of the race problem, a weakening of the moral code, and various other undesirable things. On this point Rev. W. T. Price, of Marlinton, W. Va., for 16 years a prominent citizen of Rockingham, said in a recent letter:

When the public school system [of 1870] was first mooted, the feeling quite prevalent among the more influential people was that the effect would be a very serious one upon the religious interests of the people, through secular education. . . . The first superintendent of schools [in Rockingham] was the Rev. Mr. Loose. He favored all efforts to have the teachers realize their moral responsibility. The result was that a predominating element of officers and teachers were in control of the system who realized this. The institutes were opened with prayer, the Bible was read in all the schools as a preliminary exercise, and in numerous in-

ROCKINGHAM COUNTY

stances the school would be lead in extempore prayer, or the Lord's Prayer would be recited in concert. As time passed it was to be noticed that the moral and religious features became more evident, and the baneful effects of mere secularism were in great measure prevented.

In January, 1871, it was reported that there were 7663 white and 965 colored persons in the county of school age, 5 to 21; that over 60 free schools were in operation in the county, with more than 2000 children in attendance. There were at this time two free schools in Harrisonburg for colored pupils, but as yet none for white children.

In November, 1874, there were 112 teachers of free schools in Rockingham, and about 90 were present at an institute in Harrisonburg.

The following statistics are copied from the county superintendent's report, published in September, 1876, for the year ending July 31, 1876:

Total school population, aged 5 to 21, 9815.
Total number of public schools, 157.
Average number of months taught, 4.85.
Average number of pupils enrolled monthly, 5060.
Average daily attendance, 3897.
Total enrolment for the session, 6446.
Average monthly salary of teachers, $32.56.
Amount received from the State, $10,165.
Amount received from the county, $8809.17.
Amount from district tax, $5818.95.
Amount of supplements paid teachers, $5050.50.
Value of school property owned by districts, $8985.
Number of school houses owned by districts, 24.

In 1889, 203 schools were open to white and 16 to colored pupils; 7348 white pupils and 617 colored were enrolled; 118 men and 85 women (white), 6 men and 10 women (colored), were employed as teachers; the total amount expended in the county for school purposes was $42,833.78; the total value of school property was $78,144.

According to the census of 1905, the school population of the county was 9470; the number of illiterates, 443.

A HISTORY OF

The present widely recognized excellence of the Harrisonburg public schools is mainly due to the efficient and energetic principal, William H. Keister, who came here in 1894. He has been here continuously since that time, and has built up one of the best school systems, beginning with a kindergarten and ending with a high-school following eight grades, in the State. He has stood by the school, and the progressive school board has stood by him. The people have stood by both.

In 1911 Harrisonburg and the several districts of the county voted for compulsory school attendance by large majorities—Rockingham being the second county in Virginia to adopt the compulsory rule. This year (1912) the school board of Harrisonburg has secured an aid of $250 a year for five years from the Slater Fund to introduce industrial training into the colored schools of the town.

The year 1911 also marked the opening of the splendid Waterman School in the northern section of Harrisonburg, providing for a second kindergarten and a number of the lower grades. In 1910 Mr. Albert G. Waterman of New York gave the town a fine lot of three acres or more for a school site; and the town at once erected thereon a stone building, with most approved equipment, for a school of the sort contemplated. The site commands a wide view of the town and surrounding country, and is only a few hundred yards south of the old Waterman homestead, where the house and farm buildings burned on the night of July 13, 1868.[13]

The Harrisonburg school board, composed of Messrs. W. J. Dingledine, Wm. Dean, and P. F. Spitzer, are setting a pace which, if generally followed over the State, will soon

---

[13.] Dr. Asher Waterman, already mentioned in this book, was a surgeon in the Revolution. He came to Harrisonburg about 1783. August 30, 1787, he married Sarah Lochart of Augusta County. Albert G. and Augustus Waterman were his sons, the latter probably living at the old homestead above mentioned. Annie and Isabella were his daughters, the former marrying Chas. Douglas, the latter Robt. Gray. Albert G., born at Harrisonburg, about 1800, went about 1827 to Philadelphia, where he

Joseph Salyards

(Pages 288-292, 328)
Engraving loaned by Henkel & Co.
New Market, Va.

place Virginia in the front rank of educational progress. Other recent members of the board were Hon. A. H. Snyder (1863-1910) and Dr. T. C. Firebaugh. Dr. J. M. Biedler deserves special mention for the work he has done in forwarding medical inspection in the schools of Harrisonburg and Rockingham County.

Rockingham County has had a notable history in the normal school work of Virginia. In August, 1870, E. Armfield Legg was advertising the "Harrisonburg Normal School," the next session of which was to begin the first Monday of September, in the basement of the Lutheran Church, and close the last Friday of June, 1871. Teachers' institutes were held in the county before this time, and many short summer sessions have been offered to teachers of the county for many years. From 1884 to 1891 summer normals were held at Harrisonburg under provisions of the Peabody Fund, as many as 300 teachers being in attendance at one time. From 1882 to 1884, and thereabouts, the institution now Bridgewater College was called the "Virginia Normal School."

Of all the early movements for the professional training of teachers the most notable in Rockingham, perhaps in Virginia, was carried on at Bridgewater from 1873 to 1878 by Alcide Reichenbach,[14] J. D. Bucher,[15] A. L. Funk,[16] Miss Vir-

---

died February 16, 1862, highly honored as a citizen and benefactor. For 24 years preceding his death he was on the board of managers of the Pennsylvania Institution for the Instruction of the Blind. His son, Mr. A. G. Waterman, Jr., is the honored patron of the Harrisonburg school bearing his name.

14. Alcide Reichenbach, A. M., was born in Switzerland in 1845, and enjoyed excellent advantages for training in both Europe and America. For a number of years he has been a professor in Ursinus College, Collegeville, Pa., where he still lives.

15. Dr. J. D. Bucher, still a resident of Bridgewater, was born in Pennsylvania, and has been identified for many years with various phases of educational and professional work. He had received a 4-year course of training in the Pennsylvania normal schools.

16. Prof. A. L. Funk, with Prof. G. H. Hulvey and others, continued

A HISTORY OF

ginia Paul,[17] Miss Laura O'Ferrall,[18] and others. In outlining professional courses for teachers, one covering two years, another four, catalogues of the best American and German normal schools were consulted. A model school for observation, etc., was conducted. State Supt. Ruffner, Maj. Jed Hotchkiss, Prof. S. T. Pendleton, of Richmond, Prof. E. V. DeGraff, and others were secured as special lecturers. Students were in attendance from a number of counties of Virginia, from West Virginia, and Ohio. Some of the pupils that have since become prominent in education and related work are: S. F. Lindsay, Mrs. G. B. Holsinger, Miss Fannie Lowman, Miss Fannie Speck, L. J. Heatwole, J. S. McLeod, G. R. Berlin, Cyrus H. Cline, and Rockingham Paul. In 1875 Supt. Ruffner wrote to the principal:

> Your normal school has been a most useful institution, and I am greatly pleased that you intend to continue it. You are offering advantages to teachers such as are hard to find anywhere else in reach of them. They could well afford to spend a large portion of their earnings in attending upon your school.

A detailed history of the Valley Normal School should be preserved in the educational records of Virginia. It was perhaps the first in the State to do real normal school work.

Shenandoah Normal College, G. W. Hoenshel,[19] princi-

---

normal teaching at Bridgewater and other places. He was principal of the Harrisonburg high-school in 1878-9.

[17]. Miss Virginia Paul, daughter of Peter Paul, sister of Judge John Paul, was a graduate of the State normal school at Trenton, N. J. She taught in the Valley normal school at Bridgewater from 1876 to 1878. She died at Ottobine, Nov. 14, 1879, aged 26.

[18]. Miss Laura O'Ferrall was a sister to Hon. Chas. T. O'Ferrall, governor of Virginia, 1894-8.

[19]. George W. Hoenshel was born at Mendon, Pa., Dec. 11, 1858. After graduating from the Danville, Ind., Normal School, he took steps toward organizing a similar school in Virginia. First at Middletown, then at Harrisonburg, afterward at Basic City and Reliance, he did a helpful work for the teaching profession and the cause of education. His wife was Miss Carrie Moffett, of New Market. He died at Reliance, April

ROCKINGHAM COUNTY

pal, was located at Harrisonburg, on W. Market Street, from 1887 to 1890. Other members of the faculty were A. P. Funkhouser, I. M. Groves, J. J. Cornwell, Mrs. Minnie Funkhouser, and E. U. Hoenshel. Some of the students in 1888 were D. R. Good, I. S. Wampler, T. O. Heatwole, and Orville Dechert.

When, in 1904, definite steps were proposed in the Virginia Senate for establishing another State normal school for women, Harrisonburg formally entered competition for the said school. The town council offered an appropriation of $5000, the county supervisors one of $10,000. The same year a committee of the General Assembly visited Harrisonburg, among other places, to compare the claims of the respective localities. It was not, however, until March 14, 1908, that Harrisonburg was designated, by Act of Assembly, as the place for a new State normal. April 15, 1909, the corner stone was laid; and on September 28, following, the first session began. At present (1912) there are four buildings, three of stone, one of brick, not counting several smaller structures. In all, 1343 different students, representing over 90 counties of Virginia, with a number of States outside of Virginia, have been enrolled. About 70 full graduates have been sent out—two years of work upon the basis of a 4-year high-school course being required for graduation. Two literary societies (the Lanier and the Lee) are maintained by the students, who publish a splendid annual, "The Schoolma'am." A Y. W. C. A., an athletic association, and an alumnae association are kept up, and the student body has adopted an honor system. Julian A. Burruss, formerly of Richmond, is the president and efficient organizer of the school, to whom is due the chief credit for its phenomenal success. He is assisted by a corps of 20 specialists, as instructors and administrative officers, together with a number of student assistants. Hon. Geo. B. Keezell is president of the board of trustees; Hon. Floyd W.

12, 1896. Among his published works is a 149-page volume entitled "X-Talks and Other Addresses." Dr. E. U. Hoenshel of Dayton, Va., well known as an educator, traveler, author, and lecturer, is a brother.

King is vice-president; Hon. Geo. N. Conrad is treasurer. The late Hon. A. H. Snyder was a most helpful member on the original board of trustees.

Two sons of Rockingham who long ago became famous as educators were Henry Tutwiler and Gessner Harrison, both born in Harrisonburg in 1807, one the son of the postmaster, Henry Tutwiler, the other the son of the doctor, Peachy Harrison. They both entered the University of Virginia in 1825, where, in due time, Tutwiler got the M. A. and Harrison the M. D. degree. It is said that Tutwiler was the first to receive the coveted Master's degree from the new institution. Later he went to Alabama, where his life work was given, with eminent success, to educational work. His daughter, Julia Tutwiler, is to-day accorded first honors in Alabama among the teachers and leaders of her sex. Henry Tutwiler lived till 1884.

Gessner Harrison became a professor in his alma mater, and was chairman of the faculty a number of years. He prepared serviceable text-books, and taught with the inspiring word of a leader. His motto, "Trust God and work," explains his life and character. He died in 1862. The sons of Mars dinned men's ears at the moment, but upon the quiet lawn, and among the arcades where the scholars linger, his voice is still heard.

Among the men and women, native or not, who have made notable contributions to Virginia's schools, may yet be mentioned the following: Geo. A. Baxter, of Rockingham; president of Washington College, now Washington and Lee University, 1799-1829; Hugh Tagart, first a Catholic priest, then a school-master, who died at Harrisonburg about 1840; Wm. S. Slusser (1836-1898), 40 years a teacher in Rockingham and Augusta; R. H. Sheppe, lately deceased, prominent first as an educational leader in Rockingham, then in the State at large; C. E. Barglebaugh, long well known as a teacher in the county, and still in active life; Miss Belle C. Hannah, long a favorite teacher, now the wife of Sen. G. B. Keezell; Chas. G. Maphis (1865 —), a native of Shenandoah,

ROCKINGHAM COUNTY

but from 1887 to 1890 principal of the Harrisonburg schools; now professor of education in the State University; H. M. Hays, a son of Rockingham by long residence, now on the faculty of the University of Missouri; W. T. Myers, a son by birth, now on the faculty of the University of Virginia; I. N. H. Beahm (1859—), another native, a founder of schools; H. S. Hooke, long in Harrisonburg, now in Roanoke; J. J. Lincoln, well known in the State; J. W. Basore, of Broadway and Princeton; and last, but not least, our veteran superintendent, Geo. H. Hulvey, a son of Rockingham by birth and service.

References have already been made to the colored schools of the county and county-seat. As early as December, 1866, Mrs. M. W. L. Smith, Miss Phoebe Libby, and Miss Ellen Crockett, from Maine and New Hampshire, were conducting a school in Harrisonburg for colored children: 82 being in attendance during the day, 100 at night.[20] They were teaching, it was said, in the new colored church. From time to time the school seems to have been taken from place to place. Sometimes it was held in the basement of the church (Northern Methodist, later Catholic) that stood opposite the B. & O. station; at another time it was in a back room, somewhere, upstairs, and the boys and girls to reach it had to "climb, jump, and stoop." But they did it all gladly.

In the fall of 1868 Watkins James, an agent of the Freedmen's Bureau, established a colored school at Bridgewater. Just before Christmas a lot of white fellows wrecked the furniture, but the better people condemned the act.[21]

Within the last year or two the colored people of Harrisonburg have taken notable part in repairing and enlarging their school building, which is now a handsome and commodious structure. The efficient principal is Mr. H. A. M. Johns, formerly of Hampton, who has been here since 1908. Under his direction the work is making fine progress.[22]

---

[20]. *R. Register*, Dec. 13, 1866.   [21]. *Old Commonwealth*, June 6, 1869.

[22]. I am indebted to Prof. U. G. Wilson for a most interesting paper on the Harrisonburg colored schools; it is withheld from publication here only for lack of space.

CHAPTER XVI.

CHARITABLE INSTITUTIONS.

As early as 1822 there was in Rockingham an auxiliary colonization society, endeavoring to raise money to establish and support an "Infant Colony" at Cape Misurado, on the African Coast. Robert Herron was treasurer. This society was still in existence in 1825.

The civil war of course produced many needs for charity, and was marked throughout by organized movements aiming to supply those needs. Early in the war a soldiers' aid society was organized in the county. At a meeting in Harrisonburg, September 24, 1861, the following officers were elected:

President—Miss Jeannetta Conrad.

Vice-Presidents—Mrs. Amanda Keezle, Mrs. Strother Effinger.

Recording Secretary—Miss M. Byrd.

Corresponding Secretaries—Mrs. Harriet Ruffner, Mrs. M. Harvey Effinger.

Treasurer—Mrs. Harriet Warren.

The following were chosen managers:

Mrs. James Crawford	Mrs. Margaret Wartmann
Mrs. G. Kratzer	Mrs. Rebecca Newman
Mrs. Dr. Dinges	Mrs. Henry Ott
Mrs. Nelson Sprinkel	Mrs. Annie Kenney
Mrs. Geo. Christie	Mrs. Lucy Effinger
Mrs. Col. Hopkins	Mrs. Juliet Strayer
Mrs. A. Lincoln	Mrs. Mary Kyle
Miss Anna Strayer	Maj. L. W. Gambill
Miss Rebecca Davis	Mr. Peter Woodward
Miss Annie Jennings	Mrs. Lizzie Hudson
Miss O'Brien	Mrs. Susan Bear
Mrs. L. Bryan	Mrs. Malinda Kite

ROCKINGHAM COUNTY

Most of the ladies named lived in Harrisonburg and vicinity; some were from other parts of the county. At another meeting held in Harrisonburg, October 29, the following were added to the list of solicitors for the county:

Mrs. Bramwell Rice, Rushville;
Mrs. E. Bear, North Mountain;
Mrs. Fannie Hopkins, Mt. Clinton;
Mrs. Kieffer, Mountain Valley;
Mrs. Mary Lincoln, Linvill's Creek;
Mrs. A. Brock, Linvill's Creek;
Mrs. Jane Burkholder, Linvill's Creek;
Mrs. Christian Coffman, Linvill's Creek;

Mrs. D. C. Byerly	Mrs. Huldah Heiskell
Mrs. Jacob Byerly	Mrs. Priscilla Miller
Mrs. Lenion Harman	Mrs. Rankin
Miss Mary Lewis	Miss Dolly McGahey
Miss Sarah Weaver	(Mrs. Fannie Hopkins)

The object of the society was to provide supplies of various kinds for soldiers in the field and in the hospitals.[1]

In June, 1862, C. Clinton Clapp, a Harrisonburg merchant, made the first subscription ($50) to a fund for the purpose of erecting a monument upon the battlefield where the lamented Turner Ashby fell.[2]

On April 30 and May 1, 1863, the ladies of Bridgewater gave an entertainment in the M. E. church, the proceeds to be used for the benefit of sick and wounded soldiers. In the spring of 1864 they sent 30 pairs of socks to Co. D, 10th Va. Infantry.

In February, 1864, the Misses Ewing, of near Harrisonburg, furnished an abundant supply of warm, woolen socks to Co. A, 1st Mo. Cavalry. This was the famous Woodson's Company, McNeill's Battalion, partisan rangers. About the same time D. M. Switzer offered to cut garments free for private soldiers of Rockingham in limited circumstances.

---

1. See *Rockingham Register*, Oct. 4 and Nov. 1, 1861.
2. See page 179 of this book.

The physicians made special provisions for such soldiers and their families. Some of the mills in the county did grinding for soldiers' families, free of toll.

At a meeting held in McGaheysville February 21, 1864, residents of the village and neighborhood contributed $1700 for the aid of soldiers. The meeting was addressed by Rev. J. L. Stirewalt, of New Market, who was soliciting funds to be used in purchasing artificial limbs for maimed Confederates.

November 28, 1864, at a special meeting in the M. E. church, Port Republic, conducted by Rev. J. Stirewalt and Pastor J. P. Hyde, $894.66 was taken up for the help of wounded (maimed) soldiers.

After the battle of New Market, May 15, 1864, the people of Harrisonburg and vicinity sent a lot of carriages to the battlefield, specially for the purpose of bringing the wounded men of Woodson's company to Harrisonburg, where many of them were cared for in private families.

In 1865-6 the merchants, lawyers, doctors, and mechanics of Harrisonburg formed a Thespian society, for the relief of widows and orphans of Rockingham soldiers. In May, 1866, a Thespian society was formed in Bridgewater.

In the summer of 1866, a Rockingham Memorial Association was organized by the ladies of Harrisonburg. This was probably the beginning of the Ladies' Memorial Association mentioned on pages 159, 169, 170, above. In the *Old Commonwealth* of November 28, 1872, appeared a tribute to Mrs. C. C. Strayer, president of this association.

In 1878 liberal contributions were sent from Rockingham to the yellow fever sufferers in the South. Up to October 17, $715.24 had been contributed in the county to this cause. Early in 1880 a meeting was held in the Court House to organize relief for the victims of the famine in Ireland.

A work of benevolent character that must not be overlooked in this connection was organized and led for many years by Mrs. Lucy G. Chrisman, in cleaning up, beautifying, and caring for the cemeteries of the county. This work

Rockingham County Alms House
(Page 313)

Old Folks' Home
(Page 313)

Post Office and U. S. Court House, Harrisonburg

Rockingham Memorial Hospital
(Pages 314, 315)

ROCKINGHAM COUNTY

probably centered at New Erection, but has extended far and wide with most beneficent results.

The remainder of this chapter will be devoted to five particular institutions, which typify different lines of benevolent enterprise: (1) the Harrisonburg almshouse, (2) the county almshouse, (3) the Old Folks' Home, (4) the Orphans' Home, (5) the Rockingham Memorial Hospital. The chief benevolent institution of Rockingham is the good will of her citizens; but this has crystalized in various definite forms.

The almshouse for the town of Harrisonburg is located on the Valley Pike, a short distance southwest of town, near the toll gate. It is under the supervision of a committee of three of the town council, who, with the chief of police, look after the poor of the town. The inmates usually number only five or six. The present chief of police is Frank L. Dovel; the superintendent of the almshouse is David Landes.

The almshouse for the county was formerly located near Keezletown, but for the past thirty or forty years it has been at the present site, one mile northeast of Pleasant Valley. It is on a fine farm of 323 acres, 185 acres of which are under cultivation, the balance being in timber. The number of persons cared for here is usually 46 or 47. The popular superintendent is C. W. Pence, who has had charge of the place for the past seven years.

At Timberville is located the Old Folks' Home, maintained by the Church of the Brethren. Initial steps toward providing such an institution were taken in 1888, when Michael Zigler, S. F. Miller, and N. W. Beery were appointed a committee, by the Second District of Virginia, to take the matter under advisement. The home was opened March 1, 1892, with Daniel Wine and wife in charge. The number of inmates ranges from ten to twenty-five. J. W. Lichliter is the present superintendent.

Near the Old Folks' Home, at Timberville, the Church of the Brethren maintains an Orphans' Home, established in 1905. The present building was completed in 1910. The plan contemplates a home and industrial school for orphan

A HISTORY OF

children, regardless of religious affiliation. Altogether, up to March 31, 1912, 44 children had been received at the Home. Of these, 24 have been placed in permanent homes. The original trustees of the institution were D. H. Zigler, J. W. Wampler, J. M. Wampler, M. J. Cline, and P. S. Thomas; the present trustees are D. H. Zigler, S. D. Miller, M. J. Cline, J. J. Conner, and P. S. Thomas. Mr. and Mrs. John L. Holsinger are in immediate charge.

On October 1, 1912, the Rockingham Memorial Hospital, located at the south side of Harrisonburg, adjoining the grounds of the State Normal School, was formally opened. A gift of $20,000 or more, by will, made four years ago by William G. Leake, led to the establishment of this institution. Of Mr. Leake it has been said, "He devoted his life to honest work, and his wealth to relieve human suffering. The Rockingham Memorial Hospital is his Monument." By his own request, the hospital does not bear his name, but inside the main entrance is a handsome bronze tablet, bearing the following inscription:

```
WILLIAM GLODOMORE LEAKE
         1848—1908

     THIS TABLET IS ERECTED
   TO RECORD THE GRATITUDE
              OF
        THE PEOPLE OF
      ROCKINGHAM COUNTY
              TO
   WILLIAM GLODOMORE LEAKE
    OF HARRISONBURG VIRGINIA

    FOR THE NOBLE GENEROUS
         AND FREE GIFT
        WHICH MADE THIS
   HOSPITAL BUILDING POSSIBLE
            MCMXII
```

ROCKINGHAM COUNTY

At another place in the hall is a marble tablet, inscribed as follows:

THE ROCKINGHAM MEMORIAL HOSPITAL
1910

BOARD OF TRUSTEES

J. WILTON—President
T. N. HAAS—Vice-President
J. M. BIEDLER—Secretary
E. R. MILLER—Treasurer

W. J. Dingledine	T. O. Jones
George E. Sipe	Layton B. Yancey
Elmer U. Hoenshel	John S. Funk
Walter B. Yount	John H. Hoover

BUILDING COMMITTEE

J. Wilton	W. J. Dingledine
E. R. Miller	E. U. Hoenshel
T. N. Haas	J. M. Biedler

ARCHITECTS—Corneal & Johnston
BUILDERS—W. M. Bucher & Son

At present Julian A. Burruss and Jacob S. Sellers are members of the board of trustees.

All over the county, churches, benevolent organizations, and generous individuals have made donations to the hospital. Within the past year the ladies' auxiliary of Harrisonburg has raised $2575 for the institution. The president of this organization is Mrs. Russell Bucher; Mrs. Julian A. Burruss is secretary, and Mrs. E. Purcell, treasurer. Among the number of ladies who have rendered notable service, it will not be invidious to mention the name of Mrs. B. Ney. The superintending nurse in charge of the hospital is Miss Nan Dupuy.

CHAPTER XVII.

WRITERS AND PRINTERS: BOOKS AND PERIODICALS.

A. A LIST OF WRITERS AND THEIR WORKS.

Beahm, Isaac N. H.: Born near Good's Mill, May 14, 1859; educator, traveler, and lecturer; writer on various educational and social topics; address, Trevilians, Va.

Bowman, Peter: Located in Rockingham about 1785; in 1817 published (Laurentz Wartmann, Harrisonburg, printer) a book entitled "Ein Zeugniss von der Taufe."

Braun, Johannes: From 1800 to 1850 a leader of the German Reformed Church in Rockingham; in 1818 he published (Laurentz Wartmann, Harrisonburg, printer) a 16mo book of 419 pages, entitled "Circular-Schreiben an die Deutschen Einwohner von Rockingham und Augusta, und den benachbarten Counties: Erster Band." In 1830 Wartmann printed for him "Eine kurze Unterweisung Christlichen Religion," etc., a 16mo book of 72 pages.

Brown, T. H. B.: Born in Albemarle County, Va., Sept. 25, 1835; died at his home in Bridgewater, Aug. 12, 1900; a resident of Rockingham from 1859 or 1860; a physician, a skilled journalist ("N. W. Orb"), and a contributor for many years to the *Rockingham Register* and different metropolitan papers.

Bryan, Daniel: Born in Rockingham about 1795, son of Maj. William Bryan; brother of Allan C. Bryan; named after Daniel Boone; graduated from Washington College (now W. & Lee University) 1807; merchant, lawyer, poet; colonel in War of 1812; postmaster at Alexandria many years; died in Washington City, December, 1866; author:

1813—"The Mountain Muse" (16mo, 252 pp.); printed at Harrisonburg, by Davidson & Bourne.

ROCKINGHAM COUNTY

——— —"Lay of Gratitude" (greeting to Lafayette).
1826—"Appeal for Suffering Genius."
1830—"Thoughts."
——— —"Education," etc.[1]

"The Mountain Muse," dealing in heroic verse with the adventures of Daniel Boone, was sold in no less than nine or ten States outside of Virginia. Considering the difficulties of travel, transportation, and communication in those days, we cannot help wondering how Mr. Bryan secured such a wide circulation for his little book. The matter may be explained in some measure, no doubt, by the fact that the number of books put upon the market then was small in comparison with the number that are bidding now in sharp competition for the reader's notice. In one copy of "The Mountain Muse" that the writer has seen, and in only one, is printed the list of the subscribers' names. They total about 1350, and belonged for the most part, to the people of Virginia: eastern Virginia as well as the Valley. About 150 belonged to residents of Tennessee; about 100 to residents of Ohio; while the remainder were distributed among Pennsylvania, Maryland, New York, South Carolina, North Carolina, Connecticut, Louisiana, and Mississippi Territory.

Hon. Chas. Page Bryan, ambassador to Japan, is a grandson of Daniel Bryan.

Bryan, Mrs. Emma Lyon: Native of Richmond; a resident of Harrisonburg since her marriage in 1864 to Pendleton Bryan (son of Allan C. Bryan); artist, composer, author:

1879—"My Sunflower's Fan" (illustrated by herself; published in *St. Nicholas*, December).

1892—"A Romance of the Valley of Virginia" (a story of the war of 1860-5; 12mo, 228 pp.; printed on Confederate paper).

Paintings:
1867—"Harrisonburg, Looking Eastward."

---

[1]. References: Washington and Lee Catalogue of Alumni, p. 59; Painter's Poets of Virginia, pp. 57-59; *Rockingham Register*, Jan. 3, 1867, and May 7, 1868.

1886—"Sunrise at Lover's Leap."

1886—"Where Ashby Fell" (original owned by Miss Lucy Shacklett, Harrisonburg; copies in the Confederate Museum at Richmond, and elsewhere).

Burkholder, Newton M.: Born at Fort Lynne, near Greenmount, Jan. 17, 1844; son of John Burkholder; was a C. S. A. soldier, and a telegraph operator at Harrisonburg from Jan. 1, 1863, till the close of the war; graduated in dentistry (1867) from the Balt. College of Dent. Surgery; in 1865 married Miss Ella Moore, who died in 1897; in 1899 married Miss Cornelia Switzer who survives him; he died Dec. 8, 1900, at Harrisonburg; was a frequent contributor to the *Rockingham Register*, the *Central Presbyterian* (Richmond), etc.; in 1899-1900 he wrote a series of articles for the *Richmond Dispatch*, on episodes of the war.

Burkholder, Peter: Long a resident of Rockingham; in 1816 he published a treatise on water-baptism, etc., comprising 60 16mo pages, which was printed in Harrisonburg by Laurentz Wartmann; was the author of "Nine Reflections," published in English by Joseph Funk in 1837.

Byerly, Frank Aubrey: A native of Rockingham, and many years a teacher in the county, now in West Virginia; published in 1910 "Hints, Helps, Devices, and Suggestions for School Work" (16mo, 32 pp). Has been a frequent contributor to the *Rockingham Register* and other periodicals on educational topics.

Chrisman, George: Born in Rockingham, June 2, 1832; son of Geo. H. and Martha Herring Chrisman; captain of "Chrisman's Infantry" (1861) and the "Boy Company" of cavalry (1864); married Lucy Gilmer Grattan, Nov. 13, 1867; for many years a writer on farming and stock raising.

Cline, Justus H.: Born near Timberville, Oct. 14, 1875; minister, teacher, and author:

1905—"Some Benefactors of Bridgewater College."

1912—"Geological Features of Rockingham County" (see pp. 21-31 above).

1912—"Dikes of the Shenandoah Valley" (in preparation with Dr. Thos. L. Watson).

ROCKINGHAM COUNTY

Address, Stuart's Draft, Va.

Compton, Geo. F.: Long a resident of Harrisonburg, now living in Charlottesville; wrote 27 articles on the early history of Rockingham County, published, 1885, in the *Rockingham Register*.

Conn, Miss Ruth Randolph: Born at McGaheysville, 1893; author of "Swords and Roses" (story), "The Making of the Flowers," "October Woods," "A Blink o' Rest" (poems); etc.; a contributor to this book (page 32).

Conrad, Miss Mary Lynn: A native of Rockingham, and a resident of Harrisonburg; author of "Confederate Banners" (12mo, 20 pp., illust.).

Converse, Henry Augustus: Born in Philadelphia, May 8, 1839; died Dec. 5, 1880, in Harrisonburg, where he had lived from January, 1879, and where he compiled his valuable work for the members of his profession: "Indexes to the Virginia and West Virginia Reports" (8vo, 381 pp.; Richmond, 1881).

Cox, S. K.: Born in Baltimore, July 16, 1823; died in Harrisonburg, Nov. 27, 1909; clergyman, journalist, poet. Dr. Cox came in 1888 to Harrisonburg, where he had his home the remainder of his life. In 1892 he married Miss Bryan Moffett, who survives him. For a number of years he was associate editor of the Baltimore and Richmond *Christian Advocate*; he wrote much in prose and verse, of high merit.

Daingerfield, Foxhall A.: Born in Rockingham, Feb. 8, 1839; married Nettie Gray, Nov. 4, 1863; lawyer, soldier, writer; contributor to agricultural papers, specially; residence, Castleton, Lexington, Ky.

Daingerfield, Mrs. Nettie Gray: Born in Harrisonburg, daughter of Col. A. S. Gray; wife of Capt. F. A. Daingerfield; address, Castleton, Lexington, Ky.; author:

1903—"That Dear Old Sword" (12mo, 99 pp.).

1906—"Our Mammy" (8vo, 143 pp.).

1909—"Frescati" (12 mo, 71 pp.).

Early, Henry C.: Born in Augusta County, Va., May 11, 1855; for many years a resident of Rockingham. Long a contributor to, and recently an editor of, the *Gospel Messenger*, he writes with force and grace. He is the author of Chapter 5 in "Two Centuries" (8vo, 398 pp.; Elgin, Ill., 1808).

Flory, J. S.: Born in Rockingham, March 28, 1836; in 1881 was editor of the *Home Mirror*, Longmont, Colo., in 1883, of the Longmont *Press*; the latter year he contributed a series of letters to the *Rockingham Register* on "Western Ramblings"; author:

— —"Echoes from the Wild Frontier."
1897—"Mind Mysteries" (12mo, 221 pp.).

Flory, John S.: Born in Rockingham in 1866: Ph. D. of the University of Virginia, 1907; now president of Bridgewater College; author of:

1903—"The Turleytown Blockhouse" (in U. Va. Mag., Feb.).

1903—"Gray's Relation to His Time" (in U. Va. Mag., Oct.).

1904—"The First University Planned for America" (in Southern History Magazine, Washington, Jan.).

1904—"John Wilson as an Essayist" (in Sewanee Review, Oct.).

1906—"The German Folksong" (in Sewanee Review, Jan.).

1908—"Literary Activity of the Brethren in the 18th Century" (12mo, 347 pp.).

1908—"Our Present Educational Activity" (pp. 331-339 of "Two Centuries," Brethren Pub. House, Elgin, Ill.).

1911—"The Junior and Senior Years of the College Course" (in the Inglenook, August).

Funk, Benjamin: Born at Singer's Glen, Dec. 29, 1829; died in 1909; compiled "Life and Labors of Elder John Kline," an octavo volume of 480 pages, published at Elgin, Ill., in 1900.

Funk, Joseph: Born in Berks County, Pa., March 9, 1777; died at his home in Singer's Glen, Dec. 24, 1862; teacher, author, translator, compiler, and publisher. His printing establishment, opened at Mountain Valley (Singer's

DR. GESSNER HARRISON
(Pages 308, 322)
By per. of J. S. Patton, U. Va.

ROCKINGHAM COUNTY

Glen) in 1847, is said to have been the first Mennonite printing house in America; this was kept up by himself and his sons till 1863, and then by his sons till 1878. The Ruebush-Kieffer press, established at Dayton in 1878, continues his work into the present. More concerning him is given in this chapter, in the list of Rockingham periodicals, and in Chapter 18, under the head of Rockingham singers; following is a list of his more important writings, compilations, etc.:

1816 (traditional date)—A collection of hymns, in German, set to music, entitled "Choral-Music"; 88 pages; printed at Harrisonburg by Laurentz Wartmann.[2]

1832—First edition of "Genuine Church Music," 208 pages; later called "Harmonia Sacra," the last (17th) edition appearing after 1870. The first two editions were printed at Winchester; the third at Harrisonburg (1842), by Wartmann & Way; the rest, beginning with the 4th in 1847, at Singer's Glen.

1837—"Mennonite Confession of Faith," with Burkholder's "Nine Reflections" (12mo, 460 pp.); a translation from the German; including a historical introduction, written by himself.

1857—"The Reviewer Reviewed"; a work in controversial theology, directed against Eld. John Kline's "Review" of Eld. Henry Funk's "Treatise on Baptism"; 16mo, 309 pages; printed by Joseph Funk & Sons, at Mountain Valley.

Funkhouser, Jacob: Born in Rockingham about 1833; died July, 1903; compiled and published (Harrisonburg, 1902) "A Historical Sketch of the Funkhouser Family" (8vo, 100 pp.).

Garber, Jacob A.: Born near Mt. Crawford, Jan. 25, 1879; residence, Timberville; occasional writer of prose and verse; formerly editor of Emerson College Magazine, etc.

Garber, W. A.: Minister, lecturer, writer; among other things, has published "The Passion Play Graft" (12 mo, 64 pp.; 1911); address, Dayton, Va.

---

[2]. Mr. Noah Blosser, Dale Enterprise, has kindly loaned a copy of this book. It bears no date, but Mr. John Funk, a son of the compiler, says it was published in 1816.

A HISTORY OF

Grattan, Geo. G.: Born in Rockingham, February 12, 1839; lawyer and soldier; judge of the Rockingham County Court, 1885-1904; brother of Charles and nephew of P. R. Grattan; published in 1912 "The Battle of Boonsboro Gap" (8vo, 12 pp., illust.); address, Harrisonburg.

Grattan, Peachy R.: Born in Rockingham, 1801; died near Richmond, 1881; famous in Virginia history as a statesman and as the compiler of Grattan's Reports.

Hall, J. H.: A native of Rockingham, and a resident of Dayton; compiler of "Golden Thoughts and Memoirs" (16mo, 125 pp.), published in 1905 by the Ruebush-Kieffer Company, Dayton; has in preparation a history of popular Gospel songs. —See Chapter 18, for additional facts of biography.

Harrison, Gessner: Born in Harrisonburg, June 26, 1807; died near Charlottesville, April 7, 1862; physician, educator, and author:
  1848—"On Greek Prepositions."
  1852—"Exposition of Some of the Laws of Latin Grammar."

Hays, Daniel: Born in Hampshire County, Va., now W. Va., May 16, 1839; for many years past a resident of Rockingham; postoffice, Broadway. Eld. Hays has long been recognized as one of the best writers in the Church of the Brethren, and has been a frequent contributor to the church papers, especially the Gospel Messenger. In 1908 he contributed chapter 8 to "Two Centuries," a volume of church history; the year before (1907) he, with Eld. S. F. Sanger, published "The Olive Branch" (12mo, 232 pp.); and he now has ready for the press "A Silver Thread of History in a Golden Cord of Doctrine."

Hays, Heber M.: Born in Shenandoah Co., Va., May 7, 1876; long a resident of Rockingham; Ph. D., Univ. of Chicago, 1912; member of the faculty, Univ. of Missouri; teacher and author:
  1908—"On the German Dialect Spoken in the Valley of Virginia" (in *Dialect Notes*, Vol. 3).
  1910 (?)—A genealogy of the John Myers Family (in *Penn-Germania*).

ROCKINGHAM COUNTY

1912—An edition of Hesiod's *Works and Days*, with introduction, explanatory notes, etc., comprising about 200 pages.

Heatwole, Cornelius J.: Born at Dale Enterprise, Oct. 20, 1868; teacher and educator; published "History of the Heatwole Family" (8vo, 274 pp.), in 1907; a special contributor to this volume (see Chapter 21).

Heatwole, D. A.: Published a history of the Heatwole family (16mo, 24 pp.), in 1882.—See note 7, page 224.

Heatwole, Lewis J.: Born at Dale Enterprise, Dec. 4, 1852, eldest son of D. A. Heatwole (p. 224); teacher, pastor, astronomer, author; has been a volunteer weather observer for 30 years; makes calculations annually for a large number of almanacs, etc., in the United States and Canada; is a frequent contributor to periodicals; he has published the following books:

1907—"Moral Training in the Public Schools" (12mo, 109 pages).

1908—"Key to the Almanac" (12mo, 238 pp.).

1910—"A History of the Mennonite Conference of Virginia" (8vo, 117 pp.).—The last with C. H. Brunk and Christian Good.

At present Bishop Heatwole is perfecting the "Perpetual Calendar," which has already attracted wide attention because of its simplicity, accuracy, and convenience, and which may become epoch-making in the annals of time.

Hoenshel, Elmer U.: Home address, Dayton, Va.; several years principal of Shenandoah Collegiate Institute; traveler, lecturer, and author:

1909—"My Three Days in Gilead" (16mo, 85 pp.).

1910—"By The Overflowing Nile" (16mo, 133 pp.).

1912—"The Crimson Trail" (12mo, 141 pp.).

Hoenshel, George W.: Born in Pennsylvania, 1858; died at Reliance, Va., 1896; at Harrisonburg, 1887-1890; in 1888 published "Education of Girls." In 1900 Mrs. Hoenshel published his "X-Talks and Other Addresses" (16mo, 149 pp.) at New Market, Va.

Hott, George P.: Residence, Dayton; clergyman, educator, author; a frequent contributor to magazines, and a writer of a number of excellent hymns; author of "Christ the Teacher" (12mo, 138 pp.), 1900.

Jeffries, Thomas Fayette: Known as "Crippled Fayette" and "Roaming Invalid." His home was at or near Keezletown, but he spent most of his time traveling, selling his writings, showing stereoscopic views, etc. He was a frequent contributor of travel sketches (from many different States) to the *Register*, the *Old Commonwealth*, etc., during the 60's and 70's—perhaps during the 80's also. He died in Georgia 15 or 20 years ago. He published at least two books:

1856—"Nine Years in Bed" (16mo, 72 pp.); printed by Jos. Funk & Sons, Mountain Valley.

——"Invalid's Offering" (16mo, 150 pp.); date and place of publication not known.

These books contain interesting notes of travel.

Johnston, James C.: Educator and writer; residence, Harrisonburg; contributor to periodicals, and editor of classics for school use.

Kemper, Charles Edward: Born near Cross Keys, June 5, 1859, son of Edward S. and Susan Craig Kemper; graduated in law at Washington and Lee, 1882; practiced 10 years in Staunton; in 1893 appointed Assistant and Chief Clerk in the office of the Supervising Architect, U. S. Treasury Dept.; in 1894 appointed chief of this office, holding the position till March, 1911, when he resigned on account of poor health; on July 16, 1912, re-entered the service, and, by special designation of the Secretary of the Treasury, placed on the Board of Award, to award all contracts for the construction of public buildings. During his service in the above department, Mr. Kemper has been directly connected with the erection of post-offices, courthouses, custom houses, and marine hospitals for the United States, costing in the aggregate more than $160,-000,000; and served on the U. S. Boards of Management for the expositions held at Atlanta, Nashville, and Omaha. He was a contributor to Boogher's "Gleanings of Virginia His-

ROCKINGHAM COUNTY

tory" (Washington, 1903); and edited, with valuable notes, the following:

"The Record of Peaked Mountain Church" (William and Mary College Quarterly, Vol. 14).—See pages 61-63, above.

"Moravian Diaries of Travel through Virginia" (Virginia Magazine of History and Biography, Vols. 11 and 12).—See pages 45-51, above.

"The Early Westward Movement of Virginia" (Va. Mag., Vol. 13).—See pages 35, 36, above.

In addition, he has frequently written articles of special historical interest and value.

Kieffer, Aldine S. (1840-1904): musician and poet; published "Hours of Fancy, or Vigil and Vision" (16mo, 237 pp.) at Dayton in 1881.—See next chapter for a more extended sketch.

Kieffer, H. Prime: Born at Singer's Glen, July 23, 1880, son of Rollin and Jennie Stinespring Kieffer; nephew of Aldine S.; educated in Lafayette, Indiana, high-school and Purdue University; contributor to leading magazines; traveled in Canal Zone and Europe as special correspondent for N. Y. papers; residence, New York.

Langhorne, Mrs. Orra Gray: Born in Harrisonburg, daughter of Col. A. S. Gray; lived in Lynchburg; wrote several small volumes, and was a contributor to high-class periodicals.

Lilly, Malcolm G.: Well known as a teacher at Clover Hill and other places in Rockingham; occasional writer of verse; has in preparation a volume on U. S. history and teaching devices.

Long, Isaac S.: Born near Port Republic, May 13, 1875; since 1903 a missionary in India; present address, Pimpalner; lecturer and writer on subjects relating to India.

Long, Mrs. Isaac S.: Born near Scott's Ford, Rockingham County; since 1903 a missionary in India; writer on India, Babylonia, etc.

Mauzy, Richard: Born at McGaheysville, June 17, 1824, son of Col. Jos. Mauzy; editor and journalist; from 1860 to

A HISTORY OF

1895 was owner and editor of the *Staunton Spectator;* in 1911 he published a history (8vo, 127 pp.) of the Mauzy and Kisling families (printed at Harrisonburg, bound at Dayton); he is a special contributor to this volume (see pp. 194, 195, etc). Present address, McGaheysville.

Myers, Weldon Thomas: Born at Broadway, Oct. 25, 1879; Ph. D., Univ. of Va., 1912; adjunct professor, English Literature, U. Va.; occasional writer of prose and verse.

1905—Two chapters in "Bridgewater College, Past and Present."

1908—"Aldine S. Kieffer, the Valley Poet, and His Work" (in *Musical Million*, August).

1909—An article on Amelia B. Welby, in the "Library of Southern Literature."

1912—"The Relations of Latin and English as Living Languages in England during the Age of Milton."

Neff, John H.: Born near Mt. Jackson, Va., 1842; married Miss Brownie Morrison, Nov. 1, 1883; died at Charlottesville, March 18, 1912; for many years a prominent physician of Harrisonburg and Virginia; wrote "Typhoid Fever," published by Va. Med. Soc., 1893; "The Proper Mode and Place for Inflicting the Death Penalty," published by Virginia Board of Health, 1901.

O'Ferrall, Chas. T. (See chapter XIX for sketch): Author of "Forty Years of Active Service," a volume of 367 8vo pages, published by Neales in 1904.

Palmer, Olin Austin: Of Port Republic, printer and author:

1912—"At the Mercy of Fate" (8vo, 210 pp.); a tale of the Shenandoah Valley; printed by Mr. Palmer at Port Republic.

1912—"The Mystery of Chesney Hall"; in preparation.

Paul, Mrs. K. S.: Miss Katherine Green, of Front Poyal, Va., married Hon. John Paul, of Rockingham, in 1872; compiled a list of about 500 Virginia writers in 1893 for the World's Fair; was a member of the executive committee of

ROCKINGHAM COUNTY

the board of lady commissioners; a writer of both prose and verse; address, Harrisonburg.

Price, Wm. T.: Clergyman, editor, and author; born near Marlinton, W. Va. (his present home), July 19, 1830; from 1869 to 1885 was a citizen of Rockingham—pastor at New Erection. During this period he published the *Young Virginian* (q. v.); he also took much interest in education (see page 302, above). He has contributed extensively to periodicals, and is author of:

"Memoirs of Rev. John Pinkerton" (pastor of Mossy Creek Church, Va.).
"Memoirs of Dr. J. H. Scott" (of Beverly, W. Va.).
"History of Pocahontas County."
"Semicentennial History of Greenbrier Presbytery."
"On to Grafton." Etc.

Richcreek, W. A.: A resident of Bridgewater; for many years a contributor to the press, local and national.

Rohr, Will S.: Under pseudonym "Singlesticks" wrote "The Mountaineer," a tale of the war, published as a continued story in 1866 in the *Old Commonwealth;* in 1868 was associate editor of the *Southern Musical Advocate*, in which he published "Wishtaneta," a serial, founded on a legend of the Joe's Creek Valley.

Roller, John Edwin: Born near Mt. Crawford, 1845, son of Peter S. and Frances Allebaugh Roller; graduate, Va. Military Institute, 1863; soldier, C. S. A.; member of Va. Senate, 1869-1873; appointed major-general of the 3d division of the Virginia militia, January, 1872; lawyer, lecturer, antiquarian. He has made a collection of rare books, manuscripts, etc., that cannot, perhaps, be duplicated in America. Among his published addresses are the following:

1900—"The Reformed Church in Schlatter's Day."

1907—Address before Neff-Rice Camp, U. C. V., New Market, Va.

1909—Address of welcome, made at Harrisonburg before the annual conference of the Church of the Brethren.

See page 282 above.

Roller, Robt. Douglas: Born in Rockingham, near Mt. Crawford; received degree of D. D. from W. Va. University, 1894; now rector of St. John's Episcopal Church, Charleston; has served in various honorable and responsible positions in the councils of the church; author:

"Richardson—De Priest Family" (8vo, 50 pp.); gave valuable assistance to Bishop Peterkin in the preparation of "A History and Record of the Protestant Episcopal Church in the Diocese of West Virginia" (8vo, 876 pp., 1902). Dr. Roller is a brother of Gen. John E. Roller, of Harrisonburg.

Salyards, Joseph (1808-1885): Scholar, teacher, philosopher, poet; writer of prose and verse; in 1874 his chief work, "Idothea; or, The Divine Image" (16 mo, 308 pp.), was published by Henkel, Calvert & Co., New Market.—See pages 288-292, above.

Showalter, William Joseph: Journalist and author; born near Dale Enterprise, July 10, 1878; present address, Washington City. For a number of years Mr. Showalter has been one of the best known syndicate writers of the national capital. His schooling was received at Bridgewater, Mt. Clinton, and other places in Rockingham, and his first experience in newspaper work in Harrisonburg. His great book, "The American Government" (1911), written for F. J. Haskin, is attracting unusual attention. His articles on the Panama Canal are regarded as among the best, if not the best, published. One appeared in the National Geographic Magazine for February, 1912. Mr. Showalter is now publishing a large volume on the Panama Canal. His reputation is becoming not only national, but international.

Snell, Walstein M.: Born in Harrisonburg, Oct, 7, 1888; business man and occasional author:

1911—"The New Tutor" (played in Harrisonburg; sold to a New York firm).

1912—"The Artist's Model" (played in Harrisonburg).

1912—"The Freshman's Prestige" (in preparation).

Strayer, Joseph S.: Born in Rockingham, 1853; died near Port Republic, July 25, 1896; wrote much, and very well,

ROCKINGHAM COUNTY

under the name of "Wyndham," for the *Rockingam Register*.

Wartmann, Henry T.: Born in Harrisonburg, Nov. 8, 1823, the son of Laurentz Wartmann; after more than 50 years in the place of his nativity, he moved to Citra, Fla., in 1879, where he served as school trustee, tax collector of Marion County, etc.; he died in Citra, Febr. 27, 1905. At Harrisonburg he was associated with his brother, J. H. Wartmann, in the publication of the *Rockingham Register*. For twenty years (1861-1881), perhaps longer, he was a frequent contributor to the *Register*, under the pseudonym of "Jonathan Sykes of Zekelville." A really fine wit was sharpened by a facile pen. His writings were a feature of the paper. More is given concerning him in Chapter 18.

Wenger, Joseph H.: Born near Edom, Nov. 15, 1835; now a resident of South English, Iowa; author:

1905—"Descendants of Abraham Beery" (12mo, 328 pp.).

1911—"Descendants of Nicholas Beery" (12mo, 496 pp.).

Winfield, Miss Paulina: Daughter of Capt. John Q. Winfield (p. 134); address, Broadway; author of:

"With Washington in the Valley of Virginia" (in *Things and Thoughts*, Winchester).

1909—"On the Primrose Way" (in *The People*, Franklin, Pa., Jan.).

1909—"The Incredulity of Ford's John" (in *Pictorial Review*, N. Y., March).

1910—"In Lieu of a Pig" (in *Pictorial Review*, October).

1912—"When Boys Went Forth to Battle" (to appear in *Adventure*).

And other pieces in prose and verse.

Zigler, David H.: A native of Rockingham, and a resident of Broadway; published in 1908 "A History of the Brethren in Virginia" (12mo, 278 pp.).

Bocock, John Paul: Editor and poet, born at Harrisonburg, 1856, son of Rev. J. H. Bocock. Educated for law, but turned to letters; member of staff of Philadelphia *Press*, later of N. Y. *World*; contributed to leading magazines; died

A HISTORY OF

1903. His wife issued his poems: "Book Treasures of Maecenas."

B. A LIST OF PERIODICALS.

From 1818 to 1820, etc., Ananias Davidson had a printing establishment in Harrisonburg. In 1818 he printed a second edition of "The Mountaineer" (16mo, 240 pp.); in 1820 he printed the "Life and Labors of Rev. Benj. Abbott" (16 mo, 292 pp.), for James A. Dillworth;[3] and it is said that he was printing the "Kentucky Harmony" and other musical works about 1821.[4]

1822—Rockingham Weekly Register—Harrisonburg; first issue, Saturday, July 27; 4 pages, each 10½x17 inches; Lawrence Wartmann, printer and publisher; Lawrence Wartmann was still the publisher in 1838; in 1841 Wartmann, Way, & Wartmann were the publishers. There were 86 subscribers at the start; in October, 1874, Jacob D. Williamson of Rockingham had been a subscriber 52 years, and was the only one of the original subscribers then living. In 1841 the size of the paper was 16x21. In 1833 the title was *Rockingham Register;* in 1842, *Rockingham Register and Valley Advertiser;* in 1860, *Rockingham Register and Advertiser;* in 1861 *Rockingham Register and Virginia Advertiser;* in 1862, *Rockingham Register and Advertiser;* in 1863, *Rockingham Register.*

In 1861 and 1864 it was asserted that the *Register* had a larger circulation than any other country paper in the State; in 1871 the number of subscribers was said to be over 2000. In December, 1864, the subscription price was $10; in March, 1865, $20.

In 1842 J. H. Wartmann was publisher; in 1844, J. H. Wartmann & Brothers; in 1854, J. H. Wartmann and Wm. G. Stevens; in 1863-4, J. H. Wartmann & Co.; in 1866-7, J. H.

[3.] I am indebted to the kindness of Messrs. E. M. Whitesel and Q. G. Kaylor for a loan of the two books named.

[4.] See *Rockingham Register,* Oct. 5, 1876.

ROCKINGHAM COUNTY

Wartmann & S. M. Yost; in 1867-8, J. H. Wartmann, Hern & Co.; in January, 1868, Giles Devier entered the firm, succeeding Hern and Guiheen; in October, 1875, Giles Devier succeeded J. H. Wartmann & Co.; in 1878 Devier & Dechert were proprietors; in 1883, Devier and John P. Kerr; in 1890, Devier and A. H. Snyder; in 1900 Snyder became sole owner. Since 1903 the paper has been published by the News-Register Co. In 1895 the Register was said to be the fifth newspaper in Virginia in age.

About 1868 Maj. S. M. Yost was connected with the St. Louis *Times.* In 1897 J. Harvey Wartmann was living in St. Louis.

Adolph Heller Snyder, born in Woodstock, Oct. 22, 1863, died in Harrisonburg, January 18, 1910, shortly after his election to the Virginia House of Delegates. He was a gentleman journalist.

Giles Devier was born July 24, 1820, near Bridgewater, son of Allen Devier; he died at Harrisonburg, Sept. 3, 1906, one of the best known citizens of Rockingham.

Lawrence Wartmann, founder of the *Register*, had first worked at New Market with Ambrose Henkel—probably learned his trade there. He was established at Harrisonburg as early as 1813, since in that year he printed a book containing a sermon by Rev. A. B. Davidson.[5] In 1849 J. H. Wartmann & Bros. printed a 16mo book of 476 pages, entitled "Sketches on a Tour Through the Northern and Eastern States, The Canadas & Nova Scotia," by J. C. Myers, of New Hope, Va. Funks bound this book.

Mrs. Carr gives the following interesting account of the early *Register:*

> The next building on the N. W. corner of the Main street was a large log house. The first newspaper in Harrisonburg was printed in this building, on the second floor in the S. end. The Editor, Mr. Wartman, was proprietor, printer, and everything else. I often went to look at him. He had a small folding press on a table in the middle of the room; in either hand he held a leather ball, which was used to ink the

---

[5] *Rockingham Register,* Feb. 22, 1901.

A HISTORY OF

type. Then he placed the dampened paper on the type, and turning over the top of the press, screwed it down tight, until the impression was taken; removed the paper and went on this way until one side of the edition was finished; then he set the type for the other side of the paper, and proceeded in the same way until the whole edition was finished. On Saturday Harvey, his son, about ten years old, would deliver the papers to the subscribers: I do not think there were more than one hundred. New Years some one would write an address for Harvey to deliver to the subscribers, and receive a small amount of money from them. I have so often looked at the patient old man, going through his work so systematically, and thought it [a very grand thing to be a newspaper publisher. If his spirit could visit a steam printing office and see the hundreds of thousands of papers turned out daily, it would make his hair stand on end.

1844—The Republican—Harrisonburg; first issue about June 18; published every Tuesday morning by W. S. Ward; office, opposite Pollock's Hotel, Main St. (from No. 6, Vol. I, July 23, 1844); 4 pages; in January, 1847, Maupin & Gilmer were publishers; seems to have been running in 1854.

1854—Valley Democrat—Harrisonburg; in the *Register* of May 27, Samuel T. Walker and Samuel M. Sommers announce that they will remove the office of the *Valley Democrat* from New Market to Harrisonburg soon; in 1859 Walker & Bridegame were publishing the said paper at Harrisonburg.

Col. S. T. Walker was killed at Chancellorsville, May 3, 1863 (see p. 138).

1859—The Southern Musical Advocate and Singer's Friend —Mountain Valley (Singer's Glen); monthly magazine; first issue, July; Joseph Funk & Sons, publishers; continued till March, 1861; resumed for a year or so in 1867; Aldine S. Kieffer and Wm. S. Rohr were editors in January, 1868.

The Funk printery and bindery were busy from the first. In 1848 "Sturm's Reflections," an octavo of 490 pages, bound in leather, was published. In 1850 was bound the second edition of Kercheval's History of the Valley of Virginia. In 1853 "Dialogues of Devils" (Vol. I, 16mo, 336 pp.) was given to the public by Andrew Hess and Henry A. Showalter, through the Funk press. The "Harmonia Sacra" had reached the 10th edition by 1860; in 1872 the firm brought out the 6th

ROCKINGHAM COUNTY

edition of the Mennonite Hymn Book, partly in German. These random instances will indicate the scope and volume of the work done by the Funks as printers and binders.

1862—The Stonewall—Harrisonburg; 4-page weekly; No. 4, Vol. I, was dated January 15, 1863; Saml. J. Price was editor and proprietor; it was not long continued; the editor, Mr. Price, was later in charge of the *Page Valley Courier*, Luray, Va.

1865—The Old Commonwealth—Harrisonburg; 4-page weekly; first issued about Oct. 10; Cushen & Sheiry publishers and proprietors in October, 1866; in 1870 Capt. John Gatewood and Capt. Ran D. Cushen were editors; in the fall of 1871 W. H. Effinger and W. S. Lurty took the place of Gatewood, being associated with Cushen; about Jan. 1, 1872, Effinger became sole editor; from January to May, 1873, J. N. Liggett was editor; about May 1 (1873) Chas. H. Vanderford became owner and editor; Vanderford sold to J. K. Smith and P. B. Dulaney, May, 1878; Smith was still editor in November, 1883; in 1884 the paper was sold at public auction.[6]

1866—The American Union—Harrisonburg; Geo. K. Gilmer, publisher; Smith & Gatewood reported proprietors in 1868.

Dr. Geo. K. Gilmer was appointed P. M. of Richmond in 1880.

1869—The Musical Million—Dayton; monthly magazine, devoted to music and literature; published at Singer's Glen, by Ruebush, Kieffer & Co., till 1878; then at Dayton; present editor, Joe K. Ruebush, of the Ruebush-Kieffer Co.; probably the oldest music journal in America.—Ephraim Ruebush, one of the original firm of Ruebush, Kieffer & Co., was born near Churchville, Augusta Co., Va., Sept. 26, 1833, the son of John and Mary Huffman Ruebush; he married at Singer's Glen, March 28, 1861, Virginia Kieffer, a granddaughter of

---

6. Thanks are due to Hon. Geo. E. Sipe for lending files of the *Old Commonwealth*.

A HISTORY OF

Joseph Funk, and a sister of Aldine S. Kieffer, the poet. Mr. and Mrs. Ruebush have been living at Dayton since 1878. A sketch of Aldine Kieffer, another member of the firm named above, will be found in Chapter 18.

1869—Harrisonburg Enterprise; 5-column, 4-page weekly; Gideon Sheiry, propr.; "Published every Friday morning . . . Office in Paul's Building, over C. F. Dutrow's store." —From No. 43, Vol. 4, Nov. 15, 1872. Last issue about Nov. 30, 1872. For some time, beginning about September 15, 1870, the *Enterprise* was semi-weekly, Geo. S. Null and John F. Sheiry being associated at different times with G. Sheiry; publication stopped a month by fire of Dec. 25, 1870.

"Rose Thornton," a camp novelette, was published by Harry & Sheiry, Harrisonburg, in 1864.

1872—The Lily of the Valley—Harrisonburg; a 32-page monthly magazine, historical, literary, agricultural; first issue, January; G. Sheiry & Co., publishers; still running in August.

1872—The Rural Virginian—Harrisonburg; monthly; J. S. Trout, editor; Sheiry, publisher. May issue noticed in *Register* of May 10.

1874—The Young Virginian—Mt. Clinton; 8-page monthly; first issue, January; editor W. T. Price; printed by Ruebush, Kieffer & Co., Singer's Glen; published 3 years.—Contained numerous pieces of local interest, especially sketches of Presbyterian churches in northern Virginia.

1875—The Ray of Hope—Harrisonburg; a semi-monthly, issued first Jan. 1; a temperance paper; S. J. Price and W. J. Points, editors.

1877—The Faithful Word—Mt. Clinton; 8-page monthly; first issue, January; W. T. Price, editor; Ruebush, Kieffer & Co., Singer's Glen, printers.

1878—Spirit of the Valley—Harrisonburg; weekly; first issue in September; Daniel Dechert & Son, publishers; purchased by D. S. Lewis, 1886; converted into the *Daily Times*, 1905.—Daniel Sheffey Lewis was born at Lynnwood, Oct. 17, 1843; died at Clifton Forge, Oct. 3, 1912; lawyer and journal-

ROCKINGHAM COUNTY

ist; son of Sen. John F. Lewis.—See page 127 above, and Chapter XIX, following.

1878—The Bridgewater Enterprise; 4 pages; No. 1, Vol. I, Sept. 11;[7] E. Smith Dinkle propr.; Dr. T. H. B. Brown, editor; J. E. Braithwaite, asso. ed. and bus. mgr. In 1879 Lambert & Burwell ran the paper a short time, then John B. F. Armstrong succeeded, changing the name to the *Journal*, Sept. 4, 1879.[8]

1879—The Star—Bridgewater; "a diminutive though spicy sheet"; first issue, July 4; J. B. Burwell, publisher.

1879—The Bridgewater Journal; succeeds *Bridgewater Enterprise*, Sept. 4; E. S. Dinkle, propr., J. B. F. Armstrong, editor. In September, 1880, Armstrong, who was a young lawyer, died; in October (1880) G. T. Barbee purchased the *Journal*, and published it till Nov. 30, 1883; then G. R. Berlin published it till Nov. 30, 1885.

1880 — Rockingham Advertiser — Bridgewater; semi-monthly; G. R. Berlin, publisher. *Register* announced receipt of first number, July 8.

1881—The Valley Herald—Bridgewater; weekly; published during June, July, August, by G. R. Berlin.

1881—The Pearl Press—Mt. Crawford; first issue, July; Pearl Press Pub. Co.

1881—The Watchful Pilgrim—Dale Enterprise; a religious monthly; first issue, August; Abraham Blosser printer and publisher; 24 pages and cover till December; 16 pages from December (1881) till April, 1883; after this, 8 pages, twice a month; last number seen, Dec. 15, 1886. Abram Blosser did job printing, also; he had the press that was set up by Jos. Funk & Sons, at Mountain Valley, in 1847. His paper circulated in Virginia, Pennsylvania, Ohio, Indiana, Kansas, and Ontario.[9]

---

7. Thanks are due Mr. Paul Miller, Bridgewater, for a loan of the above paper.

8. Information by Mr. S. G. Dinkle, Bridgewater.

9. Special acknowledgement is due Mr. Noah Blosser and Rev. L. J. Heatwole, Dale Enterprise, for lending files of the *Watchful Pilgrim*.

A HISTORY OF

1882—Virginia Post—Harrisonburg; published by R. B. and M. L. Robinson (colored); moved to Alexandria.

1883—The People—Harrisonburg; 4-page weekly; first issue, Dec. 8; A. P. Funkhouser and C. I. B. Brane, editors; absorbed by the *State Republican*, 1886.

1884—The Postal Card—Mt. Crawford; a semi-monthly, published by W. H. Foley; first issue in March.

1885—Farm and Home—Harrisonburg; 8-page weekly; first issued in January; J. K. Smith, editor and propr.; sold to Thomas & Yancey, 1886.—Jos. K. Smith, who had also been associated with the *Register*, died at Winchester, Va., in February, 1905.

1885—The Sentinel—Harrisonburg; H. M. Roudabush, editor; announced in September.

1886—Our Monthly—Bridgewater; G. R. Berlin, publisher; issued 12 months.

1886—The Independent—Port Republic; 48-column weekly newspaper, published by Holsinger & Bowman.

1886—The State Republican—Harrisonburg; founded by A. P. Funkhouser; W. C. Elam, editor; 1891, Funkhouser & Snavely, publishers; 1893, leased to Hughes & Hinde; 1894, Funkhouser resumed management; in June, 1899, Saml. J. Price, editor, died; W. W. Roller (1856-1897) was some time connected with the paper as associate editor, etc.

1887—People's Educational Quarterly—Dayton; published by Fries & Ruebush.

1888—The Broadway Enterprise; first issued in January; E. D. Root was publisher in 1892 and 1893—perhaps from the beginning; purchased in November, 1893, by I. C. Wade; discontinued, probably in December, 1894.

1890—The Broadway News; Geo. L. Jameson and John S. Fravel, publishers; later Kline & Kline were publishers; discontinued in December, 1893—sold to I. C. Wade, editor of the *Broadway Enterprise*.

1890—Harrisonburg Progress; a monthly.

1891—The Elkton Index; first issued in January; continued at least till June, 1892.

Oldest Known copy of *Rockingham Register*
Front page
(See pages 330-332)

ROCKINGHAM COUNTY

1891—The Shendun News; first heard of in February, 1891; the first editor and manager, L. A. Frazier, was succeeded as editor by J. A. Phillips, October, 1891; in June, 1892, it was changed from a weekly to a semi-monthly; in December, 1892, Mr. Coles was editor; ordered discontinued by directors, March, 1893.

1891—The Monthly Call—Bridgewater; 8-pages; started in April by Rev. A. R. Thompson.

1891—Harrisonburg Free Press; weekly; H. B. Miller, publisher, succeeds Miller & Snavely March, 1897; W. I. Good was business manager in 1900; the *Free Press* was made a daily about March 20, 1904. It has not been published for several years past.

1893—The Elkton News; ran at least from August, 1893, till January, 1894.

1894—The Bridgewater Herald; first issue, Feb. 2; G. R. Berlin, publisher; last issue, Sept. 15, 1906.—Mr. Berlin is a skilled job printer, as well as a publisher.

1895—The Evening Glance—Harrisonburg; 4-column afternoon daily; first issue, June 17; last, Jan. 8, 1896; Weishampel & Hinde, publishers.

1895—The Virginia Echo—Broadway; W. Grim, editor.

1896—Philomathean Monthly—Bridgewater; first issue, May; published by the literary societies of Bridgewater College; issued every month the first three years, 8 or 9 times a year since 1899.

1896—The Broadway Echo; Mr. Grim, publisher.

1898—Harrisonburg Daily News; founded by R. B, Smythe, the present manager; first called the *Evening News;* editor, 1903-10, A. H. Snyder; editor, 1910-11, James C Johnston; present editor, J. H. Robertson.

1898—Our Assistant—Mt. Crawford; 4-page monthly; Rev. A. D. Wolfinger, publisher; ran at least till May, 1899.

1898—The Illuminator—Dayton; 8-page quarterly, edited by E. U. Hoenshel and E. T. Hildebrand.

1899—College Life—Bridgewater; educational quarterly; published by the faculty of Bridgewater College.

A HISTORY OF

1905—Harrisonburg Daily Times; founded by D. S. Lewis; present publishers, Rickard & Voorhees; editor, D.S. Lewis, Jr.

1906—Old Dominion Home—Dayton; published for a few months by Taylor & Kieffer.

1907—The National Poultry Journal — Harrisonburg; monthly; founded about 1907, by C. O. Henton; continued till 1911, E. V. Crist, R. B. Smythe, R. C. Hughes, and Chas. Turner having successive parts in the enterprise; office of issue, Elkton.

1909—Our Mountain Work—Elkton; 4-page monthly; F. W. Neve and J. R. Ellis, publishers; in fall of 1911 moved to Charlottesville.

1911—The Sunday-School News—Elkton; G. M. Keezel, publisher.

1911—Rockingham Daily Record—Harrisonburg; H. W. Bertram and C. C. Herring, editors; Geo. W. Berry, business manager.

CHAPTER XVIII.

SINGERS OF ROCKINGHAM.

It has been asserted (see page 183) that there are probably more people, old and young, in Rockingham who can sing, and who love music, than in any other section with the same population in America. This assertion is, of course, beyond either proof or disproof, but it is made advisedly, and is believed to be warranted by known facts. For example, a year or two ago a dozen competent judges were asked to vote for the twelve leading singers and musicians of Rockingham, natives or long residents of the county, and to name others deemed worthy of special mention. In all, about 80 different men and women were named. So many teachers and leaders of song would not be found apart from a large number of learners and lovers of song. Most of the people of the county are church-goers, and nearly every member of every congregation sings. Singing is a common pastime in many homes, and singing classes are frequently conducted in the churches as well as in the schools. All-day singings at churches are not uncommon. Singing books were printed by Lawrence Wartmann and Ananias Davisson a century ago; Joseph Funk and Sons printed tens of thousands of music books and music journals from 1832 to 1878; and since that time the Ruebush-Kieffer Company have sent out hundreds of thousands more. The output to-day is greater than ever. The music departments of Shenandoah Collegiate Institute and Bridgewater College have attracted many students for many years; the Funk school at Singer's Glen was widely known of old; the new State Normal School at Harrisonburg has large classes in music; and occasionally, for the past forty years or more, summer normals for music teachers have been held in and near the county. For example, in the early 70's, Chester G.

A HISTORY OF

Allen, P. J. Merges, B. C. Unseld and others held several sessions of a music normal at New Market; and from 1894 to 1896 G. B. Holsinger, B. C. Unseld and others held summer music schools at Bridgewater. For three-quarters of a century Joseph Funk, his sons, his grandsons, and their pupils went all over Rockingham and neighboring counties teaching the art of song.

While the music cultivated in Rockingham has been mostly church music in its simpler forms, classical forms of music and famous musicians are not, and have not been, unknown. Within the writer's own recollection Sidney Lanier, Edward Remenyi, Creatore and his band, and the Conradis have delighted Rockingham audiences. A few famous songs have also had their genesis in Rockingham: "Twilight is Falling," by Kieffer and Unseld, and "The Everlasting Arms," by Hoffman and Showalter, have probably been sung around the world.

In November, 1867, a great musical convention was held in Harrisonburg, in Rev. T. D. Bell's (Presbyterian) church. The session continued for four days; 122 delegates from Harrisonburg, Dayton, McGaheysville, Bridgewater, New Erection, Singer's Glen, Cross Keys, Union church, and Edom, in Rockingham, and from Mossy Creek, Parnassus, Augusta church, and Bethel church, in Augusta County, were present. A constitution was adopted and a permanent organization effected. Rev. T. D. Bell was elected president; Rev. T. U. Dudley, Maj. J. H. Irvine, Emmet Guy, and Capt. J. P. Ralston, vice-presidents; H. T. Wartmann, secretary; and G. Fred Mayhew, treasurer. Subsequent meetings of the organization, which was known as the Valley Musical Association, were held at Mossy Creek (1868), Harrisonburg (1869), Bethel church (1870), and Tinkling Springs (1872). W. H. Evans was director of the chorus in 1869, etc. It may be of interest to state in this connection that an oratorio society has just been organized in Harrisonburg, with Miss Julia Starr Preston and Rabbi Schvanenfeld as directors.

The twelve singers and composers of Rockingham receiv-

ROCKINGHAM COUNTY

ing the highest number of votes in the election referred to above were the following:

J. M. Bowman.
J. D. Brunk.
Joseph Funk.
Timothy Funk.
J. H. Hall.
E. T. Hildebrand.
G. B. Holsinger.
A. S. Kieffer.
J. H. Ruebush.
W. H. Ruebush.
A. J. Showalter.
J. Henry Showalter.

Four are dead, eight are living; and, of the latter, four are now residents of the county.

Bowman, John Michael: Born near Harrisonburg, June 11, 1859; at the age of 18 attended the music normal of Unseld and Merges at New Market; has since studied with a number of America's foremost teachers. Every year he conducts a number of music normals in the Southern States. He is a skilled tuner of pianos; has written a number of popular pieces of music; and is author, or associate author, of several books of hymns, songs, and choruses. Residence, Harrisonburg.

Brunk, John David: Born near Harrisonburg, March 13, 1872, a great-grandson of Peter Burkholder (see p. 318); has had training in the New England Conservatory of Music, and in other high-class schools; he is a teacher and composer of ability, and possesses unusual skill in directing choruses; he has compiled and edited several excellent books; for the past six years or more he has been director of music in Goshen College, Indiana.

Funk, Joseph: A native of Pensylvania, but an almost life-long resident of Rockingham. On December 25, 1804, he married Elizabeth Rhodes: children, Jonathan (1806-1874), Henry (1807-1813), Elizabeth (1808-1870), Susan (1810-1815), Barbara (1812-1850); on Sept. 6, 1814, he married Rachel Britton: children, Mary (1815-1888), Joseph (1816 —— ?), David (1818-1870), Samuel (1819 ——), Hannah (1821 ——?), John (1822 ——), Timothy (1824-1909), Solomon (1825-1880), Benjamin (1829-1909).

For 46 years Joseph Funk was a teacher of music, a trainer of music teachers, and a publisher of music books and periodicals. By 1858 he and his sons, particularly Timothy, had taught music classes in at least 10 counties of Virginia, besides Rockingham; records show that by the same year his books had been sold and used in 37 counties and cities of Virginia, as well as in Georgia, Illinois, Ohio, Maryland, North Carolina, Indiana, Pennsylvania, Iowa, Missouri, and Canada West. By the 70's, between 75,000 and 100,000 copies of his famous book, "Harmonia Sacra," had been sold. It is still used in old-folks' all-day singings in Rockingham and adjacent sections.

One of the 12 men now under review (Timothy Funk) was Joseph Funk's son; one (A. S. Kieffer) was his grandson; two (J. H. and W. H. Ruebush) are his great-grandsons; two (A. J. and J. H. Showalter) are great-grandsons of his sister Elizabeth; others of the 12 are related to his family, and all have come more or less directly under his influence. He may, with justice, be called the father of song in Northern Virginia; he more than any other man, has made Rockingham a land of singers, and he was himself one of her greatest citizens.[1]

Funk, Timothy: Born at Singers Glen, Jan. 29, 1824; died at the same place in 1909; after his father, the most famous itinerant teacher of singing in the Valley of Virginia. For more than 50 years he was known in this capacity, not only in Rockingham, but far beyond her borders. He was also, for many years, a minister of the Gospel.

Hall, Jacob H.: A native of Rockingham, and one of the best known conductors of music institutes in the South, having worked in no less than 20 different States. He studied under Geo. F. Root and other famous teachers, and has been a student in Dana's Conservatory and other high-grade schools. He has written dozens of excellent pieces, and has been an editor of many popular music books. His address is Dayton.—See page 322 above.

Hildebrand, Ephraim Timothy: Born near Greenmount,

---

[1]. See pages 293, 294, above; see also "Joseph Funk, Father of Song in Northern Virginia" (4to, 12 pp.), published by The Ruebush-Kieffer Co., Dayton, Va.

A COMPILATION OF
GENUINE CHURCH MUSIC,

COMPRISING

A VARIETY OF METRES,

ALL

HARMONIZED FOR THREE VOICES;

TOGETHER WITH

A COPIOUS ELUCIDATION OF
THE SCIENCE OF VOCAL MUSIC.

BY JOSEPH FUNK.

———

WINCHESTER:
PUBLISHED AT THE OFFICE OF THE REPUBLICAN,
[J. W. HOLLIS, PRINTER.]
1832.

"*And the ransomed of the Lord shall return, and come to Zion, with songs and everlasting joy upon their heads.*"—Isaiah, ch. xxxv. v. 10

(Facsimile copy of Title-Page of Joseph Funk's famous music book, first edition; later known as "Harmonia Sacra.")

Jan. 18, 1866; teacher, composer, editor, publisher, and singer; has had training in New York Vocal Institute, the Metropolitan Conservatory, and other schools; was a member of the New York Oratorio Society, under the direction of Frank Damrousche; has written many excellent pieces, sacred and secular, among the latter being "The Hills of Tennessee." Some of the popular books he has helped to edit are "Gems of Gladness," "Crowning Day," and "Onward and Upward." Address, Roanoke, Va.

Holsinger, George Blackburn: Born in Bedford County, Pa., May 10, 1857; died in Illinois, November, 1908. From 1882 to 1898 Prof. Holsinger was director of music in Bridgewater College; from the latter year till his death he was music editor for the Church of the Brethren, but continued to have his home at Bridgewater. He was a pleasing singer and versatile composer, his pieces having been used in about 100 different publications. "Psalms and Hymns," one of the numerous books of which he was associate editor, had reached a sale of over 200,000 in 1905. His wife, who survives him, was Miss Sallie Kagey.

Kieffer, Aldine Silliman: Born in Saline County, Mo., August 1, 1840; died at his home in Dayton, Va., Nov. 30, 1904. His mother was Mary Funk, daughter of Joseph Funk, Father of Song in Northern Virginia; she married John Kieffer, May 30, 1837. On June 22, 1847, her husband died, and she returned from Missouri, to Mountain Valley (Singer's Glen), with her children. Lucilla Virginia married Ephraim Ruebush, March 28, 1861, and has handed down to her sons the gift of song; Aldine wrote songs, set them to music, and taught them to the people.

Aldine S. Kieffer founded the *Musical Million* and edited it for many years; he compiled the "Christian Harp," the "Temple Star," and many other books of song. The "Temple Star" has reached the half-million mark, and is still being sold. With his brother-in-law, Mr. E. Ruebush, he gave name and character to the publishing house transferred from Singer's Glen to Dayton in 1878, and still known as The

ROCKINGHAM COUNTY

Ruebush-Kieffer Company. He wrote the song, "Twilight is Falling," wedded to music by Unseld, and sung by thousands far and near. Many other songs he wrote, which, with or without music, have touched many hearts.[2]

Ruebush, James H.: Born at Singer's Glen, Oct. 19, 1865, son of E. Ruebush and Virginia Kieffer Ruebush, and great grandson of Joseph Funk; teacher, composer, editor, educator; has studied with such artists as H. N. Barttelb, H. R. Palmer, and F. W. Root, and has been a student in the Grand Conservatory of Music, N. Y., and other high-grade schools; is the author of many popular pieces of music, and the editor of many well-known music books—collections of songs and manuals of instruction. For a number of years he has been connected with Shenandoah Collegiate Institute and School of Music, and is at present general manager of that institution.

Ruebush, William H.: Born in Rockingham, June 4, 1873, a brother of James H.; a teacher of music in Shenandoah Collegiate Institute, a writer of popular pieces for male and mixed voices, and a skilled director of choirs and orchestras; has enjoyed excellent advantages for training in his art, and is endowed with the perception of the artist; is the author of various manuals for his profession, and the editor of a number of popular song books.

Showalter, Anthony J.: Born in Rockingham, May 1, 1858; for many years a man of mark in Georgia; head of the A. J. Showalter music publishing company, and editor of the *Music Teacher and Home Magazine*, Dalton; author of the music to "The Everlasting Arms" and hundreds of other Gospel hymns and songs; has studied under the best teachers of America, has visited the music centers of Europe, and has held more than 200 sessions of music institutes in the Southern States; he is the author of 30 music books, and the associate author of as many more.

Showalter, J. Henry: Born at Cherry Grove, Rockingham County, Nov. 2, 1864, a brother of A. J. Showalter; present

---

[2] See page 325 above; also, the *Musical Million*, Kieffer memorial number, August, 1908, and Wayland's "German Element," pp. 173-175.

address, West Milton, Ohio; singer, teacher, composer, and publisher; has studied under the best teachers, and holds high rank as a teacher and singer; has written hundreds of beautiful songs and anthems, and has compiled more than a score of music books; some of his best pieces are: "At the Golden Gate of Prayer," "The Blood of the Lamb," and "Breathe Upon Us, Holy Spirit."

John A. Showalter, born in Rockingham, Dec. 19, 1832, was for many years a teacher of singing classes in various parts of the Valley. In 1892 or 1893, while in Shenandoah County teaching a class, he said that he had kept account of the number of his classes till he had taught a hundred—then he had stopped counting. He is the father of A. J. and J. Henry Showalter.

Years ago Karl Merz, long editor of Brainard's *Musical World*, published at Cleveland, Ohio, taught music for awhile in Rockingham. In 1860 Chas. Eshman (died March 18, 1901) was a teacher of brass bands and orchestras in the county; in 1867 he organized at Harrisonburg a band of 13 or 14 members, composed mainly of men of German extraction. In 1891 he was still leading a band in Harrisonburg. Mr. Eshman was a native of Germany, and visited his Fatherland in 1883. From 1861 to 1873, perhaps longer, Prof. A. Kuhnert, a skilled musician, taught singing and piano-forte in Harrisonburg.

One of the best known musicians in Rockingham some years ago was Henry T. Wartmann, one of the sons of Lawrence Wartmann. (See page 329.). In October, 1872, his singing class from Andrew Chapel, Harrisonburg, numbering 60 or more, went upon special invitation to Baltimore and Washington, singing at St. Paul's Church, Trinity Church, Central Church, Western Female High School, and Maryland Institute in the former city, and at Mt. Vernon Place in Washington. They were termed the "Virginia Rustics." In 1873 the Choral Singers from Trinity M. E. Sundayschool, Baltimore, returned the visit of the "Rustics," singing in Harrisonburg, and visiting the Cave of the Fountains, Tay-

ROCKINGHAM COUNTY

lor's Springs, Rawley Springs, and other places of interest. In 1878 the "Rustics" were again in Baltimore and Washington. Mr. Wartmann was a talented composer, as well as a skilled director.

Among the younger pianists and teachers of music from Rockingham must be mentioned Kinzie Blakemore, of Newport News, and C. Ernest Hall, of Evanston, Ill. Perhaps the greatest singer ever born in Rockingham is Mrs. Tenney Showalter Schwerin, of Oregon City, Oregon. One of the best singers and teachers now in the county is Mrs. Imogen Avis Palmer, of Harrisonburg, who has enjoyed unusual advantages in piano playing, composition, and voice culture, and who is a poet as well as a musician. Mr. S. G. Cline of Harrisonburg is a well known teacher of music and a dealer in musical instruments; and Mr. J. Owen Long, of Melrose (R. D., Harrisonburg) is a composer and publisher of creditable music, as well as a singer and teacher of ability.

It would be a pleasure to mention all of the Eighty, but the printer's space limits the writer's lines.

CHAPTER XIX.

ROCKINGHAM STATESMEN AND JURISTS.

John Sevier, a pioneer of the Shenandoah Valley and one of the builders of Tennessee, was one of the most distinguished of all the sons of Rockingham. A tall shaft in Knoxville marks honor to his memory; his nickname, "Nolichucky Jack," is familiar on many tongues; and his native county may well learn to know him. He was born Sept. 23, 1745, the son of Valentine Sevier and Joanna Goade. He had a brother who also won distinction (see pages 63, 64).

After a short schooling in Fredericksburg and Staunton, John Sevier helped his father keep store. In 1761 he married Sarah Hawkins. After farming a short while in Long Meadows, he bought a tract of land where New Market now stands, and kept a store and an inn as part of the village he laid out. He gave the Baptist church three acres of land on which to erect a building. In 1770 he moved to Millerstown (supposedly Woodstock); but soon he became interested in the great southwest, and in 1773 moved to what is now East Tennessee, where his name was soon written large. In 1777 he was a member of the North Carolina legislature; and, for the rest, we may quote part of the inscription on his monument:

> Pioneer, soldier, statesman, and one of the founders of the Republic; Governor of the State of Franklin; six times Governor of Tennessee; four times elected to Congress; the typical pioneer who conquered the wilderness and fashioned the State; a projector and hero of King's Mountain; thirty-five battles, thirty-five victories; his Indian war-cry, "Here they are! come on, boys, come on!"

It is said that some of Sevier's early Indian fighting was

ROCKINGHAM COUNTY

done from New Market. He died Sept. 24, 1815, near Fort Decatur, Ga., while on a mission to the Creek Indians.[1]

The records thus far examined seem to corroborate the foregoing statements concerning Sevier. The Augusta County records show the name of Valentine Sevier as early as 1746, perhaps earlier. Dr. Waddell points out the fact (Annals of Augusta, pp. 45, 46) that he was a member of Peter Scholl's military company in 1742. In 1753 he was keeping a tavern near New Market and Tenth Legion (see page 49). From 1753 to 1773 he, with Joanna his wife, sold no less than eight tracts of land on Smith Creek, in the Long Meadow, and elsewhere in the vicinity, to Andrew Bird, the Holsingers, and others, as the Augusta records show. On May 10, 1765, Valentine Sevier, of Augusta, and Joanna his wife, sold to John Sevier, of Frederick (now Shenandoah), 378 acres, located on a branch of Smith's Creek, in Frederick County, adjoining the land of John Hodges, Capt. Peter Scholl, and Jane Schene; the said land having been granted to Val. Sevier from Lord Fairfax in 1749. The next day, May 11, 1765, John Sevier and Sarah, his wife, mortgaged the same tract to Alex. Wodrow and John Neilson, of Falmouth, King George County, Va. At this time John Sevier was living on the land in question. The mortgage was witnessed by Joseph Hawkins and others.[2]

The archives of Shenandoah County, formed from Frederick in 1772, record a number of real estate transctions in which John Sevier was a party. In 1782 Val. Sevier's "old house" was still a familiar landmark in the Long Meadow (see page 217). This, in all probability, was John Sevier's birthplace.[3]

---

1. See Harper's Encyclopaedia of U. S. History, Vol. 3, p. 418; Vol. 8, p. 132; Vol. 9, pp. 40-43; Roosevelt's Winning of the West, Vol. 1, pp. 223-230; Life of Gen. John Sevier, by F. M. Turner; Nolichucky Jack, by L. T. Sprague, in Outing Magazine, April, 1908.

2. See records of Frederick County, Va.

3. Inasmuch as John Sevier was a famous Indian fighter, as well as a statesman, it may be of interest to note in connection that Lewis Wetzel

A HISTORY OF

Gabriel Jones, known as "The Lawyer," was born May 17, 1724, near Williamsburg, Va., son of John and Elizabeth Jones, of Wales. Educated in London, he was admitted to the bar; in 1747 he bought land near Kernstown, Frederick County, Va., where he likely was residing the year before when he was appointed prosecuting attorney for Augusta County. October 16, 1749, he married Margaret Morton, widow of George Morton, and daughter of William Strother. August 8, 1751, he bought 244 acres of land from Christopher Francisco, the tract being on the north side of the river below Port Republic, whereon is the homestead called Bogota. He seems to have moved to Bogota about the end of 1753. There he had his home till he died, October, 1806. His wife lived till 1822, and in November of that year Charles Lewis, Sr., administrator, was arranging to make sale of the property on January 21, 1823. The property consisted of nearly 1200 acres of land, a frame dwelling house, with out-buildings, growing crops, and "upwards of FORTY very likely NEGROES," together with household furniture, elegant prints, a large and well selected library, horses, cattle, and farming utensils. The place has since been owned by the Strayers, and is at present the residence of Dr. A. S. Kemper.

Mr. Jones had five children, one of whom died in infancy. One daughter (Margaret) married Col. John Harvie; another married John Lewis, of Fredericksburg; the third married a Mr. Hawkins, of Kentucky. His son, William Strother Jones, born March 21, 1756, was a student at William and Mary, a captain in the Continental Army, and later a colonel of militia. His wife was Fanny Thornton, of Fredericksburg.

Mr. Jones was the first lawyer for Augusta, and the first

---

the famous Indian fighter of the Ohio Valley, was also a native of Rockingham. His father, Capt. John Wetzel, born in Switzerland, 1733, was brought to what is now Rockingham in 1740. Here were born John Wetzel's sons, Martin, Lewis, Jacob, George, and John. About 1769 John Wetzel moved west, settling on Wheeling Creek.—See Thwaites and Kellogg's Frontier Defense on the Upper Ohio, 1777-1778, page 296.— The Wetzel name is still familiar in Rockingham.

ROCKINGHAM COUNTY

also for Rockingham, in which he lived from its organization in 1778 (see pages 65-69). He held the office of commonwealth's attorney in Rockingham till 1795, when he resigned and was succeeded by David Holmes. He represented Augusta in the House of Burgesses in 1757, 1758, and 1771. In 1788, he, with his brother-in-law, Thomas Lewis (page 127), was a member of the Virginia convention, and zealously favored the adoption of the Federal Constitution. He was a little man, of great integrity and explosive temper. His difficulty with Henry Brewster (page 73) would indicate as much. Dr. Waddell tells of another incident, which probably occurred at Woodstock. Hugh Holmes, opposing lawyer, sharp and witty, made old Mr. Jones angry, and he exploded. It happened again. The court of justices refrained from interfering as long as possible, but finally they put their heads together, and then, after due consideration, the presiding justice announced that the court would send Lawyer Holmes to jail if he did not quit making Lawyer Jones swear so.[4]

In 1778 George Rootes was admitted to the practice of law in Rockingham (see page 71). Michael Bowyer took the oath of an attorney in 1779 (page 73). The following were admitted to the Rockingham bar on the dates indicated:

Lewis Wolf, May 23, 1797.
John Monroe, April 23, 1798.[5]
Daniel Smith, December 16, 1800.
Robert Gray, June 18, 1805.
George W. Harrison, April 22, 1807.

---

[4]. See Waddell's Annals of Augusta, pp. 81-84; Wayland's "German Element," pp. 55, 66, 73, 86, 223, 224, 271; and an article in the W. Va. Hist. Mag., April, 1902, entitled, "The Lawyer," by R.T. Barton. Mr. Barton, who lives at Winchester, is a descendant of Gabriel Jones. The *Rockingham Register* of Dec. 7, 1822, contains Chas. Lewis' announcement of the Jones sale.

[5]. Mr. Richard See, Jr., writing from Warsaw, Mo., May 20, 1911, says: "My grandfather on my mother's side, who is now dead, was Judge Joseph Monroe. He was born and raised in Rockingham Co., Va.; moved to Benton County, Mo., many years ago; was a soldier in the war with Mexico, also in the civil war."

A HISTORY OF

Daniel Smith, "a learned, pure judge and good man," was born at or near Harrisonburg, in 1779, son of John and Margaret Davis Smith, grandson of Justice Daniel Smith (pp. 54, 68); he married Frances Strother Duff, June 10, 1809; children, Margaret, Elizabeth, Lucius, Frances, Marie, John, Daniel; he died Nov. 8, 1850. In 1805 he was a member of the Virginia House of Delegates; from 1804 to 1811 he was commonwealth's attorney for Rockingham; on April 10, 1811, he was appointed a judge of the General Court, and from the same date till his death (1850) he was judge of the circuit superior court for Rockingham County. He succeeded Judge Hugh Holmes, and was succeeded by Judge Green B. Samuels. His portrait now adorns the Rockingham County court room. Judge John Paul said of him:

> No judge, perhaps, who ever presided on the Circuit Court bench in Virginia exerted a better or more lasting influence on the people within his jurisdiction. He was not only a great man intellectually, but he was great in the moral attributes necessary to the prefection of judicial character.

In the celebrated case of the National Bank against Steinbergen and others, involving over half a million of dollars, he gave a decision on Saturday in favor of the plaintiff; on Monday morning following he came into court and announced from the bench that he had erred in his former conclusions, and proceeded to reverse his decision. [6]

I have been told that Judge Smith's residence was a short distance northeast of Dayton, near the Shrum brick factory.

Robert Gray was born in Ireland, Nov. 1, 1781, but his family settled in the Shenandoah Valley about 1787. He was educated at William and Mary and at Princeton, and in 1805 located at Harrisonburg to practice law. Soon he married Isabella, daughter of Dr. Asher Waterman, and about 1812 built Collicello. (See page 192, 220.) He was a lawyer

---

[6]. See Judge John Paul's address, made Oct. 15, 1896; Boogher's Gleanings of Virginia History, pp. 339, 340; Waddell's Annals of Augusta, pp. 150-152; Compton's *Rockingham Register* sketches, No. 21.

JUDGE DANIEL SMITH
(Page 352)

From oil portrait in Rock.
Co. Court Room. Photo
by Morrison.

ROCKINGHAM COUNTY

of profound learning, an advocate and prosecutor of great eloquence. He wrote the proverbially bad hand of the lawyer (of his day). Once when he gave a check for several thousand dollars on a Winchester Bank—there were probably no banks nearer then than in Winchester—the payee had to ride back the 67 miles to Harrisonburg, the cashier having refused to cash the check, declaring the signature a forgery, because it was legible. He died Dec. 17, 1859, accounted the wealthiest citizen of Rockingham County. He had four sons, Algernon, Jouett, Douglas, and Robert (1826-1887).

Algernon S. Gray, eldest son of Robert Gray, was a lawyer with his father's gifts of eloquence, and a colonel of militia for his county, but he was most of all a philanthropist. In the Virginia convention he tried all measures to avoid secession, moving the assemblage to tears as he depicted what would be the "most mournful Iliad in the history of the world," but he did not withstand the action of the majority, or disregard the final peremptory orders from his constituents. During the war he gave much to feed the soldiers and provide for their families,—even took off his own shoes in the street to give to a Confederate soldier whose feet left bloody prints in the snow. He went to Richmond in behalf of the non-combatant Dunkers and Mennonites, of whom there were many in Rockingham. After the murder of John Kline it was said, "Colonel Gray next," and he finally yielded to the entreaty of his daughters, going with two of his brothers to Baltimore. After the war he returned to Rockingham, where he used his influence for education and progress. For a number of years he was U. S. Marshal for the western district of Virginia.—See pages 131, 132, above.

John Kenney, born in Augusta, 1791, located at Harrisonburg about 1817. He was commonwealth's attorney, in the circuit court, 1847 to 1852, and circuit judge, 1852-60. He was also a member of the Virginia constitutional convention of 1850. He died in Harrisonburg, 1873, at the home of his son, Judge James Kenney.[7]

[7.] See sketch of John Kenney in the *Register* of Feb. 21, 1873.

A HISTORY OF

Mrs. Carr says: "The lawyers of that day [about 1820] were Robert Gray, David Steele, and Thomas Clark, and some younger ones I do not remember."—See Chapter 27.

Isaac Samuels Pennybacker, one of the most distinguished sons of northern Virginia, was born at Pine Forge, near New Market, Shenandoah County, Va., Sept. 3, 1805. From 1837 to 1839 he was a representative in Congress from the 16th district of Virginia, composed of the counties of Rockingham, Shenandoah, Page, Warren, Hardy, Pendleton, and Bath. Later he was judge of the U. S. District Court, and a regent of the Smithsonian Institution. From 1845 till his death, January 12, 1847, he was a U. S. Senator from Virginia. It is said that he was offered the Attorney-Generalship of the United States by President Van Buren.

At the time of his death Senator Pennybacker's family was living in Harrisonburg, where he had resided for some time preceding. Some years later suit was brought in court for possession of the Waterman house, south side of the Harrisonburg public square, the same that is now occupied by Dr. R. S. Switzer and his sister, Mrs. Burkholder, with the lot whereon it stands. In the report of the said suit the following passage occurs:

> The plaintiff alleges in his bill that Isaac S. Pennybacker, his father, died about the year 1848, intestate, possessed of this lot, "leaving as his only heirs-at-law his widow, Sarah A. Pennybacker, and three infant children—John D., Isaac S., and your orator J. Edmund Pennybacker—to whom said lot of land descended"; . . . .[8]

This would appear to fix the place of Sen. Pennybacker's residence in Harrisonburg.

Senator Pennybacker's wife was Sarah A. Dyer, daughter of Zebulon Dyer, of Pendleton County. She died in Franklin, W. Va., June 17, 1891, aged 75. His sons, John D. and J. Ed., were both men of prominence, the former having served in the State senate, from Rockingham, from 1859 to 1863.— See pages 282, 295, above. Ex-Gov. S. W. Pennypacker, of

---

[8]. See 75th Va., page 672.

ROCKINGHAM COUNTY

Pennsylvania, is a relative of the family. Miss Kate Pennybacker, of Linville Creek, is a grand-daughter of Sen. I. S. Pennybacker, and possesses an excellent oil portrait of him.

In 1844 the *Rockingham Register* contained cards of the following Rockingham lawyers:

Herring Chrisman	Jacob P. Effinger
F. L. Barziza	E. A. Shands

In 1854 the following were advertised in the same paper:

Allan C. Bryan & John C. Woodson

E. A. Shands & S. M. Sommers

J. C. C. Brettell	J. N. Liggett

Allan C. Bryan, born at Edom, was a brother of Daniel Bryan, the poet. Pendleton Bryan, lawyer, who died in Harrisonburg, Aug. 30, 1906, was a son of A. C. Bryan.

John C. Woodson, who died in Harrisonburg, Apr. 25, 1875, aged 52, had represented Rockingham in the legislature, etc. The *Register* of Apr. 29, and May 6, 1875, contained sketches of his life.

Jacob N. Liggett was born in Harrisonburg, January 2, 1829, the son of Samuel and Romanzy Nicholas Liggett. He graduated in law from the University of Virginia. During the civil war he served in various commands; and among his papers is a note written by Ashby, commending his courage and service. In 1860 he was a Presidential elector on the Douglas and Johnson ticket. Following the war he represented Rockingham in the Virginia House of Delegates, and was elected to the convention that drew up the Underwood Constitution in 1868. From the latter body he was expelled by a partisan vote, because he did not hesitate to express his unvarnished opinion of the body and its proceedings. He was a lawyer of ability, a writer and reader of discrimination, and an orator of no mean powers. In 1852 he married Evelyn Winfield of Rockingham; following her death in 1884 he married Isabella Spence of Westmoreland County, who survives him. He died in Harrisonburg, May 8, 1912.

John Francis Lewis, born near Port Republic, March 1, 1818, came of the family of which Gen. Andrew Lewis and

A HISTORY OF

Col. Charles Lewis were earlier representatives. (See page 127, note.) He was a planter for many years. In 1861 he was one of Rockingham's delegates to the State convention, and the only member east of the Alleghanies who refused to sign the ordinance of secession. (See pages 131-3.) In 1865 he was an unsuccessful Union candidate for Congress, but in 1869 he was elected lieutenant-governor (Gilbert C. Walker, governor) by 20,000 majority. In the same year he was chosen U. S. Senator for Virginia, serving in that capacity till March 4, 1875. In 1881 he was again elected lieutenant-governor of Virginia (W. E. Cameron, governor). In 1872 he was mentioned as a possible candidate for the Vice-Presidency, on the Grant ticket. He died in September, 1895. John F. Lewis, of Lynnwood, is his son, as was also the late Daniel Sheffey Lewis (pages 334, 335).[9]

John Thomas Harris, for many years a distinguished citizen of Rockingham, well known throughout Virginia, and conspicuous in many national issues, was born in Albemarle County, Va., May 8, 1823, the son of Nathan Harris and Ann Allan Anderson. When he was five years old his parents moved to Augusta County, his early education being received in Albemarle and Augusta schools. At the age of 20 he taught school in Augusta, studying law in the meantime. Having graduated from the law school of Judge Lucas P. Thompson, he was licensed and admitted to the bar in 1845 by Judges Baldwin and Smith, and located in Harrisonburg.

In 1848 he was a canvasser for Cass and Butler, and four years later rendered effective service in Pierce's campaign. The same year (1852) he was elected commonwealth's attorney for Rockingham County, holding the office by re-election till 1859. In 1856 he canvassed Virginia as a Presidential elector for James Buchanan, and the next year was appointed a member of the board of visitors to the Virginia Military Institute. In 1859, after a memorable campaign, in which the

---

[9]. Biographical sketches, etc., of Sen. Lewis appeared in the *Rockingham Register*, Oct. 28, 1869; Jan. 14, 1875; Sept. 6, 1895.

ROCKINGHAM COUNTY

field at the start was against him, Mr. Harris was elected to Congress from the 9th district of Virginia, then composed of the counties of Highland, Bath, Rockbridge, Augusta, Rockingham, Shenandoah, Hardy, and Pendleton. He was re-elected in 1861.

Although opposed to secession, Mr. Harris promptly followed Virginia when she withdrew from the Union, and served two terms in the General Assembly during the war. From 1866 to 1869 he was judge of the 12th judicial circuit of Virginia, which included Rockingham (see pages 161-163, above). In 1870 he was elected again to Congress, this time representing the 7th district, and was continuously re-elected till 1880. In 1881 he resumed the practice of law, devoting himself chiefly to contested election cases, for which his long experience in Congress had given him special fitness. In 1888 he, with Richard F. Bierne, was an elector at large on the Cleveland ticket, and the following year was a rival of P. W. McKinney for the Democratic nomination for the Governorship. Later he was appointed by Gov. McKinney one of the commissioners for Virginia to the World's Columbian Exposition, and as a member of the executive committee took a prominent part in the great celebration. He died at his home in Harrisonburg, October 14, 1899.

On May 29, 1854, Mr. Harris married Miss Virginia M. Miller. The following children were born of the union: Anna H. Heard, 5908 Cabaune Ave., St. Louis; Emma H. MacQueary, 6809 McPherson Ave., St. Louis; Virginia O. Beall, St. Regis, St. Louis; Graham H. Harris, 1438 N. State St., Chicago; John T. Harris, Harrisonburg; Hatton N. T. Harris (died 1905); Edith Harris (died 1904); and Clement C. Harris, who died in infancy. Hatton Harris was a surgeon in the U. S. Navy; Graham H. Harris and John T. Harris are prominent lawyers.

For many years, beginning with or before the war, one of the prominent citizens of Rockingham, and for some time an influential member of the legislature, was Dr. S. H. Moffett. During the war he was a director on the board of

A HISTORY OF

the Western State Hospital, at Staunton. The *Register* of Nov. 17, 1881, and Aug. 7, 1896, contained interesting accounts of him as a politician and statesman. The same paper, in 1863, contained cards of John W. G. Smith, E. T. H. Warren, and John C. Woodson, Rockingham lawyers.

The following list, for 1866 and 1867, is made up from several copies of the *Register*, compared with a copy of the *Old Commonwealth* of Oct. 10, 1866.

James Kenney[10]
Geo. G. Grattan
J. S. Duckwall
F. A. Daingerfield[11]
Wm. H. Effinger
J. N. Liggett
Chas. A. Yancey
Thos. L. M. Chipley
G. W. Berlin
Warren S. Lurty
B. G. Patterson
Chas. E. Haas

Allan C. Bryan
Jno. C. Woodson
Wm. B. Compton[12]
Huston Handy
G. S. Latimer
A. M. Newman
Wm. S. Rohr
J. Ed. Pennybacker
Pendleton Bryan
John Paul
Granville Eastham (1834-'95)[13]
J. S. Harnsberger

Charles Triplett O'Ferrall was born in what is now Berkeley County, W. Va., Oct. 21, 1840, and died in Richmond, Va., Sept. 22, 1905. He was a Confederate cavalry officer, and rose to the rank of colonel. After graduating in law, in 1869, he located at Harrisonburg, and had his home there until December, 1893, when he moved to Richmond. From 1874 to 1880 he was judge of the Rockingham County court, and from 1894 to 1898 he was governor of Virginia. For twelve years of the interim he was a member of Congress from the 7th district of Virginia. Although not regarded as

---

10. Sketch of in the *Register* of Oct. 19, 1894.

11. See page 319; also, McDonald's History of the Laurel Brigade, pp. 379, 380.

12. Sketch of in the *Register* of July 29, 1898.

13. Sketch of in the *Register* of March 22, 1895.

HON. CHARLES T. O'FERRALL
(Pages 358, 359)

Photo by Morrison

ROCKINGHAM COUNTY

a profound lawyer, he was an efficient judge, and as a popular orator in political campaigns he had few equals.

Governor O'Ferrall's mother was Jane Laurens, born in Fauquier County, Va., in 1817. She died in Bridgewater in May, 1891, having lived there several years preceding. Her grave is in Woodbine Cemetery, Harrisonburg. She had the Spartan spirit and the tender devotion of the lady of Shunem. Few stories are more touching and stirring than the brief account Col. O'Ferrall gives of her journey to his bedside, after he had received what was supposed to be a mortal wound, near Upperville, in June, 1863.

In 1862 Col. O'Ferrall married Annie McLain; his second wife, whom he married in 1891, was Jennie Knight Danforth.

In addition to numerous political essays and speeches, he published an autobiographical volume entitled "Forty Years of Active Service" (see page 326). In this he has a number of interesting things to say of Rockingham, her people in general and his colleagues in particular. For example, he says of George E. Deneale, who was his colleague in the Virginia House of Delegates in 1871-3, "He was called 'the old man eloquent.'" In telling of the famous Lawson trial of 1877, he gives graphic descriptions of John Paul and John Roller, as follows:

> The Commonwealth's Attorney who prosecuted in these cases was John Paul, who afterwards served a term in Congress and was then appointed United States District Judge for the Western District of Virginia. He was one of the ablest prosecuting attorneys I have ever known; his congressional service was creditable, and his career as Judge from 1883 to 1902, when he died, was marked with ability and with an honesty and uprightness of purpose that drew plaudits from the bar of his district, and stamped him as a just, impartial, and incorruptible judge.
>
> The leading attorney for the defense was John E. Roller, and well did he act his part and do his duty. Astute, cautious, and watchful, never tiring, never lacking in quickness to object to what he conceived to be an improper question, and then maintaining his position with great force; searching and severe in the cross-examination of opposing witnesses, and drawing most skilfully from the witnesses for the defense every point favorable to his clients. Between the two—Paul and Roller —it was indeed a battle royal and a fight to the finish. They were

both young men, neither forty—the latter, who was the junior, not more than thirty-five. * * * * * * * *

A distinguished and highly-esteemed member of the county bar . . . , Colonel Robert Johnston, was elected as my successor.[14]

John Paul, statesman and jurist, was born near Ottobine, June 30, 1839, the son of Peter Paul and his wife, Maria Whitmer. He was commonwealth's attorney for Rockingham County, 1871-7; in 1880 he was elected to Congress; and in September, 1883, he was appointed U. S. judge for the western district of Virginia, in which capacity he served with distinction for 18 years,—till his death, Nov. 1, 1901.[15] His wife, whom he married in November, 1874, was Miss Katherine S. Green (see pages 326-7). One of his sons, John Paul, Jr., is now Virginia senator from Rockingham.

J. Samuel Harnsberger, the son of Jeremiah and Elizabeth Harnsberger, was born in the eastern part of Rockingham County, near Conrad's Store, now Elkton, November 17, 1839. In 1861, while a student at the University of Virginia, he entered the Confederate army, serving under Gen. Henry A. Wise in West Virginia; later he was a member of Co. F, 12th Virginia Cavalry, organized by Major Harry Gilmore, and afterwards commanded successively by Clarke, Figgett, and O'Ferrall. In 1862 he was a special aide to Stonewall Jackson, just preceding the famous Valley campaign. After the war he returned to the University to study law, and then located at Harrisonburg to practice his profession. About 1904 he was appointed U. S. Commissioner for the Western District of Virginia, and held this position till death, which occurred at his home in Harrisonburg, May 2, 1912. In 1871 he married Carrie V. Harnsberger, who, with two sons and a daughter, survives him. The sons are George S. Harnsberger, Harrisonburg, and Gilbert M. Harnsberger, Shenandoah City, Va. The daughter is Mrs. Bartow Jones, Point Pleasant, W. Va. During the last years of his life

---

14. See pages 206, 207 of "Forty Years of Active Service."

15. See "John Paul, 1889-1901," by John T. Harris.

JUDGE JOHN PAUL
(Pages 359, 390)

ROCKINGHAM COUNTY

Captain Harnsberger collected a large amount of material towards a history of the Harnsberger family.

Within the years 1876 to 1881, the following were among the lawyers of Rockingham:
Edwin C. Bruffey
G. F. Compton (pages VI, 319)
R. S. Thomas
Geo. A. Roszelle
Robt. B. Ragan (died 1881)
Henry V. Strayer (died 1900)
John A. Cowan
O. B. Roller (1855-1912)[16]
William Shands

In 1905, Winfield Liggett, a well known member of the bar, died.

George Bernard Keezell was born near Keezletown, July 20, 1854, son of George Keezell and his wife, Amanda Fitzallen Peale. He was an only child, and his father, who married late in life, died when his son was eight years old. He was educated in private schools and at Stuart Hall, a collegiate institution, in Baltimore. At the age of 16 he took up farming, residing with his mother at the home built by his grandfather in 1794. Shortly after he was 21 he was elected a justice of the peace; and in 1883 he was elected to the State senate, being re-elected four successive terms from 1895 to 1911. His senatorial service was the longest of any man in this generation. He was always in the thick of every fight, and was regarded as an authority on financial matters, having served as chairman of the Finance Committee a number of years. He resigned from the senate in 1910 to accept appointment as treasurer of Rockingham County, and served one year of an unexpired term. He has always been a Democrat in politics, and for 25 years was chairman of the party organization of his county. In 1901 he was a member of the Virginia constitutional convention, and was a presi-

---

16. See pages 173, 178, above.

dential elector in 1904. He has served on the State Board of Fisheries by appointment of four successive governors, Tyler, Montague, Swanson, and Mann.

Senator Keezell has always taken an active interest in education, serving many years as local school trustee. In the senate he was on the committee for Public Institutions and Education, and was patron of the bill establishing the State Normal and Industrial School at Harrisonburg. He was also a member of the committee which made the preliminary report favoring such schools, and was especially active and influential in locating the Normal at Harrisonburg. Since its establishment he has served as chairman of the Board of Trustees. In 1912 the "Schoolma'am," the 200-page annual published by the student body, was dedicated to him, with the characterization: "A Progressive Farmer, A Virginia Statesman, A Patron of Education, and A Friend of Virginia Teachers."

Mr. Keezell's grandfather, George Keezell, was the founder and patron of Keezletown (see pages 193, 194); his father, George Keezell, was a soldier in the War of 1812. In 1886 Mr. Keezell married Miss Kate M. Hannah, who died in 1902, leaving four sons and two daughters; in 1903 he married Miss Belle C. Hannah, one of the best known teachers of Rockingham.

Many of the men who have gone out from Rockingham to other counties and States have become eminent; a few examples are given.

William Taylor, born in Alexandria, began the practice of law in Rockingham; was elected a representative for Virginia to the 28th and 29th Congress; he died Jan. 17, 1846, in Washington.

Thomas H. Ford, born in Rockingham, Aug. 23, 18——; went when young to Ohio; became a lawyer; in 1855 was elected Lt. Governor; died in Washington, Feb. 29, 1868.

In 1871 Andrew J. Kearney, son of Martin L. Kearney of Rockingham, was judge of the parish court of Cameron, La., and was connected with the *Cameron Times*. At the

ROCKINGHAM COUNTY

same time H. H. Stevens, son of E. H. Stevens, was an influential member of the Louisiana legislature.

In 1880 died Judge Wm. P. Daingerfield, an eminent jurist of California. He was born in Virginia in 1824, and began the practice of law in Rockingham and Pendleton.— See page 126.

Chas. H. Lewis, secretary of the commonwealth prior to 1870, and minister to Portugal, 1870 to 1875, was a brother to Sen. John F. Lewis, of Rockingham; and Judge Lunsford L. Lewis, well known throughout Virginia, is a member of the same family.

Sylvester Lamb, of Toledo, a very distinguished member of a recent Ohio legislature, is a descendant of Peter Lam of Rockingham.

The late James W. Marshall, of southwest Virginia, famous as "Cyclone Jim," spent part of his early life in this county, having numerous connections here.

Judge Charles Grattan, a distinguished jurist of Augusta County, was a native of Rockingham, and a brother of Judge George G. Grattan.

Hon. James Hay, the distinguished member of Congress from the 7th district of Virginia, was a Rockingham lawyer and teacher from 1877 to 1879. The present circuit judge, T. N. Haas, was one of his pupils. Mr. Hay married his first wife, Miss Tatum, in Harrisonburg, Oct. 1, 1878.

Additional matter relating to this chapter is given in the Appendix.

We append here a few statements regarding certain sons of Rockingham distinguished in fields other than law and statesmanship.

Col. John W. Dunlap, born here in 1814, lived here till 1858; then he moved to Iowa; he died in Jackson County, Iowa, Nov. 5, 1869.

Rev. Dr. A. S. Gibbons, president Univ. of the Pacific, 1852-7 and 1872-9, was born near River Bank, Rockingham Co., Va., about 1822.

About 1871 Nat Ervin, who had gone from Rockingham

to Iowa some years before, came back on a visit. He had increased $1000 to $150,000 in the meantime.

In 1872 the following Rockinghamers were good citizens at and near Kingston, Ga.: James G. Rogers, Jonathan Speck, Peter Hollen, and the "Harris Boys."

In the 70's Dr. J. R. L. Hardesty, son of Isaac Hardesty of Harrisonburg, was an eminent surgeon and eye specialist of Wheeling. In 1875 the Khedive offered him a position at $7000.

Gen. C. C. C. Carr, of Chicago, was born in Harrisonburg, 1842.—See pages 120, 269, etc.

Maj. Walter Reed (1851-1902), surgeon U. S. A., hero and benefactor, spent part of his boyhood in Harrisonburg, where his father, Rev. L. S. Reed, had his home for many years.

Dr. O. C. Brunk, of Richmond, formerly superintendent of the State hospital at Williamsburg, is a native of Rockingham.

Mr. L. J. Bricker, of St. Paul, a prominent railroad official, is also a Rockinghamer.

Rev. David W. Gwin, A. M., D. D., M. D., LL. D., of Columbia, S. C., clergyman, educator, editor, and author, was born in Bridgewater, Dec. 6, 1838, the son of David S. Gwin, merchant.

In the blowing up of the *Maine*, February 15, 1898, Frank T. Kelly, of Rockingham, was killed. Dr. Lucien G. Heneberger, of Harrisonburg, was surgeon on the ship, but escaped with his life.

CHAPTER XX.

FARMS AND FARMERS.

The chief wealth of Rockingham is produced in the fields, the orchards, the stock ranges, the poultry yards, and the dairies. Ours is pre-eminently a county of farms and farmers: of productive farms, and of farmers who own their farms and live upon them. Of a total of 3528 farms reported in 1910, only 489 were operated by tenants and managers, while all the rest, 3039, were operated by the owners. Of the latter, 2480 were free from mortgage debt. It is not surprising, therefore, that Rockingham as an agricultural community holds front rank in the State and in the nation.

One of the most interesting phases of this subject is to be found in observing the changes that have taken place from earlier to later times in the kind and character of agricultural products. For example, tobacco for several generations was an important crop in Rockingham. In 1844 Gen. S. H. Lewis (page 127) began to cut tobacco on the 21st of August, and continued on September 4, 5, 6, and 7, finishing on the 16th. In February, 1861, he was preparing beds for tobacco plants. As late as 1876 much tobacco was raised in E. Rockingham and the southern part of Page. Most of it was hauled to Harrisonburg and shipped via the B. & O. railway. From the statements in the current press it appears that tobacco raising in the county was a common thing, but that the quantity that year (1876) was greater than usual. At present no tobacco, almost, is raised. In 1910 only 3 acres in the whole county were devoted to it.

One of the most interesting experiments was made in grape culture. A hundred years ago, perhaps, the Scherdlins (page 238), who lived on Paul Street, Harrisonburg, in the house now occupied by Mrs. Converse, had a vineyard on the hill eastward. In November, 1866, Hockman and Forrer were planting a 6-acre vineyard on the same hill. Within the next few years grape culture was undertaken on a large scale in many parts of the county. In 1867 Forrer and Hockman had about 5000 vines. In November, 1867, Col. John H. Hopkins, Dr. W. D. Hopkins, A. S. Byrd, and Francis Staling had formed a company for setting out large vineyards near Mt. Clinton, and had ordered 65,000 grape slips. They were also going to raise various fruits. Firebaugh & Company, at Mt. Clinton, were also preparing to set out a large vineyard.

By May, 1868, the following varieties of grapes had been planted about Mt. Clinton: Delaware, Concord, Norton's Virginia, Iona, Ives' Seedling, and Hartford Prolific. At the same time Simeon Woods had planted out a large tract in grapes near New Market, Shenandoah County.

In August, 1871, it was reported that Capt. A. S. Byrd had a vineyard near Hopkins' Mill and the North Mountain, planted in 1868, containing 5400 vines, of 14 different varieties. In September (1871) Dr. J. C. Homan had a vineyard of 15 acres near Timberville. In 1873 a quantity of wine was being made from G. T. Hopkins' vineyard, near McGaheysville; and Samuel Shank had 4½ acres in grapes on Linville Creek, near Broadway. In 1874 G. W. Berlin sold his vineyard at Bridgewater to J. W. F. Allemong (page 232).

At present there are a few grape vines on nearly every farm; but so far as known, no attempt is being made anywhere in the county to raise grapes on a large scale.

But some things have come in while others have gone out. The most striking instance of this sort is doubtless to be found in the development of fruit-growing. A century ago Dr. Peachey Harrison wrote that the apples of Rockingham were few and inferior (see Chapter 28). Now fruits of all kinds adapted to our latitude, especially apples, are produced regularly in immense quantities (see page 181). Four miles west of Harrisonburg stands a single apple tree (York Imperial) that produced in one season, a year or two ago, 15 barrels of fruit, which sold for $2.75 a barrel. The

ROCKINGHAM COUNTY

chief varieties grown are York Imperial (Johnson), Winesap, Ben Davis, Jonathan, Delicious, Rome Beauty, and Grimes' Golden. The Smokehouse and some other old varieties are going out. In November, 1911, T. N. Thompson and W. J. Dingledine were elected president and secretary, respectively, of the Rockingham Horticultural Society, a growing organization of over 100 members. The great fruit growers' convention and exhibition (16th annual meeting of the Virginia Horticultural Society), held in Harrisonburg in January, was one of the features of the year 1912.

About 1843 Joseph Funk, as shown by his letters, was cultivating apple sprouts at Mountain Valley, in order that they might be ready for his daughter to carry to Missouri for planting, when she should return from a visit to him. This may have been the beginning of the nursery business in Rockingham. From 1860 to 1866, perhaps longer, John Niswander was proprietor of the Rockingham Nursery, at Dayton. In 1869 Coffman & Son, near Dayton, were operating Cook's Creek Nursery. It was said:

> The elder Mr. Coffman is one of the early pioneers of superior fruit growing in the Valley.[1]

For a number of years past the Wenger nursery, near Dayton, has been well known. Mr. C. D. Wenger is the present proprietor. Greenhouses have been known in the county for the past 30 or 40 years; but the one advertised at Harrisonburg by John H. Bell in 1875 was referred to as a "new enterprise."

One of our most interesting and significant agricultural enterprises is the seed growing business of D. M. Wetsel & Son. In 1897 Mr. Wetsel, formerly a blacksmith, bought 15 acres of land near Port Republic, and began to raise superior seed corn. His business grew, so that in 1905 he purchased 160 acres further down the river, 120 acres lying on Green Island. Continuing his corn growing, Mr. Wetsel developed several new varieties, which are among the best yielders in

---

[1] *Rockingham Register*, Nov. 11, 1869.

the eastern States. He has enlarged his work, now growing many seeds for garden and field. His exhibits have taken a number of high prizes in the Roanoke, Richmond, Hagerstown, and Baltimore fairs. The trade of the firm extends over nearly every State east of the Mississippi River.

The leading grains of Rockingham are corn (994,436), wheat (719,090), oats (45,140), and rye (25,165); the figures indicating the respective numbers of bushels, for the year, reported in 1910. Practically all the wheat is grown from fall sowing, and different varieties, both smooth and bearded, are cultivated. Leap's prolific smooth wheat is extensively grown in the eastern parts of the county. This variety is regarded by competent authorities as probably better suited to Virginia soils and climate than any other known; and therefore it is of special interest to recall that this wheat was given to the world from East Rockingham. Mr. Leap, the original cultivator, now lives near Charlottesville.

In 1839 R. Kemper, of Cross Keys, was advertising "Italian Spring Wheat" for sale. In 1852, Gen. S. H. Lewis cut Zimmerman wheat on June 25; "purple straw," June 29, and following; Poland rye, July 8; and commenced sowing Mediterranean wheat on September 22. From 1852 to 1861 he was also raising "white wheat."

Judging from advertisements in the *Register*, Rockingham farmers were using "plaister" for fertilizer as early as 1833. In 1852 (March 31) Gen. Lewis sowed plaster on a clover field; on April 2, following, he sowed it on another field. In 1864 Nova Scotia plaster was being used in the county; in 1866 H. Heller & Son, of Harrisonburg, were selling raw bone phosphate and super phosphate of lime. During the years following much bone dust was used, large quantities being ground in the county. In 1866 it was reported that plaster had been found on the farm of Capt. D. S. Jones, near Harrisonburg, and also on the farm of Emanuel Rhodes. In 1867 Peruvian guano sold in Harrisonburg at $115 a ton; bone dust, at $70; wheat, at $2.25 a bushel; sugar, at 15 to 25 cents a pound. In 1868 G. W. Berlin was paying 50c a hundred

Senator I. S. Pennybacker
(Pages 354, 355)

ROCKINGHAM COUNTY

for dry bones (in Harrisonburg), and $15 a ton (delivered at his mill near Bridgewater), and was grinding them into bone dust for farm fertilizer. In 1871 he paid $20 a ton for bones, and sold the bone dust at $50 to $55 a ton. In 1880 he said that Maj. George Chrisman had bought from him from two to ten tons of pure ground bone nearly every year during the preceding 10 or 12 years.

The number of bushels of potatoes raised in 1910 was 122,116; of sweet potatoes and yams, 5058. In certain sections of the county, particularly about Spring Creek, Bridgewater, Mt Crawford, and Timberville, thousands of fine watermelons, etc., are grown every year. August court is known as "watermelon court," the reason being much in evidence all around the public square. The color scheme is red, white, and green, with black for variation. In 1901— the first time in many years—August court was melonless, owing to lateness of the crop.

Rockingham is a great country for hay and forage. In 1910 over 45,000 tons were reported. Timothy and clover, usually mixed, are the staple hay-grasses. Crimson clover and alfalfa are being introduced. The lands along Smith's Creek, Linville Creek, and other streams are excellent for grazing, and in consequence the cattle, horses and sheep of the county are numbered by thousands (see page 181). It is said that in 1903 Rockingham took first rank in livestock values in the U. S. census report.

By common consent, Geo. W. Rosenberger, who lived at Rosendale, on Smith's Creek, is regarded as the pioneer in bringing fine stock into Rockingham County. In 1842 he began raising improved breeds of cattle, sheep, and hogs; later, he secured the better breeds of chickens, turkeys, and ducks.[2] About 1860, a herd of 26 Durhams of his raising, 21 bullocks and 5 heifers, averaged a weight of 1773 pounds: the heaviest weighing 1985, the lightest 1500. From 1866 to 1876, etc., he was selling full-bred Cotswold sheep, as well as

---

2. *Rockingham Register*, Jan. 3, 1867, Jan. 31, 1878.

A HISTORY OF

shorthorn cattle. In 1874 he bought in Kentucky a Cotswold buck weighing 385 pounds. In 1876 he sold to John F. Lewis two sheep weighing 200 and 300 pounds, respectively.

In the 70's Peter S. Roller and Samuel Frank, of the vicinity of Mt. Crawford, had for sale Berkshire pigs and shorthorn calves. For many years past John S. Funk, John B. Bowman, and others, of the Singer's Glen neighborhood, have won numerous prizes at Staunton, Winchester, Woodstock, and elsewhere on Shropshire, Cotswold, and Southdown sheep, etc.

In January, 1867, Ephraim Wenger, near Dayton, killed a beef "which weighed over 1255 lbs. nett!" In April following, Col. John H. Hopkins, "of the North Mountain region," sold 25 head of fat cattle, to Mr. Hahn, of Shenandoah, at $95 a head. In 1871, D. H. Landis, near Harrisonburg, was raising Ohio Chesters and Berkshires. In 1880 Geo. W. Adams, of Linville Creek, bought of Daniel Byerly four cattle averaging 1802 pounds each; in March, 1891, Dr. E. A. Herring, of Cross Keys, sold two Durham cattle (twins), named Tom and Jerry, 4 years old the preceding December, that weighed respectively 2040 and 2155 pounds; and in January, 1895, John F. Myers shipped to Roanoke a hog ($\frac{3}{4}$ Poland-China, $\frac{1}{4}$ Chester) that weighed 855 pounds. (See page 89.)

After Mr. Rosenberger, the man who deserves most gratitude in Rockingham for the high standards set in stock-raising, etc., is doubtless Maj. George Chrisman. For forty years or more he has pointed out the best in these lines, and has shown how and why it is the best. It was he who introduced Poland-China and Berkshire hogs into Rockingham, following the war, bringing them from Illinois.[3] From 1877 to 1885 his thoroughbred cattle were awarded premiums at Staunton, Winchester, Culpeper, Richmond, and Washington; from 1875 to 1896 he contributed to the *Rockingham Register* no less than two dozen articles on such subjects as hog-raising, cattle-raising, Percheron horses, farming, fertilizers, etc.

---

[3]. *Rockingham Register*, May 9, 1878.

ROCKINGHAM COUNTY

As early as 1867, perhaps earlier, Sen. John F. Lewis was also engaged in raising fine stock. In the year named he brought into Rockingham the thoroughbred race-horse, Engineer, for the improvement of his own stock, with that of his neighbors. He also raised Durham cattle and fullbred sheep. His son, John F. Lewis, president of the Virginia Pure Bred Live Stock Breeders Association, keeps saddle and Percheron horses, Shorthorn cattle, and Berkshire hogs.

The first "thoroughbred" horse I have heard of in Rockingham was Sir Rubycon, advertised in March, 1833, by John W. Dunlap; the most famous one was doubtless Sam Purdy, brought to Harrisonburg in 1880 from the Pacific slope, a present to Capt. F. A. Daingerfield from his brother-in-law, James R. Keene. Sam Purdy had been at different times the property of Leland Stanford, and Keene had paid $50,000 for him. He was in Rockingham about ten years, but died in Culpeper in 1891, aged 25 years. General Miles, a Kentucky saddle-bred horse, the property of Dr. John A. Myers of Harrisonburg, has been in the county about 16 years, and has a great progeny. Thomas Herring and Joseph Clatterbuck, of Dayton, keep fine horses. St. Lorimer, owned by Mr. Clatterbuck, was sired by St. Blaze, owned by J. R. Keene and F. A. Daingerfield, and sold for $100,000. One of St. Lorimer's colts recently took blue ribbon in the free for all heavy jumpers' contest in France. Among other Rockingham gentlemen who have done notable things in promoting stock standards, specially of horses, are M. M. Jarman, Elkton, and Garber Brothers, of Harrisonburg. Harrisonburg is probably the greatest horse market in the Valley. In the *Register* of March 31, 1881, it was stated: "About 500 head of horses have been bought on our streets within the last two months." Every court day brings horses and horse buyers.

As may be supposed, the dairy and poultry products of Rockingham are very large—the quality keeping pace with the quantity. In April, 1866, it was announced in the *Register* that, since the preceding October, Forrer & Clip-

A HISTORY OF

pinger, local merchants, had shipped to Baltimore and Washington 25,000 pounds of butter, which had won such a reputation as to secure for the said firm a contract to supply $200's worth of butter, eggs, etc., per week, to the White House. During the two years ending July 1, 1871, there were shipped from Linville Depot 16,361 barrels of flour, 504,743 pounds of mill feed, 16,769 bushels of wheat, and 241 car loads of live stock. On a single day, in the fall or winter of 1873, 600 pounds of butter were received at the Cross Keys store. The annual shipment of butter from the same place amounted in value to $7000 or $8000. On April 13, 1877, J. B. D. Rhodes & Co., merchants at Spartapolis, had on hand 2000 dozen eggs. During the month of March, 1878, 10,000 dozen eggs were shipped from Broadway. May 22, 1894, "Egg Day" at the Harrisonburg express office, 371 cases, containing 11,406 dozen eggs, were shipped north. For the year ending December 31, 1894, the following express shipments were made from Bridgewater: 50,970 dozen eggs; 17,613 pounds of butter; 80,555 pounds of dressed poultry; 36,014 pounds of live poultry; 1721 pounds of chestnuts and dried fruits. And this was before the railroad came. In December, 1895, it was reported that over 8500 pounds of poultry had been shipped from Broadway and Timberville in one day. At present, the J. A. Burkholder Produce Co., Harrisonburg, is shipping about 50 cars of poultry and 75 cars of eggs a year: 5000 chickens and 6000 dozen eggs in a car. In other words, they send off each month over 20,000 chickens and 450,000 eggs.

At this rate something must be done to keep up the supply; and it is being done. Nearly everybody in the county raises chickens—people in the smaller towns and villages, as well as those on the farm. S. H. Blosser & Son, Dayton, have a hatchery with a capacity of 9900 eggs, tri-weekly becoming chicks. There is only one other in the State (the one at Riverton) of equal size. Near Dayton are also the large poultry yards of Senger Brothers; and there are many others, of varying sizes, over the county. A yearly poultry show is one of the delights of the county-seat.

ROCKINGHAM COUNTY

There was a formal movement for agricultural societies in the Valley as early as 1825-6, the General Assembly records showing; and closer or looser organization has existed among Rockingham farmers, from time to time, up to and into the present. From 1874 to 1878 the Grange was active in the county. In 1874-5 local organizations were perfected at Bridgewater, Mt. Crawford, McGaheysville, Port Republic, Conrad's Store, Zirkle's School House, Melrose, North Mountain, and Harrisonburg. On May 21, 1875, a great demonstration was made in Harrisonburg by the several granges of Rockingham and adjoining counties. Dr. J. B. Webb, of Cross Keys, was installed Master of the county grange; M. M. Sibert was made secretary, and H. B. Harnsberger, treasurer.

In March, 1878, the McGaheysville grange passed resolutions acknowledging the services of Geo. Chrisman, John F. Lewis, and Geo. Rosenberger in improving the herds and flocks of Rockingham. From 1890 to 1893 the Farmers' Alliance was much in evidence. G. T. Barbee of Bridgewater was president of the State organization in 1890.

At present there is an active Rockingham Farmers' Association. C. B. Kiser of Bridgewater is president; C. W. Wampler of Dayton is secretary; there are five directors, one from each magisterial district: D. C. Acker (Plains), W. S. Armentrout (Linville), Harry Forrer (Central), C. T. Callender (Ashby), and J. C. Armstrong (Stonewall). Another healthy and growing organization is the boys' corn club.

April 14, 1870, "Agricola," writing in the *Register*, proposed an agricultural fair for Rockingham. In November, 1892, the first annual agricultural fair of the county was held at Assembly Park, just north of Harrisonburg. In September of the next year, and perhaps for a year or two longer, this movement was kept up. In August, 1898, the first exhibition of the Rockingham Horse and Colt Show Association was held in Assembly Park; in 1901 the annual exhibition was first held on the new grounds, just west of town. These horse and colt shows were discontinued a few years ago; but now, upon the same grounds, while these lines are being written, a new county fair is being held (October, 1912). Maj. Geo. Chrisman is president; Mr. Paul Rhinehart is manager; and H. M. Strickler, Esq., is secretary.

For about ten years past an annual horse and stock show has been held at Lacey Spring; Mr. J. S. Sellers is president, and Mr. L. B. Morris is secretary.

There are dozens of particular farms in Rockingham so well situated and so well kept as to make the observer, whatever he is, long to be a farmer. Perhaps the most famous of all these farms is the one two miles west of Harrisonburg, on the Rawley Pike, until recently owned by James E. Reherd, now the property of Frank B. Showalter. This farm has been "written up" for at least three world's fairs: Chicago (1893), St. Louis (1904), and Jamestown (1907).

Organization, co-operation, and increasing efficiency are marking the progress of farming and farm life in Rockingham. Farm houses are being constructed and furnished with more regard for convenience and comfort, and the people are learning to get more pleasure and culture, as well as more money, out of their farms. Intensive farming and better selection and adaptation of farm products will soon double results on our farms and for our farmers. The following instance is presented to show what is possible in Rockingham on a very small farm.

A. J. Anderson of Bridgewater has a farm of seven acres. The land is river bottom—sandy loam. He plants field corn and potatoes in three acres; the remaining four acres he uses as a truck farm, making specialties of tomatoes, cucumbers, cantaloupes, beans, and sweet corn. Practically the whole output is sold at retail in Harrisonburg and other nearby towns. In 1911 he cleared $1100.00. This year (1912), up to August 15, his sales amounted to $600.00. He regards the total receipts from the four acres of vegetables as clear profit, since the corn and potatoes raised on the other three acres pay expenses for the whole farm.

CHAPTER XXI.

DOMESTIC ARTS AND MANUFACTURING ENTERPRISES.

In regard to manufactures, the same general conditions have existed and the same general changes have occurred in Rockingham County as in the country at large. Early times were marked by a great many and a great variety of manufactures in small establishments and in the homes of the people; the civil war stimulated these local enterprises, and called forth certain ones unknown before; the boom periods produced larger establishments than were operated before, but which were usually short-lived; the last two or three decades have seen most of the small factories give up their business to a few large ones.

The number of different industrial enterprises in our county during the last century or more has been so great that nothing more than a desultory catalogue can be attempted here, except in a few cases.

Some of the first manufacturing establishments, and some of the most important of all, were flouring mills, built on the banks of the numerous power-giving streams. The Bird, Zirkle, and Strickler mills, on Smith's Creek, Plains mill, below Timberville, Bowman's mill, on Linville Creek, Paul's mill, on Beaver Creek, Carthrea's mill, at Port Republic, and other mills on South River and tributary streams, were all likely built a hundred years or more ago. The 40 mills now in the county form one of our most important branches of industry.

Tanners, shoemakers, harness and saddle makers, cabinet makers, tailors, weavers, and blacksmiths were on the ground, of necessity, from very early days. In 1839 Wm. J. Ford was a saddler in Harrisonburg; in 1840 Henry Smals was a

A HISTORY OF

shoemaker in Bridgewater; for 50 years, beginning in 1850, John W. Jacobs was a shoemaker at the same place. In 1826 Jacob Houck and Samuel Liggett were hatters in Harrisonburg; Liggett had perhaps been at McGaheysville beforehand. The same year (1826) John Crummey had a gunshop in Harrisonburg; other gunsmiths in the same town, about 1850, were Alex. McGilvray, Geo. S. Logan, and Wm. W. Gibbs. In 1854 Isaac Stone, in Dayton, J. M. Irvine, O. C. Sterling, and J. C. Williams, in Harrisonburg, were making chairs, bedsteads, and other furniture.

A large number of tanneries were operated from time to time in various parts of the county. Soon after 1800 the following men were tanning at the places indicated: John Zigler, Timberville; Michael Wise, Bridgewater; Francis A. Hite, James Clarke, Abraham Shue, Abner Fawcett, and Jesse Bowlin, Harrisonburg. In 1870 the Zigler Tannery, at Timberville, declared to be one of the best in the Valley, was still running. Later tanners at or near Bridgewater were Geo. F. Dinkle, Philip Phares, and A. R. Hollen. In 1842 George Conrad had a tanyard in Harrisonburg; and later tanners here were H. J. Gray, Jos. Cline, J. A. Loewenbach, and Houck & Wallis. Between 1860 and 1880 the following were tanners: Jas. O'Brian, McGaheysville; S. P. H. Miller, Conrad's Store; S. Burtner, Keezletown; V. H. Lamb, near Bloomer Springs; Simon Smith, Edom; Wm. S. Downs, Port Republic; John Shutters, Cootes' Store; and somebody at Peale's Cross Roads.

In 1826 Henry Tutwiler made buckskin gloves in Harrisonburg, and kept postoffice. About the same time John Zigler had a hemp mill at Timberville. At the same time and later Nelson Sprinkel had a shop in Harrisonburg in which he made all sorts of spinning wheels, at times working 25 hands. He would send out these wheels by wagons into all the adjoining counties, trading them for flax seed, bacon, etc., as well as money. In 1839 J. Meixell & Co. were making threshing machines, corn shellers, etc., at Harrisonburg; in 1841 P. A. Clarke was manufacturing air-tight stoves at Mt.

ROCKINGHAM COUNTY

Crawford; in 1844 C. S. Weaver was advertising threshing machines and cloverseed boxes from his shop "one mile below Davie Kyle's mill on Mill Creek"; in 1854 John W. Showalter, near Mt. Crawford, was making an improved sausage machine; in 1858 Col. Henry Miller of E. Rockingham invented and patented a corn harvester; in 1866 W. H. Karicofe invented and patented the Virginia Corn Planter, a half interest in which he sold to H. J. Gray for $5000; in 1871 Miss Mary E. Long, of Lacey Spring, made a skein of fine white sewing silk, from cocoons of her own raising; in 1873 S. Loewner, at Harrisonburg, was manufacturing combs of different styles; the same year, at the same town, F. Staling was making paint; in 1877 R. H. Snyder (Hbg.) was making a specialty of grain cradles; in 1892 Calvert McGahey, of Elkton, invented, made, and patented a steam engine; in 1911 the Miller device for train control, invented by H. B. Miller, formerly of Harrisonburg, was proved a success.

For many years J. G. Sprinkel, Harrisonburg, was a skilful metal worker. In 1857 he and Basford invented and patented an engine. He made engines under his patent, and four of his make were in use in Rockingham in 1861—one of them driving the press of the *Rockingham Register*. He also made circular-saw mills. In April, 1863, he was advertising for six men to make cavalry steel spurs.

In 1862-3 Isaac Reamer, Conrad's Store, was making (by machine) shoe pegs of all sizes for sale; at the same time J. H. Long, Harrisonburg, was offering 5c each for old blacking boxes, to be used in marketing his Ivory Paste Blacking. In 1840-41 Berger & Pope, in the 60's, 70's, and 80's Chas. Eshman, and later others, all of Harrisonburg, were manufacturing cigars, etc.; and in 1888 it was stated that the town manufactured more cigars than any other in Virginia, except Richmond. Peter Bolinger, at McGaheysville, and Young & Cox, Harrisonburg, were brewers early last century. Peter Dinkel, Mt. Stevens (p. 201), in 1822, and John Bowman, Jr., near Timberville, in 1870, had distilleries; in 1867 J. R. Koogler and W. P. McCall erected on Muddy

Creek, near Rushville, a steam distillery, with a capacity of 200 to 250 gallons of whiskey a day. In the *Register* of April 8, 1875, it was said: So far this season, about 6000 lbs. of Maple sugar has been made in the upper end of Brock's Gap.

Wagon makers and potters were important in earlier days. The Rohrs made carriages and wagons in Harrisonburg for half a century; Joseph Dinkle was a pioneer carriage maker at Bridgewater. In 1826 G. Cline had a pottery in Harrisonburg; in 1830 John Zigler established one at Timberville; between 1860 and 1880 J. H. Kite, near Elkton, Ireland, Duey, & Shinnick, at Mt. Crawford, Emanuel Suter, at New Erection, and J. D. Heatwole (Potter John), on Dry River, were making all sorts of earthen ware. About 1890 large potteries were started at Harrisonburg and Broadway.

During the Revolution Coonrad Hansberger (page 93) had a woolen mill on Elk Run, site of Elkton. Prior to 1815 Jonathan Shipman owned a woolen mill at or near the site of Spring Creek; Abram Whitmore and Thomas Tousey succeeded him in ownership.[1] In the 40's Michael B. Cline, of Dayton, was doing much wool carding; Patrick Kelly was a Rockingham carder and fuller; and the Blossers, at Dayton, were operating a "Silk, Cotton, and Woolen Dyeing Establishment." Between 1860 and 1873 no less than 12 factories for carding, spinning, weaving, or dyeing wool were operated in the county: at Riverton, near Conrad's Store; Port Republic; River Bank; on Cub Run; on Beaver Creek; Hollen's Mill; Berlinton; Mt. Crawford; Bridgewater; and elsewhere. The leading promoter of these industries was J. H. Larkin; some others prominent in the business were C. M. Harlow, A. B. Tanquary, D. C. Anderson, and J. F. Bradburn.

In 1880 the Massanutten Organ Company was organized at McGaheysville, and organs were manufactured for awhile. In September, 1882, the Virginia Organ factory, at Dayton, was started in a 2-story building, 40 x 60 feet. In 1886 the factory burned, about 70 organs being destroyed. A few

---

[1]. S. H. W. Byrd has an old advertisement of this mill dated June, 1815. Probably this was the same mill operated later by Daniel Thomas.

ROCKINGHAM COUNTY

years ago S. A. Myers built at Dayton a large pipe organ, which was first used there in the United Brethren church, and which is now in the Presbyterian church of Waynesboro, Virginia.

In different parts of Rockingham large iron furnaces have been operated: In Brock's Gap, by the Pennybackers; at Paulington, by Faussett and others; east of Elkton, by Daniel and Henry Forrer and others; Mt. Vernon Furnace, in Brown's Gap; etc. Faussett probably started the furnace at Paulington prior to 1800; the Forrers were in control east of Elkton for many years before 1866; Mt. Vernon Furnace, built about 1848, was operated by the Millers, John F. Lewis, and others at intervals until 1878.[2] Mt. Vernon Forge was at Grottoes; and there have been foundries at Port Republic and elsewhere for many years. In the 70's J. Shickel & Sons had a foundry and machine shop near Rushville; from 1877 to 1885 Jos. Shickel was superintendent of the Broadway foundry and machine shop; in 1877 a foundry and machine shop were built at Natural Falls above Bridgewater.

Among the different manufacturing enterprises in Rockingham at present are the woolen mill, the canning factory, the carriage factory, and the plow factory at Bridgewater; the harness factory, working about 30 hands, the creamery, and the Shrum Brick factory at Dayton; the Fravel Sash and Door Factory, Houck's tannery, and Bradley's foundry at Harrisonburg; Paxton's lime kiln at Linville; the Timberville creamery; Cover's tannery, at Elkton, and the Elkton creamery; the Whitesel poultry coop factory, at Pleasant Valley, from which more than 65,000 coops have been sent out.

The Bradley foundry was operated in the 50's by Nelson Bradley and others; from 1866 to 1878, by P. Bradley and J. Wilton; since 1878, by P. Bradley and his sons. The Houck tannery has been developed from the earlier establishment

---

[2.] I acknowledge information concerning Mt. Vernon Furnace received from Messrs. J. H. Mace, J. W. Blackburn, and R. T. Miller; and concerning Faussett's furnace, from Messrs. John A. Armentrout and J. H. Mace.

A HISTORY OF

of J. A. Loewenbach and others. The Elkton tannery was built by John Cover in 1872. Its present output is 220 sides of heavy sole leather daily. The Miller cannery at Bridgewater, the first in the county, dates from 1888. Its products take high rank. The Bridgewater woolen mill, which alone survives of all the Rockingham woolen mills, was started in 1872. J. F. Bradburn was superintendent for many years. H. G. Miller is president; J. A. Fry secretary and treasurer. The output of its products is inadequate to the demand for them. The Bridgewater plow factory, with John P. Burke, J. A. Fry, and D. S. Thomas as president, secretary, and manager, makes a specialty of the Superior garden plows, turning out about 10,000 yearly. The Timberville creamery, E. M. Minnick president, W. C. Hoover secretary, was making 100 gallons of ice cream and 1000 pounds of butter a week during the past summer.

Besides the things already mentioned, brooms, barrels, etc., by the thousands, tanks of apple butter and bergs of ice are made in Rockingham every year.

The extent and variety of our local manufactures having thus been indicated, a detailed account is now presented of that particular manual art in which our mothers and grandmothers have most excelled. This account is a special contribution to this work.

Hand-Weaving in Rockingham County.

By Professor Cornelius J. Heatwole.

> .... The piece prepare
> And order every slender thread with care;
> The web enwraps the beam, the reed divides,
> While through the widening space the shuttle glides,
> Which their swift hands receive, then poised with lead
> The swinging weight strikes close the inserted thread."
>
> *Ovid's Metamorphoses.*

A century or more ago hand-weaving was the usual means of making the cloth used in the colonial homes from the Carolinas to New England. The hand-loom formerly

ROCKINGHAM COUNTY

used in the colonies, and occasionally still used in some homes in Rockingham county, is an historic machine of great antiquity and dignity. It is perhaps the most absolute bequest of the past centuries, which we have had unchanged in domestic use, to the present time. In some of the famous paintings of the year 1335 you can see just such looms as many of our grandparents had in their homes in Rockingham county.

The whole process of converting the wool or flax into yarn went on often in close proximity to the loom, and was carried on by some member of the household as a by-industry. The term "spinster" has come down to us from this occupation.

"The first half of the present century saw a race between spinning and weaving. The first found its evolution to machinery; and then led the way for similar means of carrying on the weaving industry. By 1850 combers, spinners, and weavers were no longer individual workers, but became a part of that great monster the *mill machinery*."[3]

When the pioneer settlers came to Rockingham county from 1730 to 1750 to make their homes, one of the first machines they set up was the old loom. It found its abiding place in one of the rooms of the main house or in a shed attached to the house; sometimes in the attic; and often a house was built especially for the loom. There are at present, particularly in the western part of the county, many homes that have a building about the premises known to this day as the "loom house." If one were to look carefully about in one of these buildings, one could find here the old loom resting in peace, as a relic of bygone days. It is sometimes even now called into service for the making of a piece of rag carpet.

The operating of the loom, together with the accessory occupations, such as spinning and carding, were duties assigned to the women of the household. The mother took

---

3. Earle's Home Life in Colonial Days, page 231.

the weaving side of the work, while the daughters did the spinning and spooling. During the spring months the loom was occupied with the making of rag carpet, while in the fall it was used for making the requisite amount of clothing and linen for the household—jeans (usually grey) for suits for the men and boys; linsey (chestnut browns, dull blues, and Scotch plaids) was the material used for the wearing apparel for the women and children. Sometimes a piece of linen for the table, towels and counterpanes, were made during the fall. The flax used in making these articles was grown in a little patch near the house, and was harvested and prepared for the loom by the women.

During one generation the old loom would turn out a number of those rare products of the weaver's art, the coverlets. The size of the family usually determined the number of these; for every ambitious housewife desired that each one of her children should have at least one of these interesting, and in many respects artistic, bed covers. These were made and carefully stored away in a chest, and were presented to the children on their wedding day. The coverlet is probably the highest form of the hand-weaver's art.

The woolen blanket was a product also of the hand-loom. Each member of the family fell heir to one, when she left the old homestead to establish a new home of her own. All the work attending the preparation of the wool for these fabrics, such as washing, combing, carding, and spinning, was done on the premises by the women.

The various colors used in dyeing these household fabrics, particularly the carpets and linseys, were usually the bright, warm colors: red, yellow, green, and blue; though sometimes the more delicate shades were obtained. These colors were arranged in patterns of stripes either in the warp, or chain, or in the woof, and sometimes in both. The sources from which these dyes were obtained were largely vegetable, and procured according to the most primitive methods. The hickory bark furnished the yellows, walnut bark or hulls made the rich browns, sumac berries produced the deep warm reds,

ROCKINGHAM COUNTY

oak yielded the shades of purple, and the cedar berries furnished the delicate dove, or lead color. The simplest method of extracting the coloring matter from these vegetables was employed. The bark was put into a large kettle and boiled for several hours, and then the wool and rags were immersed in this liquid and hung upon the line or fence to dry.

The work preparatory to the actual weaving was probably the most difficult phase of the whole process. The person planning the article to be made on the loom must have skill in handling the instruments, mathematical accuracy for grouping threads and determining the size and proportion of the piece. The aesthetic taste of the individual was shown in the choosing of the patterns and in the selection and combining of colors.

After coloring the chain, which was usually on sale at all country stores, and known as "prepared chain," the skeins were placed upon the swift and run upon spools or quills. These spools were generally made of corn cobs, and the quills of the stalk-part of the weed known to the German people as "Boova Strahl," but to others as teasel. The main reason for using these was because the pith was easily removed. Sometimes these quills were made of rolls of paper and paste.

These spools, filled to the requisite number, were placed in the spool-rack or, in the parlance of the weavers of some sections of the country, the "skarne." This is a large frame, with every few inches small sticks or wires running through, upon which the spools were placed. A thread is gathered from each one of these spools and run through holes in a paddle so that the weaver can gather the threads into "bouts" and run them upon the warping bars. The warping bars are an upright frame revolving with one end of the axle on a pivot on the floor and the other at the ceiling. The bars upon which the warp-threads were wound were one yard apart, and so the length of the threads, and also the length of the piece of cloth, was determined. One takes off twenty yards of thread if one wants to weave twenty yards of cloth. Forty warp-threads make what is called a "bout," and a warp of two hundred threads was designated as a warp of five "bouts."

From the warping bars these bouts were wound upon the warping beam of the loom. The bouts however were first passed through the "wrathe," or rake, a wooden bar with rows of closely set wooden pegs. This rake kept the bouts from becoming entangled, and gave the warp the proper width as it was wound upon the beam. This particular process of winding the warp upon the beam was known as "beaming the piece." It took two persons to do this, one to turn the beam and the other to hold and guide the warp.

The next process in the order of placing the warp upon the loom was called "drawing in." The end of each thread or group of threads was "thumbed in" with a warping needle through the eye or mail of the harness, or "heddle." The harness was commonly called "gears" by the weavers, and consisted of two rows of twine or cord stretched vertically between two horizontal bars, which were fastened above to a pulley and below to a foot-treadle.

The warp-threads were next drawn through the interspaces of the reed, or sley. This was done with a "reed-hook." Two or more warping threads were drawn through each space. The reed, or sley, was composed of a row of thin strips of cane arranged somewhat like comb-teeth, and called "dents." There might be fifty or sixty of these dents to an inch for weaving very fine cloth. The number of dents to the inch determines the fineness of the cloth. The reed when filled was placed in a groove in the heavy batten, or "lathe," which hung by two side bars and swung from an axle, or "rocking-tree," at the top of the loom. The swinging of this batten "strikes close the inserted thread," as Ovid puts it, and produces that thwacking sound heard in hand-weaving. All the threads thus drawn are brought over the front frame of the loom and fastened in the cloth-beam and wound round it. By means of ratchets connected with the cloth-beam and the warp-beam the warp is stretched up and the piece is ready for weaving.

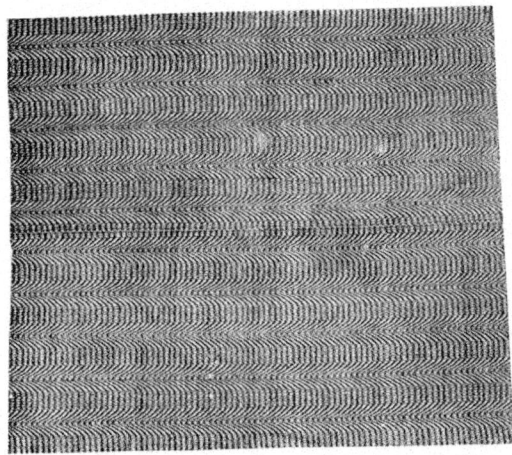
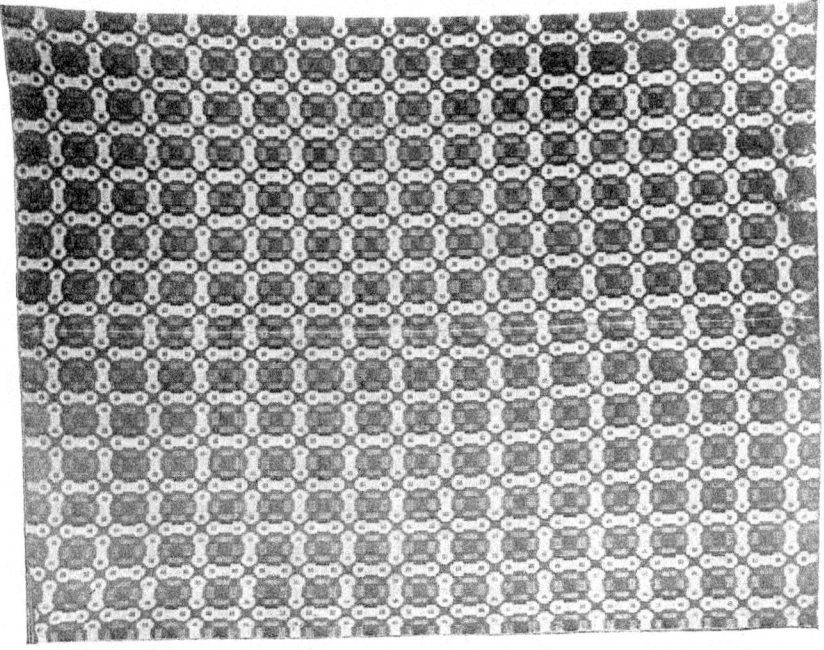

Hand-Woven Coverlets (Page 382)

ROCKINGHAM COUNTY

The temples are adjustable bars with sharp teeth-like pegs in the ends to catch in the selvage to keep the cloth uniform in width. The shuttle is an instrument that contains the woof, and is thrown from one side of the loom to the other by the weaver's hand, and by moving the harness with the foot the shuttle goes over every alternate thread. With the motion of the batten the weft-threads are crowded into place, . and thus the operation continues till the piece is finished.

Some one has calculated that in weaving three yards of close woolen cloth, which was regarded as a day's work, the shuttle was thrown three thousand times, and the treadle pressed down and the batten swung the same number of times. The number of yards regarded by the housewife as a day's work depended upon the kind of cloth. With the finer fabrics, such as linen and jeans, three or four yards was a good day's work; while with carpets as many as ten yards have been woven in a day, though six or eight yards of carpet was regarded as a good day's work. In an old copy of the *Rockingham Register*, dated March 2, 1871, it was reported that a married lady living in Harrisonburg, age fifty-seven, had woven in the past three years, on an old fashioned-loom, 1800 yards of carpet, besides attending to her domestic duties. It is safe to say there were hundreds of these old looms in Rockingham county during the last half of the nineteenth century, and thousands of yards of the various kinds of cloth and carpets were turned out annually by them. The price paid for the weaving of carpet was from ten to twelve cents per yard; for jeans, linseys, and linens the price was considerably more, probably from twenty-five cents to fifty cents per yard.

The loom was made of heavy timber, and the ordinary carpenter in the community could make it. Sometimes it happened that one person specialized in this particular line, and made looms as a business. It is known that Samuel Weaver made many looms in the western part of the county, on the farm now owned by Mr. Elias Brunk. A man by the name of Lamb made looms in the section locally known as "The Brush." John G. Heatwole also made many looms on the farm now owned by Mr. Abram Heatwole, a few miles north of Dayton. These men got any where from eight to ten dollars for doing the carpenter work on one of these looms.

Just how many of these old looms may be found now within the bounds of Rockingham county is hard to say; and how many are now and then brought out for a piece of rag carpet can hardly be ascertained without a great deal of effort. The people in the county of German extraction are still given to making rag carpets, to a great extent. The hand-looms are probably never used any more for the making of such fabrics as linen, wool blankets, coverlets, linseys, etc. Nowadays one often notices in bills of sale, particularly where an old household is being broken up, the "old loom" mentioned as one of the articles for sale, and when put up it generally goes for the meager amount of seventy-five cents, or at most for a few dollars. One was sold a few months ago at a public sale for fifty cents.

The old Rockingham county loom is fast approaching the period of its history when it will be regarded as a relic of the past. Its products, such as linen for table cloths, coverlets, and blankets, are already being treasured by the present generation, and valued for their associations. In almost every household, if you should speak of these rare products of the old loom, the housewife would go to a chest of drawers and bring out, from a safe keeping place, pieces of the various kinds of cloth woven on the old ancestral loom. It is to be hoped that some one who has a proper appreciation of the things of the past will make a collection of the old looms, their accompanying paraphernalia, and their interesting products, and preserve them in a suitable museum for the information and interest of the coming generations.

CHAPTER XXII.

BANKS AND BANKING.

First, let us notice briefly the Rockingham banks that are not now in operation.

By Act of Assembly, March 16, 1850, the Rockingham Savings Bank was chartered, being authorized to discount paper and do a general banking business. The capital stock was not to exceed $100,000. John Kenney, Ed. H. Smith, Robt. M. Kyle, Peachy R. Harrison, Robt. Grattan, Wm. G. Stevens, Abraham Smith, M. Harvey Effinger, Isaac Hardesty, and John H. Waterman were named as incorporators.

In 1852-3 several Acts were passed to establish branches of certain banks at Harrisonburg.

February 24, 1860, an Act was passed incorporating the Harrisonburg Savings Bank. The commissioners named were Saml. Shacklett, Isaac G. Coffman [page 139], Alfred Sprinkle, L. W. Gambill, Wm. D. Trout, John D. Pennybacker [page 295], Thos. L. Yancey, Saml. R. Sterling, David Kingree.

In the 60's and 70's Jonas A. Loewenbach (Dec. 25, 1828 —Dec. 22, 1907) did a good deal of banking business in Harrisonburg.

On April 2, 1873, an Act was passed incorporating Rockingham Bank, Ed. S. Kemper, B. G. Patterson, J. W. F. Allemong [page 232], M. Y. Partlow, Chas. A. Yancey, Jos. A. Hammon, J. A. Lowenbach, Jas. L. Avis, Jacob Gassman, and Wm. McKeever being named as commissioners. The bank was opened for business, July 1, 1874, in a portion of A M. Effinger's bookstore, south side of the public square, Harrisonburg. This was probably in the Switzer building. Henry Shacklett was president, Wm. Rice Warren cashier; the directors were W. D. Hopkins, J. A. Hammon, C. A.

A HISTORY OF

Yancey, Jas. L. Avis, E. S. Kemper, Andrew Lewis, J. S. Harnsberger, and G. M. Effinger.[1] Mr. Warren was cashier till his death in 1883; from 1883 to 1886 Mr. W. J. Dingledine was cashier; he was succeeded by Mr. C. D. Beard. About 1889 Rockingham Bank was succeeded by the Commercial Bank of Harrisonburg, which was in business for several years. Messrs. J. J. Hawse, Eugene West, and Wm. Loeb were connected with these institutions during the later years of their history.

In 1878 the Farmers Bank was organized at Bridgewater. A building was erected for it in 1883, at the corner of Bank Street and Main. At first the officers were: J. W. F. Allemong, president; J. S. Loose, cashier; O. B. Loose, teller. In 1889 S. H. W. Byrd was made cashier. In 1891 the directors were Jas. F. Lowman, J. W. F. Allemong, and B. M. Rice. This bank closed business in 1892.[2]

In March, 1891, a bank was opened at Shendun (Grottoes), W. P. Roberts and James Martin, of Lynchburg, being president and cashier, respectively This bank was still in operation in December, 1892.

Let us next take a glance at the nine banks now doing business in the county.

In 1853 an Act was passed authorizing the establishment of the Citizens' Bank of Virginia, in the town of Harrisonburg. Robt. Gray, Harvey Kyle, and ten other gentlemen were named as commissioners. The next Assembly changed the name to Bank of Rockingham. In 1854 A. B. Irick was president; C. C. Strayer, cashier; A. E. Heneberger, clerk and teller. It "commenced operation in the stone building next door to the Post Office" (the Waterman house—see page 192). This is said to have been the first bank in the county; but if any of those projected in 1850-3, noted above, were actually started, it may not have been the first.

In April, 1863, the Bank of Rockingham was located in

---

[1]. *Rockingham Register*, July 3 and Aug. 27, 1874.

[2]. Information given by Mr. S. H. W. Byrd.

ROCKINGHAM COUNTY

the Exchange Hotel building (C. C. Clapp, propr.).[3] This was the house on the north side of the public square, built by A. B. Irick, in which Dr. Frank L. Harris till recently had his office. In August, 1865, it was reorganized as the First National Bank of Harrisonburg, the officers continuing as named above. C. C. Strayer was cashier from 1854 to 1888; then he was succeeded by L. C. Myers.[4] Mr. L. H. Ott has the first safe used by the bank. The total on each side of the financial statement published April 13, 1866, was $247,148.11. In October, 1866, the bank was moved into its new building opposite Hill's Hotel. The present building was erected in 1903. L. C. Myers is president, Geo. E. Sipe vice-president, C. H. Chandler cashier, and C. D. Beard assistant cashier. The total on each side of the financial statement published Sept. 4, 1912, was $1,648,894.34.

The Planters Bank of Bridgewater was opened for business February 3, 1898. Jos. H. Craun was president; John W. Cline, vice-president; Jas. R. Shipman, cashier. The original board of directors were J. H. Craun, J. W. Cline, John W. Wise, Robt. J. Miller, and John S. Garber.

The present officers are: J. W. Cline, president; W. H. Sipe, vice-president; J. R. Shipman, cashier; S. H. W. Byrd, assistant cashier. The present directors are J. W. Cline, W. H. Sipe, J. Newton Wilson, J. S. Garber, G. Ed. Miller, N. B. Wise, and Ed. G. Crist. Miss Ida Thomas has been a valued assistant in the bank for a number of years.

Business was begun with a paid up capital of $4000. The balanced total in the published statement of April 18, 1912, was $145,014.57.

The Rockingham National Bank, Harrisonburg, was organized December 21, 1899. The shareholders present elected the following directors: Andrew M. Newman, Jr., Geo. G. Grattan, Aaron H. Wilson, Jesse R. Cover, and Jacob Funkhouser. These directors held their first session on

---

[3]. *Rockingham Register*, April 24, 1863.
[4]. *Idem*, Feb. 2, 1866; Apr. 30, 1897.

A HISTORY OF

January 10, 1900, and elected A. M. Newman, Jr., president, and A. H. Wilson, vice-president. They also elected W. J. Dingledine cashier and Ernest S. Strayer teller. The bank opened for business on March 15, 1900, with a capital of $50,000. The directors are: Geo. G. Grattan, Samuel Forrer, Samuel M. Bowman, A. H. Long, Jno. B. Peale, J. R. Cover, Jacob S. Sellers, T. N. Haas, Jno. I. Harnsberger, F. M. Stinespring, C. G. Harnsberger.

The officers and employees are: G. G. Grattan, president; C. G. Harnsberger, vice-president; W. J. Dingledine, cashier; S. D. Myers, assistant cashier; C. H. Mauzy, teller; E. R. Lineweaver, A. R. Ruff, R. L. Coffman, bookkeepers; A. J. Crawn, Clerk; Miss Flavia Converse, stenographer.

The capital of the bank is now $60,000: surplus and profits, $65,000; deposits, $600,000; loans $600,000; resources, $800,000.

The First National Bank of Broadway was opened for business April 24, 1903, with $25,000 capital stock. The directors were Geo. S. Aldhizer, B. F. Helbert, J. P. Miller, D. B. Sites, D. F. Geil, J. W. Grim, and T. J. Pennybacker. Mr. Aldhizer was president, Mr. Helbert vice-president, and Mr. Grim cashier. The following gentlemen now constitute the board of control, with organization as indicated: D. F. Geil, president; B. F. Helbert, vice-president; T. C. Aldhizer, cashier; G. S. Aldhizer, A. R. Miller, Jos. Shank, J. M. Kline, and A. M. Turner. The balanced total in the financial statement made Sept. 4, 1912, was $104,828.28.

The Bank of Elkton was organized in November, 1903, and opened for business February 8, 1904. James E. Leebrick was president, C. G. Harnsberger vice-president, and I. L. Flory cashier. The directors were J. E. Leebrick, C. G. Harnsberger, J. T. Heard, W. E. Kite, M. M. Jarman, W. J. Dingledine, and Geo. G. Grattan, Sr. The present officers are, C. G. Harnsberger, president; J. T. Heard, vice-president; and W. H. McVeigh, cashier. The present board of directors is composed of the following gentlemen: C. G. Harnsberger, J. T. Heard, W. E. Kite, A. P. Yancey, and I.

ROCKINGHAM COUNTY

L. Flory. The balanced total in the financial report published Sept. 4, 1912, was $99,213.77.

The Bank of Dayton was organized in 1906, by the people of Dayton, with Jno. M. Flory as principal solicitor, with a capital stock of $10,000. This was increased to $20,000 in 1910. Doors were opened for business March 2, 1906. The original officers were, E. C. Ralston, president; J. M. Kagey, vice-president; N. R. Crist, cashier; directors: E. C. Ralston, J. M. Kagey, J. M. Snell, J. M. Flory, J. Wilton, J. H. Rhodes, Jos. F. Heatwole. The present officers are E. C. Ralston, president; J. M. Kagey, vice-president; N. R. Crist, cashier; present directors: E. C. Ralston, J. M. Kagey, J. H. Rhodes, J. H. Ruebush, Joe. K. Ruebush, L. M. Hollen, E. W. Burkholder, J. N. Shrum, Jno. T. Wright. The balanced total in the financial statement published Sept. 4, 1912, was $89,472.27.

The Bank of Grottoes was opened for business February 17, 1908, J. M. Koiner, J. S. Pirkey, D. E. Ham, J. D. Alexander, G. R. Root, M. D. Eutsler, W. A. Leeth, W. C. Patterson, C. L. Weast, D. H. Patterson, and J. F. Miller being directors. Mr. Koiner was president, Mr. Pirkey 1st vice-president, Mr. Geo. M. Nicholas 2d vice-president, and Mr. Root cashier. At present the officers and directors are the following. M. D. Eutsler, president; E. L. Weast, vice-president; G. R. Root, cashier; Philip R. Cosby, assistant cashier; J. S. Pirkey, J. M. Pirkey, D. H. Patterson, W. A. Leeth, C. S. Craun, J. D. Alexander J. L. Cosby, G. K. Foster. The balanced total published Sept. 4, 1912, was $64,408.72.

The Peoples Bank of Harrisonburg was chartered in 1907, and opened its doors for business April 20, 1908. The incorporators and original board of directors were: James E. Reherd, Isaac N. Beery, John N. Mohler, James O. Stickley, Thomas J. Martin, Eugene X. Miller, Thomas P. Beery, and A. P. Eiler.

The business has increased steadily during the four years of the bank's existence, until it now has total resources of

A HISTORY OF

nearly $400,000. The capital stock is not held in large blocks, but is distributed among over 250 share-holders, who, with few exceptions, are residents of Rockingham County. The present officers, who have held their respective positions from the first, are: Jas. E. Reherd, president; I. N. Beery, J. N. Mohler, A. S. Kemper, vice-presidents; T. P. Beery, cashier; D. B. Yancey, assistant cashier.

The Farmers and Merchants Bank of Timberville was organized in March, 1908, with John H. Hoover, president; E. M. Minnick, vice-president; J. A. Garber, cashier. It was opened for business Aug. 24, 1908. The directors are John H. Hoover, W. C. Hoover, F. H. Driver, J. A. Zigler, D. S. Wampler, W. E. Fahrney, E. M. Minnick, E. E. Jones, M. F. Garber, Geo. E. Sipe, Wm. A. Pence, E. A. Andrick, and R. S. Bowers. The balanced total in the financial report published Sept. 4, 1912, was $142,061.74.

All of the Harrisonburg banks, probably some of the others in the county, have savings departments.

It is deemed appropriate, in closing this chapter, to present a few facts regarding local insurance companies.

In the early 50's several Acts of Assembly were passed chartering and amending the charter of the Rockingham Mutual Insurance Company. In 1854 the Rockingham Mutual Fire Insurance Company was granted the powers and privileges of a savings bank. E. T. H. Warren (page 139) was secretary. In 1868-9 the Rockingham Insurance Company, capital stock $100,000, was in operation. A. M. Newman was president; G. F. Mayhew, secretary; R. N. Pool was general agent for the State; Jos. H. Shue was agent for Rockingham County. It was a fire insurance company.

In January, 1869, the General Assembly chartered the Rockingham Home Mutual Fire Insurance Company, to do business in a circle radiating seven miles from Cross Keys. The original officers and directors were: Wm. Saufley, president; Ed. S. Kemper, secretary and treasurer; Jos. B. Webb, Saml. Good, Jonathan Miller, Peter Showalter, Isaac Long, Geo. W. Kemper. In 1881 G. W. Kemper was president; Geo. B.

ROCKINGHAM COUNTY

Keezell was president-elect, and J. B. Webb was secretary and treasurer. The number of members was 432; amount of property insured, $615,000. At present (1912) there are 1442 members and the amount of insurance is $3,010,000. G. B. Keezell is president; John G. Fulton, vice-president; C. T. Callender is secretary and treasurer. The plans and methods of this company have attracted wide attention.

On January 6, 1872, the West Rockingham Mutual Fire Insurance Company was organized, with David A. Heatwole (page 224) president, J. W. Minnick secretary, A. Andes treasurer. The directors were B. M. Rice, John Geil, J. H. Ralston, David Garber.[5] In the Act of incorporation, March 22, 1872, Saml. Firebaugh, Geo. Chrisman, Saml. A. Long, Jos. Click, Hugh Swope, Jas. C. Heltzel, and John H. Ralston, Jr., were named as directors. In 1886 D. A. Heatwole and H. A. Heatwole were president and secretary, respectively, and the amount of insurance was $800,000. At present John S. Funk is president and H. A. Heatwole (Mt. Clinton) is secretary-treasurer.

In January, 1874, R. H. Spindle, secretary, called a meeting of the Farmers' Mutual Fire Insurance Company at Conrad's Store. Nothing further is known of this company.

In 1897 the Cross Keys Home Mutual Fire Insurance Company was chartered and organized under the state laws of Virginia, with the following directors: C. T. Callender, T. P. Yager, G. B. Keezell, W. H. Long, J. R. Filler, A. B. Miller, and J. R. Bowman; C. T. Callender[6] being president and T. P. Yager secretary. The purpose of the company is defined in the charter as follows:

"To make insurance upon the contents of dwelling-houses, stores, barns, and all other buildings, except mills, against loss or damage by accidental fire."

This company supplements the Rockingham Home Mutual; the one insuring buildings, the other, contents of buildings.

---

5. *Rockingham Register*, Jan. 11, 1872.
6. C. T. Callender died Oct. 27, 1912, aged 53.

CHAPTER XXIII.

HEALTH RESORTS.

The inspiring elevations, the splendid mountain scenery, the health-giving waters, and the historic associations of Rockingham have long made it attractive to persons on tidewater and in the cities, specially in the days of summer. Not only do hundreds of people come hither every year, seeking health and pleasure, but many others seek to have the good things sent to them—piecemeal, of necessity, but in as large measure as possible. Not to mention other things, thousands of gallons of Rockingham mineral waters are shipped annually to many distant points.

The oldest well-known summer resort in Rockingham is located four miles east of Harrisonburg, and is now called Massanetta Springs. The old name is Taylor Springs. The original name-givers were Jonathan and William Taylor, owners at the beginning of the 19th century. They were of Irish descent, and their graves are at Cross Keys. In olden days, according to tradition, Taylor Springs were resorted to by many of the East Virginia notables—the Madisons and Monroes, among others. In 1816 they were selected as a permanent place for the annual campmeeting by the quarterly conference, Rockingham Circuit, of the Methodist Episcopal Church; and were leased at that time for ten years. On the death of the Taylors, the Springs passed into the possession of Evan Henton, who was proprietor in 1854, and thereabouts. Later, they were sold to Abraham Miller. In the early 60's they came into the hands of Geo. E. Deneale, and in 1870 Leneas Woodson became owner. In 1872 they were purchased by a company made up of John F. Lewis, Dr. Burk Chrisman, and others, and the name was changed to Massanetta. In July, 1909, they were purchased by J. R.

Rawley Springs (Pages 395, 396)

Hotel Massanetta, Looking West from the Grove (Pages 394, 395)

ROCKINGHAM COUNTY

Lupton, and in January, 1911, the Massanetta Springs Company, J. R. Lupton, manager, became the owners. The waters contain calcium carbonate, magnesium, and other valuable elements, and are widely celebrated. The hotels are filled with guests, permanent and transient, during the summer months, and large quantities of the water are sent out upon order.[1]

For a number of years past the most famous summer resort in Rockingham, and one of the most celebrated in Virginia, has been Rawley Springs, located 11½ miles west of Harrisonburg, 2000 feet above the sea level. Rawley is also old in story. The following extracts from a letter written September 24, 1881, by Benjamin H. Smith, of Charleston, W. Va., will be of interest, as to beginnings.

My father resided in Rockingham county in the year 1810. In the early part of that year my mother became diseased with chronic diarrhoea, and although she had the medical services of Drs. Harrison and Cravens, eminent physicians of that time, they failed to relieve her. My father, being much alarmed at her dangerous condition, made earnest inquiries into all the remedies from which relief could be hoped. He had for years herded his cattle in the North Mountain, and during the year before stated, or some previous year, heard of the medicinal springs on Dry River, in the mountain. Early in July of the year 1810 he resolved to try the waters of that spring. For this purpose he had a shanty of plank constructed at the Spring, and supplied with comfortable furniture and suitable cooking utensils, taken from home by wagon. To this place in July of that year, my mother was removed, with competent servants. All members of the family were occasional visitors, but I was deputed as her constant attendant, and stayed with her during parts of the months of July and August, altogether about six weeks, at which time my mother had thoroughly recovered, and her health was perfectly restored. She lived 27 years thereafter, without any recurrence of the disease.

The road from the river to the spring went up a point of the mountain next above the spring branch, and was made by the hands of my father, by cutting out the brush only, to enable our wagon to approach the bench of the mountain from which the spring issued. When we went

---

1. For information regarding the history of Taylor Springs, I am indebted to the kindness of Mr. R. L. Myers. His account has been supplemented by records found in the Methodist minute books and in the *Rockingham Register* of January 18, 1872, and other dates.

there no improvement of any kind existed, and all was a primeval forest. My father's shanty was the first dwelling ever erected on the premises, and we (my mother and myself) were the first resident visitors of the spring. Before we left the spring we had an accession of some four or five families in shanties and tents. The spring then had no name; but I recollect a Mr. Rawley lived at or about the gorge of the mountain through which Dry River runs, and I have always thought the name the spring bears was derived from this farmer, Rawley, the nearest resident of the place.

I have not visited the springs since 1810. I was nearly 13 years old at the time, and the recollection of the incidents connected with my residence there is clear and distinct.

The waters of Rawley Springs are said to be almost identical with those of Pouhon, the most noted spring of Spa, Belgium,—those of Rawley containing more carbonic acid, those of Pouhon more iron.

In 1825 Joseph Hicks was advertising "Rawley Springs"; in 1836-7 and in 1877 acts of incorporation were passed; in 1845 Miller, Sites, & Fry were proprietors; in 1861 the managers were John Sites & Son; in 1872, and thereabouts, A. B. Irick was president of the board, and Jos. N. Woodward was manager. In 1874, 1875, etc., the number of guests at Rawley frequently reached 500. In 1884, etc., J. Watkins Lee was the popular manager. In 1886 many of the buildings were destroyed by fire; and a remarkable coincidence was observed in the fact that Anthony Hockman, who had constructed the main building, died the same night.

The popular proprietor of Rawley in more recent years was Hon. D. M. Switzer; and the property is still in the hands of his heirs. It is needless to say that modern progress is found exemplified in the present equipment.

As one stands on Lover's Leap, at Rawley, and looks out eastward across the Giant's Grave upon the smiling valley, he has Union Springs two miles upon his right, and Liberty Springs two miles upon his left. The water at Union is among the best in Virginia, and the view at Liberty is one of the finest in Virginia and West Virginia.

Union Springs were resorted to as long as forty years ago; and in 1878 Miss Kate Croushorn, of Ottobine, was ad-

ROCKINGHAM COUNTY

vertising summer boarding at Union Springs. The water is chalybeate. Every year, until recently, at least a few families of the county spent part of the summer there; but a steep, stony road, with a defective title to the property, has by this time made visitors rare.

Some one writing of Liberty Springs in 1889 said that on the south side of the springs old chimneys were standing, marking the sites of cabins built before the war by William Ewing, John Beery, Abe Beery, Archibald Hopkins, Peter Good, John Gordon, and others. In connection with this, the following paragraphs from a letter written December 14, 1911, by the late Mr. D. B. Showalter, will be of interest:

In the burnt records, Deed Book 16, page 325, you will see that Augustus Waterman sold in 1843 210 acres of mountain land to Jacob Bowman, who, with his family, lies buried in the family burying ground on the farm now owned by S. F. Showalter, the said Bowman's old home farm. . . . In 1845 (Deed Book 18, page 123) Jacob Bowman sold to the Liberty Springs Company 52 acres of the 210 acre tract. The company then was composed of John Swank, John Beery, Peter Good, Joseph Burkholder, several of the Hopkinses, Henry Showalter, Jacob Dundore, an old Mr. Ewing, John and Peter Eversole, Joseph Showalter, Samuel Driver [?], and others, all of whom have passed away, and many of whom had cabins built there before the civil war. All these cabins were burnt during the war to prevent persons hiding there to keep out of the Confederate army. There are some 20 cabins there now, all of which have been built since the war. The company is now composed by our home people, who spend some time there. . . . A. H. Long is president, Frank Ralston, secretary and treasurer. The springs are near the top of the mountain; the water is fine chalybeate. The place can be reached by a good public road, built by the company in the last 12 years.

A short distance east of Liberty Springs, two miles west of Singer's Glen, at the base of Little North Mountain, is the popular resort called Sparkling Springs. The old name is Baxter's Springs. The company now in control was organized in September, 1886, and among the promoters of the enterprise were Messrs. David A. Heatwole, J. W. Minnich, Isaac N. Beery, John Funk, Timothy Funk, Daniel F. Heatwole, Lewis Driver, Michael Showalter, David Lineweaver, Henry A. Rhodes, Samuel Brunk, Abraham Weaver, Abram B.

Wenger, Noah W. Beery, and Emanuel Suter. The company was incorporated in 1900. The grounds in 1911 comprised 22 acres, and upon them were located 24 cottages, a boarding house, a fountain house, a dairy, two stone wagon bridges, one foot bridge, and a good road connecting with the county road. Among the minerals contained in these springs are iron, magnesia, and sulphur.[2]

At the western base of the Massanutten Mountain, about three miles east of Lacey Springs, are the well-known Brock's Springs, called also the Yellow Massanutten Springs. After important improvements in June, 1874, they were opened the next month to visitors. Chas. J. Brock was proprietor; W. R. Carrier, general superintendent. The waters are chalybeate and blue sulphur.[3]

Three miles north of McGaheysville, at the eastern base of the Massanutten, are Rockingham Springs, known also as Hopkins' Springs. The surroundings are beautiful, and the waters contain health-giving properties in various combinations, springs of chalybeate, sulphur, and magnesium-alum being found there. These springs, under the proprietorship of Messrs. G. T. and Edwin B. Hopkins, have been a popular resort for many years. Mr. G. T. Hopkins had made extensive improvements there as early as 1874, or earlier. In the summer of 1879 the poet Sidney Lanier, with his family, was among the notable guests.

Not far from Rockingham Springs are Bloomer Springs, opened as a health resort in or about the year 1852 by Col. Henry Miller, Dr. S. B. Jennings, and Maj. John C. Walker. Soon ten or twelve cottages were on the grounds. Frequently as many as a dozen or more families from the neighborhood would spend the summer there, and persons from a distance would endeavor to secure accomodations, but no equipment for general entertainment seems to have been provided. On

---

[2]. For aid in securing information concerning Sparkling Springs, I acknowledge special favors by Messrs. I. N. Beery and J. W. Minnich.

[3]. *Rockingham Register*, June 12, July 10, 1874; etc.

special occasions, however, a hundred or two persons would be present for the day. The springs have not been regularly attended for the past twenty years, owing mainly to change in the ownership of the property. During the years the springs were used the land about them was owned by Mr. Henry Brill.[4]

In the vicinity of Bridgewater and in other sections of Rockingham not specially mentioned in the foregoing pages, are fine springs of medicinal waters. The Bear Lithia Spring, below Elkton, must be mentioned particularly. It is connected by a special track with the Norfolk & Western Railway, and thousands of gallons of water are shipped from it every week. Elkton is a favorite summer resort, and the Elkton Hotel, in beautiful surroundings and under skilled management, affords excellent accommodations to visitors.

Another place that may properly be noticed in this chapter is Assembly Park, just a mile north of Harrisonburg. A company was chartered for managing it in March, 1892, and at frequent intervals ever since it has been the scene of large and important gatherings, such as temperance rallies, religious conferences, chautauquas, farmers' encampments, etc. The present manager is Dr. A. P. Funkhouser.

---

4. For information concerning Bloomer Springs, I am indebted to the kindness of Mr. John W. Brill, Elkton, Va.

CHAPTER XXIV.

NATURAL CURIOSITIES.

First, let us take a walk through some of the underground palaces. Rockingham has a dozen or more beautiful caves.

In point of discovery, Harrison's Cave, six miles northeast of Harrisonburg, is perhaps the oldest. Few persons in the county now know of its existence. I found a reference to it in Kercheval's old history of the Valley, and, upon inquiry, succeeded in locating it. It was discovered by David Harrison (born in 1775), and is in a cedar-covered rocky hill a short distance northeast of Melrose, and a few hundred yards west of the Valley Pike. The hill is in plain sight from the pike, and is a part of the farm of Mr. Thos. A. Moore.

Wednesday afternoon, September 20, 1911, I visited Harrison's Cave. My guide was Mr. Daniel Harrison, a grandson of the man who found the cave, so many years ago. William Harrison, a son of David, put a building over the entrance, but this went into decay before the civil war, and now the opening is altogether without protection. In fact, we had some difficulty in getting down the first ten feet, so much mud and so many leaves had washed in ahead of us.

Once in, there was plenty of room. Several of the apartments are very large. One room, near the end, is larger in circumference, I think, than any room in any other cave I have visited except, perhaps, the Grand Cathedral in Weyer's. The ceiling, however, is not higher than 15 or 20 feet.

Vandals have defaced Harrison's Cave shamefully—have broken off tons of stalactites; and the smoke from candles and torches has blackened the whole interior; yet in spite of all this it is a great wonder, and presents many striking

Washington Profile, Rawley Springs
By per. of E. G. Furry

The Giant's Grave
(Page 405)

Photo by Hammers   Cedar Cliff Falls
(Page 405)

Formation in Massanutta Cave

Diamond Lake, New Market Endless Caverns

ROCKINGHAM COUNTY

features. It contains a column thicker, I think, than any I have seen elsewhere. One great column is severed about midway from floor to ceiling. The grand "organ" has had its pipes broken off about half way up.

Hundreds—perhaps thousands—of names are to be found on the walls, ceiling, and columns. Some are cut into the stone, others are made with the smoke of candle or torch. Most of the legible dates after names fall in the year 1862. In April of that year a large number of Federal soldiers, perhaps from the army of Banks, were in the cave. I saw the names of many men from the 4th and 8th regiments, Ohio Volunteer Infantry.

The earliest date I saw was 1818. This was smoked on the wall in large figures, plainly, and apart from other dates. In all probability, 1818 was the year in which the cave was discovered.

About 200 yards southwest from the cave just described is a grotto called "Wide-mouth Cave." It is about 40 feet in diameter—a single vaulted chamber—opening widely to the surface of the earth.

On Smith's Creek, a mile or two above Rosendale, on a farm now owned by Dorilas Driver, is a cavern known as Strickler's Cave. When it was discovered is not known, but it is called an old cave.

In 1879, Reuben Zirkle and his sons, following a dog which had chased a rabbit into the rocks near the foot of the Massanutten Mountain, found a cave which is now known as the New Market Endless Caverns. It is in the rugged slope between the mountain and Smith's Creek, a short distance below Strickler's Cave, and is opposite the site of the old Zirkle mill. Rosendale is within sight.

On September 16, 1911, Mr. Harry Strickler and I visited the Endless Caverns, having for guide the owner, Mr. Harvey J. Rosenberger. Going down abruptly at the entrance for 20 or 30 feet, we entered the Anteroom, one of the handsomest apartments in the cave. Other apartments deserving special mention are Centennial Hall, Alexander's Ball Room, St.

A HISTORY OF

Paul's Cathedral, the Alpine Pass, and the Brown Room. For profusion, variety, and beauty of formations the Brown Room is unexcelled by any other I have seen.

There are many large apartments and passage ways, from which dark openings lead off, and around which bottomless chasms yawn. Many of these corridors are not covered with stalactites, but the massive limestone arches and vaulted ceilings, the huge dependent crags, with the ponderous boulders piled up on the floor or projecting in ledges, combine to form a rugged beauty and grandeur that are unusual. Interspersed with these rugged gorges come splendid apartments rich in mural and overhead decorations.

A striking feature of these caverns is found in the numerous huge, fluted columns, many of them supporting the ceiling, some cut finely off just below the ceiling, and one or more fast above and extending far downwards, but separated from the floor by the space of only a few inches. These splendid columns, large and small, make up what is perhaps the most characteristic feature of the caverns.

Among particular curiosities of special interest and beauty are Diamond Lake, the Montana Snowdrift, Snow on the Alps, the Negro Campmeeting, and the Gypsy Tent. The last and the Montana Snowdrift are unsurpassable for wonder and beauty. In the Tent is a huge horror that looks like the open jaws of a mammoth crocodile. The jaws must be three or four feet long, and the teeth are like the guards on the cutter-bar of a mowing machine. At another place is a nearly perfect ear of corn, about as tall as the average man, and weighing several hundred pounds. Not far away is a giant plowshare, which may easily be connected in imagination with the great ear of corn.

We were in the caverns two and a fourth hours, and did not go into all the apartments. They are truly endless.

Three strong, clear, cold springs gush out at the foot of the hill, only 200 or 300 yards below the cave mouth; and from the hill the prospect across the Valley, westward and northward, is glorious. The Alleghanies are in full view at

ROCKINGHAM COUNTY

the farther side of the Valley, 12 or 15 miles away, while the massive ridge of the Massanutten looms up at one's back.

In 1871 or 1872 J. Harvey Taylor discovered a cave on the land of Mrs. Clary West, about 3½ miles northeast of Harrisonburg, one mile east of the Valley Pike. It was explored for 200 yards or more.[1]

From public notices that appeared in 1874, it may be inferred that Newman's Cave, at or near Roadside, East Rockingham, was at that time being visited.

In 1890 a cave was discovered on the land of Hon. Chas. E. Fahrney, three-fourths of a mile north of Timberville. One morning Mr. Fahrney noticed a hole in the ground, such as might have been left by a stump entirely decayed; but he also noticed vapor issuing from the opening, and so made further investigation. This cave is said to contain a number of beautiful formations,—an archway hung with sparkling stalactites, a small lake, and a good-sized flag, mounted on a staff. The ceiling at some places is 30 or 40 feet high.

On November 5th, 1892, hands blasting rock for lime on the farm of Augustine Armentrout, near Keezletown, discovered the beautiful wonder now widely known as Massanutta Gertrude Cave. It contains 28 apartments, the ceilings of many being 15 feet in height, and the decorations in stalactites and stalagmites are of great profusion and variety. The illumination by means of gas and magnesia tape enhances the splendid interiors. Scientists and scholars, as well as less purposeful tourists, have come many miles to see this gem of nature. Clubs, societies, and all sorts of picnic parties find Massanutta Cave both accessible and delightful.

In Februray, 1893, a cave was discovered on the lands of Mrs. Peter Pence, adjoining Long's Hill, in East Rockingham.[2]

In the winter of 1901 it was reported in the local papers

---

1. *Rockingham Register*, January 25, 1872.
2. *Rockingham Register*, February 10, 1893.

A HISTORY OF

that boys of the Weaver's Church neighborhood had explored numerous interesting cavities in the limestone of the surrounding hills.

There are caves in Round Hill, west of Bridgewater, in a hill near Linville, and in the Roudabush and Armentrout neighborhood, between Edom and Singer's Glen. Indeed, Rockinghamers feel like claiming a share in Weyer's Cave, since it is so near the county line. Many go every year to visit it, at any rate.

One of the places in Rockingham long celebrated for a combination of rugged scenery and interesting associations is Brock's Gap, located in the northern part of the county, and affording a giant's gateway through the first ranges of the Alleghanies. The mountain walls on either side, the trees and shrubbery springing from the slopes and cliffs, and the sparkling waters that rush down fresh from the heights and hollows beyond, all lend a charm and beauty to the place that must be seen to be appreciated. Descriptions and pictures are both inadequate to convey a just impression of the varied and splendid forms in which nature has here enthroned herself.—See page 21.

What has just been said of Brock's Gap is equally true of Massanutten Peak, or Peaked Mountain, to which attention has already been directed in several connections. The Peak must be seen to be appreciated. Perhaps one should say, other things about it must be seen from it. The Peak is a great natural wonder, and it is unexcelled as an observatory.

Within the Peak is the Kettle. This is a great, deep basin, or trough, with a narrow outlet at the eastern part. This outlet is called Harshberger's Gap, and through it flow the waters gathered from the springs in the basin. One of these is far up near the head of the trough, and for a considerable distance the waters roar down through subterranean passages between the huge rocks that are heaped over the channel in wild profusion. The stream that thus heads in the Kettle is called Stony Run, or Stony Creek, and flows through McGaheysville into the South Shenandoah.

ROCKINGHAM COUNTY

On the mountain side, a short distance east of the Kettle, and just above Rockingham Springs, is White Rock. This is a high, broad-faced cliff that can be seen for miles as one passes Elkton, McGaheysville, and other places in East Rockingham. On the opposite side of the Valley, high up in the Blue Ridge, may be seen the silver arc of Cedar Cliff Falls,— the waters of Wolf Run leaping down a hundred feet or more in their hurried descent to join Elk Run, and then the Shenandoah.

Before leaving East Rockingham, a word must be said of Indian Rock, which, if it is not a natural curiosity, is nevertheless set on a wondrous pinnacle of nature. It is described by "G. T. H.," writing from McGaheysville under date of March 27, 1864, as follows:

Deeply cut in a large, flat rock that forms the extreme western projection of the peak of the Massanutten mountain can be seen the print of a moccasined foot, with the toe pointing due West. This was no doubt executed by order of an Indian council, to direct the wandering members of their tribes to the path their leaders had taken. Judging from the weatherbeaten appearance of the track, it must have been cut hundreds of years ago.

About half way between Broadway and Singer's Glen is Tide Spring, which flows out only at intervals, but whose intermittent stream is of sufficient volume to run a mill. In a wet season it flows three or four times in an hour; in a dry time, only once, perhaps, in a day.

On one of the cliffs near Rawley Springs—perhaps at Lover's Leap—is the remarkable Washington Profile; and out in the Valley a mile or so, in plain view, is the long, low ridge called the Giant's Grave.

Until comparatively recent years a great wonder was to be found on Second Mountain, about half way between Rawley and Liberty Springs. It was a huge rock, about forty feet long, thirty feet wide, and six feet thick, almost perfectly balanced on a ledge near the mountain top. About 1893 some young men dislodged it with dynamite, and thus destroyed one of the most remarkable curiosities in the county.

On the Rawley Pike, about two miles west of Dale Enterprise, is a chinkapin tree which is, so far as is known, the largest of its kind in the world. It is about 40 feet high, and two feet above the ground the trunk measures 10 feet six inches in circumference. At the ground the girth of this vegetable giant is 19½ feet.

Near Dayton until lately was a large sugar-berry tree, which was regarded as very unusual because of its size.

So much for natural curiosities. We shall now take the liberty of appending to this chapter a few notes regarding various minerals, etc., found in Rockingham County.

Tradition has it that lead was mined near Broadway and Timberville during the Revolutionary War. In 1894 signs of old workings were found about two miles west of Timberville, and specimens of lead and zinc were secured. In October, 1894, the Colonial Lead and Zinc Company, made up of W. H. Ritenour, Thompson Lennig, R. R. Douthatt, N. G. Douglass, and David B. Sites, got a charter to work these old lead mines. In 1886 a lead mine on the farm of D. P. Showalter, near Chrisman, was being worked by Pennsylvania capitalists.

In 1833, Philip Miller and J. N. Ball were advertising a "superior quality" of marble quarried on Smith's Creek, and were manufacturing it into tombstones, hearths, mantelpieces, steps, sills, etc. In 1880 marble was reported in Brock's Gap. Two years later marble was being quarried at or near Timberville by Messrs. Moffet & Moore. It seems probable that black marble may be obtained just north of Harrisonburg. At present Dr. E. D. Davis is making developments in that section.

In 1854 gypsum was reported near the line of the Manassas Gap Railway; and coal in Brock's Gap; both in Rockingham County. The Dora Coal Fields in Briery Branch Gap have already been mentioned. The presence of coal there was known as early as 1866. From 1870 to 1880 a good deal of development work was done. In January, 1880, the editor of the *Register* reported that he was using some of the Briery Branch coal, and found it "first-class."

ROCKINGHAM COUNTY

In April, 1866, it was announced that plaster beds existed on the farm of Peter Wine, two or three miles west of Tenth Legion. Plaster was being sold there at $6 a ton. It was said that certain farmers on Linville Creek had been using this plaster for the past five or six years.

In 1866 a bed of blue paint was discovered in Brock's Gap. In 1872 and 1880 finds of mineral paint were reported in East Rockingham, and serious attempts were made in the manufacture and sale thereof, but the enterprises were not permanently successful.

In 1868, as recorded by Mr. S. H. W. Byrd, John W. Click discovered onyx on the farm of John C. Miller, near Bridgewater. From time to time the onyx quarries at Bridgewater have been worked more or less successfully. There are indications of roofing slate on the river below Bridgewater. In 1894 onyx was being shipped to New York City from quarries near Hinton.

Iceland spar exists in large quantities near Broadway and Timberville. In 1889 J. P. Houck, in boring a well, presumably at or near Harrisonburg, found evidence of oil. Gold and silver in small quantities have been found at various places in the county. The late Mr. David A. Heatwole, of Dale Enterprise, records the fact that in Adams' geography, published in the earlier part of last century, it was stated that nuggets of gold had been found a short distance west of Harrisonburg, on the farm lately owned by Mr. Daniel J. Myers.

But every golden age is largely dependent on iron; and Rockingham is rich in iron. From early times iron has been worked in various parts of the county, particularly in the vicinity of Paulington, in Brown's Gap, in the districts east of Elkton, and in Brock's Gap. It is said that iron ore used to be hauled to Mossy Creek iron works from the neighborhood of Dale Enterprise.

The limestone, blue and gray, in which the county abounds, is fine for building. Some of the oldest, as well as some of the newest, houses are constructed of this native limestone, which is also converted, at many places and in large quantities, into valuable lime. At Pleasant Valley is a quarry of gray limestone, which was opened about 1873, and which has been worked regularly since 1890, tons of stone from it being sent by rail to Staunton and other places at a distance, to be used for lintels, sills, bases of monuments, etc. Mr. C. E. Loewner is the present owner of this quarry.

About two and a half miles southeast of Elkton extensive operations are now being carried on in the mining of manganese.

In 1891 parts of the skeleton of a mastodon were found one mile north of Singer's Glen, by Henry Frank, while digging out an old pond. The remains were identified by Dr. M. S. Zirkel of Edom, and were sent, probably, to the National Museum, at Washington. The find attracted a good deal of attention among scholars and scientists over the country. On July the 25, 1912, while at Singer's Glen, I saw parts of one of the great teeth, preserved by Mr. Edward Funk.

In April, 1899, two mammoth teeth were discovered in an excavation being made in Harrisonburg for Mr. Herman Wise's new store building. They weighed over a pound apiece, and were found 15 feet below the surface of the street.

CHAPTER XXV.

HUNTING IN THE WESTERN MOUNTAINS.

Near the end of the French and Indian War, to wit, in the year 1762, one of the families that moved into Rockingham from Pennsylvania was the Custer family. The head of this family was Paul Custer; and he had a young son Richard, born in Pennsylvania some five years before: that is, on June 1st, 1757. The Custers (or Küsters) settled in or near Brock's Gap, where Nature called in stirring echoes from the wooded heights, and Diana no less than Mars claimed many a rugged glen. Small wonder, therefore, that soldiers and hunters should spring from the Custer line.

Even to-day the mountains of western Rockingham often sound to the huntsman's horn, and echo to the deep baying of his dogs or the sharp crack of his rifle. Enough of the past is with us yet to make a chapter of hunting stories both interesting and appropriate; they form an integral part in the history of this great county where once the buffalo stalked the plains while the deer, bears, wolves and panthers sheltered in the hills and mountains; and we are peculiarly fortunate in having this chapter mainly from the pen of a living member of that same Custer family. The line of genealogy may be briefly indicated thus: Paul Custer, Richard Custer (1757-1837), Richard Custer (1790-1858), Jacob Custer (1817-1892), Samuel Custer (1842-   ·), Milo Custer (1880—   ).

Milo Custer is custodian of the McLean County Historical Society, with offices in the city of Bloomington, Illinois; but when he heard that a history of Rockingham County, Virginia,—the prolific land of his ancestors,—was being prepared, he had his father, Mr. Samuel Custer, to recount the hunting stories given below, that he might write them down and contribute them to this work.[1]

---

1. Early in the year 1781 Richard Custer, Sr., enlisted in the Virginia

A HISTORY OF

Tradition has it that Paul Custer, founder of the Custer family in Rockingham, once shot a buffalo at one of the salt licks in the adjacent mountains. His great-grandson, Jacob Custer, was a mighty hunter. From 1830 to 1850 he frequently

troops under Col. Nall for service against the British in the war of the Revolution. He served as a private soldier three months under Capt. George Huston, and three months under Capt. Anthony Rader. He was in the skirmishes at Williamsburg, Va., and Hot Water Creek. In 1788 he married Jane, the 17-year-old daughter of Conrad Humble. They were the parents of Richard Custer, Jr., Mrs. Sarah Fulk, Susan Custer, Gabriel Custer, Mrs. Johannah Wevner, Strawder Custer, and George Custer.

Richard Custer, Sr., received a pension for his service in the Revolution, and his widow also drew a pension after his death. He died February 14, 1837. The date of his wife's death is not known; but she was still living in Rockingham and drawing a widow's pension as late as 1841.

Richard Custer, Jr., was born on his father's farm in Rockingham about 1790. This farm lies about 4 miles north of Cootes' Store. He was by trade a gunsmith, but also farmed to some extent, and operated a sawmill. The latter was on the farm of his son-in-law, Isaac Ween, and was situated about 13 miles nw. of Cootes' Store, in the valley of Dry River. His wife, whom he married March 28, 1810, was Elizabeth Trumbo, born August 21, 1791. The Trumbos and Custers, as well as the Hesses and others in the vicinity, were of Pennsylvania-German stock. This Richard Custer served from August 29, 1814, to December 8, 1814, in the war of 1812, as a member of Capt. Thomas Hopkins' company of Virginia militia. He and his wife, who lived till 1871, are buried on the old Custer homestead, 4 miles north of Cootes' store. This farm is now owned and occupied by their son-in-law, Abram Hess.

Jacob Custer, son of Richard Custer, Jr., married Isabella Miller in 1838, who bore him five children. In 1852 he moved to McLean County, Ill., where he died in 1892. In writing of him his grandson (Milo Custer) says:

"His early life was spent among the mountains of his native county, and was in many respects typical of that rugged locality. . . . He lived upon his farm (near the Pendleton mountain) about fifteen years. Most of his land was covered with a fine growth of pine and poplar timber. Some of the trees were over a hundred feet high, and logs 60 feet long and entirely clear of limbs were cut from many of them. In the fall of the year 1852 he sold his farm to Anthony Rhodes for $800, and moved with his family to McLean County, Ill. He also owned one negro slave, a young man named Wesley, whom he sold to Samuel Cootes, the founder of Cootes' Store, for $200."

ROCKINGHAM COUNTY

ranged the mountains in the northwestern portions of the county, a terror to the fierce no less than to the fleet. The killing of deer and bears was a favorite occupation with him.

Prior to the year 1852 he owned 400 acres of land, on which he resided, at the head of Dry River, near the Pendleton Mountain. On one occasion, while at work clearing a part of his land, he heard a sharp squeal from one of his hogs. Looking up, he saw a large black bear seize one of his best brood sows in its huge arms, rear upon its hind legs, and walk away. Being some distance from his house, without his gun, and knowing he would not have time to get it, he called his dogs, seized his axe, and started after the bear. Incredible as it may seem, the bear, although hampered with the burden of the sow, whose weight was upwards of 250 pounds, could still walk about as fast as the man. The bear had seized the sow from behind; and as it walked along would gnaw her back, actually eating her alive. Custer and his dogs followed the bear up the steep sides of the mountain for nearly a mile, and finally compelled it to release the sow. The latter was able to return home, but died next day. The bear had eaten away nearly all the flesh from her back.

Each fall, during the hunting season, Mr. Custer would kill from fifteen to twenty deer. His family was always well supplied with venison. Many times he would return from a hunting trip with a deer weighing upwards of 175 pounds slung over his shoulders. He was very stoutly built, and in his younger days was a man of great physical endurance. He and his neighbors would frequently take their rifles and hunting dogs, and "run" deer on Pendleton Mountain. This mountain was then covered with heavy timber, and was a favorite haunt of wild animals.

The deer when pursued had a peculiar way of running at a gradual angle down the mountain side to the valley, and if not overtaken they would cross the Valley, swimming the stream, and then run up the side of the next mountain, taking the same gradual course as they ran. They would sometimes run as much as ten miles before they were overtaken and killed.

On one particular occasion Jacob Custer, in company with his brother Conrad, went up on the mountain to run deer. Conrad took up his station near the foot of the mountain, on the east side, to watch, and to shoot the deer as they ran by; while Jacob took the dogs and went up into the timber to chase them out. He soon started a fine buck, got him headed toward the east, the dogs giving chase; he himself followed them on the run, down the mountain side, some three or four miles. The buck soon came within the range of Conrad's rifle, and fell. Jacob, who was following, reached the animal before it ceased kicking, so closely had he followed the entire distance.

On another occasion Jacob Custer came near losing his life on one of these hunting trips. His two dogs had chased a large buck into a stream of water, and the one of them that was in the lead had overtaken and seized him. Mr. Custer coming up laid down his gun and, with his knife in hand, ran into the water and seized the deer, intending to cut his throat. But no sooner had he laid hold of the animal than the dog let go. In less time than one may tell it the enraged buck turned, dropped his head and savagely pushed Mr. Custer against the bank of the stream. Holding the animal by the horns, between the prongs of which he was pinned fast, the man pitted his strength against that of the infuriated beast. It was a life and death struggle. In the nick of time the second dog came up and seized the buck, thus turning the scale in his master's favor. Many years later, when he was an old man of more than seventy, Mr. Custer stood before the gate of the deer pasture at Miller Park in Bloomington, and told the park keeper, who was somewhat timid about coming near a fractious buck, how he had killed many a larger deer in his early days, back in the mountains of Old Virginia.

One of the well known early hunters of Rockingham was Frederick Kiester. An account of his many hunting exploits

ROCKINGHAM COUNTY

and thrilling encounters with wild animals, and a list of the number of bears and deer he had killed, was published in the *Rockingham Register* about the year 1855. He was out hunting once some where in the mountains of Rockingham, when he was attacked by a panther. The animal had hidden upon the limb of a tree which overhung the path, and had dropped down upon him as he passed underneath. Had it not been for his dogs, Kiester would have been killed. Their attack upon the panther caused it to turn its attention toward them, and give the man a chance to shoot it. As it was, he was badly injured. His clothing was torn to shreds; his body was covered with blood. The beast's claws had cut his back and the calves of his legs like knives. He bore the marks of this encounter during the remainder of his life.

Two other hunters, whose names the writer's father does not remember, once had a thrilling experience with a she-bear. One of these hunters found a couple of bear cubs, and promptly shot them. One of them made an outcry which was heard by the mother bear. She came rushing to the assistance of her young, and attacked the man before he could reload his rifle. Using his gun as a club, he managed for a while to beat her off, calling at the same time for help. His partner, who was with the dogs some distance away, was deaf and could not hear him; but the dogs heard him, came to his rescue, and held the bear at bay until the other man, who had followed the dogs, came up and shot the bear. The stock of the gun which the first man had used as a club against the bear was badly broken, and the weapon was almost ruined. He said that the bear had stood up on her hind legs and struck at him with her great fore paws, warding off his blows like a man. He was a large well-built man, and managed to get in a few terrific blows upon the animal's head and fore arms; but he said that after she was killed and skinned the places where his blows had fallen were not discolored, and seemed hardly bruised. When we take into consideration the fact that most of the guns used by those early hunters were flintlocks, which could not be loaded excep at the expense of several minutes of time, we can readily understand how those men were exposed to risks such as are not shared by huntsmen of the present day.

Richard Custer, Jr., the father of Jacob Custer, was a gunsmith, as elsewhere noted; and the site of his gun shop is still pointed out as one of the old landmarks near Cootes' Store.

Sometimes a deer that was started in Pendleton County would be chased across the mountains into Rockingham, the hunters who started it not caring to follow it so far. Under such conditions the animal might be shot by some Rockingham party; and vice versa. Occasionally the dogs would follow the deer long after their masters had given it up, and would be fed and cared for by strangers, some not getting back home for several days.

Many a hunter of those early days valued his dogs as highly as his horses. There were two classes of hunters; one class that hunted with dogs; the other without. The latter were known as "private hunters." They were much opposed to running deer with dogs, and sometimes resorted to extreme measures—destroying dogs with poison. Such proceedings of course led to much hard feeling between the two classes. Two dogs that Jacob Custer prized very highly fell victims to some "private hunter's" poison. Long afterwards, when his anger had perceptibly cooled, Custer by mere chance learned the name of the poisoner. Meeting the man one day he accused him of killing the dogs. Reluctantly the guilt was admitted. "Well," said Custer, "it is past and gone now; but if I had known it was you, then, I'd have shot you."[2]

The foregoing stories are not only true of the particular incidents recounted, but are also typical of their class, and enable us to realize vividly what the actual and frequent experiences of the mountain hunters were in days long past. Now and then a bear or deer is still found in these mountains; and

---

[2]. I am indebted to Mr. Milo Custer for much other interesting matter, which is withheld here only for lack of space.

ROCKINGHAM COUNTY

now and then, it may be at increasing intervals, the huntsman's horn still is heard:
'Sweet and far from cliff and scar,
Like horns of Elfland faintly blowing.'
But the sounds to-day are mostly echoes.

In connection with the foregoing paragraphs the following incidents have appropriate significance. They give specific information of various beasts and birds found or seen in Rockingham at various times.

The two incidents first given are related by Messrs. J. R. Shipman and S. H. W. Byrd of Bridgewater.

About 1794, when St. Michael's Church above Bridgewater was building, a young girl, later the grandmother of Mr. Jacob H. Wynant, was employed carrying dinner each day to the workmen. One day, in going from Bridgewater to the church—a distance of only 2½ or 3 miles—she saw seven deer.

About 1850, Mr. Wynant's mother, a daughter of Rev. John Brown of the Reformed Church, found a panther in the cow stable, and narrowly escaped with her life—the beast so nearly catching her as he sprang that he tore off part of her clothing.

In the winter and spring of 1865-6, James Steele and his associates killed in Rockingham County 17 red foxes and one gray fox.

In February, 1866, Mr. Geo. W. Rosenberger, who lived on Smith's Creek below Tenth Legion, shot and killed a bald eagle that measured 6 feet 8 inches from tip to tip of wings.

In December, 1867, Mr. Derrick Pennybacker killed a black eagle, measuring 6 feet 8 inches from tip to tip, on Linville Creek.

In January, 1870, William Minnick of Broadway reported that he had been in at the death of no less than 33 deer in the mountains of Brock's Gap and Rawley Springs during the past season, October 1 to January 1.

In March, 1876, a large black eagle was committing various depredations between Harrisonburg and Dayton.

A HISTORY OF

In June of the same year a black bear was killed in the vicinity of Cross Keys, and two cranes were killed elsewhere in the county.

Not always, however, were the Nimrods of Cross Keys so successful. In January, 1891, the near presence of a bear was reported at Yager's store, and there was instant commotion. The hunters sallied forth, fierce and fast. There was "racing and chasing" o'er woodland and lea; but, as in the hunt for the lost bride of Netherby, the object of dear desire ne'er did they see. The incident was made the subject of a really fine set of humorous verses by J. W. Tyler, and published in the *Register* of January 30, 1891.

In the *Register* of October 18, 1877, appeared the following paragraph:

> A few days since a gentleman in Brock's Gap went out squirrel hunting, and taking his seat upon a log, killed one hundred squirrels without moving from the spot. He says at least five hundred more passed by where he was sitting, during the day. It was not a first class day for squirrels, either. They all seemed running eastward.

In the same paper, issue of November 29, 1877, was printed a sketch of James Todd, lately deceased, who lived at or near the southwest corner of Rockingham. One paragraph of this sketch is given herewith:

> He was the most remarkable hunter in the Valley of Virginia, having killed over 2700 deer up to 1860, with one old muzzle-loading rifle, which had been bored so often that you could get your thumb in it. He had killed bears without number. He was a dead shot, and could perform the feat of putting a bullet through a hat on the opposite side of a tree every time, by placing an axe blade for the ball to glance.

From June 30, 1878, to June 26, 1879, sheep were killed in the county to the number of 165, and were paid for at the rate of $3.50 each. During the same period the county paid $129 for 86 red fox scalps, $72 for 90 gray fox scalps, and $50 for 20 wild cats scalps; not a cent, so far as reported, for the scalps of worthless dogs.

March 31, 1879, Jacob Fawley caught the "boss otter" of Brock's Gap, the said otter weighing 15 pounds, and measuring 3 feet 10 inches from end of nose to end of tail.

A Rockingham Orchard
(Peaked Mountain in the Distance)

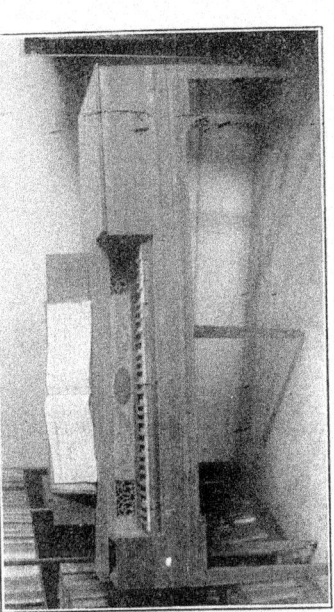

First Piano brought into Rockingham. Now in hands of Chicago Historical Society (Page 427)

Sidney Lanier Cottage, Rockingham Springs
(Pages 435, 436)

Keezletown School Building

ROCKINGHAM COUNTY

In 1879 a big crane was killed in the county.

In February, 1880, seven bears were killed in Peaked Mountain.

In Januray, 1881, Samuel Smith and his two sons killed the "daddy bear" in West Rockingham. He weighed 300 pounds dressed. In the following February a 160-pound bear was killed by Geo. W. Long in Dayton. The next month a large bear was killed near Rawley Springs.

In 1882 deer were frequently seen in the vicinity of Mt. Clinton. One was killed not ten feet from the kitchen window of one home, and another in a nearby field.

In January, 1891, it was reported that Wallace B. Minnick of Broadway had killed, during the past season, 13 bears, several of them weighing over 300 pounds each.

In February, 1891, Messrs. Wittig & Son, of Dovesville, were said to have shipped to Washington 1643 rabbits, from November to January, inclusive.

The same year Robt. Higgs shot an eagle, near Lacey Springs, which measured 5 feet 7 inches from tip to tip of wings.

During the winter of 1892-3 A. M. Turner of West Rockingham killed 10 black bears, ranging in weight from 100 to 500 pounds. The skins were sold at an average of $20 each.

In March, 1893, a gray fox attacked a child, then a woman, near McGaheysville. The woman finally killed it with a piece of scantling.

In 1897 J. C. Funkhouser shot a bald eagle near Keezletown. It weighed 9½ pounds, and measured 6 feet 10 inches from tip to tip.

CHAPTER XXVI.

BOATING ON THE SHENANDOAH RIVER.

All of us have heard or known of the days of "wagoning," when the farmer or his son would load the flour, bacon, or other products of his labor in the great wagon, and set out for Fredericksburg, Scottsville, Alexandria, or some other important market. It may not be generally known, however, that for many years hundreds of tons of flour, lumber, iron, and other articles of trade were taken down the Valley in boats on the main streams of the Shenandoah River. Concerning this river trade Mr. Richard Mauzy, a venerable citizen of McGaheysville, writes as follows:

"Between 1830 and 1840 Zack Raines[1] as leader, or 'boss,' with the soubriquet 'Commodore,' and a number of others made their living by boating to Harper's Ferry. There—the flour having been disposed of—the boats were sold for the lumber in their construction, and the boatmen would walk back to their homes.

"The floatboats used were made of heavy undressed lumber, and were guided by rudders at each end. At the dams in the river, next to the shore, chutes were placed, constructed of strong timber, for the passage of the boats. When the rise in the river was sufficient, the boats would go over the dams."

An idea of the magnitude of this river trade from Port Republic and other points in the eastern part of the county may be obtained from the following advertisement, which appeared in the *Rockingham Register* of January 16, 1841:

Notice.

The subscriber takes this method of informing his customers and the public, that he still continues the business of Boating Flour and other produce of this country to market; and, owing to the failure of crops, his terms hereafter will be—

---

[1]. "Commodore" Zachariah Raines died February 3, 1871, aged 59.

ROCKINGHAM COUNTY

For Flour taken from the neighborhood of Mt. Crawford to Georgetown, $1.25.

From Port Republic and his own neighborhood, $1.20.

And an additional charge of 12½ cents per barrel when taken to Baltimore. He will also deliver Flour at Harper's Ferry, on the Canal or Rail-road, at $1.00 per barrel.

Having a saw-mill of his own, to enable him to build his own boats, and having hands of his own to go with the water,—he will take Flour from his own yard at $1.12½ per barrel. All barrels delivered in good order—no cooperage to be charged. Last season he and his hands took through the Shenandoah locks 5,623 barrels. He was not forgotten when there was a great deal of business to do, and he flatters himself that his customers will not forsake him when there is a little to do. He avails himself of this opportunity to return his thanks to those who have heretofore encouraged him in his business, and flatters himself that his long experience and success in his business will enable him to give general satisfaction. He leaves as security for his returns, 1,492 acres of real property, and between .... and $4,000 worth of personal property. The public's humble servant,

Jacob Sipe.

This notice makes the fact obvious that Mr. Raines was not the only man in the river trade worthy to be called "Commodore."

About twelve years ago a gentleman who signed himself "Gabriel" wrote an exceedingly interesting article on the subject before us for the *Page Courier*, published at Luray, Va. We give herewith his account in full.

Old Boating Days on the Shenandoah.

The Shenandoah River used to be the great commercial highway of this Valley, and boating in those days gave employment to many men. My first recollections of the River date back to the day that my father moved on its banks near the old Columbia Bridge. The second day after we moved my father and three uncles went up the River to the Furnace (now Shenandoah City) and in a few days we heard that the fleet was in Kite's dam, so my grand-mother took me to the High Rock to see the boats come through the shoot. We got in sight just in time to see the first boat go thro, strike a great rock, split in twain, and the whole cargo of pigiron went to the bottom. Each boat was manned by six men, and when the boat broke those on it were carried to such deep water that they had to swim. There were 18 boats in this fleet, and soon the men began to wade in and gather the iron together in a pile. The broken boat was then taken to the bank and repaired, reloaded and started

A HISTORY OF

on its way again. This was in March, I think, so you can see that a River sailor had his perils and hardships. William Lowry was, I think, the steersman on the broken boat.

Nearly all boats were provided with tin horns about 8 feet long, and when they would start from stations on the River, all would blow. War songs were the favorite tunes, and the music they made would make your hair stand on end. These horns could be heard for five miles.

These boats were 9½ x 76 feet. In low water they carried 8 tons and flush water 12 tons of iron; 8 to 12 thousand feet of lumber or 110 barrels of flour made a load. Iron was then worth $60 per ton; lumber $1.80 to $2.25 per 100; flour $8 per barrel. A great deal of bark, hoop-poles, rails, shingles, posts, apples, brandy, potatoes, and corn was boated off also; tho iron, flour, and lumber were the principal exports in those days.

Boats sold at the journey's end for from $18 to $25. Boatsmen got from $14 to $18 for the trip. It generally took from 5 to 7 days to make the trip—3 or 4 to take the boat down and 2 or 3 to walk back.

The stations along the River had names just like our railroad stations. Here are some of them: Starting at Shenandoah, we came first to Welfley's Mill, then Wm. Kite's Mill, Roland Kite's Mill, and so on, each of which all the way down the River old boatsmen and residents along the River will remember; but I have not space to mention them here. The deepest water in the River those days between Port Republic and Harper's Ferry was at Gray Horse Eddies, below Castleman's Ferry. [Castleman's Ferry is in Clarke County.]

These are the names of some of the old boatsmen: Hamp Miller, Frank Rucker, Coronee Comer, Billie Melton, Alec Kite, Bud Cave, Wm. Strickler, Merrell Comer, Bud, William, Cap, Dick, Dan, George, Ben, John and Al Dofflemoyer; Ben and Dug Dovel; Columbus Kite, Jack Kite, Commodore Turner, William, Reuben, Dick, and Henry Lucas; Fred Phillips, Wm. and Jack Alger; M. V. Louderback, John Gaines, Bogus Lucas, James Bateman, Shinnol Croft, Bax Bugan, Ton Morris, James, Sim, and Davy Keyser; Chris, Aleck, Charley and Jacob Hilliard; W. M. Lowry, Reuben, Joseph, Peter, Martin, John, Isaac and Abram Painter; James W. Foltz, Sharp Good, Adam, John W., Noah, David, Jacob, and Newton Seakford; Joel Decker, Joe and John Burner, Wm. Price, Jas. and George Webster; John and Dan Martin; W. M. Martin, Sr., Wm. Martin, Jr., George W. Seakford, Buck, Dick, Harrison and Hutch Cameron; Wm. Stoneberger, Alf Kite, and Robert, Isaac, and Billy Aleshire.

The last three boats that ever went down the River were built for Adam Seakford on the James Bumgardner place, three miles southwest of Rileyville, about 11 years ago. They were loaded with plank, which was sold at Riverton. They were run off by Adam Seakford, James Webster, and J. R. Seakford, the stern hands being Martin Painter, Buck Cameron, and Newton Seakford.

ROCKINGHAM COUNTY

This ended the boating business in Page.

There may more occur to me later on this subject, and if it does I may write another chapter about it, as it covers an important era in the history of our county.[2]

From Mr. J. H. Mace of Port Republic the following facts relating to transportation on the Shenandoah have been obtained. For some time in the early days Port Republic was the highest point on the river from which boats started. Later, the channels being sufficiently cleared, they started farther up: on the South River, at Mt. Vernon Forge, now Grottoes; on Middle River, at Mt. Meridian; and on North River, at Bruback's Mill.

The boats were called "gundalows," the accent being on the first syllable. They were frequently or generally nine feet wide and 90 feet long. The main side board was 2 inches thick and 14 inches high, this height being increased—perhaps doubled—by a second board on top, one inch thick, called the "splash board."

Occasionally, perhaps frequently, boats started on North River as high as Mt. Crawford and Bridgewater. Gen. John E. Roller tells me that he used to see Com. Raines and his men taking flat boats down the river past Mt. Crawford. In Martin's Gazetteer of Virginia (1835), it is stated in the sketch of Mt. Crawford, "The North River is navigable for flat boats, about three miles above this village." A point three miles above Mt. Crawford is almost exactly the site of Bridgewater. Henry Howe, in his history of Virginia (1852), says that Mt. Crawford was near the head of boat navigation. The fact that Bridgewater was formerly called "Bridgeport" is thus explained.

Hon. Geo. E. Sipe tells me that he has seen as many as 1000 barrels of flour in one convoy on the Shenandoah. He also states that the government expended some money in opening the river for navigation. As early as 1798 the feasi-

---

[2]. From the *Page Courier* of May 24, 1900. The paper from which the above was copied was loaned to the author by Ed. S. Conrad, Esq., of Harrisonburg, Va.

bility of making it navigable was being discussed in the Virginia General Assembly. In 1824 and 1831 Acts were passed declaring certain parts thereof a public highway. In 1831 an Act was passed directing a survey of the Shenandoah River to the highest points of navigation, for the purpose of determining the practicability and expediency of improving the said river by means of dams, locks, etc., or of building a railroad through the adjacent valley.[3]

April 11, 1867, some one, who evidently knew a good deal of the subject, was writing in the *Rockingham Register* urging that steps be taken to open North River for navigation from Port Republic to Bridgewater. This could be done, he thought, for about $2400.[4]

Doubtless the improvement of the river, like the making of fords and the building of bridges, had to be repeated from time to time, owing to destructive freshets.

What Rockingham Boatmen Can Do.

The following will show what our hardy, persevering boatmen are capable of doing:

A fleet of boats, loaded with iron, was taken down the Shenandoah River, from Port Republic to Harper's Ferry, 165 miles, by the following named boatmen, viz.: Zachariah Raines, Capt.; Samuel May, Henry Pirkey, Alexander Pirkey, Jacob Raines, Reuben Raines, Jacob Hudlowe, George Rodeheffer, Henry Raines, Wm. Jones, Wm. Knight, James Anderson, privates, 12 in number. The boats were run through in four and a half days, and had in them one hundred and ten tons, (110,) making over nine tons to each man. They lashed the boats together, in twos, which were thus taken down the river. A portion of the trip was accomplished when the river was very high, making the management of the boats very difficult and dangerous. The fleet was commanded by that veteran navigator and sailor, Captain Zachariah Raines, living at the head of navigation, whose knowledge of the dangerous reefs and shoals and quicksands of the raging Shenandoah is perfect, he having passed over the same watery path for many years past, making several hundred trips.[5]

---

3. See Hening's Statutes and the Acts of Assembly.

4. In the *Rockingham Register* of March 8, 1888, is an article relating to Port Republic, headquarters of the old "Flatboat Brigade," and pointing out the natural advantages of the place.

5. From the *Rockingham Register* of March 21, 1867.

ROCKINGHAM COUNTY

The following item, copied from the *Register* of January 27, 1870, will show that navigation was not unknown in days of yore on the north fork of the Shenandoah. So far as is known, however, the trade in Rockingham on this branch of the river never reached large proportions.

A New Era!

Messrs. Editors:—Navigation has been opened on the North Branch of the Shenandoah River, from Brenneman's saw-mill, in Brock's Gap, to Cootes' Store. First boat, King Fisher, Capt. W. F. Turner, laden with shingles, deer-hides, furs, &c., also passengers, arrived to-day at the latter place, at 3 o'clock, P. M. Hurrah for the first improvement on the admission of the old State!

Jan. 20, 1870.   Brock's Gap.

CHAPTER XXVII.

COURT DAYS OF LONG AGO.

Court day in Rockingham has been a great day in the calendar for more than a century. Even now, after the absorption of the county court by the circuit court, court day is still perpetuated and religiously observed. All who have a horse to sell, a horse to buy, a man to see,—anything to be seen: those with business of all sorts, and chiefly those with none of any sort,—those and these all come to town on court day. Court day may be termed an institution: a social and economic institution. It doubtless has an educational as well as a general social value. To be on court square, or near it, on court day makes one dream of the agora at old Athens and the forum at Rome.

In the following paragraphs, taken from Mrs. Maria Graham Carr's charming reminiscences, one gets a vivid idea of the court square and the court days of 1820, and thereabouts.

About eighty feet in front of her [Mrs. Effinger's] corner house was located the Court House, nearly in the middle of the square. I think I remember a log or frame court house, that stood in the same place. I certainly remember a stone building with a large door on the east end, as well as a large bull's-eye, or round window, near the roof, and other windows on the second floor to light the jury rooms. A stone jail with grated windows stood a few paces southeast of the court house. Mr. Fletcher, an old man, was the jailer then. Behind the court house, about 20 feet from it, was a small one-story building called the clerk's office. Between it and the court house was a roof of shingles, supported by wooden pillars. Under this beef was sold; it was called the market-house. A whipping post was near the east end of it. The whole was enclosed by a strong wooden fence, made of

ROCKINGHAM COUNTY

three horizontal rails set into posts securely planted in the ground, all painted Spanish brown. I do not think the color was ever noted for its beauty, but for its durability.

The lawyers of that day were Robert Gray, David Steele, and Thomas Clark, and some younger ones I do not remember. Court day once a month was looked upon as a great event; every one that could leave home was on hand. It was a day of great interest; farmers coming in with their produce, such as butter, eggs, and other articles which they exchanged for groceries and dry goods. The streets around the court house were thronged with all sorts of men; others on horse-back, riding up and down trying to sell their horses. Men in home-made clothes, old rusty hats that had seen several generations, coarse shoes and no stockings, some without coats or vests, with only shirts and pants. I have seen a rich man come in from his country home, riding a fine horse. The man was dressed in home-spun linen shirt and pants, coarse shoes, no stockings, and an old slouch hat or straw hat. He had a large yellow silk bandana handkerchief, with a pocket-book filled with bank-notes rolled in it. He placed the handkerchief under his arm, with the two ends tied over his shoulder. He made money by buying deeds and other papers, or loaning money on notes—this was called shaving paper; and many men got rich by this business.

This was also a day to settle all grudges. When a man got too much whiskey he was very quarrelsome, and wanted to fight. Others would follow suit, and go in pell-mell. It was a dreadful sight to see them beat one another—I used to run off and hide.

It was also a great day for ginger-bread and molasses beer. The cake sellers had [tables] in front of the court house, spread with white cloths, with cakes piled high upon them, and kegs of beer nearby. I have seen the jurymen let their hats down from the window above, get them filled with ginger-bread, and a jug of beer sent up by a rope. About four or five o'clock the crowd began to start for home.

CHAPTER XXVIII.

SOME INTERESTING INCIDENTS.

Spotswood's Expedition of 1716 and the University Pageant of 1909.

All Virginians, and doubtless all Americans, are familiar with the expedition Gov. Alexander Spotswood, with a party of 20 or 30, made across the Blue Ridge in 1716, leaving Williamsburg August 20, and reaching Williamsburg, on the return, September 17.

John Fontaine, one of the party, tells in his journal of the party drinking the health of the King and the royal family on top of the mountain, Sept. 5, and of their coming down into the valley in the evening. On the 6th they crossed the river; on the 7th they went back over the mountain.

There is some confusion in Fontaine's account; but it is generally agreed that Spotswood and his party came over the Ridge at Swift Run Gap, and down to the river at or near Elkton. Says Fontaine:

> We crossed the river, which we called Euphrates. It is very deep; the main course of the water is north; it is fourscore yards wide in the narrowest part. We drank some healths on the other side, and returned; after which I went a swimming in it. We could not find any fordable place, except the one by which we crossed, and it was deep in several places. I got some grasshoppers and fished; and another and I, we catched a dish of fish, some perch, and a fish they called chub. The others went a hunting, and killed deer and turkeys. The Governor had graving irons, but could not grave any thing, the stones were so hard. I graved my name on a tree by the river side; and the Governor buried a bottle with a paper inclosed, on which he writ that he took possession of this place in the name and for King George the First of England. We had a good dinner, and after it we got the men together, and loaded all their arms, and we drank the King's health in Burgundy, and fired a volley, and all the rest of the Royal Family in claret, and a volley. We drank the Governor's health and fired another volley. We had several sorts of

Rockingham County Teachers in the University of Virginia Historical Pageant, 1909, Commemorating Spotswood and the Knights of the Horseshoe
(Page 427)
Photo by Holsinger

ROCKINGHAM COUNTY

liquors, viz., Virginia red wine and white wine, Irish usquebaugh, brandy, shrub, two sorts of rum, champaign, canary, cherry, punch, water, cider, etc. — *From John Fontaine's Journal of Sept. 6, 1716.*

In 1724 Hugh Jones wrote of the Spotswood expedition as follows:

Governor Spotswood, when he undertook the great discovery of the Passage over the Mountains, attended with a sufficient guard, and pioneers and gentlemen, with a sufficient stock of provision, with abundant fatigue passed these Mountains, and cut his Majesty's name in a rock upon the highest of them, naming it Mount George; and in complaisance the gentlemen, from the Governor's name, called the mountain next in height Mount Alexander.

For this expedition they were obliged to provide a great quantity of horse shoes, (things seldom used in the lower parts of the country, where there are few stones;) upon which account the Governor, upon their return, presented each of his companions with a golden horse shoe, (some of which I have seen studded with valuable stones, resembling the heads of nails,) with this inscription on the one side: *Sic juvat transcendere montes;* and on the other is written the tramontane order.

This he instituted to encourage gentlemen to venture backwards, and make discoveries and new settlements; any gentleman being entitled to wear this Golden Shoe that can prove his having drunk his Majesty's health upon Mount George.

Tradition says that Stephen Harnsberger came over with Spotswood, or shortly after him. The Harnsbergers were among the early settlers about Elkton. Stephen Harnsberger, it is said, gave his gold horseshoe to a younger Stephen Harnsberger, who went to Georgia in 1792 or 1793. Jos. M. C. Harnsberger, late of Port Republic, saw this horseshoe while on a visit to Georgia.[1]

In 1909 the teachers of Rockingham, in attendance upon the University of Virginia summer school, personated Spotswood and his knights in the 4th of July historical pageant, participated in by 1000 persons from more than 20 different States. Prof. C. J. Heatwole played the Governor. A song written for the occasion, "Rockingham," was sung to the tune, "Die Wacht am Rhein."[2]

---

1. Related to me by Capt. J. S. Harnsberger (page 360).
2. On Spotswood's expedition, see Wayland's "German Element," pp.

A HISTORY OF

The Coming of the Lincolns.

In 1903 Mrs. Mary Elizabeth Lincoln Pennybacker (page 295) told me that some time prior to the Revolution John Lincoln came from Pennsylvania and bought land on Linville Creek. The place is a short distance below Wenger's Mill. The house now occupied by Mr. S. M. Bowman, built about 1800 by Capt. Jacob Lincoln (1751-1822), is at or near the original Lincoln homestead. The old Lincoln graveyard is nearby on the hill.

John Lincoln had five sons, Abraham, John, Jacob, Thomas, and Isaac. Jacob (Capt. Jacob), grandfather of Mrs. Pennybacker, was the only one of the five to remain in Virginia. Abraham, with his little son Thomas, aged about 4, went in 1781 or 1782 to Kentucky. Abraham Lincoln, later President, was born in Kentucky Feb. 12, 1809, when Thomas was about 31.

Daniel Boone on Linville Creek.

In the spring of 1750, when Daniel Boone was 15 or 16, his parents left Pennsylvania for North Carolina. It was autumn, 1751, a year and a half later, before they reached their destination. Tradition says they tarried for a year or more in what is now Rockingham County, Va.—on Linville Creek, six miles north of Harrisonburg.[3] It is understood that the Boones and the Lincolns were acquaintances in Pennsylvania. If the Lincolns had already come to Virginia, the Boones were doubtless their guests on Linville Creek; if the Lincolns followed, they may have been directed to Linville Creek by the Boones. The Bryans were also early residents on Linville Creek, and the William Bryan who married Boone's sister probably went to North Carolina from this section. There is also a tradition that Henry Miller, founder of Miller's

---

7, 8; on the 1909 pageant see Charlottesville *Daily Progress*, July 9, 1909; Richmond *Times-Dispatch*, July 11, 1909; U. Va. *Alumni Bulletin*, October, 1909.

[3]. Thwaites' Daniel Boone, pp. 15-17; Bruce's Daniel Boone and the Wilderness Road, pp. 13, 14.

ROCKINGHAM COUNTY

Iron Works on Mossy Creek, was a cousin to Boone, and hunted and trapped with him over this region about 1750.[4]

Valentine Sevier's Sale Bill.

Reference has already been made (p. 349) to Valentine Sevier's numerous land sales on and near Smith's Creek and Long Meadow from 1753 to 1773. The following document, recorded at Staunton, is apropos. It shows, for one thing, that Sevier (father of Gen. John Sevier) was in 1763 a resident of what is now Shenandoah County. Possibly this was about the time his son founded New Market.

Know all men by these presents that I Valentine Severe of Frederick County & Collony of Virginia farmer for & in Consideration of the sum of forty two pounds Ten Shillings and Seven pence Current Lawfull money of Virginia to me in hand paid by Andrew bird of Augusta County in Colony aforesd. Miller[5] where of I do hereby acknowledge the Receipt and my Self therewith fully & Entirely Satisfied have Bargained Sold Set over & Delivered and by these presents in plain & open market— according to the just and true form of Law in that case made and provided do bargain Sell Set over and Deliver into the sd. Andrew Bird and his heirs Exrs. admrs. and assigns The Following Cattle Goods and Chattles Viz five Cows one with a young calf a two year Old heifer & three yearlings four feather Beds with all their Coverings & furniture to them belonging withall my hogs and all my wearing apparral and all the Pewter and all other my housefurniture withall my Iron pots and pans & three Smooth Bore Guns And every part and parcel of my movable Estate too tedious to mention in particulars all my Tools and Implements of Husbandry &c To Have and to Hold the said Bargained premises unto the said Andrew Bird his heirs Exrs. Admrs. & Assigns to the only proper use and Behoof of the said Andrew Bird his Exrs. Adminrs. and Assigns forever And I the sd. Valentine Sevire for myself my heirs Exrs. & adminrs. the said Bargained Premises unto Andrew Bird his heirs Exrs. & Administrators and assigns against all and all manner of persons Shall and will warrant and for ever Defend by these presents In Witness whereof together with the Delivery of these premises I have hereunto Set my hand and Seal This Eighteenth Day of April in the year of our Lord one Thousand Seven hundred and Sixty three 1763

    Sealed and Delivered   Valentine Sevire (L. S.)
in presence of
    Nicholas Zeehon
    John Phillips

---

4. See Wayland's "German Element," page 206.

5. Bird's mill was on Smith's Creek, a short distance above New Market, just across the line in what is now Rockingham County.

A HISTORY OF

The Influenza of 1807.

In December, 1807, Dr. Peachy Harrison, of Harrisonburg, wrote a scientific paper for the Philadelphia *Medical Museum*. More than a hundred years later, without my searching for it, or even having known of it, a copy of this paper came to my hand. It deals mainly with the influenza epidemic of 1807, but also gives many interesting facts about Rockingham a hundred years ago. Accordingly, certain paragraphs, chiefly the first, are herewith presented.

Rockingham, of which Harrisonburg is the county-town, and distant from Philadelphia about 260 miles, is bounded on the north-west by the North Mountain, from which the Shenandoah River derives several important branches; and on the south-east by the Blue Ridge, which are distant from each other between twenty and thirty miles. The soil, throughout a great portion of the county, is calcareous, and is well adapted to the cultivation of wheat, rye, maize, red clover, and, in the low grounds formed by the small creeks, where argil predominates, timothy and blue grass constitute excellent meadows. This district of country abounds with perennial springs; but the water they yield holds so much lime in solution, or, to use the common phrase, is so hard, as to require *breaking*, before it is fit to be used in washing clothes; for, when this precaution is not taken, the soap is decomposed, and its cleansing power entirely destroyed. Fruit of every kind is an uncertain crop, except along the mountains, and there, apples in many orchards are rendered unfit for use, by what is called the *bitter rot*, a disease of which the cause, so far as I have been able to learn, has not been well ascertained. Whether the default in the fruit arises from some cause inherent in the tree, or some external source unconnected with the condition of the tree, is matter, it seems to me, of great doubt. The evil, however, is a serious one; and one that renders the rearing of an apple orchard, in this country, at this time, a labour of uncertain advantage.[6] This disease of apple orchards was unknown till of late years. Orchards are said to have been much less injured by it this season than they were several seasons past.

South winds are generally the precursors of our rains; northeastwardly winds bring our deep snows; and those from the north-west accompany dry, and are perhaps the cause of our coldest weather; these prevail through a large portion of the year. All our hurricanes come

---

[6]. Science, or blind chance and time, controlled by a beneficent Providence, has certainly wrought encouraging changes in Rockingham orchards since 1807.

ROCKINGHAM COUNTY

from this direction; they were more frequent and destructive last spring than they were ever known before in this country. Bilious fevers are not natives of our soil. We had our share of them, however, in the extraordinary autumn of 1804. In common seasons, pure remittents and intermittents are scarcely known, at least as generated by causes existing in our own country: they have been caught in other places. We are occasionally visited by fevers, but they mostly prevail in cold weather, and are of typhous character. In the winter of 1805-6, cases of this fever were frequent, and, in every instance of which I had any knowledge, they appeared to me to be the offspring of domestic filthiness. They occurred, in every instance, in circumstances favourable to the accumulation and putrification of human excretions, viz: in crowded and unventilated cabins, and in families not remarkable for their cleanliness.7

The winter of 1806-7 was among the severest ever experienced in this latitude. In the months of March and April, a catarrh, accompanied with more or less pneumonic symptoms, prevailed pretty generally through the town and its vicinity. It resembled, in almost every important particular, the late influenza. The most remarkable differences were, more acute pains of the thorax, a more obstinate cough, and requiring a more free use of the lancet.

It was remarkably healthy, both in town and country, from the last of April until the appearance of the influenza, which was about the 8th of September. My colleague, Dr. Cravens, and Mr. Benjamin Smith, were the first subjects of it, within the circle of my acquaintance and observation. They had returned, on the evening of the 5th, from Tyger's Valley, distant from this, in a north-west direction, about a hundred miles. On the evening of the 8th Dr. Cravens was seized with chilliness, soreness in his muscles, pains in his head and bones; coryza, fever, and cough soon succeeded. The pain of the head was seated over the right eye, and was the most distressing of all his symptoms. On the morning of the 9th, Mr. Benjamin Smith, who lives two miles out of town, saw him; in the evening of the same day he was seized with symptoms of influenza. They saw on their journey no complaint similar to, or what they had a right to believe was the influenza. They saw no one labouring under it after their return. From this time until the 11th, I knew of no other cases in either town or county, and have good reason to believe there were none; for at this time we had begun to expect its appearance, having heard that it had successively attacked Winchester, Woodstock, and New Market. * * * * * Very soon after its appearance in town [Harrisonburg], it fell on the adjoining neighborhoods, and, by the 12th of October, it was only heard of in the remotest parts of the county,

---

7. It is hoped and believed that the progress of a century in Rockingham has been attended with as much improvement in domestic conditions as in fruit growing.

A HISTORY OF

and had entirely disappeared by the 23rd of this month. The comet was not observed in this place until about the 26th of September, and was no more to be seen after the 12th of November. There was a deficiency of rain during the months of October and November. The wind generally stood north-west.

A Case of Body Snatching.

An extract from the reminiscences of Maria Graham Carr. The time referred to is about 1820.

There were two men hanged in Harrisonburg. Ben Hopkins was hung on top of the hill where Sherdlins' vineyard was afterward located.[8] Sprouce, who killed his wife in Fluvanna Co., was brought to Harrisonburg, tried, condemned, and hung in the woods back of Mr. Rutherford's house [east of town]. I saw the procession pass on its way to the gallows: Sprouce, with several preachers, among them Mr. Smith, who sat beside him on the coffin, talking to him. As it was raining, Mr. Smith took off his overcoat and put it around Sprouce's shoulders, talking to him and trying to make him understand his condition; but Sprouce took no heed, but was looking at the crowd. His wagon was surrounded by fifty mounted soldiers, well armed. Then came hundreds of men and women whipping up their horses, trying to get as near as they could to the wagon. I could not bear to look at it, only for a few moments. The medical students came from Staunton, with a covered carry-all, determined to have Sprouce's body. As soon as the hanging was over they buried the body right under the gallows. The Harrisonburg students wanted the body and were determined to have it if they had to fight for it. The Staunton students took up the body as soon as the people were gone, and hid it in some brush wood. The Harrisonburg students, after having searched for some time, found the body, put it across a horse, and went four or five miles around on the west side of the town, and hid the body in Mr. Gibbon's tan house. Afterwards the body was taken to the log house where I went to school, where it was then skinned and [the skin] tanned. The Presbyterian prayer meeting was held every Wednesday evening in this log house, and we did not know that Sprouce's body was above us.

A Rockinghamer's Visit to Philadelphia in 1847.

We took the cars about 14 miles below Cumberland [they had ridden horseback to that point from West Rockingham] and went the same day to Baltimore, a distance of 160 or 170 miles: the scenery on the road was highly interesting, varied—and sublime. Baltimore is a place of great trade—the shipping is very extensive. In the morning when we left

---

[8]. See pages 238, 365.

Ruins of Mt. Vernon Furnace
[Page 379]

Where Meigs Fell [Pages 149, 434]
The spot is marked by the children

Round Hill, The Falls, and the Wool Mills, Bridgewater
By permission of E. G. Furry

A Glimpse into Brock's Gap   (Page 21)

Lincoln Graveyard

Silver Lake, Dayton, and Mole Hill

ROCKINGHAM COUNTY

Baltimore, we passed many Wharfs with immense shipping, for the distance of between one and two miles.—The scenery, from Baltimore to Philadelphia was beautiful and sublime. Much of the way you have the Chesapeake bay in view, and cross a bridge 1¼ miles long over a river, or rather arm of the bay; and another Bridge of ¾ miles long. Soon after, we crossed the Susquehannah River on a steam boat, and ere long came in sight of Delaware River, which we had often in view until we arrived at Philadelphia. This is a city—the beauty and grandeur of which baffles description—the elegance and size of its houses—the beauty and cleanliness of its streets—and the handsome and splendid manner which they have in displaying their goods, through window lights of from 4 to 7 feet long and proportionably wide! Here we also saw ships of an enormous size: many more things might be mention(ed) among which are the State House, Gerard College and the Fairmount Waterworks, where by machinery, the water is elevated up a prodigious height into basons, to supply the whole City with water. Should I be spared and blest with health a few years longer I think of visiting Philadelphia once more: especially if I succeed in selling my Musical Map or Scale.—*From a letter written March 26, 1847, by Joseph Funk of Rockingham County, Va., to his daughter in Missouri.*

Death of Ashby: 1862.

On the evening of June 6, 1862, Gen. Turner Ashby was shot and killed while leading an infantry charge against the Pennsylvania Bucktails. The place of his death, now marked by a monument, is about two miles south of Harrisonburg. (See pages 141, 179, 318.) Gen. Thos. L. Kane, commanding the Bucktails, a brother of the famous arctic explorer, Elisha Kent Kane, was captured; and at the same time, in a cavalry fight near at hand, Ashby's men, led by Munford, captured Sir Percy Wyndham, whose highest ambition was to capture Ashby.

Ashby's body lay next day in the house of Dr. Geo. W. Kemper, Port Republic, wrapped in the Confederate flag. Col. O'Ferrall says that at evening the flag and bier were wet with the tears of strong men. The next day, Sunday, June 8, while Cross Keys was being fought, the body was taken to Charlottesville and buried.

On October 10, 1912, when the Daughters of the Confederacy of Virginia, in convention at Harrisonburg, went out to decorate the Ashby monument, there was in the company one,

A HISTORY OF

Mrs. J. E. Alexander, who, fifty years before, had followed Ashby's body to the grave at Charlottesville.

Stonewall Jackson at Port Republic.

It is said that on the morning of June 8, 1862, before the battle of Cross Keys opened, Jackson, who was at Madison Hall, the guest of Dr. G. W. Kemper, was cut off from the North River bridge at Port Republic by a detachment of Shields' men, who seized the village and planted a battery at the village end of the bridge; and that Jackson, wearing a rain-coat over his uniform, dashed up, ordered the battery to another position, and thus got the opportunity to cross the bridge to his own men.[9] Whether he actually got the Federal battery moved by his order or not, there seems to be no doubt that he most narrowly escaped capture.

The Killing of John Kline: 1864.

Elder John Kline, a prominent minister of the Dunker Church (page 250), was distinguished for high character and good works, but his goings and comings upon missions of his office aroused the suspicions of an evil time, and when he did not heed either the threats of foes or the warnings of friends he was waylaid and shot. The deed was committed near his home, near Broadway, June 15, 1864. He was a martyr to duty and the works of peace.[10]

The Death of Meigs: 1864.

The three Confederate scouts referred to on page 148, above, were Frank Shaver, Campbell, and Martin. Shaver, who lived near Pleasant Valley, and who died in 1895, was the one who killed Meigs. He and his companions were planning to get on the high hills between the Warm Springs Pike and the Valley Pike, to locate the Federals by their night campfires, and would gladly have ridden away from Meigs and his companions without firing a shot. Shaver,

---

[9]. See Mauzy's Genealogical Record, pp. 37, 38; also, pp. 142, 143, above.

[10]. See Zigler's History of the Brethren, pp. 143, 144.

SIDNEY LANIER.
Page (435)

ROCKINGHAM COUNTY

Campbell, and Martin left the Pike, by the old east-going road, near D. T. Click's. Meigs and his men followed, crossed the line now occupied by the C.-W. Railroad, and mounted the first terrace of the hill. Then the Confederates turned, and in a moment the fight was over. Martin was wounded. He was taken by Shaver and Campbell to Robt. Wright's, near Spring Creek, where he was attended by Dr. T. H. B. Brown (page 316).[11]

The Thurman Movement.

Wm. C. Thurman, who died in Richmond almshouse in 1906, was a notable figure in Rockingham for many years. First a Baptist, he joined the Dunker Church at Greenmount in 1865, and was at once put into the ministry. Soon he began to preach new doctrines, and to fix a time, near at hand, for the second Advent. He won followers—perhaps a hundred—chiefly good people; and in time he was expelled from the church. He and his followers continued their activities, and the movement culminated in September, 1868, when, upon the appointed day, the saints assembled at a farm house near Dayton, to await the Lord's coming. The day passed, the evening came, but not the fulfilment of the leader's prophecy. A second time was fixed, and a second expectation failed, when, in April, 1875, a small company waited long at a well known home near Harrisonburg. Thurman was in the county occasionally as late as 1878, perhaps later.

Sidney Lanier at Rockingham Springs.

Sidney Lanier, the great Southern poet and musician, spent six weeks at Rockingham Springs, near McGaheysville, in the summer of 1879, and wrote there his splendid book, "Science of English Verse." The cottage he and his family occupied is still standing, and the room in which he worked is very much as he left it. The summer was full of varied

---

[11] See *Rockingham Daily Record*, April 8, 1912; O'Ferrall's Forty Years of Active Service, pp. 128, 129.

incidents that give charm and color to the poet's notable achievement. In literature, Rockingham has had no more pleasing distinction than that conferred upon her those rich summer days by Sidney Lanier.[12]

A Fence-Corner Council.

In 1885, one evening in the dark, eight young men met in a fence corner, near Dale Enterprise, and sat on a log. They were tired but not exhausted; they were in the dark, but were seeking light. They organized a society for mutual improvement: they decided to buy books and read them, and to talk together of what they read. In Hartman's carpenter shop, in Heatwole's wash house, somewhere they continued to meet, some walking three miles to the place. Their motives were misunderstood, their aims questioned, the outcome dreaded, and they were often in straits; but finally a man built them a house, and a woman became their "god-mother." The society lived about 20 years, and grew in numbers and in favor.

This is history, not a fairy tale. One of the original eight is dean of the dental department of the University of Maryland; another was lately chairman of the board of supervisors of Rockingham County; another is an educator known over Virginia. Of those who came in later, one is a distinguished pulpit orator, another a writer of national reputation; and many are filling honorable places worthily. I give as many names as I have been able to find:

The Eight: T. O. Heatwole, Frank A. Heatwole, C. J. Heatwole, Aldine Heatwole, John J. Heatwole, John R. Swartz, Wm. T. Swartz, L. F. Ritchie.

Of those who came in later: D. Hopkins Ralston, W. J. Showalter, D. I. Suter, P. G. Suter, E. J. Suter, Chas. Senger. Henry Senger.

Miss Tyreetta P. Minnich, a teacher, was god-mother; and Mr. David A. Heatwole built the house.—See page 224.

[12.] See "Sidney Lanier at Rockingham Springs," an illustrated volume published in 1912 by Ruebush-Elkins Co., Dayton, Va.

ROCKINGHAM COUNTY

The first piano in Rockingham (John Graham's) was bought in London in 1805 for £100. Mrs. M. G. Carr, Graham's granddaughter, gave it in 1888 to the Chicago Historical Society.

It is said that the successful conclusion of the War of 1812 was celebrated by the people of Rockingham in a barbecue on the top of Mole Hill. An ox-roast was the chief feature, the poor beast having been spared long enough to carry his own weight to the summit.[13]

In 1842 an Act of Assembly was passed allowing Henry Juett Gray, son of Robt. Gray, to have a slave, Randolph, taught to read and write. Young Gray was blind. Wishing to become a teacher of the blind, he needed a servant who could read and write. His father, Robert Gray, undertook to indemnify the public against any possible injury which might result from the slave's misconduct.

During the last year 2,000 lbs. of walnut kernels were shipped by rail from Broadway depot in this County. They sold in the Baltimore market at 30 cents per pound, bringing the handsome sum of $600 for these small and seemingly worthless things. These walnut kernels were gathered mainly by poor children in Brock's Gap who had no other way in which to turn an honest penny. They are used in making candy.— *Rockingham Register*, January 10, 1873.

In April, 1875, Lewiston, the brick mansion below Port Republic, formerly the home of Gen. S. H. Lewis, was burned.

In June, 1878, "the crop of hay on the Court House Green brought three dollars and the purchaser gathered it."

On November 27, 1878, Peter Paul was drowned in Dry River; four days later William Lewis, brother of Sen. John F. Lewis, was drowned in the South Shenandoah River.

As late as 1879 pig iron was hauled to Harrisonburg from Shenandoah Iron Works (Page County). In early days iron ore was hauled from Dale Enterprise to Miller's Iron Works on Mossy Creek.

In 1879 the Moffett Liquor Law of Virginia was adopted in Texas, and the Moffett bell-punch register was ordered from Virginia in large quantities.—Moffett was a Rockinghamer (pages 357, 358).

---

13. Rev. L. J. Heatwole, of near Mole Hill, relates this.

A HISTORY OF

At the January court, 1881, 476 sleighs were reported in Harrisonburg. (See page 174.)

In the summer of 1909 the annual meeting of the Church of the Brethren brought together at Assembly Park, near Harrisonburg, over 30,000 people—the largest assembly ever in the county.

In this connection it may be appropriate to chronicle the visits of certain famous men to Rockingham County.

Mrs. Carr heard Lorenzo Dow preach in the northeast corner of the court yard, and saw the Grand Duke of Saxe-Weimar, Andrew Jackson, and Henry Clay pass through Harrisonburg.

In March, 1866, and April, 1881, Dr. Geo. W. Bagby lectured in Harrisonburg; in October, 1866, B. J. Lossing was in Harrisonburg, at Cross Keys, Port Republic, and other places preparing his illustrated history of the war. In May, 1868, Gen. D. H. Hill lectured in Harrisonburg on "Southern Literature and the Southern People." In September, 1868, Gen. Th. L. Price of Missouri was a visitor in the county; and in September, 1869, Gen. John B. Magruder lectured in Harrisonburg on "Mexico, Maximilian, and Carlotta." In June, 1874, President Grant passed through, stopping a few minutes at the railway station. In July, 1879, Gen. Wm. Mahone visited Harrisonburg, and in August following Gen. Beauregard was at Rawley Springs and Harrisonburg. In September, 1880, Zeb B. Vance made a couple of political speeches in Harrisonburg; in October, 1883, Fitzhugh Lee spoke on Court Square; and in 1884 Dr. J. L. M. Curry lectured in Harrisonburg. In 1884 Dr. T. DeW. Talmage was at Rawley, and on July 29, 1896, he spoke at Assembly Park. Sam Jones was here frequently in the 90's. John W. Daniel spoke in the county in 1891, 1894, 1896, and 1897. In August, 1895, Gen. John B. Gordon delivered his lecture, "Last Days of the Confederacy," at Assembly Park. On Oct. 15, 1897, Eduard Remenyi played in Harrisonburg. In May, 1899, President McKinley passed through the Valley, stopping awhile in Harrisonburg.

CONCLUSION.

The best conclusion to any book is doubtless the one that the intelligent reader draws for himself after reading the book. Accordingly, not many words by the author are deemed necessary in this place. It is hoped that the resources of the County, together with the versatility of the people, have been effectively indicated, if not adequately detailed. The wealth and scope of both have been a growing wonder from the beginning of this study to the end. Our county has great resources, and our people have great powers: both facts have been proved sufficiently to be a stirring prophecy for the future, and to set a call of duty and responsibility ringing in the soul of every man and woman, every boy and girl, within these wide borders.

Not merely our flocks and farms, but our churches, our schools, and our homes have made Rockingham a goodly land in which to dwell. These are the bulwarks of our safety and happiness, and the towers of our strength to help Virginia and the world. It was free manhood and true womanhood that enabled Rockingham to rise so quickly in new strength from "wild war's desolation"; it is free manhood and true womanhood that must ever be our best resource, either in the face of external foes or in the midst of internal dangers.

APPENDIX.

It must be understood that the lists of sheriffs and members of the General Assembly are more or less incomplete and subject to correction. The original records are all difficult, and some are incomplete. While all the following lists are known to be correct in most cases, it has not been possible to verify them in some instances.

SHERIFFS OF ROCKINGHAM.

1778: Silas Hart
1778-9: Josiah Davison
1779: Abraham Smith
1780: George Boswell
1781: Thomas Hewitt
1782: Isaac Hinckle
1783-5: John Thomas
1785: William Nalle
1786: Robert Davis
1787: Benj. Harrison
1788: John Davis
1789: William Herring
1790-2: Andrew Shanklin
1793: Wm. Dunlap
1794-5: Layton Yancey
1796-9: Ezek. Harrison
1800: John Ewin
1801-2: Benj. Harrison
1803-4: Andrew Shanklin
1805: William Herring
1806-7: Joseph Baxter
1808-9: Asher Waterman
1810-12: St. C. Kirtley
1812-14: Charles Lewis
1814-16: Ezek. Harrison
1816-18: George Huston
1818-20: Walter Davis
1820-22: Arch. Rutherford

1822-24: George Dove
1824-26: Peachy Harrison
1826-28: Giles Turley
1828-30: Jonathan Shipmar
1831-32: Joseph Baxter
1833-34: Daniel Mathews
1835-36: David Henton
1837: R. P. Fletcher
1838: David Henton
1839-40: R. P. Fletcher
1841-42: J. D. Williamson
1843-44: J. H. Campbell
1847-48: S. H. Lewis
1849-50: Anderson Moffett (?)
1851-52: G. W. Kemper
1853-56: A. S. Byrd
1857-60: J. R. Koogler
1861-64: Y. C. Ammon
1865: J. R. Koogler
1866-68: S. R. Allebaugh
1868-70: O. C. Sterling
1870: J. A. Hammen
1870-73: J. P. Ralston
1874-83: D. H. Ralston
1883-87: J. H. Shipp
1887-95: V. H. Lam
1895-07: J. A. Switzer
1908—: E. J. Carickhoff

COUNTY TREASURERS.

Prior to 1870 the sheriffs handled the county money.

1871-76: S. R. Allebaugh
1877-85: S. R. Sterling
1886-98: P. W. Reherd

1899-1911: E. W. Carpenter
1911: Geo. B. Keezell
1912—: P. W. Reherd

JUDGES OF COUNTY COURT.

From 1778 to 1852 the county court was composed of a number of justices appointed by the Governor; from 1852 to 1869 it was composed of a similar body of justices elected by the people; from 1869 to 1870 the body of justices held office by military appointment, under the Reconstruction Acts; and in April, 1870, the system of county courts, presided over by a single justice, went into operation.

James Kenney, 1870-1873
Chas. T. O'Ferrall, 1874-1879

Robert Johnston, 1880-1885
George G. Grattan, 1886-1904

JUDGES OF CIRCUIT SUPERIOR COURT.

Hugh Holmes, 1809-1811
Daniel Smith, 1811-1850

G. B. Samuels, 1850-1852

A HISTORY OF

JUDGES OF CIRCUIT COURT.

John Kenney, 1852-1860
J. W. F. Allen, 1860-1865
Richard Parker, 1865-1866
John T. Harris, 1866-1869
Thomas S. Hargest, 1869-1870

Robert H. Turner, 1870-1875
Mark Bird, 1875-1883
J. G. Newman, 1883-1884
William McLaughlin, 1884-1898
S. H. Letcher, 1898-1906
T. N. Haas, 1906-——

CLERKS OF COUNTY COURT.

Peter Hog, April 27, 1778, to about Jan. 1, 1782
Thomas Lewis, pro tem., Feb. 18, 1782
Richard Mathews, pro tem., Feb. 25, 1782
Henry Ewing, Feb. 25, 1782, to 1792
Samuel McWilliams, 1792-1817

Henry Jewett Gambill, 1817-1847
L. W. Gambill (pro tem.), 1848
Erasmus Coffman, 1848-1852
L. W. Gambill, 1852-1869
Robert A. Gray, 1869-1870
A. St. Clair Sprinkel, 1870-1871
Wm. McK. Wartmann, 1871-1872
Joseph T. Logan, 1872-1885
Joseph S. Messerley, 1885-1904

CLERKS OF CIRCUIT COURT.

Henry J. Gambill, April 24, 1809, to May 11, 1847.
Littleton W. Gambill, May 11, 1847, to July 1, 1852.
A. St. Clair Sprinkel, 1852-1869.

A. L. Lindsey, 1869-1870.
F. A. Daingerfield, 1870-1872.
L. W. Gambill, 1872-1875.
Joseph H. Shue, 1875-1883.
A. N. Black, 1883-1887.
D. H. Lee Martz, 1887-——.

ATTORNEYS FOR THE COMMONWEALTH.

Gabriel Jones, 1778-1793.
David Holmes, 1793-1797.
James Allen, 1797-1804.
Daniel Smith, 1804-1811.
Robert Gray, 1811-1847.
Herring Chrisman, 1847-1852. (Co. Ct.)
John Kenney, 1847-1852. (Cir. Ct.)
John T. Harris, 1852-1859.

Thomas L. Yancey, 1859-1862.
John C. Woodson, 1862-1865.
Wm. H. Effinger, 1865-1869.
Chas. H. Lewis, 1869-1870.
J. N. Liggett, 1870-1871.
John Paul, 1871-1877.
Geo. G. Grattan, 1877-1881.
Chas. D. Harrison, 1881-1899.
Geo. N. Conrad, 1899-1912.
Chas. D. Harrison, 1912-——.

SUPERINTENDENTS OF SCHOOLS.

1870-2—Geo. W. Holland.
1872-5—Jos. S. Loose.

1876-83—Jasper Hawse.
1883-6—A. P. Funkhouser.
1886-——Geo. H. Hulvey.

COUNTY SURVEYORS.

1778-1789: Thomas Lewis.
1789-1825: Alexander Herring.
1825-1835: Gordon McWilliams.
1835-1849: Joseph Mauzy.
1849-——: H. B. Harnsberger.
——1853: Peter Paulsel.
1853-1863: H. B. Harnberger.

1863-1870: J. H. Ralston.
1870-1872: Geo. J. Kisling.
1873-——: A. C. Bear.
——-1883: Edw. S. Kemper.
1883-1887: Wm. B. Yancey.
1887-1903: Jasper Hawse.
1903-——: Jos. G. Myers.

MEMBERS OF HOUSE OF DELEGATES.

1779—John Smith, Silas Hart.
1780—Silas Hart, John Grattan.
1781-3—Wm. Nalle, Benj. Harrison.
1784—Gabriel Jones, John Hopkins.
1785-7—Gawen Hamilton, John Hopkins.
1788—John Hopkins, Geo. Huston.
1791—Francis Kertley, Geo. Baxter.
1793—John Hopkins, George Huston.

ROCKINGHAM COUNTY

1794—Geo. Baxter, Geo. Huston.
1795-7—Geo. Kirtley, John Wayt.
1797-8—John Koontz, Walter Davis.
1799-03—Geo. Huston, Benj. Harrison.
1803-06—H. J. Gamble, Daniel Smith.
1807-11—Arch. Rutherford.
1810-16—Arch. Rutherford, Wm. Bryan.
1817-18—J. D. Williamson, Wm. Bryan.
1818-19—Jos. Mauzy, Andrew Moffett.
1820-21—Daniel Mathews, John Henry.
1822-23—John Koontz, R. P. Fletcher.
1824—Arch. Rutherford, John Koontz. (?)
1825—Arch. Rutherford, Jos. Cline.
1826—Jos. Cline, Wm. McMahon.
1827—Samuel H. Lewis, Jos. Cline.
1828—Samuel H. Lewis, Wm. McMahon.
1829-33—Wm. McMahon, Jos. Cline.
1834—J. J. Moorman, A. Waterman.
1835—J. J. Moorman, Jos. Cline.
1836—A. Moffett, J. Conrad.
1837—A. Moffett, Saml. Cootes.
1838—S. Cootes, Isaac Thomas.
1839—Isaac Thomas, Ed. H. Smith.
1840-42—Ed. H. Smith, Jas. C. Shipman.
1842-3—S. Cootes, Geo. E. Deneale.
1844-5—S. Cootes, Hiram Martz.
1846—Hiram Martz, St. C. D. Kirtley.
1847—Naason Bare, ———— Brown.
1848—Naason Bare, H. Martz.
1849—H. Martz, Addison Harper.
1850-51—H. Martz, W. B. Yancey.
1852-53—H. Martz, N. Bare, W. G. Stevens.
1853-55—H. Martz, W. G. Stevens, J. M. R. Sprinkle.
1857—J. M. R. Sprinkle, J. G. Brown, W. B. Yancey.
1858—H. Martz, A. Harper, W. G. Stevens.
1861—Chas. Grattan, Reuben N. Harrison.
1862-3—Chas. Grattan, John C. Woodson, J. H. Hopkins.
1864-5—John T. Harris, John C. Walker, Jas. Kenney.
1866-7—J. C. Woodson, H. B. Harnsberger, W. G. Thompson.
1869-70—H. B. Harnsberger, Philo Bradley.
1871-2—Geo. E. Deneale, Chas. T. O'Ferrall.
1873-4—T. N. Sellers, E. J. Armstrong.
1875-6—E. J. Armstrong, W. M. Sibert.
1877-80—S. H. Moffett, R. N. Harrison.
1881-2—H. B. Harnsberger, P. Herring.
1883-4—Geo. G. Grattan, John F. Soule.
1885-6—John Acker, J. B. Webb.
1887-8—J. B. Webb, J. E. Sanger.
1889-90—Thos. K. Harnsberger, W. H. Blakemore.
1891-93—W. H. Blakemore, C. E. Fahrney.
1895-96—B. G. Patterson, W. H. Zirkle.
1897-8—W. H. Blakemore, D. M. Switzer.
1899-00—B. G. Patterson, W. H. Blakemore.
1900—Frank Ralston.
1901-2—Geo. E. Sipe, J. T. Robson.
1903-4—J. T. Robson, H. M. Rogers.
1905-8—H. M. Rodgers, P. B. F. Good.
1909-10—P. B. F. Good, A. H. Snyder.
1911-12—C. H. Ralston, Geo. N. Earman.

MEMBERS OF STATE SENATE.

1780—Sampson Mathews.
1786-7—Thomas Adams.
1791—Sampson Mathews.
1797—Alex. St. Clair.
1798—John Oliver.
1799-1800—Archd. Stuart.
1805—James Allen.
1811-17—Chapman Johnson.
1820—Daniel Bryan.
1821—Robert Allen.
1822—Daniel Bryan.
1823-26—Robert Allen.
1827-30—Moses Walton.
1831-33—Jos. Cravens.
1834-37—Wm. McMahon.
1838-45—A. Moffett.

A HISTORY OF

1846-58—Geo. E. Deneale.
1859-63—John D. Pennybacker.
1864-65—Samuel A. Coffman.
1866-68—A. S. Gray.
1869-73—John E. Roller.
1874-77—S. H. Moffett.
1878-80—John Paul.

1881-83—J. B. Webb.
1884-87—Geo. B. Keezell.
1888-91—John Acker.
1892-95—Thos. K. Harnsberger.
1896-1911—Geo. B. Keezell.
1912------John Paul, Jr.

MEMBERS OF STATE CONVENTIONS.

1788—Gabriel Jones, Thomas Lewis.
1829—J. D. Williamson, Peachy Harrison.
1851—John Kenney, ————————.
1861—S. A. Coffman, J. F. Lewis, A. S. Gray.
1867—J. N. Liggett, John C. Woodson.
1901—Geo. B. Keezell, Geo. N. Earman.

EARLY MARRIAGE RECORDS IN ROCKINGHAM COUNTY.

The following items are taken from the records of the Peaked Mountain Church:

Jacob Kropp	Anna Barbara Metzer	March 2, 1762
Peter Miller	Margaret Kropp	March 2, 1762
George Shillinger	Anna Elisabeth Horning	October, 1762
George Adam Mann	Elisabeth Herrmann	Dec. 7, 1762
Jacob Schaefer	Daughter of P. Bietfisch	June 27, 1796
Christian Geiger, sr.	Widow Dindore	Sept. 6, 1796
Christian Geiger	Emilia Schmidt	Sept. 25, 1796
George Schaefer	Elisabeth Vogt	Sept. 30, 1796

The following list is compiled from the records in the Rockingham County Clerk's office.

Wm. Ireland	Jennet Miller	Aug. 21, 1778
John Brown	Frances Gartra	Aug. 25, 1778
Alexr. Hannah	Mary Laird	Sept. 21, 1778
Robt. Gamble	Catharine Grattan	Feb. 6, 1779
John Clough	Frances Price	Feb. —, 1779
William Hogshead	Sarah Robertson	May 25, 1779
Josiah Harrison	Mary Cravens	July 23, 1779
James Harris	Sarah Whitesides	July 26, 1779
Jos. Haynes	Jane Young	Oct. 9, 1779
John Gregor	Christian Huston	Oct. 26, 1779
Thomas Hughes	Jane Lewis	Nov. 6, 1779
Zerah Osborn	Mary Doniphan	Dec. 10, 1779
James Sims	Sarah Sommers	Feb. 19, 1780
John Arckenbright	Elizabeth Bowen	March 28, 1780
David Hogshead	Agness Ralston	March 28, 1780
Wm. Holeman	Agness Shepherd	April 14, 1780
Jacob Lincoln	Darcus Robinson	Aug. 29, 1780
Joseph Hall	Edith Herring	Sept. 26, 1780
James Dyer	Jane Rolestone	Oct. 13, 1780
James Allen	Mary Herniche (?)	Nov. 17, 1780
William Bell	Ann Baird	Jan. 1, 1781
Jno. Hawkins	Anna Gabriella Jones	Jan. 15, 1781
John McWilliams	Margaret Coffey	Feb. 22, 1781
James Assent	Christian Swan	March 5, 1781
William Rice	Eleanor Denison	March 9, 1781
John Hopkins, jr.	Elizabeth Hopkins	March 20, 1781
Samuel Johnston	Mary Fulton	April 27, 1781
James Magill, jr.	Jane Fulton	May 28, 1781
John Hunter, jr.	Elizabeth Ozman	May, 1781
John Fulton	Jennet Dunn	June 23, 1781
John Lewis	Mary Elsee	Aug. 17, 1781
Thomas Mackelvain	Frances Price	Sept. 3, 1781
Peter Coger	Mary Mackelvain	Sept. 3, 1781
Jno. Cowan	Mary Craig	Sept. 11, 1781
Jacob Kester	Margaret Lear	Oct. 1, 1781
Richard Reins	Theodisia Eastridge	Oct. 12, 1781
Henry Nul	Marget Arey	Nov. 8, 1781

ROCKINGHAM COUNTY

Groom	Bride	Date
Arnold Custard	Margaret Woldredg	Nov. 21, 1781 (?)
John Slavin	Sarah Wade	Nov. 23, 1781
Frederick Nesslerod	——Fulmore (Vallmer)	Nov. 23, 1781
Isaac Hankle	Mary Cunningham	Nov. 26, 1781
Arnold Kester	Margaret Lair	Nov. 28, 1781
Zachariah Lee	Jean Bright	Dec. 3, 1781
Fredrick Boot	Christina Long	Dec. 4, 1781
Robert Weeb	Elizabeth Breeding	Dec. 18, 1781
William Leach	Margaret Marks	Jan. 2, 1782
Engel Bours	Catren Burckes	Jan. 3, 1782
Andrew Shanklin	Abigal Herring	March 16, 1782
Elijah Gartan	Sarah Boid	March 16, 1782
Denis Lanahan	Margaret Cravens	March 18, 1782
Philip Hinckel	Barbara Vallmer	April 5, 1782
William Crow	Hester Pettejohn	April 13, 1782
Handle Vance	Rebeckah Thomas	April 15, 1782
Wm. Ralston	Mary Hopkins	April 16, 1782
Brewer Reeves	Martha Smith	April 21, 1782
Wm. Dunlap	Catharine Sites	May 18, 1782
Robt. Poage	Mary Hopkins	June 17, 1782
David Hogshead	Cathrine Black	June 25, 1782
Benjamin Erwin	Sarah Bruster	July 23, 1782
Wm. Devier	Elizabeth Ewin	July 27, 1782
Joseph Dunlap	Mary Black	July 29, 1782
Bethuel Herring	Mary Miller	Aug. 16, 1782
Nathan Lamb	Nancy Ralston	Aug. 24, 1782
John Swartz (Black)	Barbara Sanger	Aug. 26, 1782
Thos. Karr	Jean Lewis	Sept. 12, 1782
David Garvin	Ann Cloverfield	Sept. 17, 1782
Thomas Lincoln	Elizabeth Casner	Sept. 23, 1782
Alexander Gilmer	Esther Magill	Sept. 24, 1782
George Pence	Margaret Carpenter	Oct. 12, 1782
Ferdinand Lair	Susanah Custard	Oct. 15, 1782
Stephen Ruddell	Sarah Bags	Oct. 20, 1782
Jacob Custar	Pheby Cutnar	Oct. 21, 1782
George Argenbright	Elizabeth Black	Oct. 25, 1782
Henry Barler	Jane Marshall	Nov. 3, 1782
Samuel Magill	Martha Shannon	Nov. 4, 1782
George Rush	Mary Bushang	Nov. 9, 1782
John Brock	Ann Jones	Nov. 26, 1782
Henry Gibson	Sarah Hester Gilbert	Dec. 2, 1782
John Shankling	Cathrine Franklin	Dec. 4, 1782
William Blain	Margret Chesnut	Dec. 23, 1782
Robert Belshe	Mary Claney	Jan. 3, 1783
John Pence	Barbara Zimerman	Jan. 10, 1783
John Rice	Rebeckah Elliott	Jan. 18, 1783
David Rolstone	Sarah Henton	Jan. 18, 1783
Ludwick Stephen	Anne Carpenter	Feb. 1, 1783
Peter Ferrel	Jane Wilard	Feb. 1, 1783
Peter Ferrol	Jean Whyatt	Feb. 8, 1783
John Heaton	Sarah Warden	March 7, 1783
Christian Rispe	Mary Spears	March 22, 1783
Robert Henry	Margaret Magill	March 28, 1783
Thomas Gordon	Catherine Davis	April 2, 1783
Frederick Hance	Franey Coffman	April 5, 1783
John McElheney	Mary Lewis	April 21, 1783
Thomas Gilmer	Elizabeth Lewis	April 21, 1783
Jacob Roadarmour	Katy Argabright	May 3, 1783
John Lauk	Barbara Woolrige	May 10, 1783
James Denison	Hannah Fulton	May 12, 1783
Jacob Hammond	Elizabeth Guise	June 2, 1783
Richard Smith	Mary Dickey	June 23, 1783
Charles McClean	Margaret Dictum	Aug. 8, 1783
John Riddel	Deborah Bryan	Aug. 13, 1783
Henry Sites	Mary Dunlap	Aug. 15, 1783
Adam Bible	Modelean Shumaker	Sept. 17, 1783
Andrew Johnston	Else Black	Oct. 11, 1783
Benja. Henton	Sarah Hopkins	Oct. 13, 1783
John Knave	Susannah Shaver	Oct. 20, 1783
Danl. Benj. Bailey	Lydia Goodpasture	Oct. 22, 1783

A HISTORY OF

Isaac Kiser	Mary Harrison	Oct. 23, 1783
David Stephenson	Mary Davies	Nov. 11, 1783
Michael Foizle	Elizabeth Bush	Nov. 16, 1783
John Kesterson	Elizabeth Whiteman	Nov. 29, 1783
Ebenezer Henton	Emele Mathews	Dec. 12, 1783
George Knave	Fany More	Dec. 19, 1783
Philip Keplinger	Barbara Mauk	Jan. 1, 1784
Anthony Alison	Mary Hatfield	Jan. 17, 1784
Daniel Harrison	Ann Patton	Jan. 29, 1784
Michael Harrison	Margret Ragan	Feb. 9, 1784
Jesse Harrison	Elizabeth Wilson	March 5, 1784
Cristian Miller	Dorothy Bradshaw	March 18, 1784
Matt. Boyers	Ann Morris	April 3, 1784
Gideon Harrisson	Mary Brian	April 24, 1784
John Devier	Mary Collins	May 24, 1784
Wm. Lusby	Easter Hair	May 24, 1784
Charles Sparkes	Jane Neilson	July 19, 1784
Conrad Keller	Elizabeth Helfrey	July 21, 1784
John Hair	Sarah Stinson	July 27, 1784
Benj. Wheaton	Mary Wease	Aug. 9, 1784
John Gristley	Elizabeth Redman	Aug. 18, 1784
Robt. Harrison	Polly Harrison	Sept. 11, 1784
Robert Young	Jean Burley	Oct. 5, 1784
Henry Black	Elizabeth Hammer	Oct. 16, 1784
John Hays	Marey Ragan	Nov. 22, 1784
Jacob Argabright	Mary Fifer	Dec. 4, 1784
John Flack	Mary Crow	Dec. 6, 1784
David Smith	Isabella Duncason	Dec. 13, 1784
Hugh Guin	Margret Fairbern	Sept. 27, 1785
Jacob Rape	Cathrine Howel	Sept. —, 1785
Robert Harnsberger	Christeny Miller	Dec. 30, 1785
Josiah Harrison	Margret Miller	Jan. 4, 1786
Elijah Russell	Katy Armentrout	Jan. 23, 1786
Michl. Hennesey	Anny Lang	Feb. 9, 1786
James Doak	Jenet Fulton	Feb. 20, 1786
Benjamin Berry	Johanna Berry	Feb. 21, 1786
Frederick Swartz (Black)	Mary Argabright	March 25, 1786
Henry Ceplinger	Barbary Harpole	March 27, 1786
Abraham Louderback	Margaret Ammon	April 10, 1786
David Brumfield	Patience Tallman	April 12, 1786
John Daniel Moyer	Nancy Culburt	April 24, 1786
John Rimel	Margaret Lincoln	April 26, 1786
Mathias Lung	Elizabeth Munger	April 28, 1786
John Bair	Elizabeth Pup	April 28, 1786
George Ruddell	Mary Goar	May 4, 1786
John Wiseman	Sarah Green	May 8, 1786
William Bryan, jr.	Nancy Celley	May 13, 1786
William Tallman	Phebe Henton	May 30, 1786
Henry Nicholas	Molly Coffelt	June 12, 1786
John Blizard	Catherine Kester	June 16, 1786
Henry Hammer	Mary Davis	June 21, 1786
George Sirkel	Cathrine West	July 24, 1786
James McMichal	Nelly Cranny	July 28, 1786
John Ridenhouse	Christian Sumervalt	Aug. 1, 1786
Thomas Woodward	Elizabeth Chesnut	Aug. 2, 1786
John Johnston	Margret Greimes	Aug. 5, 1786
Spencer Breeding	Elizabeth Finney	Aug. 5, 1786
Henry Hauk (?)	Margaret Thomas	Aug. 22, 1786
John Patton	Mary Hopkins	Aug. 29, 1786
John Taylor	Ann Gilbert	Aug. 31, 1786
Adam Shillinger	Elizabeth Man	Sept. 22, 1786
William Kiser	Charety Fridley	Sept. 25, 1786
Abraham Beary	Modlenah Rife	Sept. 28, 1786
John Geabhart	Rachel Allin	Sept. 29, 1786
George Dice (Tice)	Mary Dice	Oct. 2, 1786
Henry Armentrout	Elizabeth Argabright	Oct. 20, 1786
John McDonald	Elizabeth Crawford	Nov. 7, 1786
George Springer, jr.	Catherine Earhart	Nov. 11, 1786
Jacob McLey	Catherine Ogan	Nov. 13, 1786
Jacob Cowger	Catherine Harpole	Nov. 16, 1786

ROCKINGHAM COUNTY

Michael Keller	Barbary Roadarmor	Nov. 17, 1786
Thomas Fitzwater	Mary Been	Nov. 17, 1786
George Bowers	Cathrine Tulee	Nov. 18, 1786
Jacob Runkle	Rebeccah Price	Nov. 25, 1786
David Garvin	Sarah Bush	Nov. 26, 1786
Stophel How	Elizabeth Harman	Nov. 27, 1786
James Gamble	Margaret McHenry	Dec. 13, 1786
Peter Nicholas	Euly Boshang	Dec. 20, 1786
Christian Leeah	Elizabeth Armentrout	Dec. 21, 1786
George Prise	Mary Runkle	Dec. 25, 1786
John Pitner	Elizabeth Fifer	Nov. 16, 1788
John Matheas	Elizabeth Lokey	Nov. 13, 1789
Gulhery Homes	Sally Cooper	Jan. 27, 1790
Andrew Shankling	Sarah Huet	Feb. 15, 1790
Wileam Shaklen (?)	Ruth Hareson	Feb. 25, 1790
Samuel Smallridg	Ann Jarrel	March 10, 1790
Jessy Oneal	Barbary Rambo	July 11, 1790 (?)
Jacob Rambo	Cathene Hnlen	July 19, 1790
John Hoof	Deaborah Hatheway	Aug. 24, 1790
Franses Sanford Settles	Elisabeth Armstrong	Aug. 30, 1790
Heanery Caster	Hannah Smith	Nov. 24, 1790
Thomas Harysen	Sally Oliver (?)	Dec. 22, 1790
James Brown	Nancy Shpman	Jan. 4, 1791
Edward Evins	Ann Heanicy	April 24, 1791
Rubin Harison	Mary Mathes	April 26, 1791
James Lang	Eleoner Hansford	July 24, 1791
Thomas Loky	Sarah Reaves (?)	Sept. 13, 1791
Bazilia Ragin	Jean Ditums	Oct. 3, 1791
Jephtheh Moore	Nancy Ragin	Nov. 14, 1791
James Graham	Jean Beard	Nov. 24, 1791
George Fridley	Sarah Woolford	Dec. 20, 1791
Abraham Nickemon	Mary Stephenson	Dec. 31, 1791
Nathaniel Harrisson	Mary Woodly	Date illegible
Samuel McWilliams	Edith Harrison	Jan. 16, 1792
Matthias Long	Mary Heastand	Jan. 31, 1792
Daniel Ragin	Rhebe Harrison	Mar. 1, 1792
Henry Smith	Margaret Cravens	Apr. 2, 1792
Adam Flower	Mary Weaggy	April 9, 1792
Benjamin Smith	Mary Ewin	April 19, 1792
James Mohoney	Sarraih Berry	Apr. 21, 1792
David Garvin	Barbara Maggart	Apr. 23, 1792
Aaron Sollomon	Susanah Rader	Sept. 1, 1792
John Carthrea	Sophia Lewis	Sept. 24, 1792
John Travis	Elizabeth Oliver	Sept. 26, 1792
Henry Ewin	Abigail Davisson	Sept. 29, 1792
John Reader	Sally Spears	Oct. 2, 1792
Patrick McGuyer	Nelly Huston	Oct. 3, 1792
Andrews Woolf	Hannah Kyror	Oct. 24, 1792
John Swick	Catterena Shafer	Nov. 9, 1792
Henry Rolestone	Sarah Sempil	Nov. 20, 1792
Charles Wheafer (?)	Keatren Shafer	Dec. 6, 1792
Benjamin Grace	Catherine Lair	Dec. 15, 1792
Elias Vicars	Phebe Loid	Dec. 19, 1792
Abraham Crumpacker	Mary Rife	Dec. 25, 1792
Jacob Johnson	Betsy Church	Dec. 28, 1792
John Lauk	Susanna Moore	Dec. 29, 1792
Lewis Sheridan	Mary Joseph	Dec. 30, 1792
Henry Kite	Elizabeth Heastand	Jan. 1, 1793
Henery Barrot	Mary Lukes	Jan. 1, 1793
George Brown	Barbara Upleman	Jan. 3, 1793
David Dudley	Keziah Short	Jan. 8, 1793
Samuel Pullins	Jane Henry	Jan. 22, 1793
John Kagy	Margaret Fridley	Mar. 10, 1793
Alexr. Keran	Peggy Smith	March 14, 1793
John Meineck	Catrin Rader	March 19, 1793
Joel Crumbaker	Elizabeth Rife	March 31, 1793
John Laundrice	Catherine Coffman	Apr. 7, 1793
William Lowry	Sarah Herrings	Apr. 9, 1793
Peter Winegord	Eve Hooke	Apr. 13, 1793
Thomas Waren	Elizabeth Harrison	May 2, 1793

A HISTORY OF

John Palmer	Leodosia Eaton	May 13, 1798
Asa Webb	Mary Shanklin	May 16, 1793
James Molloy	Sarah Shepherd	May 25, 1793
James Dickey	Eliz. Burges	May 27, 1793
Jacob Christman	Barbara Paulson	May 28, 1793
George Wells	Jane Reagan	May 28, 1793
Wm. Thomson	Jennet Shanklin	June 13, 1793
George Philips	Rachel Hinton	July 22, 1793
William Kite	Elizabeth Grims	July 28, 1793
Conrad Helmer	Fanny A. Mulatto	Aug. 3, 1793
John Spears	Margret Chrisman	Aug. 30, 1793
William Baily	Elinor Gum	Sept. 8, 1793
John Argubright	Anne Smith	Sept. 9, 1793
Henry Funk	Susenna Frey	Sept. 12, 1793
Samuel Chandler	Elizabeth Nezbet	Sept. 25, 1793
Joseph Snapp	Margaret Cravens	Oct. 1, 1793
Joseph Thornton	Catharine Snap	Oct. 3, 1793
Elliot Rutherford	Barbara Miller	Oct. 21, 1793
John Sellers	Heany Smith	Oct. 28, 1793
Jonathan Newman	Hannah Spears	Nov. 1, 1793
Philip Royer	Keaty Keller	Nov. 5, 1793
David Noftsinger	Hannah Crumpacker	Nov. 14, 1793
Leonard Berry	Magdalene Sibeley	Dec. 31, 1793
Daniel Spangler	Nancy Dictom	Jan. 2, 1794
James Harrison	Anne Mellon	Jan. 27, 1794
William Cravens	Jane Harrison	Jan. 29, 1794
Thos. Pullins	Jane Henry	Feb. 18, 1794
John Segfried	Eliz. Black	Feb. 24, 1794
Christian Keagy	Mary Peepler	March 17, 1794
James Burgess	Mary Beard	March 20, 1794
Adam Howard	Keaty Bumgardner	March 20, 1794
George Huston	Susanna Snap	March 20, 1794
David Spangler	Margaret Snap	March 20, 1794
William Reans	Eve Stonebuck	March 24, 1794
Christian Denice	Barbara Roller	March 27, 1794
John Wright	Elizabeth Erwin	April 3, 1794
George Snowden	Elizabeth Rice	April 10, 1794
Aron Turley	Rebecca Howland	April 12, 1794
James Shanklin	Hannah Hopkins	May 13, 1794
George Millar	Sarah Custerd	May 24, 1794
Philip Kennerly	Jane Carthrae	June 19, 1794
Isaac Depoy	Anna Yeakley	July 8, 1794
Jacob Twitwiler	Anna Aldoffer	July 9, 1794
Henry Bear	Barbara Howman	July 24, 1794
George Surphos	Christianna Long	July 28, 1794
Leonard Oliver	Rosanna Dashner	Aug. 1, 1794
George Robins	Catherine Laulcer	Aug. 9, 1794
James Bggs	Marey Custer	Aug. 28, 1794
Isaac Norman	Hannah Herring	Sept. 2, 1794
Marten Heggins	Cateren Ember	Sept. 3 (?), 1794
David Gilmor	Margrat Smith	Sept. 3 (?), 1794
William Robeson	Barbra Cofman	Sept. 3 (?), 1794
James Green	Nancy Yeates	Sept. 3 (?), 1794
John Davis	Sarah Dokerty	Sept. 19, 1794
John Hudlow	Elizabeth Croft	Oct. 2, 1794
Samuel Day	Hannah Bowen	Oct. 22, 1794
Jacob Johnston	Freelove Wilcocks	Oct. 23, 1794
William Mitchel	Eve Nestreete	Oct. 26, 1794
Jacob Fulks	Margreat Dispenett	Nov. 2, 1794
Jacob Percy	Abbigail McDowell	Nov. 6, 1794
Jacob Deppoy	Elizabeth Lemon	Nov. 11, 1794
John Shafer	Mary Pence	Nov. 25, 1794
Thomas Travis	Margaret Miller	Dec. 16, 1794
John Armontrout	Charlotte Helfreegh	Dec. 16, 1794
Alexander Graham	Anna Herdman	Dec. 30, 1794
John Green	Amelia Mathews	————, 1794
Christian Fry	Elizabeth Minnick	————, 1794
John Johnston	Mary Wooledge	————, 1794
Joseph Carercy	Pheby Sheffing	————, 1794
Arnold Ford	Mary Runion	————, 1794

ROCKINGHAM COUNTY

LARGE LANDOWNERS OF ROCKINGHAM CO. IN THE YEAR 1789

Lists compiled from the Original Manuscripts in the County Clerk's Office.

The number preceding the name of each individual indicates the militia-company district to which he belonged; the number following his name shows the number of acres of land he owned.

LIST BY RALPH LOFTUS, COMMISSIONER

4 Amond, Mathias, 1180.
5 Argabright, Martin, 508.
2 Berry, Benjamin, 901.
2 Baxter, George, 1196.
3 Butt, Windle, 557.
4 Beard, James, 1365.
6 Briant, Thomas, Sr., 954.
6 Burkholder, Peter, 543.
7 Baker, Michael, 581.
2 Crawford, Geo. A., 800.
4 Cathrea, John, 890.
5 Cravens, Robert, 539.
1 Douglass, Joseph, 975.
1 Dever, William, 575.
1 Dever, Hugh, 506.
1 Davies, John, 1380.
2 Davison, Josiah, 980.
4 Donaghe, Hugh, 734.
5 Dever, James, Land Co., 1283.
2 Cruins, John, Sr., 875.
5 Cuins, Henry, 1101.
4 Fisher, Abraham, 514.
2 Green, Francis, 703.
8 Grattan, Jn., 2047.
6 Grattan, John, 915.
1 Heart, Silas, 704.
1 Hamilton, Gawin, 952.
3 Hopkins, Arch, Jr., 586.
2 Hopkins, Arch, Sr., 1551.

2 Herdman, John, Jr., 572.
2 Harrison, Jess, Sr., 544.
3 Herring, William, 516.
4 Huston, George, 703.
4 Houlder, Michael, 680.
5 Harrison, Benjamin, 1024.
5 Harrison, Robert & Reuben, 1620.
5 Harrison, Thomas, 860.
5 Hemphill, Samuel, 653.
6 Kesler, Woolery, 550.
1 Miller, John, 748.
1 Miller, Henry, 671.
4 Machall, John, 1282.
5 Miller, Samuel's exrs., 636.
1 Rice, John, 861.
3 Roler, Peter, 1033.
6 Ruddle, Cornelius, 704.
1 Smith, William, 858.
1 Smith, Henry, 1053.
1 Smith, Joseph, 582.
2 Shanklin, Thomas, 853.
3 Shanklin, Edward, 575.
4 Snap, John, 629.
5 Stephenson, Caster, 879.
5 Smith, Benjamin, 955.
7 Shoemaker, George, 500.
6 Thomas, John, 683.
1 Walker, Thomas, 900.
5 Winger, Henry, 500.

LIST BY REUBEN MOORE, COMMISSIONER.

8 Josiah Harrison's Company.
9 Ezekiel Harrison's Company.
10 Richard Ragan's Company.
11 John Rush's Company.
12 Casper Hains' Company.
13 Henry Miller's Company.
14 Michael Rorick's Company.
9 Andrews, Andrew, 600.
9 Bear, John, Sr., 836.
3 Crim, Peter, 516.
10 Crow, Walter, 759.
10 Crotzer, Joseph, 641 1-2.
11 Craig, John, 1314.
12 Carsh, Matthias, 680.
12 Conrad, Peter, 890.
12 Conrad, George, 844.
13 Davis, William, 841.
9 Fifer, Adam, Sr., 602.
8 Harrison, Reuben, 1204.
8 Harrison, Zebulon, 575.
8 Harrison, Matthew, 900.
9 Hoover, Jacob, 516.
10 Harrison, John, 933.
10 Hagay, Godfrey, 730.
10 Harned, David, 795.

12 Headrick, John, 625.
11 Jones, Gabriel, 1004.
10 Kessle, George, 810.
11 Kislinger, Jacob, 615.
12 Kirtley, Francis, 824.
14 Kisore, Michael, 566.
8 Lokey, Thomas, 530.
11 Lewis, Thomas, Sr., 2050.
8 March, Sabaston, 515.
8 Moore, Thomas, Sr., 1070.
9 Moore, John Quaker, 1088.
13 Miller, Henry & Elizabeth, 1315.
14 Null, Henry, 695.
8 Phillips, John, Sr., 540.
11 Pence, George, 703.
11 Perkey, John, 515.
11 Perkey, Henry, 515.
11 Price, Augusteen, Sr., 531.
10 Ragan, Richard, 736.
11 Rush, Charles, 553.
8 Sircle, Ludwick, 932.
10 Smith, Jane, Sr., 500.
10 Smith, Benjamin, 500.
11 Swisher, John, 676.
12 Sellers, Adam, 1154.

MUSTER ROLLS OF ROCKINGHAM SOLDIERS.

A list of Captain William Nall's company of volunteers from Augusta County, in the campaign to Point Pleasant, 1774.

A HISTORY OF

William Nalle, Capt.
Martain Nalle, Lt.
Jacob Pence, Ensign
William Bush, Ser.
John Bush, Ser.
Barnod Crafford, Ser.
Shadrick Butler
William Feavil
Robert Rains
Moses Smith
Steven Washburn
Israel Meader
Henry Owler
John Grigsby
Richard Welsh
Zacarias Lee
John Goodall
Bengaman Petty

Michael Gurden
Bruten Smith
James Todd
William Spicer
James Washbun
Charles Brown
James Alexander
George Rucker
Joseph Roay
William Scails
John Pright
Yenty Jackson
John Owler
George Fuls
James Miller
George Harmon
John Chism
Adam Hansburger 1

Henry Cook
John Breden
Thomas Brook
Henry Miner
Chesly Rogers
Sefniah Lee
Zacarias Plunkepel
Mecagh Smith
William Smith
John Deek (Deck)
John fy (Fry?)
John Williams
Joseph Butler
James Selby
James Reary
Abraham Rue
Jacob Null
John Null 2

CAPT. DANIEL MATHEWS' CO., 116TH REG. VA. VOLS.
(Entered service July 7, 1813.)

Daniel Matthews, capt.; William Woodward, lt.; John F. Effinger, ensign; Daniel Pickering, 1st ser.; Warner Peters, 1st cor.; William F. Brown, 2d cor.; George Hill, 3d cor.; Fredrick Hartman, 4th cor.; Elisha Hooke, 5th cor.; John Henning, 6th cor.; John Haney, drummer; Henry Rader, fifer.

William Heavener
William Lacrost
Thomas Brown
James Bogers
Andrew Brown
Abram Bushong
John Berry
George Berry
Kinley Berry
Elisha Bryan
Reuben Bogan
John Bible
Henry Baker
Philip Carey
Mayberry Curry
Henry Carrico
Jacob Crim
Thomas Clemmings
Thomas Deane
Philip Eary
John Feagle
John Farris

Henry Fisher
Isaac Flemming
William Graves
Jacob Groves
Samuel Huling
Henry Heddecker
Peter Hinton
John Haudley
Joseph Holland
Fredrick Hartman
Elisha Hooke
John Heavener
Silas Hinton
John Jack
Nelson Kimbrough
Joseph Laten
William Doyd
Henry Miller
John Miller
James Montague
Peter Michael
Jacob Messick

Andrew Orebaugh
Stephen Oglesby
Philip Peach
Christian Rankle
John Rust
Abram Rust
George Rumsey
George Rue
William Rutledge
David Swisher
Jacob Silknetter
Samuel Suelling
Mathias Snider
William B. Smith
William Souveraine
John Stubs
Jesse Thorp
Alexander Trout
Mathew Trumbo
Andrew Wesley
Jacob Wither
John Wright

CAPT. THOS. HOPKINS' CO., 116TH REG. VA. VOLS.
(Entered service July 7, 1813.)

Thomas Hopkins, capt.; John McLaughlin, lt.; John J. Salvage, 1st ser.; Silas Hinton, 2d ser.; Jesse Harmer, 3d ser.; William Heavener, 4th ser.; Matthew Snider, 1st cor.; Jacob Massie, 2d cor.; Michael Markwood, drummer; Henry Rider, fifer.

Rinley Berry
Elisha Berry
Reuben Bryan
John Berry
George Berry

John Bible
John Crim
John Faris
John Fink
George Fultz

Joshua Fate
William Fitzwater
Isaac Hare
John Hill
Nelson Kimbrough

---

1. Adam Hansburger was the grandfather of Capt. J. Sam'l Harnsberger.

2. The above list is made up from the list of Captain Nall's company as given on page 405 of Thwaites and Kellogg's Documentary History of Dunmore's War; and the company was made up chiefly, if not entirely, from what is now Rockingham.—See pages 63, 64, above.

ROCKINGHAM COUNTY

Isaac Lincoln
Arthur McCord
George Messick
John Miller
Abram Orebaugh

Andrew Orebaugh
John Wright
John Stiles
William B. Smith
John Stully

Christian Souverine
Alexander Trout
Jacob Whetzel
Jacob Witt

CAPT. ROBT. HOOKE'S CO., 58TH REG. VA. VOLS.

(Entered service July 8, 1813.)

Robert Hooke, capt.; James Hooke, lt.; Richard S. Emmitt, ensign; Charles Burton, 1st ser.; Charles Blaine, 2d ser.; Charles Hudlow, 3d ser.; Jacob Fisher, 4th ser.; John Rust, 1st cor.; Jacob Rust, 2d cor.; Thomas Rice, 3d cor.; John Fisher, 4th cor.; Stephen Oglesby, 5th cor.; Thomas Deane, 6th cor.; George Baker, 7th cor.

William Armentrout
George Armentrout
John Baker
George Baker
John Burnett
Henry Baker
Peter Bowyer
Jacob Chrisman
David Crickenberger
Benjamin Cash
William Campbell
William Cline
Henry Sipe
John Fisher
John Feagle
Joseph Holland
Jacob Harnesberger

John Harnesberger
John Hedrick
John Hanley
James A. Hooke
Christian Hawk
John Hanna
Peter Kesler
Daniel Kesler
Henry Keller
Lewis Keller
John Lammon
Thomas Lewis
George Middleberger
Adam May
Alexander Ogg
Henry Probst
John Pence

Jacob Pence
Adam Pence
Edward Price
Jacob Ritter
Michael Ritter
George Rumsey
George Reece
Abram Rust
Christian Bowyer
John Shipp
Jacob Shirley
Samuel Swisher
Nathaniel Swisher
Henry Sack
George Shank
Jesse Thompson
Henry Ulstaw
Henry Winkle

CAPT. ROBT. MAGILL'S CO., 38TH REG. VA. VOLS.

(Entered service July 8, 1813.)

Robert Magill, capt.; John McLaughlin, lt.; Jacob Spader, ensign; Abram Smith, ord. ser.; George Mallow, 2d ser.; John Lawson, 3d ser.; John Viger, 1st cor.; Augustine Allen, 2d cor.; John Irwin, 3d cor.; Henry Gilmore, 4th cor.

Richard Rankin
Jacob Amole
Christian Boody
Aaron Back
Fredrick Cupp
John Cahoon
Benjamin Cove
Jacob Ditmer
David Dofflemire
William Davis
Adam Howdyshell
Isaac Hare
Christian Kite
David Dosburne
Peter Freysinger
George Fultz
William Fitzwater
Joseph Gladen

William Graves
Samuel Gross
John Harnesbarger
Peter Ryler
Philip Linsay
James Lady
Simon Lucas
Matthias Lore
David Loush
Isaac Lincoln
Peter Lindsay
John Matheny
Conrad Morrice
John Morrice
Jacob Maiden
Ephriam Meadows
Arthur McCord
Adam Orebaugh
Henry Peterfish

George Peterfish
Patrick Reins
Bennett Reigns
Abram Roots
Samuel Rites
William Rutledge
Moses Sutton
John Shank
Joseph Snider
Emanuel Sherman
Emanuel Sipe
John Stilt
Joshua Tate
Jacob Whitsell
Charles Weaver
Joseph Waggoner
Christian Ulster
Samuel Utes
John Yorges

CAPT. WM. HARRISON'S CO., 1ST VA. VOLS.

(Entered service August 29, 1814.)

Wm. Harrison, capt.; Peter Sprinkle, 1st lt.; Zephaniah Wade, 3d lt.; John Sheets, 1st ensign; Thomas Hinton, 2d ensign; Philip Armentrout, 1st ser.; Henry Armentrout, 2d ser.; Benjamin Fawcett, 3d ser.; John Cowen, 4th ser.; David Armentrout, 5th ser.; Daniel Witts, 6th ser.; Moses Cummings, 1st cor.; Abram Flesher, 2d cor.; Martin Martz, 3d cor.; John Wade, 4th cor.; Joseph Wade, 5th cor.; David Wallace, 6th cor.; Jacob Sheets,

A HISTORY OF

7th cor.; James Dean, 8th cor.; Abram Armentrout, drummer; Matthew Miller, fifer.

Fredrick Armentrout
Jacob Armentrout
Jacob Alstat
Felix Albert
Christian Argabright
Philip Armentrout
Thomas Bachelor
Augustus Armentrout
Michael Beaver
Joseph Blain
Henry Bare
Jacob Bare
R. W. Berkhead
Voluntine Bolton
Thomas Beard
Henry Cowen
Thomas Cottrel
Conrad Cove
Jacob Crider
Michael Clinepelter
William Cherryhomes
Andrew Doreman
David Doreman
Chrisley Doreman
Thomas Dehart
James Duffy
Christopher Eighinger
George Fridley
Charles Fridley
John Fuzet
Jacob Flock
John Fogle
Jacob Fogle
Caleb Fitzpatrick
John Fisher
William Flint

Joseph Fifer
Peter Grout
David Grout
Jacob Heidecker, sr.
Gasper Haynes
George Hiniker
Michael Hilbert
Jacob Heidecker, jr.
Joseph Huling
John Huffman
Bernard Huffman
George Hammon
Peter Hinton
George Hiser
Samuel Jewell
George Rifer
Abram Knopp
Reuben King
Henry Kiser
David Kisley
William Layman
John Layman
David Layman
Adam Lash
Fredrick Long
Paul Long
Mathias Long
Abram Lauderback
Sebastian Martz
Jacob Martz
George Miller
Jacob Miller
Daniel Moyers
George Moyers
John Miller
John Nave

John Overholt
George Overholt
Henery Peters
William Pickering
Henry Pirkey
Jacob Pirkey
John Roadcap
Jacob Rhodes
Michael Roller
William Richwine
George Rader
Philip Reedy
George Spinkley
George Smith
John Sellers
Gasper Stoutmeyer
George Smith
Daniel Smith
Christopher Schooltz
Peter Stone
George Siles
John Sheets
Crisian Sipe
Joseph Stock
Rodey Tate
Moses Tomah
William Terry
Jacob Trout
David Timberlake
John Whitmore
John Wise
Daniel Wise
David Whitmore
Peter Williams
Charles Weaver
John Zimmers
Christly Zimmers

CO. B, 10TH VA. VOL. INF.
(Rockingham Rifles.)

James Kenney, capt.; Isaac G. Coffman, 1st lt.; Wm. D. Trout, 2d lt.; David A. Jones, 3d lt.; Wm. H. Waesche, 1st ser.; Samuel M. Jones, 2d ser.; Jos. H. Kelley, 3d ser.; Lewis J. Cordell, 4th ser.; Jos. A. Rice, 1st cor.; B. F. Hughes, 2d cor.; J. H. Helphenstine, 3d cor.

Thos. W. Basford
Joseph Bezanzon
James Bowles
Wm. Brown
B. F. Caldwell
W. McK. Coffman
A. Crow
James Curry
Geo. C. Everding
Robt. B. Ewan
Oliver Ferrell
Francis Flick
James J. Fultz
James B. Fultz
James Furry
John Gaither
W. C. R. Gray
Jacob R. Grove
W. A. B. Haney
Wm. P. Kemper
Wm. M. Kemper
Geo. B. Kemper

John Kenney
A. Koontz
Robt. Koontz
E. B. Knipple (Aug. Co.)
Andrew Lewis
Geo. R. Lewis
Jas. A. Lewis
Wm. M. Lewis
Chas. T. Liggett
Robt. Long
Jno. C. Mauck
A. B. Martz
James May
Wm. Miller
James Moore
L. R. McCauley
John McCrary
L. Mohler (Aug. Co.)
Henry Murray
J. B. Odor
Asbury B. Payne
Wm. H. Payne
James W. Payne

James E. Phillips
H. J. Pritchard (Fred.Co.)
Robt. B. Ragan
Lewis W. Reherd
J. D. S. Reamer
George Rimel
James Roadcap
John Roadcap
John Roadcap of P.
J. K. Ryan (Aug. Co.)
Geo. W. Salyards
George Sipe
David Smith
J. G. Sprenkel
R. Steele
Isaac Timmons
Joseph Waters
W. H. H. Wheeler (A.C.)
John T. Wilkins
James Williams
James H. Wolfrey
C. Yeakle
Jacob H. Yost

—From Rockingham Register, August 16, 1861.

ROCKINGHAM COUNTY

CO. D, 10TH VA. VOL. INF.

(Bridgewater Grays.)

Brown, John S., capt.; Brown, Wm. R., 1st lt.; Smals, Adam H., 2d lt.; Pool, G. H., 3d lt.; Linhoss, Fred., ord. ser.; Messick, B. F., 2d ser.; Berry, D. N., 3d ser.; Childress, M. B., 4th ser.; Harmon, B. F., 1st cor.; Chandler, R. C., 2d cor.; Thompson, J. L., 3d cor.; Wheeler, Peter, 4th cor.

Brown, M. H.
Byrd, L. S.
Bricker, Abner
Bricker, G. W.
Berry, S. K.
Cave, Hamilton
Click, J. B.
Cook, John
Coffman, T. R.
Coffman, J. S.
Copenhaver, G. E.
Decker, R. S.
Furry, Wm. J.
Flemming, Harrison
Herring, Philander

Haney, G. W.
Haney, John
Hatfield, John
Howdishell, Jacob
Holland, Peter
Jordan, A. J.
Jones, Thomas
Kibler, Charles
Longley, Charles
Linhoss, D. H.
Long, John
Lash, Andrew
Mowry, J. A.
Minnick, James
Minnick, Elijah

Peterson, J. J.
Rogers, Albert
Rohr, Stansberry,
Srecker, F. W.
Smals, N. M.
Sheets, Christian
Sandy, R. W.
Shiflett, Noah
Stinespring, W. H.
Taylor, G. W.
Taylor, J. E.
Terrell, A. J.
Terrell, St. C.
Vance, A. H.
Wise, R. J.

—From Hardesty's Encyclopedia, p. 398.

CO. C, 10TH VA. VOL. INF.

(Organized January, 1862.)

Robt. C. Mauck, capt.

Lieutenants.

Melhorn, John W.
Brown, Milton
Riddleberger, H. H.
Donaghen, John

Privates.

Amiss, George
Armentrout, J. P.
Ball, James
Bamber, William
Berry, Samuel
Bowman, John R.
Bowman, Noah W.
Brown, Frank
Carroll, James
Cave, Wesley A.
Coffman, Wm. McK.
Crow, John
Dovel, Daniel D.

Falls, William
Fearneyhough, Wm.
Fisher, Burt
Fletcher, John
Gaither, Geo. W.
Gibbs, Charley
Gibbs, William
Gowl, William
Gray, George
Hern, Samuel
Hurley, Daniel
Jones, H. Clay
Kirkpatrick, John
Kirkpatrick, Thos.
Lamb, Allen
Leehan, Jack
Logan, N. W.
Long, Joseph
Long, Wm. C.
Lowery, Joseph
McCreary, Douglass

Manning, Wm.
Miller, Benj.
Morris, Silas
Moss, Rial
Nisewarner, John
Phillips, Frederick
Phillips, Thad.
Polen, James
Ragan, John G.
Rhinehart, Algernon
Roadcap, James
Roadcap, John
Shifflet, D.
Shifflet, Robert
Summers, David
Swanson, Joseph
Terrell, Calvin
Vanpelt, Arch
Ward, John
Way, Ferdinand
Way, Frank
Way, G. W.

—From Col. D. H. Lee Martz's rolls.

CO. E, 10TH VA. VOL. INF.

(Mustered in June 30, 1863.)

Yancey, Wm. B., capt.; Kisling, W. G., 1st lt.; Hawkins, J. H., 2d lt.; Mauzy, T. G., 3d lt.; Rush, J. B., 1st ser.; Hammon, C. E., 2d ser.; Dunnivin, James, 3d ser.; Wyant, Augustine, 4th ser.; Leap, E. A., 1st cor.; Sipe, J. F., 2d cor.; Wyant, D. W., 3d cor.; May, S. A., 4th cor.

Breedin, Calvin
Booze, John
Boyers, Jacob
Bauserman, Joseph
Bauserman, G. W.
Britt, Wm.
Carikoff, Peter

Dennet, G. R.
Davis, John
Hamer, J. M.
Harman, B. F.
Johnson, David
Lamb, H. J.
Lilly, H. B.

Lafferty, Addison
Michaels, W. F.
Morris, Harrison
Royer, Noah A.
Whitmer, J. S.
Wyant, Isaac
Williams, George
Williams, Joseph

—From Hardesty's Encyclopedia, p. 398.

A HISTORY OF

CO. G, 10TH VA. VOL. INF.
(Valley Guards.)

Captains
Sprinkel, C. A.
Martz, D. H. Lee
Campbell, Chas. F.

Lieutenants
Walker, Samuel T.
Hardesty, J. N. A.
Bryan, Pendleton
Eastham, C. Byrd
Guiheen, Maurice
Smith, Dorman L.
Houck, John W.
Shank, Gabriel

Privates
Armentrout, Geo. D.
Braithwaite, W. S.
Braithwaite, Jacob N.
Billhimer, Wm. M.
Bowman, Robert
Black, Joseph M.
Bear, John
Blakemore, Wm. H.
Brown, Wm. G.
Braithwaite, Newton H.
Coffman, M. D.
Cootes, B. F.
Crickenberger, Daniel
Dice, P. H.
Devier, Newton
Dice, Thomas H.
Effinger, G. M.
Fletcher, A. K.

Funkhouser, David
Gordon, James H.
Garrison, James
Greiner, N. Lee
Grandstaff, H. P.
Giles, Samuel N.
Guyer, Peter
Gray, James H.
Good, Wm. H.
Harrigan, Daniel
Houston, Jno. W. C.
Hutchens, Sam'l W.
Heatwole, David H.
Heatwole, Gabriel S.
Hooke, Elisha
Irvine, A. J.
Johnson, Eliphalet
Jennings, Wm. G.
Kelley, John H.
Kenney, Robert
Kavanaugh, James M.
Long, B. Frank
Layton, John H.
Layton, Gibbons
Landes, James H.
Layman, Preston
Layman, Jack
Lincoln, A. C.
Lambert, E. L.
Murphy, James M.
McGilvray, L. T.
McAllister, Wm. C.
Miller, Brown
Miller, B. Frank

Miller, C. B.
Miller, Chas. L.
Miller, J. Wesley
Mayhew, Geo. F.
Martz, Addison B.
McAllister, J. W.
Martz, M. J.
Moon, Jack
Newman, Wm. A.
Phillips, George
Pollock, S. W.
Pennybacker, J. D.
Robinson, Wm. H.
Richards, B. F.
Rohr, Wm. S.
Richards, Chas. L.
Ruff, John J.
Rogers, Jonathan G.
Rice, John B.
Shacklett, Edw. P.
Simmons, John W.
Sites, John A.
Sterling, Thos. O.
Sterling, Andrew
Van Lear, Ed. F.
Wilson, James H.
Weaver, Rich. W.
Whitmer, David
Elderdice, Eugene (Md.)
Fleming, (Md.)
Bowers, (Shen. Co.)
Henkel, D. (Shen. Co.)
Moore, I. (Shen. Co.)

—From Col. D. H. Lee Martz's rolls.

CO. H, 10TH VA. VOL. INF.
(Chrisman's Infantry.)

Chrisman, Geo., capt.

Lieutenants
Rolston, J. P.
Rolston, John H.
Myers, Lycurgus

Sergeants
Mauck, J. W.
Rolston, M. A.
Atchison, Wm.
Heatwole, H. A.

Corporals
Showalter, A. J.
Frank, John H.

Privates
Applegate, Chas.
Andes, John
Atchison, Thos. J.
Bear, A. J.
Bear, M. H.
Bennett, Geo.
Bennett, John
Burkholder, Ira
Burkholder, Martin

Burkholder, John N.
Brunk, John W.
Bowers, J. T.
Coffman, Dan
Coffman, Samuel
Custer, Richard
Miller, Eli
Dove, Franklin
Donovan, William
Flemming, John
Ford, Reuben
Firebaugh, Samuel A.
Ford, Joseph
Frank, Jacob
Gunner, William
Glick, John
Gaither, George
Hughes, Wm.
Hopkins, Peachy
Hopkins, Ant. C.
Hopkins, Archibald
Hopkins, Jesse
Gaines, John
Keiffer, Aldine S.
Keister, Isaac
Keesayer, John
Long, A. H.
Long, John F.

Lowman, John I.
McCloud, John
Minnick, J. Wallace
McCloud, Nicholas
McLaughlin, Jos.
Minnick, John B.
Minnick, Dallas
Miller, Henry
Miller, Peter
Pifer, Morgan D.
Pittington, Samuel
Rice, Joseph
Rolston, David H.
Roadcap, Madison
Rice, James
Ritchie, Addison
Rolston, William
Showalter, Ananias
Shoemaker, Wesley
Sheets, Joseph
Sheets, Strother
Swartz, George
Shepp, Solomon
Secrist, David
Secrist, John
Secrist, Thomas
Summers, David

—454—

ROCKINGHAM COUNTY

Van Pelt, Martin
Van Pelt, James
Whitmore, Bowman
Whitmore, John
Whitmore, Benj.
Whitmore, James C.
Winegord, John
Winegord, Joseph
Whitmer, Wm. C.
—From Col. D. H. Lee Martz's rolls.

CO. I, 10TH VA. VOL. INF.
(Riverton Invincibles.)

Covington, W. D. C., capt.

Lieutenants.
Kite, Jos. H.
Miller, J. G. H.
Crawford, Wm. J.
Sigler, Wm.
Huffman, John P.
Sellers, Samuel A.
Miller, Hiram H.
Jennings, W. K.

Privates.
Bridges, A. P.
Bear, N. W.
Carrier, Henry F.
Caton, Richard H.
Coffman, Wm. T.
Cook, Jeremiah
Crickenberger, B. F.
Davis, Wm. H.
Eppard, Jos. Calvin
Eppard, Strother
Eddins, Wm. A. O.
Elliot, Francis W.
Grove, Jacob N.
Grove, John W.
Grove, Miles M. G.

Hammer, Henry C.
Hall, Christian
Harnsberger, Chas. W.
Harnsberger, Robt.
Harris, James A.
Harris, Wm. E.
Huffman, D. W.
Huffman, George
Huffman, James
Hitt, Silas
Kiblinger, Wm. C.
Kite, Chas. N.
Lamb, Isaac
Lamb, Lewis
Lewis, Ellis
Lewis, John L. A.
Long, Thomas
Long, Wm. C.
Louderback, J. Philip
Marshall, John H.
Marshall, Montgomery
Marshall, Robert F.
Marshall, Wm. H.
McCauley, Daniel
Merica, Geo. S.
Monger, John B.
Monger, Joseph
Phillips, James M.

Powell, Albert
Powell, Elias
Powell, Moses F.
Price, John H.
Propst, H. F.
Pulliam, James,
Rhine, John
Secrist, David A.
Secrist, Philip
Sellers, John M.
Sellers, Peter J.
Sellers, John N.
Shepp, Chas. N.
Shifflet, Edmund
Shifflet, Geo. W.
Shifflet, Jos. N.
Shifflet, Sampson
Shifflet, Theophilus
Short, Wm. J.
Smith, John Jeff.
Southard, John
Stanley, Isaac N.
Stover, David H.
Stover, Joseph H.
Wimbigler, Geo. H.
Wolfe, Jos. H.
Wolfe, Thurston
Wyant, Alexander
—From Col. D. H. Lee Martz's rolls.

CO. I, 33RD VA. VOL. INF.
(Stonewall Brigade.)

Jones, John R., capt.

Lieutenants
Huston, George
Whitescarver, L. C.
Eastham, Geo. C.
Huffman, Daniel

Sergeants
Ott, L. H.
Lindon, M.
Martin, D. A.

Privates
Argenbright, A. A.
Argenbright, Branson
Armentrout, John Adam
Armentrout, Preston
Beery, Joseph
Berry, Bert
Bertram, Samuel
Bird, Isaac
Black, John
Brannaman ———
Branner, John
Brown, Henry
Calterton, James
Carroll, John
Carver, William

Chapman, Milton
Chapman, Thos.
Click, Daniel
Cline, Daniel
Cook, John
Crickenberger, A.
Cromer, Joseph
Custer, George
Derrer, Harvey
Derrer, Robert
Donahue, John
Donahue, William
Donovan, Daniel
Donovan, Washington
Fadely, William
Foley, James
Foley, W. H.
Garber, Daniel
Gilkerson, William
Glover, Derrick
Glover, Jack
Grandle, Emanuel
Hannah, Samuel
Harman, Samuel
Harnsberger, Joseph
Harvey, Jewett
Hasler, George
Hasler, Jacob
Hasler, Philip

Hasler, William
Heatwole, John D.
Helms, Jacob
Hinton, Joseph
Hiser, Edward
Holcomb, Fletcher
Holland, Rev. George
Hudlow
Jones, Albert
Keplinger, George
Kratzer, Christian
Landis, Washington
Lewis, William
Long, John
Lutholtz, Christian
Lutholtz, Noah
McLeod, James P.
Meyerhoeffer, John
Miller, Sylvanus
Minnick, Wm.
Nicely, Isaac
Painter, Johnson B.
Patterson, John
Pence, John W.
Pence, Peter
Perry, Joseph
Reed, Griffin
Riddle, Harrison
Riddle, James

A HISTORY OF

Riddle, Thomas
Scanlon, Bat ("Big")
Scanlon, Bat ("Little")
Secrist, Harvey
Shipp, Albert
Shipp, George
Sheets, John B.
Sheets, Simon P.
Showalter, Buck
Simmers, Jacob A.
Sipe, Archibald

Sipe, Levi
Slusser, W. S.
Summers, William
Switzer, S. C.
Switzer, V. C.
Switzer, Wm. O.
Taylor, Albert
Taylor, Harvey
Taylor, Hiram
Thomas, John
Van Lear, Chas. A.

Vawters, Emanuel
Wean, John
Weller, John
Whitmer, Benj. J.
Whitmer, James
Whitsel, Peter
Wilhite, Joseph
Wilhite, Peter
Wise, Adam
Wise, Harvey
Wise, James
Wise, Wm. N.

—From Col. D. H. Lee Martz's rolls.

THE RIVER RANGERS.

(Troop of cavalry from East Rockingham.)

E. S. Yancey, capt.; C. M. Kemper, 1st lt.; A. J. Sigler, 2d lt.; R. F. Weaver, 3d lt.; J. H. Berry, 1st ser.; J. H. Royer, 2d ser.; R. B. Ergenbright, 3d ser.; Robt. Hooke, 4th ser.; A. H. Harris, ensign.

John Burkhard
J. L. Bocock
J. J. Bent
J. S. Burner
Jonathan Bateman
Edward Brown
Peter McCauley
George W. Davis
G. R. Ergenbright
T. M. Groves
George Tally
W. W. Hedrick
Wm. P. Kyle
Geo. W. Hedrick

C. L. Hedrick
A. L. Hansberger
R. J. Hooke
A. S. Hooke
J. B. Huffman
W. F. Harris
Wm. M. Hansberger
J. N. Humes
Benj. Powell
John Keister
Thos. J. Keran
S. H. Kayler
J. H. Larkin
Warfield Lee

Harrison Maupin
S. C. Nicholas
G. M. Nicholas
O. F. A. Pirkey
A. H. Pirkey
S. H. Pence
George Powell
Henry Raines
Reuben Raines
Jacob Raines
Michael Scott
Emanuel Sellers
Wm. S. Showalter
William Scott
F. H. Weaver

—From Rockingham Register, May 31, 1861.

CO. B, 7TH VA. CAVALRY.

Captains.
Winfield, John Q.
Magruder, J. H.
Humphries, David

Lieutenants.
Liggett, J. N.
Jordan, S. B.
Pennybacker, J. S.
Kennon, P. P.
Acker, Jacob
Neff, E. R.
Mason, Henry
Riddle, J. N.
Mullen, S. F.
Stickley, C.
Funk, T. W.
Showalter, Jos.
Moore, John W.
Pennybacker, D. D.
Bowers, W. F.
Ritchie, Isaac
Taylor, Edwin
Ritchie, I. F.
Zirkle, Harvey

Privates.
Acker, Peter
Acker, Isaac
Ashby, Richard

Alger, Harvey
Bowman, George
Bowman, Michael
Baker, D. S.
Burkholder, Geo. B.
Bull, A. V.
Beam, John
Byrd, Jerry
Bush, Henry
Baxter, Jacob T.
Black, Richard
Brock, Wm.
Brock, Godfrey
Beam, Jacob
Barb, Daniel
Barb, Simon
Barb, Noah
Carpenter, Newton H.
Custer, Isaac
Cromer, David
Coffelt, J. B.
Carpenter, John
Coffman, Geo. C.
Dwyer, A. W.
Devier, Giles
Devier, Hiram K.
Emswiller, Samuel
Emswiller, W. T.
Emswiller, J. T.
Emswiller, Noah
Fulk, John G.

Fetzer, Cyrus
Funk, Milton E.
Funk, H. N.
Funk, James
Funk, William
Funk, A. B.
Grabill, C.
Grabill, N. C.
Good, Jacob
Hollar, S. B.
Helsley, W. G.
Harris, John A.
Hupp, C. T.
Hulva, Jonathan
Hulva, David
Hulva, S. B.
Hulva, Josiah
Jones, Isaac
Keyes, Eras. L.
Lindamood, Sylvanus
Lindamood, James
Leedy, John
Miller, Isaac
Miller, John
Miller, William
Minnick, Wm.
Minnick, Levi
Messick, Wm.
May, George
Miller, George
Mullen, Emanuel

ROCKINGHAM COUNTY

Mullen, S. F.
Moore, George
Moore, Samuel
Moore, Joseph
Neff, John H.
Neff, Michael D.
Phillips, J. M.
Pennybacker, Isaac
Pennybacker, B. N.
Pennybacker, John
Ritchie, Isaac
Rader, Peter
Rader, George
Rader, J. S.
Rader, C. S.
Reedy, Isaac
Ritchie, Solomon
Swanson, Wm.
Scott, J. C.
Stickley, Daniel
Showalter, Michael
Simmers, John
Sylvanus, Uriah (?)
Turner, Jacob
Thomas, John H.
Toppin, Wm.
Wean, E. J.
West, John W.
Will, Chas. B.
Wood, Geo. M.
Wean, Abram
Wean, Jacob
Zirkle, David P.
Barglebaugh, John M.

CO. H, 10TH VA. CAVALRY.

Captains
Brock, John P.
Poage, George
Pennybacker, Thos. J.
Dovel, Jos. M.
Newham, Samuel K.

Lieutenants
Yancey, Richard
Rhodes, John H.

Sergeants
Branner, Casper
Sites, D. B.
Bowman, S. S.
Armentrout, B. F.

Privates
Andes, John W.
Argenbright, John
Armentrout, Harrison
Armentrout, B. John
Baker, Joseph
Baugher, P. H.
Bazzle, A. W.
Bear, Benjamin
Billhimer, John H.
Blakemore, Henry
Bowman, Michael
Bowman, Joseph
Bradford, James
Branner, James
Brock, Chas. J.
Brock, Michael
Breen, James
Carrier, Moses
Carrier, Shelton H.
Calhoun, Preston
Cavanaugh, James
Chapman, James
Crawford, A. G.
Cummings, Thos.
Davis, Marion
Dillard, Frank
Drewry, William
Earman, John W.
Earman, David
Flook, Harvey
Fults, John
Fults, J. K.
Foley, Michael
Frank, Wm. H.
Frank, Isaac
Faucett, George
Garber, Jacob
Graham, Thomas
Grandle, Christley
Grable, G. W.
Handley, Perry
Harrison, Robert
Harrison, J. Polk
Harrison, Tiff
Hawkins, Wm.
Henkle, L. P.
Henkle, L. M.
Henkle, J. C.
Hinegardner, Jacob
Higgs, Isaac
Higgs, Jackson
Henton, John M.
Holsinger, D. C.
Holsinger, Perry
Homan, Herod
Homan, S. J. C.
Huffman, Madison
Jennings, G. W.
Johnson, E. A.
Johnson, Montgomery
Johnson, Wellington
Koontz, R. F.
Knupp, William
Knupp, John A.
Lambert, E. L.
Lincoln, B. F.
Long, Erasmus
Loker, Thomas
Loker, David
Loker, Rash
Lowman, James
Martz, Michael
Martz, H. C.
Martz, D. G.
Martz, Isaac C.
Minnick, Edward
Minnick, David
Minnick, Samuel
Minnick, Harvey
Misener, Robert
Moyers, Ambrose
Mooney, Asbury
Mooney, Robert
Moore, David H.
Moore, R. W.
Neff, Chas. A.
Neff, Michael
O Conner, James
O'Rreak, Branson
O'Roark, Branson
Pickering, D. H.
Pickering, Abraham
Pickering, Daniel
Reedy, David
Rhodes, Wilson A.
Rhodes, J. N.
Rhodes, J. M.
Rhodes, Preston
Roller, John
Rosenberger, John W.
Rosenberger, G. W.
Ruffner, Robert
Ruffner, Mark
Reed, Abraham
Sellers, Jacob S.
Shank, George
Shirkey, Samuel
Shirkey, G. B.
Silvius, Joseph
Simmers, Jacob
Sites, Wm. H.
Sites, J. W.
Simpson, James
Stearn, J.
Strickler, S. G.
Strickler, John
Stinebuck, Fred
Stephens, Wm. G.
Summers, Jacob
Summers, Michael
Summers, John
Thomas, Mark
Thomas, John R.
Tutwiler, Addison
Varner, Jacob
Voorhees, John S.
Whissen, J. H.
White, Christley
Wood, John D.
Wood, Calvin
Wetsel, Jack
Whitmire, Louis
Wilson, ———
Yates, Jackson

—From Col. D. H. Lee Martz's rolls.

A HISTORY OF

CO. H, 12TH VA. CAVALRY.

Sipe, E., capt.

Lieutenants
Randolph, E. C.
Simpson, A.
Kratzer, Jos. W.
Keller, John
Horn, O. P.

Sergeants
Huffman, J. W.
Arehart, W. S.
Garber, Daniel
Arey, J. W.
Holsinger, Martin
Perry, Thos J.
Altaffer, J. W.

Corporals
Baker, Jacob
Brunk, A. D.
Bowman, Solon M.
Crawn, S. M.

Privates
Altaffer, William
Altaffer, Martin
Alford, Robert
Arehart, Nason
Adams, Geo. W.
Archer, C. R.
Arehart, W. H.
Arehart, Casper H.
Baker, Isaac
Baker, Samuel
Brooks, John
Brooks, Hez.
Bateman, Elijah
Bowman, David H.
Bowman, J. M.
Bowman, Socrates
Bowman, John S.
Bowman, Ephriam
Bowman, Benj. T.
Bowman, F. M.
Bowman, Alpheus M.
Bare, Daniel
Bowman, Paul C.
Bowman, Samuel
Bright, John
Cool, Littlington
Carpenter, W. H.
Crawn, John S.
Dundore, David
Dinkle, Calvin
Davis, David
Dovel, Lucius
Life, Jerry
Fitch, Buck
Frankum, Walker
Fadely, Silvanus
Frankum, John
Gowl, David
Gowl, Peter
Grandstaff, Branson
Glovier, Madison
Gilmer, J. H.
Grove, W. H.
Holsinger, John D.
Holsinger, Samuel
Holsinger, Noah
Holsinger, Peter P.
Holsinger, Abraham
Holsinger, Silas J.
Huffman, Jos. H.
Hile, Samuel
Hinegardner, Jacob
Hawkins, W. H.
Hawkins, Jacob
Hidecker, William
Jones, Adam
Jamison, John W.
Jennings, Dallas
Keller, Philip
Kelley, John
Lackey, Robert
Loker, Thomas
Lairey, John
Long, Conrad
Long, Isaac
Dundore, Samuel
Myers, E. P.
Moore, John H.
Moyerhoeffer, James
Masters, John
May, Josiah F.
Miller, Jacob
Norris, Patt
Neff, Washington
Orebaugh, W. A.
Oakis, Dick
Painter, Allen
Painter, Romanus
Painter, Uriah
Phillips, Nathaniel
Phillips, John
Plecker, W. H.
Ryman, Samuel A.
Roller, Henry
Roller, Emanuel
Roller, Peter
Rinker, Erasmus
Ritchie, Polk
Ritchie, George
Ritchie, Joseph
Rice, Bram
Rogers, Joseph
Strickler, B. F.
Slusser, Samuel L.
Slusser, William
Saufley, William
Sherman, D. W.
Saufley, Joseph
Showalter, Samuel
Stone, James
Silvius, Moses
Spader, John
Smith, Allen
Trobaugh, Harrison
Treaby, J. C.
White, Milton
Whitesell, Jacob
Wine, J. M.
Wine, William

—From Col. D. H. Lee Martz's rolls.

CO. A, 3D BAT. VIRGINIA RESERVES

(Chrisman's Boy Company.)
(Mustered into service April 3, 1864.)

George Chrisman, capt.; Wm. A. McCue, 1st lt.; Harden A. Van Lear, 2d lt.; J. W. Showalter, 3d lt.; Wm. Ed Kite, 1st ser.; Jas. Royer, 2d ser.; Can Ralston, 3d ser.; Jac. Rush, 4th ser.; Daniel S. Harrison, 5th ser.; Joe A. Earman, 1st cor.; John G. Moore, 2d cor.; J. W. Neff, 3d cor.; W. Harvey Arehart, 4th cor.

Altaffer, Jos.
Argabright, John M.
Argabright, J. C.
Argabright, J. H.
Arey, Sam
Blosser, J. H.
Bowman, F. M.
Bowman, S. G.
Bowman, B. F.
Bontz, Geo. W.
Baker, Dan
Bent, Geo. W.
Baker, Wm.
Carrier, R. M.
Cook, John R.
Chandler, St. Clar.
Coffman, Isaac
Cline, Daniel
Clatterbuck, Jos.
Crider, Wm.
Dillard, Jas. D.
Dovel, Jno.
Flick, Silas
Fridley, John
Gowl, Adam G.
Gentry, Benj. W.
High, Grafton
Hoover, Jno.
Hartman, Dav.
Huffman, J. S.
Hilliard, Jas. C.
Harner, J. N.
Hinkle, Jacob

ROCKINGHAM COUNTY

Holland, Elias
Hahn, Geo.
Hammer, Wm. H.
Hook, Jno. C.
Higgs, Jno. W.
Hedrick, H. C.
Hinton, Jno.
Koontz, Morgan
Kyger, Jac. A. S.
Lineweaver, Chas.
Lineweaver, Wm. T.
Lemon, Eli
Lilly, John H.

Leap, J. Sam.
Miller, J. F.
May, Lewis
Morris, C. S.
Michael, R. D.
Monger, Geo. W.
Naylor, Geo.
Rosenberger, H. J.
Roller, W. H.
Silvius, Uriah
Sibert, J. M.
Sellers, Jac. B.
Summers, J. W.
Scott, Geo.

Meyerhoeffer, J. W.
Showalter, W. P.
Sowers, Jos.
Spitzer, Cyrus
Shifflet, W. H.
Showalter, P. H.
Shickle, J. C.
Trobaugh, J. H.
Wood, Wm.
Wright, Wm.
Weaver, Thos.
Wise, J. H.
Whitmore, J. B.
Wine, J. H.

—From Col. D. H. Lee Martz's rolls. 2

ROCKINGHAM COUNTY DIRECTORY.
(See also Pages 183-5 and 193-207, Above).
POSTOFFICES AND POSTMASTERS.

(Note abbreviations, as key to addresses in subsequent lists.)

Beldor (Bdr.)—J. L. Marshall
Bridgewater (Bwr.)—J. A. Riddel
Broadway (Bdy.)—Jas. Williams
Concrete (Con.)—Mrs. Hattie Raines
Cootes Store (CSt.)—Mrs. Ida Cootes
Criders (Crd.)—Jos. Stultz
Dale Enterprise (DEn.)—J. W. Minnich
Daphna (Dph.)—F. M. Stinespring
Dayton (Dtn.)—J. W. Thompson
Dovesville (Dvl.)—C. L. Souder
Edom (Edm.)—C. H. Masters
Elkton (Ekn.)—H. B. C. Gentry
Fulks Run (FR.)—J. D. Custer
Furnace (Fur.)—Ida B. Smith
Genoa (Gen.)—A. D. Breneman
Goods Mill (GdM.)—Not a P. O.
Greenmount (Gmt.)—Not a P. O.
Grottoes (Grt.)—Bessie R. Fulton
Harrisonburg (Hbg.)—W. L. Dechert
Hinton (Htn.)—L. O. Moubray
Island Ford (IF.)—C. J. Kite
Keezletown (Kzn.)—Cora White
Lacey Spring (LSp.)—L. C. Neff
Linville Depot (LD.)—Levi Rhodes
Lynnwood (Lwd.)—John F. Lewis (?)
McGaheysville (MGl.)—W. R. Bader
Mt. Clinton (MCl.)—W. F. Myers
Mt. Crawford (MCr.)—E. H. Sherman
North River (NR.)—E. F. Rhodes
Palos (Pal.)—S. E. Hoover
Penn Laird (PLd.)—C. S. Earman
Port Republic (PRp.)—C. H. Palmer
Rawley Springs (RS.)—
Rockingham (Rkm.)—T. J. Johnson
Singers Glen (SGl.)—J. R. Baer
Spring Creek (SpC.)—N. A. Spitler
Swift Run (SwR.)—J. E. F. Hughes
Timberville (Tvl.)—Virginia Driver
Yancey (Yan.)—Ashby Wyant

3. For copying rolls and for giving assistance in various capacities in the collection of materials for this book, acknowledgment is gratefully made to Miss Ella C. Heatwole, of Mt. Clinton.

A HISTORY OF

PREACHERS AND PASTORS.

BAPTIST.

Cook, Geo. F., Hbg.
Davis, E. C., SGl.
Hubbard, W. J., Bdy.
Taylor, C. E., Bdy.

BRETHREN.

Garber, W. A., Dtn.

CHRISTIAN.

Andes, A. W., Hbg.
Dofflemyre, J. W., Ekn.
Lassiter, L. L., Bdy.
Moore, H. C., Hbg.
Truitt, H. E., Ekn.
Williamson, R. L., Hbg.

CHURCH OF THE BRETHREN.

Bixler, E. C., Bwr.
Bowman, J. H., Hbg.
Bowman, S. I., Hbg.
Bowman, S. L., Bwr.
Brady, Geo. W., FR.
Cline, M. J., Dtn.
Coffman, J. B., Dtn.
Coffman, J. M., Bwr.
Conner, W. K., Hbg.
Dove, Addison, Dvl.
Dove, Geo. L., Dvl.
Driver, J. F., Tvl.
Flory, John S., Bwr.
Fulk, G. H., Genoa
Garber, Jacob A., Hbg.
Garber, P. I., Hbg.
Glick, Jacob D., Dtn.
Hays, Daniel, Bdy.
Hoover, W. C., Tvl.
Kagey, Jos. M., Dtn.
Kline, J. H., Bdy.
Landes, B. S., Hbg.
Lantz, J. W., Criders.
Long, C. E., PLd.
Long, Emanuel, Bwr.
McCann, S. N., Bwr.
Miller, Benj., Hbg.
Miller, B. B., Gmt.
Miller, H. G., Bwr.
Miller, Wm. I., SGl.
Miller, J. C., Tvl.
Miller, L. S., Hbg.
Miller, M. B., SpC.
Miller, O. S., Bwr.
Moyers, Henry, Dvl.
Myers, I. C., Gmt.
Nair, C. E., Bdy.
Pence, Joseph, PRp.
Pence, Samuel, NR.
Petry, Samuel, PRp.
Roller, J. S., Tvl.
Ronk, Chas., Bwr.
Thomas, A. S., Bwr.
Thomas, P. S., Hbg.
Turner, D., Genoa.
Wampler, Jos. W., Hbg.
Zigler, D. H., Bdy.
Zigler, I. N., Bdy.
Zigler, S. D., Hbg.

CHURCH OF CHRIST.

Minor, G. C., Hbg.

EPISCOPAL.

Ellis, J. R., Yancey.
Jackson, J. L., Hbg.

JEWISH.

Schvanenfeld, J., Hbg.

LUTHERAN.

Conder, I., MGl.
Folk, E. L., Hbg.
Hausenfluck, J. W., NR.
Shuey, Geo. E., Dtn.

MENNONITE.

Burkholder, A. B., Hbg.
Coffman, J. W., Dtn.
Geil, J. W., Bdy.
Good, Christian, Hbg.
Heatwole, Amos, Dtn.
Heatwole, L. J. (Bp.), DEn.
Heatwole, M. J., Dtn.
Heatwole, P. S., DEn.
Heishman, A. S., Bdy.
Martin, J. S., Dtn.
Rhodes, S. H., Hbg.
Shank, Joseph, Bdy.
Shank, Lewis (Bp.),Bdy.
Shank, P. E., Bdy.
Showalter, George, Bdy.
Suter, J. E., Hbg.
Weaver, S. S., MCl.

MENNONITE, OLD ORDER.

Heatwole, Emanuel, Dtn.
Heatwole, G. D., Dtn.
Heatwole, Simeon (Bp.), Dtn.
Wenger, J. D. (Bp.), Dtn.

ROCKINGHAM COUNTY

METHODIST.

Burch, Thos. A., PRp.
Potter, C. L., MCr.
Richardson, G. W., Kzn.

Sherman, H. H., Hbg.
Tabler, M. T., Ekn.
Thrasher, J. C., Bwr.

PRESBYTERIAN.

Borthwick, H. R., Bwr.
Williams, L. McC., Bdy.

Wilson, B. F., Hbg.
Young, H. A., MCl.

REFORMED.

Garrison, J. S., Hbg.
Lerch, C. D., MCr.

Stonesifer, J. B., MCr.

UNITED BRETHREN.

Brunk, J. H., Hbg.
Dyche, C. P., Rkm.
Funkhouser, A. P., Hbg.
Hammack, A. S., Dtn.
Hoenshel, E. U., Dtn.
Hott, Geo. P., Dtn.

McMullen, E. W., Dtn.
Rau, W. S., Ekn.
Sampsell, W. H., LSp.
Secrist, A. J., Dtn.
Skelton, S. D., Htn.

PHYSICIANS AND SURGEONS.

Alfred, R. H., Dtn.
Armstrong, Howard, Edm.
Biedler, J. M., Hbg.
Beydler, B. H., Bwr.
Brewer, S. W., SGl.
Byers, A. C., Hbg.
Conger, C. E., Rkm.
Conrad, Charles, Hbg.
Davis, E. D., Hbg.
Dunsford, J. C., Bdy.
Deyerle, J. H., Hbg.
Fahrney, W. E., Tvl.
Firebaugh, T. C., Hbg.
Fultz, G. S., Bdy.
Geil, D. F., Bdy.
Gilmer, H. D., Ekn.
Gordon, W. A., Ekn.
Graves, A. W., LSp.
Hall, E. G., CSt.
Hammer, L. A., MGl.

Holler, G. F., Dtn.
Jones, T. O., Hbg.
Kemper, A. S., PRp.
Klinger, J. M., Hbg.
Koontz, W. W. SpC.
Lewis, Lunsford, Ekn.
Lincoln, J. E., LSp.
Marshall, J. L., Htn.
Miller, E. R., Hbg.
Miller, F. J., GdM.
Miller, J. D., Bwr.
Painter, R., Dtn.
Ralston, C. H., MCl.
Smith, Edward, MCr.
Turner, Ashby, Hbg.
Vaughan, W. A., Tvl.
Weaver, Z. L., Ekn.
Wissler, W. F., Grt.
Wright, J. F., Kzn.
Yancey, L. B., MGl.

DENTAL SURGEONS.

Baugher, W. L., Hbg.
Bucher, J. D., Bwr.
Dodd, R. A., Bdy.
Fahrney, W. B., Tvl.
Gambill, J. R., Hbg.
Garrison, E. C., Dtn.
Kale, Z. T., Ekn.

Lineweaver, W. T., Hbg.
Nicholas, C. E., Hbg.
Pennington, R. B., Ekn.
Sprinkel, C. C., Hbg.
Strickler, R. E. L., Bwr.
Switzer, M. D., Hbg.
Switzer, R. S., Hbg.

VETERINARY SURGEONS.

Bell, F. G., Bwr.
Bowers, B. B., Tvl.
Myers, John A., Hbg.

Will, E. J., Hbg.
Williams, G. E., Hbg.
Wittig, H. J., Dvl.

ATTORNEYS-AT-LAW.

Bertram, H. W., Hbg.
Blackburn, J. F., Hbg.
Conrad, Ed. S., Hbg.
Conrad, Geo. N., Hbg.
Conrad, Laird L., Hbg.
Crawford, E. B., Hbg.
Dechert, D. O., Hbg.
Downing, John H., Hbg.
Earman, D. W., Hbg.

Grattan, Geo. G., Sr., Hbg.
Grattan, Geo. G., Jr., Hbg.
Haas, T. N. (Judge), Hbg.
Hammer, Chas. A., Hbg.
Harnsberger, Geo. S., Hbg.
Harris, John T., Hbg.
Harrison, Chas. D., Hbg.
Keezell, Walter G., Kzn.
Martz, Ed. C., Hbg.

A HISTORY OF

Ott, E. D., Hbg.
Paul, John, Hbg.
Roller, John E., Hbg.
Sipe, Geo. E., Hbg.

Stephenson, Jas. B., Hbg.
Strickler, H. M., Hbg.
Swank, Ward, Hbg.
Switzer, J. Robert, Hbg.
Winfield, Chas. R., Bdy.

Special Note:—With much labor and no little expense, the author has collected data for extending this directory much further, but the size of the book has already exceeded, by a number of pages, the limits assigned.

BIBLIOGRAPHY.

A List of Books, Magazines, and Newspapers Containing Information Concerning Rockingham County and Rockingham People.

Armstrong, J. E.: Old Baltimore Conference; 12mo, 543 pp.; Baltimore, 1907.
Asbury, Francis: Journal; 3 8vo vols.; N. Bangs and T. Mason, New York, 1821.
Acts of Assembly of Virginia; contain much valuable material relating to Rockingham County.
Boogher, W. F.: Gleanings of Virginia History; 8vo, 450 pp.; Washington, 1903.
Braun, Johannes: Circular Schreiben; 16mo, 419 pp.; Harrisonburg, 1818.
Broadway: Prospectus of Improvement Company; 8vo, 18 pp.; published about 1890.
Burkholder, Peter: Treatise on Baptism, etc.; 16mo, 60 pp.; written 1815, translated 1881; printed by Abraham Blosser, Dale Enterprise. Contains sketch of Burkholder family.
Burnaby, Andrew: Travels through North America; 8vo, 265 pp.; A. Wessels Co., N. Y., 1904.
Cartmell, T. K.: Shenandoah Valley Pioneers; 4to, 594 pp.; Winchester, 1909.
Census: Heads of Families, 1790; 4to, 189 pp.; Govt. Printing Office, Washington, 1908.
Custer, Milo: Alexander Miller and Descendants; 8vo, 36 pp.; Bloomington, Ill., 1910.
Daily News: Rockingham County, Its Past and Present; 4to. 52 pp.; Harrisonburg, 1909.
Denton, Benjamin: The Separate Arminian Union Church; 32mo, 58 pp.; printed by Jos. Funk & Sons, 1849.
Dingledine, W. J.: Harrisonburg and Rockingham County; 24 pp.; Harrisonburg, 1911.
Eckenrode, H. J.: Revolutionary Soldiers of Virginia; 8vo, 488 pp.; Richmond, 1912.
Evening News: Harrisonburg and Rockingham County; 16mo, 24 pp.; Harrisonburg, 1900.
Foote, W. H.: Sketches of Virginia; 8vo, 610 pp.; J. B. Lippincott, Philadelphia, 1856.
Fretz, A. J.: Funk Family History; 12mo, 874 pp.; Mennonite Pub. Co., Elkhart, Ind., 1899.
Funk, Benjamin: Life of John Kline; 8vo, 480 pp.; Brethren Pub. House, Elgin, Ill., 1900.
Funkhouser, Jacob: Funkhouser Family History; 8vo, 100 pp.; Harrisonburg, 1902.
Gilmer, Geo. Rockingham: Sketches of Some of the First Settlers of Upper Georgia; 8vo, 587 pp.; D. Appleton & Co., N. Y., 1855. Tells of Gilmers, Grattans, Lewises, and other Rockingham families.
Hale, J. P.: Trans-Allegheny Pioneers; 12mo, 330 pp.; Charleston, W. Va., 1886.
Hardesty, H. H.: Historical and Geographical Encyclopedia; Rockingham edition; 4to, 430 pp.; Richmond, etc., 1884.
Harris, John T.: John Paul, 1839-1901; 8vo, 10 pp.; Harrisonburg, about 1901.
Hartzler and Kauffman: Mennonite Church History; 8vo, 422 pp.; Scottdale, Pa., 1905.

ROCKINGHAM COUNTY

Hays and Sanger: The Olive Branch; 12mo, 243 pp.; Brethren Pub. House, Elgin, Ill., 1907.

Hays, Heber M.: German Dialect in the Valley of Virginia; 8vo, 16 pp.; from Dialect Notes, Middletown, Conn., 1908.

Heatwole, Cornelius J.: Heatwole Family History; 8vo, 274 pp.; Harrisonburg, 1907.

Heatwole, David A.: Heatwole Family History; 16mo, 24 pp.; Dale Enterprise, 1882.

Heatwole, Brunk, and Good: Mennonite Conference of Virginia; 8vo, 117 pp.; Mennonite Pub. House, Scottdale, Pa., 1910.

Hening, W. W.: Statutes at Large, of Virginia; 16 8vo vols.; Richmond. Rich sources for county history.

Henkel, Socrates: History of Lutheran Tennessee Synod; 8vo, 275 pp.; New Market, Va., 1890.

Hoenshel, G. W.: X-Talks and Other Addresses; 16mo, 149 pp.; New Market, Va., 1900. Contains matter of local and personal interest.

Holsinger, H. R.: History of Tunkers and Brethren; 8vo, 826 pp.; Lathrop, Cal., 1901.

Hopkins and Harrison: A Chapter of Hopkins Genealogy, 1735-1905; 8vo, 396 pp.; Lakeside Press, Chicago, 1905.

Howe, Henry: Historical Collections of Virginia; 8vo, 544 pp.; Charleston, S. C., 1846.

Huddle, W. P.: Hebron Lutheran Church; 8vo, 126 pp.; Henkel & Co., New Market, Va., 1908.

Hull, Susan R.: Boy Soldiers of the Confederacy; 12mo, 256 pp.; Neale Pub. Co., N. Y., about 1910. Contains sketches of some Valley of Virginia men.

Johnston, F.: Virginia Clerks; 12mo, 425 pp.; J. P. Bell Co., Lynchburg, 1888. Pages 344-354 relate to Rockingham.

Jones, Calvin: Wier's Cave, with map; 7 pp.; published in Johnson & Warner's Va. Almanac for 1816.

Keagy, Franklin: Kagey Family History; 8vo, 675 pp.; Harrisburg, Pa., 1899.

Kemper and Wright: Kemper Family History; 8vo, 267 pp.; G. K. Hazlitt & Co., Chicago, 1899.

Kercheval, Samuel: History of Valley of Virginia; 8vo, 403 pp.; 3d ed.; J. H. Grabill, Woodstock, Va., 1902.

Koiner: Koiner Family History; 8vo, 171 pp.; Staunton, Va., 1893.

Lake, D. J.: Rockingham County Atlas; folio, 72 pp.; Philadelphia, 1885. Copy loaned by Mrs. David Driver, Timberville.

Lederer, John: Journal and Map; 8vo, 30 pp.; G. P. Humphrey, Rochester, N. Y., 1902.

Long, Chas. M.: Virginia County Names; 12mo, 208 pp.; Neale Pub. Co., N. Y., 1908.

McDonald, W. N.: The Laurel Brigade; 8vo, 499 pp.; Baltimore, 1907.

Martin, Joseph: Gazetteer of Virginia, 1835; 8vo, 636 pp.; Charlottesville, Va. Pages 432-434 relate to Rockingham.

Maury, Ann: Memoirs of a Huguenot Family; 12mo, 512 pp.; G. P. Putnam & Sons, N. Y., 1872. Pages 245-310 contain Fontaine's journal covering Spotswood expedition.

Mauzy, Richard: Mauzy and Kisling Families; 8vo, 127 pp.; Harrisonburg, 1911.

Meade, William: Old Churches, Ministers, and Families; 2 8vo vols.; Philadelphia, 1872.

Morton, O. F.: History of Pendleton County, W. Va.; 8vo, 500 pp.; printed by Ruebush-Elkins Co., Dayton, 1910.

Morton, O. F.: History of Highland County, Va.; 8vo, 419 pp.; Monterey, Va., 1911.

Neff, John H.: Typhoid Fever as Met With in Harrisonburg and Vicinity; in Transactions of Med. Soc. of Va., 1893.

Newcomer, Christian: Life and Journal; 16mo, 330 pp.; F. G. W. Kopp, Hagerstown, 1834.

O'Ferrall, C. T.: Forty Years of Active Service; 8vo, 367 pp.; Neale Pub. Co., N. Y., 1904.

Painter, F. V. N.: Poets of Virginia; 12mo, 336 pp.; B. F. Johnson Pub. Co., Richmond, 1907.

Paul, John: Address at Cornerstone-Laying, Rockingham Courthouse, 1896; 8vo, 19 pp.; Harrisonburg.

Peyton, J. L.: History of Augusta County; 8vo, 402 pp.; S. M. Yost & Son, Staunton, 1882.

Roller, John E.: Michael Schlatter Memorial Address; 8vo, 24 pp.;

A HISTORY OF

Daniel Miller, Reading, Pa., 1900.
Ruffner, W. H.: The Waterman Lands; 16mo, 35 pp.; Harrisonburg, 1859.
Scott, W. W.: History of Orange County; 8vo, 292 pp.; Richmond, 1907.
Semple, R. B.: History of Baptists in Virginia; 8vo, 454 pp.; Richmond, 1810.
Shuey, D. B.: Shuey Family History; 12mo, 279 pp.; Lancaster, Pa., 1876.
Smith, C. H.: Mennonites of America; 8vo, 484 pp.; Scottdale, Pa., 1909.
Spencer, A. C.: Geology of the Massanutten Mountain; 8vo, 54 pp.; Washington, 1897.
Thwaites and Kellogg: Dunmore's War; 12mo, 500 pp.; Madison, Wis., 1905.
Travis, Joseph: Autobiography; 12mo, 238 pp.; Nashville, 1856. Tells of great revival in Harrisonburg, 1802.
Turner, F. M.: Life of John Sevier; 12mo, 226 pp.; Neale Pub. Co., N. Y., 1910.
Waddell, J. A.: Annals of Augusta; 4to, 545 pp.; Staunton, Va., 1902.
Waddell, J. A.: Scotch-Irish of the Valley of Virginia; pp. 79-99, Proceedings of 7th Congress of Scotch-Irish Society.
Wayland, J. W.: German Element of the Valley of Virginia; 8vo, 272 pp.; 1907.
Wayland, J. W.: Sidney Lanier at Rockingham Springs; 8vo, 54 pp.; Ruebush-Elkins Co., Dayton, 1912.
Wayland, J. W.: Joseph Funk, Father of Song in Northern Virginia; 4to, 12 pp.; Ruebush-Elkins Co., Dayton, 1912.
Wayland and Garber: Bridgewater College, Past and Present; 8vo, 298 pp.; 1905.
Webster, Richard: Presbyterian Church in America; 8vo, 720 pp.; Philadelphia, 1857.
Weekley and Fout: Our Heroes, Vol. II; Otterbein Press, Dayton, Ohio, 1911.
Wenger, Jonas: Wenger Family History; 12mo, 259 pp.; Elkhart, Ind., 1903.
Wenger, J. H.: Descendants of Abraham Beery; 12mo, 328 pp.; South English, Iowa, 1905.
Wenger, J. H.: Descendants of Nicholas Beery; 12mo, 496 pp.; South English, Iowa, 1911.
Wilson, B. F.: Historical Year Book, 1911-12, Harrisonburg Presbyterian Church; 34 pp.
Wilton, Dwyer, and Conrad: History of Rockingham Union Lodge. A. F. & A. M.; 8vo, 46 pp.; Harrisonburg, 1889.
Woods, Edgar: History of Albermarle County; 8vo, 412 pp.; Charlottesville, Va., 1901.
Zigler, D. H.: Brethren in Virginia; 12mo, 278 pp.; Brethren Pub. House, Elgin, Ill., 1908.

B. Articles in Newspapers and Magazines.

American Motorist, March, 1912: The Grottoes of the Shenandoah, by J. S. Grasty.
Baltimore Sun, Feb. 13, 1909: The Lincolns of Virginia.
Blue and Gray, May, 1894: The First Provost-Marshal of Harrisonburg, by C. W. Boyce.
Bridgewater Herald, Nov. 29, 1895: Some Valley History.
Sept. 27, 1901: Col. E. Sipe obituary.
Century Magazine, June, 1885: Stonewall Jackson in the Shenandoah, by J. D. Imboden.
March, 1887: Lincoln's Ancestors in Virginia, by J. T. Harris.
Gospel Messenger (Elgin, Ill.), Nov. 30, 1907: Ministers of Long Ago, by Daniel Hays.
Mar. 14, 1908: Sketch of the Klein Family, by Daniel Hays.
Dec. 25, 1909: W. C. Thurman in the Shenandoah Valley, by J. H. Stover.
Harrisonburg Daily News, June 20, 1903: J. W. Howe obituary.
July 10, 1903: First County Court.
July 13, 1903: First Murder Case.
April 6, 11, 22, 24, 1907: Valley Soldiers in French and Indian War, by J. W. Wayland.
April 23, 1908: Famous Old Music Book, by D. Hays.

ROCKINGHAM COUNTY

April 16, 1909: Normal School Cornerstone Laying.
May 8, 1909: Sketches of Rockingham, Harrisonburg, Normal School, etc.
May 22, 1909: History of Timberville.
Dec. 1 (?), 1909: Elkton Methodist Church.
Jan. 8, 1910: J. S. Messerley obituary.
Jan. 12, 1910: Harrisonburg Church Statistics.
March 23, 1910: The Miller Family, by Milo Custer.
April 2, 4, 5, 6, 1910: The Old Church on the Hill, by James Kenney.
Aug. 21, 1911: Meyerhoeffer Family Reunion.
Oct. 3, 1911: Harrisonburg Methodist Church, by H. H. Sherman.
Mar. 7, 1912: Roller Military Records.
Oct. 29, 1912: Kiracofe Family Reunion.
Harrisonburg Daily Times, Aug. 6, 1907: The Germans in the Valley, by D. S. Lewis.
Jan. 12, 1910: Harrisonburg Church Statistics.
Sept. 29, 1911: J. H. Ralston obituary.
June 3, 1912: New Church at New Erection.
Harrisonburg Free Press, Feb. 14, 1900: The Germans in Rockingham and the Valley, by C. E. Kemper.
May 23 to July 27, 1900: History of Rockingham County, by J. H. Floyd.
May 28, 1904: Day-Break on the Massanutten, by J. A. M., in the Richmond News-Leader.
June 4, July 2, 1904: Harrisonburg War History, by Mrs. Emma Lyon Bryan.
Musical Advocate (Singer's Glen), August, Sept., Oct., Nov., 1868: Wishtaneta, by Will S. Rohr.
Musical Million (Dayton, Va.), August, 1908: Aldine S. Kieffer and His Work, by W. T. Myers.
August, 1911: The Ruebush-Kieffer Co., by O. F. Morton.
Old Commonwealth (Harrisonburg), Feb. 13, 1867: · Battle of Port-Republic, by John Esten Cooke, from Old Guard.
Dec. 23, 1868: Completion of the M. G. Railroad.
Jan. 12, 1870: East Rockingham.
April 13, 1870: Fine Rockingham Stock.
Oct. 5, 12, 1870: The Great Flood.
Dec. 28, 1870: Big Christmas Fire.
May 2, 1872: Re-Division of County into Townships.
May 29, 1873: The Great Valley of Virginia, reprinted from Staunton Spectator.
April 22, 1875: Dora Coal Fields.
Aug. 23, 1877: Yellow Massanutten Springs.
Nov. 29, 1877: The Flood of 1877.
Sept. 27, 1883: Union Veterans in Harrisonburg.
Old Dominion Home (Dayton, Va.), November, 1906: Legend of Cook's Creek, by L. J. Heatwole.
Our Assistant (Mt. Crawford), May, 1899: History of Brown Memorial Church, by A. D. Wolfinger.
Our Church Paper (New Market, Va.), August 27, 1902: 82d Annual Lutheran Tennessee Synod at Rader's Church.
Outing Magazine, April, 1908: Nolichucky Jack, by L. T. Sprague.
Page News (Luray, Va.), Dec. 13, 1907: Milnes and the Flood of 1870.
Aug. 25, Sept. 1, 8, 15, 22, 1911: Diary of John W. Mauck, Co. K, 10th Va. Inf.
Penn-Germania (Lititz, Pa.), October, 1911: Joseph Funk, Father of Song, by John W. Wayland.
Philadelphia Medical Museum, Vol. 5, No. 1, 1808: The Rockingham Influenza of 1807, by Peachey Harrison.
Philomathean Monthly (Bridgewater), Jan., 1912: Origin of the Massanutten Mountain, by H. N. Glick.
Presbyterian Journal (Philadelphia), June, Sept., Dec., 1903: First German Reformed Colony in Virginia, by W. J. Hinke.
Religious Herald (Richmond), August 15, 1912: Baptists of Rockingham, by C. S. Dodd.
Richmond Dispatch, July 22, 1900: The Barn-Burners, by N. M. Burkholder.
Richmond Times-Dispatch, July 2, 1911: A Home Institution, by J. S. Flory.
Rockingham Daily Record, Sept. 16, 1911: Harrisonburg Schools, Rockingham Roads, State Normal School.

A HISTORY OF

Sept. 18, 1911: Methodism in Harrisonburg, by H. H. Sherman; Rockingham Memorial Hospital.
Oct. 2, 1911: Harrisonburg Baptist Church, by J. C. Staples.
April 8, 1912: How Shaver Killed Meigs, by S. N. Callender.
Rockingham Register (Harrisonburg), Jan. 2, 1863: Joseph Funk obituary.
May 9, 11, 1863: 10th Regiment's Killed and Wounded in the Battle of Chancellorsville.
Feb. 9, 1866: Catholics in the Valley.
June 28, 1866: Sketch of Bridgewater.
Oct. 11, 18, 1866: East Rockingham.
April 11, 1867: Beaver Creek People and Works.
Nov. 21, 1867: Valley Musical Association.
Nov. 18, 1869: The Tunkers.
Jan. 6, 1870: Hedrick, Flory, and others on the Thurman Movement.
Oct. 6, 13, 20, 1870: The Great Flood.
Dec. 12, 1873: On Cross Keys Battle, etc.
Jan. 23, Feb. 20, Apr. 3, June 26, 1874: Interesting Sketches of Rockingham, by Roaming Invalid.
June 5, 1874: East Rockingham; Tearing Down the Old Courthouse.
May 27, 1875: Grange Demonstration.
Sept. 21, 1876: Rockingham Schools, by J. Hawse.
Oct. 5, 1876: Harrisonburg 50 Years Ago.
April 26, 1877: St. Michael's Church.
Nov. 29, 1877: Terrible Flood.
Dec. 13, 1877: Flood at River Bank.
Jan. 31, 1878: Farming at Rosendale, from the Baltimore Sun.
Feb. 6, 1879: Port Republic.
May 1, 1879: Methodism in Old Times.
Dec. 4, 1879: New Market Cave.
Dec. 8, 1881: New Erection; Linville Creek.
Jan. 26, 1882: Along the Moorefield Road, by N. M. Burkholder.
March 3, 1882: Samuel Cootes obituary.
May 3, 1883: Mt. Crawford.
July 5, 1883: McGaheysville.
Feb. 5 to Aug. 27, 1885: 27 articles on Rockingham County, by G. F. Compton.
Dec. 22, 1887: Col. B. H. Smith obituary.
June 14, 1888: The Old Kline House.
Jan. 31, 1889: First Piano in Rockingham.
March 14, 1890: Brock's Gap, by J. L. Campbell.
Dec. 19, 1890: Timberville Cave.
March 27, 1891: Shendun; Frederick A. Berlin.
Jan. 20, 1893: W. B. Compton's Escape from McHenry.
Feb. 17, 1893: Kyd Douglas's Ride.
Jan. 5, 1894: Roller Family History.
Jan. 22, 1894: Lead and Zinc in Rockingham.
July 20, 1894: Who Burned the Bridges? by Luther Coyner; from Staunton Spectator and the Galveston News.
Aug. 31, 1894: Kagey Reunion at Dayton.
Feb. 8, March 1, 22, 29, 1895: Friedens Church.
May 24, 1895: Cook's Creek Church.
June 14, July 26, 1895: Valley Mennonites, by L. J. Heatwole.
Aug. 16, 1895: Killing of Meigs, by N. W. Orb.
July 17, 1896: Trumbo Family History.
Aug. 28, Sept. 4, 1896: Roller Family Reunion.
Oct. 2, 1896: Destructive Floods.
Nov. 20, 1896: Friedens Church.
Feb. 19, Mar. 12, 19, 1897: Friedens History.
April 16, 1897: Life in Rockingham in 1865.
Sept. 24, 1897: How Ashby Died, by E. C. Bruffey, from Atlanta Constitution.
Oct. 1, 1897: Courthouse Opening.
Feb. 4, 1898: Where Turner Ashby Fell.
May 13, 1898: History of McGaheysville.
June 10, 17, 1898: Ashby Monument Unveiling.
Sept. 30, 1898: Harrisonburg Guards Return from Florida.
Jan. 13, 1899: German-Virginians, by J. E. Roller.
March 10, 1899: Rockingham Historical Society.

ROCKINGHAM COUNTY

July 6, 1900: Hunter's Raid in the Valley.
July 13, 1900: Sheridan's Raid in the Valley.
Jan. 2, 1903: Rockingham Revolutionary Pensioners, by C. E. Kemper.
Feb. 20, 1903: A Tradition of War Branch.
Feb. 27, 1903: More Traditions of War Branch.
Jan. 26, 1904: The Old County Court, by J. E. Roller.
Dec. 30, 1904: Myers Family History.
Shenandoah Valley (New Market, Va.), Jan. 2, 1908: St. John's Lutheran Church (Rock. Co.), by T. H. Fansler.
March 24, 1910: Huffman Family Reunion.
Sept. 25, 1910: Valley Rangers at Lacey.
Spirit of the Valley (Harrisonburg), Aug. 15, 1902: J. C. Wheat obituary.
Staunton Daily Leader, June 16, 1912: Local Newspapers, by Newton Argenbright.
Virginia Magazine of History and Biography (Richmond), April, July, October, 1902: The Germans of the Valley, by J. W. Wayland.
July, 1902: Adam Mueller, First White Settler, by C. E. Kemper.
October, 1903, January, April, July, October, 1904, January, 1905: Moravian Diaries of Travel through Virginia, by W. J. Hinke and C. E. Kemper.
January, 1905: The Dunkers and the Sieben-Taeger, by J. W. Wayland.
April, July, October, 1905, January, April, 1906: Early Westward Movement of Virginia, by C. E. Kemper.
Washington Herald, May 16, 1912: Sketch of Harrisonburg.
West Virginia Historical Magazine, April, 1902: The Lawyer (Gabriel Jones), by R. T. Barton.
William and Mary College Quarterly, Vol. IX: First Settler in the Valley, by Lizzie B. Miller.
Vols. XII, XIV: Peaked Mountain Church, by W. J. Hinke and C. E. Kemper.
Young Virginian (Mt. Clinton), February, 1874: History of Harrisonburg Presbyterian Church.
November, 1875: Cooke's Creek Church.
April, 1876: Mossy Creek Church.
September, 1876: The Old and New Side.

INDEX

---, Elizabeth 126 Nicholas 60
ABBOTT, Benjamin 330
ACKER, D C 373 Isaac 456 Jacob 456
    John 443-444 Peter 456
ADAM, Miller 38
ADAMS, 407 George W 370 458 John 183
    Thomas 443
AIDOFFER, Anna 448
AIRY, C W 161
AKER, D S 456
ALBERT, Felix 452
ALBRECHT, Lisa 13
ALBRIGHT, John 122
ALDERSON, John 9 John Fr 244 John Sr
    244
ALDHIZER, G S 390 George S 390 H H
    184 T C 390
ALER, Anthoney 60
ALESHIRE, Billy 420 Isaac 420 Robert
    420
ALEXANDER, J D 280 391 James 450
    Mrs J E 434
ALFORD, John 55 Robert 458
ALFRED, John 122 R H 461
ALGER, Harvey 456 Jack 420 William
    420
ALISON, Anthony 446
ALLABAUGH, Jacob 122
ALLABOUGH, John 120
ALLEBAUGH, John 198 S R 441
ALLEMONG, Hannah Payne 232 J W F 225
    232 366 387-388 388 John 232 John
    Edwin 232
ALLEN, Augustine 451 Chester G 339-
    340 J W F 442 James 442-444 R Lee
    193 Robert 443
ALLIN, Rachel 446
ALSTAT, Jacob 452
ALTAFFER, J E 193 J W 458 Joseph 458
    Martin 458 William 458
AMAN, Matthias 195
AMISS, George 453
AMMON, Margaret 446 Y C 301 441
AMOLE, Jacob 451

AMON, Mathias 196
AMOND, Mathias 449
ANDERS, John 122
ANDERSON, A J 374 Ann Allan 356 D C
    378 James 422
ANDES, A 393 A W 247 280 460 Abram
    224 Andrew 213 John 454 John W 457
ANDREW, Fletcher 115
ANDREWS, Andrew 449 Joseph 155 222
ANDRICK, E A 392
APPLEGATE, Charles 454
ARCHER, C R 458 James 60
ARCHKENBRIGHT, John 444
AREHART, Abram 151 Casper H 458
    George 151 Harvey 458 Jacob 151
    Nason 458 W H 458 W S 458
AREY, G P 199 J W 458 Marget 444 Sam
    458
ARGABRIGHT, Adam 96 Christian 452
    Elizabeth 446 J C 458 J H 458
    Jacob 446 John M 458 Katy 445
    Martin 96 449 Mary 446
ARGEBRIGHT, Abraham 122 John 122
ARGENBRIGHT, A A 455 Branson 455 F J
    184 George 445 John 457
ARGUBRIGHT, J L 121 John 448
ARIE, Cutlip 60
ARKENBRIGHT, Jacob 82
ARKINBRIGHT, Jacob 59
ARMENTROUT, 241 Abram 452 Augustine
    403 Augustus 452 B F 457 B John
    457 Christopher 52 David 451 E R
    206 Elizabeth 447 Frederick 93 99
    Fredrick 452 George 81 451 George
    D 454 Harrison 457 Henry 59 99 446
    451 J P 453 Jacob 122 452 John 92
    John A 379 John Adam 455 Katy 446
    Philip 451-452 Preston 455 R 208 W
    S 373 William 451
ARMONTROUT, Frederick 59 Jno 60 John
    448
ARMSTRONG, E J 443 Elisabeth 447
    Howard 461 J C 373 Jno 98 John B F
    335

ROCKINGHAM COUNTY

ARNOLD, 84 General 103
ASBURY, Bishop 10 187 283 286
ASHBY, 355 434 General 141 Richard 456 Turner 11 141 179 433
ASHER, Waterman 441
ASSENT, James 444
ATCHISON, Thomas J 454 William 454
ATTKISSON, Mary L 295
AVIS, J L 297 Jas L 387-388
BACHELOR, Thomas 452
BACK, Aaron 451
BADER, A J O 194 A S 185 195 J H 298 Mr 264 W R 459
BAER, J R 459 Jacob 96 Jacob Sr 48
BAGBY, George W 438
BAGS, Sarah 96 445
BAILEY, Daniel Benjamin 445
BAILY, William 448
BAIR, John 446
BAIRD, Ann 444 James 97
BAIRET, James 216
BAKER, Dan 458 Daniel 269 George 451 Henry 451 Isaac 458 John 451 Joseph 457 Michael 213 Michael 86 97 213 449 Samuel 458 William 458
BALDWIN, John 291 John B 165 Judge 356
BALL, J N 406 James 453
BALMAINE, Mr 251
BAMBER, William 453
BANKS, General 136
BANNEKER, Benjamin 219
BARB, Daniel 456 John H 296 Noah 456 Simon 456
BARBEE, G T 335 373
BARE, C Coffman 281 Daniel 458 Henry 452 Jacob 21 452 John 21 N 443 Naason 119 443 Wesley 119
BARGLEBAUGH, C E 308 John M 457
BARKER, Henry 450
BARLER, Henry 445
BARNES, Mrs 195
BARNET, Thomas 59
BARR, David 254
BARROT, Henery 447
BARTON, R T 351
BARTTELB, H N 345
BARZIZA, F L 355
BASFORD, Thomas W 452
BASHAW, Darwin 194
BASHOR, S H 246
BASORE, J W 203 309
BATEMAN, Elijah 458 James 420 Jonathan 456
BAUGHER, C W 185 G W 185 J L 180 P H 457 W L 461
BAUSERMAN, G W 453 Joseph 453

BAXTER, Captain 73 George 72 89 99 216 442-443 449 George A 308 Jacob T 456 Joseph 441
BAZZLE, A W 457
BEAHM, I N H 309 Isaac N H 316
BEALL, Virginia O 357
BEAM, Jacob 456 John 456
BEAR, 37 A C 442 A J 454 Benjamin 457 Harriet 293 Henry 448 Jacob 37 95 102 Jno 101 John 213 454 John Sr 449 John W 281 M H 454 Mrs E 311 N W 455 Susan 310 Westely 123
BEARD, C D 388-389 James 18 55 83 449 Jean 447 Mary 448 Thomas 452 William 302
BEARY, Abraham 446
BEASLEY, Jeremiah 79
BEASLY, Jeremiah 66
BEAUREGARD, 438
BEAVER, G W 204 Michael 452
BEAVERLY, Frances 101
BEAZLE, Jere 94
BEEN, Mary 447
BEERY, 241 Abe 397 Abraham 329 Dewitt C 248 H C 248 Henry 199 I N 392 398 Isaac N 391 397 John 397 Joseph 302 455 N W 313 Nicholas 329 Noah W 398 T P 392 Thomas P 391
BEESLIE, Captain 85 Jeremiah 84
BEEZLY, Jere 94
BELL, F G 461 H M 207 J M 207 John H 367 Mr 272 N 49 Shendun 207 T D 253 268-269 340 Thomas D 293-294 William 444
BELSHE, Robert 445
BENNETT, George 454 John 454
BENNINGER, Henry 52
BENS, Jacob 63 John 63
BENT, George W 458 J J 456
BERCKE, Jacob 62
BERKHEAD, R W 452
BERLIN, F A 159 280 G R 306 335-337 G W 225 232 358 366 368
BERRY, Benjamin 446 449 Bert 455 D N 453 Elisha 450 George 450 George W 338 J H 456 James 60 Johanna 446 John 450 Kinley 450 Leonard 448 N W 234 Rinley 450 S K 453 Samuel 453 Sarraih 447 Thomas 60
BERTRAM, H W 298 338 Samuel 455
BERY, David 217
BESSELLY, Jere 94
BEVERLY, 38 Robert 37 William 37 39 43
BEYDLER, B H 200 461
BEYERLY, Jacob 37

BEZANZON, Joseph 452
BGGS, James 448
BIBLE, Adam 445 John 450
BIEDLER, J M 183 305 315 461
BIERNE, Richard F 357
BIETFISCH, P 444
BIG, Jack 57
BILLHIMER, J 120 John H 457 William M 454
BIRD, Abram 259 Andrew 73 349 429 Captain 73 Isaac 455 Mark 442 William 122
BIXIO, Joseph 272
BIXLER, E C 460
BKER, Jacob 458
BLACK, 236 A N 442 Cathrine 445 Elizabeth 445 448 Else 445 G R 184 Henry 446 John 455 Joseph M 454 Mary 445 Richard 456
BLACKBURN, F J 461 J F 183 J W 379
BLAIN, John 102 Joseph 452 William 445
BLAINE, 176 Charles 451
BLAKE, E A 230
BLAKEMORE, Henry 457 John L 267 Kinzie 347 W H 443 William H 454
BLETCHER, James 98
BLIZARD, Beerton 66 John 446
BLOOM, Bernard 258
BLOSE, Adam 59 Adam Jr 122 George 59 Jacob 123
BLOSSER, Abraham 335 J H 458 Noah 321 335 S H 372
BOCOCK, J H 269 329 J L 456 John Paul 329
BOEHM, 274
BOGAN, Reuben 450
BOGERS, James 450
BOGGS, Captain 70 Captain 73 Thomas 69
BOHK, Robert 51
BOID, Sarah 445
BOLINGER, Peter 194 377
BOLTON, Voluntine 452
BONDS, 224
BONTZ, George W 458
BOODY, Christian 451
BOOGHER, 324
BOONE, 429 Daniel 316-317 428 Geo 40
BOOT, Frederick 445
BOOZE, John 453
BORDA, Eugene 167
BORST, P B 230
BORTHWICK, H R 461
BOSHANG, Euly 447
BOSWELL, George 55 65-67 70-71 73-74 83 87 95 441 William 60

BOUDE, A P 260 293 A Poe 282 293-295
BOURDEN, Benjamin 39
BOURNE, 316
BOURS, Engel 445
BOWELL, George 65
BOWEN, Elizabeth 444 Hannah 448 Richard 219 Thomas 214
BOWERS, 454 B B 461 George 447 J T 454 R S 203 392 W F 456
BOWLES, James 452
BOWLIN, Jesse 376
BOWMAN, 205 241 Alpheus M 458 Benjamin 249 Benjamin T 458 Daniel 247 David 151 David H 458 Ephriam 458 F M 203 458 George 456 Godfrey 102 J H 460 J M 341 458 J R 235 393 Jacob 397 John 91 John B 370 John J 158 John Jr 377 John Michael 341 John R 453 John Rice 269 John S 458 Joseph 457 Michael 456-457 Noah W 453 Paul C 458 Peter 41 316 Robert 454 S G 458 S I 460 S L 460 S M 428 S R 184 S S 457 Samuel 458 Samuel M 390 Socrates 458 Solon M 458
BOWMN, B F 458
BOWYER, Avonas 59 Christian 451 John 59 Michael 73 351 Peter 451
BOYCE, Upton L 230
BOYD, A H H 269
BOYER, Alwintus 62
BOYERS, Jacob 453 Matthew 446
BOYLAN, Frank 252
BRADBURN, J F 378 380
BRADDOCK, 51
BRADFORD, Jack 180 James 457
BRADLEY, J S 193 Nelson 379 P 379 Philo 160 443
BRADSHAW, Dorothy 446
BRADY, George W 460
BRAITHWAITE, J E 335 Jacob N 454 Newton H 454 W S 454
BRAMHAM, John 40
BRANDMUELLER, 47 49
BRANE, C I B 336
BRANNAMAN, 455
BRANNER, Casper 457 J J 183 James 457 John 455
BRANUM, John 95
BRAUN, Johannes 316
BREDEN, John 450
BREEDEN, Allison 194
BREEDIN, Calvin 453
BREEDING, Elizabeth 445 Spencer 446
BREEN, James 457
BRENEMAN, A D 459
BRETT, W T 295

BRETTELL, J C C 355
BREWER, S W 204 461
BREWSTER, Henry 66 73 351 Thomas 71
BRIAN, Mary 446
BRIANT, Thomas Sr 449
BRICKER, Abner 453 G W 453 L J 364
BRIDGES, A P 455
BRIGHT, Jean 445 John 458
BRILL, George 194 Henry 399 John W 399
BRITT, William 453
BRITTON, Rachel 341
BROACK, Godfrey 456
BROCK, Charles J 398 457 Elsie 21 George 21 Henry 21 John 445 John P 21 123 457 Julia 21 Michael 457 Mrs A 311 Rudolph 21 William 456
BROOK, Thomas 450
BROOKING, Robert U 254
BROOKS, Hez 458 John 458
BROWER, John 249
BROWN, 167 443 Andrew 450 Charles 450 Edward 456 Father 272 Frank 453 George 447 Henry 192 269 293 455 J G 443 James 104 447 John 75-76 95 104 111-112 134 259 271 415 444 John S 453 M H 453 Milton 453 T H B 316 335 435 Thomas 450 Tyree R 122 William 452 William F 450 William G 454 William R 453
BRUCE, Philip A 70
BRUFFEY, Edwin C 361
BRUISTER, James 54
BRUMFIELD, David 446
BRUNK, A D 458 C H 183 208 235 263 323 Elias 385 J D 341 J H 461 John 224 John David 341 John W 454 O C 364 Samuel 397
BRUNOMER, Anthony 59 Peter 59
BRUSTER, James 60 90 95 Sarah 445
BRYAN, 178 A C 190 355 Allan C 117 316-317 355 358 Charles Page 317 Daniel 10 111 316-317 355 443 Deborah 445 Elisha 450 Emma Lyon 13 317 John Jr 66 Mr 317 Mrs L 310 Pendleton 355 454 Reuben 452 Thomas 213 William 316 428 443 William Jr 446
BUCHANAN, John 211
BUCHER, J D 305 461 Mrs Russell 315 W M 178 315
BUCK, Charles 289
BUGAN, Bax 420
BULL, A V 456
BULLET, John 101
BUMGARDNER, Keaty 448
BUNTING, O S 254

BURCH, Thomas A 461
BURCKES, Catren 445
BURD, Abram 120
BURGES, Elizabeth 448
BURGESS, James 448
BURGOYNE, 70
BURK, John 95
BURKE, John P 380
BURKHARD, John 456
BURKHOLDER, A B 460 Cornelia S 155 E W 391 George B 456 Ira 454 J A 372 Jacob Jr 247 Jane 311 John 241 248 318 John N 454 Joseph 397 Martin 241 247 261 454 Mrs 354 N M 234 Newton M 318 Peter 261-262 318 341 449
BURLEY, Jean 446
BURNER, J B 456 Joe 420 John 420
BURNETT, John 451
BURNSIDE, 138 William 120
BURNSIDES, William 120
BURRUSS, Julian A 307 315 Mrs Julian A 315
BURTNER, George P 302 H L 215 S 376
BURTON, Charles 451
BURWELL, J B 335
BUSH, Elizabeth 446 Henry 456 John 450 Sarah 447 William 66 450
BUSHNANG, Mary 445
BUSHONG, A 151 Abram 450 Jesse 151
BUTCHER, James 76
BUTLER, 356 Joseph 450 S H 176 Shadrick 450
BUTT, Windle 449
BYERLY, Daniel 370 F A 300 Frank Aubrey 318 Jacob 302 Mrs D C 311 Mrs Jacob 311
BYERS, A C 461
BYRD, A S 366 441 Andrew 9 Collo 81 James 17-18 Jerry 456 L Ls 453 M 310 S H W 177 199 199-200 200 271-272 293 296 388 388-389 407 415
CAHOON, John 451
CAIN, Cornelius 83 87
CAIRN, Nicholas 83 Nicolas 214
CALDWELL, B F 452
CALHOUN, Preston 457
CALLENDER, C T 184 373 393
CALTERTON, James 455
CAMERON, Buck 420 Dick 420 Harrison 420 Hutch 420 W E 356
CAMPBELL, 434-435 C F 140 Charles F 454 Hugh 218 J H 441 Lachlan 239 Robert 84 87-88 S L 296 Thomas 76 214 W G 296 William 60 216 239 451
CANTY, Colonel 143
CAPLINER, George 52

CAPLINGER, Jacob 302
CARE, Thomas 99
CARERCY, Joseph 448
CAREY, Philip 450
CARICKHOFF, E J 183 441 T A 183
CARIKOFF, Peter 453
CARLILE, J S 120
CARN, Nicolas 218
CARNES, Mr 202
CARNS, Michael 101
CARPENTER, 142 236 Ann 100 Anne 445
 Banabas 94 Captain 144 E W 178 441
 George 97 100 John 456 Margaret
 445 Newton H 456 W H 458
CARPINTER, George 193
CARR, C C C 120 364 Maria Graham 120
 201 424 432 Mrs 121 202 238 266
 269 287 331 354 438 Mrs M G 437
CARRICO, Henry 450
CARRIER, Henry F 455 Moses 457 R M
 458 Shelton H 457 W R 398
CARROLL, James 453 John 455
CARSH, Matthias 449
CARTER, Mary Nicholas 134
CARTHRAE, Jane 448
CARTHREA, John 447
CARVER, William 455
CASH, Benjamin 451 Jno 72 Rachel 72
CASNER, Elizabeth 445
CASS, 356
CASTER, Heanery 447
CATHREA, John 449
CATON, Richard H 455
CAVANAUGH, James 457
CAVE, Bud 420 Wesley A 453
CELLEY, Nancy 446
CEPLINGER, Henry 446
CESAR, Smiths 57
CHANDLER, C H 389 Charles 122 R C
 453 Samuel 448 St Clair 458
CHAPEL, Andrew 293
CHAPMAN, A A 234 James 457 Milton
 455 Thomas 455
CHERRYHOMES, William 452
CHESNUT, Elizabeth 446 Margret 445
 William 214
CHILDRESS, M B 453
CHIPLEY, Thomas L M 358
CHISM, John 450
CHRISMAN, B 232 Burk 394 Burke 135
 George 75 84 134 300 318 369-370
 373-374 393 454 458 George H 318
 Herring 355 442 Jacob 451 Lucy G
 312 Margret 448 Martha Herring 318
CHRISTIE, Mrs George 310
CHRISTMAN, Jacob 448
CHURCH, Betsy 447

CIRCLE, Lewis 96
CLANEY, Mary 445
CLAPP, C Clinton 311
CLARK, George 55 P A 119 Thomas 118
 354 425
CLARKE, 360 James 376 P A 376
CLATTERBUCK, Joseph 371 458
CLAY, H M 233 Henry 438 Henry M 167
 232 Jones H 453
CLEMMINGS, Thomas 450
CLEMON, Christian 40
CLEVELAND, 176
CLICK, D T 435 Daniel 455 J B 453 J
 W 234 John W 407 Joseph 393
CLINE, 241 Cyrus H 306 Daniel 455
 458 David 150 G 378 George 189 J W
 389 John 122 John W 389 Joseph 188
 288 376 443 Justus H 22 26 318 M B
 E 203 M J 314 460 Michael B 378
 Reverend 281 S G 347 William 451
CLINEPELTER, Michael 452
CLIPPINGER, 371-372
CLOUGH, Frances 83 John 83 444
CLOVERFIELD, Ann 445
COCHRAN, James 240
COE, W W 230
COFFELT, J B 456 Molly 446
COFFEY, Margaret 444
COFFMAN, 132 367 Catherine 447 Dan
 454 Erasmus 442 Franey 445 George
 C 456 I G 11 139 Isaac 458 Isaac G
 387 452 J B 460 J M 460 J S 453 J
 W 460 M D 454 Martin 41 Michael 41
 Mrs Christian 311 R L 390 Robert
 123 S A 131 444 Samuel 261 454
 Samuel A 444 T G 453 W Mck 452
 William Mck 453 William T 455
COFMAN, Barbra 448
COGER, Captain 70 Michael 73 85
 Peter 444
COILE, William 60
COLE, Rev Mr 287
COLES, Mr 337
COLHOON, James 75
COLLICK, Thomas 98
COLLINS, Mary 446 T J 178
COMER, Coronee 420 Merrell 420
COMPTON, G F 13 297 361 George F 220
 George L 319 William B 358
CONDER, I 460
CONGER, C E 461
CONN, Ruth 32 Ruth Randolph 319
CONNER, J J 314 W K 460
CONRAD, Charles 461 Ed S 461 Ed W
 421 Eva 195 G O 297 George 376 449
 George N 129 220 308 442 461

ROCKINGHAM COUNTY

CONRAD (cont.)
  George O 281 J 443 J M 281
  Jeanetta 289 Jeannetta 310 Joseph
  119 Joseph H 301 Laird L 461 Mary
  Lynn 319 Peter 449 Stephen 84 212
CONROD, Captain 85 George 59 Henry
  122 Jacob 123 Peter 83 Stephen 79
CONVERSE, Flavia 390 Henry Augustus
  319 Mrs 365
COOFMAN, Jacob 101
COOK, George F 460 Henry 59 450
  Jeremiah 455 John 453 455 John R
  458
COOL, Littington 458
COONROD, George 101 Jacob 107 Peter
  101 Stephen 101 104 Wooley 54
  Woolrey 52
COOPER, J C 184 Peter 171 Sally 447
COOTES, 414 423 B F 454 Dr 232 Ida
  459 Mr 118 Samuel 117 119-120 204
  410 443
COPENHAVER, G E 453
COPLINGER, George 54
CORDELL, Lewis J 452
CORNELL, O H P 231
CORNWALLIS, 64
CORNWELL, J J 307
COSBY, J L 391 John 254 Philip R 391
COTTREL, Thomas 452
COUGER, Michael 92-93 95
COUNCE, Balser 91
COUTES, John 58
COVE, Benjamin 451 Conrad 452
COVER, J R 197-198 390 Jesse R 389
  John 12
COVINGTON, W D C 135 455
COWAN, James 54 Jno 444 John A 361
COWEN, Henry 452 John 120 451
COWGER, Jacob 446
COX, 377 Dr S K 176 Miss Bryan 319 S
  K 319
COYNER, S B 197
CRAFFORD, Barnod 450 John 91
CRAIG, John 60 101 107 239 449 Mary
  444
CRAIGE, George E 122
CRANNY, Nelly 446
CRAUN, C S 391 J H 389 Joseph H 389
CRAVEN, Captain 73 Robert 67
CRAVENS, Captain 70 Dr 395 431
  Joseph 265 283 283-284 443
  Margaret 101 445 447-448 Mary 101
  444 Robert 65 72 449 William 216
  283 448
CRAVEORS, Robert 98
CRAWFORD, A G 457 E B 461 Elizabeth
  446 George A 449 Marshall 155

CRAWFORD (cont.)
  Martin 60 Mrs James 310 William J
  455
CRAWN, A J 390 John S 458 S M 458
CRENSHAW, C A 184 Charles 115
CRICKENBERGER, A 455 B F 455 Daniel
  454 David 451
CRIDER, Jacob 452 W R 209 William
  458
CRIM, Jacob 450 John 450 Peter 288
  449
CRING, John 91
CRISMAN, George 107
CRIST, B F 202 E V 338 Ed G 389 N R
  391
CROCKETT, Ellen 309
CROFT, Elizabeth 448 Shinnol 420
CROMER, David 456 Joseph 455
CROOMER, Martin 247 Molly 247
CROTZER, Joseph 449
CROUSHORN, D E 183 Kate 396
CROW, A 452 Benjamin 102 John 453
  Mary 446 W 58 Walter 97 101-102
  449 William 77 445
CRUINS, John Sr 449
CRUMBAKER, Joel 447
CRUMMEY, John 376
CRUMPACKER, Abraham 447 Hannah 448
CRYTER, Michael 41
CUINS, Henry 449
CULBURT, Nancy 446
CUMMINGS, Moses 451 Thomas 457
CUNNINGHAM, Mary 445
CUNROD, John 52 Walter 52
CUPP, Fredrick 451
CURRY, Alexander 239 J L M 438 James
  452 Mayberry 450 Nicholas 97
  Samuel 239
CUSHEN, Ran D 288 333
CUSTAR, Jacob 445
CUSTARD, Arnold 445 Joseph 66
  Susanah 445
CUSTER, 411 Conrad 412 Gabriel 410
  George 410 455 Isaac 456 Isabella
  410 J D 459 Jacob 409-410 412 414
  Marey 448 Milo 186 270 409-410 414
  P M 294-296 Paul 409-410 Richard
  409 454 Richard Jr 409-410 414
  Richard Sr 410 Samuel 409 Strawder
  410 Susan 410
CUSTERD, Sarah 448
CUTNAR, Pheby 445
DADNUM, E T 280
DAINGERFIELD, F A 358 371 442
  Foxhall A 319 Leroy 126 Nettie 319
  Nettie Gray 14 William 126 William
  P 363

DAMROUSCHE, Frank 344
DANFORTH, Jennie Knight 359
DANGERFIELD, Foxhall A 252
DANIEL, John W 178 438
DANNER, William 122
DASHNER, Rosanna 448
DAVIDSON, 316 A B 269 331 Ananias
  330 Josaih 68 Josiah 65-67 69 74
  85 Robert 85
DAVIES, John 449 Mary 446
DAVIS, 58 Captain 74 Catherine 445
  David 458 E C 460 E D 406 461
  George W 456 James 77 84 John 74
  79 81-83 85 90 101 441 448 453
  Marion 457 Mary 446 N Wilson 191
  Rebecca 310 Robert 65 72 101-102
  441 Walter 441 443 William 100 449
  451 William H 455
DAVISON, Josiah 65 216 441 449
DAVISSON, Abigail 447 Ananias 189
  339
DAY, Samuel 448
DAYTON, 11
DEAL, Philip 122 W E 198
DEAN, James 452 M 201 William 304
DEANE, Thomas 450-451
DECHERT, 331 D O 461 Daniel 334
  Orville 307 W L 178 459
DECK, Henry 59 Jacob 59 119 John 59
DECKER, Joel 420 R S 453
DEEK, John 450
DEGRAFF, E V 306
DEHART, Thomas 452
DENEALE, George E 119 359 394 443
  443-444
DENESTON, Jno 58
DENICE, Christian 448
DENISON, Eleanor 444 James 445
DENISTON, John 98
DENNET, G R 453
DENNY, Joseph 283
DENTON, Benjamin 267 C L 155 John
  267
DEPOY, Isaac 448
DEPPOY, Jacob 448
DEPRIEST, 328
DERRER, Harvey 455 F I 184 Robert
  455
DETAMORE, St Clair 123
DETRICK, John 241
DEVER, H 76 Hugh 449 James 83 449
  John 76 William 66 449
DEVIER, 105 205 D C 193 Giles 176
  331 456 Hiram K 456 Hugh 99 James
  99 103 217 John 446 Margret 91
  Newton 454 William 445
DEVIR, William 91

DICE, George 446 Mary 446 P H 454
  Thomas H 454
DICKEY, James 448 Mary 445
DICKTOM, Joseph 55
DICTAM, Joseph 67 83 213-216
DICTOM, Nancy 448
DICTUM, Joseph 218 Margaret 445
DICTUMS, Joseph 72
DIER, James 102
DILLARD, Frank 457 James D 458
DINDORE, Widow 444
DINGES, G H 232 George H 167 L R 300
  Mrs Dr 310
DINGLEDINE, W J 182 280 304 315 367
  388 390
DINKEL, Peter 377
DINKLE, 259 Calving 458 E A 200
  George F 376 Jacob 199 John 119
  199 John Sr 199 Joseph 378 S G 199
  335 Smith 335
DISPENETT, Margreat 448
DITMER, Jacob 451
DITUMS, Jean 447
DIVER, Charles 54 Hugh 52 54 William
  91
DOAK, James 446
DODD, C S 243 R A 461
DOFFILMIRE, Martin 59
DOFFLEMIRE, David 451 Michael 59
DOFFLEMOYER, Al 420 Ben 420 Bud 420
  Cap 420 Dan 420 Dick 420 George
  420 John 420 William 420
DOFFLEMYRE, J W 247 460
DOKERTY, Sarah 448
DONAFIN, William 92
DONAGHE, Hugh 449
DONAHUE, John 455 William 455
DONAPHAN, John 103
DONGAHEN, John 453
DONIPHAN, Mary 444
DONOVAN, Daniel 455 P H 204
  Washington 455 William 454
DOOLEY, Thomas 58
DOOLIN, Thomas 60 239
DOREMAN, Andrew 452 Chrisley 452
  David 452
DORSSON, Berryman 122
DOSBURNE, David 451
DOUGHTY, Moses 86
DOUGLAS, 355 Charles 304 Hugh 238
DOUGLASS, Joseph 449 N G 406
DOUTHATT, R R 406
DOVE, Addison 460 C W 184 Franklin
  454 George 441 George L 460 Henry
  96
DOVEL, Ben 420 Daniel D 453 Dug 420
  Frank L 313 James 122 Jno 458 John

ROCKINGHAM COUNTY

DOVEL (cont.)
  122 Joseph M 457 Lucius 458 Tandy 122
DOW, Lorenzo 438
DOWNING, John H 193 461
DOWNS, William S 376
DOYD, William 450
DRATZER, Joseph W 458
DREWRY, William 457
DRIVER, C 234 Dorilas 401 F H 203 392 J F 460 Jacob 262 John W 150 Joseph N 262 Lewis 397 Samuel 397 Virginia 459 Widow 150
DUCKWALL, J S 358
DUDLEY, David 447 T U 282 340 Thomas Underwood Jr 253-254
DUEY, 378
DUFF, Frances Strother 352
DUFFY, James 452
DULANEY, P B 333
DUMORE, John 199
DUNAHOE, Hugh 101
DUNAHOR, Hugh 239
DUNAPHANS, William 104
DUNCASON, Isabella 446
DUNDORE, David 458 Jacob 397 Samuel 450
DUNLAP, John W 363 371 Joseph 445 Mary 445 Robert 102 217 William 441 445
DUNN, James 90 Jennet 444
DUNNIVIN, James 453
DUNSFORD, J C 461
DUPUY, Nan 315
DUTROW, C F 334
DWYER, A W 456 J H 155
DYCHE, C P 461
DYE, Jacob 53 Mary 53
DYER, James 65-66 70 74 77 85 101 107 444 Roger 52 54 Sarah A 354 William 52 54 Zebulon 354
DYERLE, J H 461
EADIE, John 239
EARHART, Abraham 52 Catherine 446 Martin 193 Michael Jr 52
EARLY, General 139 Henry C 319 Jonas 150
EARMAN, C S 459 D W 461 D Wampler 184 David 457 G N 185 George N 443-444 Jacob 122 Joe A 458 John W 457
EARY, Philip 450
EASTHAM, C Byrd 454 G R 235 George C 455 Granville 358
EASTRIDGE, Theodisia 444
EATER, William 122
EATON, Leodosia 448 William 122

EBERMAN, Jacob 52 Michael 52
EDDINS, William A O 455
EDDY, John 102
EDWARDS, T Jervis 254
EFFINGER, A M 188 387 G M 388 454 Jacob P 355 John F 189 450 John G 281 Lucy 310 M H 189 M Harvey 387 M Hite 189 Margaret D 242 Mrs 424 Mrs M Harvey 310 Mrs Strother 310 W H 333 William H 252 358 442
EIGHINGER, Christopher 452
EILER, A P 391
EILLIOTT, Rebeckah 445
EITOR, David 122
ELA, Mr 165
ELAM, W C 336
ELDERDICE, Eugene 454
ELLIOT, Francis W 455 James 97 Robert 55 92 99 102 213
ELLIOTT, 108
ELLIS, J R 255 338 460
ELLSWORTH, Jacob 66
ELSEE, Mary 444
ELZEY, Arnold 135 General 143-144
EMBER, Cateren 448
EMICK, Reuben 119
EMMITT, Richard S 451
EMSWILLER, J T 456 Noah 456 Samuel 456 W T 456
EPPARD, Joseph Calvin 455 Nancy 295 Strother 455
ERGEBRECHT, Jacob 62 Jacob I E 62
ERGENBRIGHT, G R 456 R B 456
ERHART, Michael 52 54
ERMENTRAUT, Christopher 63 Frederick 62 Henry 62 John 63 Philip 62
ERRRING, Edith 444
ERTRAM, H W 461
ERVIN, France 91 Nat 363
ERVINE, F M 302
ERWIN, Benjamin 269 445 Elizabeth 448 Frances 97
ERWINE, Gerard 76
ESHMAN, Charles 346
ESTILL, 108
EULER, Peter 63
EUTSLER, M D 207 391
EVANS, C F 184 Evan 54 238 Jonathan 60 238 Nathaniel 54 Rhoda 54 W H 340
EVERDING, George C 452
EVERSOLE, David 122 John 397 Peter 397
EVINS, Edward 447 Evan 60
EWAN, Robert B 452
EWELL, 136 143 General 142-144 146 148

EWIN, Elizabeth 445 Henry 105 217
447 John 97 441 Mary 447
EWING, Henry 65-66 70 75 81-83 85 88
239 442 Mrs 311 William 239 397
EWINS, Henry 102 John 102
FADELY, Silvanus 458 William 455
FAHRNEY, C 202 C E 178 443 Charles E
203 403 W B 203 461 W E 392 461
FAIRBERN, Margret 446
FAIRFAX, Lord 67 349 Thomas Lord 18
FALLS, William 453
FANSLER, T A 184
FARIS, John 450
FARRIS, John 450
FATE, Joshua 450
FAUCETT, George 457
FAUSSETT, 379
FAWCETT, Abner 376 Benjamin 451
FAWLEY, Charles R 183 G W 209 Jacob 416
FEAGLE, John 450-451
FEARNEYHOUGH, William 453
FEAVIL, William 450
FECHTIG, Louis R 265
FERREL, Peter 445
FERRELL, Oliver 452 William 41
FERROL, Peter 445
FETZER, Cyrus 456
FIE, John 104
FIELD, Ann 95
FIFER, Adam Sr 449 Elizabeth 447
Joseph 452 Mary 446
FIGGETT, 360
FILLER, J R 393
FINK, John 450
FINLEY, W W 228
FINNEY, Elizabeth 446
FIREBAUGH, Samuel 393 Samuel A 454 T C 305 461
FISHER, Abraham 449 Burt 453 Henry
450 Jacob 451 John 122 451 451-452
William 122
FITCH, Buck 458
FITZPATRICK, Caleb 452
FITZWATER, Jno 74 John 65-66 70 73
80 88 93 97 216 239 Thomas 447
William 96 450-451
FLACK, John 446
FLAHAVAN, Patrick 239
FLEMENS, Albert 151
FLEMING, 454
FLEMMING, Harrison 453 Isaac 450
John 454
FLESHER, Abram 451
FLETCHER, 424 A K 454 John 453 R P
441 Richard 287 Richard P 288
Thomas 126

FLICK, Francis 452 Silas 458
FLINN, Michael 239
FLINT, William 452
FLOCK, Jacob 452
FLOOK, Harvey 457
FLORY, D C 299 I L 197 390 390-391 J
M 391 J S 320 Jno M 391 John S 204
299 320 460
FLOWER, Adam 447
FLOYD, James 75 John 117
FOGLE, Jacob 452 John 452
FOIZLE, Michael 446
FOLEY, James 455 Michael 457 W H 336 455
FOLK, E L 460 Lodowick 54
FOLTZ, James W 420
FONTAINE, John 426
FORD, Arnold 448 Joseph 454 Reuben
454 Thomas H 362 William J 375
FORRER, 366 371 Daniel 379 Harry 373
Henry 379 Samuel 390
FOSTER, G K 391
FOUGHT, Adam 100
FOUT, H H 275
FOWLAND, Jacob 97
FOWLER, Bridget 67 71 76 James 54
John 67 71 76 Jonathan 214 William 218
FOY, Charles 59 John 59
FRANCISCO, 42 Christopher 350
FRANCISCUS, Christopher 42
Christopher Jr 42 Ludwig 42
Stopfel 47
FRANCISKI, 42 Christopher 41
FRANK, A A 184 Daniel 125 Henry 408
Isaac 457 Jacob 454 John H 454
Samuel 370 William H 457
FRANKLIN, B H 204 Cathrine 445
FRANKUM, John 458 Walker 458
FRAVEL, John S 336
FRAZER, Captain 73
FRAZIER, 239 Captain 70 John 213 L A
337 Patrick 55
FRAZOR, John 95
FREDERICK, Jacob 122
FREED, John D 267
FREMONT, 143 196-197 General 142
FREY, Susenna 448 William 201
FREYSINGER, Peter 451
FRIDLEY, Charety 446 Charles 452
George 59 447 452 John 248 458
Margaret 447
FRIES, J N 235
FRIZOR, John 60
FROGG, John 56
FRY, 396 Christian 448 J A 380 John 450

ROCKINGHAM COUNTY

FUDGE, Coonrod 92 David 92-93 Jacob 52 John 93
FULK, G H 460 John G 456 Sarah 410
FULKERSON, Colonel 142
FULKS, Jacob 448
FULMORE, 445
FULS, George 450
FULSE, John 52
FULTON, Bessie R 459 Hannah 445 Jane 444 Jenet 446 John 444 John G 393 John Jr 66 Mary 444 Thomas 214
FULTS, George 52 John 60
FULTZ, G S 204 461 George 450-451 J K 457 Jacob 194 James B 452 James J 452 John 457
FUNK, 241 A B 456 A L 305 Barbara 341 Benjamin 245 320 Colonel 145 David 341 Edward 408 Elizabeth 242 341 341-342 H N 456 Hannah 341 Henry 261 321 341 448 James 456 John 49 242 245 321 341 397 John R 242 John S 184 315 370 393 Jonathan 341 Joseph 11 125-127 204 245 262 293 297 318 320-321 324 332 334-335 339-341 341 341-343 345 367 433 Joseph R 204 Mary 341 344 Milton E 456 Rachel 341 S 260 Samuel 242 341 Solomon 245 341 Susan 341 T W 456 Timothy 10 245 341-342 Timothy 341 Vada 280 W C 204 William 456
FUNKHOUSER, 241 A P 307 336 399 442 461 A Paul 296 C A 297 C H 184 David 454 J C 417 J H 201 Jacob 206 321 389 Minnie 307
FURRY, James 452 William J 453
FUTCH, Jno Jr 59 John 59
FUZET, John 452
FYE, John 101
GAINES, John 420 454
GAITHER, George 454 George W 453 John 452
GAMBILL, Henry J 117 196 442 Henry Jewett 442 J R 461 L W 281 310 387 442 Littleton W 442
GAMBLE, J H 443 James 447 Robert 444
GARBER, 241 371 Daniel 455 458 David 393 J A 203 210 392 J N 297 J S 389 Jacob 203 457 Jacob A 321 460 John S 389 M F 392 P I 460 Solomon 249 W A 321
GARISON, E C 461
GARNSBERGER, George S 360
GARRETT, John 194
GARRISON, J S 272 280 461 James 454
GARTAN, Elijah 445
GARTNER, George 91 Peter 21

GARTRA, Frances 444
GARVER, Martin 250
GARVIN, David 445 447
GASSMAN, J 282 Jacob 387
GATEWOOD, John 333
GAY, Samuel 86
GEABHART, John 446
GEIGER, Christian 62 444 Christian Sr 444
GEIL, D F 390 461 J W 460 John 393
GENTRY, Benjamin W 458 G B C 459 J B 228
GEORGE, King Of England 426
GIBBON, 37 Mr 432
GIBBONS, A S 363 James 272 R A 206 S B 11 134-136 176 Samuel 123
GIBBS, Charley 453 William 453 William W 376
GIBSON, Henry 445
GILBERT, Ann 446 Felex 96 Felix 54 54-56 58 60 64 69 107 187 213 217-218 239 Sarah Hester 445
GILES, Samuel N 454
GILKERSONWILLIAM, 455
GILLILAN, James 239
GILMER, Alexander 445 Algernon E 267 George 109 195 George K 154 253 333 George Rockingham 10 108 110 H D 461 J H 458 Peachy 57 Thomas 445
GILMOR, David 448
GILMORE, David 194 George 196 Harry 360 Henry 451 Peachy 95 Zebulon 194
GIST, Captain 78
GIVENS, John 195
GLADEN, Joseph 451
GLASGOW, 108
GLASPIE, Jacob 98
GLICK, Jacob D 460 John 454
GLOSSBRENNER, J J 273
GLOVER, Derrick 455 Jack 455
GLOVIER, Madison 458
GOADE, Joanna 348
GOAR, Mary 446
GOOCH, Governor 44 William 35
GOOD, 241 Christian 263 323 460 D R 307 J H S 199 J S 184 Jacob 456 M A 300 Peter 397 Samuel 207 392 Sharp 420 W I 337 William H 454
GOODALL, John 450
GOODPASTURE, Lydia 445
GOODWYN, James B 11 252
GORDON, J B 140 James H 454 John 397 John B 438 Thomas 72 214 445 W A 197 461
GOTTLOB, Brother 50
GOTTSCHALK, 37 Brother 45-47

GOWL, Adam G 458 David 458 Peter 458 William 453
GRABILL, C 456 N C 456
GRABLE, G W 457
GRACE, Benjamin 447 Jacob 60 James 101
GRAHAM, 437 Alexander 448 D C 184 Harriet 269 James 447 John 189 269 437 John H 281 Mrs 125 Thomas 457
GRANDLE, Christley 457
GRANDSTAFF, Branson 458 H P 454
GRANKLE, Emanuel 455
GRANT, 167 356 General 139 President 438
GRATTAN, Catharine 444 Charles 322 363 443 G G 390 George 270 George G 75 175 322 358 363 389-390 441-443 George G Jr 461 George G Sr 390 461 John 86 239 442 449 Judge 280 Lucy Gilmer 318 P R 322 Peachy 117 Peachy R 322 Robert 293 387
GRATTEN, John 65-67 74-75
GRAVES, A W 461 J E 207 William 451 William 450
GRAY, 132 A S 131 173 281 319 325 444 Algernon 192 Algernon S 252 353 Charles D 281 Douglas 353 George 453 H J 376-377 Henry Juett 437 Isabella 352 James H 454 Jouett 353 Nettie 319 R A 190 Robert 10 173 192 239 270 304 351-354 388 425 437 442 Robert A 442 W C R 452
GREELYEY, 167
GREEN, Francis 214 449 James 448 John 448 Katherine 326 Katherine S 360 Sarah 446
GREGG, William 81
GREGOR, John 444
GREIMES, Margret 446
GREINER, N Lee 454
GRIGSBY, John 450
GRIM, J W 390 Peter 125 W 337
GRIMS, Elizabeth 448
GRISTLEY, John 446
GROSS, Samuel 451
GROUT, David 452 Peter 452
GROVE, Jacob N 455 Jacob R 452 John W 455 Miles M G 455 Tobias M 196 W H 458 William H 200
GROVES, I M 307 Jacob 450 T M 456
GRUB, Jacob 52
GRUBB, Daniel 81 Jacob 56
GUIHEEN, Maurice 454
GUIN, Daniel 96 239 Hugh 446 John 97 239 Patrick 95 239
GUISE, Elizabeth 445

GUM, Ann 77 Anne 82 Claypole 77 83 Elinor 448 John 52 Marten 213
GUNNER, William 454
GURDEN, Michael 450
GUSTARD, Paul 213
GUY, Emmet 340
GUYER, Peter 454
GWIN, David S 364 David W 364
HAAS, Charles E 358 T N 183 315 363 390 442 461
HADRICK, John 59
HAGAY, Godfrey 449
HAHN, George 459 Mr 370
HAILMAN, Sarah C 232
HAINES, Casper 212 Frederick 212 Joseph 84
HAIR, Easter 446 John 446
HALE, H C 200
HALINS, Casper 449
HALL, C Ernest 347 Christian 455 E G 461 J G 206 J H 246 322 341 Jacob H 342 James 188 Joseph 444 Stuart 361
HALSTEAD, Richard 296
HAM, D E 391 William 55
HAMAKER, J D 251
HAMER, George 52 J M 453
HAMILETON, Godferry 91
HAMILTON, Captain 70 Cave 453 G 214 Gawen 67 73 75 77-78 215 442 Gawin 57 69 75 97 103 106-107 214 449
HAMMACK, A S 275 297 461
HAMMEN, J A 441
HAMMER, C A 155 Charles A 461 Elizabeth 446 Henry 241 446 Henry C 455 Isaac 123 Jacob 59 John 123 L A 461 Lee 246 William H 459
HAMMON, C E 453 George 452 J A 387 Joseph A 387
HAMMOND, Abraham 82 Jacob 445
HAMNER, T L 269
HAMPHILL, Samuel 94
HAMRICK, William H 224
HANCE, Frederick 445
HANCKLE, Isaac 74
HANCOCK, General 139
HANDLEY, Perry 457
HANDY, H 295 Huston 358
HANEY, G W 453 John 450 453 W A B 452 William 59
HANFRUP, Vitus 45
HANKLE, Abraham 216 Isaac 86 445
HANLEY, John 451
HANNA, John 451
HANNAH, Alexander 444 Belle C 308 362 Joseph 95 Kate M 362 Samuel 455

ROCKINGHAM COUNTY

HANSBARGER, Henry 122
HANSBERGER, A L 456 Adam 59 93
  Coonrod 93 Stephen 59 William M
  456
HANSBURGER, Adam 450
HANSBURGHER, Stephen 52
HANSFORD, Eleoner 447
HARDESTY, 189 Isaac 189 364 387 J
  190 J N A 454 J R L 364
HARDMAN, John 59
HARE, Isaac 450-451
HARESON, Ruth 447
HARGEST, Thomas S 442
HARISON, Ezekiel 218 Rubin 447
HARLOW, C M 378
HARMAN, B F 453 Elizabeth 447 M G
  228 Mrs Lenion 311 Samuel 455
HARMER, Jesse 450
HARMON, B F 453 George 450 Jacob 101
HARNBERGER, H B 442
HARNED, David 449
HARNER, J N 458 J P 298
HARNESBARGER, John 451
HARNESBERGER, Jacob 451 John 451
HARNET, David 76 92 220
HARNETT, David 213
HARNSBERGER, 37 241 C D 207 C C 390
  Captain 361 Charles W 455 Carrie V
  360 Conrad 264 Coonrad 378
  Elizabeth 360 George S 461 Gilbert
  M 360 H B 207 373 442-443 443
  Henry B 174 J S 220 282 358 388
  427 J Samuel 360 450 Jacob E 281
  Jeremiah 360 Jno I 390 Joseph M C
  427 Joseph 455 Mrs W I 207 Robert
  446 455 Stephen 115 427 Thomas K
  443-444 W I 206-207
HARPER, Addison 118 443 John 196
HARPOLE, Barbary 446 Catherine 446
HARRELL, G R 302
HARRIGAN, Daniel 454
HARRIS, A H 456 Ann 356 Anna H 357
  Clement C 357 Edith 357 Emma H 357
  Frank L 280 389 Graham H 357
  Hatton N T 357 James 444 James A
  455 John A 456 John T 55 161 357
  360 442 442-443 461 John Thomas
  356-357 M H 281 302 Michael H 117
  Nathan 356 Thomas 50 Virginia M
  357 Virginia O 357 W M 456 William
  E 455
HARRISON, 176 Benjamin 63 63-64 66-
  67 69 74 79 81-82 88 98 105 214
  214-215 215 217 283 283-284 441
  441-443 449 Captain 70 Carrie 294
  Charles D 183 442 461 Daniel 53
  63-64 400 446 Daniel S 458 David

HARRISON (cont.)
  400 Dr 395 Edith 447 Elizabeth 447
  Ezekial 441 Ezekiel 102 104 215-
  217 449 George W 265-266 351
  Gessner 64 287 308 322 Gideon 52
  89 James 448 Jane 54 338 Jeremiah
  97-98 213-214 Jess Sr 449 Jesse 75
  216 446 John 52 92 215 217 449
  Josiah 79 88-89 104 444 446 449 M
  H 183 Mary 446 Matthew 449 Michael
  446 Nathan 52 Nehemiah 101 215
  Peachey 10 265 366 Peachy 64 115-
  116 118-119 198 308 430 441 444
  Peachy R 387 Polly 446 R N 443
  Reuben 69 81 93-95 101 104 187 213
  263 265 283 449 Reuben N 443
  Reubin 283 Rhebe 447 Robert 83 101
  187 263 283 446 449 457 Ruben 54
  Thomas 9 50 74 74-76 78 83 100-102
  187-188 188 193 215 283 449 Thomas
  Sr 74 Tiffin 287 W C 174 William
  111 400 451 Zeb 83 96 213 Zebulon
  88 213 449
HARRISSON, Gideon 446 Nathaniel 447
HARSON, Sarah 74
HART, Major 257 Silas 17 65 67 75
  75 76 82-83 85 99 245 441-442
HARTER, Henry 96
HARTMAN, 436 Dav 458 Fredrick 450
HARVEY, Jewett 455
HARVIE, John 350 Margaret 350
HARYSEN, Thomas 447
HASKIN, F J 328
HASLER, George 455 Jacob 455 Philip
  455 William 455
HATFIELD, John 453 Mary 446
HATHEWAY, Deaborah 447
HAU, Christopher 63
HAUDLEY, John 450
HAUK, Henry 446
HAUSENFLUCK, J W 460
HAUSMAN, John 62
HAVENER, Jacob 80
HAWK, Christian 451
HAWKINS, 350 B A 295 J H 453 Jacob
  458 Jno 444 Joseph 349 Sarah 348 W
  H 458 William 457
HAWSE, J J 388 Jasper 442
HAY, James 282 363
HAYES, 170-172
HAYNES, D F 210 Frederick 59 Gasper
  452 Joseph 63-64 64 444
HAYS, Colonel 145 Daniel 250 322 460
  H M 309 Heber M 322 John 446
HEADRICK, John 449
HEANICY, Ann 447

HEARD, Anna H 357 J T 185 197-198 390
HEART, Silas 449
HEASTAND, Elizabeth 447 Mary 447
HEATON, John 445
HEATWOLD, Daniel F 397 David A 397 L J 306 460
HEATWOLE, 241 436 A S 183 Abram 386 Aldine 436 Amos 460 C J 299 427 436 Cornelius J 323 380 D A 323 393 David A 224 393 407 436 David H 454 Ella C 459 Emanuel 460 Frank A 184 436 G D 460 Gabriel S 454 H A 393 454 J D 378 J W 199 John D 455 John G 386 John J 436 Joseph F 391 L F 437 L J 14 181 212 263 267 282 335 Lewis J 323 M J 460 P S 460 P X 199 Simeon 460 T O 307 436
HEAVENER, John 450 William 450
HEDDECKER, Henry 450
HEDRICK, Adam 52 C L 456 Fayette 298 G W 204 George 52 George W 456 H C 459 John 451 W W 456
HEGGINS, Marten 448
HEIDECKER, Jacob 452 Jacob Jr 452
HEINRICHS, Lieutenant 144
HEISHMAN, A S 460
HEISKELL, Mrs Huldah 311
HELBERT, B F 390
HELFREEGH, Charlotte 448
HELFREY, Elizabeth 446
HELLER, H 368 Herman 256 Jonas 256
HELMER, Conrad 448
HELMS, Jacob 455
HELPHENSTINE, J H 452
HELSLEY, W G 456
HELTZEL, Jas C 393
HEMPHILL, John 97 Samuel 52 216 449
HENDERSON, Archibald 99
HENDRICKS, 172
HENEBERGER, A E 189 388 Lucien G 364 Mrs A E 176
HENKEL, Ambrose 331 Benjamin 271 D 454 Elon O 288-290 Paul 260 S A 203
HENKLE, J C 457 L M 457 L P 457
HENNESEY, Michael 446
HENNING, John 450
HENRY, Jane 447-448 John 443 Patrick 65 256 Robert 445 S 189 Sam 269 Susanna 255
HENSELL, John C 271
HENSLEY, James L 275
HENTON, Benjamin 445 C O 247 338 David 118 120 441 Ebenezer 446 Evan 394 James 105 John 75 99 John M 457 Phebe 446 Sarah 445

HERDMAN, Anna 448 John 72 102 214 John Jr 449
HERING, Alexander 54
HERMAN, Adam 63
HERN, Samuel 453
HERNDON, W T 247
HERNICHE, Mary 444
HERRING, Abigal 445 Alexander 101 442 Bethuel 445 Bethuell 101 C C 298 338 E A 370 Hannah 448 J A 255 John A 198 Leonard 93 P 443 Philander 199 453 Thomas 371 William 67 73 82 82-83 83 88 93 105 214 441 449
HERRINGS, Sarah 447
HERRMANN, Elisabeth 444
HERRON, Leonard 52 Robert 310 William 79
HERSHMAN, Woolry 95-96
HESS, Andrew 332
HESSE, Julius 293
HETH, Robert 58
HETRICH, Adam 62
HETRICK, John 62
HEWIT, Captain 70 Thomas 81 85
HEWITT, Thomas 65-66 69 101 441
HICKS, Jno 100 Joseph 396 Thomas 72
HIDECKER, William 458
HIGGENS, John 247
HIGGINS, John 126
HIGGS, Isaac 457 Jackson 457 Jno W 459 Robert 417
HIGH, Grafton 458
HILBERT, Michael 452
HILDEBRAND, 341 E T 337 Ephraim Timothy 342
HILE, Samuel 458
HILING, Joseph 452
HILL, A P 135 D H 438 George 450 Homer M 183 J N 152 John 450 Robert 60 71 Thomas 40
HILLIARD, Aleck 420 Charley 420 Chris 420 Jacob 420 James C 458
HINCKEL, Isaac 65 Philip 445
HINCKLE, Isaac 66 70 441
HINDE, 337
HINEGARDNER, Jacob 457-458
HINER, Young J 119
HINIKER, George 452
HINKE, W J 61 William J 45
HINKLE, Jacob 458
HINTON, Estor 76 Jno 459 John 71 75-76 90 102 Joseph 216 455 Peter 450 452 Rachel 448 Silas 450 Thomas 451
HIRE, Leonard 54
HISER, Edward 455 George 452

ROCKINGHAM COUNTY

HITE, 39 Francis A 376 Isaac 202
   Jost 34 T M 232
HITT, Dr 194 Nirod 123 Silas 455
HLEBERT, B F 390
HNLEN, Cathene 447
HOBSON, George 39
HOCKMAN, 366 Anthony 396
HODGE, B L 296
HODGES, John 349
HOENSHEL, E U 14 307 315 337 461
   Elmer U 315 323 G W 306 George W
   306 323 Mrs 323
HOFFMAN, 259 Frederick 201
HOG, Captain 78 80-81 Elizabeth 98
   Peter 66 68 75 77 86 88 98 217 442
HOGSHEAD, David 444-445 William 444
HOLBROOK, 196
HOLCOMB, Fletcher 455
HOLEMAN, William 444
HOLLAND, 260 Elias 459 G W 260 296
   George 455 George W 442 Joseph
   450-451 Peter 453
HOLLANDER, 238
HOLLAR, D M 204 S B 456
HOLLEN, A R 376 L M 391 Peter 364
HOLLER, G F 461
HOLMAN, Daniel 21
HOLMES, David 110 351 442 Hugh 108
   351-352 441 Julius C 168
HOLSINGER, 241 D C 457 David 9 G B
   340-341 George 344 H R 246 John D
   458 John L 314 Martin 458 Michael
   9 218 Mrs G B 306 Mrs John L 314
   Noah 458 Perry 457 Peter P 458
   Sallie 344 Silas J 458 Samuel 458
HOMAN, Herod 457 J C 366 S J C 457
HOME, G 40
HOMES, Gulhery 447
HOOD, P B F 443
HOOF, John 447
HOOFMAN, George 59 Michael 59
HOOK, Elijah 60 James 60 Jno C 459
   Robert 95 101 239 Robert Sr 60
   William 60 90 99-102
HOOKE, A S 456 Elisha 450 454 Eve
   447 H S 309 James 451 James A 451
   R J 456 Robert 111 451 456
HOOKER, 138
HOOPER, John 60
HOOVER, B 151 Jacob 449 Jesse 199
   Jno 458 John 288 John H 315 392 S
   E 459 Samuel 288 Sebaston 96
   Samuel 125 W C 380 392 460
HOPKENS, John 216
HOPKIN, 37
HOPKINS, 241 397 Anthony C 454
   Archibald 52 89 99 102 215 302 397

HOPKINS (cont.)
   454 Archibald Jr 449 Archibald Sr
   449 Ben 432 Captain 70 Edwin B 398
   Elizabeth 444 Fannie 311 G T 366
   398 Hannah 448 J H 443 Jesse 454
   John 52 89 99 102 215 442 John A
   120 John Fr 444 John H 366 370
   Luther 298 Mary 445 445-446 Mrs
   Col 310 Peachy 454 Sarah 445
   Thomas 111 410 450 W D 366 387
HORN, O P 458
HORNIGN, Anna Elisabeth 444
HOTCHKISS, J 147 Jed 11 21 306
HOTT, G P 297 George P 323 461
HOUCK, 376 379 Alice 294 J P 191 233
   278 407 Jacob 376 John W 454
HOULDER, Michael 449
HOUSTON, George 193 J W C 301 Jno W
   C 454
HOVER, Pasley 101 Sebastian 72 77
HOW, Stophel 447
HOWARD, A A 184 Adam 448 David 289
HOWDISHELL, Jacob 453
HOWDYSHELL, Adam 451
HOWE, Henry 114 186 205 421 John
   Williams 275
HOWEL, Cathrine 446
HOWLAND, Rebecca 448
HOWMAN, Barbara 448
HOWVER, J P 184
HUBBARD, W J 460
HUDLOW, 455 Andrew 95 Charles 451
   John 448
HUDLOWE, Jacob 422
HUDSON, Lizzie 310
HUET, Sarah 447 Thomas 60
HUFFMAN, 241 Bernard 452 D W 455
   Daniel 455 George 212 455 J B 456
   J S 458 J W 458 James 455 John 122
   452 John P 455 Joseph H 458
   Madison 457 Nicholas 54 Samuel H
   122
HUFMAN, Hamilton I 122 Honicle 52
   Philip 52
HUGHES, 168 B F 452 J E F 459 R C
   338 S 40 Thomas 444 William 454
HUGHS, William 283
HULING, Samuel 450
HULVA, David 456 Jonathan 456 Josiah
   456 S B 456
HULVAH, Coonrod 95
HULVEY, G H 305 George H 144 183 278
   309 442 Otey C 300
HUMBLE, Conrad 410 Conrod 216 Jane
   410
HUMES, J N 456
HUMPHRIES, David 456

HUNTER, 236 General 150 John Jr 444
   S M 288
HUPP, C T 456
HURLEY, Daniel 453
HURRAH, P M 423
HUSHMAN, Ullry 59 Ullry Jr 59
HUSTON, Archibald 54 Christian 444
   David 122 George 66 80 100 122 196
   215 410 441-442 442-443 443 448-
   449 455 James M 117 John 84 215
   Nathan 122 Nelly 447
HUTCHENS, Samuel W 454
HYDE, J P 312
HYTE, Joost 39
IMBODEN, General 148
INGLE, Paul 212
IRELAND, 378 John 244 William 444
IRICK, A B 388-389 D 119 David 122
   194
IRISH, Robert Hook 60
IRVINE, A J 454 France 101 J H 340 J
   M 376
IRWIN, D C 269 John 451
ISELEY, E T 246 248
JACK, John 450
JACKSON, 136 138 434 Andrew 438
   General 137 141 148 256 J L 460
   Jno 60 John L 254 Stonewall 20-21
   196-197 360 T J 147 Yenty 450
JACOBS, J W 232 John W 232 376
JAMES, Watkins 309
JAMESON, George L 336
JAMISON, John W 458
JARMAN, M M 371 390
JARREL, Ann 447
JAYS, Stephen 58
JEFFERSON, 70 106 110 Thomas 83
JEFFRIES, Thomas Fayette 324
JENNINGS, Annie 310 Dallas 458 G W
   457 S B 398 W K 295 455 William C
   293 William G 454
JEWELL, Samuel 452
JEWETT, C A 231
JOHNS, H A M 309 John 253
JOHNSON, 355 Captain 85 Chapman 443
   Colonel 141 David 453 Edward 136
   139 Eliphalet 454 H H 292 Jacob
   447 L B 269 Montgomery 457
   President 160 T J 459 Wellington
   457
JOHNSTON, Andrew 72 86 445 Captain
   74 General 168 Jacob 448 James C
   324 337 John 446 448 Joseph E 135
   Mary 221 Robert 360 441 Samuel 444
JONES, Adam 458 Albert 455 Ann 445
   Anna Gabriella 444 D S 190 368
   David A 452 David S 124 168 E E

JONES (cont.)
   392 Elizabeth 350 Fanny 350
   Gabriel 9 54 57 65 69 73 76-77 86
   95 98 213 225 255 350-351 442 444
   449 Harriet Yost 168 Hugh 427 I N
   183 Isaac 456 J R 168 J W 298
   Jacob 126 John 350 John R 252 455
   John Robert 168 Margaret 350 Mrs
   Bartow 360 Robert S 224 Sam 438
   Samuel M 452 T O 315 461 Thomas
   453 William 422 William Strother
   350
JONSON, E A 457
JORDAN, A J 453 Captain 281 S B 456
   William N 147-148 242
JOSEPH, Mary 447
JUNK, Joseph 344
KAGEY, 177 241 J M 391 Joseph M 460
   Sallie 344
KAGY, John 447
KALBERLAND, 49
KALE, Z T 461
KANE, 141 Elisha Kent 433 Father 272
   Thomas L 433
KARICOFE, W H 377
KARN, Nicholas 217
KARR, Thomas 445
KAUFFMAN, Michael 261-262
KAUFMAN, Michael 36-38
KAVANAUGH, 108 James 289
KAVANGAUGH, James M 454
KAYLER, S H 456
KAYLOR, 113 241 D M 121 George 122 Q
   G 155 186 330
KEAGY, Christian 448 Franklin 177 J
   R 289
KEARNEY, Andrew J 362 Martin L 362
KEENE, James R 371
KEES, Frances 100
KEESAYER, John 454
KEEZEL, G M 338
KEEZELL, Amanda Fitzallen 361 Belle
   C 362 G B 308 393 George 362
   George B 307 392-393 441 444
   George Bernard 361 Kate M 362
   Senator 362 Walter G 461
KEEZLE, Amanda 310
KEIFFER, Aldine S 454
KEILER, Frederick 101
KEISELL, George 193 Mr 193
KEISTER, Isaac 454 John 456 William
   H 304
KEITER, J W 183 199
KELLAR, George 123
KELLER, 260 Conrad 446 Henry 451
   John 458 Keaty 448 Lewis 451
   Michael 447 Philip 458

KELLEY, John 458 John H 454 Joseph H 452
KELLY, Emanuel 80 Frank T 364 Jemima 80 Patrick 239 378
KELSLE, George 94
KEMPER, 37 168 241 A S 185 350 392 461 C E 61 C M 456 Charles A 37 Charles E 35-36 45 48 Charles Edward 324 E S 388 Ed S 387 392 Edward S 324 442 G W 392 434 441 George B 452 George W 302 392 433 George W Jr 252 R 368 Susan Craig 324 William M 452 William P 452
KENNEDY, W S 295
KENNERLY, Philip 448
KENNEY, Annie 310 James 134 159 168 191 229 239 287 353 358 441 443 452 John 118 126 353 387 442 444 452 Judge 169 172-173 231 297 Robert 454
KENNON, P P 456
KENNY, John 119
KEPLINGER, George 455 John 213 Philip 446
KERAN, Alexander 447 Thomas J 456
KERCHEVAL, A W 232 292 Samuel 51
KERR, John P 331
KERSH, Mathi 59 Mathias 99
KERTLEY, Francis 442 St Clair 123
KERTLY, Francis 122
KESLER, Daniel 451 Peter 451 Woolery 449
KESSLE, George 94 449 Gorge 94
KESTER, Arnold 445 Catherine 446 Frederick 101 Jacob 444 Joseph 77
KESTERSON, John 446
KEYES, Eramus L 456
KEYSER, Davy 420 James 420 Sim 420
KEZLE, Georg 94
KIBLER, Charles 453
KIBLINGER, Jacob 95 122 Jacob Jr 122 William C 455
KIEFFER, 321 338-339 A S 341 A S 13 342 Aldine S 325-326 332 334 344 Aldine Silliman 344 H Prime 325 Jennie Stinespring 325 John 344 Lucilla Virginia 344 Mary 344 Mrs 311 Rollin 325 Virginia 333 345
KIESTER, Frederick 412-413
KIGER, William 293
KILLBUCK, Chief 51
KILLE, Mrs Thomas 210
KILLIAN, C M 209 Melville 298
KILPATRICK, Abner 269 Abner W 288
KIMBROUGH, 450
KIMLER, A C 13 298 Abram C 299
KING, Floyd W 307-308 Reuben 452

KINGREE, David 387
KINNEY, John 190
KIRACOFE, William H 233
KIRKPATRICK, John 453 Thomas 453
KIRTLEY, Francis 52 449 George 443 St C 441 St C D 443
KISER, C B 200 373 George 242 Henry 452 Isaac 446 William 446
KISLEY, David 452
KISLING, 326 George J 167 442 W G 453 Whit 139
KISLINGER, Jacob 449
KISORE, Michael 449
KISSLING, Jacob 63
KITE, Alec 420 Alf 420 C J 459 Charles N 455 Christian 451 Columbus 420 Gabriel 52 George 52 Henry 447 J H 197 378 Jack 420 Jacob 53 186 Joseph H 455 Malinda 310 Roland 420 Valentine 53 W E 390 William 53 420 448 William Ed 458
KIZE, Peter 101
KLEMAN, Christian 42
KLINE, 241 J H 460 J M 390 John 12 250 320-321 353 434
KLINGER, J M 461
KLUG, George S 260 George Samuel 46 Mr 47
KNAVE, George 446 John 445
KNIGHT, William 422
KNIPPLE, E B 452
KNOPP, Abram 452
KNUPP, Claude 204 John A 457 William 457
KOCH, David 60
KOHLER, Henry 62
KOINER, 241 J M 391
KOOGLER, J R 377 441
KOOK, James 122
KOONTZ, A 452 John 187 202 244 443 Lurty 183 Morgan 459 P P 301 R F 457 Robert 452 W W 461
KRAHN, Frederick 122
KRATZER, Christian 455 John Sr 247 Mrs G 310
KROPF, Daniel 62 Jacob 62
KROPP, Jacob 444 Margaret 444
KUHNERT, A 346
KYGER, J A S 184 197-198 Jacob A S 459
KYLE, Davie 377 Harvey 232 388 Jerry 189 270 Mary 310 Mrs P 190 Robert M 387 St Clair 281 William P 456
KYROR, Hannah 447
LACKEY, Robert 458
LACROST, William 450

LADY, James 451
LAFAYETTE, 64
LAFFERTY, Addison 453
LAGO, F H 201
LAIR, Catherine 447 Ferdinand 445
  Margaret 445
LAIRD, David 80 100 102 James 94 239
  Mary 444
LAIREY, John 458
LAM, J M 210 Peter 363 V H 441
LAMB, 386 Allen 453 H J 453 Isaac
  455 Lewis 455 Mr 289 Nathan 445 V
  H 376
LAMBERT, C L 299 E L 185 206 454 457
LAMMON, John 451
LANAHAN, Denis 445
LANDES, B S 460 Barbara 127 David
  313 James H 454
LANDIS, D H 370 Washington 455
LANG, Anny 446 James 447
LANGHORNE, Mrs Orra Gray 325
LANIER, Sidney 13 340 398 435-436
LANTZ, J W 460
LARKIN, J H 378 456
LARKINS, J H 206
LASALLE, 33
LASH, Adam 452 Andrew 453
LASSITER, L L 460
LATEN, Joseph 450
LATIMER, G S 358
LAUDERBACK, Abram 452
LAUK, John 445 447
LAULCER, Catherine 448
LAUNDRICE, John 447
LAURENS, Jane 359
LAWMAN, David 247
LAWN, John 59
LAWSON, John 451
LAYMAN, David 452 Jack 454 John 452
  M A 235 O A 201 Preston 454
  William 452
LAYTON, Gibbons 454 John H 454
LEACH, William 445
LEAKE, William G 314
LEAP, E A 453 Jacob 194 John 194 J
  Samuel 459 Mr 368 Nicholas 259
LEAR, Joseph 213 Margaret 444
LEAS, Mathias Jr 66
LEDERER, John 33
LEE, Boler 58-59 Fitzhugh 438
  General 137-138 140 J Watkins 396
  Robert E 106 Sefniah 450 Thomas 39
  Warfield 456 William 60 William Jr
  60 Zacarias 450 Zachariah 60 445
  Zephaniah 60
LEEAH, Christian 447
LEEBRICK, J E 197 390 James E 390

LEEDY, John 456
LEEHAN, Jack 453
LEETH, J L 207 W A 391
LEGG, E Armfield 305
LEMON, Eli 459 Elizabeth 448 J W 207
LENNIG, Thompson 406
LEONARD, Solomon 122
LERCH, C D 461
LETCHER, S H 442
LEVERING, 178
LEVERTS, Windal 59
LEWIS, 108 132-133 143-144   S H 365
  Andrew 127 252 355 388 452
  Benjamin 195-196 Charles 109 127
  351 356 441 Charles H 363 442
  Charles Sr 350 D S 338 D S Jr 338
  Daniel Sheffey 334 356 Elizabeth
  445 Ellis 455 George R 452 J F 444
  James A 452 Jean 445 Jane 444 John
  34 43 127 350 444 John F 127 131
  174 252 335 356 363 370-371 373
  379 394 437 459 John Francis 355
  John L A 455 Lunsford 461 Lunsford
  L 363 Mary 311 445 Mr 67 S H 125
  368 437 441 Samuel H 127 252 443
  Samuel H Jr 252 Sophia 447 Thomas
  9 42 57 88 107 127 255 351 442 444
  451 Thomas Sr 449 William 196 437
  455 William M 452
LIBBY, Phoebe 309 Phoeby 12
LICHLITER, J W 313
LIFE, J F 185 Jerry 458 John 298
LIGGETT, 131 190 Charles T 452
  Evelyn 355 Isabella 355 J N 123
  281 333 355 358 442 444 456 Jacob
  N 355 Mr 126 P 281 Romanzy
  Nicholas 355 Samuel 189 355 376
  Winfield 361
LIGHTFOOT, G 41
LILLY, H B 453 John H 459 Malcolm G
  325
LINAWEAVER, Jacob 122
LINCOLN, 202 A C 454 Abraham 9 428 B
  F 301 457 Captain 70 David 120
  Isaac 428 451 J E 461 J J 309
  Jacob 56 83-84 218 295 428 444
  John 106 428 John Jr 428 Margaret
  446 Mary 311 Mrs A 310 Thomas 428
  445 Virginia C 295
LINDAMOOD, James 456 Sylvanus 456
LINDON, M 455
LINDSAY, Peter 451 S C 296 S F 306
LINDSEY, A L 442
LINEWEAVER, Charles 459 David 397 E
  R 390 W J 235 W T 280 461 William
  T 459
LINGAL, Paul 95

ROCKINGHAM COUNTY

LINGLE, Jacob 62 Jacob Jr 59 John 59 Paul 59 Philip 60
LINHOSS, D H 453 Frederick 123 453
LINSAY, Philip 451
LISKEY, George W 68
LITTELL, William W 293
LITTLE, Jack 55-57
LOCHART, Sarah 304
LOEB, William 240 256 388
LOESCH, 49
LOEVENSTEIN, Corad 63
LOEWENBACH, J A 376 380 Jonas A 387
LOEWENBACK, Jonas 240
LOEWENER, Charles 258
LOEWNER, A M 193 C E 408 S 377 Samuel 256-257
LOFTIES, Ralph 91
LOFTUS, Ralph 106
LOGAN, George S 376 Joseph T 253 280 442 N W 453
LOHR, George 150
LOID, Phebe 447
LOKER, David 457 Rash 457 Thomas 457-458
LOKEY, Elizabeth 447 Thomas 449
LOKY, Thomas 447
LON, Mrs Isaac S 325
LONG, 241 A H 390 397 454 B Frank 454 Benjamin 123 C E 460 Christianna 448 Christina 445 Conrad 458 D A 246 248 251 Daniel 53 Emanuel 460 Erasmus 457 Fredrick 452 George 91 George W 417 Henry 53 95 Isaac 249 392 458 Isaac S 325 J H 377 J Owen 280 347 John 53 453 455 John F 454 Joseph 453 Mary E 377 Mathias 452 Matthias 447 Mrs 195 Paul 36 38 452 Philip 36 38 42 48 101 Robert 452 Samuel A 393 T A 233 Thomas 455 W E 208 W H 393 William 53 62 William C 453 455
LONGLEY, Charles 453
LOOSE, J S 12 233 296 388 Joseph S 442 Mr 302 O B 388
LORE, Matthias 451
LOSSING, B J 438
LOTT, Reeves 105
LOUDERBACK, Abraham 446 J Philip 455 M V 420
LOUSH, David 451
LOVE, Daniel 56 58 91 Ephraim 53 102 Joseph 54
LOWENBACH, J A 387
LOWERY, Joseph 453
LOWMAN, Fannie 294 306 James 457 Jas F 388 John I 454

LOWNER, Emanuel 256 Samuel 256
LOWRY, Philip 151 W M 420 William 420 447
LUCAS, Bogus 420 Dick 420 Henry 420 Reuben 420 Simon 451 W E 198 William 420
LUKES, Mary 447
LUNG, Henry 212 Mathias 446 Philip 48-49
LUPTON, J R 394-395
LURTY, 174 W S 333 Warren S 358
LUSBY, William 446
LUTHOLTZ, Christian 455 Noah 455
LYNES, Robert 60
MACE, J H 379 421
MACHALL, John 449
MACHEN, E C 231
MACKALLS, John 107
MACKELVAIN, Mary 444 Thomas 444
MACKEY, John] 34
MACQUEARY, Emma H 357
MADDAY, James 59
MADISON, 394 Bishop 58 George 255-256 James 9 255 John 58 255 Richard 98 Rowland 255 Susanna 255 Thomas 255
MAGART, Hans 95
MAGGART, Barbara 447
MAGILL, Esther 445 James 101 214 217 James Jr 444 John 66 82 Margaret 445 Robert 111 451 Samuel 445 William 66 97 99
MAGOT, Samuel 59
MAGRUDER, J H 456 John B 438 Virginia 139
MAHONE, William 438
MAHOY, Joseph 122
MAIDEN, Jacob 451 James 78 Theodisia 78
MALLO, George Jr 62 George Sr 62 Michael 63
MALLOW, George 53 60 82 95 100-101 451 Michael 53
MAN, Elizabeth 446
MANN, 362 George Adam 444 John 62
MANNING, William 453
MAPHIS, Charles G 308
MARCH, Sabaston 449
MARKS, Margaret 445
MARKWOOD, Bishop 275 Michael 450
MARR, Gideon 40-41
MARSHAL, William 97
MARSHALL, J L 459 461 James W 363 Jane 445 John H 455 Montgomery 455 Robert F 455 W H 209 William 96 William H 455
MART, Sebastian 213

MARTIN, 434-435 D A 455 Dan 420 J S 460 James 388 John 420 Joseph 205 Thomas J 391 W M Sr 420 William Jr 420
MARTZ, 241 A B 452 Addison B 454 D G 457 D H Lee 134 176 183 280 442 453-459 Ed C 134 220 461 H 443 H C 457 Hiram 443 Isaac C 457 Jacob 452 M J 454 Martin 451 Michael 457 Sebastian 452
MASON, Henry 456
MASSIE, Jacob 450 John E 245
MASTERS, C H 459 John 458
MATHEAS, John 447
MATHENY, John 451
MATHES, Mary 447
MATHEWS, Amelia 448 Daniel 443 Emele 446 Richard 91 99 442 Sampson 443 Solomon 99
MATHEWWS, Daniel 441
MATHIAS, Selzer 36
MATTHEWS, C L 181 Daniel 111 450 George 98 Richard 88
MAUCH, Jno C 452
MAUCK, J W 454 Robert C 136 453
MAUK, Barbara 446
MAUPIN, Harrison 456
MAUZY, 37 224 238 326 C H 390 George 289 Henry 194 J P 235 Joseph 111 194 325 442-443 Mr 126 Richard 123 194-196 242 289 298 325 418 T G 453
MAY, Adam 451 George 456 James 452 John 122 John W 184 Josiah F 458 Lewis 459 S A 453 Samuel 422
MAYHEW, G F 392 G Fred 340 Geo F 454
MCALLISTER, J W 454 William C 454
MCBRIDE, 81 Francis 75
MCCABE, James D 254
MCCALL, W P 377
MCCANN, S N 460
MCCARTHREY, John 195
MCCAULEY, Daniel 455 L R 452 Peter 456
MCCLANAHAN, 260 Captain 81
MCCLEAN, Charles 445
MCCLELLAN, 137
MCCLOUD, John 454 Nicholas 454
MCCOMMON, S B 209
MCCORD, Arthur 451
MCCORMICK, 196
MCCOY, William 78 119
MCCRARY, John 452
MCCREARY, Douglass 453
MCCUE, William A 458
MCDONALD, John 446 Randall 82 Ruth 82

MCDOWELL, 136 Abbigail 448 William 65-66 73-74 77 85
MCDUGAL, John 102
MCELHENEY, John 445
MCGAHEY, Alice 195 Calvert 377 Dolly 311 Tobias Randolph 10 194-195
MCGILL, J B 281 James 215 Right Rev Bishop 272 William 215 239
MCGILVRAY, Alexander 376 L T 454
MCGINTY, M J 192
MCGLAHING, Jno 98
MCGUIRE, Father 272
MCGUYER, Patrick 447
MCHEL, William 63
MCHENRY, Margaret 447
MCINTOSH, 64
MCKEEVER, William 387
MCKENLEY, Daniel 105
MCKINLEY, 178 President 14 438
MCKINNEY, Governor 176 357 P W 357
MCLAIN, Annie 359
MCLAUGHLIN, John 450-451 Joseph 454 William 442
MCLEOD, J S 306 James P 455
MCLEY, Jacob 446
MCMAHON, Colonel 121 William 288 443
MCMICHAL, James 446
MCMULLEN, E W 461
MCQUAIDE, Mary J 272 Mollie 294
MCSWYNY, Dennis 55
MCVEIGH, W H 198 390
MCVEY, James 73 215
MCWILLIAMS, Gordon 442 John 102 444 Samuel 187 283 442 447
MEADE, General 139
MEADER, Israel 450
MEADOWS, Ephriam 451
MEEM, Dr A R 153
MEIGS, 149 John R 148
MEINECK, John 447
MEIXELL, J 376
MELHORN, John W 453 R D 207
MELLON, Anne 448
MELTON, Billie 420
MENZIES, 79 Robert 78
MERGES, P J 340
MERICA, George S 455
MERZ, Karl 346
MESEROLE, Jacob 231 233
MESSERLEY, Joseph S 442
MESSERLY, J S 176
MESSICK, B F 453 George 451 Jacob 450 William 456
METZER, Anna Barbara 444
MEYERHOEFFER, Charles 183 J W 459 John 455
MGAHEY, Tobias R 186

ROCKINGHAM COUNTY

MICHAEL, Peter 450 R D 459
MICHAELS, W F 453
MIDDLEBERGER, George 451
MILDEBARLER, Nicholas 53
MILDEBERGER, John 62 Nicholas 62
MILELR, Charles L 454 J G H 455 John 451
MILES, General 371
MILLAR, George 448
MILLER, 37 241 336-337 396 A B 393 A R 390 Abraham 258 394 Adam 9 34-35 35 35-36 36-37 40 48 53 Alex Jr 216 Alexander 94 96 268 270 B B 460 B Frank 454 Barbara 448 Benjamin 122 126 453 460 Bettie Neff 127 Brown 454 C Armand 261 C B 454 C E 204 Christeny 446 Christian 60 Colonel 264 Cristian 446 David 53 E R 278 280 282 315 461 Eli 454 Elizabeth 449 Elizabeth B 35 Eugene X 391 F J 461 G Ed 389 George 452 456 George W 135 H B 234 337 377 H G 380 460 Hamp 420 Henry 59 93-95 212 377 398 428 449 449-450 454 Hiram G 299 Hiram H 455 Isaac 456 Isabella 410 J C 460 J D 461 J F 391 459 J G H 140-141 J I 260-261 J J 281 J P 390 J Wesley 454 Jacob 53 452 458 James 450 Jennet 444 John 53 59 100 122 208 449-450 452 456 John C 407 Jonathan 392 Joseph I 260 L S 460 L V 200 Leonard 95 M B 460 Margaret 448 Margret 446 Martin 249 Mary 445 Matthew 452 Nicholas 122 O S 460 O W 200 Otho 183 Paul 335 Peter 53 122 260-261 444 454 Peter Jr 95 Peter Sr 95 Philip 406 Priscilla 311 R T 206 379 Robert J 389 S D 314 S F 313 S P H 158 197 376 Samuel 120 449 Sylvanus 455 Thomas 123 V C 197 Virginia M 357 W H 200 William 452 456 William I 460
MILLS, William 100
MILNES, William 229
MILROY, General 136
MINER, Henry 450
MINGE, Mr 115
MINNICH, J W 184 397-398 459 Tyreetta P 436
MINNICK, Dallas 454 David 457 E M 380 392 Edward 457 Elijah 453 Elizabeth 448 Harvey 457 J W 393 J Wallace 454 James 453 John B 454 Levi 456 Matthias 151 Samuel 457 Wallace B 417 William 415 455-456

MINNIS, Robert 81 216
MINOR, G C 460 George C 251 J G 225
MITCHEL, William 448
MOFFET, 406 Anderson 84
MOFFETT, A 443 Anderson 441 Andrew 244 288 443 Carrie 306 George 150 Miss Bryan 319 S H 357 443-444 Samuel 288
MOFFITT, Anderson 120 125 John 244
MOHLER, J N 392 John N 391 L 452
MOHONEY, James 447
MOLLOY, James 448
MONGER, George W 459 Henry 99 John B 455 Joseph 455 William 264
MONOR, J G 232
MONROE, 394 John 351 Joseph 351
MONTAGUE, 362 James 450
MONTGOMERY, James 100 Samuel 100
MOOMAU, Dr 117
MOON, Jack 454
MOONEY, Asbury 457 Robert 457
MOOR, John 218 Samuel 122
MOORE, 406 Anna 288 D H 178 David H 457 Ella 318 George 457 H C 460 I 454 James 452 Jephtheh 447 John G 458 John H 295 458 John Quaker 449 John W 456 Joseph 457 R W 457 Reuben 449 Samuel 457 Susanna 447 Thomas 90 Thomas A 400 Thomas Sr 449
MOORMAN, J J 443
MORE, Fany 446 Jonathan 214 Reuben 66 84
MORGAN, Gerard 265 Gideon 196 Moragan 39
MORRICE, Conrad 451 John 451
MORRIS, Ann 446 C S 459 Harrison 453 L B 374 Silas 453 Tom 420
MORRISON, Brownie 326
MORRISS, William 238
MORTON, George 350 Margaret 350 W J 254
MOSS, Rial 453
MOUBRAY, J F 204 L O 459
MOWRY, J A 453
MOYER, Jacob 59 101 John Daniel 446 Joseph 122 Philip 122
MOYERHOEFFER, James 458 W F 201
MOYERS, 241 Ambrose 457 Daniel 452 George 452 Henry 460 Jacob 53 96 Joseph B 225
MUELLER, Adam 48-49 Peter Sr 62
MULATTO, Fanny A 448
MULLEN, Emanuel 456 S F 456-457
MUNFORD, 433
MUNGER, Elizabeth 446 Henry 58
MUNGOR, John 59

MURPHY, James M 454
MURRAY, Henry 452
MURRY, John 239
MYERS, 241 B F 184 Daniel J 407 E P
  184 458 G W 142 I C 460 J C 331
  Jacob 245 John 322 John A 371 461
  John F 370 Joseph G 183 223 442 L
  C 389 Lycurgus 454 R L 395 S A 379
  S D 390 S H 150 Samuel H 250 W F
  459 W T 309 Weldon Thomas 326
NAIR, C E 460
NALL, 410 William 96 104 107 449
NALLE, Martain 450 William 63-65 69
  73 76 86 441-442 450
NASMUS, Peter 59
NATHANAEL, Brother 50
NAVE, J H 204 John 452
NAWL, Colonel 97 William 93 99
NAYLOR, George 459
NEAD, Peter 250
NEFF, Abe 127 Brownie 326 E R 456
  George A 184 Henry 167 302 J W 458
  John H 326 457 L C 459 Mary 128
  Michael 457 Michael D 457
  Washington 458
NEICE, Michael 259
NEIF, Charles A 457
NEILSON, Jane 446 John 349 Johnston
  97
NEIR, Martin 147
NELSON, Adam 86 Kimbrough 450
NESSLEROD, Frederick 445
NESTREETE, Eve 448
NEVE, F W 338
NEWCOMER, Bishop 10 Christian 274
NEWHAM, Samuel K 457
NEWMAN, 131 A M 358 392 A M Jr 390
  Alexa 122 Andrew M Jr 389 Hattie
  120 J G 442 Jonathan 448 Rebecca
  310 S F 207 Samuel 21 288 William A
  454
NEWPORT, John 41-42
NEY, B 256-258 Joseph 256 258 Mrs B
  315
NEZBET, Elizabeth 448
NICELY, Isaac 455
NICHOLAS, 241 C E 461 Charles 122
  Edwin 196 F F 193 G M 456 George
  122 George M 391 Henry 446 Jacob
  48 59 94 100 John 122 Peter 94 447
  S C 456
NICHOLASS, Peter 193
NICHOLS, Thomas 41
NICKEMON, Abraham 447
NICLAS, Jacob 62 Peter 62
NICOLAS, John 82
NISEWANDER, Abram 261

NISEWRANER, John 453
NISWANDER, 241 John 367
NOFTSINGER, David 448
NORMAN, Isaac 448
NORRIS, Patt 458
NOSTER, Boston 59
NUCKOLS, E M 161
NUL, Henry 444
NULL, George S 334 Henry 59 449
  Jacob 450 Jno 59 John 450 Nicholas
  53
NYE, Mrs 121
OAKIS, Dick 458
OBRIAN, Jas 376
OBRIEN, Miss 310
OCONNER, James 457
ODOR, J B 280 452
OEHLER, Anthony 62
OESTREICHER, Simon 256 256-258
OFERRALL, 360 433 435 Annie 359
  Charles T 306 326 441 443 Charles
  Triplett 358 Governor 359 Jennie
  Knight 359 Judge 225 Laura 306
OGAN, Catherine 446
OGG, Alexander 451
OGLESBY, Stephen 450-451
OKEEFE, Father 272
OLDHAM, 108
OLER, Henry 60 John 60 William 60
OLIVER, Elizabeth 447 John 443
  Leonard 448 Sally 447
ONEAL, Jessy 447
OREBAUGH, Abram 451 Adam 451 Andrew
  450-451 Oscar 204 W A 458
OROARKE, Branson 457
OSBERNE, R B 230
OSBORN, Zerah 444
OTT, E D 462 L H 296 389 455 Mrs
  Henry 310 William 188
OTTERBEIN, 274
OUNGST, David 122 Henry 122 Joseph
  122
OUR, Christopher 214
OVERHOLT, George 452 John 452
OWLER, Henry 450 John 450
OZMAN, Elizabeth 444
PAGE, John 97
PAINTER, Abram 420 Alexander 259
  Allen 458 Chrisly 102 Isaac 420
  John 420 Johnson B 455 Joseph 420
  Martin 420 Peter 420 R 461 Reuben
  420 Romanus 458 Uriah 458
PALMER, 178 C H 459 E P 269 H R 345
  Imogen Avis 347 John 448 Olin
  Austin 326
PARKER, Richard 442
PARROT, Samuel 87

ROCKINGHAM COUNTY

PARTLOW, M Y 387
PATTEN, Mrs 202
PATTERSON, B G 176 358 387 443 D H
  391 John 455 L D 206 W C 391
PATTON, Ann 446 General 143 James
  211 John 446 Mathew 101
PAUL, Isaac 152-153 John 18 178 185
  306 326 352 358-360 442 444 462
  John Jr 360 444 Katherine S 360
  Maria 360 Mrs K S 176 326 Peter
  223 247 306 360 437 Rockingham 306
  Virginia 305-306
PAULSEL, Peter 442
PAULSON, Barbara 448
PAXTON, J C 14
PAYNE, Asbury B 452 James W 452
  William H 452
PEACH, Philip 450
PEAL, Jonathan 122
PEALE, Amanda Fitzallen 361 Jno B
  390 John B 234
PEEPLER, Mary 448
PEIRCE, George 98
PENCE, 241 Adam 60 451 C W 313
  Captain 70 George 60 96 445 449
  Henry 60 96 Jacob 53 60 81 450-451
  John 60 101 213 445 451 John Jr 60
  John W 455 Joseph 460 Mary 128 448
  Mrs Peter 403 Peter 455 S H 456
  Samuel 460 Valentine 48 W P 108
  William 60 101 128 William A 392
PENDLETON, Bryan 358 S T 306
PENINGER, Henry 53-54 72 76
PENN, Major 145
PENNINGTON, R B 461
PENNIREY, Elizabeth 69 Thomas 69
PENNYBACKER, B N 457 D D 456 Derrick
  415 I S 117 295 355 Isaac 457
  Isaac S 192 Isaac S Jr 354 Isaac
  Samuels 354 J D 454 J Ed 282 295
  358 J Edmund 354 J S 456 John 457
  John D 295 354 387 444 Kate 355
  Mary Elizabeth Lincoln 428 S W 354
  Sarah A 354 T J 390 Thomas J 457
PERCY, Jacob 448
PERKEY, Henry 195 195-196 449 Jacob
  99 John 449
PERKIE, Jacob 213
PERKY, John 96
PERRY, Joseph 455 Thomas J 458
PETERFISH, George 451 Henry 451
  William 123
PETERISH, Gunrod 53
PETERS, Abram 101 Henery 452 Jacob
  95 Warner 450
PETERSON, J J 453
PETMUS, Matthew 59

PETORFISH, Conrod 59
PETRO, Martin 99
PETRY, Samuel 460
PETTEJOHN, Hester 445 William 102
PETTY, Bengaman 450
PHARES, Philip 376
PHILIPS, John 212
PHILLIPS, Fred 420 Frederick 453
  George 448 454 J A 337 J M 457 J W
  269 James E 452 James M 455 John
  429 458 John Sr 449 Nathaniel 458
  Thad 453
PICKERING, Abraham 457 D H 457
  Daniel 450 457 J W 184 R 119
  Richard 118 William 452
PIERCE, 356 John 193 William A 203
PIFER, A M 201 Morgan D 454 William
  F 200
PINKERTON, John 327
PIPER, George 120
PIRKEY, A H 456 Alexander 422 Henry
  422 452 J M 206-207 391 J S 391
  Jacob 194 452 O F A 456 Solomon
  118 194
PITNER, John 447
PITTINGTON, Samuel 454
PLECCKER, D A 232
PLECKER, D A 153 232-233 W H 458
PLUMB, Jacob 72
PLUNKEPEL, Zacarias 459
POAGE, George 457 Robert 445
POAGUE, 142 145 Captain 144
POINTS, W J 334
POLEN, James 453
POLK, James K 148
POLLOCK, S W 454
POLSER, Daniel 97
POOL, G H 453 R N 167 232 392
POPE, 138 John 137
POST, Virginia 336
POTTER, C L 461
POWELL, Albert 455 Benjamin 456
  Elias 455 George 456 Moses F 455
PREISCH, Augustine 62 Augustine Jr
  63 Conrad 63
PRESTON, Julia Starr 340
PRICE, Augusteen Sr 449 Augustian 60
  Augustine 82 101 Daniel 59 Edward
  451 Frances 444 Frederick 81 Henry
  59 101 John H 455 Joseph D 164
  Rebeccah 447 S J 334 Samuel J 333
  Samuel J 336 Sterling 48 Thomas L
  438 W T 270 302 334 William 420
  William T 327
PRIGHT, John 450
PRISE, George 447
PRITCHARD, H J 452

PROBST, Henry 451
PROPST, H F 455 Reuben 122
PRUPECKER, John 40 Margaret 42
PUGH, P W 203 232 R E 183
PULLIAM, James 455
PULLINS, Samuel 447 Thomas 448
PUP, Elizabeth 446
PURCELL, Mrs E 315
PURDY, Sam 371
PURKEY, Henry 60 Jacob 60 John 60 Margaret 60
PURKY, Jacob 58
RADER, Adam 233 Anthony 70 410 C S 457 Catrin 447 George 452 457 Henry 450 J Js 457 Jane 410 Peter 457 Susanah 447
RAGAN, 239 Jeremiah 218 John G 453 Marey 446 Margret 446 Richard 188 449 Robert B 361 452
RAGIN, Bazilia 447 Daniel 447 Nancy 447
RAGON, Darby 96 239 Jeremiah 96 99
RAINES, Henry 422 456 Jacob 422 456 James Jr 60 Mrs Hattie 459 Reuben 422 456 Zachariah 422 Zack 418-419
RAINS, Robert 450
RALSTON, Agness 444 C H 185 443 461 Can 458 Charles H 235 D H 441 D Hopkins 436 David 101 248 E C 391 Frank 184 397 443 J H 190 393 442 J P 340 441 Jesse 302 John H 140 John H Jr 393 John Hinton 276 Mr 277 Nancy 445 William 123 445
RALSTONE, David 75
RAMBO, Barbary 447 Jacob 447
RANDOLPH, E C 458
RANKIN, Mrs 311 Richard 451
RANKLE, Christian 450
RAPE, Jacob 446
RAU, W S 461
RAUHOF, J P 183
RAWLEY, 396
RAYNES, James 60
READER, Adam 83 Anthony 73 85 John 447 Matthew 214
REAGAN, James 215 Jane 448 Jeremiah 213 283 Richard 79 215
REAGEN, Jeremiah 214 Richard 67
REAMER, Isaac 377 J D S 452
REANS, William 448
REARY, James 450
REAVES, Sarah 447 Thomas 122 William 122
REDER, H 49
REDLICKSBERGER, Christian 41
REDMAN, Elizabeth 446
REECE, George 451

REED, Abraham 457 Griffin 455 L S 364 Walter 364
REEDY, David 457 Isaac 457 Philip 452
REES, John Thomas 217
REEVES, Brewer 96 102 218 445 Bruer 88 James 103
REHERD, James E 374 391 Jas E 392 Lewis W 452 P W 231 234 441 Peter W 183
REICHENBACH, Alcide 305
REIDER, Adam 259
REIGNS, Bennett 451
REINS, Patrick 451 Richard 444
REISCH, John 62
REMENYI, Eduard 438 Edward 340
REUTZ, 47
RHINE, John 455
RHINEHART, A R 248 Algernon 453 D C 248 Lewis 101 Michael 36 38 Paul 374
RHODES, 241 Anthony 410 David 261 E F 459 Elizabeth 341 Emanuel 368 Frederick 261 Henry 261 Henry A 397 Henry E 158 J B D 372 J H 199 391 J M 457 J N 457 Jacob 452 John 37 46 John H 457 Levi 459 Preston 457 S H 460 Wilson A 457
RICE, B M 388 393 Bram 458 Elizabeth 448 James 454 John 67 98 215 449 John B 454 Jon 445 Jonathan 214 Joseph A 452 Joseph 454 Mrs Bramwell 311 Thomas 451 William 98 444
RICHARDS, B F 454 Charles L 454
RICHARDSON, 328 G W 461
RICHWINE, William 452
RICKARD, 338 W H 231 William 234
RIDDEL, J A 459 John 445
RIDDLE, Harrison 455 J N 456 James 455 Thomas 456
RIDDLEBERGER, H H 453
RIDENHOUSE, John 446
RIDER, Henry 450
RIDGEWAY, Peachey 107
RIFE, Daniel 122 Elizabeth 447 John 150 Mary 447 Modlenah 446
RIFER, George 452
RIMEL, George 452 John 446
RIMERL, Philip 194
RINEHART, Lewis 59
RINKER, Erasmus 458 Joel 184
RISCH, Charles 62 Jacob 63
RISPE, Christian 445
RITCHIE, Addison 454 George 458 I F 456 Isaac 456-457 Joseph 458 L F 436 Polk 458

ROCKINGHAM COUNTY

RITCHIS, Solomon 457
RITENOUR, Mrs W H 159 W H 231 406
RITES, Samuel 451
RITTER, Jacob 451 Michael 451
ROADARMOR, Barbary 447
ROADARMOUR, Jacob 445
ROADCAP, James 452-453 John 452 Madison 454
ROADCAPJOHN, 453
ROARICK, Michael 92
ROAY, Joseph 450
ROB, Frederick 92
ROBERTS, John 123 W P 388 W T 254
ROBERTSON, J H 337 James 63 Sarah 444
ROBESON, William 448
ROBINS, George 448
ROBINSON, Darcus 444 M L 336 William H 454
ROBISON, David 101 John 101
ROBSON, J T 443
ROCK, Rubin 60
RODEHEFFER, George 422
RODES, 108
RODGERS, H M 443 James 81
ROEDER, Adam 47
ROGERS, Albert 453 H M 443 James G 364 Jonathan G 454 Joseph 458
ROGGERS, Chesly 450
ROGINSON, R B 336
ROHR, Jacob Jr 189 S C 129 Stainsberry 453 Will S 327 William S 332 358 454
ROLELR, J S 460
ROLER, John Edwin 327 Peter 122 449
ROLESTONE, Henry 447 Jane 444 Matthew 53-54 William 53-54
ROLLER, Barbara 448 E 282 Emanuel 458 Frances Allebaugh 327 General 188 Henry 458 J E 261 270 J J 207 John A 203 John E 50 167 192 282 284 300 328 359 421 444 462 John 457 Michael 452 Michael J 180 O B 173 178 361 P S 289 Peter 458 Peter S 327 370 Robert Douglas 328 W H 459 W W 336
ROLSTO, J P 454
ROLSTON, David H 454 John H 454 M A 454 Samuel 53 William 454
ROLSTONE, David 445
RONK, Charles 460
ROOD, Hans 36-38
ROOT, E D 336 F W 345 G R 391 George F 342
ROOTES, George 71 351
ROOTS, Abram 451
RORICK, Michael 449

ROSENBERGER, G W 457 George 291 373 George W 369 415 H J 459 Harvey J 401 John W 267 457
ROSS, D 289
ROSZELLE, George A 361
ROUDABUSH, H M 336
ROWTZ, Michael 122
ROYER, David 122 J H 456 Jacob 122 James 458 John 122 Noah A 453 Philip 448 Samuel 122
RUCKER, Frank 420 George 450
RUDDEL, George 218
RUDDELL, George 446 John 213 Stephen 445
RUDDLE, Captain 73 Cornelius 449 George 72 101
RUE, Abraham 450 George 450
RUEBUSH, 321 339 E 344-345 Ephraim 333 344 J H 297 341-342 391 James H 345 Joe K 155 245 254 275 333 391 John 333 Lucilla Virginia 344 Mary Huffman 333 Mr 334 Mrs 334 Mrs E 129 Virginia 333 345 W H 341-342 William H 345
RUFF, A R 390 John J 454
RUFFNER, 306 Harriet 310 Mark 457 Robert 457 W H 297
RUMPLE, J W 206
RUMSEY, George 450-451
RUNCKLE, Lewis 101 Peter 102
RUNION, Mary 448
RUNKLE, Jacob 447 Mary 447
RUPE, Mary 71 Nicolas 71
RUSH, Captain 73 Charles 60 101 449 George 445 J B 298 453 Jacob 118 458 John 59-60 72 449 Jonathan 122
RUSSELL, Elijah 446 W 40
RUST, Abram 450-451 Jacob 451 John 450-451
RUTH, Samuel 228
RUTHERFORD, Archibald 441 443 Eliot 448 Elliot 66 Elliott 80 James 94 John 83 Joseph 79 Mr 432 Robert 77 215 215-216 218
RUTLEDGE, William 450-451
RYAN, J K 452
RYDER, Anthony 65-66 69
RYLER, Peter 451
RYLIE, John 76 Mary 76
RYMAN, Samuel A 458
SACK, Henry 451
SALLING, John 34
SALVAGE, John J 450
SALYARD, Joseph 242
SALYARDS, George W 452 Joseph 11 288-290 328 Mr 291
SAMPLES, Alexander 102

SAMPSELL, W H 461
SAMUELS, G B 441 Green B 352
SANDY, R W 453
SANFORD, George W 197
SANGER, Barbara 445 J E 443 Mr 19 S F 322
SAUFLEY, William 392 458
SAUFLEY,JOSEPH, 458
SAXE-WEIMAR, Grand Duke 438
SCAILS, William 450
SCANLON, Bat 456
SCHAEFER, George 444 Jacob 444 John 63
SCHAUB, Matthias 47-49
SCHENE, Jane 349
SCHILLINGER, George 62
SCHLATTER, Michael 270
SCHMIDT, Emilia 444
SCHNEIDER, Martin 63
SCHNELL, 47-49 Leonard 45
SCHOLL, Peter 21 53 211 259 349
SCHOOLTZ, Christopher 452
SCHVANENFELD, J 258 460 Rabbi 340
SCHWERIN, Mrs Tenney Showalter 347
SCOTT, Colonel 145-146 E H 294 George 459 J C 457 J H 327 Jacob 60 James 60 Michael 456 Mr 269 Nat 60 Robert 55 Robert Jr 60 Thomas 187 189
SEAKFORD, Adam 420 David 420 F R 420 George W 420 Jacob 420 John W 420 Newton 420 Noah 420
SEAWRIGHT, George 213
SEBRELL, T E 193
SECRIST, A J 461 David 454 David A 455 George 123 Harvey 456 John 454 Philip 455 Thomas 454
SEE, Richard Jr 351
SEEVER, Benjamin 248
SEGFRIED, John 448
SEISS, Joseph A 260
SELBY, James 450
SELLER, John 53
SELLERS, Adam 95 99 449 Emanuel 456 J S 374 Jacob B 459 Jacob S 315 390 457 John 101 448 452 John M 455 John N 455 Peter 92 Peter J 455 Samuel A 455 T N 443 William 301
SELSER, Mathias 40
SELZER, Mathias 38 Matthias 46-47
SEMPIL, Sarah 447
SENGER, 241 372 Charles 436 Henry 436
SETH, Jacob 91
SETTLE, V L 245
SETTLES, Franses Sanford 447

SEVIER, Joanna 9 348-349 John 9 49 53 63 77 348-349 429 Sarah 348 Valentine 9 53 63 77 238 348-349 429 Valentine Jr 64
SHACKLETT, Henry 174 387 Lucy 318 Samuel 189
SHAFER, Catterena 447 John 448 Keatren 447
SHAFFER, G W 204
SHAKLEN, Wileam 447
SHANDS, 130 E A 355 S A 355 William 361
SHANK, 259 C F 204 Gabriel 454 George 451 457 Henry 261 John 451 Joseph 390 460 Lewis 460 P E 460 S T 289 Samuel 261-262 366
SHANKLIN, Andrew 83 105 283 441 445 Edward 53 449 James 448 Jennet 448 John 53 445 Mary 448 Richard 53 Thomas 449
SHANKLING, Andrew 447
SHANKLINS, Edward 218
SHANLING, Thomas 91
SHANNON, Martha 445
SHAVER, 241 434-435 E B 246 Frank 434 George 60 J E 235 Joseph E 155 Susannah 445 W H 184
SHCKLETT, Edward P 454 Samuel 387
SHEETS, Christian 453 J W 184 Jacob 451 John 451-452 John B 456 Joseph 454 Simon P 456 Strother 454
SHEFFING, Pheby 448
SHEFFY, Hugh 291
SHEIRY, G 334 John F 334
SHELBY, Evan 63
SHEPHERD, Agness 444 Sarah 448
SHEPP, C W 209 Charles N 455 Katie 241 Solomon 454
SHEPPE, R H 298 308
SHERDLINS, 365
SHERIDAN, 148-150 General 158 Lewis 447
SHERMAN, D W 458 E H 459 Emanuel 451 H H 265 267 282 287 461
SHEVER, Paul 53
SHICKEL, J 379
SHICKLE, J C 459
SHIELDS, 137 General 142-144
SHIFFLET, D 453 Edmund 455 George W 455 Joseph N 455 Robert 453 Sampson 455 Theophilus 455 W H 459
SHIFFLETT, J A 199
SHIFLETT, Noah 453
SHILLINGER, Adam 446 George 53 444
SHINNICK, 378
SHIPMAN, Elizabeth 91 Isaiah 53 Isiah 92 99 J R 210 299 389 415

ROCKINGHAM COUNTY

SHIPMAN (cont.)
 James C 443 Jas R 389 John 101
 Jonathan 98-99 378 Josiah 53 Nancy
 447
SHIPMAR, Jonathan 441
SHIPP, Albert 456 George 456 J H 178
 441 John 451
SHIRKEY, G B 457 J H 235
SHIRKEYSMAUEL, 457
SHIRLEY, Jacob 451
SHOANFARBER, Dr 257
SHOCKMAN, Adolph 240
SHOEMAKER, George 449 Wesley 454
SHOOLER, Mathias 59
SHORT, William J 455
SHOWALTER, 241 A J 341-342 346 454
 Ananias 454 Anthony J 345 D B 235
 397 D P 406 David 262 Frank B 374
 George 460 Henry 397 Henry A 332 J
 H 342 J Henry 341 345-346 J W 458
 John A 346 John W 377 Joseph 397
 Michael 397 457 P H 459 Peter 392
 S F 397 Samuel 122 W J 436 W P 459
 William Joseph 328 William S 456
SHOWLATER, Joseph 456 Samuel 458
SHOWLTER, Buck 456
SHRUM, J N 199 391
SHUE, Abraham 376 Joseph H 392
 Joseph H 442
SHUEY, 241 George E 460
SHULENBERGER, Elizabeth 71 George 71
SHULER, Michael 18
SHULL, Tobias 202
SHUMAKER, Modelean 445
SHUMATE, Augustus 194 John 194
 Thomas 224
SHUTTERS, John 376
SIBELEY, Magdalene 448
SIBERT, J L 288 J M 459 M M 373 Mrs
 M M 159 W M 443
SIGLER, A J 456 William 455
SILES, George 452
SILKNETTER, Jacob 450
SILLER, Adam 59 Henry 59 John 60
 Michael 59 Peter 59
SILVIUS, Joseph 457 Moses 458 Uriah
 459
SIMERMAN, Nana 95
SIMMERMAN, Barnabas 94
SIMMERS, Harvey 248 J H 184 Jacob
 457 Jacob A 456 John 457
SIMMONS, John W 454
SIMON, Mordecai 40
SIMPSON, A 458
SIMS, James 444
SINK, Daniel 59

SIPE, Archibald 456 Captain 142
 Crisian 452 E 248 458 Emanuel 142
 451 George 452 George E 186 315
 389 392 421 443 462 Henry 451
 Henry E 206 J F 453 Jacob 419 Levi
 456 W H 389
SIPSON, James 457
SIRCLE, Ludwick 449
SIRKEL, George 446
SITES, Catharine 445 D B 390 457
 David B 406 Garnett C 181 Henry
 445 J W 457 John 396 John A 454
 William H 457
SKELTON, S D 461
SKIDMORE, James 53 John 53 63-64 64-
 65 67 Joseph 53 215 Samuel 66 215
SLATER, V R 193 258
SLAUGH, Thomas 56
SLAUGHTER, Lawrence 95 Robert 95 101
SLAVIN, John 445
SLODSER, Lodowick 53
SLUSSER, Samuel L 458 W S 456
 William 458 William S 308
SMALLRIDG, Samuel 447
SMALS, Adam H 453 Henry 375 N M 453
SMITH, 190 Abraham 53-54 65-66 74-76
 79 83 170 387 441 Abram 69 84 97
 451 Allen 458 Anne 448 Benjamin 77
 218 283 431 447 449 Benjamin H 395
 Brustor 59 Bruten 450 C H 263
 Conrad 97 Daniel 11 17 54 63-65
 67-71 74 76-78 81 83 86 95-97 108
 213 213-214 214-215 242 293 351-
 352 352 441-443 452 Daniel Jr 69
 David 66 446 452 Dorman L 454 Dr
 298 Ed H 387 Edward 461 Edward H
 117 443 Elizabeth 352 Frances 352
 George 452 Hannah 447 Heany 448
 Henry 53 447 449 Ida B 459 J H 269
 J K 333 336 Jane Sr 449 Jno 92
 John 39 53 79 96 352 442 John
 Green 293 John Jeff 455 John W G
 358 Joseph 67 77 102 215 269 287
 449 Judge 356 Lucius 352 Margaret
 352 Margaret Davis 352 Margrat 448
 Marie 352 Martha 12 445 Martha
 Reid 170 Marthew 89 Mecagh 450
 Mijah 59 Moses 450 Mr 110 432 Mrs
 M W L 309 N Calvin 123 Peggy 447
 Richard 445 Robert 79 Samuel 417
 Simon 376 William 59 67 75 88 97
 123 449-450 William B 450-451
 William Jr 59
SMTIH, Daniel 84
SMUCKER, C J 203 Samuel C 203
SMYTHE, R B 337-338

SNAP, Catharine 448 John 449
  Margaret 448 Susanna 448
SNAPP, John 193 Joseph 448
SNAVELY, 336-337
SNELL, J M 193 231 391 Walstein M
  328
SNIDER, Joseph 451 Joshua 122
  Mathias 450 Matthew 450
SNODDING, George 218
SNODING, William 95
SNOWDEN, George 448
SNYDER, 260 A H 305 308 331 337 443
  Adolph Heller 331 R H 377
SOERS, Joseph 459
SOLLOMON, Aaron 447
SOMMERS, S M 355 Samuel M 332
SOMMRES, Sarah 444
SORT, Keziah 447
SOUDER, C L 459 L P 184
SOULE, John F 443
SOUTHARD, John 455
SOUVERAINE, William 450
SOUVERINE, Christian 451
SOWTER, Henry 41
SPADER, Jacob 451 John 458
SPANGENBERG, 47
SPANGLER, Daniel 448 David 448
  Frederick 187
SPARKES, Charles 446
SPEARS, George 99 Hannah 448 John
  448 Mary 445 Sally 447
SPECK, Captain 120 Fannie 306
  Jonathan 364
SPEIR, W E 178
SPENCE, Isabella 355
SPENCER, Mr 286
SPICER, William 450
SPIERS, George 217
SPIKEARD, Elizabeth 77 Julius 77
SPINDLE, R H 393
SPINKLEY, George 452
SPITLER, N A 459
SPITZER, Cyrus 459 P F 304
SPOTSWOOD, Alexander 426 Governor 34
  427
SPRENKEL, J G 452
SPRINGER, George Jr 446
SPRINKEL, A St Clair 442 C A 233 301
  454 C C 461 Charles A 302 Henry A
  193 J G 377 Mrs Nelson 310 Nelson
  189 376
SPRINKLE, Alfred 387 J M R 443 Peter
  451
SPROUCE, 432
SPYKEARD, George 77
SRECKER, F W 453
STALING, F 377 Francis 366

STANFORD, Leland 371
STANLEY, F W 277 Isaac N 455
STAPLES, J C 278 280
STAUNTON, 49
STCLAIR, Alexander 443
STEARN, J 457
STEELE, David 117 354 425 James 415
  R 452
STEIN, Ludowick 41 Ludwig 41-42
STEMPHLEY, David 127 206
STEPHEN, Ludwick 445
STEPHENS, William G 457
STEPHENSON, Caster 449 David 446
  Easther 102 Ester 95 James B 116
  300 462 John 81 213 Mary 447 Wm 97
STERLING, Andrew 454 O C 376 441 O C
  Jr 288 S 119 S R 166 441 Samuel R
  387 Thomas O 454
STERNE, Rabbi 258
STEUART, George H 139
STEVANS, General 98
STEVENS, Edward 115 Edward H 252 H H
  363 Jacob R 281 Mrs E 190 W G 443
  William G 281 330 387
STEVINS, Francis 73
STEWART, Frances 94 100-101 Francis
  83 General 143-144 George H 141
STICKLEY, C 456 Daniel 457 James O
  391
STILES, John 451
STILT, John 451
STINE, Ludwig 41
STINEBUCK, Fred 457
STINESPRING, F M 390 459 John 198
  Rev C W 155 W H 453
STINSON, Sarah 446
STIREWALT, J L 312 J P 260
STOCK, Joseph 452
STOLPH, Henry 91
STONE, Henry 72 95 101 Isaac 248 376
  J A 199 James 458 Ludwick 40 Peter
  452
STONEBERGER, William 420
STONEBUCK, Eve 448
STONESIFER, J B 461
STONEWALL, 175
STOUTMEYER, Gasper 452
STOVER, 37-39 41-42 David H 455
  Frank 296 Jacob 35 35-36 38 40-42
  Joseph H 455 Joshua 138 Major 137
STRATTON, Captain 85 Seruiah 81
  Zeruiah 83 85
STRAUSS, M 259
STRAYER, Anna 310 C C 388-389
  Crawford C 170 Ella V 232 Ernest S
  390 Henry V 361 Joseph S 328
  Juliet 170 310 Juliet Lyle 170 Mrs

ROCKINGHAM COUNTY

STRAYER (cont.)
  C C 159 312
STREIT, Christian 259
STRICKLER, 241 H M 107 Abraham 41
  Abram 36-38 B F 458 C N 235 H M
  374 462 Harry 401 John 457 Joseph
  102 R El 461 Reuben 245 S G 457
  William 420
STROTHER, Margaret 350 Miss 255
  William 350
STUART, A H H 291 Archibald 443
STUBS, John 450
STULLY, John 451
STULTZ, Joseph 459
STUMP, Michael 101
STUMPS, Leonard 216
SUELLING, Samuel 450
SULLIVAN, E J 239 E W 178
SUMERVALT, Christian 446
SUMMERS, David 453-454 J W 459 Jacob
  457 Michael 457 William 456
SUMMERSETTS, William 59
SUMMRES, John 457
SURPHOS, George 448
SUTER, D I 300 436 E J 184 436
  Emanuel 378 398 J E 460 P G 436
SUTTON, Moses 451
SWAN, Christian 444
SWANK, J Newton 183 John 397 S H 204
  Ward 462
SWANSON, 362 Joseph 453 William 457
SWARTZ, 236 Frederick 446 George 454
  John 445 John R 436 William T 436
SWATS, John 123
SWICK, John 447
SWISHER, David 450 John 193 449
  Nathaniel 451 Samuel 451
SWITZER, Charles 169 Cornelia 318 D
  M 192 311 396 443 J A 441 J Robert
  462 John A 235 Morgan 281 R S 354
  461 S B 235 S C 456 V C 456 W C
  235 William O 456
SWOPE, Hugh 224 393 Jacob 110 Reuben
  224
SWORD, John 101
SWTZER, M D 461
SYBERT, Charles Fred 71 Mary 71
  Nicholas 72
SYKES, Jonathan 329
SYLVANUS, Uriah 457
TABLER, M T 461
TACK, Henry 58 Jacob 59 Jno 58
TAGART, Hugh 239 308
TALIAFERRO, General 142 146 W B 135-
  136
TALLMAN, Patience 446 William 446
TALLY, George 456

TALMAGE, T Dew 438
TAMWOOD, Henry 59
TANNERY, Zigler 376
TANQUARY, A B 378
TATE, J W 210 Joshua 451 Mr 102
  Rodey 452
TATUM, Miss 363
TAYLOE, John 39
TAYLOR, 338 Albert 456 C E 460
  Conrad 59 Edwin 456 Esther 55 G W
  453 General 143 145-146 Harvey 456
  Hiram 456 J E 453 J F 198 J Harvey
  403 J T 210 John 446 John W 12
  294-295 295 Jonathan 394 Nancy 295
  Virginia C 295 William 362 394
  Zachary 295
TERRELL, A J 453 Calvin 453 St C 453
TERRY, 140 William 452
TETER, Christian 59 George 216
THOASM, Mark 457
THOMAS, A S 460 B B 167 D S 380
  Daniel 378 Ida 389 Isaac 125 288
  443 Jno 86 John 65-66 66-67 71 73
  93 101 441 449 456 John H 457 John
  R 457 Margaret 446 Mrs P S 280 P S
  250 314 460 R S 361 Rebeckah 445
  Reed 214 Rees 216 Reis 93 Rev
  Daniel 153 Robert C 167 Rowland 57
  Thornton 150
THOMPSON, A R 337 J L 453 J W 459
  Jesse 451 John 246 Lucas P 356 T N
  193 367 W G 443 William 125
  William G 151 202 242
THOMSON, William 448
THORNHILL, John 78 Samuel 78
THORNTON, Fanny 350 Joseph 448 Rose
  334 William M 176
THORP, Jesse 450
THRASHER, J C 461
THURMAN, William C 159 435
THURMOND, R W 293
TICE, Mathias 54
TILDEN, 170-172
TIMBERLAKE, David 452
TIMMONS, Isaac 452
TODD, James 416 450
TODHUNTER, Mrs Ryland 107
TOMAH, Moses 452
TOPPIN, William 457
TOUSEY, Thomas 378
TRAUT, Jacob 62
TRAVIS, John 447 Thomas 448
TREABY, J C 458
TRIGG, 108
TRIMBLE, General 143-144 146
TROBAUGH, Harrison 458 J H 459

TROUT, Alexander 450-451 J S 334 Jacob 452 Michael 60 William D 387 452
TRUITT, H E 460
TRUMBO, Benjamin 302 Elizabeth 410 Mathew 450
TSCHAPPAT, S 150
TUCKER, Dallas 254
TULEE, Cathrine 447
TULEY, Christian 54
TURLEY, Giles 204 441
TURLYE, Aron 448
TURNER, 108 A M 183 390 417 Ashby 461 Charles 338 Commodore 420 J H 296 Jacob 457 Robert H 442 W F 423
TUSSING, Moses 151
TUTWILER, Addison 457 Henry 10 287 308 376 Julia 308
TUTWILLER, Henry 186
TWICHET, Samuel 60
TWITWILER, Jacob 448
TYLER, 362 J W 416 Madison 267
ULSTAW, Henry 451
ULSTER, Christian 451
UMBLE, Gunrod 54 Martin 54 Ury 54
UNSELD, B C 340
UPLEMAN, Barbara 447
URNER, Clarence H 297
UTES, Samuel 451
VALLMER, Barbara 445
VANBUREN, 119 President 354
VANCE, A H 453 Handel 97 101 Handle 445 Zeb B 438
VANDERFORD, Charles H 333
VANEMAN, Peter 54
VANLEAR, Charles A 456 Ed F 454 Harden A 458
VANPELT, Arch 453 D S 204 James 455 Martin 455 R A 120
VARNER, Jacob 457
VAUGHAN, W A 461
VAWTERS, Emanuel 456
VENABLE, Dr 298
VICARS, Elias 447
VIGER, John 451
VIQUESNEY, Charles 293
VOGT, Elisabeth 444
VOORHEES, 338 John S 457
VOSS, Ephraim 54
WADDELL, Alexander W 254 Dr 349 351 J A 34
WADE, B F 295 I E 336 John 451 Joseph 451 Lind 98 Sarah 445 Zephaniah 451
WAESCHE, William H 452
WAGGONER, Joseph 451
WAGNER, A L 209

WALKER, 137 Gilbert C 356 James 55 John C 398 443 S T 332 Samuel T 135 138 332 454 Thomas 57 449
WALLACE, 108 David 451 John 122 Lew 140
WALLIS, 376
WALSH, John 106 284 Mr 286
WALTER, I N 246
WALTERS, J W 200
WALTON, Moses 443
WAMPLER, C W 373 D B 300 D S 203 392 I S 299 307 J M 314 J W 314 Joseph W 460
WARD, John 453 W S 332
WARDEN, Sarah 445
WAREN, Thomas 447
WARENS, Michael 217
WARICK, Jacob 102
WARREN, 130 Colonel 137-139 E T H 11 135 358 392 Edward Tiffin Harrison 139 Harriet 310 James Magruder 139 Michael 215 Mr 388 Virginia 139 William Rice 387
WARRIN, Abijiah 98 Michael 218
WARTMAN, Henry T 281 J H 163
WARTMANN, 347 H T 340 Harvey 331-332 Henry T 329 346 J H 329-331 331 Laurentz 318 321 Lawrence 10 111 189 330-331 339 346 Margaret 310 W Mck 281 William Mck 442
WARVEL, Mrs Christopher 121
WASHBUN, James 450
WASHBURN, Steven 450
WASHINGTON, D N 183
WATERMAN, 191 354 A 443 A G 220 A G Jr 305 Albert G 304 Annie 304 Asher 10 187 192 196 220 304 352 Augustus 117 304 397 Dr 188 270 Isabella 304 352 John H 387 Mr 118 Sarah 304
WATERS, Joseph 452
WATRTMANN, Laurentz 329
WATSON, Thomas L 26 318
WATTS, Samuel 58
WAY, Ferdinand 453 Frank 453 G W 453
WAYLAND, J W 14
WAYT, James 55 John 443
WEAER, R F 456
WEAGGY, Mary 447
WEAN, Abram 457 E J 457 Jacob 457 John 456
WEASE, Mary 446
WEAST, C L 391 E L 391
WEATHERHOLT, Nicolas 72
WEAVER, A L 461 Abraham 397 C S 377 Charles 451-452 David 122 158 F H 456 Floyd W 298 George 99 John 99

ROCKINGHAM COUNTY

WEAVER (cont.)
  261 Richard W 454 S S 460 Samuel
  385 Sarah 311 Thomas 459
WEBB, Asa 448 J B 174 373 393 443-
  444 Joseph B 392
WEBSTER, Daniel 117 George 420 James
  420 Jas 420
WEEB, Robert 445
WEED, Father 272
WEEKLEY, W M 275
WEEN, Elizabeth 410 Isaac 410
WEIR, John 95
WEISHAMPEL, 337
WELBY, Amelia S 326
WELLER, John 456
WELLS, A H 276 George 283 283-284
  448 Joshua 284
WELSH, Richard 59 450
WENGER, 241 Abram B 397-398 C D 235
  367 Ephraim 370 Henry 262 J D 460
  Joseph H 329
WESLEY, Andrew 450 John 284
WEST, Cathrine 446 Eugene 388
  Madison 301 Mrs Clary 403
WESTJOHN, W 457
WETSEL, D M 367 Jack 457
WETZEL, Christopher 194 George 350
  Jacob 350 John 350 John C 242 John
  Jr 350 Lewis 349-350
WEVNER, Johannah 410
WEZEL, Martin 350
WHEAFER, Charles 447
WHEAT, John C 252
WHEATON, Benjamin 446
WHEELER, 172 Peter 453 W H H 452
WHETON, Ban 91
WHETZEL, Jacob 451
WHISLER, Henry 101
WHISSEN, J H 457
WHITE, Benjamin 95 Brock T 183
  Christley 457 Cora 459 John Jr 60
  John Sr 60 Milton 458 William 99
WHITEMAN, Elizabeth 446
WHITENER, Milton 203
WHITESCARVER, L C 455
WHITESEL, E M 186 330 Henry N 278
WHITESELL, Jacob 458
WHITESIDES, Sarah 444
WHITMER, Benjamin J 456 David 454 J
  S 453 James 456 Maria 360 William
  C 455
WHITMIRE, Louis 457
WHITMORE, Abraham 122 Abram 378
  Benjamin 455 Bowman 455 C R 204
  David 452 J B 459 Jacob 216 James
  C 455 John 452 455
WHITSEL, Peter 456

WHITZELL, Jacob 451
WHYATT, Jean 445
WIECE, Jacob 54 Joseph 54
WIITTS, Daniel 451
WILARD, Jane 445
WILCOCKS, Freelove 448
WILDES, General 150 Thomas F 149
WILHITE, Joseph 456 Peter 456
WILILAMS, G E 461
WILKIN, Hannah 156
WILKINS, John T 452
WILL, Charles B 457 E J 461
WILLIAMS, Abram S 200 Dr 232 Edward
  96 George 453 J C 376 James 452
  459 John 122 126 450 John C 248
  Joseph 453 Joseph T 240 L Mcc 461
  Peter 452 Robert 92 Samuel C 203 W
  N 204
WILLIAMSON, Abraham 202 C B 231 J D
  202 441 443-444 Jacob D 330 John
  123 R L 460 Thomas L 289
WILLIS, Major 92
WILSON, 167 457 A H 390 Aaron H 389
  B F 270 461 Benjamin 269 Charles
  77 Elizabeth 446 Ephraim 60 J Mark
  153 294 J Newton 389 James H 454
  John 58 320 R B 198 U G 309
WILTON, J 254 280 282 315 379 391
  Joshua 252
WIMBIGLER, George H 455
WINDER, 145 General 142 144 146
WINE, Daniel 313 J H 200 459 J M 458
  O W 200 Peter 407 William 458
WINEGORD, John 455 Joseph 455 Peter
  447
WINFIELD, 130 203 C R 204 Charles
  134 Charles R 462 Dr 232 Dr
  Richard 134 Evelyn 355 Jno 302
  John Q 134 232 329 456 Paulina 210
  329
WINGER, Henry 449
WINKLE, Henry 451
WIPE, W H 155
WISE, 259 Adam 456 Adolph 256-258
  Albert 256 Daniel 452 Harvey 456
  Henry A 252-254 360 Herman 234 256
  258 408 J C 201 J H 459 James 456
  John 452 John W 389 Leopold 256
  Michael 199 376 N B 389 Peter 302
  R J 453 William N 456
WISEMAN, John 446
WISSLER, W F 461
WITHER, Jacob 450
WITSEL, Marten 213
WITSELL, Henry 216 Martin 72 216
WITT, Jacob 451
WITTIG, 417 H J 461 J Luther 184

WODROW, Alexander 349
WOHLFARTH, Michael 34
WOLDREDG, Margaret 445
WOLF, Lewis 351
WOLFE, Joseph H 455 Thurston 455
WOLFINGER, A D 337
WOLFREY, James H 452
WOOD, Calvin 457 George M 457 Isaac 96 John D 457 John I 184 William 459
WOODING, 142
WOODLEY, Jacob 213
WOODLY, Jacob 217 Mary 447
WOODS, John 159 198 John W 197 200
WOODSON, 131 J C 443 Jno C 358 John C 163 355 358 442-444 Leneas 394 R Lee 193
WOODWARD, Joseph N 396 Peter 310 Thomas 446 William 450
WOOLEDGE, Mary 448
WOOLF, Andrews 447
WOOLFORD, C W 228 Sarah 447
WOOLRIDGE, Barbara 76 George 76
WOOLRIGE, Barbara 445
WRIGHT, J F 461 James 293 Jno T 391 John 448 450-451 Robert 435 William 459
WYANT, A E 155 Alexander 455 Ashby 459 Augustine 453 C N 298 D W 453 Isaac 453
WYNANT, Jacob H 415
WYNDHAM, Sir Percy 433
XAVIER, Francis 49
YACOME, Filey 54
YAGER, 236 T P 393
YANCEY, 37 130 A P 390 Albert 122 C A 387-388 Charles 122 Charles A 358 387 D B 392 E S 456 John G 182 John G Jr 193 L B 461 Layton 441

YANCEY (cont.)
  Layton B 315 Richard 457 Thomas L 387 442 W B 138-139 206 443 William 298 William B 134-135 301 442
YANCY, William B 453
YANKEY, W H 183
YARDLEY, Benjamin 17-18
YATES, Jackson 457
YEAGER, L F 198
YEAKEL, David 190
YEAKLE, C 452
YEAKLEY, Anna 448
YEATES, Nancy 448
YERGER, O M 254
YORGES, John 451
YOST, Jacob H 452 S M 163 331
YOUNG, 377 Conrod 59 H A 461 Jane 444 Robert 446 William 93 98 217
YOUNT, Daniel 249 W B 299 Walter B 315
YOUST, William 122
YURNER, D 460
ZANE, Elizabeth 58 Isaac 58
ZEEHON, Nicholas 429
ZIGLER, D H 250 314 460 David H 329 I N 460 J A 392 John 118 125 202 249 376 378 John P 179 Michael 203 313
ZILER, S D 460
ZIMERMAN, Barbara 445
ZIMMERMAN, 236 George 62
ZIMMERS, Christly 452 John 452
ZIRKEL, M S 408
ZIRKLE, B F 203 David P 457 Harvey 456 M Harvey 184 Reuben 401 W H 443